HUNTING THE FALCON

HUNTING THE FALCON

Henry VIII, Anne Boleyn, and the
Marriage That Shook Europe

JOHN GUY
AND JULIA FOX

An Imprint of HarperCollinsPublishers

HarperCollins books may be purchased for educational, business, or sales promotional use. For information, please email the Special Markets Department at SPsales@harpercollins.com.

Originally published in Great Britain in 2023 by Bloomsbury Circus.

FIRST U.S. EDITION

Library of Congress Cataloging-in-Publication Data has been applied for.

ISBN 978-0-06-307344-9

23 24 25 26 27 LBC 5 4 3 2 1

Contents

THE PARKERS

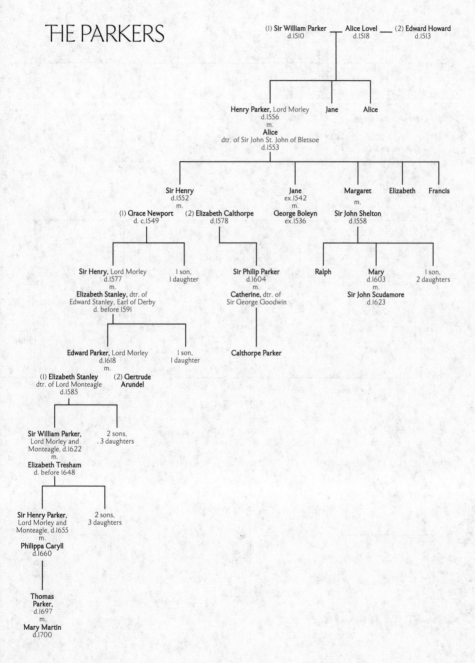

(1) Sir William Parker ——— Alice Lovel ——— (2) Edward Howard
d.1510   d.1518   d.1513

Henry Parker, Lord Morley   Jane   Alice
d.1556
m.
Alice
dtr. of Sir John St. John of Bletsoe
d.1553

Sir Henry   Jane   Margaret   Elizabeth   Francis
m.   ex.1542   m.
                              m.   Sir John Shelton
                        George Boleyn   d.1558
                        ex.1536

(1) Grace Newport   (2) Elizabeth Calthorpe
d. c.1549   d.1578

Sir Henry, Lord Morley   1 son,   Sir Philip Parker   Ralph   Mary   1 son,
d.1577   1 daughter   d.1604   d.1603   2 daughters
m.   m.   m.
Elizabeth Stanley, dtr. of   Catherine, dtr. of   Sir John Scudamore
Edward Stanley, Earl of Derby   Sir George Goodwin   d.1623
d. before 1591

Edward Parker, Lord Morley   1 son,   Calthorpe Parker
d.1618   1 daughter
m.

(1) Elizabeth Stanley   (2) Gertrude
dtr. of Lord Monteagle   Arundel
d.1585

Sir William Parker,   2 sons,
Lord Morley and   3 daughters
Monteagle, d.1622
m.
Elizabeth Tresham
d. before 1648

Sir Henry Parker,   2 sons,
Lord Morley and   3 daughters
Monteagle, d.1655
m.
Philippa Caryll
d.1660

Thomas
Parker,
d.1697
m.
Mary Martin
d.1700

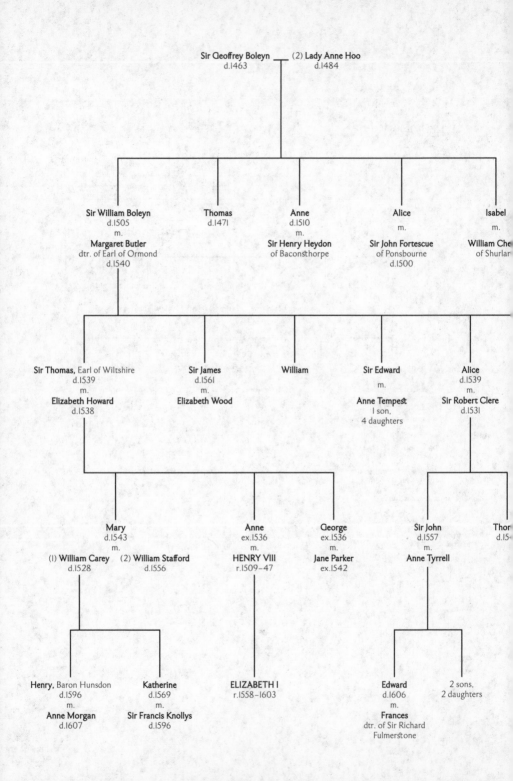

Sir Geoffrey Boleyn   (2) Lady Anne Hoo
d.1463   d.1484

Sir William Boleyn
d.1505
m.
Margaret Butler
dtr. of Earl of Ormond
d.1540

Thomas
d.1471

Anne
d.1510
m.
Sir Henry Heydon
of Baconsthorpe

Alice
m.
Sir John Fortescue
of Ponsbourne
d.1500

Isabel
m.
William Che
of Shurlar

Sir Thomas, Earl of Wiltshire
d.1539
m.
Elizabeth Howard
d.1538

Sir James
d.1561
m.
Elizabeth Wood

William

Sir Edward
m.
Anne Tempest
1 son,
4 daughters

Alice
d.1539
m.
Sir Robert Clere
d.1531

Mary
d.1543
m.
(1) **William Carey**   (2) **William Stafford**
d.1528   d.1556

Anne
ex.1536
m.
HENRY VIII
r.1509–47

George
ex.1536
m.
Jane Parker
ex.1542

Sir John
d.1557
m.
Anne Tyrrell

Thor
d.15

Henry, Baron Hunsdon
d.1596
m.
Anne Morgan
d.1607

Katherine
d.1569
m.
Sir Francis Knollys
d.1596

ELIZABETH I
r.1558–1603

Edward
d.1606
m.
Frances
dtr. of Sir Richard
Fulmerstone

2 sons,
2 daughters

THE BOLEYNS

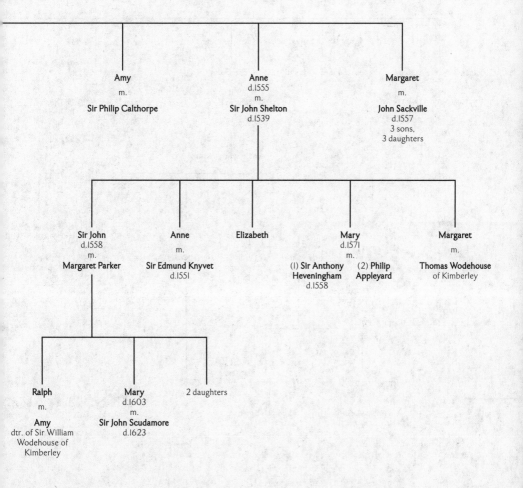

Amy
m.
Sir Philip Calthorpe

Anne
d.1555
m.
Sir John Shelton
d.1539

Margaret
m.
John Sackville
d.1557
3 sons,
3 daughters

Sir John
d.1558
m.
Margaret Parker

Anne
m.
Sir Edmund Knyvet
d.1551

Elizabeth

Mary
d.1571
m.
(1) Sir Anthony   (2) Philip
Heveningham   Appleyard
d.1558

Margaret
m.
Thomas Wodehouse
of Kimberley

Ralph
m.
Amy
dtr. of Sir William
Wodehouse of
Kimberley

Mary
d.1603
m.
Sir John Scudamore
d.1623

2 daughters

THE HOWARDS

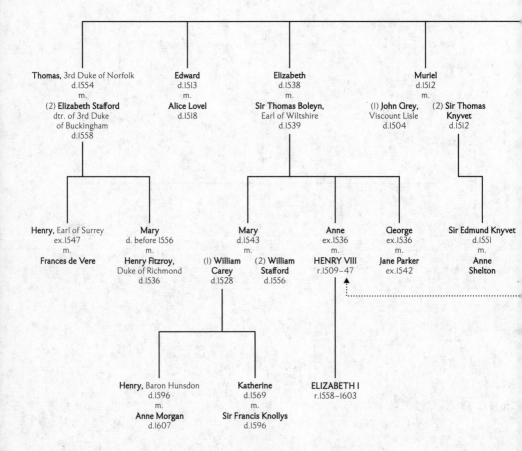

Thomas, 3rd Duke of Norfolk
d.1554
m.
(2) Elizabeth Stafford
dtr. of 3rd Duke
of Buckingham
d.1558

Edward
d.1513
m.
Alice Lovel
d.1518

Elizabeth
d.1538
m.
Sir Thomas Boleyn,
Earl of Wiltshire
d.1539

Muriel
d.1512
m.
(1) John Grey,
Viscount Lisle
d.1504

(2) Sir Thomas
Knyvet
d.1512

Henry, Earl of Surrey
ex.1547
m.
Frances de Vere

Mary
d. before 1556
m.
Henry Fitzroy,
Duke of Richmond
d.1536

Mary
d.1543
m.
(1) William
Carey
d.1528

(2) William
Stafford
d.1556

Anne
ex.1536
m.
HENRY VIII
r.1509–47

George
ex.1536
m.
Jane Parker
ex.1542

Sir Edmund Knyvet
d.1551
m.
Anne
Shelton

Henry, Baron Hunsdon
d.1596
m.
Anne Morgan
d.1607

Katherine
d.1569
m.
Sir Francis Knollys
d.1596

ELIZABETH I
r.1558–1603

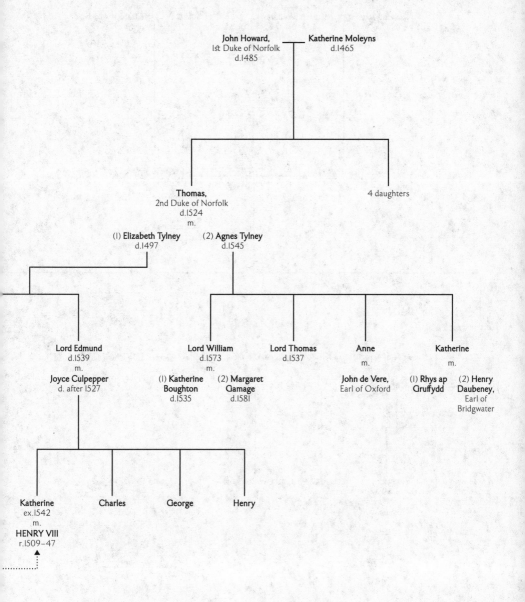

John Howard,
1st Duke of Norfolk
d.1485

Katherine Moleyns
d.1465

Thomas,
2nd Duke of Norfolk
d.1524
m.

4 daughters

(1) Elizabeth Tylney
d.1497

(2) Agnes Tylney
d.1545

Lord Edmund
d.1539
m.
Joyce Culpepper
d. after 1527

Lord William
d.1573
m.
(1) Katherine
Boughton
d.1535

(2) Margaret
Gamage
d.1581

Lord Thomas
d.1537

Anne
m.
John de Vere,
Earl of Oxford

Katherine
m.
(1) Rhys ap
Gruffydd

(2) Henry
Daubeney,
Earl of
Bridgwater

Katherine
ex.1542
m.
HENRY VIII
r.1509–47

Charles

George

Henry

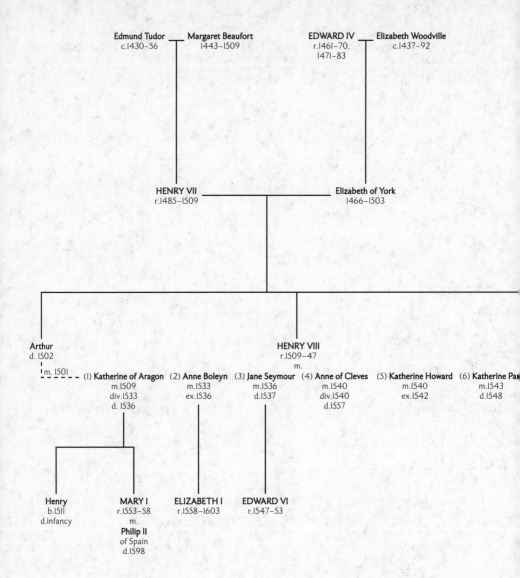

Edmund Tudor
c.1430–56

Margaret Beaufort
1443–1509

EDWARD IV
r.1461–70,
1471–83

Elizabeth Woodville
c.1437–92

HENRY VII
r.1485–1509

Elizabeth of York
1466–1503

Arthur
d. 1502

m. 1501

(1) Katherine of Aragon
m.1509
div.1533
d. 1536

HENRY VIII
r.1509–47
m.

(2) Anne Boleyn
m.1533
ex.1536

(3) Jane Seymour
m.1536
d.1537

(4) Anne of Cleves
m.1540
div.1540
d.1557

(5) Katherine Howard
m.1540
ex.1542

(6) Katherine Par
m.1543
d.1548

Henry
b.1511
d.infancy

MARY I
r.1553–58
m.
Philip II
of Spain
d.1598

ELIZABETH I
r.1558–1603

EDWARD VI
r.1547–53

THE TUDORS

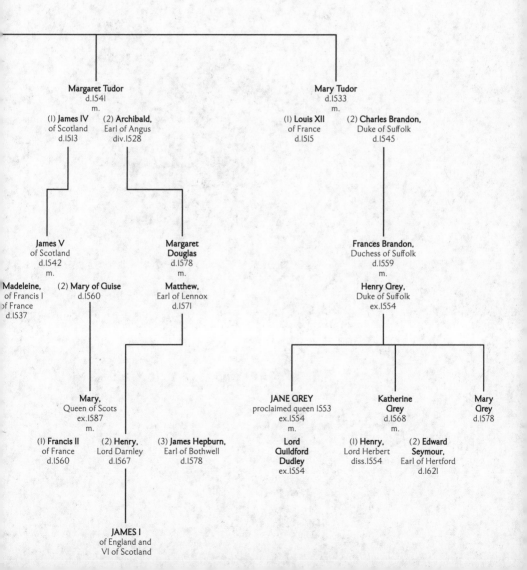

Margaret Tudor
d.1541
m.

(1) **James IV**
of Scotland
d.1513

(2) **Archibald,**
Earl of Angus
div.1528

Mary Tudor
d.1533
m.

(1) **Louis XII**
of France
d.1515

(2) **Charles Brandon,**
Duke of Suffolk
d.1545

James V
of Scotland
d.1542
m.

**Margaret
Douglas**
d.1578
m.

Frances Brandon,
Duchess of Suffolk
d.1559
m.

Madeleine,
of Francis I
of France
d.1537

(2) **Mary of Guise**
d.1560

Matthew,
Earl of Lennox
d.1571

Henry Grey,
Duke of Suffolk
ex.1554

Mary,
Queen of Scots
ex.1587
m.

JANE GREY
proclaimed queen 1553
ex.1554
m.

**Katherine
Grey**
d.1568
m.

**Mary
Grey**
d.1578

(1) **Francis II**
of France
d.1560

(2) **Henry,**
Lord Darnley
d.1567

(3) **James Hepburn,**
Earl of Bothwell
d.1578

**Lord
Guildford
Dudley**
ex.1554

(1) **Henry,**
Lord Herbert
diss.1554

(2) **Edward
Seymour,**
Earl of Hertford
d.1621

JAMES I
of England and
VI of Scotland

Dramatis Personae

THE TUDORS

Henry VIII, King of England

Henry VII, King of England, father of Henry VIII

Elizabeth of York, eldest child of King Edward IV and Elizabeth Woodville; wife of Henry VII and mother of Henry VIII

Margaret Beaufort, Countess of Richmond, daughter and heir of John Beaufort, Duke of Somerset; mother of Henry VII and grandmother of Henry VIII

Margaret Tudor, elder sister of Henry VIII; married (1) James IV, King of Scotland; (2) Archibald Douglas, Earl of Angus; (3) Henry Stewart

Mary Tudor, known as 'The French Queen', younger sister of Henry VIII; married (1) King Louis XII of France as his second wife; (2) Charles Brandon, Duke of Suffolk

Katherine of Aragon, youngest daughter of Queen Isabella I of Castile and King Ferdinand II of Aragon; married (1) Arthur, Prince of Wales; (2) Henry VIII as his first wife

James V, King of Scotland, son of Margaret Tudor and James IV

Margaret Douglas, Henry VIII's niece; only child of Margaret Tudor and Archibald Douglas, and a leading contributor to the Devonshire Manuscript

Princess Mary, daughter of Henry VIII and Katherine of Aragon

Princess Elizabeth, daughter of Henry VIII and Anne Boleyn

Henry Fitzroy, Duke of Richmond, Duke of Somerset, Earl of Nottingham; illegitimate son of Henry VIII by Elizabeth Blount; married Mary Howard

THE BOLEYNS

Sir Geoffrey Boleyn, Lord Mayor of London, great-grandfather of Anne Boleyn

Sir William Boleyn, son of Sir Geoffrey Boleyn and grandfather of Anne Boleyn

Margaret Butler, wife of Sir William Boleyn and grandmother of Anne Boleyn; daughter and co-heir of Thomas Butler, Earl of Ormond

Sir Thomas Boleyn, son of Sir William Boleyn and Margaret Butler; father of Anne Boleyn; later Viscount Rochford, Earl of Wiltshire

Elizabeth Howard, daughter of Thomas Howard, Earl of Surrey and 2nd Duke of Norfolk; wife of Sir Thomas Boleyn, mother of Anne Boleyn

Sir James Boleyn, brother of Sir Thomas Boleyn, uncle of Anne Boleyn and her chancellor as queen

Elizabeth Boleyn, wife of Sir James Boleyn; one of Anne Boleyn's ladies-in-waiting

Anne Boleyn, daughter of Sir Thomas Boleyn and Elizabeth Howard; second wife of Henry VIII

Mary Boleyn, sister of Anne Boleyn; married (1) William Carey; (2) William Stafford

George Boleyn, brother of Anne Boleyn; later Viscount Rochford

Jane Parker, wife of George Boleyn, daughter of Henry Parker, Lord Morley; one of Anne Boleyn's ladies-in-waiting

Lady Anne Shelton (*née* Boleyn), Anne Boleyn's aunt, mother of Mary and Margaret Shelton, custodian of Princess Mary

HENRY'S COURT

Anthony Anthony, groom of the king's chamber, Surveyor of the Ordnance in the Tower

Sir Thomas Audley, Lord Keeper of the Great Seal in succession to Thomas More; Lord Chancellor from 1533

William Benet, church lawyer, diplomat, ambassador to Rome

Gertrude Blount, second wife of Henry Courtenay; close friend and lady-in-waiting to Katherine of Aragon

Charles Brandon, Duke of Suffolk; married (1) Anne Browne, daughter of Sir Anthony Browne; (2) Henry VIII's younger sister Mary, widow of Louis XII; (3) Lady Katherine Willoughby

William Brereton, groom of the privy chamber, chamberlain of Chester; dominant royal servant in Cheshire and North Wales

Urian Brereton, younger brother of William, groom of the privy chamber

Sir Anthony Browne, gentleman of the privy chamber; half-brother of Sir William Fitzwilliam

Sir Francis Bryan, cousin of Anne Boleyn, gentleman of the privy chamber and diplomat; later known as the 'Vicar of Hell'

Niccolò de Burgo, theologian and Franciscan friar born in Florence; lectured in Oxford and assisted with Henry VIII's divorce campaign

Dr William Butts, royal physician

Sir Nicholas Carew, gentleman of the privy chamber, diplomat, supporter of Princess Mary; brother-in-law to Sir Francis Bryan

William Carey, husband of Mary Boleyn, gentleman of the privy chamber; died of the sweat

Sir Thomas Cheyne, gentleman of the privy chamber, early protégé of Anne Boleyn

William Compton, groom of the stool until 1526; died of the sweat

Henry Courtenay, Earl of Devon, Marquis of Exeter; eldest son of William Courtenay, Earl of Devon, and Katherine, sister of Elizabeth of York; nobleman of the privy chamber

Thomas Cranmer, Cambridge scholar and early protégé of the Boleyns; Archbishop of Canterbury from 1532

Thomas Cromwell, self-trained lawyer and servant of Wolsey; parliamentary manager, Master of the Jewels and principal secretary to Henry VIII; later Vicar-general and Lord Privy Seal

John Fisher, friend of Thomas More, Bishop of Rochester

Sir William Fitzwilliam, courtier and privy councillor; diplomat, treasurer of the royal household in succession to Sir Thomas Boleyn; half-brother of Sir Anthony Browne

Edward Foxe, Cambridge scholar and early protégé of the Boleyns; diplomat, later Bishop of Hereford

Stephen Gardiner, Wolsey's secretary, briefly Henry VIII's secretary; diplomat, Bishop of Winchester from 1531, ambassador to France

Cornelius Hayes, goldsmith and jeweller to Henry VIII

Sir Thomas Heneage, gentleman usher and trusted servant of Wolsey; gentleman of the privy chamber; replaced Henry Norris as groom of the stool

Hans Holbein the Younger, artist born in Augsburg who worked in Basel, Switzerland, before leaving for England in 1526

Thomas Howard, Earl of Surrey, 2nd Duke of Norfolk, victor of Flodden; father-in-law of Sir Thomas Boleyn

Thomas Howard, Earl of Surrey, 3rd Duke of Norfolk, Anne Boleyn's uncle, brother of her mother Elizabeth Howard

Henry Howard, Earl of Surrey, courtier, poet; son of Thomas Howard, 3rd Duke of Norfolk

Lord Thomas Howard, lover of Margaret Douglas; a leading contributor to the Devonshire Manuscript; younger brother of

Lord William Howard; stepbrother of Thomas Howard, 3rd Duke of Norfolk

John Husee, court agent to Viscount and Lady Lisle

Sir William Kingston, Constable of the Tower of London

William Knight, royal chaplain, archdeacon of Richmond, prebendary of St Stephen's Chapel, Westminster; one of Henry VIII's secretaries

Edmund Knyvet, eldest son of Sir Thomas Knyvet and Muriel, daughter of 2nd Duke of Norfolk; kinsman of Mary Shelton

Henry Knyvet, minor courtier, younger brother of Edmund

Lady Honor Lisle, second wife of Arthur Plantagenet, Viscount Lisle; known as 'Lady Lisle'

Thomas More, lawyer, diplomat, author of *Utopia*; one of Henry VIII's secretaries 1518–25; Lord Chancellor 1529–32

Henry Norris, gentleman of the privy chamber, groom of the stool from 1526

Richard Pace, Dean of St Paul's, diplomat, one of Henry VIII's secretaries

Sir Richard Page, Wolsey's chamberlain, gentleman of the privy chamber

Richard Pate, archdeacon of Lincoln, ambassador to Charles V

Sir William Paulet, courtier and privy councillor, Master of the Wards, comptroller of the royal household from 1532

Henry (or Harry) Algernon Percy, eldest son of 5th Duke of Northumberland; Anne Boleyn's first love; 6th Earl of Northumberland from 1527

Arthur Plantagenet, Viscount Lisle, illegitimate son of Edward IV; married (1) Elizabeth Grey; (2) Honor Grenville; Lord Deputy at Calais

Sir John Russell, protégé of Wolsey and gentleman of the privy chamber

Mark Smeaton, musician and groom of the privy chamber

Edward Stafford, 3rd Duke of Buckingham, eldest son of Henry Stafford, 2nd Duke of Buckingham, and Katherine Woodville, sister-in-law of Edward IV

Elizabeth Stafford, daughter of the 3rd Duke of Buckingham, maid of honour and later lady-in-waiting to Katherine of Aragon; estranged wife of Thomas Howard, 3rd Duke of Norfolk

John Stokesley, royal chaplain and confessor, diplomat; later Bishop of London

Pietro Vannes, Wolsey's and later Henry VIII's Latin secretary; diplomat

Robert Wakefield, Hebrew scholar; later Regius Lecturer in Hebrew at Oxford

Walter Walsh, groom of the privy chamber

William Warham, Archbishop of Canterbury, Lord Chancellor to 1515; died 1532

Sir Francis Weston, gentleman of the privy chamber

Dr Richard Wolman, church lawyer, archdeacon of Sudbury, servant of Wolsey; Dean of Wells and royal chaplain

Thomas Wolsey, Archbishop of York, Cardinal and papal legate, Lord Chancellor to 1529; died 1530

Sir Thomas Wyatt, courtier, poet, diplomat; Anne Boleyn's admirer

ANNE BOLEYN'S COURT*

Jane Ashley, later Lady Mewtas, gentlewoman

Sir Edward Baynton, vice-chamberlain

John Barlow, chaplain to Sir Thomas Boleyn who undertook assignments for Anne

Nicholas Bourbon, evangelical French refugee poet whom Anne recruited as a tutor to the children in her circle

*See also under 'The Boleyns'.

Elizabeth Browne, Countess of Worcester, lady-in-waiting; sister of Sir Anthony Browne

Lady Jane Calthorpe, lady-in-waiting; formerly Princess Mary's governess

Margaret Coffyn, lady-in-waiting

Sir William Coffyn, Master of the Horse; married to Margaret Coffyn

'Nan' Cobham, role in Anne's household unknown

Margaret Gamage, gentlewoman; later married Lord William Howard as his second wife

Anne Gaynesford, gentlewoman; married George Zouche

Elizabeth Hill (*née* Isley), gentlewoman

Elizabeth ('Bess') Holland, mistress of the 3rd Duke of Norfolk, gentlewoman

Margery Horsman, gentlewoman; later married Sir Michael Lyster

Mary Howard, Anne's cousin, daughter of the 3rd Duke of Norfolk; wife of Henry Fitzroy; lady in-waiting; contributor to the Devonshire Manuscript

Mary Kingston, wife of Sir William Kingston, lady-in-waiting

Hugh Latimer, one of Anne's chaplains; later Bishop of Worcester

William Latymer, one of Anne's chaplains; author of 'A Brief Treatise or Chronicle of the Most Virtuous Lady Anne Boleyn'

Matthew Parker, one of Anne's chaplains; later Archbishop of Canterbury

John Scut, tailor

Jane Seymour, gentlewoman, third wife of Henry VIII

Nicholas Shaxton, one of Anne's chaplains, her first almoner; later Bishop of Salisbury

Mary Shelton, Anne's cousin, gentlewoman, contributor to the Devonshire Manuscript

Margaret Shelton, Anne's cousin, Mary Shelton's sister

John Skip, one of Anne's chaplains and her second almoner

George Taylor, receiver-general

Harry Webb, sewer

Bridget Wilshire, lady-in-waiting; married (1) Sir Richard Wingfield; (2) Sir Nicholas Harvey; (3) Robert Tyrwhitt

SPAIN AND THE HABSBURGS

Isabella I, Queen of Castile, mother of Katherine of Aragon

Ferdinand II, King of Aragon, father of Katherine of Aragon

Juana of Castile, sister of Katherine of Aragon, married Philip the Handsome, Duke of Burgundy; Queen of Castile

Charles of Ghent, Duke of Burgundy (as Charles II) from 1506; King of the Spanish kingdoms (as Charles I) from 1516; Holy Roman Emperor (as Charles V) from 1519; son of Juana of Castile and Philip the Handsome

Maximilian I, Archduke of Austria, King of the Romans from 1486; Holy Roman Emperor from 1508; Philip the Handsome's father

Margaret of Austria, daughter of Maximilian I, sister of Philip the Handsome, aunt to Charles V, regent of the Low Countries; died 1530

Eleanor, sister of Charles V, widowed Queen of Portugal; married King Francis I of France as his second wife

Marie of Hungary, sister of Charles V, widowed Queen of Hungary, succeeded Margaret of Austria as regent of the Low Countries

Philip the Handsome, Duke of Burgundy, King of Castile; died 1506

Íñigo López de Mendoza, Cardinal, Archbishop of Burgos, Charles V's ambassador to London, 1526–29

Eustace Chapuys, Charles V's ambassador to London from 1529

FRANCE

Louis XII, King of France

Francis I, King of France; married (1) Claude; (2) Eleanor, sister of Charles V

Louise of Savoy, widow of Charles d'Orléans, Count of Angoulême; mother of King Francis I

Claude, Queen of France, elder daughter of King Louis XII by his second wife, Anne, Duchess of Brittany

Marguerite of Angoulême, daughter of Louise of Savoy, sister of King Francis I

Anne, Duke de Montmorency, Grand Master of France

Giovanni Gioacchino di Passano, maître d'hôtel to Louise of Savoy; ambassador to London, 1525, 1526–27, 1528, 1530–31, 1531–32

Jean Brinon, Chancellor of Alençon, ambassador to London, 1525–26

Gabriel de Gramont, Bishop of Tarbes to 1534, Archbishop of Bordeaux from 1529, Bishop of Poitiers from 1532; ambassador to London, 1527; French agent at the Vatican

François de la Tour, Vicomte de Turenne, ambassador to London, 1527

Jean du Bellay, Cardinal, Bishop of Bayonne by 1526, Bishop of Paris from 1532; ambassador to London, 1527–29, 1530, 1531, 1533–34

Gabriel de la Guiche, ambassador to London, 1530–31, 1534

François de Tournon, French agent at the Vatican

Jean de Dinteville, Bailly of Troyes and Seigneur de Polisy, ambassador to London, 1533, 1535, 1536

François de Dinteville, elder brother of Jean; Bishop of Auxerre from 1530; French ambassador to Rome

Georges de Selve, Bishop of Lavaur, friend of Jean de Dinteville

Gilles de la Pommeraye, ambassador to London, 1531–32, 1534

Philippe Chabot, Seigneur de Brion, Admiral of France, ambassador to London, 1534

Palamèdes Gontier, King Francis I's secretary, assistant to Chabot in 1534; ambassador to London, 1535

Antoine de Castelnau, Bishop of Tarbes from 1534, ambassador to London, 1535–37

Lancelot de Carle, secretary to Antoine de Castelnau, poet

ROME

Giuliano della Rovere, Pope Julius II

Giovanni di Lorenzo de' Medici, Pope Leo X

Adriaan Florensz Boeyens, Pope Adrian VI

Giulio de' Medici, Pope Clement VII

Alessandro Farnese, Pope Paul III

Lorenzo Campeggi, Cardinal and papal legate

Rodolfo Pio da Carpi, Bishop of Faenza, papal nuncio to France

Uberto Gambara, papal prothonotary and nuncio to England

Gregorio Casali, Henry VIII's agent in Rome

Prologue

Shortly after dawn on Friday 19 May 1536, Sir William Kingston, Constable of the Tower of London, left his quarters near the eastern perimeter of the fortress and set out around the west side of the White Tower. Passing through the Coldharbour Gate, the great tower and gateway built by Henry III in around 1240 to guard the entrance to the royal apartments, he gained admission to the innermost ward. Arriving at the queen's lodgings, he mounted the stairs at the south end of the building, and then passed through the recently rebuilt Presence Chamber. After he reached the door of the more intimate privy chamber, he gently knocked.[1]

A lady-in-waiting opened it, and beyond was a slim, thirty-five- or thirty-six-year-old woman of average height with dark, flashing eyes and a long, slender neck – Queen Anne Boleyn, second wife of King Henry VIII. This was not the first time that Kingston had visited her at this hour. She had sent for him early in the morning on Thursday, after keeping an anxious vigil since 2 a.m., kneeling in prayer with John Skip, her trusted almoner. Under sentence of death, she had summoned Kingston while she received the holy sacrament of the Mass and protested her innocence of the heinous crimes of which she was accused: incest, quadruple adultery and plotting to kill her husband. Swearing twice on the sacrament that she spoke God's truth, she declared that she was 'a good woman' and had never been unfaithful. Her belief was that she would die shortly after 8 a.m., the customary hour for such executions. Steeling herself to walk to the scaffold, she had spent many long hours of waiting that night, reconciling herself to what was to come.[2]

She so readied herself, because one of the four former ladies-in-waiting whom her husband had redesignated as her custodians and whom she detested – possibly her aunt, Lady Elizabeth Boleyn – had informed her that she would die that day. It was a cruel misunderstanding. The date and time of execution had not yet been fixed.[3] When nothing happened, she became sorely distressed. Sending for the Constable again, she said: 'Master Kingston, I hear say I shall not die afore noon, and I am very sorry therefore, for I thought then to be dead and past my pain.' Unbeknown to her, Henry would not approve her death-warrant until later that same Thursday. When the writ was finally sealed, it instructed Kingston that 'immediately on receipt of these presents, you bring the said Anne upon the Green within our Tower of London, and cut off the head of the said Anne, and in this omit nothing.'[4]

There were other reasons for a delay. During daylight hours, the gates of the Tower were left open to permit visitors to access the outer ward. Not wishing to arouse suspicions, but keen to restrict independent reports of the manner of Anne's death from travelling abroad, Thomas Cromwell, the king's principal secretary and chief enforcer, had ordered Kingston to expel some thirty foreigners from the Tower precincts before the execution could begin. Cromwell appointed his staunch ally, the merchant-banker Richard Gresham, soon to be Lord Mayor of London although he was one of the most hated men in the city, to take charge of security and make sure only those whom the king wished to see his wife die should be allowed to enter 'because of [the] wondering of the people'. Equally, Henry, who was planning everything from afar in the minutest detail, intended everyone who mattered to be there. Given the initial uncertainty as to the date and time, Kingston worried that 'if we have not an hour certain [as it may] be known in London, I think here will be but few and I think a reasonable number were best.' On that score, he need not have feared.[5]

A man not without some human sympathy, Kingston tried to divert Anne's attention from the muddle over the timetable. 'It should be no pain,' he answered, 'it is so subtle.'

'I heard say', she replied, 'the executioner was very good, and I have a little neck.' At this, she 'put her hand about it, laughing heartily.' All through her life, she had never lacked courage and it did not fail her now. 'I have seen many men and also women executed,' Kingston informed Cromwell, 'and all they [i.e. all of them] have been in great sorrow, and to my knowledge this lady hath much joy and pleasure in death.' With her marriage and her reputation destroyed, Anne had put her faith in a redeeming Christ.[6]

By Friday morning, everything was ready. Anne had spent a second night with Skip, kneeling in prayer, too exhausted to sleep. As dawn broke, Kingston reappeared to tell her she would die that day and to give her a purse containing £20 which she was to distribute, according to tradition, as alms before her death. Sometime after 8 a.m., he returned: the moment was approaching.[7]

Anne dressed herself with the greatest care for her final appearance on a public stage. As a teenager at the court of Queen Claude of France, she had learnt about the power and symbolism of beautiful clothes. The occasion demanded sobriety, not flamboyance, and so today she chose a gown of grey damask lined with fur, over which she wore an ermine mantle. Her choice is telling, because dark or neutral shades of silk or satin rarely found a place in her wardrobe. She had never worn grey or black: colours too closely associated with her predecessor as queen, Katherine of Aragon. She then tied up her still lustrous dark brown hair, over which she wore an English gable headdress, another unusual choice for her as she tended to prefer the more fashionable and flattering French hoods. We should not overlook the significance of her hood. Anne had been a Francophile from a young age: her tastes and values were radically different to those of previous royal consorts – but this was an occasion to protest her loyal Englishness.[8]

Attended by Lady Boleyn and the three other ladies, she left her privy chamber for the last time and went downstairs into the open air. Crossing the inner courtyard of the palace area out of the queen's lodgings, she passed through the Coldharbour gate and around the White Tower to arrive at the Green before the 'House of Ordnance'. This was the place where the king's soldiers often practised archery and shooting, and where a 'new scaffold' had been hastily erected – for today the killing would be real.[9]

No more than three feet high, the scaffold was mounted by four or five steps.[10] It ought to have been draped in black canvas, but whether the Tower officials had managed to do this in time is uncertain. Around it ranged rows of hastily constructed seating for the more important spectators, notably Anne's stepson, the seventeen-year-old Henry Fitzroy, Duke of Richmond, the king's illegitimate son, perhaps there to represent his father. Anne had treated Fitzroy badly, and he was going to enjoy seeing her die. Close by sat the Duke of Suffolk, Sir Thomas Audley (the Lord Chancellor), Cromwell and most of the king's privy councillors, supported by members of the House of Lords. Behind them sat the Mayor and Aldermen of London, with the leaders of the city's livery companies, headed by the Master and Wardens of the Mercers' Company, further back craning for a view.[11] A Tower official noted that many of the London contingent brought their wives and that, despite the strict prohibition, some 'strangers' (i.e. foreigners) had managed to slip through the cordon.[12] One of Cromwell's future servants said, with pardonable exaggeration, that a crowd of a thousand had gained entry. More likely it was around half that number.[13]

Once Anne reached the foot of the scaffold, Kingston led her up the steps. By now it was almost 9 a.m., and as was the usual protocol, he gave her permission to speak briefly. Audiences had fixed opinions as to what condemned prisoners should say. They were to make peace with their accusers and the world by confessing their faults, trusting in the mercy of God, asking the crowd to pray for them and then dying bravely. Obedience to the king's will and submission to his justice was expected. No one was allowed to question the justice of their sentence or impugn the king – indeed, it was customary to praise him as a just and gracious lord. Above all, they should acknowledge that they were sinners, as all mortals were in the sight of God, and that they deserved to die.[14]

Anne was not someone to conform blindly to the rules if she did not feel they were right. Barely three weeks before, she had been the most influential woman in the country. Advancing to the edge of the scaffold 'with a goodly smiling countenance' to address the crowd, she unburdened herself of the lines she had carefully prepared:

> Good Christian people, I am come hither to die, for according
> to the law and by the law I am judged to die, and therefore
> I will speak nothing against it. I am come hither to accuse no
> man, nor to speak anything of that whereof I am accused and
> condemned to die, but I pray God save the king and send him
> long to reign over you, for a gentler nor a more merciful prince
> was there never: and to me he was ever a good, a gentle and
> sovereign lord. And if any person will meddle of my cause,
> I require them to judge the best. And thus, I take my leave of
> the world and of you all, and I heartily desire you all to pray for
> me. O Lord, have mercy on me, to God I commend my soul.[15]

What stunned the crowd into silence was not what she said, but what she failed to say. She offered no public admission of sin, no confession that she had wronged her husband, not even a hint that she was guilty of the crimes against God and nature of which royal justice had convicted her. One seventeenth-century reader, after transcribing her words in the Bodleian Library, Oxford, annotated them as 'The queen's oracular and ambiguous speech.'[16]

The speech over, Anne's ladies removed her mantle but left her wearing her gown. This was possible because the fashionable low square neckline would not have impeded access to her neck. Taking off her gable headdress herself, she tucked her hair into a coif. She next fastened 'her clothes about her feet', ensuring that if her skirts moved, her legs were not visible. She then 'knelt down upon her knees'. Her only visible sign of emotion was to glance over her

shoulder several times.[17] Was this an understandable moment of
fear, perhaps that the headsman would strike before she was ready?
Or was it more poignant? She had previously told Kingston that
though she had been harshly treated at the time of her arrest: 'I
think the king does it to prove me.'[18]

Did she hope against hope for a last-minute reprieve? Was she
looking over her shoulder for a messenger? Henry had the power
to spare her – if he chose to. Although she had been in France at
the time, she cannot but have heard of the king pardoning some
400 prisoners taken after the so-called 'Evil May Day' uprising
in London in 1517, when the houses of Italian and other foreign
merchants were looted and burned. While twenty men were sent
to the gallows, the rest, dressed only in their shirts and with halters
already around their necks, knelt before the king in his full majesty
in Westminster Hall. When they begged for mercy, Henry allowed
himself to be persuaded into granting it. He waited until the last
possible moment and would do the same a mere six days after Anne
mounted the scaffold in the case of a friar known as 'Peretrie'. It
had already been decided to pardon him, but, theatrically, Henry
ordered that 'the law should proceed upon him even till the last
point of execution.' Only as the hangman was about to kick the
ladder away from the gallows would a messenger arrive with the
letters of pardon. But if Anne dreamed that her former lover would
save her, she barely knew him.[19]

There was no need for a block since Anne was to be killed not
with an axe, but with a two-handed sword in the French manner.[20]
For a beheading to go smoothly, it needed someone skilled enough
to sever the head with a single blow. In Henry's England, unlike in
France, the common hangman wielded the axe. Because such men
had more experience with the grislier tasks of hanging and 'drawing'
(i.e. disembowelling) their prisoners before cutting off the head
and quartering the corpse, they often bungled beheadings, leaving
dying victims in agony until a final stroke killed them. Commonly
the hangman used his axe as a meat-cleaver to hack through the
more obstinate sinews.

Anne did not have to face these horrors. Possibly as a last concession to the woman he had once called his 'own sweetheart', or perhaps as a sardonic reminder of her love of France, Henry had sent to Calais for a specialist headsman said to be an expert with a two-handed sword. At a price of 100 gold crowns of the sun (over £23,000 in modern values: see Dates, Spellings, Units of Currency, page 518), the man would not come cheaply.[21]

While one of her ladies placed a blindfold over her eyes, Anne said repeatedly, 'To Christ I commend my soul; Jesu, receive my soul.'[22] Those words were the executioner's cue. On hearing them, his sword hissed through the air and he sliced off her head with a single blow. Sir John Spelman, one of the royal justices present, who confided his impressions to his private notebook, says, 'He did his office very well ... the head fell to the ground with her lips moving and her eyes moving.' A French report adds the blow came 'before you could say a paternoster [Lord's Prayer]'.[23] Nothing is said about the crowd's reaction beyond that she died 'boldly', but it is hard to believe they did not gasp. Anyone who harboured doubts had to mask them. No one dared grieve openly for the dead queen lest they share her fate. Henry's conscience was clear: she had paid, quite rightly, for her wickedness and treachery.[24]

As soon as her head was off, one of the women threw a linen cloth over it, while the others wrapped the body in a bedsheet.[25] They then carried the body with the head some seventy or so yards along the path to the Chapel of St Peter ad Vincula at the north-west corner of the site. Inside the chapel, Anne's clothing was stripped off – the Tower officials claimed her valuable fabrics as perquisites – before the women laid the corpse in an elm chest which had once contained bow staves destined for Ireland. Someone had perhaps forgotten, or more likely not dared, to attempt to measure Anne for a coffin, so the elm chest became a substitute.[26]

At noon, the coffin was buried without ceremony under the floor of the chancel in the chapel beside the high altar.[27] There she lay undisturbed until 1876 when, during restoration work, human remains said to be hers were exhumed at the request of Prince Albert, who ordered the bodies buried there to be properly identified and reinterred with name plaques. At a depth of two feet, bones were uncovered, said to belong to a woman in the prime of life, and of moderate height. The forehead and lower jaw were small and well formed. The skeletal vertebrae were unusually petite, especially one joint (the atlas) next to the skull, which the onlookers said was testimony to Anne's 'little neck'.[28]

Henry famously had six wives: 'Divorced, beheaded, died; divorced, beheaded, survived' is a jingle that schoolchildren learning about them chant around the world. Why, of all these relationships, does this one bear fresh scrutiny? Part of the answer is personal and political: with none of his other wives would Henry rekindle the intense passion, and genuine respect, he felt for this one woman. For the love of Anne, he alienated his family, many of his courtiers and his subjects; for her he destroyed and even killed men whom he had once regarded as his supporters and friends; for her he broke with the pope, used Parliament to enact matters that affected people's faith, ended centuries of tradition and risked war in Europe.

The other part of the answer is cultural and psychological: none of Henry's queens is etched into the popular imagination so deeply as is Anne. Her story exerts a perennial fascination and is the inspiration for countless biographies and works of fiction, for plays, poems, films and websites, even for a Donizetti opera. Anne Boleyn costumes, dolls, necklaces and rings are sold online. Hever Castle's shop offers an Anne Boleyn rubber bath duck in a French hood. Hers is a story that everyone thinks they know; and yet, do we fully comprehend who she was and what she stood for, and if so, how do we set about understanding why a man who was so besotted that he could hardly bear to be away from her for more than an hour could calmly summon a swordsman to strike off her head and believe himself to be in the right?

Too often it is forgotten that Anne and Henry's relationship, far from being a one-dimensional story of passionate love followed by a failed marriage, was dynamic and multi-layered, evolving over a period of nine or so years, six of which came before they were able to marry. For this reason, this book gives more attention than is conventional to their backstories and early lives, notably to the seven eventful years Anne spent in France before setting foot in the English court.

Moreover, fresh archival discoveries, along with sources hidden in plain sight, deepen and enlarge our understanding of their relationship. Some of these relate to the composition of Anne's side of the royal court as queen and especially to the women around her. Others help us to dispel lingering and latently misogynistic assumptions about Anne which anachronistically presumed that a sixteenth-century woman could exert little to no influence on the politics and beliefs of a patriarchal society. Hints of this were present from the very beginning of their affair when Anne was briefly allowed to conduct a parallel diplomacy to his. And as their relationship blossomed, his letters to her began to place her on a par with, and then above, his most trusted male advisers. He never wrote to Katherine in this way and never did so again to any of his other wives.

Most of all, however, further new archival discoveries illuminate for the very first time the scale, depth and inner workings of the game Henry and Anne played out on an international stage. We learn for the first time not simply of Anne's love of and commitment to France, but how she took the powerful women she met there as role models, and how far her outlook was shaped by the ideas, especially religious ones, to which these women introduced her. Her Francophile tendencies worked greatly to her advantage in the early stages of her and Henry's courtship, only to rebound when attitudes changed.

Throughout our research we have gone back to the archives, deciphering the handwritten letters of the leading characters, the reports of councillors and ambassadors, the records meticulously compiled by small armies of secretaries and clerks. Wherever possible, the aim is to let Henry and Anne speak for themselves, to reconstruct how and why they acted as they did, but also to recreate their world, and to consider why the stories of some of their contemporaries are so strikingly different from those of others about the very same events.

HUNTING THE FALCON

Henry: Childhood and Adolescence

Henry VIII was not born to be king. He was a second son, the spare, not the heir: it was his elder brother, Prince Arthur, who was meant to rule. But on the morning of an idyllic Midsummer's Day in 1509 it would be Henry who, just a few days short of his eighteenth birthday, was crowned and anointed King of England in a ceremony of glittering pomp in Westminster Abbey. His wife of barely two weeks, the Spanish princess Katherine of Aragon, was crowned beside him. At that moment Henry – handsome, precocious, supremely gifted, with a round, beaming face and mop of ginger hair – seemed to be the king of dreams, of fairy tales, of chivalry, of honour, of justice. He certainly looked the part going by the measurements of his first suit of armour, standing at least six feet one inch tall but with no less than a forty-two-inch chest measurement and a waistline of thirty-five inches. The Venetian ambassador described him as 'magnificent, generous and a great enemy of the French'.[1]

The new king's parents were Henry Tudor, Earl of Richmond, and Elizabeth of York. A descendant of an illegitimate child of Edward III's son, John of Gaunt, Duke of Lancaster, by Katherine Swynford, Henry Tudor grew up in a hard school, forced into exile in 1471 during the turmoil and bloodshed of civil wars. These wars, better known as the 'Wars of the Roses', began in 1455 after Richard Plantagenet, Duke of York, sought to oust the weak and ineffectual Henry VI. In 1460, Richard was slain in battle, but within a year his son was crowned Edward IV, only to lose his position in 1469 before recovering it two years later. With Edward on the offensive after his return to power, Henry Tudor, who had his own small claim to the throne, sought refuge in Brittany and France.

When in 1483 the sybaritic Edward suddenly died, his calculating brother Richard, Duke of Gloucester, sprang into action, imprisoning his two young nephews, the uncrowned Edward V and his younger brother Richard, now the Duke of York, in the Tower from where they shortly disappeared. Usurpers came cheap in the fifteenth century. When Gloucester made himself king as Richard III, Henry Tudor's opportunity arrived. The result, with French aid, was the Battle of Bosworth in August 1485, which left Henry triumphant and Richard lying dead upon the field. A York–Tudor marriage had been secretly mooted since the closing days of Edward IV's reign. Now plans could be made in earnest. Edward's eldest daughter, Elizabeth of York, had better dynastic credentials than Henry: by marrying her three months after he was crowned king as Henry VII, he could recast himself as the true heir to the throne. As a chronicler remarked, the 'red rose' of Lancaster became the avenger of the 'white rose' of York.[2]

Despite beginning as one of convenience, the marriage was soon to prove much deeper. The couple came to like, even love, one another. They were two very different personalities. Henry was astute, wary, prudent, indefatigable, ruthless: a tyrant in the making whom it was dangerous to cross. Elizabeth was as cultured, intelligent and sophisticated as she was beautiful. Affectionate, accessible, charming, a peacemaker, she brought harmony to the royal family and was the perfect counterpoise to her distant, dispassionate husband.

Prince Henry was born on 28 June 1491 at Greenwich, five years after his elder brother Arthur, and baptised in the adjacent Franciscan friary church. The palace was then little more than a Thameside manor house, but once rebuilt in brick with a suitably regal riverside range for feasting and entertainments, chapel, stables, library and tiltyard it would end up as the child's favourite home. Henry scarcely knew Arthur, since long before he was fully weaned and learning to walk, his brother would be made Prince of Wales and installed in his own household. Queens and noblewomen alike sought to govern their children's early years, but royal protocol dictated that the king alone had charge of the heir to the throne. Arthur, whose very name invoked the ancient prophecies of Merlin, left the royal nursery at the tender age of three, when male tutors and servants were first assigned to him. Only Henry and his sisters Margaret, two years older, and Mary, five years younger, stayed in their mother's care, attended by her gentlewomen, nurses and rockers.[3] In this at least, the young Henry was blessed: he gained from Elizabeth of York the stability and affection he always ruefully remembered and would forever crave, and with her he was happy. Later in life, it would be said of him that 'he frequents ladies' company for mirth as a man nurtured among them.'[4]

These years with his mother, whom he adored but who cosseted and spoiled him, shaped Henry psychologically. As late as age twelve, he still lived in the royal nursery with its attached schoolroom in Eltham Palace, a short ride from Greenwich. His first tutor was the poet and satirist John Skelton, but it was his mother who taught him to read and write. His schoolroom copy of Cicero's *De officiis* ('On Duties'), printed in 1502, contains an ownership inscription in his bold, clear, highly distinctive handwriting which reads 'Thys Boke is Myne, Prince Henry', and the letter forms are almost identical to Elizabeth's own.[5]

Under Skelton's tutelage, Henry studied French and Latin grammar, history and chronicles, poetry, and tales of chivalry and courtly love. This had been the model for princely education since 1468, when Edward IV's sister, Margaret of York, married Duke Charles the Bold of Burgundy. Famously, the fifteenth-century Burgundians wrote the rules for courtly etiquette and manners throughout Western Europe. Their court prized luxury, ritual, magnificent dress, art patronage and book and manuscript collecting; music, dancing and ceremonial display; hunting and outdoor sports. Urban centres such as Bruges, Ghent and Brussels boasted grand palaces designed to host tournaments, banquets, masques and 'disguisings'. By the 1490s, Franco-Burgundian language and literature, dress styles, pageantry, art and interior decoration were as integral to English vernacular taste as Geoffrey Chaucer's works.

From a young age, Henry was a particular fan of Jean Froissart's thrilling *Chroniques de France et d'Angleterre*, a work he ordered as king to be translated into English. From it he learned much about the Hundred Years' War against the French – about Edward III's fabled victory at Crécy and Henry V's at Agincourt, leading in 1420 to the famous Treaty of Troyes by which Henry was to marry Princess Catherine de Valois and be recognised as heir to the French throne. All of this helped to give him something of a phobia about France as a country. While revelling in Franco-Burgundian culture and its richness, he regarded the kingdom of France, certainly the areas of northern France most recently occupied by Henry V, as part of the rightful, hereditary possessions of the kingdom of England.[6]

Where chivalry and honour were concerned, Skelton urged his young pupil to think of himself as a knight of King Arthur's Round Table. Whether he gave him Sir Thomas Malory's *Morte D'Arthur* in Caxton's monumental 1485 edition to read is uncertain, but there was in any case no need, as Henry already had access to multiple versions in manuscript of the Arthurian stories in his father's library at Richmond Palace. For an impressionable young pupil, this was the stuff of romance. According to the legends, after winning the throne with the help of his magical sword Excalibur and uniting Britain through a series of bitterly fought wars, the teenage King Arthur's first action is to marry the incomparably beautiful Guinevere. He fights the Romans when they demand tribute and, when victorious, is himself crowned emperor by the pope. Later chapters tell the stories of Sir Lancelot, Sir Tristram and Sir Galahad, showing how Lancelot becomes the greatest knight in the world, fighting battles, slaying dragons, rescuing maidens, seeking the Holy Grail and playing 'games of love' with the women of the court. He is Guinevere's favourite and champion in the lists: the final stories in the sequence chart the catastrophe of his fatal love affair with her.[7]

In 1502, when Henry was eleven, Skelton was replaced by John Holt, a brilliant Latinist and highly experienced schoolmaster steeped in the new values of the Italian Renaissance. Almost certainly it was Holt who first turned his pupil's mind towards the works of Cicero and ancient philosophy, and to the study of classical rhetoric (or the art of speaking persuasively), theology, geometry and astronomy. It would be partly thanks to his teaching that Henry, as an adult, became a keen amateur theologian and mathematician, and an ardent astronomer.[8]

Meanwhile, in the French lutenist, Gilles du Wés, the young prince had a tutor who taught music and conversational French to all the royal children for some thirty or so years. With him, Henry first tried his hand at keyboard instruments, before taking up the recorder, flute and cornet, which he studied with one 'Master Guillam', his 'schoolmaster at pipes'. As king, he presided over a court where music and dancing occupied most winter evenings. He built up a large collection of musical instruments and sought out star performers from as far away as Venice and southern Spain.[9]

Always a passionate sportsman, Henry rode, hunted and hawked, and would become an accomplished jouster. He played tennis, learned to shoot a crossbow and to pole-vault. His father, ever cautious, refused to allow him to learn how to joust until he was seventeen, and even then, only to do what was known as 'running at the ring' – to practise catching a suspended metal ring on the point of a lance while running down the lists on horseback. His grandmother, the redoubtable Margaret Beaufort, who ordered and paid for his earliest saddle and harness, came to watch him perform in the tiltyard.[10]

Henry did not study or play competitive sports by himself. When he was eight or nine, his mother recruited her chamberlain's stepson, William Blount, Lord Mountjoy, as a mentor. He was thirteen years older than Henry, but boys closer in age were brought in too: William Fitzwilliam, who spoke fluent French and was the scion of a noble family on his mother's side, arrived at the age of ten, later joined by his younger stepbrother Anthony Browne. Throughout their lives, the pair stayed close to Henry.

Elizabeth of York's nephew, Henry Courtenay, heir to the earldom of Devon, was another young recruit. The prince's cousin and 'one who hath been brought up as a child with his grace in his chamber', Courtenay would still be jousting, playing tennis and shovelboard* or throwing snowballs with Henry when they were in their twenties.[11]

A chance encounter gives us an insight into Henry's earliest priorities. Erasmus of Rotterdam, the most stellar intellectual north of the Alps, had tutored Mountjoy in Paris, and in 1499 his former pupil arranged for the great scholar to visit the prince's schoolroom, accompanied by a lawyer friend, Thomas More. Erasmus, a sound judge of character, was instantly struck by Henry's adolescent charm and 'kingly demeanour' and when, after the visit, he composed a Latin ode of 150 lines to present to him along with a dedicatory letter, he addressed him as if he – and not his brother – was heir to the throne, advising him that only heroic individuals who were also men of letters could win immortal fame. Erasmus – himself no shrinking violet – had discerned that the quest for fame would be what motivated Henry as an adult.[12]

Despite his luck at Bosworth, Henry VII's hold on the crown was shaky. That nobody knew for certain whether Elizabeth of York's two brothers were dead or how they died left an open door for disgruntled Yorkists to promote the cause of imposters. The first, Lambert Simnel, was defeated and captured before Prince Henry was born, but the second, Perkin Warbeck – who posed as Richard, Duke of York, the younger of the two missing princes in the Tower – proved more threatening. To counter Warbeck's claims, Henry VII knighted the three-year-old Prince Henry, declared him to be the 'true' Duke of York and conferred on him the offices of Lord-Lieutenant of Ireland and Warden of the Scottish Marches. But Warbeck could be bewitchingly persuasive, and his supporters infiltrated the king's inner circle. So great was

---

*A game in which a coin or other disc is driven by a blow with the hand along a highly polished board, floor or table (sometimes ten yards or longer) marked with transverse lines.

the danger that, during the Cornish Rebellion in June 1497, when Henry was six, his mother rushed him and his terrified sisters to their grandmother's house in London, then to the safety of the innermost ward of the Tower for five days – a crisis that ended only when Warbeck paid for his ambition with his head. That no king could be complacent about dynastic security was a chilling lesson for the pampered prince. He would never forget it.[13]

Prince Arthur's marriage in 1501 offered his brother a chance to steal the limelight. When searching for a wife for his elder son, his father turned to Spain, choosing Katherine, the youngest daughter of Queen Isabella I of Castile and King Ferdinand II of Aragon. For Henry VII, such a marriage brought prestige and legitimacy to his fledgling regime and a ready-made ally against both France and future imposters. What made Ferdinand and Isabella doubly attractive to their contemporaries, if not to us, was their 'Crusade for the Catholic faith' to expel Muslim Moors and Jews from their country. Katherine had been on campaign with her parents while scarcely more than a babe in arms. At the age of six, she was with them when they defeated Abu Abdallah Muhammad XII, the last Nasrid ruler of Granada, and made their triumphal entry into the Alhambra, his red-walled citadel. To obtain such a bride for Arthur was a major coup, especially as Katherine came with a generous dowry.

Once Katherine was fifteen, her parents decided that she was old enough to begin her new life. Central to the celebrations, which began soon after she landed at Plymouth, was the ten-year-old Henry. Here was no self-effacing younger son, but a needy extrovert striding across his brother's stage. In arrangements masterminded by Bishop Richard Fox, Katherine was escorted from Kingston upon Thames to St George's Fields in Southwark by Edward Stafford, Duke of Buckingham. But it was Prince Henry's task to accompany her when she entered the city of London.[14] It was the first time he met the woman he would himself later marry.

On Friday 12 November 1501, the young Henry led Katherine 'in the most royal wise' over London Bridge and through the streets of the capital.[15] Riding confidently at her right hand, he waved to the crowds, stopping every so often to admire the carefully choreographed tableaux which the citizens laid on. It entirely eluded him that the people were marvelling at Katherine, not him; praising her for her soft, 'sweet' face and yielding lips and for her composure and refinement as she rode perched uncomfortably on a mule with her fair hair hanging down about her shoulders. Like her elder sister Juana, with whom her portraits are often confused, Katherine's nose was long and straight, her blue eyes large, deep and soulful, her mouth an almost perfect cupid's bow, her fingers slim and delicate. She had stage presence, and Thomas More found her entrancing: 'Take my word for it,' he said, 'she thrilled the hearts of everyone. She possesses all those qualities that make for beauty in a very charming young girl.'[16]

The following Sunday brought Henry another task: to escort Katherine into a packed St Paul's Cathedral for her wedding.[17] Then, after the marriage, he attended the nuptial Mass in the sanctuary, before walking Katherine back to the bishop's palace across the churchyard and to the threshold of the bridal chamber, where Arthur awaited her. Amongst those watching as the couple were ceremonially 'put to bed' was the twenty-eight-year-old William Thomas, one of the grooms of Arthur's privy chamber whose tasks included helping their master to dress and undress and guarding him at night.[18]

Henry was too young to compete in the 'jousts royal' which shortly followed. He was restricted to watching from the cloth-of-gold-draped stands as the Duke of Buckingham took centre-stage as 'challenger' in the lists, and as a seventeen-year-old esquire, Charles Brandon, who would soon become young Henry's closest friend, held everyone in thrall. Brandon was hearty and sensual, rough of speech and a known lady-killer. Before long, he would be promising to marry Elizabeth of York's maid, getting her pregnant, then ditching her in favour of his own widowed aunt, only to asset-strip her lands and have their marriage annulled.[19]

But once the jousting was over, it was Prince Henry whose appearance hit the headlines. At the masque and banquet held in Westminster Hall, he stepped forward to perform two *baas* dances with his sister Margaret. Originating in Spain and Flanders, this was one of the more fashionable dances for couples at the time. Although relatively sedate, it involved complicated steps forwards, backwards and to the side. To everyone's delight, Henry threw himself into it, casting off his gown and dancing uninhibitedly in his jacket.[20]

When, a fortnight later, the king decided that Arthur should live at Ludlow Castle on the Welsh borders so that he could take up his duties as Prince of Wales, there was lengthy, acrimonious debate over whether it was safe for Katherine to go with him. He was only fifteen, she just sixteen, and a school of thought held that too much sex while young could be hazardous. Despite such concerns, Henry VII went ahead with the move.[21]

The couple reached Ludlow in January 1502 with a baggage train of a hundred packhorses and dozens of attendants. All seemed well until the closing weeks of March, when Arthur sickened with a mystery illness. Whatever it was, possibly bubonic plague, influenza or an unidentified fever, he deteriorated rapidly, dying on 2 April.[22] Masses were said in every church in London for his soul and he was buried with all pomp in a special chapel in the Benedictine priory in Worcester (now the cathedral), near to the high altar and the tomb of King John. With his passing, Henry's life was changed for ever: now he would be king.

Arthur's death devastated his parents. We have touching descriptions of each comforting the other after they received the news, of Elizabeth of York reassuring her husband that they were young enough to have more children and of her reminder that Henry lived. He was, she is reported to have said, 'a fair, goodly, and a towardly [i.e. promising, hopeful] young Prince'.[23]

Less than a year after Arthur's death, on the night of 2 February 1503, the feast of Candlemas, Elizabeth, who was once more pregnant, 'travailed of [a] child suddenly, and was delivered of a daughter'.[24] She died soon afterwards, as did her baby. Henry agonised over his mother's death, calling it the worst event of his life. Nothing ever shook him more, he wrote some years later, than first hearing that she was gone and he would never see her again. Just an incidental, casual reference to his bereavement, he explained, could 'reopen a wound that time had begun to heal'.[25] Raised separately from his older brother, he had not been able to find grief in his heart for him, but he mourned his mother intensely. She had moulded the way in which he imagined women. Hers had been the love he wanted and the love he needed. The rest of his life would be a quest to rediscover it.

Tragedy reshaped Henry's father too: his hair whitened, his eyesight started to fail and he underwent a personality change, turning into a lean, mean, gimlet-eyed Argus, overseeing every aspect of the lives of his nobles and courtiers. As a ruler who lacked charisma and had acquired the throne largely through good fortune and the failings of others, he felt bound to stifle any possibility of deposition through chance or conspiracy.

His concern for his only surviving son became obsessive. Unlike Arthur, the new Prince of Wales was not sent to Ludlow. Shortly after he was thirteen, his father brought him from the schoolroom to live at court, where he saw for the first time the dark underbelly of politics, with underlings too venal or frightened to challenge the king even when he manifestly did wrong. When a newly arrived Spanish ambassador described the scene, he explained how the Prince of Wales was kept in an apartment 'from which there was neither an entrance nor an exit except through the chamber of the king'. He was unable to go out except through a private door that led into a park, where he was closely guarded. 'He does not speak a word except in reply to what the king asks him.'[26]

Henry now became in many respects a victim of his childhood. Still shaken by the suddenness of his mother's death, he found his father distant and domineering, bestowing trust or withdrawing approval and affection based solely on performance. It was a tense relationship, which imprinted an insatiable need for validation on the young Henry's psyche, along with an anxiety that whatever he achieved, it would never be enough.

Henry VII's visibly declining health encouraged courtiers privately to speculate on the succession. When he lay sick for several weeks at Wanstead, it was said in the garrison in Calais, the last of England's Continental possessions and an important trading gateway, that 'the king's grace is but a weak man and sickly, not likely to be no long-lived man.' No one spoke of the younger Henry as the next king, as if the dynasty would die with its creator.[27] Such loose talk provoked in his father a reign of terror in which the young Henry learned about the fragility of power and with it the 'shoulds' of royal rule, rather than the 'woulds'. He saw at first-hand how iron-fisted his father could be; how far he needed to be that way; how far he operated on the margins of the law while still managing to stay within it. He discovered fear to be a proven method of control: how the king's faithful apparatchiks, Richard Empson and Edmund Dudley, used spies, blackmail, perjury, threats and rapacious fines to silence opposition even where it did not exist. Anyone who crossed the older Henry would not just lose the chance of a job or peerage: the king would seek to ruin or destroy them. And it was by soaking up all these introjects that his son learned how to govern.[28]

After Arthur's death, Katherine had returned to London to convalesce. The question was what to do with her when she was recovered. The answer was plain to her parents: she should marry Prince Henry. They had been in a similar position in 1498 after the death in childbirth of their eldest daughter, Isabella, Princess of Asturias, Manuel I of Portugal's wife. To continue their alliance with Portugal, they obtained a papal dispensation to allow Manuel to marry his dead wife's younger sister, Maria. They saw no reason why the same solution could not be applied again.

Henry VII found the idea appealing. On 23 June 1503, a revised marriage treaty was agreed and he organised what in many eyes passed for a wedding between Katherine and his son.[29] Except this was a sham. Despite having almost all the elements of a true marriage, it lacked the crucial one: it was not to be consummated on the grounds that the young prince was still below the age of consent, which by church law was fourteen for a boy and twelve for a girl. The canny king did it this way to extract the maximum benefit from the Spanish alliance and retain Katherine's dowry, without fully committing himself.[30]

For the wedding to be valid, a dispensation would be needed
'after the manner of the Roman curia', since church law forbade
a man from marrying his brother's widow. On 26 December 1503,
Pope Julius II issued a holding document known as a 'Brief' to
reassure Katherine's reputedly dying mother that a suitably worded
dispensation would soon be forthcoming. For reasons of speed and
convenience, it said that Katherine and Arthur's marriage had been
fully consummated. In reply, Ferdinand raised objections based on
information sent to Spain by Katherine's chief gentlewoman, and
so the bull of dispensation, when it finally arrived, had the word
forsan ('perhaps') inserted, making it a fudge: the notion that the
marriage had only been 'perhaps consummated' left the matter
ambiguous.[31]

But, with Queen Isabella ailing, Henry VII did not intend to
persist with the marriage of his only surviving son to Katherine
if he thought Spain might break apart. He was wise because the
union of the crowns of Aragon and Castile was only personal. When
Isabella died in November 1504, Spain was thrown into confusion.
Ferdinand's title as King Consort of Castile lapsed and he became
merely the acting governor of that kingdom. Isabella's heir in
Castile was Juana, Katherine's elder sister, wife of the vain, coercive,
philandering Philip the Handsome, Duke of Burgundy. The son of
the Habsburg Maximilian I, King of the Romans and soon to be
Holy Roman Emperor, Philip ruled the so-called 'Low Countries',
the rump of the territories once possessed by Charles the Bold from
1467 to 1477, before Louis XI of France's annexations. Straddling
boundaries, these lands comprised parts of north-east France and
most of what we think of today as the Netherlands, Belgium and
Luxembourg.

Ferdinand had no living son, so Isabella's death set in motion a
struggle for the Spanish succession. Until that was resolved, Henry
VII meant to leave open the choice of his son's future bride.[32] So
it was that Prince Henry – on the eve of his fourteenth birthday –
summoned a notary and read out a solemn protest, declaring that
he had entered the marriage contract while still underage, and so
was not bound by its conditions, rendering it 'null and void'.[33]

Katherine took this badly. 'No woman, of whatever station in life,' she complained to her father, 'can have suffered more than I have. None of the promises made to me on my marriage have been kept.'[34]

Her pleas went unheard. Dynastic security was Henry VII's overriding concern. Soon after Katherine arrived in England, Edmund de la Pole, Elizabeth of York's cousin, had fled abroad and Henry wanted him back. His opportunity came in January 1506, when Philip and Juana set off by sea from the Low Countries to claim their Castilian inheritance, leaving their children, notably their five-year-old son and heir, Prince Charles of Ghent, to be brought up by his aunt, Margaret of Austria. By then, de la Pole was under Philip's protection. When a violent storm drove Philip's ship to seek shelter off the Dorset coast near Weymouth, Henry VII enticed the Burgundians ashore, showered them with gifts and hospitality at Windsor Castle, and in return Philip agreed to extradite de la Pole on condition the English king solemnly swore that his life would be spared. There followed a treaty on trade and an exchange of orders of chivalry during which Philip created the fourteen-year-old Prince Henry a Knight of the Golden Fleece.[35]

The young Henry shadowed Philip throughout his stay. The duke was his godfather, so it was natural that the two should spend time together. Sent to Winchester to welcome him on his journey to Windsor, Henry took him to the great hall of the Norman castle, where he proudly showed him the massive round wooden disc believed to be the original Round Table of King Arthur and his Knights, which as king he would have repainted.[36] The twenty-seven-year-old Philip was a fine sportsman, and his godson was visibly in awe of him, treating him as the father he had always really wanted. Twenty years later, he continued to rhapsodise about him, telling the Spanish ambassador: 'I still have his portrait in one of my rooms called Philip's room, which I like more than the others in my palace, not just because of its name, but because I was his godson.' It was something he never forgot and in the last months of his life, Henry would still be purchasing 'perfumes for Duke Philip's chamber'.[37]

Philip, however, would not live long after he left England: he
died of a fever within six months of arriving in Castile, making
Juana both Queen of Castile in her own right and Ferdinand's
heiress in Aragon. To secure control of Castile, Ferdinand forced
her to retreat to a convent near Burgos, and later to the castle
in Tordesillas, allowing him to rule in her place. In so doing, he
ensured that in the longer term, the heir to a united Spain was
likely to be Charles of Ghent, still in the care of his aunt Margaret,
whom Maximilian made regent of the Low Countries.[38]

In response, Henry VII tilted his diplomacy more towards
Maximilian and the emerging Habsburg dynastic complex
in Northern Europe, a move calculated in the light of wider
international developments. In 1494, the face of Europe had been
transformed when Charles VIII of France invaded Italy with a
massive army. For the next seventy-five years, Italy became the
cockpit of international politics. The Duchy of Milan, ruled by
Duke Ludovico Sforza, then claimed by Charles, and Naples, also
claimed by him but conquered by Ferdinand, were the principal
battlegrounds. Rivalry was as strong between individual Italian
cities as between them and the great powers: Florence and Pisa,
where the pickings were rich, fought each other for decades;
Venice, ideally situated on the Adriatic, powerful, envied and even
wealthier through trade in the Mediterranean and far beyond, was
a formidable ally or opponent but often the butt of attack. Added
to the mix was that the pope was both a spiritual and temporal
leader, the ruler of a great swathe of central Italy known as the Papal
States, often willing to countenance, even encourage, war. Finally,
Maximilian, although Austrian by birth, claimed rights in several
Italian cities. After Philip's death, he talked openly of driving the
French from Lombardy, and of coming to Rome or Bologna to be
crowned Holy Roman Emperor by the pope.

Pressures closer to home also played a part. No English city
or region was more commercially or politically engaged than
London, where mercantile interests tilted strongly towards the
Habsburg Low Countries. This was because the international trade
networks and banking systems of northern Europe were centred

on and around the so-called 'mart' (market) towns of Antwerp and Bergen-op-Zoom in the Low Countries, where London's Company of Merchant Adventurers won privileges to sell their cloths at the quarterly fairs. By 1500, Antwerp had consolidated its position as northern Europe's premier credit market. For centuries, English rulers had financed their wars using a mixture of short-term borrowing in Antwerp and special licences to export large quantities of unfinished English cloths for sale in the 'mart' towns without paying the usual customs duties.[39]

Keen to secure his legacy, Henry VII made proposals for fresh dynastic marriages. All hit the buffers save two: shortly after his wife's death, his elder daughter, Margaret, left Richmond Palace to begin her thirty-three-day journey to Edinburgh to marry James IV of Scotland. More spectacularly, in December 1507, he successfully arranged with Maximilian to betroth his younger daughter, Mary, to Charles of Ghent, with the wedding to take place as soon as Charles reached the age of consent. He considered this to be his crowning achievement and disbursed more than £260,000 in bribes and subsidies to the Habsburgs to accomplish it.[40]

The end for Henry VII came in 1509. His devoted mother, Margaret Beaufort, moved to be near him as he lay fatally sick at Richmond. By 31 March, he was said to be 'utterly without hope of recovery'.[41] A week later a scribe was paid for writing his last will, but he lingered on until 11 p.m. on Saturday 21 April. Worn out by the almost impossible demands he had placed upon himself, he died at just fifty-two.

Prince Henry's day had dawned.

2

Henry: Apprentice King

Henry VII's final years had been marked by a mounting wave of unease and apprehension, as if to confirm suspicions that, after all, he was a false king and a usurper. Seeking instant applause, the young Henry VIII announced a clean break with the past. He would be an 'affable' prince, the harbinger of a different kind of rule. His schoolroom mentor, Lord Mountjoy, captured the mood: 'Heaven smiles, earth rejoices, all is milk, honey and nectar. Avarice is well and truly banished. Generosity sprinkles wealth with an open hand.' Henry, he extravagantly predicted, had a passion for 'justice and honesty'. A prince blessed with almost superhuman talents, he would be the country's 'deliverer'. His reign would usher in a new Golden Age.[1]

Not everyone was convinced. Piero Pasqualigo, a Venetian granted an audience early in the reign, depicted him revelling in a life of spectacle. Arriving at Richmond in time for breakfast on St George's Day, Pasqualigo found Henry leaning against his gilded throne, wearing a mantle of thick purple velvet lined with white satin and with a train four yards long, sporting his regalia as sovereign of the Order of the Garter. 'Very close round his neck he had a gold collar, from which there hung a diamond, the size of the largest walnut I ever saw, and to this was suspended a most beautiful and very large round pearl.' His fingers were 'one mass of jewelled rings'.[2]

Henry did remedy some of the wrongs of his father's reign, but he carried out no wholesale repudiation of his methods. On his deathbed, Henry VII had granted a general pardon to those in fear of ruin from his fiscal demands. His son amplified that pardon, encouraging all those who were wronged to come forward and receive 'impartial' justice free of influence from the rich and powerful. It sounded almost too good to be true, and it was. Henry reversed a handful of his father's oppressions, but even people offered genuine relief could be burdened by fresh penalties. The Duke of Buckingham, whom Henry believed to have threatened him on his accession by asserting a hereditary right to be Lord High Constable of England (the greatest office of state, with quasi-regal powers in an emergency) had a bond for £400 cancelled but was wrongfully charged with debts exceeding £7,000 and lost a further £3,500 in expenses. Four years later, Buckingham won a legal battle over his claim to be Constable, but Henry refused to allow him to exercise functions which he said were 'very high and dangerous'.[3]

Most surprising, and most consequential, was Henry's impulsive decision to marry Katherine of Aragon, despite first 'marrying' her before, and then formally rejecting her. Somewhat evasively, he claimed at one moment that he was deeply in love, at another that he was fulfilling his father's dying wishes.[4] Six years older than he was, Katherine was never quite the mother figure, but she seemed safe and reassuring, and above all she seemed to represent the fastest way to secure the dynasty and his throne. In making his choice, Henry overruled the Archbishop of Canterbury, William Warham, who warned him that in view of his legally registered protest withdrawing from the marriage contract, the papal bull of dispensation secured by his father to overcome the prohibition on marrying his dead brother's widow might prove to be insufficient in law.[5]

The wedding took place in Elizabeth of York's private oratory. If death meant Henry's mother could not be there, he still needed to feel her presence. The ceremony was a low-key affair with just a handful of witnesses. Did Henry have scruples of conscience over marrying his brother's widow? If so, he dismissed them at the time. His father had drilled into him the harsh 'shoulds' of royal rule: monarchies and dynasties are not built on virtue or reputation alone. They are rooted in families, marriages and the birth of legitimate heirs and successors. Only when the new king had fathered children of his own might it be said that the dynasty was safe. Katherine was royal, available and the terms of her dowry had long been agreed, but for Henry to claim, as he did, that she had swept him off his feet romantically after months and years in which he had ignored her was an illusion, a sign of his ability to deceive himself when it suited him to do so.[6]

For her part, Katherine had set her mind on marrying Henry ever since her parents first suggested it after Arthur's death. She considered a royal marriage to be her destiny, and having achieved it, she would never willingly relinquish it. She too professed herself smitten, loving her new husband 'much more', she declared, than herself.[7]

In November 1509, Henry appointed an almoner, a specialised chaplain to assist him with his prayers and oversee his charitable gifts. This was Thomas Wolsey, an urbane, artful, ingratiating, nimble, masterfully efficient genius some twenty years the king's senior, who did what he could to train him in the art of kingship. Overcoming his humble origins as an Ipswich butcher's son, Wolsey had studied at Magdalen College, Oxford. Graduating as a Bachelor of Arts aged fifteen, he was elected, in 1497, a Fellow and later Bursar of the college, but was severely criticised for (allegedly) overspending on the building works that ensured the completion of Magdalen tower. Ordained a priest in 1498, he acquired several parish benefices, before becoming a chaplain to Henry VII. Suitably impressed by his abilities, the king had sent him on missions to Scotland and the Low Countries, where his efforts secured his early promotion to the deaneries of Lincoln and Hereford.

As the king's almoner, Wolsey now was attached to the Chapel Royal. Besides hearing Henry's confession and saying Mass, he sat as a junior councillor, mainly sorting and hearing petitions, but often joining in more important discussions of policy. He rose rapidly in favour, outclassing all potential rivals. His gentleman-usher and earliest biographer, George Cavendish, reports in his *Life of Wolsey*, written in the 1550s, that of all the councillors, the almoner was the 'most earnest and readiest ... to advance the king's only will and pleasure without any respect to the case. The king therefore perceived him to be a meet instrument for the accomplishment of his devised will and pleasure.'[8]

Wolsey, says Cavendish, had no guiding political principles. Instead, he taught Henry how to use war, balance-of-power politics and peace in any combination. What he most had to offer was a will to serve the king and to succeed, coupled with 'a special gift of natural eloquence with a filed tongue to pronounce the same'. By this and other means, 'he was able with the same to persuade and allure all men to his purpose.' His influence was pervasive. As Polydore Vergil, a resident papal tax-collector and reliable eyewitness, noted:

> Every time he wished to obtain something from Henry, he introduced the matter casually into his conversation; then he brought out some small present or another ... and while the king was admiring the gift intently, Wolsey would adroitly bring forward the project on which his mind was fixed.[9]

With his almoner always on hand, the young Henry could indulge himself doing what he liked best. A song he composed around this time begins:

> Pastime with good company,
> I love and shall until I die.
> Grudge who list but none deny,
> So God be pleased, thus live will I.
> For my pastance:
> Hunt sing and dance.
> My heart is set.
> All goodly sport
> For my comfort.
> Who shall me let [forbid]?[10]

Writing in Latin (as he spoke no Spanish and Ferdinand no English) he told his father-in-law: 'I spend most of my time enjoying myself: hawking, hunting and in other healthy recreations, and in jousting, tourneying and other honourable sports, and all the while travelling around and taking stock of my kingdom.'[11] He insisted that he would not 'neglect affairs of state', but this was very much an afterthought. When his older, wiser councillors tried to restrain him, he brushed aside their pleas: a pattern was taking shape as he showered gifts and rewards on his friends, paid for from his father's coffers.

All was not benign. To help feed his hunger for popularity, Henry had Empson and Dudley arrested, putting his father's agents on trial on trumped-up treason charges, then locking them away in the Tower while he worked out whether they could be useful to him or not. By August 1510, the torrent of complaints against them had turned into a tsunami. Abdicating responsibility for their actions, Henry had the pair beheaded while he rode out hunting.[12] Taking the blame when things went wrong was never on his agenda.

In these early years, Katherine did her best to assume an English identity, but it never fully worked. While still with her parents in Spain, she had signed herself 'Catalina' with a 'C'. After marrying Henry, she changed this in her Spanish letters to 'Katherina' and in English ones to 'Katherine' with a 'K', or sometimes just 'La Reyna'.[13] She had herself painted wearing a gold pendant in the shape of the letter 'K'. She did her best to learn English, but always spoke it haltingly and was most at ease when surrounded by her loyal Spanish gentlewomen. She also tried to position herself politically as a champion for Spain, her father's secret weapon in his diplomacy. Since her arrival in England, she had been in constant, often meticulously ciphered communication with him.[14] Her most trusted confidants were those who arrived with her from Spain and, perhaps most of all, Fray Diego Fernández, her Catholic confessor, with whom she prayed every day.[15]

On New Year's Day, 1511, it looked as though her prayers had been answered when she gave birth to a boy at Richmond. Henry, overwhelmed with joy, set out at once to offer his thanks at the

shrine of Our Lady at Walsingham in Norfolk, a round trip of
about 200 miles and the first of at least three pilgrimages he would
make over the next ten years.[16] The baby, named Henry after his
father and grandfather, was baptised in the Franciscan friary church
at Richmond, with Margaret of Austria a godparent, represented at
the ceremony by a proxy.

For seven whole weeks, the country rejoiced, with services of
praise and thanksgiving to God in the churches, civic bonfires
and free wine. Following tradition, Henry organised a two-day
tournament in the child's honour, sparing no expense. He led
the 'challengers' dressed as 'Loyal Heart', with his young friends,
notably Charles Brandon, among the 'answerers', while Katherine
sat watching him fondly. On the evening of the second day came
pageants, music and dancing and a banquet, for nothing would be
too good for Henry's son. There was even a magnanimous response
when an unruly mob broke through a safety cordon and rushed
in to snatch the solid gold 'H' and 'K' badges which adorned the
stunningly clad courtiers. One man managed to sell his loot for
£4, more than most artisans could earn in a year and enough to
purchase two acres of meadow.[17]

Henry's rapture would be short-lived. Just fifty-two days after
the birth, little Prince Henry fell sick and died at Richmond.
Katherine came from stern stock – her mother Isabella had greeted
the death of her only son by stating stoically that 'the Lord hath
given, and the Lord hath taken away.'[18] All the same, the pain was
severe. Experiencing his own grief, but manfully suppressing it, as
he claimed, for his wife's sake, all that Henry could do was to give
his son a princely funeral.[19]

Over the years, visiting diplomats picked up hints of Katherine's
later pregnancies.[20] In 1513 she was pregnant again, but in September
or October she was delivered of a premature son who died within
hours; another boy was stillborn in November or December 1514;
other children would be lost in 1515, 1517 and 1518.[21]

Henry assumed his wife's gynaecological difficulties to be her
fault. However, two modern medical experts believe the cause was
blood group incompatibility. Katherine's pregnancy misfortunes fit

the symptoms of haemolytic disease of the new-born, caused by a genetic mismatch between the blood groups of the parents. If one of them was positive for an antigen known as Kell, while the other was negative, then a couple could very rarely produce more than a single living child. Henry would have been responsible for the couple's problems if he were positive and Katherine – like 90 per cent of Caucasian populations – was negative. That is a persuasive theory, since Katherine's sisters filled their nurseries with ease. Whether it casts light on Henry's reproductive history more generally is not a question that can be answered in the present state of knowledge.[22]

About four o'clock in the morning on Tuesday 18 February 1516, to the royal couple's considerable relief, the queen produced a healthy daughter christened Mary. Katherine rejoiced, as did Henry, telling the Venetian ambassador that 'if it was a daughter this time, by the grace of God the sons will follow' since he and his queen were 'still young' – he was rising twenty-five and she was thirty.[23]

But if settling the succession was critical for Henry, so was securing his place on the international stage, which is where Wolsey took the lead, eclipsing Katherine. After his coronation, Henry swore to wage war on France as soon as the opportunity arose. On greeting a special French ambassador who said he wished to renew the existing peace, and that he made his request in response to a letter from one of the king's senior councillors, Henry stormed, 'Who wrote this letter? Should I ask peace of the king of France, who dare not look me in the face, still less make war on me?'[24] His older, more seasoned advisers, notably Warham, advocated peace, whereas young bloods like Charles Brandon and the king's 'groom of the stool' (chief personal body-servant) William Compton, urged him to fight.

With all the ardour of youth, Henry dreamed of emulating Henry V by leading his army in battle to claim the French throne.[25] This was in tune with the mood of his subjects. And there is more. Already aware of the significance of Italy in international affairs, and especially of the crucial role of Julius II as a military leader, he declared himself to be 'the pope's good son'. This was more than canny self-presentation: he really meant it. From an early age, he had coveted a papally conferred title such as 'Protector of the Holy See' to match the French king's 'Most Christian King', and in reward for his devotion, Julius sent him a consecrated Golden Rose (a papal honour) at Easter 1510, soon followed by 100 Parmesan cheeses and barrels of wine. Henry reciprocated by sending Cornish tin for roofing works at the pope's new basilica of St Peter's in Rome, then under construction.[26]

Henry's war strategy first emerged when Louis XII of France threatened Julius. With French armies occupying much of northern Italy and poised to invade the Papal States, Julius, better known as the 'warrior pope', began organising a Holy League of European powers to force them back. When Louis replied by renouncing his ties with the pope and convoking a schismatic General Council of the Church in Pisa to depose him, Henry was scandalised: he could not stand idly by if the Catholic faith was endangered.[27]

Julius was driven from Bologna in May 1511, but by October the Holy League was in place. Henry and Ferdinand were jointly to invade Aquitaine from the south; papal forces were to recover the Emilia-Romagna; Maximilian was to occupy Verona, and with the Swiss and Venetians expel the French from Lombardy. When the League's army suffered a humiliating defeat on Easter Sunday 1512, Wolsey sent 10,000 troops to Aquitaine and a flotilla of eighteen ships to pillage the coast of Brittany. The invasion of Aquitaine failed after Ferdinand backed out, but the League, overall, achieved its purpose, since its operations compelled Louis to return to France.[28]

Over the ensuing winter, Henry decided to intensify the war and fulfil his adolescent dreams by leading his 'army royal' into battle in a full-scale invasion of northern France. Wolsey masterminded the deployment of troops, military equipment and victualling, winning rapid promotion. Within a year, the archbishopric of York would fall vacant and he was elected. He became Dean of York, then Bishop of Lincoln. Soon afterwards, Henry began lobbying the Vatican to make him a cardinal. That would finally be secured in September 1515, after which Henry appointed him as his Lord

Chancellor and chief minister. So complete would his influence become that Richard Pace, one of Henry's secretaries, described him as *quasi alter deus* ('almost another God') and as *alter rex* ('second king'), soubriquets that stuck.[29]

In the spring of 1513, Henry had several more decisions to make before he left to invade France. One was to have Edmund de la Pole, held in the Tower ever since his extradition, summarily executed – this despite Henry VII's promise to keep him alive. Another was to appoint Katherine as regent while he was abroad. In theory, he gave her huge powers, but he was unsure whether he trusted in her ability enough and so, to her dismay, named a group of senior councillors to oversee her. He put Thomas Howard, Earl of Surrey, in command of such forces as he left behind, in case James IV of Scotland took advantage of his departure: despite Henry's elder sister's marriage to James, relations with Scotland remained tense. Howard had backed the wrong side at the Battle of Bosworth, but with the young king's accession, he successfully rehabilitated himself.

On 13 June, Henry landed in Calais, gloriously arrayed in his newly commissioned, jewel-encrusted battle armour, then rode into Artois at the head of 30,000 men, a larger number than Henry V had led across the Channel. The moment was opportune. By now, Julius had died and been replaced as pope by the much younger, less belligerent Leo X, which emboldened the main French army to cross the Alps again and overrun much of the Duchy of Milan. Their success would be brief. Routed by the Swiss, they could not regroup and return home in time to pose a serious threat to Henry.

Within a fortnight, Henry's vanguard had marched forty miles to reach the walls of Thérouanne, a fortress town near the frontier of the Low Countries, where after delays caused by heavy rain, an artillery bombardment began. The arrival of Maximilian's allied forces gave fresh impetus to the siege, but serious progress was made only when Henry arrived with his main battle army and blocked the town's supply lines. On the morning of 16 August, a French relief column was surprised and took flight at such a pace that the skirmish was called the 'Battle of the Spurs'. Henry regarded it as a famous victory, even though he personally missed the main action. A week later the town surrendered.

Flushed with success, Henry and Maximilian went together to inspect the fortress and discuss its fate. They found few buildings of any note beside the cathedral, and had the English decided to retain possession, they would have had to maintain a large garrison. It was far simpler to destroy the place, a decision greeted with hearty approval from Maximilian as it had long been a thorn in his side. After making a triumphal entry into the town, Henry handed it over to Maximilian, who razed it to the ground. Only the cathedral and adjacent houses of the clergy were spared.[30]

Flushed with success, Henry ordered his main battle army to march some seventy miles east towards Tournai, another frontier city and a second gateway to the Low Countries, while he and Maximilian diverted to Lille. Henry entered Lille on his warhorse, attended by his nobles and 200 men-at-arms. A delegation of citizens presented the keys of the gates to him, after which in the first of three face-to-face meetings in these weeks, Margaret of Austria and her ladies entertained the visitors in festivities lasting for several days. On the first night, Henry flaunted his musical talents, singing and playing on the flute and the cornet, before casting off his shoes and dancing in his jacket, just as he had at Prince Arthur's wedding banquet. He then started to flirt, beginning with Marine de Bourgogne, known as 'Madame the Bastard', the natural daughter of a Portuguese noblewoman. Once done with her, he whispered 'sweet nothings' (*belles choses*) and 'other blandishments' (*paroles*)* to another of Margaret's women, Étienne de la Baume, promising her a substantial dowry when she married.[31]

News then arrived from Katherine that the Scots had indeed tried to move against England in Henry's absence, but that Surrey had routed an invading Scots army at the Battle of Flodden, near Branxton in Northumberland – a fearful, bloody encounter lasting

---

*The usage here masks a sexual innuendo as in the phrase *donner paroles*, by which a suitor in the game of courtly love 'offers service' to a mistress.

until after dusk, which left James IV and the bulk of his nobility lying dead upon the field. As tangible, vivid proof, Katherine sent her husband the bloodstained coat of the slain Scottish king as a trophy. Rashly, she ranked this victory above Henry's. Writing to him for the first time in her own hand, and in English, she declared, 'To my thinking, this battle hath been to your grace and all your realm the greatest honour that could be, and more than ye should win all the crown of France.' Wisely, she claimed no personal credit. 'Thanked be God of it,' she insisted, even though, far from letting her husband's councillors take the lead, she had mobilised a reserve force of 40,000 men and was marching north with it in case Surrey's army was defeated, for this was her war too.[32]

In Tournai, the beleaguered citizens appealed to Margaret of Austria to intercede for them. They knew she was conflicted, because the city – a prosperous trading centre, renowned for its fine tapestries and wines, and strategically positioned, boasting fine bridges across the Scheldt – was culturally Flemish and claimed by Maximilian. Margaret did her best to avoid bloodshed, but Henry refused to listen. According to the well-informed Burgundian chronicler, Robert Marquéreau, he was deeply affronted by what he claimed were libellous ballads and songs lampooning him, which emanated from the city. 'With God's help,' he declared, 'I'll avenge these lies and insults.' One of these satires, a slight on his lineage, especially enraged him. Turning animatedly to Margaret in the council of war, he ordered her to be silent, then stalked out of the council chamber.[33]

After inspecting the double walls of Tournai with their ninety-five towers and seven thick gatehouses, Henry ordered his troops to take up their positions. On 16 September, the bombardment began. For all its fortifications, the city lacked a professional garrison and the walls were no match for Henry's siege guns. With their supplies low and communications severed, the citizens chose to surrender. Wolsey offered a parlay, at which he made plain that, this time, there was no question of destroying the place or surrendering it to Maximilian. Henry was the lawful king of France: Tournai was part of his dominions and must yield to him. After further talks, the matter was settled. On Sunday 25 September, ten days after inspecting his troops, Henry made his *entrée royale* into Tournai.[34]

Maximilian reappeared shortly afterwards, soon to be joined by Margaret, who brought Prince Charles of Ghent, and stayed for ten days. After attending Mass together, Henry and Maximilian agreed that Charles's wedding to Henry's younger sister Mary should take place in Calais before 15 May next, and that after the nuptials, Maximilian should declare Charles to be old enough to succeed to his inheritance. The thirteen-year-old Charles then joined Maximilian and Henry at 'jousts royal', staged by the English in pouring rain.

In the tiltyard, Henry and Charles Brandon charged all comers, and 'upon the king attended twenty-four knights on foot in coats of purple velvet and cloth of gold.' The impresario of the tournament was Sir Thomas Boleyn, who received the huge sum of £40 (over £40,000 in modern values) for his services. A banquet followed with a hundred separate dishes, accompanied by music, dancing and indoor pageants on courtly themes.[35]

Watching from the sidelines was Boleyn's twelve- or thirteen-year-old daughter Anne, one of Margaret of Austria's maids of honour, whom her father had sent to join her court in Mechelen and who had also been in Lille when Henry and Maximilian arrived there after the fall of Thérouanne. This must have been the first time Henry saw her, but it is unlikely that he even glanced in her direction as he was far too busy flirting with the older women and hoovering up the attention he believed was rightfully his as a conquering hero.

3

Anne: Childhood and Adolescence

Anne Boleyn was born to marry upwards. She came from a family keen to better themselves by gaining wealth and status, one which understood the multi-generational nature of building a dynasty. Geoffrey Boleyn the elder, her great-great-grandfather, had lowly origins, but prospered sufficiently in the textile industries in Salle, eight miles west of Blickling, near Aylsham in Norfolk, to be able to marry Alice Bracton, an heiress. Geoffrey placed his first-born son, another Geoffrey, as an apprentice with a London hatter and sent his second son, Thomas, to study at Gonville Hall in Cambridge, where he was elected first a Fellow, then Master.[1] The younger Geoffrey won fame and fortune in trade, rising to become a leading member of London's Mercers' Company, the oldest and most prestigious of the civic livery guilds. In 1453, he threw a lavish supper at his fine mansion close to Cheapside in an opening bid to become Lord Mayor. He made his first fortune as a wholesaler selling English cloths in the Flemish 'mart' towns, using the profits to purchase silk, velvet, pepper and other luxury goods for resale at home. Soon he was able to focus less on everyday trading and concentrate on making a second, larger fortune as a banker, extending credit and mortgages to courtiers, nobles and fellow merchants, buying and selling bills of exchange and taking on the debts of the Genoese mercantile community in London whom he charged interest at the punitive rate of 14 per cent.[2]

The great leap forward – legendary in the family – was Geoffrey's second marriage. After the death of his first wife, Denise, sometime before 1448, his great wealth made him eligible to marry Lady Anne Hoo, the eldest daughter and co-heir of Sir Thomas Hoo, who had fought bravely in the Hundred Years' War and was ennobled as Lord Hoo and Hastings. A man with large estates in Bedfordshire and Norfolk, Hoo was a favourite of Henry VI, as well connected to the royal court as anyone in the age of the Wars of the Roses. By this marriage, Anne's great-grandfather took the Boleyns to a more exalted level in society. No longer were they simply merchants who aspired to be landowners.

Geoffrey was chosen as a member of Parliament for London in 1449 and as Lord Mayor in 1457, when he was also knighted. Already he was investing heavily in land, which he knew to be the currency of power, and purchased the manor of Blickling from the ailing Sir John Fastolf in 1452. A veteran of the Battle of Agincourt whose name, suitably amended, Shakespeare borrowed for his comic hero in *Henry IV*, Fastolf sold at a loss on condition Anne's great-grandfather granted him a generous annuity to boost the price. Boleyn gambled on Fastolf's early death and lost: Sir John lived until 1459, dying just as the Wars of the Roses took a turn for the worse.[3]

The manor house had been built in the 1380s or 1390s by Sir Nicholas Dagworth, who died in 1401 and is commemorated by a fine memorial brass in St Andrew's parish church in Blickling, little more than a stone's throw away. Fastolf does not seem to have improved the property greatly, as he lived chiefly at Caister Castle or in his other houses in Norwich and Southwark. By the time he decided to sell, the house was a castellated dwelling of modest size surrounded by a moat, built largely of timber-framed construction infilled with brick around a rectangular courtyard.[4]

Fastolf declined to sell Boleyn the manor of Guyton, six miles north-west of Blickling, despite having promised to do so, probably because of ill-feeling caused by Boleyn's late payments of the annuity. Anne's great-grandfather made a further attempt to purchase Guyton from Fastolf's executors in 1460 but failed again.

Instead, early the next year, and for an undisclosed amount, he and others acting as a syndicate purchased the manor of Hever, near Sevenoaks in Kent, complete with its idyllic rolling estates and other lands in the parishes of Hever and Chiddingstone. The seller was Sir William Fiennes, Lord Say and Sele, and Geoffrey Boleyn had the inside track on the deal as an existing trustee of the Say and Sele estates. He took for himself the manor of Hever, and by the time the purchasers gained possession of their properties, Edward IV had become king. Geoffrey acquired other houses in Sussex, Norfolk, Kent and London, but it was Blickling that Anne's great-grandfather chose to make his home.[5]

Geoffrey Boleyn and Anne Hoo had two sons, Thomas and William, and three daughters, Alice, Isabel and Anne. Thomas died in his early twenties, leaving William to inherit his father's estates, including Blickling and Hever.[6] Geoffrey died in 1463 and was buried with considerable pomp in the church of St Lawrence Jewry, close to his London mansion. He was munificent in death, leaving his widow a large cash sum and his daughters 1,000 marks (£666) each for a dowry; £100 went to the parish of St Lawrence Jewry and £20 to Blickling church. He earmarked funds to feed prisoners in London, for leper houses, for the 'sick and feeble' in hospitals throughout the city and for poor widows. He left money to support a divinity scholar in Cambridge, always providing he studied and preached, and paid a priest a salary to say Masses quarterly for his soul for twenty years and to spend the rest of his time teaching or 'preaching the word of God'. The residue of his estate was for the relief of the poor, for setting up schools for children, and for 'other works and deeds of mercy and piety'. In all, his charitable bequests approached £1,000 (well over £1 million today).[7]

William Boleyn, Anne Boleyn's grandfather, briefly attended Lincoln's Inn and joined the Mercers' Company. After gaining a rudimentary knowledge of commercial law, he continued his father's business in the cloth trade for a while, before winding it down and milking his position as a landowner. He too married upwards, choosing Margaret, daughter and co-heir of Thomas Butler, Earl of Ormond, a wealthy Anglo-Irish peer. In or about 1475, they began their life together at Blickling and had ten children, six boys and four girls. Their eldest son was Queen Anne Boleyn's father, Thomas, born in 1477. Other sons included James and Edward, who were knighted and served on the fringes of the Tudor courts until Anne rose to prominence, when James's fortunes changed. Their daughters all married well: the eldest, another Anne, wed Sir John Shelton, a Norfolk landowner from the village of Shelton, some ten miles south of Norwich, and two of their daughters would later play crucial roles in the Boleyn story.[8]

William's marriage to Margaret Butler was a matrimonial coup of the first order. At the outset, it did not quite look that way since her father had backed the losing side at the Battle of Towton in 1461. Full rehabilitation came only after Bosworth, when Ormond received a pardon and Elizabeth of York made him her chamberlain. With his title and lands fully restored, Ormond settled down largely in Essex, where his properties included New Hall, near Boreham, and Rochford Hall, near Leigh-on-Sea. In 1491 he acquired a licence to renovate and crenellate New Hall and create a deer park of 1,000 acres.[9]

William Boleyn was never shy to mix business with family. After marrying Margaret Butler, he lent money to his father-in-law to settle his debts, investing in his own future by gaining control of portions of Ormond's English estates. And he repeated these tactics with members of his mother's family. In a series of murky transactions, he anticipated the extinction of the Hoo male bloodline, taking over the valuable manor of Luton Hoo in Bedfordshire in 1484. This defied the law, because it was not until 1486, when Lord Hoo's half-brother Thomas died, that the Boleyns' right of inheritance came into effect.[10]

William also learned to play the courtier. In 1483 Richard III had made him a Knight of the Bath, but he quickly adjusted to the new Tudor regime after Bosworth. In 1494 he attended the young Prince Henry's creation as Duke of York; in 1501, he was among those stationed alongside the prince in St George's Fields in Southwark to greet Katherine of Aragon on her arrival from Spain.[11]

Thomas Boleyn, Anne's father, went considerably further. Born and brought up at Blickling, he too briefly studied law before arriving on the national stage, aged twenty, when he took up arms with his father against the Cornish rebels. In or about this time, he married the beautiful Elizabeth Howard, the Earl of Surrey's eldest daughter by his first wife, Elizabeth Tylney. Since the Howards ranked among the country's most important old nobility, it was another extraordinary match. The downside was that the bride came with a minimal dowry, an expensive deficiency the Boleyns had to remedy for themselves.[12] Almost certainly the couple were married by 1498, for on 22 August that year, the anniversary of Bosworth, Henry VII, who was travelling through Norfolk on a royal progress (a summer break involving hunting and visiting, in which a court slimmed down by half or more moved from place to place in easy stages), spent the night at 'Mr Boleings', meaning Blickling. A royal visit, even just for one night, was a signal honour: that the host was Thomas can be deduced from the fact that his father was known as 'Sir William', not 'Mr' Boleyn.[13]

Once Thomas was married, his father surrendered Blickling to him and moved to Luton Hoo. But without the family's former income from trade to rely on, Thomas struggled financially and had to borrow in London.[14] As he afterwards explained, 'When I married my wife, I had but fifty pounds [a year] to live on for me and my wife as long as my father lived.'[15] He did not let this stop him. In 1501 Thomas and Elizabeth attended Prince Arthur's wedding. Two years later, Thomas joined the Earl of Surrey's retinue escorting Henry VII's daughter Margaret to Scotland for her wedding to James IV and was an honoured guest 'at the high feast with the queen'.[16]

After Henry VIII's accession, Thomas Boleyn's infiltration of the court and access to the benefits it brought dramatically increased. A versatile, cosmopolitan, highly talented linguist with near-perfect French and a good knowledge of art and literature, horses, hawks and bowls, he had the makings of a perfect courtier. Wearing a special livery of black mourning cloth, he joined Henry VII's funeral cortège. On the eve of the new king and Katherine's coronation, he was dubbed a Knight of the Bath and his wife, Elizabeth, was appointed one of the queen's ladies-in-waiting.[17]

He performed with great distinction as an answerer in the grand tournament celebrating the birth of little Prince Henry in 1511. And on the baby's death, he was one of the bearers accompanying the tiny, black-draped coffin as it was rowed along the Thames from Richmond and carried into Westminster Abbey.[18]

Thomas and his wife had three children while they lived at Blickling: Mary, Anne and George. Their respective birth dates, until recently, were a subject of fierce controversy among Anne's biographers. Parish registers recording dates of births, marriages and deaths were not ordered to be kept until 1538 and are seriously deficient before the 1560s. The Blickling parish registers only begin in 1559. Since 2004, the consensual view has been that Anne was the younger of the two sisters. And fresh evidence, hidden away in the library of The Queen's College, Oxford, and never previously brought to bear on the controversy, supports this reasoning (see Appendix 1). All things considered, birth dates of around 1499 for Mary, 1500 or 1501 for Anne and 1503 or 1504 for George are likely to be correct. Fortunately, there is almost complete unanimity in accepting George as the youngest Boleyn sibling.

As a baby, Anne would have been carried the short distance to Blickling church and christened in the octagonal font by the west door. Still in its place, and decorated on every side with a lion rampant, the cistern holding the holy water rests on a stone plinth flanked by four sitting lions with angel corbels above. She was brought up with her siblings in the manor house until at least 1505, although what, if anything, she remembered of those earliest years cannot be known. We might imagine her spending time with her sister, brother, mother, nurse or servants; we can speculate romantically as to whether she was led on a pony as a three-year-old around the glorious park attached to the manor house with its woods and grassy meadows stretching as far as the eye could see. What we can say with confidence is that building works were going on while she was there. With their characteristic skill with property, the Boleyns transformed the manor house into a substantial mansion with two courtyards and a long gallery. What we know best concerns the west wing, where the service rooms lay. These comprised on the ground floor a porter's lodge at the south end, two adjoining rooms towards the north, the kitchen, two larders, a pantry and washing house, and on an upper floor 'the corner chamber and ten chambers more'.[19]

In October 1505, the Boleyn children faced a sudden upheaval: their grandfather William Boleyn fell sick in Luton Hoo and was dead within a month. In his will, he specified that Thomas Boleyn, as the principal heir, should pay his mother, Margaret Butler, an annuity of 200 marks (£133), but more invasively that she was 'to have her dwelling for herself and her servants convenient within the site or mansion of my said manor of Blickling'.[20] Thomas was not keen: protracted negotiations began between him and his mother that would drag on for the next seven years. In the meantime, the family upped sticks and moved to Hever.

There can be no question that, from around Christmas 1505 onwards, Anne and her siblings spent their childhood in Kent. In 1538 Thomas wrote a letter from Hever in his own inimitable scrawl stating categorically that he had lived in 'this country', meaning Kent, for thirty-three years – in other words, since 1505.[21] How popular he was in Kent is a moot point. Witness statements, admittedly taken from victims of his strict enforcement of his hunting rights, suggest that the new master of Hever was seen as a man of 'some extremity' and 'not beloved in the country'.[22] His critics claimed 'He had no love of the country neither' – whether that meant his heart had stayed in Norfolk or just that he was intolerant of the traditional latitude granted to Kentish poachers is left ambiguous.[23]

Hever was – and still is – a visually stunning, relatively compact moated castle dating back to the fourteenth century, nestling in the heavily wooded Weald of Kent. The building's interior had been left to rot by the Fiennes family, requiring the Boleyns to undertake renovations. By the time Anne arrived, the original layout of the square keep and the footprint of the medieval hall, gatehouse, kitchen and scullery were little changed. A fireplace and windows had been inserted in the hall, which was foreshortened to make space for a parlour beyond the screens passage. Elsewhere, separate, more comfortable living rooms were carved out. A gallery was contrived, accessed by a staircase, by the simple expedient of giving a ceiling to the hall and other rooms on the north side of the keep and making use of the roof space above. Barns and outbuildings were constructed outside the moat, to provide stabling and servants' quarters. Of the three original portcullises, two still stand today. However, the present-day drawbridge of stout old English oak, which appears to be medieval, is in fact modern: it replaces a utilitarian brick bridge used in the eighteenth and nineteenth centuries, which itself replaced an older wooden drawbridge.[24]

We can identify several local families with whom the Boleyns were connected when Anne was a child.[25] The roster begins with the Isleys of Sundridge and the Wilshires of Stone Castle, near Dartford, an old Norman seat on rising ground a short distance from the high road from London to Dover. Thomas Isley of Sundridge, the father of ten sons and three daughters, lived a mere eight miles from Hever, and with Anne's father was notably active as a magistrate.[26] He rarely ventured out of his home county other than to consult his lawyers, unlike Sir John Wilshire, who was regularly absent in Calais where he was comptroller, leaving his wife Margaret and daughter Bridget behind in Stone. Although Bridget was at least ten years older than the Boleyn siblings, she came to know them to the point where Anne could later say that 'next mine own mother, I know no woman alive that I love better.'[27] When Sir John fell mortally ill in 1526 and was preparing his tomb in St Botolph's church by Aldgate in London, he appointed Anne's father as the overseer of his will. As a testimony to their friendship, he bequeathed him a precious ring 'which I have duly worn of long continuance'.[28]

Others from the Boleyns' social network were the Cheynes of Shurland on the Isle of Sheppey and the Brookes of Cobham, near Gravesend, and Cooling Castle, near Rochester. In both cases, the families had kinship ties. Recently the link to the Cheynes has been disputed, but an inscription on Anne's great-aunt Isabel's memorial brass in Blickling church proves that she married 'William Cheyne, Esquire, of the Isle of Sheppey in the County of Kent' as his first wife.[29] Thomas Brooke, who became 8th Lord Cobham and for much of the time was the only resident peer in Kent, was the son-in-law of Anne's great-aunt Anne Heydon.[30] Whether Anne was ever invited as a child to the family's home at Cobham Hall is not documented, but she certainly got to know the Brookes later and would insist that Anne, the wife of Thomas Brooke's eldest surviving son, George, rode in her coronation procession.[31]

But it was the Wyatts of Allington Castle, some three miles north-west of Maidstone, whom the Boleyns perhaps knew best. Sir Henry Wyatt, Henry VIII's Master of the Jewels and a leading coordinator of royal finances, whose estates ran from Maidstone in the south to Gravesend in the north, had first encountered them when they still lived at Blickling. Since 1485, he had been accumulating property in Norfolk and Kent, purchasing Allington in 1492 in a run-down state and renovating it.[32] A royal councillor since 1504 and an executor of Henry VII's will, Wyatt had the closest ties to Anne's father from at least 1511, when they were jointly appointed as constable and keeper of Norwich Castle, supervising the gaol there and arranging for the transfer of prisoners to and from the assizes twice a year.[33]

In 1511, when Anne was ten or eleven, Thomas Boleyn finally reached an accord with his mother that settled in advance the disposition of such lands as she would inherit on the death of her father, the Earl of Ormond, who was now over eighty years old. Although Margaret would not lose her father for four more years, Thomas persuaded her to sign a legal agreement whereby, in exchange for a life estate in the manors of Blickling and Luton Hoo, he would inherit everything 'that comes by the death of the said Earl of Ormond', notably his two prize Essex properties, New Hall and Rochford Hall.[34]

The explanation for this thoroughly shabby arrangement is that Thomas Boleyn was living beyond his means. With the regular income from his estates insufficient to keep the family afloat, or at least living in the style to which they had become accustomed, he resorted to mortgaging, selling off or leasing plots of land or borrowing on the security of his future share of the Ormond inheritance. The Boleyns were rich – just not rich enough. So far, royal service had not been without its rewards. Henry made Anne's father keeper of the currency exchanges in England and Calais for an annual rent of £30 6s 8d. If well managed, his profit could have approached £100 a year. Thomas and his father-in-law Surrey also obtained a valuable lease. But such gifts were insufficient to meet the expenses he and his wife incurred which were not reimbursed by the king, especially their fine clothing and Thomas's jousting and hunting equipment.[35] The family lived in glorious surroundings and moved in the highest social circles but banked on Henry's largesse. They also had to find a property in London for when the king was away and needed them there on call. Its exact location is uncertain, but wherever it was, it was on the river since Henry once stopped there when travelling by barge to Greenwich. Most likely it was a house Thomas rented from the Corporation of London, possibly close to Baynard's Castle beside Blackfriars Stairs, bordering the Thames.[36]

If Anne was to prosper in the world and gain a husband in line with Boleyn traditions, she needed a courtly education. An opportunity for this arose in the spring of 1512 when Henry sent her father, quite unexpectedly, to Margaret of Austria's palace in Mechelen, charged with shoring up Emperor Maximilian's support on the eve of the joint English-Spanish invasion of Aquitaine. As a fluent French speaker with an enviable knowledge of classical literature and all the courtly arts, Boleyn was well equipped for a diplomat's role. While the success of this mission really mattered to Henry, for the Boleyns, and especially for Anne, it would turn into a make-or-break opportunity.

4

Anne: Apprentice Courtier

Thomas Boleyn arrived in Mechelen in the third week of May 1512.[1] Located on the river Dyle, the city was a prosperous port town, well defended by a series of moats and walls. Margaret's palace, much of it still under construction, encompassed a complex of old and new buildings known as the 'Hof van Savoyen'. Only the late-gothic first phase of building work, with its diaper-patterned brickwork, cruciform windows, turrets and stepped dormer windows, was so far completed. Work had begun on Margaret's library, but the Renaissance-styled northern range of the palace would not be started until the 1520s.[2] Maximilian, when in the Low Countries, occupied a larger, even more luxurious palace known as the Coudenberg in Brussels, fourteen or so miles away. With its spacious rooms, fountains, labyrinth and menagerie, it was more suited to his imperial vision of rule.

On or about the 28th, Boleyn rode with Sir Richard Wingfield, a fellow courtier already experienced in Low Countries affairs, to meet Maximilian secretly on horseback. After they had exchanged pleasantries, Maximilian talked evasively about the Holy League, promising to resume the conversation next day. Instead, as Henry had feared, he gave audience to the French and then withdrew from sight.[3] In her father's absence, Margaret took over the negotiations. In mid-June Boleyn hurried home for further instructions, but was back in Brussels by the 26th, where Margaret's court had temporarily moved. Summoned next day, he heard evensong in the chapel and afterwards watched Prince Charles of Ghent shoot with a longbow. He 'handles his bow right well favourably', as Boleyn reported back to Henry, who was keenly interested in anything about the youth whom he believed would one day become his brother-in-law.[4]

Henry kept Boleyn and Wingfield on call in Mechelen for the best part of a year. Their mission was finally completed on 5 April 1513 when, just in time for Henry's invasion of northern France, Maximilian agreed to join the English king as a signatory of a second Holy League under the auspices of the new Pope Leo.[5] His work done, Boleyn left for Calais a few days after the treaty was ratified and was spotted in the harbour there on 11 May. He was back in London by the middle of the month, but quickly returned to Hever to raise a retinue of 100 soldiers to serve in the vanguard of Henry's army. He and his men took ship for Calais sometime in the second half of June, ready to join in the action.[6]

While in attendance on Margaret, Boleyn struck up an easy rapport with her. He found her to be a glamorous, utterly confident woman fully in control of her own destiny. Twice married for reasons of political convenience, twice widowed by the age of twenty-four and keenly aware of the special status and dignity she enjoyed as a single woman, she wore a widow's coif to signal her independence from men, choosing as a motto *Fortune Infortune Fort Une* ('Changes in fortune make a woman stronger'). Another motto she took from the old Dukes of Burgundy: *Groigne qui groigne et vive Burgoigne* ('Grudge if you like, and long live Burgundy').[7] She knew how to charm visiting diplomats, often with a wink and a smile. She clearly liked Boleyn, whom she found to be an incisive, no-nonsense negotiator. When she invited him to bet that her letters of authority from Maximilian to conclude the treaty would arrive within ten days, he quickly accepted, saying as they shook hands on it that he would gladly lose the wager to her. If she lost, Margaret was to give him a Spanish warhorse. If she won, she was to have a 'hobby' (a small ambling or pacing horse).[8] She lost, and it was at some point after this that Anne's father plucked up the courage to ask if she would make his daughter Anne one of her maids of honour as a personal favour, and she agreed.

Anne left Hever to travel to Mechelen most likely during the summer of 1513. Quite possibly Claude Bouton, Seigneur de Courbaron, an equerry to Margaret, came to fetch her in a Flemish ship, or maybe one of Boleyn's own servants accompanied her and she was merely formally presented to Margaret by the equerry. An undated letter from Margaret to Boleyn, written in French and last seen in the archives at Lille in 1839 when it was partially printed before disappearing, names Bouton. 'I have received your letter', she wrote, 'by the equerry Bouton, who presented your daughter to me.'

> She is most welcome to me, and I hope to treat her in a way
> that will make you very happy. Take care that until your return
> there need be no other intermediary between you and me,
> other than she; and I find her so bright and pleasant for her
> young age, that I am more beholden to you for having sent her
> to me than you are to me.[9]

From the beginning, Anne stood out from the crowd.

She could not have found a better place to study French and courtly accomplishments. An apprenticeship in Mechelen enabled her to master these skills while observing at first hand a politically agile woman exercising power as a regent. She was also able to perfect her French, for this was the principal language spoken at Margaret's court, and to study etiquette while learning to live alongside, and how to speak to, royalty. She discovered how to dress, for Mechelen was a hotbed of fashion. She almost certainly began to learn the lute and the virginals. She would also have been taught courtly dances, and more specifically dances popular in masques and 'disguisings'.[10]

Margaret of Austria had spent ten of the most impressionable years of her life at the French court. Betrothed to Charles VIII of France at the age of three and jilted at eleven before finishing her education in the Low Countries, she had gone on to marry first in Spain and then in Savoy. Although just as hostile politically to France as Henry, she had learned how to dress and conduct herself, to paint, draw, write poetry, dance, sing and play the lute as an adolescent in France.[11]

A prolific patron of the arts, Margaret amassed an astonishing collection of paintings, tapestries, decorative and devotional objects, Venetian glassware, fine books and manuscripts, along with one of the earliest collections of ethnographic artefacts from the New World. She owned 100 tapestries, over 50 sculptures and almost 200 paintings, featuring masterpieces by Jan van Eyck, Rogier van der Weyden, Hans Memling, Jan Gossaert and Hieronymus Bosch. When she gave the celebrated Nuremberg artist, Albrecht Dürer, a guided tour on his visit in 1520–21, he gasped in awe before voicing his disappointment at being unable to obtain from her a much-prized sketchbook of Italian drawings. For her chapel she commissioned polyphonic motets from Josquin des Prez, whose fame stretched across Europe. Her library contained books from Italy, Spain, France, Savoy and Germany as well as Flanders: the collection ran to about 380 bound volumes, only twelve of them printed, the rest manuscripts, many of them opulently illustrated. Some fifty were romances and works of fiction: others were songbooks, manuals on dancing, hunting or warfare, philosophical texts and Greek and Roman literature. Roughly a quarter were devotional, including thirty or so illuminated Books of Hours, aids to worship which included scriptural texts, psalms and prayers to be used at specified times of the day. Many had velvet covers, secured by gold clasps. Several were kept in her bedchamber, where she allowed her women to read them.[12]

Apart from Anne, the *filles d'honneur* and maids in Margaret's service came from Germany, Spain, France and the Low Countries. A newly discovered list of some of them includes the name 'Bullan'.[13] To help further their educations, Margaret allowed them to sit in on the schoolroom lessons of her young nieces Eleanor, Isabella and Marie, the future queens respectively of Portugal (and later of France), Denmark and Hungary. They worked and slept communally, accompanying Margaret wherever she decided to go. In overall charge was Anne, Countess of Hoogstraten, wife of Philippe de Lalaing, Governor of the Duchy of Guelders. Her deputy was 'Madame de Verneuil', whose identity is obscure. Household ordinances, reissued in 1525, but based on a template from Anne's time in Mechelen, record that Verneuil's stipend was 200 *livres tournois* a year (worth around £22,000 today). Nine *filles d'honneur* received between 50 and 100 *livres*, the two principal maids got 30 (£3,300) and the rest were rewarded at Margaret's discretion.[14]

It was not unknown for a girl of roughly Anne's age to become a maid of honour at royal or ducal courts. In 1509 Elizabeth Stafford, the Duke of Buckingham's eldest daughter, joined Katherine of Aragon's household as a maid of honour when she was twelve, although the usual age was between thirteen and fifteen. We know this from a letter Maximilian wrote to remind his daughter of his promise to Don Diego de Guevara, maître d'hôtel to Prince Charles, that Don Diego's niece should join her household, and that Don Diego had asked him to fulfil his promise now that she was thirteen. This suggests Anne's birth date is more likely to have been 1500 than a year later, but there is no certainty. The Spanish-born de Guevara had been maître d'hôtel to Philip the Handsome and Juana of Castile. He presented Margaret with Jan van Eyck's *Arnolfini Portrait*, believed to depict Giovanni di Nicolao Arnolfini, known as Giannino, and his second wife. Margaret adored the painting, still renowned as one of the most famous and intriguing works of Flemish art in the world, marking it in her inventory as *ung tableau fort exquis*. She took care to protect it, giving orders to fit the wings which were then attached to it with a replacement hinge, so that they closed properly. It is a painting Anne may well have seen and admired.[15]

Of the 150 or so persons who served Margaret, only a few lived with her in the 'Hof van Savoyen'. Her women servants were among the privileged few. The others were housed in the city, arriving early in the morning when the gates of the palace were opened, and leaving before they shut in the evening, but everyone ate dinner in the palace, which in royal courts was served from around noon.[16] As the great hall was not large enough for everyone to eat at the same time,

Margaret dined first, and if honoured guests or ambassadors were present, they were invited to join her. Afterwards, the officials and servants of the household ate in groups according to their station. The *filles d'honneur* and maids dined and supped together: the daily meal allowance for their table included thirty-four loaves of bread, six bottles of wine, three joints of beef, three of boiled mutton and two of roast mutton, three hens or six chickens, along with assorted soups and pastries, and platters of cheese, fruits and vegetables. To vary their diets when desired, equivalent quantities of duck, geese, pigeon, wildfowl, pork and so on could be requested. As in all royal and noble households, fish dishes would be substituted for meat in Lent, on Fridays and on certain fast days. Allowances were increased at Easter and at other festivals and celebrations.[17]

Discipline was strict throughout the palace. Only authorised persons had access to Margaret's person and the innermost rooms, while regulations prescribed how many paces nobles of varying ranks should advance to welcome a guest. Gentlemen-in-waiting were not to depute their duties to others, and Margaret kept a strict eye on the women. Conversation and deportment had to be correct: gossip or flirting with the younger gentlemen or pages was forbidden. While Margaret was thoroughly proficient herself in the game of courtly love, it had to be played by the rules. In one of her verses, she laid out the standard she expected from her *filles d'honneur* and maids if approached by men.[18]

> Trust in those who offer you service?
> Unless you first use your head, my *demoiselles*,
> You'll discover yourselves joining all those
> Who've been deceived.
> They choose for their smooth talk
> Words softer than the tenderest of virgins.
> Trust in them?
> In their hearts they harbour many tricks to deceive,
> And then when they've had their wicked way
> Everything will be as if it never happened.
> Trust in them?[19]

Not so long after her arrival, Anne wrote a letter to her father in reply to one of his, using rudimentary, but easily recognisable French. She wrote, she said, from 'Veure' or 'La Veure', the French name given to a 700-acre park close to Brussels, known in Flemish as Tervuren.[20] Here was a château which served as a summer palace and hunting lodge, where Margaret often stayed with Prince Charles and his siblings. Maximilian spent the summer at Tervuren in 1512, and in 1513 Margaret visited it again.[21]

Anne wrote (the original French text is so ungrammatical that the translation has partly to be conjectural):

Sir, I understand from your letter that you desire me to be an entirely virtuous woman when I come to the court, and you tell me that the queen will condescend to converse with me, and it gives me great joy to think of talking with such a wise and virtuous person. This will make me all the keener to persevere in speaking good French, especially as you have so enjoined it on me, and with my own hand I inform you that I will observe it the best I can. Sir, I beg you to excuse me if my letter is badly written, because I assure you, that and the spelling is all out of my own head, while the letters are shaped by my hand alone. Samonnet left me to compose the letter by myself that nobody else may know what I am writing to you ... I promise you that my love is based on such great strength that it will never grow less, and I will make an end to this my study (*mon pourpens*), after having commended myself right humbly to your good grace. Written at Veure by your very humble and very obedient daughter,

  Anna de Boullan.[22]

A word sometimes considered impossible to decipher is almost certainly meant to be *pourpens*, which meant 'great thought', 'care', 'study', 'task' or (in the case of students) 'written exercise': and this helps to make sense of earlier passages of the letter. A standard method of teaching languages was for advanced students to write short essays known as 'themes' on topics prescribed by their tutors, and for novices to write letters, since an epistolary style was easiest to acquire and the best way for a student to begin. The content was dictated at first by the tutor, and it seems likely this is the earliest letter Anne was allowed to compose herself. She names her tutor as 'Samonnet' (possibly Symonnet or Simonette), almost certainly male, since in 1510 Maximilian recommended a person of this name for a place in Margaret's household as an archery tutor to Prince Charles. Symonnet, it seems, was not employed as a language tutor, but could well have acted as such on a part-time basis to any of the maids who arrived in Mechelen knowing little or no French.[23]

Anne's remark, 'you tell me that the queen (*la reine*) will condescend to converse with me' is worth unpacking. Generally, it is taken to mean that her father planned on her return to place her in Katherine of Aragon's household alongside her mother, but Margaret as the regent of the Low Countries was herself sometimes referred to as 'the queen', even though she was strictly an archduchess. Most notable, however, is the likely date. Anne almost certainly wrote her letter while lodged at Tervuren in the summer of 1513, and it was directly from there that Margaret and her ladies travelled to Lille to visit Maximilian and Henry after the fall of Thérouanne.[24]

Later, during the festivities celebrating Tournai's capitulation which Margaret and her ladies attended, Anne could hardly have failed to learn of a scandal. While playing games of courtly love, the exuberantly over-sexed Charles Brandon – cheered on by Henry – compromised Margaret. So embarrassed and insulted did his wanton behaviour make her feel, she registered a written protest. Nineteenth-century archivists muddled up the sheets of this candid document and some portions may be lost, but Brandon clearly overstepped the mark, first by touching her; then, when she asked him to stop, by

> put[ting] himself upon his knees before me, and in speaking and him playing, he drew from my finger the ring, and put it upon his, and since showed it [to] me, and I took to laugh, and to him said that he was a thief ... And I prayed him many times

to give it [to] me again, for that it was too much known. But
he understood me not well.[25]

The exchange of symbolic jewellery, or 'tokens', played an
important part in the chivalric rituals of love.[26] Such a 'gift' would
be made by a woman to a lover to whom she had pledged her heart.
Margaret found Brandon's seeming incomprehension to her requests
to return her stolen ring infuriating, as he was able to communicate
well enough in French when he wanted something. He kept the ring
until the next day, when she appealed for help to Henry, unwisely
offering to exchange it for a bracelet which she always wore. A gift of
a bracelet was itself compromising, if less so than a ring: Brandon's
flaunting it might still speak of commitment and possession. What
considerably soured things was when, after the swap was made,
Henry pruriently asked Margaret whether she fancied taking
Brandon to bed now love tokens had been exchanged.[27]
    Neither Henry nor Brandon, it seemed, had encountered
a woman in control of her own life: they mistook Margaret's
sociability as stemming from sexual desire. Henry did not hold
it against Brandon: after they returned to England, he raised
his friend to the highest level of the peerage as Duke of Suffolk.
The promotion – matched on the same day by others in which
Thomas Boleyn's father-in-law, Thomas Howard, the victor of
Flodden, became 2nd Duke of Norfolk and the eldest of Howard's
eight sons, another Thomas, replaced him as Earl of Surrey – was
designed to equip Brandon to marry Margaret. His spectacular
elevation encouraged courtiers and London citizens alike to wager
large sums on the wedding date. In the May Day jousts of 1514,
when Henry and the new duke were answerers in the lists 'against
all comers', Brandon carried his lance, as he proclaimed, 'for my
lady Margaret of Austria', and wore her colours. Now incensed by
his presumption, she insisted Henry scotch the rumours, and the
king, much put out, reluctantly obliged.[28]
    Suddenly, Anglo-Habsburg relations cooled, bringing the young
Anne Boleyn's apprenticeship at Margaret's court to a premature
end. Prince Charles's betrothal to Henry's sister Mary had been the

ultimate prize of Henry VII's diplomacy, and when Maximilian, without warning, repudiated it, the English accused him of treachery. By then, Henry's plans for his sister's wedding were already well advanced. Her wardrobe had been chosen, appointments made to her household and orders given for the jousts in Calais to celebrate the nuptials.[29] On 6 July 1514, Margaret warned Maximilian that without the wedding, Henry would switch sides in Maximilian's rivalry with France.[30]

Her judgment was sound. Barely was the month out before Mary solemnly repudiated Charles. A week later, the gouty, toothless, libidinous but passionately art-loving Louis XII of France, who at fifty-two was almost three times her age, accepted defeat in Italy and offered a dowry of 1 million crowns for her hand. She would be his third wife. He had been a widower for six months since the death of his second wife, the indomitable Anne, Duchess of Brittany. He had secured an annulment of his first marriage to Jeanne de Valois after she agreed to retreat to a nunnery.

With Ferdinand of Spain now making warlike noises, Pope Leo wanted peace between France and England as a counterbalance, and so on 7 August, Henry signed the marriage contract. On the 11th, heralds proclaimed the terms. Mary would marry Louis and make herself the first English princess to be Queen of France. The following day while Mary reclined naked in bed, Louis d'Orléans, the Duke de Longueville, King Louis's proxy, lay down beside her in his jerkin 'with one leg naked from the middle of the thigh downwards', touching her leg with his bare leg, a symbolic act intended to signal her agreement to cohabitation.[31] None of this meant that Henry had abandoned his innate animosity to France. Just a year before, he had captured Thérouanne and Tournai in emulation of Henry V. Now he made peace just as his hero had done, in a marriage pact which bound his dynasty directly to the crown of France.[32]

On 14 August, Anne's father wrote to Margaret of Austria from Henry's court at Greenwich. Describing Margaret as his *très chère et très redoubtée dame* ('Most dear and most redoubted lady'), he said he hoped she would be very pleased to know that the sister of his master, 'Madame Marie, queen affianced of France', desired to have with her his daughter, *la petite boulain*, and so he very humbly begged his *très redoubtée dame* to be pleased to grant her permission to return 'with his people' (*avec mes gens*) whom he had sent to her. Boleyn's letter has not been seen since 1895, when it was sold at Sotheby's auctioneers in London: a transcript made and published at the time, however, indicates that Anne's father was disoriented, even shellshocked by the turn of events, writing in (for him) unusually clumsy French. Only his *très redoubtée dame*, it seemed, could get him off the hook with Henry, who insisted his sister was satisfied in the matter. 'To this request', he pleaded, 'I could not, nor did I know how to refuse, and it is to my most redoubted and dreaded lady that I appeal in case it is her pleasure to give and grant leave to my daughter to permit her to return.'[33]

It is easy enough to understand why Henry's sister might have wanted the young Anne to join her retinue. Despite taking lessons from John Palsgrave, one of the most distinguished language tutors in England, and having a young Frenchwoman, Jeanne Popincourt, as a schoolroom mentor, Mary could read in French, but 'did not know how to speak French intelligibly enough'.[34]

Ever since a transcript of Boleyn's letter appeared in the public domain, Anne's biographers have struggled to explain her movements over the next few months. A majority believe she hurried back to England. There, on 2 October, it is claimed, she was able to join the ladies of the household of the new French queen as they boarded their ship at Dover.[35] She would then have been present when an equinoctial storm turned their Channel crossing to Boulogne into a terrifying ordeal. The ships were scattered far and wide: one was wrecked on the French coast and several hundred men drowned. The flagship held its course but failed to enter the harbour at Boulogne, so Henry's sister and her retinue were ferried ashore in a dinghy.[36] The women continued some fifty miles riding on palfreys or in carriages to Abbeville, where on the 9th the royal wedding took place. A list of names unearthed in a dusty manuscript in Paris in 2004 confirms that Anne's sister, Mary Boleyn, was among them.[37]

There was no mention of Anne.

5

Focus on France

Margaret of Austria was not in Mechelen or Brussels to receive Thomas Boleyn's letter recalling his younger daughter. On 19 August 1514, she left for Bergen op Zoom, some fifty miles away, where she attended the Estates.[1] Boleyn's couriers might just have reached her by then, but it is likely they did not. Even if they did, and even if Margaret cooperated and released her promptly it hardly left enough time for Anne to travel back to England to prepare for her new life at the French court.[2]

Some of Anne's biographers argue that, instead of first returning to Hever and her family, she was hastily shuttled from one ship to another in the port of Dover to join the courtiers who, on 2 October, sailed for France. Was Anne's father among them? If he was, that explanation might carry more conviction: there would have been less need to return home to see her family if her father was already in Dover. Edward Hall, the fullest, most reliable contemporary chronicler of Henry VIII's reign, says that he was, but the original list on which he based his claim gives the name of Sir Thomas Botrym, not Boleyn.[3] No solid evidence exists to show that Anne crossed the Channel with her elder sister: the fact that Henry's sister requested *la petite boulain* to join her does not mean that Anne did so yet. A hint that she might have been on the ship comes early on in a French poem, called in its original handwritten versions 'La histoire de la royne Anne Boullant d'Angleterre' ('The

History of Queen Anne Boleyn of England'). The poem's author
is one Lancelot de Carle (or Carles), a secretary to Antoine de
Castelnau, later the French ambassador in London.[4] He begins by
observing:

> Anne Boleyn first departed
> From this country [England], when Mary Tudor left
> To go and find the King in France
> To cement the two rulers' league of friendship.
> At that time, Boleyn who was young
> When she came to court, wisely listened to
> Maids of honour, trying hard to use
> All her wits to imitate them well,
> And she employed her senses with such spirit
> That in a short time she learned the language.[5]

De Carle would have some interesting things to say about the
events of Anne's fall, which occurred while he was in London, but
his knowledge of her early adolescent years is hazy. He did not
arrive in England until de Castelnau himself did so in May 1535, so
before then, what he says about Anne can only be based on hearsay
or rumour.

Anne's name is not on the official roster of the new French
queen's female attendants. This was vetted by Louis: he signed his
copy 'Loys' and the date is added in an English hand.[6] The day after
the wedding, he ordered back to London anyone not approved on
his copy. A 'Mademoiselle Boleyne' is on the roster and stayed in
France, but she is not Anne.[7] Fresh discoveries in Paris put it beyond
question. Two copies of the official list of the *Officiers domestiques
de la Reyne Marie d'Angleterre* for the three months from 1 October
to 31 December 1514 survive in the French archives. Both name
'Marie Boulonne' as one of the queen's *demoiselles* at a salary of 240
livres (worth around £26,600 today). Again, Mary not Anne.[8]

Louis, who had been 'licking his lips and gulping his spittle' at
the mere sight of his beautiful young bride, was said to be 'very
joyous' on his wedding day.[9] On 5 November Henry's sister was

crowned in the royal abbey of Saint-Denis on the outskirts of Paris, and she made her triumphal entry into the capital next day. Mary Boleyn rode in the procession.

But just eleven weeks after the wedding, everything changed. Louis died on New Year's Eve 1514, shortly before midnight, reputedly of a surfeit of sex. The twenty-year-old Francis, Duke of Angoulême, the husband of the fifteen-year-old Claude, Louis XII's elder daughter, succeeded as Francis I.

Just five days later, letters from Maximilian were read out in Brussels which declared the fifteen-year-old Prince Charles able to govern his lands and lordships in the Low Countries personally.[10] The political landscape of Europe had transformed in the space of a week.

Within a few months, Anne was in France as Queen Claude's *demoiselle*. For this, we have the unimpeachable testimony of Claude's sister, Renée – discovered in the archives in London – who went on to marry Ercole II d'Este, Duke of Ferrara, and lived to a ripe old age. In 1561, recently widowed and back in France, she informed Sir Nicholas Throckmorton, then Queen Elizabeth I's ambassador to Paris, who had travelled to Orléans to interview her, that Elizabeth's mother, Anne Boleyn, had been very well known to her, because 'there was an old acquaintance betwixt [her] and me when she was one of my sister Queen Claude's maids of honour.'[11]

When and how could Anne have arrived in France? She would have needed a chaperone, since single women of her status could not travel alone. The roads and the inns where horses could be hired, or lodgings found, were too unsafe. The solution lies in the events in Paris after Francis's accession. Once Louis was dead, his widow moved into the Hôtel de Cluny on the south bank of the Seine. Her removal there was to fulfil the obligations of what the French called the *deuil blanc*. Clad from tip to toe in a white veil superimposed over her black mourning dress, she kept to her bedchamber with darkened windows, secluded from the world, until it became certain that she was not pregnant with a potential heir. Only then could Francis's title as king be legally registered by the Parlement of Paris.

Or so it was meant to be. Except that during these days and weeks, Charles Brandon, the new Duke of Suffolk, who had travelled to Paris to joust in Francis's coronation tournament, was a frequent visitor to the Hôtel de Cluny. Unabashed by his rejection by Margaret of Austria, he now plied his suit to Mary, or rather perhaps, she plied hers to him. Rumour said, not without justification, that they were so much in love, they raced to the bedroom the moment Louis was in his coffin, where they enjoyed uninhibited sex. The lovers secretly exchanged wedding vows in the second week of February 1515. The officially announced date in France was over a month later, but this was all a part of Suffolk's smokescreen.[12]

From Suffolk's perspective, however, wooing and marrying Mary carried deadly risks, since he had sworn a solemn oath to Henry that he would try no such tricks. Fully informed as ever, and sensing an opportunity to make the newlyweds his future allies for life as he climbed to a position of power, Wolsey ghost-wrote a grovelling apologia for Mary to copy out and send to her brother. But as he warned Suffolk, Henry would need far more than fair words, 'having also such an affianced assurance in your truth, that for all the world (and to have been torn by wild horses) ye would not have broken your oath'. 'Cursed be the blind affection and counsel that hath brought you hereunto,' for Suffolk was 'in the greatest danger that ever man was in'.[13]

Guided by Wolsey, the duke settled matters after agreeing to surrender to Henry as much of his new wife's plate and jewels as could be prised back from Francis's clutches, along with a large cash sum and half the pension of 55,000 *livres* to which Mary was entitled as a dowager queen of France. In the end, money talked and Suffolk won his reprieve.[14]

The special ambassador sent to France by Henry to inform Francis that Suffolk was forgiven was Thomas Boleyn. At the Christmas revels in 1514 at Henry's court he and Anne's mother had played leading roles in a mummery.[15] His arrival in Paris shortly after, where 'he tarried a while', is described by the French chronicler Robert de La Mark, Seigneur de Florange, in a long-overlooked passage.[16] Boleyn's embassy achieved no diplomatic breakthrough beyond easing Mary and Suffolk's journey home – they finally left Paris in mid-April – but he did succeed in placing Anne as a *demoiselle* to Queen Claude.[17] If Anne was already in France having travelled there via Dover or perhaps directly from Mechelen with her father's couriers after being released from Margaret of Austria's service, then it would have been a straightforward move from Mary's entourage. If she were not, and she had returned to Hever too late to travel to France with Mary, then the most likely explanation is that her father had brought her with him once ordered to set out on his mission, knowing that she could never return to Margaret and there was every chance that he could exploit his diplomatic access to Francis to achieve his aim.[18] Whatever the truth, Anne was now securely placed in Paris and the French court.

Paris would have made a deep impression on Anne. A city more populous than London in the 1510s, it had around 100,000 inhabitants compared to London's 80,000 and was far larger than Mechelen or Brussels. The Cité, on its island in the middle of the Seine, was the oldest part. At the eastern end stood the cathedral of Notre-Dame, and at the opposite end was the Palais-Royal, or old royal palace, occupied by the Parlement and other sovereign courts. The university and its famous Faculty of Theology in the Sorbonne were on the left bank along with the printers and booksellers, enclosed by the medieval wall. What struck English travellers was that Paris was 'fairer built and better situate[d]' than London. The streets were just as narrow, but smells and drainage were less irksome.[19]

When Anne joined her household, she and Queen Claude were of a similar age. Claude, already pregnant with her first child, was said to be sweet, gentle, graceful and eloquent, but plain, dumpy and below average height. Like her late beloved mother, Anne of Brittany, she was popular with the ordinary people, and it is said that greengages (still known today in France as *reine claudes*) were named after her. She was fiercely protective of her identity and used methods that Anne would remember, placing her badges and 'C' monogram on the wall panelling, masonry and ceilings of her apartments and on her gold and silver plate, her coffers and chests, her books and manuscripts. Her badges soon became as defining as Katherine of Aragon's pomegranate and 'K' monogram. One was a swan pierced by an arrow, another an ermine; others included *cordelières* (or friar's knots) and armillary spheres, an astrological device which came to symbolise the belief that visible things are the mirror of things invisible.

Unlike Henry's relationship with Katherine, which at this stage was still loving, that between Claude and Francis was a mixture of mutual respect, collaboration and occasional mistrust. Claude was the sole heir to her parents' personal fiefdoms, which included Blois, Brittany and the French claim to the Duchy of Milan. Francis did not marry her for love, but to build his dynasty.[20] Her attitude to him is best evinced in her willing toleration of his mistresses, but absolute refusal to give him a key to the magnificent library in her favourite château of Blois, where she vigilantly guarded her mother's unrivalled book and tapestry collections from what she feared would be his predations.[21]

On his accession, Francis appointed his mother, Louise of Savoy, some twenty-three years older than Claude, to his *conseil privé*, where she remained until her death. Louise, not Claude, would be Francis's first choice as regent whenever he was out of the country. He trusted her implicitly; she conducted her own independent diplomacy and exercised a vice-like grip over the royal court, where her apartments were those closest to her son's. She was a lynx-eyed, ruthless politician in her own right, a woman with a razor-sharp mind and a venomous tongue if suitably aroused, who could steer Francis and guide his policies often against the advice he received from his more established male advisers.

Francis's sister, Marguerite of Angoulême, was another formative influence. Tall, slim, witty, charming and vivacious, she too was a shrewd, versatile politician, less ruthless than Louise, but an acute, clear-headed, discerning observer of all that went on in royal courts, with a searching intelligence fully equipped to counter or repulse the slippery, deceitful devices of ambitious, predatory men. Now in her early twenties, she had been married, at age seventeen, to Charles, Duke of Alençon, a rather stupid man who rarely left his ducal centre except when on military campaigns and whom she could safely forget about. A talented writer with a keen interest in literature, theology and the creative arts, Marguerite would later win recognition for her incisive, sardonic, biting sense of humour.[22]

Louise and Marguerite resoundingly gave the lie to those who believed that women had no place in the government and politics of a patriarchal society; Claude may not have matched them as a politician, but she was also able to hold her own.[23] The impressionable Anne found herself in a world in which women could exercise power in strikingly differing ways. What she witnessed was a revelation: she had a unique vantage point on how women could navigate their way through the thickets of the court and international affairs. Her experiences helped to transform her outlook and her life. She could contrast them to the way that women were not regarded as political actors in England, where Henry never once sought his sister Mary's advice and where Katherine and her ladies increasingly withdrew to pray and read devotional works, sing, dance, listen to minstrels, do embroidery, play chess and occasionally cards, or in wet weather enjoy games of indoor bowls or ninepins with ivory skittles.[24]

Although smaller than her husband's, Claude's household still numbered a staff of 120 or so. In charge was the *première dame d'honneur*, Gillette d'Acigné, the wife of a Breton nobleman, followed by twelve *dames de l'hôtel*, the unmarried *filles* and the younger *demoiselles d'honneur*, after whom came the *femmes de chambre*, *filles de chambre* and so on, who served as chambermaids, linen maids, nurses and washerwomen. Of the *demoiselles*, Anne must have encountered d'Acigné's daughter, Marie, as they joined the household at around the same time. She would also have known Gillette de Gigny, a girl from a humbler background, whose dowry Claude paid on her marriage.[25]

Something else Anne would have discovered was that French courtly protocol differed from English. In both countries, queen consorts adhered to a similar spatial hierarchy to their husbands in lodgings separately located in the royal palaces, but their social etiquette was markedly different in the two countries. In France, the sexes could intermingle relatively freely in both the queen's *chambre à parer* (Presence Chamber) and *chambre de retrait* (privy chamber), whereas in Katherine's household, the only men allowed in, unless invited for specific purposes, were her husband and her own officers or relatives. In France, casual visits from men were forbidden only in the queen's bedchamber or, depending on the limitations of palace architecture, the more private space towards the back of her *chambre de retrait*, with its writing desk and *dressoir* to set gold and silver plate on, and where cushions were set out for her *demoiselles* to sit. It was there that Claude, imitating her mother, often held what the men disparagingly dubbed the 'court of the ladies'.[26]

If Claude followed her mother's example, she knew to take special care of the *demoiselles* in her charge, ensuring they received an education designed to equip them for courtly life. A prized item which she kept in the library at Blois was a deluxe copy of the Dominican monk Antoine Dufour's *Vies des femmes célèbres*, a copy still counted as one of France's greatest treasures and now in the Musée Dobrée in Nantes. The book was a compilation of ninety-one biographies of famous women, including Joan of Arc, that with a few exceptions presented models of virtue, but also role models for female empowerment.

Claude herself was educated by a team of women. One of her ladies-in-waiting, Anne de Graville, a noted proto-feminist, rewrote classic texts by men, recasting women as individuals with the right to govern their own lives, to object to philandering husbands, even to marry the man of their choice.[27] Among the rewrites she did for Claude while Anne was in her service was the fifteenth-century Alain Chartier's classic poem on courtly love, *La belle dame sans merci*, in which the lady refuses to yield. Another was the *Beau romant des deux amans Palamon et Arcita*, a French adaption of Giovanni Boccaccio's epic romance poem *Teseida*, telling of the love of the two Theban rivals Palamon and Arcite for the beautiful and wise Emilia. Now in the Bibliothèque Nationale in Paris, the verso of the first folio has an outstanding image of Claude, seated on her throne, attended by her *demoiselles*.[28]

As in Mechelen, artists and musicians flourished in France. Claude employed François Clouet to draw (and probably paint) her children. Like her husband, she was a connoisseur of Italian as much as of Franco-Burgundian art. When in 1518 the pope presented paintings to the royal couple, Claude's gift was Raphael's *Holy Family of Francis I*, a depiction of Jesus, Mary, Joseph, St Elizabeth, an infant St John the Baptist and two angels, now in the Louvre. And when the Venetians followed suit, they commissioned Sebastiano del Piombo, judged to be the best painter in Rome after Michelangelo and Raphael, to paint *The Visitation of Mary and Elizabeth*, also now in the Louvre, although it was intended 'to hang perpetually in the chamber of the Very Christian Queen of France'. Anne must have seen both works, as they arrived while she was present. It is even just conceivable that she saw something by Leonardo da Vinci, who from about 1516 until his death was Francis's pensioner, living on an annuity of 500 *livres* a year at the manor of Cloux, near Amboise.[29]

De Carle, who would have known far more about events in France at this time than in England, says that while with Queen Claude, Anne mastered courtly skills to perfection:

Wherein her graces she so refined
That no one ever judged her English
In her ways, but native French:
She knew how to sing and dance well
And to put her words together wisely,
To play the lute and other instruments
To chase away sad thoughts.[30]

The sources do not permit a decoupling of which musicians were employed by Francis and which by Claude. More likely, they were shared. But one closely linked to Claude was Jean Mouton, whose work Anne knew.[31] While in France she acquired a manuscript containing thirty-nine Latin motets and five French chansons in which someone inscribed her name: 'M^{res} [Mistress] A. Bolleyne nowe thus', followed by three musical notes with stems going

upward and a longer one with its stem downwards. ('Now thus'
was a Boleyn family motto; the significance of the notes has yet to
be satisfactorily explained.) Of the known composers in the book,
Mouton wrote eight, possibly nine of the pieces. Three popular
chansons by Claudin de Sermisy were added to it in or about the
year 1520.[32]

Something Anne must have reflected on in France was the
relative ease with which Claude learned to live with her husband's
mistresses. In these early years, this was less of a problem for
Katherine of Aragon as Henry had fewer of them. In 1510, he was
rumoured to have made advances to Anne Hastings, one of the
Duke of Buckingham's sisters, and in the summer of 1515, when
Katherine was pregnant, he began some sort of liaison with Jeanne
Popincourt. He grew tired of her, because within a year he shipped
her off back to France with a payoff of £100 (worth over £100,000
today) to take up a new post in the joint household of Francis's
daughters.[33]

Whereas Henry had some inhibitions about extra-marital sex,
Francis, who was regularly depicted in court entertainments as
Jupiter, the most promiscuous of the gods, had none. His first
official mistress, Françoise de Foix, was at court by June 1516.
Starting out as one of Claude's *dames de l'hôtel*, she rose at Francis's
insistence to be *première dame d'honneur* on a salary of 1,200 *livres*,
three times more than anyone else. Besides his official mistresses,
Francis had his so-called 'privy band' of women who shadowed
him on his hunting expeditions, which he held to be an aperitif
to sex.[34]

Claude quickly learned that she empowered herself by not
becoming jealous. Her security came from her dynastic inheritance
and her fecundity. By producing seven children in almost as many
years, she would make her position impregnable. As hers, all along,
had been a marriage of convenience, why should she object to her
husband's lovers? She knew that jealousy would simply eat her up,
and life for a queen had more to offer than that.

She also found herself a role model. If Francis was to be Jupiter,
then she would be Esther, the virtuous wife of the Old Testament

King Ahasuerus, whose faith, fidelity and untarnished integrity are the foil to male misdeeds. Claude's choice was no accident, since Esther had also been her mother's moral exemplar. In Claude's deluxe illuminated copy of Dufour's *Vies des femmes célèbres*, a masterly illustration by the renowned Paris illuminator, Jean Pichore, shows Esther dressed as a queen of France, kneeling in intercession before Ahasuerus's throne, watched by her *demoiselles*, while the king gently touches her with a golden sceptre to validate her unassailability.[35]

With her lands, her status, her children and her beloved château of Blois with its rich library, tapestries and other glorious treasures, Claude did not need and did not ask for more.

6

The Queen's *demoiselle*

Unlike Henry VIII's court, which rotated in the winter months between the so-called 'standing palaces' – those bordering the Thames which were kept permanently furnished – and only travelled more widely on a royal progress during the summer, Francis's ranged far and wide across France. When Queen Claude was not in Paris, she and her *demoiselles* could usually be found in the Loire Valley, often at Blois or at Amboise, two of France's more historic palaces (see Appendix 2). We can be confident of Anne's dependency on Claude: the only home she had in France was in the queen's court. Where Claude was, there too was Anne. Commonly held theories that Anne had inherited property in the parish of Brie-Comte-Robert, twenty miles from Paris, or in Briis-sous-Forges, a staging-post on the road between Paris and Chartres, are pure invention.[1]

Anne's first extended journey outside Paris began in 1515 shortly after her arrival in France. On 24 April, Francis, Claude, Louise of Savoy and their attendants set out for Blois, first travelling in the royal barges down the Seine before riding overland to reach the Loire with its wide, sprawling banks and slow-flowing current. Disembarking beside Blois on 23 May, they made an *entrée royale* into the town, before ascending into the château with its beautiful terraces and gardens.[2]

After a fortnight, Francis left. He was impatient to make his mark on the European stage by marching across the Alps to recover Milan.

He made his mother the regent of France, leaving the pregnant Claude with her *demoiselles* at Blois, where on 8 August she gave birth to a daughter, who was named Louise after her grandmother.[3] Soon Francis reached the plain of Piedmont, heading for Turin. After crossing the Ticino, his army made camp at Marignano (now Melegnano) on the outskirts of Milan. The great battle, fought on 13–14 September against a Swiss army in the pay of an anti-French coalition, led to the defeat and capture of Duke Massimiliano Sforza of Milan and left Francis in control of large areas of Piedmont and Lombardy. Fully aware that retaining these conquests depended on papal support, he travelled to Bologna to meet Pope Leo and heal the breach caused by Louis XII's Council of Pisa. In a historic concordat with the pope, Francis agreed to restore papal primacy in France so long as royal jurisdiction over disputes arising in the French Church was retained: he further pledged to join the pope in a crusade against the Ottoman Turks if God gave him a son.

Discussing Francis's victory with the French ambassador in London, Henry was decidedly tetchy. Katherine, on the other hand, took the long view. Her father, Ferdinand, was not a young man, and when he died, her nephew Charles would inherit a united realm, adding Spain to his recently granted territories in the Low Countries and beyond. Katherine believed the power politics of Europe would swing decisively back in favour of Spain and the Habsburgs and against France.[4]

In late October, eager for Francis's return, Claude and Louise of Savoy left the Loire Valley with the court, including Anne, and wagon-loads of luggage, hoping to greet him in Marseille or Aix-en-Provence. After stops in Lyon, Orange and Avignon, they sought out the tomb of St Martha, the sister of Lazarus, the man whom, according to St John's Gospel, Christ had raised from the dead.[5] Still without news of Francis, they headed for Aix, the ancient capital of Provence. Along the way, they made a diversion to see relics reputedly of Mary Jacobi and Mary Salome, two of the Three Marys said to have been present at Christ's Crucifixion, quickly moving on towards the year's end to Saint-Maximin-la-Sainte-Baume and the shrine of St Mary Magdalene, the third Mary.

Nestling at the foot of a mountain-ridge, the town and its medieval basilica had been a place of pilgrimage since a sarcophagus was discovered reputedly containing the saint's skull.

On arrival, Claude, Louise and their women entered the crypt of the basilica, where they prayed before the skull. Visibly moved, Claude made a munificent offering of 200 *livres* annually for ten years towards the costs of the shrine. Next day, she walked for two hours along a steep forest path, hastily repaired by local craftsmen for the occasion, to reach the upper part of the cliff to see the *grotte* or cave where the saint was said to have lived. There she was equally generous, giving money to the adjacent Dominican priory and to build a portal for the cave.[6]

These visits inspired Louise to call upon François du Moulin de Rochefort, her Franciscan chaplain, to investigate the legends of Mary Magdalene, and to verify the credibility of the miracles by which she had saved her devotees from prison, blindness or drowning, or guaranteed them eternal salvation after lives of debauchery. Not feeling up to this hazardously iconoclastic task, du Moulin summoned his mentor, the early French evangelical reformer Jacques Lefèvre d'Étaples. He boldly took on the challenge, closely testing his findings against the Gospel texts and judging 'Mary Magdalene' to be a conflation of more than one person and the miracle stories substantially fakes. During what amounted to impromptu seminars with Claude and Louise on the subject back in Paris and Amboise, Lefèvre brought along his protégé Denys Briçonnet, the reforming Bishop of Saint-Malo and elder brother of Lefèvre's more famous patron Guillaume, another sceptic of the miracles. The court was buzzing with all this, and Anne had no need to eavesdrop, since Claude's *demoiselles*, seated on their cushions, would have been in attendance in the *chambre de retrait* while Lefèvre or Briçonnet was speaking. What she saw and heard then would shape her outlook on questions of reform for the rest of her life and on religious matters she would, in future, look to France for guidance.[7]

When, between 1517 (the same year in which Martin Luther posted his Ninety-Five Theses) and 1519, Lefèvre published a

major work discrediting the miracle stories, Louise rescued him
from the inquisitors of the Sorbonne who judged his findings
to be heretical. Claude, meanwhile, gave her patronage to Louis
Chantereau, another Lefèvrist sympathiser, whom she made her
confessor. An illuminated prayer book she commissioned for her
sister Renée suggests that she too shared the ideal of a purified
Christianity founded on a return to the Gospels. Soon a convinced
reformer, Claude took a keen interest in the reform of the religious
life. Hearing of scandals in the Benedictine nunneries of Yerres and
Gercy, she twice wrote to the Parlement of Paris, demanding urgent
action to give France the benefit of 'good prayers and orations
which will be made by reforming the nuns'. Within a week or
so of leaving Saint-Maximin-la-Sainte-Baume, she wrote again,
expressing impatience over the delays. In 1516, she completed the
reform of the Dominican convent of Saint-Pierre de Lyon, which
her mother had begun. And in 1521, she rebuilt the Augustinian
convent of Saint-Jean of Blois for nuns known as the 'Véroniques',
who specialised in educating women.[8]

Shortly before Anne would leave France in December 1521,
Francis's sister, Marguerite, stepped forward to protect Guillaume
Briçonnet, by then Bishop of Meaux. She intervened to save his
celebrated preaching team, known as the Cercle de Meaux, from the
persecutors at the Sorbonne, promising to share their expositions
of true doctrine with those at court whom 'I find eager for it'.
Lefèvre's ideas struck a chord with her too.[9]

For the Lefèvrists, the main goal was to foster a living faith
among the laity. Faith was to be found not in fraudulent miracles
or rituals such as pilgrimages and the veneration of images, but in
the Gospels and the epistles of St Paul. Good works alone were not
a pathway to salvation as the Church insisted: what mattered was
the motive and mindset of those making the gifts. In Lefèvre's way
of thinking, a revitalised understanding of charity was the outward
sign of a truly living inner faith. This meant making devotional
works readily available in print or manuscript, preaching true
doctrine, financing schools, founding orphanages, reforming
monastic houses, devising better systems for poor-relief, inspecting

prisons to ensure humane treatment, revising legal codes and forgiving enemies.[10]

All this was still to come, however. After a ten-day stay in Saint-Maximin-la-Sainte-Baume, the women hastened on to Sisteron, where on 13 January 1516 they welcomed Francis home. Everyone then made the short journey to the port of Marseille, the oldest city in France, where on the 22nd the triumphant king made his *entrée royale*, which the citizens marked with a pageant of some 2,000 children dressed in white. The next day Louise and Claude, flanked by their ladies and *demoiselles*, made a separate *entrée*. Afterwards, Claude climbed the hill to the cathedral of Notre-Dame-de-la-Garde, another popular pilgrimage site, where until dusk she prayed to the Virgin Mary to be blessed with a son.[11]

On the return journey, Claude's entourage stopped in Lyon, where they received important news: the elderly Ferdinand had indeed died, and been succeeded as king of all Spain by Charles.[12] Claude attended a requiem Mass for Ferdinand. By the beginning of April, she was pregnant again. She withdrew with her *demoiselles* first to Blois, then to Amboise and was still there when her baby, Charlotte, arrived in late October. Twice now, Anne Boleyn had seen Claude produce a baby girl rather than the hoped-for Dauphin of France, but Francis was unruffled. Already he had dreamed up a scheme to marry his elder daughter Louise, barely fifteen months old, to Charles.[13]

After the Christmas festivities and New Year revelry, when gifts or *étrennes* were exchanged in the more intimate space of the *chambre à parer*, plans turned to Claude's coronation. Postponed on account of her second pregnancy, it was arranged for Sunday 10 May 1517 in the abbey of Saint-Denis, to be followed by her *entrée royale* into Paris. As one of Claude's *demoiselles*, Anne sat in the gallery overlooking the sanctuary during the ceremony. On the day of the *entrée*, she rode towards the end of the procession in one of three designated carts emblazoned with Claude's heraldic badges.[14]

During the entry into Paris, Claude travelled down the rue Saint-Denis and on towards the cathedral of Notre-Dame, and from there to the Palais-Royal, where a banquet awaited. First came

monks and clergy accompanied by trumpeters and clarion players
marching in their serried ranks, then a royal guard of archers and
crossbowmen clad in their short silver coats. Pageants with actors
on stages were mounted at seven different stopping places along
the route, where a narrator called an 'expositeur' explained the
meaning of the scene.[15]

At the Porte Saint-Denis to the west of the city and the first stop
on the route, the display centred on the heroic role of women in
the Old Testament. Claude's chosen characters were Sarah, Rachel,
Rebecca, Deborah, Leah and, of course, Esther. The backdrop
to the scene depicted Claude ('La Royne') surrounded by these
biblical prototypes of virtue, supported by nuns played by actors,
who stood admiringly beneath them and represented the four
cardinal Virtues (prudence, justice, fortitude and temperance). All
seemed complete, until to the astonishment of the audience, the
Holy Ghost in the shape of a clockwork dove descended, flapping
its wings, out of a heavenly cloud painted on a canvas ceiling, and
placed a crown on the head of the queen, echoing the liturgical
story of the Virgin's coronation on her Assumption into heaven.[16]

At the banquet in the great hall of the Palais-Royal, trumpeters,
oboists and other wind instrumentalists played from a specially
erected gallery, while the queen dined with the great lords and
ladies of the realm. After over a hundred different dishes were
offered, special desserts were served, one presented in the shape
of Francis's famous salamander badge, another in that of Claude's
ermine. The climax came when the queen ordered a large wine
jar filled to the brim with money to be handed to the heralds-
at-arms, who marched around the hall crying 'Largesse, largesse',
while throwing the coins into the crowd. There followed masques
and entertainments, after which Claude finally rose and took her
leave, accompanied by her *demoiselles*. For Anne, who was there
throughout, this would be a day she would always remember.[17]

Afterwards, the royal couple began an extended tour of Picardy
and Normandy.[18] Early in September, Claude and her women
spent eight days at the château of Gaillon, near Louviers, which
Cardinal d'Amboise, lately deceased, had built on the site of an

old castle with the help of a Veronese architect and a Neapolitan priest and garden designer. The château was the earliest and one of the most palatial Renaissance buildings in France. At the centre of the main court stood the finest fountain in France, commissioned from Genoese sculptors. By comparison, work on the new royal lodging at Blois with its grand staircase and fine loggias inspired by Bramante would not be finished before Anne returned home.[19]

In October, Francis and Claude were the guests for three weeks in Argentan of Claude's sister-in-law, Marguerite of Angoulême. Anne must already have seen, if not actually met, Marguerite as Francis's sister shuttled relatively freely between her own apartments and those of Louise and Claude. The women often spent days or hours together, especially when Francis was away on his hunting trips. Anne would certainly have noticed Marguerite at Claude's coronation, but their first opportunity to speak may well have come at Argentan.[20]

Like Margaret of Austria, Marguerite understood the pleasures and subversions of princely courts. Another avid bibliophile who commissioned fine illuminated Bibles, Books of Hours and manuscripts, and loved poetry and paintings as much as Anne came to do, she too was a proto-feminist. Most notably, she wrote *nouvelles* and poems that were completely honest in their discussions of relations between the sexes. Many of her writings post-date Anne's departure from France, but solid grounds exist to believe that the opinions she expressed about men and sex in her *nouvelles* were shaped much earlier. Specifically, Marguerite had been plagued while Anne was still in France by the unwanted attentions of Guillaume Gouffier, Seigneur de Bonnivet, a favourite of Francis and the Admiral of France, who attempted to rape her.[21]

Marguerite made it clear that the rules governing sexual relationships are never the same for men and women. In her view, men pursue their *amours* in only two ways: by seduction or brute force. In either case, women are in a bind. Their fathers, husbands and male relatives expect them to be chaste virgins or faithful wives; on the other hand, what *serviteurs* or 'servants' (meaning male suitors according to the code of courtly love) really want is sex without strings, whether a woman is married or not. Women must be constantly on their guard and look to religion for succour and guidance. Caution is essential. Priests, friars and monks can be as bawdy and dangerous as laymen, entering the bedrooms and cells of their female confessants to take advantage of the intimacy and secrecy of confession. They are no better than the rapists: in fact, says Marguerite, they are worse, because they knew nobody would believe a woman who says they are guilty, which is just another of the ways by which society enforces women's subordination to men.

Equally, true love cannot lie hidden for long between lovers who are neither circumspect nor sufficiently discreet. Rarely can women occupy the high moral ground. At royal courts, they should avoid the love that becomes too powerful to be concealed, and must temper their feelings, lest they be publicly shamed. Dissimulation is the most effective shield to a woman's reputation.[22]

On 11 October, in an impromptu ceremony in the park in Argentan and with Anne present, Francis created his sister Duke of Berry in her own right. About this there can be no mistake, despite its omission from almost all modern writings on Marguerite: a full text of the royal ordinance survives, and it proves that the king made Berry a *duché-pairie* (ducal peerage) and elevated his sister alone to the title, entitling her to sit on both the king's council and the *conseil secret*. By making Marguerite a duke in her own right, Francis gave her the legal status of a male, as if she were the king's brother. It was a tangible, highly visible example of the interplay of masculine and feminine elements in French political life. What's more, the ordinance conferring the duchy specifically excluded Marguerite's husband, who also had no claim upon the 24,000 *livres* pension that Francis bestowed upon her. Nothing Anne had seen or read so far in France could have demonstrated more clearly to her that a woman could rise to a position of power in a man's world.[23]

The court returned to Amboise for Christmas, since Claude was pregnant again.[24] Now Francis made no secret of his desire for a son. Determined for God to oblige him, he trudged fifteen miles on foot to the shrine of St Martin in Tours to pray. He was rewarded, since at around five o'clock on the afternoon of 28 February 1518, Claude gave birth to a healthy boy.[25]

The child was christened Francis, with Pope Leo as godfather. Standing as the pope's proxy was his twenty-five-year-old nephew, Lorenzo, Duke of Urbino, but Francis wanted a double celebration. Since the New Year, his ambassadors in Rome had been discussing terms for a dynastic marriage to mark the concordat agreed with the pope in Bologna. This came to fruition on 2 May, when Lorenzo, already riddled with syphilis, married the twenty-year-old Madeleine de la Tour d'Auvergne, Francis's cousin, with the king and Claude presiding.[26] For the reception, the courtyard in Amboise was transformed into a magnificent banqueting hall for dancing and feasting until 2 a.m. A tournament followed, lasting over a month: its climax was a mock siege with multiple blasts of live cannon, accidentally killing several of the participants.[27]

The Dauphin's birth was the pope's cue to call on Francis to redeem his pledge to join a crusade against the Turks. Leo also appealed to Henry for his support, whereupon Wolsey threw stardust into everyone's eyes, aiming to use an international league of peace to reposition England at the centre of European affairs. All serious talk of a crusade soon faded, but on the pretext of preparing for one, Wolsey set about binding all the greater powers and many of the lesser ones into a Treaty of Universal Peace.[28]

As Wolsey's diplomacy nudged forwards, Leo sent a special legate (or plenipotentiary), Cardinal Lorenzo Campeggi, to London to assist him. At this time, the only wider obstacle to peace seemed to arise from the activities of Martin Luther, a formerly obscure, thirty-three-year-old Augustinian monk and professor at the University of Wittenberg in Germany, who in 1517 attacked the abuses of the papacy and the Catholic Church and claimed that humans are justified and redeemed by faith in Christ alone. When he posted his Ninety-Five Theses on a church door for academic debate, copies travelled swiftly to London, where they caused great alarm, and then to Paris. Warned by Bishop Cuthbert Tunstall of London, one of his councillors and an ambassador to Charles, about the heresy of Luther's writings, Henry began to reimagine a role for himself as a papal champion; Francis did not yet see Luther as a serious threat.[29]

In early June 1518, Anne departed with Claude and her ladies towards Brittany, lingering for over a month near Angers while Francis went hunting, reaching Nantes in the first week of August.[30] In a ceremony on the 8th, a young girl, carried in a crystal bowl by two actors dressed as lions, presented Claude with the keys of the town, after which the royal couple, joined by Louise of Savoy, made a combined *entrée*. It was the Breton custom for citizens to offer live ermine with jewelled collars to their overlords on their entry into towns, but the citizens of Nantes played safe – the ermine could bite – and gave Francis a silver-gilt ship weighing 16 lbs 8 oz. Judging by its weight, this was a table jewel whose meaning was that his subjects were safe in storms so long as he was at the tiller. It was a motif as ancient as Plato's use of the term 'pilot of the ship of state' to describe the leadership of the Athenian Republic and one Anne would remember. To Louise, they gave twelve cups with lids, subtly enamelled with vermillion. Claude received a heart of solid gold weighing 3 lbs, borne aloft by two golden ermines.[31]

According to the municipal accounts in Nantes, these gifts cost 2,615 *livres* at a time when the town's annual budget was only around 5,000 *livres*. Considering her gift to be more than the citizens could afford, Claude graciously thanked them, then promptly donated it back. Unlike her husband, she won a reputation for charitable giving and works of piety. Later, when Francis demanded 22,000 *livres* from the citizens of Nantes towards the costs of his wars, they petitioned Claude to intercede, remembering her earlier generosity, and the demand was dropped.[32]

The royal party lingered in Nantes before moving on to Rennes, after which Francis went his own way. Claude, Louise and their women retired for two months to the château of Plessis-de-Vair, near Ancenis. Claude needed to rest – she was pregnant once more. And it was there that tragic news arrived: her daughter Louise, who had not been travelling with the royal progress but had remained at the court in Amboise, had died shortly after her third birthday.

By the Treaty of Noyon, Louise had been betrothed to Charles. With that plan now in tatters, a door opened for Henry and Wolsey. First, they persuaded Leo to appoint Wolsey as a papal legate, a privilege renewed in 1519 and again in 1521, and finally in 1524 for life. His credentials established, on Sunday 3 October, he and Campeggi proclaimed the Treaty of Universal Peace during a special High Mass in St Paul's. Coupled with it were subsidiary treaties by which Tournai would be sold back to France for 600,000 gold crowns of the sun and the nine-month-old Dauphin betrothed to the two-year-old Princess Mary.[33]

With parallel formalities due in Paris, Claude and Louise were back in the capital by December, where Francis took his solemn oath in Notre-Dame and swore with Claude to observe the subsidiary treaties. A magnificent fête followed in the courtyard of the Bastille, which presented Francis as a conquering hero. These were occasions of great excitement for Anne, since her father, whom she had not seen for over three years, was one of Henry's six ambassadors. Led by the elderly Charles Somerset, 1st Earl of Worcester, a descendant of John of Gaunt and a cousin of Henry's grandmother, the ambassadors were accompanied by 'seventy knights, gentlemen and yeomen to the number of 400 and above'.[34]

In Paris, Francis received the ambassadors in the Palais-Royal, where he embraced every gentleman.[35] At the fête, held on 22 December, no expense was spared. Francis had thrown up a temporary banqueting house for the occasion: its timber roof, eighty feet high, was lined with blue canvas, thickly waxed to stop rain coming in, and on every side stood three tiered galleries, held up by pillars festooned with antique designs, the fronts 'curiously wrought' with heraldic arms, finials and other ornaments. A canvas ceiling, painted to represent the heavens with all its planets and constellations, was studded with gilded stars and had mirrors suspended beneath the rafters to reflect light from over 200 candelabras. Francis presided at the top table, shaped like a horseshoe, with his sister Marguerite in the place of honour as the new Duke of Berry. It is often claimed, without evidence, that Anne acted as an interpreter for those English guests whose French was inadequate. Much likelier is that she sat with her fellow *demoiselles* watching from the gallery.[36]

Jousts and yet more banquets were to come, after which Anne's father hastened to visit the Dauphin in his nursery. The only blip in the proceedings came when some of the English visitors disgraced themselves: several got into drunken brawls, and one 'lieth sick and is in very evil case ... with the hunting of harlots'. Two of Henry's closest buddies and gentlemen of the privy chamber, the small group of intimates who attended to his personal needs, were among those named and shamed. Mischievously suborned by Francis, Francis Bryan and his brother-in-law Nicholas Carew had ridden through the streets in disguise, 'throwing eggs, stones and other foolish trifles at the people'. This was 'much discommended and jested at'. If that was not enough, 'these young gentlemen', when they came home, were said to be 'all French, in eating, drinking and apparel, yea, and in French vices and brags'. 'Nothing by them was praised, but if it were after the French turn.'[37]

Despite the Anglo-French treaty, public opinion in England was still overwhelmingly Francophobe, as this reaction to the courtiers' new airs shows. To be French in manners and fashion went against the grain of what was believed to be English. Wolsey struggled to strike a balance between these two opposing viewpoints. He had long seen Bryan and Carew as a threat, especially Bryan. A man with the shrewdest of minds and Anne's cousin (their mothers were half-sisters), Bryan fully grasped the opportunities and the pitfalls offered by royal courts, which he once likened to a maze – a 'perpetual dream, a bottomless whirlpool, an enchanted fantasy' – where flattery, lies and deceit bred peril and confusion.[38] His fierce intelligence, dissolute lifestyle, puckish wit and fearless speech later earned him the soubriquet 'the Vicar of Hell'.[39] When the rumours flew far and wide that such men 'after their appetite governed the king', Wolsey dismissed them, replacing them with older, wiser heads. One was Sir Richard Wingfield, now married to the much younger Bridget Wilshire, Anne's childhood friend.[40]

When the other ambassadors returned in February 1519, Anne's father stayed in France. For the next seventeen months, he served as the resident English ambassador, shadowing the French court and gaining privileged access to Louise of Savoy, with whom he got on famously and who promised (as he said) that 'she will make me privy of such news as she shall hear of from any place'. He wrote weekly reports to Henry and Wolsey, and before long had open invitations to visit Francis and Marguerite of Angoulême, often at the shortest of notice or even unannounced.[41]

Henry's decision to keep Anne's father in France was prompted by another death among the older generation of European monarchs: Maximilian had died, meaning an election for a new Holy Roman Emperor to replace him was imminent.* The vacancy brought the rivalry between Francis and Charles, so far muted, into the open. Boleyn's task was to assess the chances of Francis's candidature and foster the illusion that English policy regarding the election was pro-French or neutral. This was a challenging brief, given that Richard Pace would soon be sent to Germany with instructions to advance Henry's own candidature.[42]

Pope Leo at first backed Francis. He then hesitated, fearing a violent confrontation if either Charles or Francis won. It was when he trawled the courts of Europe for a third candidate that Henry optimistically stepped forward, hoping to win at least prestige by being paraded as a candidate and perhaps with a flicker of hope of success. In the end, Charles triumphed by spending 1.5 million florins (some £187,500 sterling) on bribes and by hiring an army of mercenaries whom he told to camp as close as possible to Frankfurt where the votes would be cast. His election put him in charge of an empire that included Germany, Savoy and the Austrian lands, the whole of Spain, the Low Countries, Naples and Sicily, and

---

*The title of Holy Roman Emperor was elective (although there were only seven electors, a mixture of bishops and noblemen) and candidates did not need to be German. Success required the votes of at least four of the seven members of the electoral college drawn from a territorial aggregation that stretched across central Europe and northern Italy.

which was already spilling over into north Africa and large tracts of the New World. Katherine had been right. The power politics of Europe were swinging back in Charles's favour.[43]

At the very least from now on, Francis and Charles, who styled himself the Emperor Charles V, would be equally matched. To defeat the other, each would need Henry as an ally. Charles's success marked the beginning of a fresh chapter in Henry's life and ambitions, and in the fullness of time had consequences which transformed Anne's life too.

7

Looking to the Future

On 11 March 1519, the heavily pregnant Claude left Paris with her ladies for the old palace of Saint-Germain-en-Laye, some fifteen miles distant, to prepare for her latest *accouchement*. Along the way, she was forced to rest at the village of Porte de Neuilly. Thomas Boleyn was the first foreign diplomat to report that she was 'very sickly, more than she has been of any other child here aforetime' – his informant was probably Anne. That night, he continued, 'she was in great danger'. False rumours abounded, first that she was dead, later that she had been delivered. His prediction, which proved to be accurate, was that when she was strong enough, the women would abandon the horse litters in which they rode and be quietly ferried in a closed barge along the Seine to Saint-Germain.[1]

Hastening there, Anne's father heard that the queen 'looketh her time every hour', an opinion he confirmed after Louise of Savoy invited him to peep into the darkened lying-in chamber. The waiting was over on the 31st, when Claude gave birth to her second son, called Henry, Duke of Orléans. The baptism was on 5 June, when Thomas Boleyn, acting as proxy for Henry VIII who had been named one of the child's godparents, held the child over the font and presented gifts of a gold salt cellar, cup and ewer. This gave Anne and her father an opportunity to meet and catch up on family news.[2]

After Charles was elected emperor, Thomas continued to shadow the French court. His latest instructions required him to arrange a summit between Henry and Francis on the frontier between England and France near Calais, a project first mooted in Wolsey's diplomacy of the previous year. Anne's father opened the negotiations at Saint-Germain but did most of the work over the summer in the Loire Valley, where Francis retreated on account of plague. Claude had already fled with her baby and her *demoiselles* to Blois, around which a *cordon sanitaire* was thrown.[3]

The following year, for three weeks in February and March 1520, Anne and her father were reunited in the Valois-Angoulême ancestral seat of Cognac in south-western France, where Francis and his sister Marguerite had been brought up. The king had taken the whole court there, after celebrating Christmas in Poitou. Travelling on by way of Saint-Jean-d'Angély, a pilgrimage town on the route to Santiago de Compostela in Spain, the royal convoy arrived in Cognac to a fanfare of trumpets. Francis made his *entrée* on the morning of Sunday 18 February, a time of carnival to mark the weekend before Shrove Tuesday. The next day, and in the presence of Anne's father, Louise arranged a second *entrée* in honour of Claude. All eyes were fixed on the queen as she rode in her finery through the streets in a horse litter borne by mules. Greeted by an actor dressed as Mercury, she graciously acknowledged the cheers of the crowds while more actors dressed as gods and goddesses stepped forward to pay her homage. Behind her, riding in liveried carts as during Claude's coronation procession, were Anne and her fellow *demoiselles*.[4]

This was the last occasion on which Anne saw her father as resident ambassador. We can be sure of this, because Claude and Louise wrote independently to Henry to inform him that 'le sieur Boulan' would deliver their latest news to him in person. Their letters were triggered by Henry's, or more likely Wolsey's, decision to recall and replace Boleyn with Sir Richard Wingfield. Joining the court in Cognac, Wingfield accompanied Boleyn to an audience with Francis, where the new ambassador delivered his credentials. No evidence exists to suppose that Anne's father was recalled for any other reason than that his work in organising the upcoming summit was done. The event was to take place in May or June 1520, the date having been shifted forward after Claude announced that she was pregnant for the fifth time and expected her baby in late July or August.[5]

Now all was set for what was to become the dazzling chivalric extravaganza known to contemporaries as the Field of Cloth of Gold. So keen an interest did Wolsey take in the event that he personally designed an Italian-style temporary *palazzo* for Henry and Katherine to entertain in, and ordered jousts, masques, Masses, fireworks, fairy-tale banquets, displays of art treasures and prodigious quantities of free wine to keep everyone busy while behind closed doors the serious talking took place. Costs would be colossal. Henry ordered vast quantities of cloth of gold – which, since legislation enacted in 1463, had been permissible only for royalty and the nobility to wear – and bales of silk from suppliers in Florence and paid for clothes for courtiers and their wives and daughters. On his side, Francis matched much of this spending. Wolsey did the same for members of his own household and gave his chamberlain, Richard Page, a 'great chain' of gold to wear.[6]

For Anne, this was to become a family reunion. Besides her father and mother, her sister Mary would be attending and probably her brother George too, even though his name did not appear on Wolsey's original lists. Mary now had a husband. On 4 February 1520, a fortnight before Anne arrived in Cognac, she had married the twenty-year-old William Carey, Henry's distant cousin and a fast-rising courtier with glittering prospects, in a ceremony at Greenwich with the king as guest of honour.[7] The newly weds were assigned lodgings close to the king's own.[8]

For Henry and Francis, the summit was meant to reset European affairs for a generation, with their meeting as the climax. At least 3,000 nobles and courtiers were to accompany each of them, with another 2,500 or so from the retinues of their nobility. Not far short of 2,000 women were to join them, since Katherine and Claude were to play extensive roles in the exchanges of hospitality. Henry was to be received by Claude, and Francis by Katherine. Claude would preside regally over banquets honouring Henry and would sit in the position of honour on Katherine's right in the stands in the tiltyard when the jousting began. Despite being seven months pregnant, her attendance was obligatory, even in the pouring rain.[9]

But before he made it to Calais, Henry double-crossed Francis. Spurred on by Katherine, who longed to meet her nephew Charles, the new emperor, in the flesh, he arranged a rendezvous with Charles, who was sailing from Galicia in Spain to Flanders with a fleet of sixty ships and took the opportunity to drop anchor off the port of Hythe, beside Dover.[10]

On 26 May, Wolsey welcomed Charles ashore, and after supper led him to a suite of apartments made ready for him in Dover Castle. Early next morning, Whitsunday, Henry bounded in and kissed Charles while still on the stairs, after which the two monarchs rode side-by-side to Canterbury Cathedral. There, they visited the shrine of the murdered Archbishop Thomas Becket in the Trinity Chapel behind the high altar and kissed a relic of the True Cross to the music of the hymn 'Veni Creator Spiritus' ('Come Holy Ghost') sung in plainsong by the choir, after which they went to a late breakfast in the archbishop's palace.[11]

Always opposed to a French match for her only daughter and exhilarated at the prospect of bringing together her nephew and her husband, Katherine played her part to the full. For her, friendship with France was one thing, friendship with her native Spain quite another: a return to an Anglo-Spanish alliance would rekindle everything she had come to England to foster.

Watched anxiously by Anne's father, who was also in Canterbury and feared what might come, the royal guests dined and danced with their hosts, interspersing the festivities with exploratory talks. Early in the morning of the 31st, Charles made his farewells and boarded his ship for Flanders. The very same day Henry, Katherine and their retinues, including the whole of the Boleyn contingent, sailed from Dover to Calais to begin the summit with Francis, who was fully aware of Henry's deceptions but preferred not to show it.[12]

For all its pomp and pageantry, the summit was no great success. Lasting from the 4th to the 24th of June, it began when Henry rode with Wolsey by his side into the courtyard of his temporary palace. The main event, the meeting of the two sovereigns, took place on the 7th in the so-called 'Golden Valley' linking the frontier towns of Guînes and Ardres. A shot fired from Guînes Castle, quickly followed by another from Ardres, gave the signal that each monarch should advance.[13] When in sight of each other, the two kings, each dressed in cloth of silver and gold studded with diamonds and rubies, spurred their horses; then, to carefully orchestrated applause, they doffed their hats, embraced three times, and on dismounting did so again before walking arm in arm to a tent of cloth of gold where only Wolsey and Admiral Bonnivet, Francis's own confidant, could join them.[14] Nobody knew exactly what they said as they talked for about an hour, but any agreement was not to last.[15]

After the meeting came the tournament, which lasted for eleven days. When the trumpets blew to summon everyone to the tiltyard, both kings stepped forward, but to emphasise their bond they jointly captained the team of challengers who competed against some 200 answerers. Among the English contestants were several from Henry's privy chamber: Mary Boleyn's new husband, William Carey; Francis Bryan and Nicholas Carew, both now reinstated; and Henry Norris, increasingly a key figure. Contrary to legend, the two kings did not fight each other, but did engage in an impromptu wrestling match. Henry initiated it, only to be humiliated when Francis threw him to the ground in a classic manoeuvre known as the 'Breton turn'.[16]

Claude and Katherine jointly presided over the jousts, enthroned inside a richly furnished pavilion. Both entered the tiltyard in ceremonial horse litters: Claude's was covered with cloth of silver bedecked with gold tassels, and behind it rode her *demoiselles* on palfreys. As the ladies of the tournament, the queens were the focus of its chivalric rituals, greeting each other with all courtesy before the competitors were presented to them. On the final day, they presented the prizes, among them a large diamond and a ruby, set in two rings, for a triumphant Henry.[17]

Anne watched from the side of the lists. She may also have been among Claude's attendants at sumptuous banquets she hosted for

Henry on 10 and 17 June in a chamber lined with cloth of gold ribbed with Claude's signature *cordelières*. Just as probable is that she joined those of Claude's women who, on those same days, accompanied Francis to dine with Katherine.[18]

Something ambassadors expressly remarked on was how elegantly dressed the French were compared to the English. Katherine, for example, wore an old-fashioned, clumsy English gable headdress to watch the tournament (confused by some with a Spanish headpiece), so named because of its heavy pointed arch at the front and metal hoops. Claude's women, on the other hand, dressed in the latest styles. According to the Mantuan ambassador to France, they always 'look better and are more beautiful' *(le francese erano meglio et più belle)*. For their headwear they chose delicately wrought French hoods, consisting of a close-fitting textile cap with jewelled bands and borders set in gold or embroidered. Not covering the front portion of the wearer's hair, which was usually combed with a centre parting, such hoods were still rare in England, although not unknown. Henry's younger sister Mary continued to wear one after she became the Duchess of Suffolk, and Katherine purchased one for her young daughter to mark her betrothal to the Dauphin. It is thus untrue, as is often claimed, that Anne would introduce French hoods into England, although they certainly would become her sartorial trademark.[19]

On 25 June, the summit broke up. Anne left with the rest of Claude's women, returning to Saint-Germain-en-Laye where, six weeks later, Claude would give birth to a daughter, called Madeleine. Henry, meanwhile, left with Katherine to meet Charles again, this time on his own territory. To make their discussions more inclusive, Charles invited Margaret of Austria to join them. Now that he was Holy Roman Emperor as well as King of Spain, he had reappointed her as regent of the Low Countries.[20]

On 10 July, Henry, accompanied by Wolsey, the Dukes of Buckingham and Suffolk, and about 300 courtiers and retainers, including Anne's father, set off towards Gravelines, about twenty miles west of Calais, just inside Charles's territory. It had been agreed that Charles would lead the English into the town, having met them along the route. Their aim was to conduct what the Venetian ambassador called a 'political conversation' (*abochamento*). Two days later, it was Henry's turn to reciprocate in Calais, where the finest buildings, the Staple Hall on the main square and the nearby Exchequer off the High Street with its royal lodgings complete with a gallery, tennis court and king's and queen's gardens, had been lavishly furnished in readiness.

Not everything went to plan. The roof of a temporary great theatre designed to house a spectacular entertainment blew off in a storm, much to its architect's chagrin, but several banquets still took place and Henry dined and danced to his heart's content. The talks themselves ended inconclusively, much as they had done with Francis. Henry and Charles spoke face-to-face for a long time, 'with the king of England talking almost in the ear of the Emperor'. They then 'embraced very affectionately, their hats in their hands', and went their separate ways.

Henry, to Katherine's disappointment, was not quite ready yet to commit. This was a setback for Charles, whose plans had less to do with restoring the Anglo-Spanish alliance as he professed, than with drawing Henry into a war against France.[21]

Could Anne's father have glimpsed war on the horizon and warned his daughter at the Field of Cloth of Gold that she might soon have to return home? This seems unlikely. It was not until the late autumn of 1520 that Francis saw the threat, when Charles devised what he called his 'Great Enterprise'. This aimed to couple the conquest of Milan with the recovery of the old Duchy of Burgundy, centred on Dijon and annexed by Louis XI. Cross-border communications were the key to Charles's strategy: he reasoned that if he could control Milan and the old Burgundian dominions, he could ship troops from Cartagena or Barcelona in Spain to Genoa, and then march them through Lombardy and the Tyrol and into Germany or through Burgundy to the Low Countries.[22]

The next spring, Francis received a shock of a different type. Pope Leo proclaimed his intention to ally with Charles, with the aim of expelling all French forces from Italy. A calamity then befell the

French garrison in Milan: an ammunition dump in the castle was struck by lightning, causing a huge explosion and devastating the defences there. Charles saw his chance. One of his armies attacked the north-east frontier of France, intending to march towards Reims; another laid siege to Milan. Europe was suddenly aflame.[23]

In August 1521, Wolsey offered to arbitrate between the rivals, recruiting Anne's father and Henry's new secretary, Thomas More, to join him on an embassy to Calais and Bruges. His approach was compelling: with the Treaty of Universal Peace now superseded by events, Henry should make himself the chief mediator of international affairs. As Wolsey explained this to Henry, 'In this controversy betwixt these two princes, it shall be a marvellous great praise and honour to your grace so by your high wisdom and authority to pass between and stay them both, that ye be not by their contention and variance brought on to the war.'[24]

This, at least, was the starting point, but as the mission developed, Wolsey steadily steered Henry towards backing Charles against Francis, which meant the threat of war reappeared. On 8 September, during an awkward audience with Antoine Duprat, Chancellor of France, Anne's father was asked to explain why Henry was posturing as a mediator while mustering ships and troops. 'My master', he replied hollowly, 'is always repairing his ships according to the many needs that he has. It is the custom to do this sort of thing at this time of year, and as to the military musters, he would only find that such manoeuvres were customary for that time of year.'[25]

Such weak denials left Francis unconvinced. After this mission, much of Boleyn's credibility with the French king and his mother evaporated for several years. Explanations were left to the new resident ambassador in France, Sir William Fitzwilliam, Henry's schoolroom friend, who fared little better.[26] Then, when Charles's forces besieged Mézières from the east and Tournai from the north, advancing into the Pas-de-Calais and razing Ardres to its foundations after it was left deliberately undefended by Francis in response to an English request, Fitzwilliam was accosted by an irate Marguerite of Angoulême. 'See ye not', she demanded accusingly, watched approvingly by Louise of Savoy, 'how the Cardinal is ever treating of peace almost to the day of battle? Our enemies come still upon us ... what say ye to that? And as for trust, that is past.'

When Fitzwilliam answered sheepishly, 'I assure you that the king, my master, is no dissimuler,' Marguerite retorted that she would take him at his word, but if she found otherwise, 'I will never trust man after.' She then urged him, 'I pray you, write the best of everything ye can, and advertise the king, your master, and my lord Cardinal how the Englishmen were [complicit] at the pulling down of Ardres, and desire them to see some punishment done upon them, to the intent that men may see it was against your master's will.'[27]

Francis struck back, capturing Fuenterrabía in the Basque Country, relieving Mézières and assembling a large army at Reims, poised to do battle with Charles. Anxious not to end up in a war on the losing side, Wolsey proposed a truce, sending Anne's father with Sir Thomas Docwra, another fluent linguist, to Charles, where their instructions were to say that Henry was not ready for a fight, but within weeks, the situation had changed again. Francis's attempts to relieve Tournai were destined for failure. In Italy, the war was going well for Charles. On 19 November, his troops broke through Milan's defences and captured the city, leaving only a small French garrison holed up in the castle.[28]

Three days later, Wolsey signed the secret treaty of Bruges, which committed England to enter a war against France on Charles's side during the next two years. What's more, Charles was to marry his cousin, Henry and Katherine's daughter, the infant Princess Mary, who was currently betrothed to the Dauphin. Rumours of an impending treaty of this sort caused a panic among the English community in Paris: scholars studying in the university there hastily packed their bags and abandoned their lodgings. Anne's father, fully aware of the danger, ordered a courier to escort his daughter home.[29]

His timing is established by the instructions Francis gave his ambassadors in the opening days of 1522, skilfully intercepted by Wolsey's spies. 'The whole question', Francis said, 'is whether my

good brother [i.e. Henry] intends to maintain his fraternal love
... As to the suspicions which he says have arisen, I have done
nothing openly or covertly against the amity between us.' 'I trust',
he continues, 'that the suspicions ... which I might have against
him, are unfounded; yet I think it very strange that this treaty of
Bruges was concealed from me, [and] that the English scholars that
were in Paris are all returned home, also the daughter of Monsieur
Boullan.'[30]

Summing up his perception of Henry's motives, Francis
concluded:

> I do not know if he finds it difficult to maintain the friendship
> of myself and the emperor elect [i.e. Charles, who was
> technically only 'emperor elect' as he had not yet been crowned
> by the pope], considering the enmity between us; but he must
> choose between neutrality and a declaration for one or the
> other. As to neutrality, I should not be dissatisfied; but if he
> were to declare against me, I should consider it a great wrong,
> after all the familiarities, oaths and treaties between us.[31]

Anne may just have been home from France in time for
Christmas 1521. If so, she would have heard all the news of the
'high feasting' and the 'many sumptuous and gorgeous disguisings,
interludes and banquets' held this year at Henry's favourite palace
of Greenwich.[32] Her parents were there, so were her sister Mary
and her husband. So was her brother George, who in 1514 had first
appeared in the Christmas revels with his parents and stayed on as
a royal page. Like many of the Boleyns, George was a fluent French
speaker, possibly tutored in Oxford and then in Paris. It was not
uncommon for the sons of aspiring Englishmen to attend lectures
at the Collège de Calvi (known as the 'little Sorbonne') or study
with private tutors.[33]

Anne was not invited that Christmas for the king's revelries, but
may have felt it no great loss, given her close ties to France. She
would need time to reorient herself, and had every chance of doing
so successfully. Her mother had been one of Katherine of Aragon's

principal ladies-in-waiting since early in the reign.[34] Her father, although close to Louise of Savoy and Marguerite of Angoulême, had deftly detached himself as the wind changed, shuttling between the rival negotiating teams at Calais and Bruges in an ostensibly neutral capacity, while happily sharing confidential dispatches from France with Charles.[35]

During the past seven years, Anne had travelled far and wide across France and had some amazing experiences. She had made invaluable personal connections, seeing how the world worked when it was governed by men, but also how notable women like Claude, Louise and Marguerite could exercise power and influence in their very different ways. It had been an education which far surpassed anything conventional tutors could have provided. But where did her future lie?

8

First Encounters

Anne Boleyn's personality was first remarked on after her return from France. In an apparent reference to the skills which she had mastered on the Continent, Wolsey's gentleman-usher, George Cavendish, speaks of 'her excellent gesture and behaviour'. It is a rare compliment to her, made in his *Life of Wolsey*, which centres on the catastrophe she was about to bring to Wolsey. Cavendish was an eyewitness to much of what he describes: his characterisations are wonderfully compelling, but he wrote from memory and his recollections could be faulty. Sometimes he gets things wrong or his chronology is muddled: he is, for instance, mistaken in claiming that Anne's father's career had barely begun by the time Henry fell in love with her, and that she stayed in the French court until the summer of 1524.[1]

Once Henry decided to divorce Katherine of Aragon, fuller descriptions of Anne would follow. The first was in February 1528, when Lodovico Ceresari, the Duke of Milan's agent in Paris, assured the Venetian Signoria that she was 'very beautiful' (*bellissima*).[2] The French diplomat Lancelot de Carle, who first saw her after his arrival in England in May 1535, when she was Henry's queen, agrees:

She was beautiful and had an elegant figure,
And still more appealing were her eyes,

Which she knew how to use well,
Holding them sometimes in repose,
Other times sending a message with them
To carry the secret witness of her heart.[3]

John Barlow, a short, red-haired chaplain to Anne's father, was less gushing. He told a Flemish diplomat in Leuven in 1532 that she 'is very eloquent and gracious', but only 'sufficiently beautiful' ('competement belle') although she came 'of a good family'.[4] Simon Grynée, whom Henry would later invite to England with a view to canvassing Swiss opinions in favour of his divorce, shared Barlow's doubts: he found her 'young, good-looking, of a rather dark complexion'.[5]

Anne's features would divide contemporaries. In her favour was that she was slim, confident, full of life, with a long, slender neck and dark, flashing eyes that made the recipient of her gaze feel that they alone mattered to her. Less appealing were her dark hair and skin: she was a natural brunette at a time when the preference was for fair-haired, porcelain-skinned women. Thomas Wyatt, whose family had known the Boleyns since Anne was a child, would give her the poetic name 'Brunet' and remark on her 'fair neck'.[6] As Marino Sanuto, a Venetian historian and diarist drawing on diplomatic dispatches, explained in 1532:

> Madame Anna is not one of the most beautiful women in the
> world. Her height is average, her skin is unusually dark, she
> has a long neck, a wide mouth, and relatively flat breasts. In
> fact, she has nothing but the great appetite of that king and her
> eyes, which are black and beautiful and exert a greater effect on
> servants than the queen's when she was in her prime.[7]

Shortly before, Sanuto had praised her flowing head of hair, saying she often liked to wear it 'hanging down loose'.[8]

Anne had to be careful if she wished to secure a coveted place in Katherine's household, the career her parents most likely planned for her. On the plus side, her family's fortunes and status had much improved. In February 1516, her father had sold Henry the manor of New Hall and its hunting park for £1,000. He could sell because his maternal grandfather, the Earl of Ormond, had died some months before: Ormond's death brought into effect the legal accord which Thomas Boleyn had reached with his mother in 1511. Delighted with the purchase, which he renamed Beaulieu,* Henry paid the money there and then, starting rebuilding work at once and allowing the conveyancing to be completed afterwards. At the same time, he promised to make Anne's father treasurer or comptroller of the king's household the next time a vacancy arose.[9]

The New Hall sale alone did not solve the family's money worries. From 1516 until soon after Anne's return, her father borrowed heavily from Richard Fermour, a wealthy London merchant. Boleyn finally settled with Fermour by quietly selling him the manor of Luton Hoo. He did this despite knowing that by doing so, he was defrauding his mother, to whom he had granted the use of that property for life alongside Blickling.[10]

In terms of status, the great leap forward came just six weeks before Anne came home, when Henry appointed her father to the coveted treasurership, which put him and his deputy, the comptroller, in charge of most of the daily operational aspects of the king's palaces.[11] The treasurer occupied lodgings close to Henry's own apartments. He was an ex officio royal councillor, creating yet another step up for Anne's father, although he had already been invited to council meetings and had sworn his councillor's oath.[12]

If Anne dreamed of joining her parents at Henry and Katherine's court, it was important that her family kept on the right side of Wolsey. This they did: a commonly voiced suggestion that they quarrelled with him over the treasurership is misplaced: rooted in a misreading of a letter Boleyn sent from Poissy in May 1519, the mistake was to believe Henry's decision to appoint an alternative candidate that spring on an interim basis had come through Wolsey's malign interventions. In fact, the issue arose only because

*Not to be confused with Beaulieu in Hampshire.

Henry needed Anne's father to stay in France to complete the planning for the Field of Cloth of Gold.[13]

Wolsey, indeed, was making plans that intimately involved the Boleyns. Whether Anne personally was aware that Wolsey, shortly after the Anglo-French summit, sought to marry her off to the twenty-four-year-old Sir James Butler, son and heir of Sir Piers Butler, a powerful Irish magnate, cannot be known, but her parents were aware. These plans were shaped after Sir Piers, vehemently opposed by Anne's father, had laid claim to the title and Irish estates of the earldom of Ormond, sparking a bitter feud.

Matters came to a head in October 1520. On the advice of the Earl of Surrey, son of the victor of Flodden whom Henry had sent to Dublin to reform the government of Ireland, Wolsey proposed to settle the quarrel by marrying Anne to Piers's heir. In this way, he believed, both sides would win in the next generation.[14] Henry gave his approval, informing Wolsey that he would 'advance' it with Anne's father. As it turned out, no marriage took place. If this was due to resistance from the Boleyns, they prevailed, and their objections did them no harm. In the meantime, Wolsey recruited James into his retinue, taking him with him on his embassy to Calais and Bruges and keeping him close.[15]

But, even with her parents' influence, it was far from certain that Anne would gain a place in Katherine's service. She was Francophile in every possible sense, and on the wrong side of Henry and Katherine's current view of the world. That applied equally to her views on religion after running across the early French evangelical reformers with Queen Claude and Louise of Savoy.

Henry's religious position was very different, at least at this point in his life. While he and Francis were at the Field of Cloth of Gold, Pope Leo had excommunicated Luther. On returning home, Henry vigorously defended the Catholic faith in a book entitled *Assertio Septem Sacramentorum* ('A Defence of the Seven Sacraments'), which he dedicated to the pope. The idea came from Wolsey, who recruited Thomas More and Richard Pace to help Henry finish the manuscript. On Sunday 12 May 1521, following a passionate outdoor sermon by Bishop John Fisher of Rochester in St Paul's

Churchyard, Wolsey held a handwritten draft aloft to the cheers of the crowd, while signalling to a torchbearer to light a huge bonfire of Lutheran books.[16] Soon the Church authorities would be putting suspected heretics on trial for their lives. In recognition, Leo granted Henry the title 'Defender of the Faith'. Katherine's resolve was just as tenacious: encouraged by her new Spanish confessor, Alfonso de Villasancta, she saw herself as the 'Defendress of the Faith'.[17]

All this neatly meshed with events in Germany, where in packed sessions of the *Reichstag* (the imperial representative assembly) in Worms during April, Luther was questioned in Charles's presence and his doctrines and writings condemned. He was allowed to return home under a safe conduct, but it was said that an arrest and trial were imminent, until the sympathetic Elector Frederick III of Saxony arranged for him to be hidden away and protected.[18]

It was fortunate that the Boleyns kept on the right side of Wolsey because Anne made her debut by his invitation. The occasion was the Shrove Tuesday masque on 4 March 1522, when she was twenty-one years old. Shrove Tuesday, like May Day, was a day of celebration associated with romantic love. This year Wolsey hosted the festivities in the great hall of his principal residence at York Place. Bordering the Thames close to Westminster Abbey and some 200 feet to the east of the narrow street that ran between Westminster and Charing Cross, York Place was Wolsey's town house, belonging to him as Archbishop of York, where he stayed during the legal terms when his presence was required in the law courts.

International affairs again framed the event. Charles, preparing to make a state visit to ratify with Henry the agreements Wolsey had made in Bruges, had sent ambassadors to England. The hospitality laid on for these honoured guests began on Shrove Tuesday Eve with a joust on the theme of 'Unrequited Love' in which Henry entered the lists sporting the motto 'She hath wounded my heart'. On the night of the masque, Wolsey led the ambassadors into a 'great chamber' lit by hundreds of candles, its walls lined with vibrantly coloured tapestries, many echoing the action about to be performed. Attention quickly moved to the far end of the hall, where an elaborate timber castle with battlements shimmering with green tinfoil called the Château Vert was installed. It had one great tower and two lesser ones, each with a different banner suggestive of the power that women could exert over men. One was of three broken hearts, another of a woman's hand gripping a man's heart, the third of a woman's hand turning a man's heart upside down. Looking out from the towers were eight damsels identified as 'Beauty', 'Honour', 'Perseverance', 'Kindness', 'Constancy', 'Bounty', 'Mercy' and 'Pity'. Each wore a gown of the finest Milanese satin, her hair held in place by a golden net beneath a close-fitting cap studded with jewels.

From below, the castle was defended by another, far less attractive group of women said to be 'Danger', 'Disdain', 'Jealousy', 'Unkindness', 'Scorn', 'Malebouche' ('slander' or 'bad-mouthing') and 'Strangeness' (i.e. unapproachability). In fact, they were not women at all but choirboys from Henry's Chapel, dressed 'like to women of India'. The action began when a posse of lusty males, Henry among them, clad in cloaks of blue satin with golden hats, assailed the defenders of the castle to capture the women in the towers. Henry took the role of 'Amorous', and the posse was led by an actor representing 'Ardent Desire' – he was probably William Cornish, the Master of the Choristers, who scripted the masque and appeared in crimson satin adorned with gold badges depicting burning flames. When 'Ardent Desire' invited the women to come down to meet his companions and they refused, the fun began. In what was almost slapstick comedy, the assault consisted of a 'siege' with salvos of mock gunfire and the hurling of dates and oranges at the defenders, who responded with arrows and fake shot from their imitation bows and muskets, while from the towers the eight women showered the men with 'comfits' (sugared confections) and rose water.[19] Finally, the castle fell, and the defenders fled, leaving the men to bring the women down from the towers as their 'prisoners', and all 'danced together very pleasantly' before everyone removed their masks. Wolsey then conducted everyone into a banqueting chamber, where sweet wines and desserts were served.[20]

Most of the women's identities can be traced in the Revels Accounts. Henry's sister, the Duchess of Suffolk, played 'Beauty' and Gertrude Blount, Lord Mountjoy's daughter and now the wife of the king's cousin Henry Courtenay, was 'Honour'. Elizabeth Browne took the part of 'Bounty', while Elizabeth Dannet represented 'Mercy'. Browne was a sister of Anthony Browne, the youngest of Henry's schoolroom associates. She would soon become one of Anne's best friends. Dannet was the wife or daughter of Gerard Dannet, an esquire of the body. She and Browne were with Katherine at the Field of Cloth of Gold.[21] But it was the lives of the last three which were destined to become most entwined. Jane Parker, Lord Morley's daughter, who before long would be betrothed to the young George Boleyn, was 'Constancy'. Anne's sister, Mary, was 'Kindness', while Anne herself played 'Perseverance'.[22]

In choosing the motto 'She hath wounded my heart' and identifying himself as 'Amorous', Henry had an ulterior motive. Shortly after the masque, if not before, he took a Boleyn as his mistress – not Anne, whom he had still barely noticed, but her more nubile sister. Her father raised no objection. A man unperturbed by robbing his mother in her old age, Sir Thomas Boleyn had no scruples about using his children to achieve wealth and power for the family. More decisive is likely to have been William Carey's attitude, and he did not hesitate. To fast-track his career, he willingly laid down his wife for his king.

Whether Mary herself was easy prey is far from certain. If a taunt attributed to Francis widely reported by Rodolfo Pio da Carpi, papal nuncio to France, is to be believed, she had already 'done service' to him and his courtiers, earning a reputation as 'una grandissima ribalda, et infame sopra tutte' ('a very great bawd, and infamous above all'). The problem is that when the original dispatch is traced among a cache of diplomatic documents once held in Castel Sant'Angelo and now in the Vatican, no proof exists that Francis ever used those words. He was simply said to have done so in March 1536 during a vitriolic smear campaign aimed less at Mary than at Anne. Without better evidence, the question of Mary's morals must be left open.[23]

Mary was not Henry's first mistress, and the inside story of his liaisons now began to unfold. His earlier trysts had quickly fizzled out, but after Katherine was delivered of a stillborn daughter in 1518, he took Elizabeth Blount, a daughter of one of his men-at-arms, as a mistress in an affair lasting less than a year.[24] Some said that William Compton was his pimp.[25] Elizabeth (or 'Bessie') was one of Katherine's maids. It was in comparison with her universally recognised good looks that John Barlow would later say of Anne that she was only 'competement belle'.

It was from that affair that Henry had a son, born in about June 1519. As Bessie's lying-in approached, Henry sent her to a secluded Essex manor house. Wolsey handled the arrangements while Katherine pretended not to notice, finding it all beneath her dignity. Her father Ferdinand and brother-in-law Philip the Handsome's open infidelities had been notorious enough. Whether Katherine already harboured her own insecurities is hard to know. Unlike Queen Claude in France, she could hardly claim to be fecund, even if the fault was not her own. Probably she sublimated her anxieties: any suggestion that her husband was unfaithful had the effect of reinforcing her steely commitment to Catholicism and to her marriage. She would hold to this position until her dying day.[26]

Once Henry heard from Wolsey that the child, who became known as Henry Fitzroy, was a healthy boy, he acknowledged him and made generous provision for his upbringing and education, but quickly divested himself of Bessie, marrying her off to Gilbert Tailboys, a wealthy young heir. He had proved that he could father a living son but had no intention being caught in such a scandal again.[27] For this reason, a married woman like Mary was safer as a lover: contraception would be less of an issue as the law would presume any child of the liaison to be her husband's.[28]

As Marguerite of Angoulême had so prudently warned, secrecy in sexual affairs was impossible. News of the king's affairs trickled down in hints and backstairs whispers. It is repeatedly said how Henry appeared to court publicity for his adultery with Mary Boleyn by naming a royal navy ship of 100 tons after her, but scrutiny of the handwritten roll in the British Library suggests otherwise. The ship, in fact, was a Boleyn merchant vessel, a hangover from the days when the family was still in the cloth trade. Henry's Vice-Admiral had bought it for £352 8s 6½d for transporting military supplies to Calais. Another Boleyn ship, the *Anne Boleyn*, was purchased or hired for transporting supplies, for which the Paymaster at War paid £115 4s 0d. The second payment relates to a transaction in 1522 or 1523, a time when nobody has suggested that Henry and Anne were lovers.[29]

To coincide with the Shrove Tuesday masque, Henry gave William Carey, the husband of his new mistress, the keepership of the former Boleyn property of Beaulieu, along with numerous other perquisites, the first of a succession of grants.[30] The keepership gave him and his wife the freedom of what was tantamount to a royal palace, since it entitled them to live there rent free when Henry was elsewhere. A sudden, dramatic event then substantially increased the Boleyn property portfolio further. For reasons we do not fully understand, Henry had become suspicious of the mighty Duke of Buckingham and, in a handwritten letter, instructed Wolsey to 'make a good watch' upon him.[31] Something had triggered the sense of insecurity the king often felt when under pressure and he lashed out furiously, exercising power without any form of self-control and without remorse. As he grew older, he could shift seamlessly from a beatific gentleness towards murderous violence. And, in Buckingham's case, he did so with a speed and vindictiveness which shocked the country.

In the show trial of 1521, Buckingham was accused of treason because, the prosecution alleged, he was plotting to seize the throne and, or so a disgruntled servant maintained, kill Henry. The duke protested that the trial was rigged – as indeed it was, as Henry had personally coached or threatened the witnesses – but the guilty verdict was a foregone conclusion.[32] Buckingham was beheaded in a ghastly bungled execution on Tower Hill. The executioner took several strokes of the axe to sever the head as the agonised duke bravely recited verses from the psalms with blood streaming down his neck. For three days afterwards, mourners went to dip their handkerchiefs in what remained of it, 'reputing him as a saint and a holy man' and 'saying that he died guiltless'. Accusing them of 'mutiny and sedition', Henry sent Thomas More to warn the citizens that they had incurred the king's 'great suspicion, and he will not forget'.[33]

Amongst those to benefit from Buckingham's spectacular fall was Thomas Boleyn, to whom the king allocated the high stewardship of Penshurst, just one of the late duke's properties now forfeit to the crown, together with a grant of various offices and lands connected to it. Penshurst lay within easy reach of Hever, so was ideal for the Boleyns.[34]

This grant, coming just after another, that of the manor of Fobbing, near Thurrock in Essex, made the Boleyn family wealthier than many of the peerage. As with the Careys at Beaulieu, the Penshurst grant gave them the use of an additional home, putting them in charge of the property's upkeep at the king's expense, and allowing them to live in the manor house unless Henry was there, which was almost never.[35] Possibly the family regarded Penshurst as their second home, since a boy named Thomas, 'son of Sir Thomas Bwllayen', who died young, was interred in the church beside the manor house around this time. A small memorial cross commemorates his short life, almost identical to another in the church at Hever, which is inscribed to Henry, 'son of Sir Thomas Bwllayen'. Two sons, it appears, had been born to Anne's parents after their move from Norfolk to Kent, but they had lost them both.[36]

Soon after the Penshurst grant, Henry took Anne's brother George into service in his privy chamber, where he joined William Carey, probably starting out as an usher.[37] Now nineteen and fully able to join in the sporting and social functions of the king's side of the court, it became clear that George's love of music, art and poetry and his deep and genuine interest in the new religious ideas that were buzzing around Europe marked him out. Like most Boleyns, he was worldly wise. He too shared in the spoils after the Duke of Buckingham's execution.[38]

Her sister's affair also greatly improved Anne's chances of gaining a place in Katherine's household, or so it seems. But the sources differ on this. Although several files or books of wardrobe and household accounts survive for these years documenting Katherine's expenditure on clothes and other items for herself, her daughter and her women, none mentions Anne. The fullest roster of Katherine's staff, which Wolsey began to compile in the summer of 1525, names each of her ladies-in-waiting individually but unhelpfully lumps together the lesser rank of 'the queen's maidens' as a generic entry.[39]

Cavendish, on the other hand, tells us that almost as soon as Anne had made her debut, 'this gentlewoman ... being again with her father, he made such means that she was admitted to be one of Queen Katherine's maids.'[40] Polydore Vergil, watching from his lodgings beside St Paul's, agrees, saying that Anne was one of the queen's maids.[41] William Camden makes the same claim in the first volume of his *Annals of Queen Elizabeth* published in 1615.[42] So does George Wyatt, grandson of Thomas Wyatt the poet, who devoted his later years to verifying the evidence for her life and career. Writing a *Life of Anne Boleyn* somewhere between 1595 and 1605, he says that after her arrival at Henry's court, she was 'waiting on the queen'.[43]

The probability is that they are correct, and Anne did now leave Hever and take up residence at court as Katherine's maid. It was the beginning of a remarkable journey.

9

Anne in Love

On Monday 26 May 1522, Wolsey and a retinue of 300 waited on the sands at Dover, ready to greet Charles, who was due to arrive for a state visit. As soon as the twenty-two-year-old emperor landed, Wolsey embraced him and led him up the path to the castle, where the guns boomed out a deafening salute. Charles was triumphant. Almost exactly a month earlier, his Italian army had defeated Francis's forces at the Battle of Bicocca, finally giving him control of the Duchy of Milan and much of Lombardy. After Henry, who had been on standby in Canterbury, arrived, he took Charles on board his flagship, the *Henry Grace à Dieu*, and they sailed off to inspect the main body of his Channel fleet at anchor nearby.[1]

After an official reception in Canterbury, Charles and Henry rode at a leisurely pace into Gravesend, where thirty barges were ready to transport them along the Thames to Greenwich Palace. Their business was to ratify the secret treaty agreed by Wolsey at Bruges: Henry would join Charles in the war against France, and Charles would marry his cousin, Princess Mary, when she was twelve.[2] As a signal of Henry's goodwill, Mary, now six, was brought from her nursery and given a gold brooch to wear on her bosom with her cousin's name picked out in jewels. Three months before, in preparation for Charles's visit, the little girl was encouraged to believe she had fallen in love with him, taking him as her 'valentine' on St Valentine's Day. Henry afterwards memorialised the visit by commissioning a miniature portrait of his daughter wearing the brooch from the Flemish immigrant artist Lucas Horenbout.[3]

When Charles reached Greenwich, Katherine and Mary met him at the door of the great hall. As described by Edward Hall, Charles 'asked [for] the queen's blessing, for that is the fashion of Spain between the aunt and the nephew'.[4] During the jousts and other sporting events laid on over the next two days, Charles and Katherine looked on from a gallery, and after supper she entertained her nephew with a banquet and a masque. Starting to relax and enjoy himself, Charles on the last day put on 'rich apparel' and joined Henry in the tournament yard 'so that all men had great pleasure to behold him'. Katherine watched with delight as the two most important men in her life behaved like kinsmen and allies.[5]

On 6 June, while Katherine and Mary stayed behind, Charles and Henry moved to Bridewell Palace in London, where – as a woodcut map made between 1561 and 1566 clearly shows – the royal gallery fronted directly onto the Thames.[6] Although Henry had refurbished it for the occasion, it proved to be too small, and Charles moved into the adjacent Dominican Priory of Blackfriars. Dressed identically, the two monarchs then joined a triumphal procession through the city, riding side by side.[7]

On Whitsunday, two days later, Wolsey celebrated a special High Mass before the two kings in St Paul's. Henry and Charles then travelled by barge to Hampton Court and onwards to Windsor Castle, where on the evening of the 15th, a long, reputedly boring play of 'love and peace' was staged for the visitors – supposedly a farce ridiculing France and likening Francis 'to a wild and unruly horse whom only Charles and Henry were able to bridle'.[8]

Next day, Charles and Henry concluded a general offensive and defensive alliance. Already Henry had sent a herald to visit Francis in Lyon, where he presented him with a declaration of war.[9] On the 20th, Charles and Henry swore to observe their treaty before the altar in St George's Chapel, Windsor, under pain of excommunication if either party defaulted, and a *Te Deum* was sung. Anne's father witnessed the treaty in his capacity as treasurer of Henry's household.[10] Finally, the two monarchs signed a subsidiary treaty by which they agreed to delay their Great Enterprise for a year to allow each side extra time to prepare, after which Henry took Charles to Winchester to view King Arthur's Round Table, just as he had taken his father, Philip the Handsome, twenty years before.[11]

It was very likely around this time that Anne Boleyn first met the Earl of Northumberland's eldest son, the young Henry (or Harry) Percy, who was in service to Wolsey. In his household of around 450 people, the great cardinal found space for nine or ten young lords who served him as pages. Percy was one of them. And, as Cavendish explains, while in and about the court at this time he 'fell in dalliance' among Katherine's maidens, one of whom was Anne. Roughly the same age (Percy's birth date is not recorded, but was no later than 1502), the couple fell deeply in love: 'there grew such a secret love between them that at length they were ensured together, intending to marry.'[12]

As a marriage prospect, Percy was spectacular. Heir to a substantial fortune and to vast English estates, he would have been a magnificent catch for Anne. Too much so, it seems. For all the upward mobility the Boleyns had achieved since Anne's great-grandfather made his bid to become Lord Mayor of London, a social gulf still separated them from the Percys, one of the country's most powerful families.[13]

When the news broke, as it was bound to do given the lack of privacy in royal courts, Wolsey summoned Percy to his gallery in York Place, where within earshot of his servants, including Cavendish, he upbraided him. 'I marvel not a little', he is reported as saying, 'of thy peevish folly that they would'st tangle and ensure thyself with a foolish girl yonder in the court, I mean Anne Boleyn. Dost thou not consider the estate that God hath called thee unto in this world?'[14]

In answer to Wolsey's charge, Percy first wept, then steeled himself, retorting: 'I considered that I was of good years and thought myself sufficient to provide me of a convenient wife whereas my fancy served me best ... And though she be a simple maid and having but a knight to her father, yet she is descended of right noble parentage.' Here Percy explicitly referenced Anne's maternal grandfather, the victor of Flodden, and the late Earl of Ormond.[15]

Wolsey had a low opinion of Percy not only for his choice of partner, but for his profligacy. Although his family enjoyed a gross rental income approaching £5,000 a year and his father left an accumulated debt of only £1,761 at his death, young Harry would owe the Lucchese banker, Antonio Buonvisi, who headed up the firm's London branch, more than £8,000 by the time he reached his early thirties.[16] He has gone down in history as weak and wayward, but where his love for Anne is concerned, he stood fast. Ordered by Wolsey to renounce his engagement, he replied, 'In this matter I have gone so far before so many worthy witnesses that I know not how to avoid myself nor to discharge my conscience.'[17] If that is really what he said, then he was 'precontracted' to Anne in a kind of engagement which church lawyers called an espousal *de futuro*. Percy would have said, 'I will take thee to be my wife', and Anne would have replied, 'I will take thee to be my husband'. If both were of marriageable age, as Anne and Percy were, then such an exchange of vows would be considered binding.[18]

Wolsey's furious response was to summon Percy's father to veto the match. The timing is uncertain: it could have been as early as the summer or autumn of 1522 or as late as June 1523 before the earl reached York Place. His relationship with his son, whom he too considered to be a wastrel, was already bad, and about to become worse. Since at least 1516 he had been planning an arranged marriage for him with Mary Talbot, the Earl of Shrewsbury's daughter. The obstacle was that Shrewsbury was heavily in debt and so could not afford the sort of dowry that such a marriage normally justified.[19]

Once Percy's father arrived, a different picture emerged.[20] It was not so much Wolsey as Henry who was the barrier to young Harry's courtship – or so says Cavendish. Much better acquainted with the Boleyn sisters since he began his affair with Mary, the king, Cavendish explained, was preparing to make his own move on Anne; but was he? A longstanding controversy surrounds this question: the problem is Cavendish's chronology. Proof of Henry's interest in Anne cannot be found before the winter months of 1525–26. Anything earlier relies on Cavendish's memory.

Nevertheless, between them, Wolsey and the Earl of Northumberland bludgeoned Percy into breaking off with Anne and marrying Mary Talbot, although the wedding did not take place quickly. The negotiations dragged on through the autumn and winter of 1523: the ceremony was planned for the New Year, but a handwritten agreement which Percy made with his tailor for money proves that he was still single in March 1525.[21] The likely wedding date was August 1525, around which time the earl was forced to borrow the exceptional sum of 500 marks (worth over £333,000 today) to pay for some great event, presumably the wedding festivities. The marriage failed within four years and the couple separated; so strongly did Percy resent his wife, he refused to give either her or her servants an adequate allowance.[22] Wolsey's objections to Percy's courtship of Anne had, Cavendish said, been rooted in the king's desire 'to have preferred her unto another person with whom the king hath travailed already' – that is, that the king and Wolsey already had someone else in mind for her.[23] Writing in the 1550s, Cavendish again assumed this meant Henry himself, but what he overlooks is a revival of Wolsey's earlier plans for the Butler marriage, which were resurrected in the winter of 1521–22.[24] By then, the Earl of Surrey's reforms in Ireland had failed, and he was pleading to be recalled, after which Henry and Wolsey switched to a policy of influencing Irish affairs by appeasing the Butlers, dangling before them the prospect of recovering the Ormond lands if James Butler married Anne. While this played out, she would have to stay single.[25] Somewhat brutally, Wolsey forcibly ordered Percy to avoid Anne's company. And to be sure they stayed apart, he had her rusticated to Hever, 'sent home again to her father for a season, whereat she smoked'. If Cavendish is trustworthy, she ranted and raged, saying that 'if it lay ever in her power, she would work the cardinal much displeasure'.[26]

At the time Anne was sent away, her father was returning from another embassy, this time to Spain. Henry gave him secret instructions to discover how warmly Charles was viewed by his

Spanish subjects, whether they supported his plans for the Great Enterprise and whether they would grant him sufficient funds to pursue it. Boleyn was also to report in cipher, as a matter of urgency, how seriously Charles regarded overtures from Portugal to ditch his engagement to Princess Mary and marry instead his first cousin, the Infanta Isabella, daughter of Manuel I of Portugal and his second wife Maria of Aragon. There was a plausible logic to the match: she was closer to him in age (only three years his junior), fluent in Spanish (although Charles rarely spoke it except when in Castile, preferring French) and came with a dowry of 800,000 ducats.[27]

Boleyn arrived home in May 1523. He reported that Charles would struggle to raise enough in taxes for the Great Enterprise, that his forces were inadequate and that despite his many fair words, he could probably not be trusted on his betrothal to Mary. This dampened Henry's ardour for a full-scale invasion of France – that is, until the unexpected happened.[28] In August, Charles, Duke of Bourbon, the Constable of France and the country's richest and most powerful nobleman, offered to rebel. His treason stemmed from a clash following the death of his wife, when Louise of Savoy, her first cousin and nearest blood relative, laid claim to her inheritance. Louise's claim lacked merit and could only be sustained by an arbitrary and selective interpretation of the legal documents, but this did not deter her.[29]

With Bourbon defecting to Charles's side, Henry agreed to launch the Great Enterprise without delay. While Charles attacked France from the south and Bourbon from the east, Henry would advance from the north, aiming for Paris, where he planned to be crowned King of France, after which the victors would divide the spoils. For Henry it seemed to be the opportunity of a lifetime and soon Wolsey began shipping an army of 11,000 troops across the Channel under the Duke of Suffolk's command.[30]

To their dismay, Bourbon's revolt misfired and Suffolk's march on Paris, after an initial rapid advance to within fifty miles of the city, ended in ignominious failure. After these twin humiliations, Henry's commitment to the Great Enterprise markedly waned as cash reserves ran low. Final hopes were dashed when news arrived that Charles had scaled back his invasion plans. He too lacked sufficient funds because the Cortes of Castile insisted on him marrying Isabella and making Spain his permanent headquarters and was refusing to grant the necessary taxes.[31]

As the year ebbed to its close, Charles proposed that he and Henry should instead focus on Italy, a move for which the English were expected to pay. Henry, on the other hand, preferred a plan by which Bourbon would reinforce what was left of Suffolk's army and march on Paris. After lengthy discussions, Bourbon advanced into Provence and laid siege to Marseille, but retreated when his troops mutinied for lack of pay. Charles ordered his generals to drive the remaining French garrisons out of Lombardy, only to find that Francis had made his mother regent of France and crossed the Alps for a second time. In October, he recaptured Milan. As Charles's forces began to melt away, Francis forced what was left of them to take refuge inside the walls of Pavia, where he began a siege.[32]

Back in London, Anne was at court by Christmas 1524, and, according to Cavendish, once more in Katherine's household, where she soon rose 'in great estimation and favour', still nursing 'a privy indignation unto the cardinal'. Psychologically it seems her entanglement with Percy made a lasting mark on both lovers, one that would never fully heal. Inwardly, Anne had toughened up: now about twenty-three, her experience with Percy thrust her into full adulthood.[33]

The great event in that holiday season was to be a grand feat of arms, the most spectacular of the reign and the last on this scale. In late October, a group of younger courtiers began the preparations. Henry, delighted with their plan, instructed Richard Gibson, the Master of the Revels, to construct a mock timber fortress in the tiltyard at Greenwich, complete with towers and turrets, to their exact specifications. Defended by a drawbridge, deep ditches and ramparts, the fortress, standing twenty feet square and fifty feet high, was called the 'Castle of Loyalty'. On a nearby mound, a white unicorn, made of papier-mâché pasted over a wire frame and painted over, stood guard over a tree of chivalry from which hung armour and knights' shields. That Harry Percy was first allowed, and then forbidden to be 'one of them which shall assault the Castle', suggests that Anne would be taking part.[34]

On 21 December, a herald proclaimed in Katherine's great chamber that Henry had entrusted the castle to four 'maidens' of her court. Being without husbands, they were weak and defenceless, for which reason a captain and fifteen noble gentlemen had come to their rescue. An actor playing a herald issued their challenge, which was to defend the castle 'against all comers, being gentlemen of name and arms'. There were to be various types of combat, culminating in a general assault on the castle.

On the 29th, two boys on palfreys disguised as ladies rode into the tiltyard, leading two 'ancient knights with beards of silver' who petitioned Katherine to be allowed to answer the challengers. When she assented, these knights 'threw away' their disguises and were revealed as Henry and his brother-in-law, the Duke of Suffolk. Close behind stood Francis Bryan, Nicholas Carew and Henry Norris, along with 'five others', one of whom was very likely Anne's brother, George.[35]

Once the challengers had been 'answered', the fighting could begin. Henry threw all his energy into the contest, astonishing everyone by breaking seven spears on the first day. After that, he was largely content, until the final day of the competition, to sit out the combats as a spectator and let others do the hard work.[36] The combats continued until 8 February, when Henry returned to the fray, tourneying with Anthony Browne, putting his full force into the attack, his sword almost severing his opponent's neck shield, 'his strokes were so great'.[37]

Who were the four maidens in the castle? Anne, it is generally agreed, was one.[38] Another may have been Jane Parker, for whose impending marriage to George Boleyn a pre-nuptial contract had been drawn up just three weeks before the plans for the 'Castle of Loyalty' were announced.[39] Other candidates include Elizabeth Darrell, one of Katherine's maids. Alternatively, the maidens could have been any of those from the Château Vert masque two years before who had not married since, which still puts Anne and Jane at the top of the list.[40]

One of the chief impresarios of these festivities was the twenty-year-old Thomas Wyatt, Sir Henry Wyatt of Allington Castle's son. With his full beard, high forehead and searching, darting blue-grey eyes, he was the most accomplished of Henry VIII's young bloods. A lover of all things Italian, acclaimed at his death by his friends as the English Petrarch, he was the ideal courtier: witty and winning, lethally charming, a diplomat, a sportsman, a fluent linguist and arguably the finest lyric poet between Chaucer and Shakespeare, even if his poems circulated solely in handwritten form in his lifetime.

Roughly the same age as Anne's brother, who shared his interests and some of his poetic skills, Wyatt had only been nine or so when Anne left for Mechelen, but the Boleyns and Wyatts were well acquainted, and Allington Castle was barely twenty miles from Hever. When sixteen or seventeen, Wyatt had gone through an arranged marriage to Elizabeth Brooke, his neighbour Lord Cobham's daughter, a woman he came to loathe. They had two children: Thomas, born in about 1521, and a daughter, Frances; but their marriage was unhappy, and around 1526 Wyatt accused his wife of adultery and they separated. More than a decade later, he refused to apportion equal blame, telling his son that 'the fault is both in your mother and me, but chiefly in her.' He advised his son to 'Love well and agree with your wife', but never managed it himself. Instead, he sent Elizabeth away and, like Harry Percy, refused to see her or grant her an allowance. Where she went for much of the next two decades is unknown, since her family disowned her too. As to Wyatt, he looked for a mistress, admitting with characteristic pith, that 'I do not profess chastity, but yet I use not abomination.'[41]

Wyatt had perhaps made occasional visits to Henry's court before the autumn of 1524.[42] His first royal duties were in October and November 1523, when his father sent him twice to York with the enormous sums of £2,000 in gold 'for the king's affairs in the North'.[43] Then, coinciding with the plans for the 'Castle of Loyalty', his father vacated one of his offices to him, the clerkship of the Jewel House.[44] This was the man with whom Anne Boleyn would next become entangled. How and when their relationship would begin, and what precisely it involved, is as uncertain and beguiling as any other riddle connected to her. But become entangled she did, and their brief liaison makes most sense if it began sometime after the events of the 'Castle of Loyalty' and ended a year or so later.

10

An Anxious Year

On 24 February 1525, Charles V's generals used the cover of night to breach the wall of the French siege-works outside Pavia and hide hundreds of their Spanish marksmen in nearby trees. Detecting their advance, Francis led his heavy cavalry in several charges at dawn, but one by one the marksmen picked them off using their arquebuses. The garrison of Pavia then sallied forth to drive the French infantry into the river Ticino, whose bridges had been destroyed. Some 3,000 were drowned and another 10,000 captured, including Francis himself. Scarcely able to believe his luck, Charles held him in Lombardy for three months, then led him to Genoa and afterwards to the fortress of Madrid.[1]

Henry was exultant. This was the opportunity he had waited for: France lay prostrate before him. After ordering a solemn High Mass in St Paul's, he sought to revive the Great Enterprise without delay. 'Now is the time', he excitedly told Margaret of Austria's ambassadors, 'for the Emperor and myself to devise the means of getting full satisfaction from France. Not an hour is to be lost.'[2]

But Charles refused. Low on cash and hungry for peace, he felt himself under no obligation to share his victory: one which, in his view, Henry had not meaningfully aided. With Francis a prisoner, this was his chance to recover the old Burgundian territories annexed by France. No longer did he need the King of England.

Henry was outraged at what he saw as Charles's treachery. Europe, meanwhile, was becoming enveloped in a new crisis. In 1521, the Ottoman Turks under their new leader, Sultan Suleiman, had advanced with a massive army up the Danube, capturing Belgrade and extending the Turkish empire's frontier to the borders of Hungary. In June 1522, Suleiman's fleet laid siege to Rhodes, which fell by the end of the year. The papacy was unable to respond. Leo X, Henry's supporter, had died of a fever, and his successor, Adrian of Utrecht, was stricken with kidney failure. When the cardinals then chose Giulio de' Medici, an experienced Vatican insider who took the name of Clement VII, he made the fatal error of joining the Venetians in an alliance with Francis just six weeks before Charles's victory in Pavia.[3]

Katherine was aghast: her nephew's snub to her husband had gravely undermined her. Having miscalculated politically, she was also facing the advancing passage of time. Almost forty and prematurely aged by at least four stillbirths or miscarriages, she was plumper and flabbier than the young girl who had so enchanted everyone when she arrived from Spain. Believing that she had passed the menopause, she stopped sleeping with Henry some months before the preparations began for the 'Castle of Loyalty'. By the summer of 1525, this was sufficiently well known for Cuthbert Tunstall, writing from Toledo, daringly to warn Henry:

> The queen's grace hath long been without child, and albeit
> God may send her more children, yet she [is] past that age in
> which women most commonly are wont to be fruitful and have
> children. For which cause the only hope of posterity to come of
> your body rest[eth] in the person of my Lady Princess.

The problem was that Princess Mary was betrothed to Charles, who insisted that she be brought up in Spain in readiness for their marriage, assuming he married her at all.[4]

Just thirty-four, and with his diplomacy in tatters, Henry gradually began to take fuller personal control. He relied less on Wolsey and was quicker to overrule him when their opinions differed.[5] He became more controlling, dictating lengthy dispatches in which he ventriloquised the precise words his ambassadors should use in multiple potential situations. One of the earliest examples is a forty-page briefing he gave to Tunstall who, when sounding out Charles's plans for Francis, was to begin by discovering whether he meant to imprison him for ever, or else ransom and restore him. Supposing the first, Tunstall was given the four main arguments he should advance as to why and how Henry himself should be crowned King of France, each backed up by fistfuls of sub-arguments: supposing the second, he was to follow an alternative script, justifying Henry's claims to Normandy, Aquitaine, Brittany and Picardy, and was in all cases to 'stick' on his right to Picardy.[6]

For Henry, the extent of the victory at Pavia reawakened the insecurity rooted in him during childhood, a feeling always exacerbated by what he saw as betrayal. If Charles was not checked, he would come to dominate much of western Europe. When Tunstall reported that Charles had indeed asked to be released from his engagement to Princess Mary, Henry did not hesitate. With his cash reserves exhausted and his subjects in revolt in Suffolk and other eastern and Midlands counties at the costs of the war, he renounced Charles after the briefest of discussions with Wolsey and looked to Louise of Savoy, who now ruled France as regent for her son. His request for a truce pushed at an open door: Louise urgently needed a settlement. On 7 June 1525, she instructed Giovanni Gioacchino di Passano, a Genoese Cistercian priest and maître d'hôtel in her household, and Jean Brinon, Chancellor of Alençon, to set out for London.[7]

While Anne was still smarting from the veto placed on her relationship with Harry Percy, Thomas Wyatt began to try his luck with her. Of the pair's first meeting, his grandson, George, says:

The knight, in the beginning, coming to behold the sudden
appearance of this new beauty, came to be holden and surprised
somewhat with the sight thereof; after much more with her
witty and graceful speech, his ear also had him chained unto
her, so as finally his heart seemed to say, 'I could gladly yield to

be tied forever with the knot of her love', as somewhere in his verses hath been thought his meaning was to express.[8]

Wyatt fleetingly described their courtship in his sonnet 'If waker care', where he barely conceals its autobiographical content by referring to his inamorata as 'Brunet'. In the handwritten version of the text, the pertinent lines read:

If thou ask whom, sure since I did refrain
Her that did set our country in a roar
Th'unfeigned cheer of Phyllis hath the place
That Brunet had. She hath, and ever shall.[9]

Brunet, it seems, was a woman Wyatt had either decided to forget, or by whom he had been denied. In later revisions, he found it prudent to alter the line 'Her that did set our country in a roar', to 'Brunet that set my wealth in such a roar'. Since Anne is the only brunette who can be accused of setting 'our country in a roar', it is unsurprising that he masks her identity. We know that during his life, he loved two women: one the not-so-mysterious Brunet, the other Elizabeth Darrell, Katherine's maid and later gentlewoman, who one day would be his mistress and the mother of a son and is likely to be 'Phyllis'.[10]

Wyatt went on to express his feelings in 'Whoso list to hunt', where he adapts one of Petrarch's most notable sonnets:

Whoso list to hunt, I know where is an hind,
But as for me, helas, I may no more.
The vain travail hath wearied me so sore,
I am of them that farthest cometh behind.
Yet may I by no means my wearied mind
Draw from the deer, but as she fleeth afore
Fainting I follow. I leave off therefore
Sithens in a net I seek to hold the wind.
Who list her hunt, I put him out of doubt,
As well as I may spend his time in vain.

And graven with diamonds in letters plain
There is written her fair neck round about:
'*Noli me tangere* for Caesar's I am,
And wild for to hold though I seem tame.'[11]

In courtly literature, sexual pursuit is likened to the hunting of
a deer with its thrill of the chase and power of the kill: the violence
of the hunt is displaced onto the chase of the bedchamber. The
popular ballad 'Blow thy horn, hunter!' by William Cornish, who
played 'Ardent Desire' in the Château Vert masque, was scarcely
more than an open invitation to sex, incorporating bawdy puns
and the sound-plays of forester's songs.[12]

Using Petrarch as his source, Wyatt recasts the story of Actaeon
and Diana from Ovid's *Metamorphoses*, making it open season on
the hind (a female deer in or after its third year), who fends off
the hunters by wearing a jewelled collar saying, 'Noli me tangere'
('Touch me not'). Those words, taken from the Latin Vulgate
edition of St John's Gospel, are coupled with the warning 'For
Caesar's I am,' proclaiming that she is the king's.[13] The whole line
corresponds to an apocryphal story that Julius Caesar kept deer in
England, marked with the words 'Noli me tangere, quia Caesaris
sum ' ('Touch me not, for I am Caesar's').[14]

In Wyatt's poem, the hind, with her 'fair neck' – Anne's most
charming feature, as many had noted – is 'wild for to hold', implying
danger and the erotic. Chasing her is like catching the wind in a
net, a metaphor invoking what his contemporaries called 'hunting
into toils': trapping the fleeing deer in waiting nets, either to restrict
their direction of flight once they are released and make them easier
prey for the hounds, or else to enable the hunter to slaughter them
on the spot within a fenced enclosure.[15] The narrator's exhaustion
(the 'vain travail'; 'fainting I follow') recalls Ovid's version of the
tale: after casting his eyes on Diana while she was bathing, Actaeon
was changed into a stag and torn apart by his own hounds.[16]

When later Catholic authors set about smearing Anne with a
salacious backstory, they used the roguish figure of Wyatt to spice
up their narratives. One of them, Nicholas Harpsfield, writing in

the 1550s, and the author of *A Treatise of the Pretended Divorce of Henry VIII*, tells us that Wyatt, on hearing of Henry's intention to marry Anne, cautioned him that she was 'not meet to be coupled with your grace'. This, he said, he knew 'by my own experience as one that have had my carnal pleasure with her'.[17]

The author of the unreliable *Spanish Chronicle*, written in Antwerp around the same time, claims how, shortly before Henry married her, Wyatt warned him that 'she was a bad woman', for which he found himself banished for two whole years. At the time of Anne's fall, he supposedly reminded the king of their conversation, adding that at one of his nocturnal trysts with Anne, she had kissed him, and might have gone much further but for the sound of heavy footsteps in the chamber above.[18] Almost certainly, this adapts what, by the time the *Chronicle's* author was writing, was known to be a genuine, if different incident in Wyatt's career, when, in a dispatch from Ghent in 1540, he congratulated the king on not marrying the sixteen-year-old Christina of Denmark two years before. 'I cannot but rejoice', he told Henry then, 'in the escape that you made there.'[19]

To detoxify these legends, George Wyatt gives a more innocent, playful version, telling us how one day his grandfather simply did to Anne what the Duke of Suffolk had done to Margaret of Austria in Tournai, and no more. While flirting with her, he snatched a locket hanging from her pocket by a ribbon as a love token, which he refused to return. Afterwards, while the king was 'sporting himself at bowls' with Suffolk and Francis Bryan, Henry claimed the contest, making the double point that he had won the game and Anne's love. This he did by gesticulating with his finger 'whereon he wore her ring' towards the bowls the players had just cast. Staring Wyatt in the eye, he said knowingly, 'I tell thee it is mine.' When Wyatt produced the locket, Henry turned ashen and stomped off muttering that he was deceived. Afterwards, Anne 'with good and evident proof' was able to explain to him how Wyatt had stolen the locket, and all ended well.[20]

Is the story true? The records show that Henry did play bowls with Bryan around this time, losing money to him.[21] The trouble is that Henry's palaces were hotbeds of intrigue, gossip and fake news, and Anne's traducers made it their mission to stitch together disparate snippets of tittle-tattle to blacken her name. In May 1530, it was reported that 'The Duke of Suffolk is sent away for a while' for warning Henry that Anne 'has been caught *au délit* [possibly best translated here as "smooching"] with a gentleman of the court'. Irresistibly tempting as it may be to assume that this means Wyatt, it hardly can, since in or about September 1529, Henry had made him Marshal of Calais, where he lived for the next fifteen months. In any case, 'other chatter' attributed Suffolk's absence 'to different causes'.[22]

Rumour also told of a previous incident when the same, or perhaps a different, courtier was chased away 'on suspicion' of some kind of amorous connection with Anne.[23] If dated to the autumn or winter of 1527, the delinquent then – if indeed there really was one – *could* have been Wyatt, who disappeared from court after returning with Sir John Russell from a mission to Italy, where he had acquired the latest edition of Petrarch's poetry. Lying low in Allington, he occupied his time reading and writing *The Quyet of Mynde*, an English translation from the French scholar Guillaume Budé's Latin version of a work by the Greek author Plutarch, which he presented by messenger to Katherine as a New Year's gift in 1528.[24]

It seems likeliest, then, that Wyatt offered Anne 'service' according to the chivalric code, but got carried away and fell deeply in love, but nothing on her side suggests anything more than flirting, teasing, perhaps even taunting – of which she would certainly become capable as her character evolved.[25] Whatever his attractions for her, Wyatt had two insuperable drawbacks: he was poor and already married. If she would not easily succumb to the married Henry's advances when he made them, why would she yield to Wyatt's? As George Wyatt says, 'For that princely lady, she living in court where were so many brave gallants at that time unmarried, she was not like to cast her eye upon one that had been then married.' Cavendish, as hostile a witness as anyone by the time he put pen to paper, felt utterly confident that Anne was 'a maiden' when Henry first discovered her.[26]

While Wyatt tried his luck with Anne in the summer of 1525, Louise of Savoy's envoys arrived to begin their talks. Di Passano reached London in June, but Brinon would be delayed until 26 July. By then, Henry's mind was already asserting the 'shoulds' of royal rule. Tunstall had alerted him to the danger of a disputed succession. As things stood, his heir was Princess Mary, and he was resolutely opposed at this point in his life to the idea of a female successor. No woman had ever been acknowledged as queen regnant of England, and the basic duties of a monarch, such as leading armies into battle, were traditionally masculine. If a woman ruler married an Englishman, he would (as Henry once put it) be her 'governor and head, and so finally shall direct the realm'. If she married a foreigner, she risked drawing the country into thraldom. He believed a woman ruler would be an open invitation to a succession crisis or a civil war.[27]

Henry did, however, have a son. On 18 June, at Bridewell Palace, well away from Katherine but in full view of everyone else, Henry elevated Henry Fitzroy, his natural son, to the foremost rank of the nobility. First created Earl of Nottingham, the six-year-old boy then knelt again before his father, to be invested as Dukes of Richmond and Somerset. Soon afterwards, Henry made him titular Lord-Lieutenant of Ireland and Warden of the Scottish Marches.[28]

Such dignities were portentous. Henry's own father had been Earl of Richmond when he won the crown at Bosworth. The dukedom of Somerset was last held by his Beaufort ancestors, the progeny of the illicit relationship between John of Gaunt and Katherine Swynford. The last Earl of Nottingham was Richard, Duke of York, the younger of the ill-fated princes in the Tower. For Katherine, everything pointed to the same thing: her daughter's exclusion from the throne.

And she was right. Bastardy could be reversed: the four natural children of Gaunt and Swynford had all been legitimised by papal bull and a royal charter in 1396–97. Katherine, always protective of her nine-year-old daughter's status and titles, did not flinch in expressing her disgust, but all she did was infuriate her husband.[29]

Henry's generosity did not stop with Fitzroy. On the same day, he raised his cousin, Henry Courtenay, to be Marquis of Exeter, while his nephew Henry Brandon, the Duke of Suffolk's son, was made Earl of Lincoln, although aged only two. Several of the king's jousting companions were promoted, but above all, Anne's father was created Viscount Rochford. Finally, the family had reached the upper echelons of the peerage for themselves, rather than marrying into them. Thomas now stood down as treasurer of Henry's household.[30]

Boleyn's ennoblement was good news for Anne's brother, George, now heir to the title. Already a groom of the privy chamber and rising fast in Henry's esteem, George had married Jane Parker earlier in the year, with the king contributing the lion's share of her generous dowry of 2,000 marks (worth over £1.3 million in modern values).[31] Their wedding gifts included six silver dishes and four silver platters, later embossed with the new family crest and engraved with the letters 'I' (which doubled for 'J') and 'B'.[32]

An outbreak of plague now caused a general exodus from the capital and Henry spent the rest of 1525 on a protracted hunting trip, beginning in Windsor Forest and continuing in a leisurely arc through Buckinghamshire and Hertfordshire towards Ampthill in Bedfordshire. Wherever he went, his privy chamber servants followed, among them George Boleyn.[33] Sometimes Henry slept overnight in his manor houses and hunting lodges, moving quickly from one to another; at other times in apartments specially kept for him in monasteries such as Reading and Waltham Abbeys or Dunstable Priory, all royal foundations. Sometimes he returned briefly to the more comfortable surroundings of Windsor Castle. Katherine accompanied him for part of the route, before retreating to Woburn Abbey, leaving him free to suit himself.

Wolsey too left York Place for his house at The More (or Moor Park), a spectacular moated property near Rickmansworth in Hertfordshire. There, in receipt of Henry's instructions relayed by messenger, and closeted for weeks with di Passano and Brinon, he pulled off the first stage of a seismic shift in international affairs – the direct result of the king's anger against Charles for his treachery after the Battle of Pavia and for not properly supporting him over the Great Enterprise. In exchange for guarantees of peace and future military cooperation, Louise agreed to pay Henry 2 million gold crowns of the sun (worth over £½ billion today) – 50,000 crowns upfront and the rest by instalments – along with a share of the profits of the lucrative rock salt trade. This was to be the prelude to joint Anglo-French action against Charles.[34]

Perhaps hoping to forestall the settlement, Charles offered to repay some of the debts he owed to Henry but confirmed that he intended to marry his cousin Isabella of Portugal. The wedding was to take place in the Alcázar in Seville in the New Year. When the news arrived, Henry could feel that his rapprochement with France was fully justified.[35]

Christmas 1525 was a subdued affair. Since plague was still afflicting the capital, Henry and Katherine spent the season in Eltham with a reduced court.[36] Early in the New Year, he continued to move about his kingdom with just a few attendants, finally returning to Greenwich at the end of January.[37] He had plenty to reflect on: Mary Boleyn, whom he had taken as a mistress, was pregnant. Her son, named Henry in the king's honour, although he was most likely not Henry's son but that of Mary's husband, William Carey, would be born in March. The date is often questioned, but the discovery of three independent reports of his age given at the time of William's death securely fixes it.[38]

Henry would have known about, or suspected, Mary's pregnancy for several months. The sources are silent, but two possibilities arise for why he ended the affair. The likelier one is that he dropped her the moment her pregnancy was confirmed. He already had an illegitimate son (albeit one he was potentially moving to legitimise) and did not want another – assuming the child was his.[39] Alternatively, the liaison simply fizzled out, and she went back to her husband. Either way, Henry no longer had a mistress and was looking for another. Katherine's appetite for sex might have waned, but his had not.

Better news was that events in Europe were shifting Henry's way. The newly installed Pope Clement, who greatly feared the Duke of

Bourbon's forces in Italy, had called for an anti-Habsburg alliance. To be known as the League of Cognac, its purpose was to expel Charles's armies from the Italian peninsula.[40] In the spring of 1526, the League was fast taking shape. After the disaster of Pavia, Francis had signed the Treaty of Madrid with Charles by which he agreed to abandon his Italian claims, hand over Burgundy and deliver up his two eldest sons as hostages for his good faith in exchange for his freedom. These conditions were harsh, but Francis scarcely had a choice. When Marguerite of Angoulême, braving the long and difficult journey to see her brother, had travelled to Madrid and offered 3 million crowns for his ransom, Charles refused. Francis capitulated, but before doing so, he made a secret legal protestation before a notary, vowing not to honour any concessions compromising the territorial integrity of France.[41]

Within hours of crossing the frontier to be reunited with his mother, Francis expressed his gratitude to Henry for not invading France while he had been a prisoner and for his efforts to free him. In words recorded and translated by John Taylor, Wolsey's trusted envoy, he declared how 'My kind brother of England, whom after God I thank of my liberty ... hath bounded me ever, and all mine, to do him service ... And howbeit that there was war moved betwixt us, I know right well that it was but ceremoniously done.'[42]

It was at this turning point in Henry's political and personal life, with his mind now firmly fixed on what, for him, was the breathtakingly counter-cultural idea of moving towards a far broader, more comprehensive understanding with France than anything he had considered before, that he noticed Anne, the epitome of all things French. He had never paid her much attention before, and had international affairs not taken this dramatic shift, he might never have sought her out. Suddenly she appeared to him in a completely fresh light – he was smitten, as he said himself, 'by the dart of love'.

II

Henry in Love

Once more Henry chose Shrove Tuesday to make his move. Just as when pursuing Mary Boleyn, he first held a joust. Then, he had taken part in the Château Vert masque with the motto, 'She hath wounded my heart.' This time, he rode into the lists displaying symbols of a man's heart gripped inside a press and surrounded by flames – again, an echo of his affair with Mary. His motto, in French, said it all. Playfully both explicit and deniable, it read, 'Declare je n'ose' meaning 'Declare I dare not'. In the evening, he held a banquet, ostensibly for Katherine, at which he insisted on serving his wife and, more to the point, the women around her – who included Anne – with their food and drink. At the time, the day was memorable for the joust in which Francis Bryan lost one of his eyes. Afterwards, it was the banquet that was remembered. Having finished with one Boleyn sister, Henry now yearned for the other. Anne had bowled him over, flinging open the doors of his perception.[1]

Henry was thirty-four, Anne about twenty-five, and both were in their prime. Henry had revisited his 'shoulds' with Fitzroy's ennoblement, but those 'shoulds' reflected the expectations of his nobles and courtiers who knew that Katherine was now infertile and demanded the security that only the prospect of a stable, male succession could provide. Now his 'woulds' had come to the fore, and chief among them was desire for Anne.

At first, he had no intention of making her more than another mistress and saw no reason why she would not succumb to his charms – and his generosity – as her sister had done. All he can have wanted was a sexual adventure with a passionate Francophile at a moment when he was resolved to use France to put Charles on notice. Divorcing his wife and marrying Anne was not then on his agenda, but within months that would radically change. He fell for her just as Harry Percy and Thomas Wyatt had before him. She would become the love of his life, the only woman who dared to answer him back or tell him he was mistaken and get away with it. Despite, and probably because of this, he came to love her with an ardour and intensity he never found elsewhere. It was as if his life was about to begin all over again.

Many things would draw Henry to Anne: her lively intelligence and quick repartee, her linguistic and dancing skills, her poise, her fashion sense, her sheer vivacity, her free spirit, her ability to light up a room. She was never the prettiest woman at court: but it was that mesmerising chic she had acquired during her seven years in France which intoxicated him – this and her dark, flashing eyes.

That, at least, is how their relationship has always been depicted, but there is more to it. Henry also felt this way because he found himself nudging closer to the momentous watershed when he would be older than his mother when death snatched her away. In other words, he was himself changing. He yearned for something new: someone spellbindingly glamorous who was as much a collaborator as a companion, a trophy wife and mother of his sons, but one who understood his brilliance and, crucially, was personally invested in it. That this woman could be Anne was not something of which he was yet entirely sure, but he was swept away by her. Caught between Katherine's barren familiarity and Charles's betrayals, it seemed to him as if Anne might finally offer him the love he both wanted and needed. He made his move on Anne as if she was a particular deer he was hunting, expecting a swift conclusion to the chase.

His impatience put Anne on the horns of a dilemma. She had returned from France expecting to find a husband. That she would suddenly become the object of the king's lust would never have occurred to her. If she followed her sister's example, she could expect lands and grants to be showered upon her family, but there was a crucial difference between the two sisters: Mary had been safely married to William Carey during her relationship with Henry whereas Anne was single. She wanted an advantageous match, which would be severely jeopardised should Henry's affections wane. She knew just how fickle he could be. Quick to distance himself from Mary when she became pregnant, he had previously married off Elizabeth Blount to a wealthy nonentity after Henry Fitzroy was born. Neither prospect appealed to Anne. We do not know what role Mary played at this stage, or whether their father, with an eye to his wealth, tried to pressure her into the king's arms. But Anne knew her own mind: becoming the king's mistress was not for her. She refused to imperil her future. If he insisted on having her, his only alternative would be to marry her.

It was a breathtaking gamble, but as the great-granddaughter of Lady Anne Hoo, she was well versed in the story of how Elizabeth Woodville, in 1464, had resisted the attentions of the lovelorn Edward IV until he promised to marry her. In a patriarchal society, Woodville's had been an astounding feat. Her marriage to Edward was a love match of no immediate dynastic or political advantage to the king. The widow of a humble knight, she became Queen of England and the most important person after the king.

Anne's ambition had been roused. While with Queen Claude, she had witnessed the influence of Louise of Savoy and Marguerite of Angoulême at close quarters, just as she had watched Margaret of Austria at Mechelen. With a relationship with Henry now in prospect, these women became role models – she saw an opportunity to make an indelible mark on England and the monarchy. She just had to play her cards in the right order. We should make no mistake. Anne was never going to be a Cinderella figure, star-struck by the attentions of her prince. She was biding her time, seeing how things played out, working out what she wanted from such an unexpected turn of events.

For Anne, marriage to Henry would need to be about shared values and partnership, not just sex and presents. In the early years of her marriage, Katherine had revelled in her time as regent and tried to reinvent herself as her father's ambassador, but when Wolsey supplanted her, she settled down to the humdrum domesticity of an English queen consort. Anne, however, should she ever become queen, did not mean to do the same. She would refuse to wait patiently for the king to visit her, or for times when her musical, chess or needlework talents were to be put on show for visiting diplomats. If ambassadors were at the court, she would sit beside Henry at the council table with them, or even receive them alone. If she felt like going out hunting with Henry, she would ride out with him, unaccompanied by an escort of ladies or a larger group of his cronies if she chose to do so.

It was still too early for Anne to know if she could come to love Henry. The spark that had ignited her romance with Harry Percy was clearly not there, but this was not a world in which immediate love was an expected part of marriage, and everything her family had taught her about marrying up would have persuaded her that, in time, she could love him. She just needed first to be sure of him. Already she had grasped a key element of his psychology: if she was to achieve her aims, she needed to keep under her control the one thing he most desired. Then he would want her even more. She was prepared to exchange letters and tokens with him, but even when she moved to her own apartments in his palaces, she refused to sleep with him. To find the right time to yield would be crucial. She had to be sure he was serious, and that she was not going to be brushed aside after just a one- or two-night stand.

No sooner were the Shrove Tuesday jousts over than Henry found himself in uncharted territory: his happiness, his peace of mind, his future, all lay at the mercy of a woman who played to her strengths, blowing hot and cold, keeping him guessing until she could be sure of him. That we can give this much psychological detail on Henry's infatuation is a piece of historical good fortune. Remarkably, the sources allow us intimate access into this intensely personal stage of Henry's life. For lying in the Vatican Library is one of the most extraordinary series of seventeen letters that perhaps any king has ever written.[2]

That Henry wrote them at all is astonishing – this, after all, is the ruler who made no secret of the fact that 'writing is to me somewhat tedious and painful.' The story of the survival of these letters, nine of which are in French and eight in English, is also extraordinary. They were not seized from Anne as was usually routine with the papers of those suspected of treason; Henry never managed to retrieve them when his passion for her turned to such malevolent hatred that he simply wanted her gone. Clearly, Anne chose to keep the letters with her, so they must have disappeared before her arrest. The usual, most likely the correct, explanation is that one of Katherine's supporters purloined them from a hidden drawer in Anne's cabinet and smuggled them out of the country as evidence in Henry's divorce suit. Once in Rome, their journeys were not over, for when Napoleon Bonaparte's armies swept through Italy in 1797, fifteen of them were amongst papers looted and sent to Paris where they were studied and transcribed by French scholars. There they remained until the emperor's defeat at Waterloo, after which they were returned to the Vatican.[3]

Within the letters, Henry pours out his innermost feelings to Anne in a way that almost strips him naked. He calls her 'mine own darling', his 'good sweetheart', 'the one woman in the world whom I most esteem'. Her prolonged absence while she is away from him is 'almost intolerable'. Invoking the familiar tropes of courtly romance literature, he casts her as his 'mistress' and himself as her 'true servant', gently chiding her for not writing to him as she has promised, for, he says, 'it has not pleased you to remember the promise you made me when I was last with you, that is to say, to hear good news from you.' He makes great play with the fact that he writes in his own hand, not by dictation – in this matter he is, he says, his own secretary. Almost all his letters close with an avowal that they are 'written by the hand of him which I trust shortly shall be yours', or 'by the hand of the secretary who in heart, body, and will is your loyal and most assured servant'.[4]

To none of his other wives nor, as far as anyone knows, to any of his handful of mistresses, did Henry surrender himself so completely. His raw emotion, his fears that his feelings are not reciprocated, his constant need for reassurance and support are naively, almost endearingly visible. His was the sort of love which is heady and obsessional. He holds nothing back. His longing for Anne in her absence is sometimes even sad, yet occasionally he gives a dark hint of the other Henry who needs to get his own way without question or objection, a man who looks for, and demands, obedience and makes his impatience menacingly clear.

Scrutinising this amazing trove presents readers with two problems: Anne's letters to the king have disappeared (as perhaps have some of his to her) and not one of the letters is dated so various transcribers and historians tend to order them differently. We can, however, deduce a good deal about her style and approach from what Henry says to her in reply – all of which helps us better to envision her character as she spun her ineffable magic. And several letters contain clues or references to contemporary events, which enable dates and places of composition to be assigned with some confidence.[5]

No great imaginative leap is needed to gauge Anne's initial reactions to Henry's advances. The first of the surviving letters shows that she had by then gone back to Kent with her mother to think over what he had already said to her, most likely to Hever but possibly to Penshurst.[6] Writing in French, the vernacular of romance literature, Henry appeals for her return. Using a metaphor from astronomy, he contrasts his own fidelity with his fears about her constancy. 'The longer the days are', he says, 'the farther off [i.e. higher] the sun is in the sky and yet the hotter; so it is with our love, for although by absence we are parted, it still retains its fervency, at least in my case, and hoping the same of yours.' To shore up his 'firm hope of your unchangeable affection', and since he cannot be with her in person, he sends her the next best thing: 'my picture set in a bracelet with the whole device [badge, motto] which you already know'. Henry hopes that by persuading Anne to wear this piece of jewellery, she will remember and display her commitment to him.[7]

Anne was unmoved by the king's gift. She adopted a high-risk strategy, ignoring his appeal, believing silence would draw him out. And she was right. Sure enough, he was soon entreating her again for 'good news of you and to have an answer to my last letter'. Since he wished to be her 'true servant', he begged her to 'advise me as to your well-being'. And to move things on, he tried another, bolder tactic. 'To put you even more often in mind of me', he explained, 'I send you by this bearer a buck, killed very late yesterday evening by my own hand, hoping that when you eat it, it will remind you of the hunter.'[8]

Anne reputedly had a gourmet's palate acquired in France, relishing all kinds of rare meats – but no contemporary could have failed to grasp that the gift was intended to remind her that Henry the lover was hunting a different kind of quarry.[9]

The king's letter was written, he says, 'by the hand of your servant, who often wishes you here instead of your brother'.[10] In other words, George Boleyn was one of those closest to the king on his hunting trip, which meant the Boleyns could operate on a triple front. Anne was with her mother in Kent, her father was commuting between there and London, gathering all the news, and her brother could report throughout on Henry's state of mind. Was this how Anne was able so finely to calculate her responses to the love-struck king? Here was a family that had already proved it knew how to operate as a business and a political force.

The mention of George also matters for another reason. Over the winter of 1525–26 in Eltham, Wolsey issued reforming Ordinances for the Royal Household, aiming to reduce the size and influence of Henry's privy chamber.[11] William Compton was ousted and made under-treasurer of the Exchequer; Sir William Kingston, already Constable of the Tower, gained further promotion as Captain of the King's Guard. Henry Norris replaced Compton as groom of the stool and keeper of Henry's privy purse, while Bryan and Carew were expelled again. Wolsey's attempt to marginalise 'young Boleyn' (meaning George) was not successful. As compensation he was 'to have £20 yearly above the £80 he hath gotten to him and his wife to live thereupon, and also to admit him to be one of the cupbearers when [the] king dineth out'.[12] But George was almost immediately back in Henry's inner circle as the king's letter proves, a foreshadowing of the waning of the cardinal's influence that was destined to come.

Not all, however, went to plan with the Boleyns' calculations. Of the next two of Henry's letters, both in French, one strikes a more insistent note of appeal. He needs to know where he stands as he is in 'great agony' through not being sure whether her responses are to his 'advantage' or not, since they appear to him to veer from side to side. He really must know, as he has been 'for more than a year struck by the dart of love'. If her love is more than just 'an ordinary love' and she is ready to give herself 'body and soul' to him as is the 'duty of a true, loyal mistress and friend', then she will be his 'sole mistress' and he will care only for her.[13]

The other letter moves away from mere pleading, trying a more assertive approach. Henry makes Anne unambiguously aware that she has failed to give him the reassurance he craves, and this situation cannot continue. His letter shows a sinister change of tone and frames itself around an unpleasant rumour that has reached him. 'I have been advised', he said, 'that the opinion in which I left you has been wholly changed, and that you will not come to court, either with Madam your mother or in any other way, which report, if true, I cannot enough marvel at.' 'Marvel at' are the words Henry routinely used in his official letters as a reprimand to subjects he believed to be disobeying or thwarting him. When Anne saw them, she would have understood they were a red flag.

It is not his fault that she keeps him at a distance, Henry continues, as he has 'never placed' her 'in a false position', so it seems a 'very small return for the great love' he has for her. He is frankly astonished that she does not suffer as he does. Then comes the punchline: she must acquiesce, or he will give up on his suit, despite the deep emotional hardship that will cause him. 'Ponder well, my mistress', he warns, 'that absence from you is very grievous to me, hoping that it is not by your will that it is so; but if I understood that in truth you yourself wished it, I could do no other than complain of my ill fortune while abating little by little my great folly.' Here surely lies a thinly veiled threat.[14]

When Anne read this, she knew it was the point of decision: she had to make up her mind. At last, she answered affirmatively. She had weighed things up, she said, and was willing to return. Although her letter is lost, its contents are obvious from the king's brief reply. Should he wish to visit her, she must have said, he could do so, but it would be 'in her capacity as a servant'. He would be the 'master', she the 'servant' – that was how it was in real life as opposed to his romantic fantasies. At this, Henry mildly protested, but said he would comply if that was her wish.[15]

Henry's reply ends with a cryptogram. The characters comprising the riddle can clearly be seen in the handwritten original in the Vatican Library, but only one scholar has correctly transcribed them: they read 'v.n.A.1.de A.o.na.v.e.r'.[16] The most persuasive suggestion as to what they mean is that they depend on a series of multilingual plays involving Anne's name, which commemorate Henry's attempts to win her heart over the course of a year – 'Anno' being the Latin for 'in the year', which is often abbreviated as 'A^o', and 'un an' (in Latin the letter 'u' is represented by a 'v') meaning 'one year' in French. (None of this, however, accounts for the presence of a final 'r' character in the cryptogram.)[17]

On 18 October 1526, Henry returned to Greenwich Palace, where he stayed until Christmas. According to Edward Hall, he again celebrated the holidays in high style 'with great plenty of victual, revels, masques, disguisings and banquets'. On New Year's Eve, he held 'an enterprise of jousts' until 3 January, when he came to Bridewell Palace to change for another masque. Oarsmen then rowed him in the royal barge to Wolsey's house at York Place, where a great company of lords and ladies were at supper, 'and then the masquers danced and made goodly pastime, and when they had well danced, the ladies plucked away their visors and were all known.'[18]

Anne would have been among the revellers, because two days before, on New Year's Day, she made a move of her own. As throughout Europe, seasonal gifts were exchanged not on 25

December, but on New Year's Day. She was well acquainted with
the rituals from her time with Queen Claude. In France, New
Year's gifts had their own special word: *étrennes*. They were formally
laid out for inspection on buffets in the *chambre à parer* (Presence
Chamber) as evidence of the ruler's prestige. At Henry's court,
the king and queen each had their own buffet and between late
November and early December, the royal carpenters 'made trestles
and boards for the king's New Year gifts to stand upon'.[19]

And it was such a gift that Anne gave to Henry. He was overjoyed
because its symbolism was transparent. She had remembered her
journey around Brittany with Claude and Louise of Savoy in the
summer of 1518, when the citizens of Nantes had presented Francis
with a silver-gilt ship jewel whose meaning was that his subjects were
safe in storms so long as he was at the tiller. Now she gave Henry
a smaller, modified version of the same device: a 'fair diamond' set
in a 'ship in which a solitary damsel is tossed about'. As the means
to convey a message, it was brilliantly choreographed. Henry wrote
immediately to thank her, using the word *étrenne* to describe it and
exclaiming how it delighted him, not only as a perfectly chosen gift
but also 'for the fine interpretation and too humble submission which
your kindness has made of it'. This appears to have come in the form
of a motto or cipher, probably enamelled or engraved on it.[20]

The jewel's meaning is plain: Anne portrays herself as the woman
in danger in a ship in stormy seas, who will be safe once she is in
Henry's arms. It provides the first signal we have of her moving
their relationship on to the next stage. Henry, she indicates, has her
permission to woo her, but must do so in earnest, not just in the
exaggerated language of courtly love, and not simply so that she
could replace her sister in his bed.

Henry had met his match. The idea of Anne being his lover was
no longer an option. She would be his wife, his queen and the
mother of his sons. It would be she, not Katherine, who would
give him the legitimate male heir he craved, who – unlike the
illegitimate Fitzroy – could be certain of succeeding to the throne.

Anxious lest his earlier badgering had upset her, Henry then
asks that 'if at any time I have offended you, you will give me the

same absolution as you yourself demand'. Finally, he makes his declaration:

> Henceforth my heart shall be dedicated to you alone, greatly
> desirous that my body could be also thus dedicated, which
> God can do if he pleases, to whom I pray every day to that end,
> hoping that my prayer will be heard.

And at the end, squeezed into the middle of his signature line 'H[enry] autre ne cherche R[ex]' ('King Henry seeks no other'), he draws her interlaced initials 'AB' inside a heart, like a lovesick youth carving his beloved's name on a tree.[21]

Since Henry was pierced by the 'dart of love' for over a year before Anne gave her answer, the only possible date for her New Year's gift is the first day of 1527: the previous year would have been too early and the next too late.[22] Other evidence supports this conclusion. Amongst Sir Thomas Boleyn's accounts, covering the last two months of 1526, is a payment of £4 to Cornelius Hayes, the king's Flemish goldsmith, coupled with a separately itemised amount of £3 12s 6d. for 'Mistress Anne's bill'.[23] Could either or both relate to the ship? If so, they corroborate not just the date of the gift, but also the part Anne's father played in easing her route to the crown. In a seventh letter written around the spring of 1527, Henry will protest that if her father does not hasten Anne's return to court by two days 'or at least on the day already determined upon', he will 'think he has no wish to serve the lovers' turn as he said he would, nor accord with my expectation'.[24]

How can we visualise the ship's size and design? Assuming at least one of the payments in the Boleyn accounts relates to this purchase, Anne's ship was not a table ornament like the far more expensive gift given to Francis in Nantes and is likely to have been a brooch or maybe a pendant. Although a mock-up appeared in the Sony Pictures TV series *The Tudors*, the jewel has long since vanished. Anne's gift, like her letters, would have been abhorrent to Henry after her fall. Within the Victoria and Albert Museum's collections in London, however, is the so-called 'Hunsdon Jewel', a ship pendant which was said to be Elizabeth I's New Year's gift to her cousin Henry Carey, Mary Boleyn's son: Anne's gift must have looked similar. It has a wooden hull mounted in enamelled gold, a gilded mast and gilded rigging strung with pearls. Its hull bristles with gilded cannon and a winged figure of Victory sounds a golden trumpet. Suspended by a golden clasp, it measures 72mm high and 51mm wide.[25]

Anne's New Year's gift set the scene for what was to become the slowest-burn royal courtship in British history. She had finally taken stock, gauged the true extent of Henry's interest in her and realised where it might lead. The irony is that while he had been hunting her, she was hunting him. For a reigning monarch to wed a commoner was a huge risk. Apart from Edward IV, a king of England had never taken a subject as his wife since before the Norman Conquest. Henry did not even dare to tell Wolsey what he was planning. First, he thought, he would overcome the difficulties himself.

How little either Anne or Henry knew of what would be in store for them over the next six years.

12

The 'Secret Matter'

By the close of 1526, Wolsey meant to replace the upheavals that had defined England's relations with France for so long with a new golden age of eternal friendship. The catalyst came when the victorious Emperor Charles, now married to Isabella of Portugal, encouraged his sister Eleanor to marry Francis. Unlike the English king, Francis was single again: Queen Claude, exhausted by her many pregnancies, had died at Blois in July 1524, leaving six living children.[1] Seeing the danger posed by a Franco-Habsburg dynastic alliance, Wolsey meant to take the Anglo-French rapprochement agreed by the Treaty of the More to a new level.[2]

He had grounds for optimism. On 23 March, Charles had issued letters to the German princes and imperial free cities forbidding religious innovations, only to find Luther's supporters in revolt in the Reichstag. And on the eastern fringes of the Holy Roman Empire, Sultan Suleiman had killed Louis II, King of Hungary, and the flower of his nobility in a desperate battle at Mohács, sweeping into Hungary afterwards. When the Turks occupied Buda, Charles's territories became prey to the incursions of Suleiman's cavalry.[3]

Henry's *schadenfreude* was unconcealed. After coming back from hunting a stag, he exclaimed, '[I] reckon surely the Emperor's affairs in Italy do stand in as evil case as may be.'[4] Seeing an opportunity, Pope Clement sent Uberto Gambara, an experienced, fleet-footed papal prothonotary, to pressure Henry into joining the League of

Cognac. Gambara respected Henry but had no love of Wolsey's pomp and show, and while the king was eager for the League to expel Charles from Italy and see him accept a fair ransom to free Francis's two sons, he had no plans to join or contribute financially. No longer, it seemed, could Henry be wholly relied on as 'the pope's good son'.[5]

In November 1526, Wolsey proposed that Francis, or perhaps the Dauphin as had previously been arranged in 1518, should marry Princess Mary. Discussions began in Poissy between Francis, Louise, Wolsey's confidential agent John Clerk and Sir William Fitzwilliam. From the outset, Louise ruled out the Dauphin, refusing to allow him out of France once he had been safely recovered from his time in Spain serving as surety for Francis himself. If Francis declined to marry the young princess, her preferred candidate was her seven-year-old second grandson, Henry, Duke of Orléans.[6]

In February 1527, a high-powered French delegation arrived in London, led by Gabriel de Gramont, the Bishop of Tarbes, and François de la Tour, Vicomte de Turenne, a *gentilhomme de la chambre* and favourite of Francis. Wolsey pushed for Francis, rather than the duke, as Mary's bridegroom. The obstacle was her age: although Mary was now almost twelve, Henry did not want her married until she was fourteen. Louise's delegation calmly suggested both kings meet in Calais, where after the marriage ceremony, Francis 'might abed himself for an hour or less with my Lady Princess'. She said her son 'was a man of honour and discretion and would use no violence'. That way 'her son might be assured of his wife' and would 'make everything sure that neither party should now vary'. Henry could then take his daughter back home 'till she should be accounted more able'.[7]

So keen were Henry and Wolsey to take this political opportunity that Louise's idea was not rejected out of hand. On 30 April, the Treaty of Westminster was agreed in York Place. Leading the English delegation were Anne's father, the newly minted Viscount Rochford, and her uncle, the younger Thomas Howard, 3rd Duke of Norfolk since 1524. A landmark in Henry's reign, the treaty sealed his diplomatic volte-face. Princess Mary was to marry either

Francis or his second son (the choice was to be left open), and Henry promised to send an embassy to Spain to press for the ransom of the French king's sons and for a general peace. In return for the betrothal, Henry also agreed to moderate the financial conditions of the Treaty of the More. Francis would now pay him no more than 1 million crowns by instalments.[8]

On 5 May, Henry ordered celebratory jousts and revels to begin immediately at Greenwich Palace. Their aim was to prove to the world he was now a Francophile, and to allow Anne to make her first public appearance with him. She was, says Cavendish in his *Life of Wolsey*, by this time looking 'very haughty and stout [proud, determined], having all manner of jewels, or rich apparel, that might be gotten with money'.[9]

Henry had been planning the Greenwich celebrations for weeks, ever since pledging himself to Anne. We know this, because, on 8 February 1527, 'Master Hans' started work inside a large, canvas-roofed temporary banqueting suite where the festivities were to be held.[10] 'Master Hans' was none other than the acclaimed Hans Holbein the Younger, a German émigré artist and portraitist born in Augsburg, who had moved to Basel in 1515 and arrived in London in 1526, bearing a recommendation from Erasmus of Rotterdam to Thomas More.[11] He was to paint the ceiling of the theatre where the masque was to be staged, along with a majestic triumphal arch separating the theatre from the banqueting hall. The ceiling, lit by candles and mirrors and creating the illusion of the heavens with all the stars and planets and signs of the zodiac, was consciously designed to rival and surpass the one hung over the courtyard of the Bastille for the banquet in honour of the English ambassadors in 1518. So too was the triumphal arch, which had a painting on the back graphically, if not tactfully, depicting the English victory at the Battle of the Spurs.

On 5 May, the jousts were followed in the evening by a banquet, songs and a pageant, this time culminating in a masque scripted around the theme of damsels rescued from a rugged mountain. At the banquet, Katherine sat with Henry and the Duchess of Suffolk under a cloth of estate (or throne canopy fixed to the wall) while dish after dish was served on solid gold plates. Anne's brother, George, poured Henry's wine. When the meal was over, everyone processed through Holbein's triumphal arch into the theatre.[12]

Many different diversions were enjoyed that night, but for the French and the Boleyns, it was only the finale that counted. Shimmering in the candlelight in their costumes of cloth of gold and wearing black velvet slippers, Henry and de Turenne danced until dawn with the women in the masque. (All eight of the chief male maskers wore these slippers out of deference to Henry, who had injured his foot playing tennis.) De Turenne partnered the young Princess Mary, but Henry sought out Anne.

For the French delegation, the king's choice was the highlight of the evening, the one event singled out in the original handwritten journal of Claude Dodieu, a lawyer in the Parlement of Paris, who diarised Turenne's mission. The journal, recently acquired by the Bibliothèque Nationale in Paris, records:

> Et Monsieur de Turenne par commandement du dict Seigneur Roi dansa avec Madame la Princesse, et le Roi avec Mestresse Boulan, qui a esté nourrie en France avec la feu Royne. ['And Monsieur de Turenne, by the king's command, danced with Princess Mary, and the king with Mistress Boleyn, who was brought up in France with the late Queen (Claude).'][13]

Whereas much of the splendour of the banquet and entertainments passed Dodieu by, this is the crucial detail he seizes on. Anne was not Henry's wife yet, but she was the woman he preferred to partner over his Spanish spouse, and one known to have close links with France. And as a further signal of intent, it was Anne's father whom the king sent to Paris to witness Francis's ratification of the treaty. On arrival, he was once again sought out by Louise and her son and invited to confer with them privately.[14]

The diplomacy surrounding the Treaty of Westminster has wider significance. The negotiations were the first of many occasions on which Henry claimed it was de Gramont who alerted him to the potentially incestuous state of his marriage to Katherine and thus to the question of their daughter's possible illegitimacy, given that he had married his dead brother's wife. Was Julius II's fudged bull of dispensation allowing the wedding, de Gramont had asked him, sufficient to overcome something so emphatically forbidden by church law?[15]

De Gramont's concern was tremendously convenient for Henry and Anne. A genuine reason to justify an investigation of the validity of the king's first marriage now appeared to exist, and they would be quick to pursue the idea.[16] On 7 April, while the French ambassadors were still locked in their negotiations with Wolsey, Henry sent Dr Richard Wolman, Doctor of Laws, to interrogate the seventy-nine-year-old Richard Fox, who had organised Katherine's wedding to Arthur and led the negotiations with Ferdinand and Isabella.

Wolman was a shrewd, sharp church lawyer talent-spotted by Wolsey, who moved to Henry's service in 1526 and was appointed a royal chaplain.[17] His visit to Winchester to question Fox did Henry little good. Unlike Archbishop Warham, Fox harboured few doubts about Henry's right to marry his dead brother's widow, but the line of questioning shows how the king's mind was working. Fox, now blind and almost deaf, said he had been present at what had first passed in 1503 for a wedding between Henry and Katherine, and had afterwards drafted the reluctant bridegroom's protest. As far as he could remember, Henry had registered his protest at his father's command, without expressly consenting to or dissenting from a future marriage to Katherine. As to Pope Julius II's dispensation, he said that copies existed in London and in Spain, and he believed they were both 'true and sufficient'. The bull of dispensation may well have been flawed, but none of its potential ambiguities was fatal.[18]

As soon as the Greenwich revels were over, Henry informed Wolsey that he had 'deep scruples' about the validity of his marriage but disingenuously said nothing of his intentions regarding Anne. It was a deception both would come to rue. Wolsey drew the wrong conclusion, believing that if Henry was considering an annulment, then his future spouse would be Princess Renée, Queen Claude's sister. Politically, that would have been a perfect match: she was already approaching the age of seventeen and on the marriage market. Acting swiftly on this belief, he secretly summoned Henry to appear before a special church tribunal.

On 17 May, just twelve days after Henry had danced with Anne and barely five months since she had presented him with his New Year's gift, Wolsey, flanked by Warham, opened the first session of a special church court to test the lawfulness of Henry and Katherine's marriage. The difficulty was to establish whether Katherine's marriage to Arthur had been consummated. If it had, as Henry resolutely maintained, no reason existed to prevent the court reaching judgment, because then he and Katherine were related in the first degree of affinity (the relationship that exists between a person and the immediate relatives of their spouse) and should never have married.[19]

But in a rare moment of indecision, Wolsey stepped back from the brink. An honest man where religion was concerned, he worried that this was not merely a matter of law, but also one of theology in which he was not a specialist. He adjourned the tribunal, citing the need to consult expert theologians, chief among them John Fisher.[20]

Then the unexpected happened. On 2 June, shocking reports arrived from Italy that mutinous troops from the armies of the Duke of Bourbon had attacked and sacked Rome.[21] After regrouping his forces in the vicinity of Milan, Bourbon had demanded the duchy in recompense for his confiscated French estates. When Charles failed to comply or to pay Bourbon's troops their promised arrears, they marched on Rome.

Bourbon's attack began at about 4 a.m. on 6 May with a battery of gunfire while his troops placed scaling ladders against the city walls. The duke, easily identifiable by his trademark white surcoat, rode out in front of his troops and was scythed down as he led them forward. Had he lived, he would perhaps have been able to keep the army under control. As it was, Rome was subjected to a merciless and catastrophic sack. Women and nuns were raped, almost a third of the city and all its major palaces and religious buildings looted or burned. Torture was used to gain knowledge of hidden treasure. Raphael's incomparable tapestries of the *Acts of the Apostles*, which had cost five times as much as the whole of Michelangelo's ceiling, were stripped from the walls of the Sistine Chapel, never to return undamaged. St Peter's became a stable for Bourbon's cavalry. As Pope Clement quickly hurried along the covered way from the Vatican to Castel Sant' Angelo to seek refuge, he could see the battle raging below and was even fired at by Bourbon's troops. For the next six months he would be a prisoner.[22]

Disclaiming responsibility for Bourbon's actions, but seizing his chance, Charles demanded indemnities from Clement for his role in establishing the League of Cognac and a ransom of 400,000 ducats for the pope's freedom. This knocked Henry for six. With Clement under the control of Katherine's nephew, he knew that divorcing Katherine was going to get much harder. To punish him for allying with Francis, Charles could easily rediscover his family loyalties.

Wolsey had other reasons to worry. On 22 June, with the tribunal still formally undecided, Henry had brazenly confronted Katherine with the news that they had been living in mortal sin for eighteen years and must separate.[23] When she burst into floods of tears, he sheepishly claimed he merely sought to 'search and try out the truth' in response to 'doubts moved therein by the bishop of Tarbes'.[24] The disclosure had dramatic consequences. Never slow to defend her interests, Katherine sent a loyal Spanish servant, Francesco Felipez, to Charles with a message, telling him what her husband was planning. Charles reacted swiftly.[25] 'Her cause is ours,' he instructed his ambassador in London to warn Henry. He also alerted Clement, suggesting he persuade Henry to drop the whole business. Should the king persist, then Clement should revoke Wolsey's ecclesiastical powers and hear the suit in Rome.[26]

Charles's intervention turned Henry's private life into an embarrassing international issue. This was not the way the secret tribunal was meant to go. On 1 July, Dr Wolman arrived in York Place with portentous news for Wolsey. The king, he informed the cardinal menacingly, doubted his loyalty: by his decision to adjourn the proceedings, trial of the 'secret matter' had been delayed, hindering Henry's plans. In one respect, Henry was right. This was as close as he would get to an annulment of his marriage in the next six years. What's more, Katherine 'stiffly and obstinately' denied her marriage to Arthur had been consummated, thereby contradicting the most important of Henry's contentions. She too had called for legal counsel and intended to 'impeach' her husband's case in Rome and to 'make all the counsel of the world, France except, as a party against it'.[27]

Henry and Anne had underestimated Katherine, who instantly saw that this could escalate into a fight not just for herself and her daughter but for the preservation of the 'Holy Catholic Faith'. To her, repudiating her marriage was repudiating papal authority, which in turn would mean repudiating the entire Church. Like her mother, Isabella of Castile, she would not flinch from her duty. Catholic recusant hagiography misleadingly came to depict her as a 'patient Griselda', quietly waiting for her husband to come to his senses.[28] Nothing could be further from the truth. If Henry would not cease from risking his own soul and the souls of the people entrusted by God to his care, then she must oppose him every step of the way.

Wolsey hastily assured Henry of his commitment to his cause. 'I take God to record', he avowed, 'that there is nothing earthly that I covet so much as the advancing thereof.'[29] On 2 or 3 July, the great cardinal mounted his mule and left York Place, accompanied by Thomas More, John Clerk, Francis Bryan and a large retinue of gentlemen and servants. Joining a grand cavalcade extending for three-quarters of a mile, he headed for Dover with the seeds of a daring plan germinating in his mind.[30] His first intention was to amplify the Treaty of Westminster, upgrading it into a full military alliance against Charles. His second, secret objective was to convene a powerful group of cardinals in the papal territory of Avignon, as large as could be mustered, and take over the government of the Church while Clement was a prisoner. There would be two popes – the captive Clement in Rome and Wolsey as an effective acting pope in Avignon, in which capacity he could confront Charles and attempt to strike a deal over Henry's divorce.[31]

Wolsey embarked for France on the 11th. A week later, the Treaty of Amiens was signed.[32] Brilliantly illuminated, the various documents included miniature portraits of Henry and Francis wearing their crowns and clutching sceptres, along with their royal coats of arms. Francis pledged to drive Charles out of Italy and into peace talks if Henry would assist him and share the costs. Princess Mary was to marry the Duke of Orléans, and if war spread to the Low Countries, English merchants should be allowed to trade in France on the same favourable conditions as they enjoyed in the Flemish 'mart' towns. To emphasise their friendship, the two kings would exchange orders of chivalry: Henry was to be admitted to the Order of St Michael and Francis to the Order of the Garter.[33] As to Henry's future marriage plans, Wolsey mentioned them to Francis 'after such a cloudy and dark sort that he shall not know your grace's utter determination and intent in that behalf'. For this, the cardinal had a very good reason: he did not know them himself.[34]

Afterwards in Compiègne, Wolsey, assisted by three French cardinals and a papal nuncio, hammered out a document to be sent to Clement, giving notice of their intention to deal with Church affairs while he was incapacitated.[35] Not surprisingly, the plan came to grief when the Italian cardinals flatly refused to make Wolsey a caretaker pope, and Wolsey could only turn back for England.[36]

By the time Wolsey returned from France in late September, the situation had developed rapidly without him, and his position was under serious threat. Sir William Fitzwilliam, keenly aware of the advantages of backing both sides, had been the first to warn him. Writing to him on 31 July from Beaulieu, he cautioned: 'the king's highness keepeth here a very great and a chargeable house, for there is at this time lodged within the Duke of Norfolk and his wife, the Duke of Suffolk, the Marquis of Exeter, the Earls of Oxford, Essex and Rutland, the Viscounts Fitzwalter* and Rochford.' Henry was 'merry and in good health'. He 'daily passeth the time in hunting,

---

*Robert Radcliffe, later 1st Earl of Sussex.

and at all times suppeth in his privy chamber.' And on all these evenings, 'there suppeth with him the Dukes of Norfolk and Suffolk, the Marquis of Exeter and the Lord of Rochford.'[37]

Henry had summoned a council of war while Wolsey was out of the way. At Beaulieu, work and pleasure could be combined. The property was now palatial: Henry had spent some £17,000 upgrading it (worth over £17 million today) since purchasing the old New Hall site from Anne's father. Its footprint had been massively expanded. With its luxurious new lodgings, gallery, gatehouse, stables and service buildings, chapel, tennis courts and fresh water supply, it was now one of the few royal residences that could accommodate the entire court of around 600 people.[38] Henry had arrived there a few days before from Hunsdon in Hertfordshire, a manor house less than thirty miles away, which he had refitted as a 'palace royal', then gave to Anne. Katherine was with him. Although some reports said that he was eager to depart without her, in fact he 'tarried' for her, 'and so they rode forth together'. Anne, however, was not kept away. Two days after the royal party arrived in Beaulieu, Henry had Cornelius Hayes deliver her an emerald ring there, followed soon afterwards by a ruby.[39]

Outwardly, Norfolk, Suffolk, Rochford and Exeter, the gang of four who every evening 'suppeth with him in his privy chamber', spoke as one on Henry's divorce. Inwardly, their unity was paper thin. Rochford, Anne's father, did not waver in support of his younger daughter. Norfolk, her uncle, took his lead from the king. Short and lean, with black hair, a thin face and an unreliable temper, it was said of him, 'he can speak fair, as well to his enemy as to his friend.'[40] His wife, Elizabeth Stafford, on the other hand, one of Katherine's longest serving ladies, would soon be slipping her letters from Rome, hidden in oranges. Her outlook would be sharply reinforced by the fact that in 1527, Norfolk took a mistress, Elizabeth (or 'Bess') Holland, whose wardrobe was generously stocked with French gowns and who later gravitated to Anne. One day, the duke would find himself on the sharp end of his niece's tongue. He knew he had to bear it, but if Henry ever changed his mind about her, he would willingly keep him company.[41]

Charles Brandon, Duke of Suffolk, faced a dilemma. He owed his career to Henry and a considerable debt to Wolsey. As a man of the world, his sympathy for Henry's passion might be presumed, but as the husband of the king's sister, he had to follow his wife's lead. The titular head of Katherine's household, the duchess had known Katherine for most of her life. A king's daughter, a king's sister, Queen of France albeit briefly, she did not take kindly to Katherine's supplanter. She considered the Boleyns *arrivistes* and especially loathed Anne, possibly because of the raunchy gossip Anne had picked up in Paris about her and Suffolk's bedroom antics after Louis XII's death.[42]

Henry Courtenay, Marquis of Exeter, was another of the queen's partisans. So was his wife, Gertrude Blount, one of her most senior ladies-in-waiting and closest friends. She would later enrage Henry by passing on sensitive intelligence gleaned from her husband to Charles's ambassador for which, at Anne's request, the king would rusticate her briefly from court. But for the moment, she and her husband had to muffle their dissent.[43]

One thing did unify this group: resentment against Wolsey, the butcher's son who for so long had lorded it over them. Until now, it had been less the substance of Wolsey's decisions that had affronted them, and more the way he monopolised power. But since Amiens, the mood had changed: Norfolk, Suffolk, Exeter and many more were paid-up Francophobes, each with grave reservations about the Anglo-French alliance despite the king's enthusiasm for it. And public opinion was on their side. There would be uproar when Wolsey announced the terms of the Treaty of Amiens to the Londoners. When he forbade the Merchant Adventurers to market their cloths in the fairs of the 'mart' towns to frustrate Charles, but to sell them in Calais instead, exports collapsed. Once it was known that Princess Mary was to be pledged to the Duke of Orléans, handbills circulated in the streets, cautioning Wolsey 'that he should not counsel the king to marry his daughter into France, for if he did, he should show himself enemy to the king and the realm.'[44]

Wolsey had glimpsed the danger before leaving France, sending Clerk on ahead to assure Henry that 'all such things as have been done and concluded here, with such expeditions as be devised to be sped at Rome concerning your secret affair' were to the king's 'surety, benefit and advantage'.[45] An hour or so later, he scribbled a grovelling second letter, protesting the success of 'your secret matter' to be 'my daily study and most inward desire', and that every day separated from Henry felt like a year. He signed the note 'with a rude and shaking hand of your most humble subject, servant and chaplain'.[46]

Barely had Clerk departed when Wolsey discovered that Henry intended to appeal directly to Clement behind his back. It was the start of an entirely fresh trail – and the great disrupter would be Anne.[47]

13

Anne Makes Her Mark

On 1 September 1527, Henry sent his new secretary, William Knight, on a special mission to Rome – one Wolsey 'should not know about'. He was to stop first in France, where Wolsey still was (he would return only at the end of the month), to allay his suspicions. On reaching Italy, he was to hand Clement the draft of a dispensation allowing the king to proceed to a second marriage, even if his first had not yet been annulled. Just as Henry and Anne had hunted each other and still hunted deer and game for pleasure, now they were on a hunt of a different sort: their quarry was the pope's consent to their marriage.[1]

Wolsey heard of the plan when news leaked. Ominously, Henry claimed to have identified his source – 'by whose means I know well enough'. Henry then appeared to change tack in the light of Wolsey's scepticism. Except this was a second duplicity: far from recalling Knight, the king sent him a heavily revised version of the document for the pope to sign, to be shown only to Clement and those whom Henry 'was sure will never disclose it to no man living for any craft the cardinal or any other can find'.[2]

A copy of the second draft does not survive, but Knight's instructions show it was to be a dispensation which already assumed Henry's first marriage to be unlawful and left him free to marry a woman related to him in the first degree of affinity, meaning one with whose sister he had already slept. Henry, in other words, did not want to be declared unmarried so that he might marry Princess Renée. When Wolsey, despite Henry's efforts, once again learned of the content of the new draft, it dawned on the startled cardinal that it was Anne whom Henry wanted as his wife.

In December, matters took a fresh turn. Now fully apprised of the situation and believing Knight's task to be beyond him, Wolsey took charge and enlisted an Italian born in Rome around 1498 who had lived for a time in England, Gregorio Casali, to represent Henry at the Vatican. Casali was as cunning as a fox, a larger-than-life character with *sprezzatura* and Machiavellian tendencies, who had risen from relatively humble origins to become an intimate of popes and cardinals. While in London, he offered advice on hunting and cavalry tactics to Henry's young bloods and supplied fine steeds and hawks to the king. Knighted by Henry, he had received a pension for life plus a gold collar.[3] Working with his cousin Vicenzo, he was now to obtain a bull commissioning Wolsey, or any other cardinal who was not pro-Habsburg, to consider Henry's suit for divorce and give a final sentence. He was to receive the princely sum of 10,000 ducats for his expenses plus a salary of 3,000 crowns a year, more than a bishop.[4]

The courier carrying these letters between Henry and Italy was the red-haired John Barlow, a chaplain to the Boleyns.[5] Barlow first tracked down Knight in Parma awaiting the arrival of Gambara.[6] About the same age as Anne, Barlow was born in Essex and was a Fellow of Merton College, Oxford, until poached by Anne's father and brought to Hever where he would be made rector of St Peter's parish church in 1525.[7]

As the urgency and decisiveness with which this mission was arranged shows, Anne was now a force to be reckoned with. As Charles's new ambassador in London, Íñigo López de Mendoza, reported in a fully ciphered dispatch, no longer was it a secret why Henry wanted a divorce. The whole court, he says, buzzed with stories that he meant to marry Anne. Already de Mendoza suspected that she had supplanted Wolsey. To illustrate his point, he explained that when Wolsey had returned from France, he sent a servant to Richmond Palace to request an audience with Henry. The servant found Anne sitting beside the king, and when he asked where Wolsey should come to meet him, it was Anne, not Henry, who answered first. 'Where else is he to come?', she quipped. 'Tell him that he may come here, where the king is.' 'She is', de Mendoza added, 'a woman who entertains no great affection for the cardinal.'[8]

Some weeks later, Thomas More, who had stayed behind in France to tidy up loose ends, arrived at Hampton Court. Henry saw him alone in the gallery, where (as More reports) he 'brake with me of his great matter', explaining that his marriage to Katherine 'was not only against the positive laws of the Church and the written law of God but also in such wise against the law of nature'. The defects of the marriage were so serious that 'it could in no wise by the Church be dispensable'.[9] Henry then laid the Old Testament Book of Leviticus in front of More, pointing to a passage which he claimed prohibited marriage to a dead brother's wife:

If a man shall take his brother's wife, it is an impurity. He
hath uncovered his brother's nakedness: they shall be childless'
(Leviticus 20:21).

As Henry assured More, this was God's law that no pope could lawfully alter. He dismissed out of hand a seemingly contrary text from the Book of Deuteronomy, denying its relevance on the grounds that it merely reflected an ancient Jewish custom known as the 'levirate' by which the brother of a deceased man was bound, if himself unmarried, to marry the widow. This, Henry declared, applied only to the Jews and was not binding on Christians.[10]

Henry understood the divine retribution threatened against illicit marriage partners according to Leviticus to be gender specific: 'they shall be childless' meant 'they shall not have *sons*'. And he went further, claiming that sexual intercourse with a brother's widow was incest pure and simple, and 'in such high degree against the law of nature'. Who put such notions into his head?

We know the source to have been Robert Wakefield, a Fellow successively of Clare and St John's Colleges in Cambridge, and the foremost Hebraist of the day. Fluent in Latin, Greek, Hebrew, Arabic and Aramaic, he believed that only a mastery of the Old Testament in its original languages allowed an accurate interpretation of Scripture. But Wakefield did not spring from nowhere. The ultimate source of these revolutionary ideas was the Boleyns, who first identified Wakefield and brought him to Henry's attention: Anne's father was Wakefield's patron and her uncle Sir James Boleyn had been one of his Cambridge students.[11]

There was another, overlapping, connection. As far back as February 1527, Richard Pace, the king's former secretary, then recuperating from illness at Syon Abbey in Isleworth on the Thames, had written to the king. Along with his letter, he sent a Hebrew alphabet to be delivered to Edward Foxe, a Fellow of King's College, Cambridge, and another scholar close to the Boleyns.[12] Foxe's appearance in the narrative chimes perfectly with More's recollections. When Henry invited More, during their conversation at Hampton Court, to verify for himself the accuracy of the king's interpretation of the scriptural texts, he ordered him 'to commune further with Master Foxe ... and to read a book with him that then was in making for that matter.'[13]

Reginald Pole's recollection is hazier, but similar. A serious young man and Henry's kinsman for whose education in Oxford and Italy the king had paid, he began by supporting the 'secret matter', but later vehemently opposed it and fled to Italy. In 1536, he set down his opinions in an open letter, handwritten in Latin and running to 280 pages.[14] Halfway through, he claims it was Anne, and not Henry, who had first found the arguments for the divorce, saying,

> She sent her priests (*sacerdotes suos*), weighty theologians, as pledges of her manifest will, both to affirm to you [Henry] that it was not only lawful to send her [Katherine] away, but also to tell you that you were sinning mortally to keep her even for a single moment, and to denounce it as the most grievous crime against God unless you repudiated her at once.

Only Anne could impress on Henry the cogency of Wakefield's arguments and persuade him to believe them. For her and her

ANNE MAKES HER MARK 151

family, there could be no turning back. In the light of this, Henry's attempt to bypass Wolsey, whose position the Boleyns could not be sure of, by sending Knight to Rome, using Barlow as the courier, makes perfect sense. She and the king were jointly in the driving seat – she had made her mark.[15]

Christmas 1527, which intervened while Knight was away, was a subdued affair. The main topic of conversation was how Wolsey, anxious about the threat posed to the Catholic Church, had conducted a purge over the past twelve months of those preachers and laymen he suspected of Lutheranism. His chief concerns were the import of Luther's books and of a highly readable English version of the *New Testament* made by William Tyndale, an expatriate who had found refuge in Antwerp. That these works, printed at a time when vernacular Bibles were forbidden, were smuggled into London by merchants of the German Hanseatic League, led to raids on their warehouse and living quarters near London Bridge, the arrest of five of the merchants and another public book burning at which 2,000 copies of Tyndale's English translation were cast into the flames.[16]

The merchants were not the only ones to feel the full force of Wolsey's zeal. Two Cambridge evangelical preachers and a yeoman usher of the king's chamber had been forced to abjure their beliefs under threat of burning at the stake, as had the London curate Thomas Garrett, who supplied many 'fardels' (heavy pallets) of Lutheran books to students in Oxford. In this, Garrett was aided and abetted by his superior Dr Robert Forman, the rector of the parish of All Hallows in London's Honey Lane. Another Cambridge reformer, Robert Barnes, punished once before for an inflammatory sermon, was trapped again for selling copies of Tyndale's *New Testament*. Put into solitary confinement in Northampton, he staged a spectacular escape, leaving a pile of clothes beside the river Nene and a suicide note for Wolsey before taking ship and joining Luther.[17]

In the event, Knight's mission failed. A few days after he slipped stealthily into Rome where the main thoroughfares were closely patrolled by sentries, Clement fled to Orvieto, a perfect natural fortress built on volcanic rock and a refuge for earlier popes. Wolsey felt confident that Casali would help Knight to gain an audience. And he did – but all Clement gave him was a general commission to examine the king's case without powers to grant a final sentence. The document was entrusted to Gambara to deliver to London while Barlow continued to shuttle between Casali in Italy and Knight, whom Wolsey detained in Paris. Once Gambara had delivered his packet in late January 1528, it was clear for all to see that the most vital clauses, forbidding Katherine's appeal to Rome, had been struck out.[18]

Anne continued to resent Wolsey for the way he had separated her from Harry Percy but she needed his help to get Henry his divorce. She therefore wrote him an emollient letter in her own hand. She began in all apparent humility:

> My Lord, after my most humble recommendations, this shall
> be to give unto your grace, as I am most bound, my humble
> thanks for the great pain and travail that your grace doth
> take in studying, by your wisdom and great diligence, how to
> bring to pass honourably the greatest wealth that is possible to
> come to any creature living; and in especial remembering how
> wretched and unworthy I am in comparing to his Highness.
> And for you, I do know myself never to have deserved by my
> deserts, that you should take this great pain for me; yet daily of
> your goodness I do perceive by all my friends; and though that
> I had not knowledge by them, the daily proof of your deeds
> doth declare your words and writing toward me to be true.

With her grovelling out of the way, Anne modulated her tone, hinting at the rewards Wolsey might obtain, should he achieve the outcome she and Henry so desired.

> Now good my Lord, your discretion may consider as yet how
> little it is in my power to recompense you, but all only with
> my goodwill, the which I assure you, that after this matter
> is brought to pass, you shall find me, as I am bound in the

meantime, to owe you my service and then look what thing in this world I can imagine to do you pleasure in, you shall find me the gladdest woman in the world to do it. And next unto the king's grace, of one thing I make you full promise, to be assured to have it, and that is my hearty love, unfeignedly during my life.

In this vein she ended 'this my rude and true meanyd [meaning] letter ... written with the hand of her that beseeches your grace to accept this letter as proceeding from one that is most bound to be, your humble and obedient servant, Anne Boleyn.'[19]

Wolsey was not one to be taken in by weasel words, but knew he needed to keep on the right side of her. On 12 February, he sent two new agents to see Clement. One was his secretary Stephen Gardiner, the other Edward Foxe. They knew each other from Cambridge days and agreed from the outset that Gardiner would take the lead and Foxe defer 'as our old amity and fast friendship doth require'.[20] They were to travel to Orvieto as fast as they could, taking John Barlow as their courier.[21]

In meticulously drafted instructions running to sixty-four closely written pages, Wolsey ordered Gardiner and Foxe to secure a full dispensation for Henry to marry again, with a special commission for himself and another cardinal-legate, or for one legate only, to settle the divorce finally. If Clement feared Charles's reprisals, they were to tell him that Henry was ready to risk his blood and his treasure in the pope's defence.

In pitching their case, Gardiner and Foxe were to emphasise the prohibition in Leviticus. Henry did not seek an annulment of his marriage 'out of a vain affection or undue love' for another woman, but because his conscience was stricken. He wished to marry Anne only because of

the approved, excellent virtuous [qualities] of the said gentlewoman, the purity of her life, her constant virginity, her maidenly and womanly pudicity, her soberness, chasteness, meekness, humility, wisdom, descent of right noble and

high through regal blood, education in all good and laudable
[qualities] and manners, apparent aptness to procreation of
children, with her other infinite good qualities, more to be
regarded and esteemed.[22]

On their way to Dover, Gardiner and Foxe were to detour to
Hever and brief Anne, who for appearance's sake had left court on
the day before Gambara's return from Italy. As Henry now wrote
to her (in English), 'Darling, these shall be only to advertise you
that this bearer and his fellow be dispatched with as many things
to compass our matter and to bring it to pass as our wits could
imagine or devise.'[23]

A few days later, Henry wrote again, decidedly annoyed
('perplexed' as he said) because his longing for her had become the
source of gossip. As he complained, it 'is better known at London
than with any that is about me, whereof I not a little marvel'.
He suspected 'lack of discreet handling must needs be the cause
thereof.' 'No more to you at this time', he ended, 'but that I trust
shortly our meetings shall not depend upon other men's light
handling but upon our own.' Later he complained further of how
his private affairs were talked of in every alehouse.[24]

This time, Anne's brother George brought her the letter: his
discretion, at least, could be relied on. So much so that Henry
gave him the rest of his message verbally to report to Anne. Those
things, he informed her, 'your brother shall on my part declare
unto you, to whom I pray you give full credence, for it were too
long to write'.[25]

By now, Anne was becoming a divisive figure. Her brother
George and brother-in-law, William Carey, were her champions in
Henry's privy chamber, as was Sir Thomas Cheyne, newly appointed
as a gentleman there in Wolsey's Eltham Ordinances. She knew
she could count on all three, but others saw her differently. Sir
John Russell, another recent arrival in this inner sanctum of the
court, was Wolsey's man. Anthony Browne, by now a pronounced
Francophobe, actively disliked her.[26] When choices had to be made,
Browne would prove loyal to Katherine and her daughter, as would

Nicholas Carew, who had once more recovered his place. For now, such splits were still no more than a speck on the horizon. Men like this were adept dissimulators. Like Henry Norris, who was rising fast in Henry's esteem, they aimed to keep on good terms with everyone for as long as they could.[27]

As soon as Gambara, his errand accomplished, set off back to Italy, Henry and Anne were reunited at Windsor Castle, where she took over the rooms below his. To keep a watch on her, Wolsey planted Richard Page and Sir Thomas Heneage, his most senior household officials, close by. Both joined the privy chamber, where Heneage ranked alongside Norris. His brief was to spy on Anne.

In his first report, dated 3 March, he describes how she deliberately set out to needle him. For instance, when her mother ordered 'a morsel of tunny [fish]' for her from the king's privy kitchen and it failed to arrive, she reported the lapse to Henry. And that evening, when Heneage duly appeared 'with a dish' for her supper, she mischievously asked him to sit down and share the meal with her, saying how pleasant it would be, seeing it was Lent, to have some fine carp or shrimps from Wolsey's fishponds. Heneage ended his 'scribbled' note by begging the cardinal's pardon, but he was not used to being toyed with like this – 'it is', he added disparagingly, 'the conceit and mind of a woman.'[28]

But it would be Anne's quest for patronage for her friends and supporters which tells us most about her character. According to Cavendish, 'it was ... judged by and by through all the court of every man, that she being in such favour, might work masteries with the king, and obtain any suit of him for her friend[s].' Like Louise of Savoy, whose interventions Anne had observed as a young *demoiselle*, she knew that exercising patronage was more than a way of distributing rewards: it was a way to demonstrate her power.[29]

The earliest example comes from Heneage's second report to Wolsey, a stray from the archives that unexpectedly resurfaced in 2022 in a Sotheby's auction.[30] On 15 March, Heneage explained that Cheyne had petitioned to receive a royal grant of £400 in cash within a week or ten days, or as an alternative might rent for sixty years some lucrative salt marshes, probably in Kent or Sussex

where he had similar interests.[31] Anne backed his suit and lobbied
Wolsey, who resisted. Wary of alienating her completely, however,
the cardinal sent Heneage a gift for her, 'for the which she heartily
thanks your grace, and she is sorry that she knew not before her
suit made under your grace ... what manner [of] thing it was.'
As a sweetener, she sent Wolsey a token in return, but only as the
prelude to another request on behalf of a candidate she backed for
the vacant post of abbot of Peterborough. Since Wolsey had his
own favoured candidate whom he arranged to be elected, this was
a non-starter, but even if she had failed this time, Anne's appetite
for power was whetted.[32]

When shortly afterwards, Cheyne and Russell quarrelled over
the wardship of the latter's two stepdaughters,* Anne took up the
cudgels. Normally, rights of wardship were sold to the highest
bidder because whoever acquired them had the unofficial right to
asset-strip lands and arrange marriages for their charges, a tactic
able to yield fabulous profits. Cheyne was insistent that he wished
to gain at least one of these wardships, whereas Russell wished to
recover the girls on his wife's behalf, especially the younger one, as
she was 'all her [mother's] joy in this world'.[33]

When Cheyne's bid was rejected, Anne dictated a message to
Heneage for him to pass on to Wolsey:

Mistress Anne ... thanketh your grace for your kind and
favourable writing unto her, and sayeth she is most bounden
unto your grace; and as your most bounden bedewoman
[i.e. one who prays for the soul or welfare of another], she
commanded me to write unto your grace, humbly desiring the
same to be good and gracious lord unto Sir Thomas Cheyne.
And she is marvellously sorry that he should be in your grace's
displeasure, and also she sayeth that the same Sir Thomas

*Should a man of property die while his heirs were still minors, feudal law decreed that
they became legal wards of the king, and this was Anne Russell's predicament after her
first husband's death.

Cheyne is very sorry in his heart that he hath so displeased your grace, more sorry than if he had lost all [his] good[s].[34]

The dispute rumbled on for over a year: Anne refused to let the matter drop. When Wolsey thought he had mastered the situation and rusticated Cheyne from court, Anne brought him back. In the end, Wolsey yielded: he had met his match. The elder of Russell's stepdaughters passed into Cheyne's control, and the younger one married the dashing Lord William Howard, the elder stepbrother of Anne's uncle, the Duke of Norfolk. Russell and his wife, the actual mother, got nothing.[35]

The gossipmongers suspected that if Anne and Henry spent too much time together his passion for her would wane, a prediction that would prove to be false. With their relationship out in the open, Henry did nothing to cloak his feelings. He heard Mass every day in his private oratory and joined his courtiers in the Chapel Royal on Sundays, on major festivals such as Christmas, Easter and Whitsuntide, and some forty-five other feast days. Sitting apart in an elevated pew known as his 'great' or 'holy day closet', he often signed documents or wrote messages during services, and around this time he scribbled one to Anne in a lavishly illuminated Book of Hours she had acquired from Bruges or Ghent, later in the possession of Bess Holland.[36] Seeking to convey the torment he suffered, he wrote in French 'If you remember my love in your prayers as strongly as I adore you, I shall hardly be forgotten, for I am yours, Henry R always.' Somewhat sacrilegiously, the message appears directly beneath a miniature of Christ as the 'Man of Sorrows', kneeling before a tomb and wearing a crown of thorns with blood streaming from his wounds.[37] Anne reciprocated with a couplet in English: 'By daily proof you shall me find / To be to you both loving and kind.' With calculated significance, she chose to write beneath a depiction of the Annunciation: the angel Gabriel telling the Virgin Mary that she would bear a son.[38]

On 21 March, Gardiner and Foxe arrived in Orvieto, drenched, mud-spattered and with no clothes beyond those they rode in.[39] On securing an audience with Clement, their discussions turned on just one point: would he concede a commission allowing the legates to deliver a final sentence on Henry's case, and with no appeal? In support of their arguments, they handed Clement a copy of what they called 'the King's Book' to study: early drafts can still be traced in the archives. The differing hands they contain proves that Foxe and Gardiner, assisted by the king's new confessor and chaplain John Stokesley, and (for the final stages of revision only) an Italian friar named Niccolò de Burgo, were its principal co-authors.[40]

After almost a month of haggling, the pope agreed to seal a fresh dispensation for Henry to marry Anne, along with a commission addressed jointly to Wolsey and Lorenzo Campeggi, empowering them to investigate the king's marriage and pass sentence upon it. Should they find the marriage invalid, Henry and Katherine were to separate and might remarry.[41]

Foxe left Orvieto immediately, enduring some frustration in Calais where it took four days to find a ship. On 2 May he landed at Sandwich on the Kent coast and reached Greenwich by 5 p.m. the next day. Henry sent him at once to Anne's chamber, now temporarily relocated to the tiltyard gallery on account of an outbreak of smallpox. He wanted her to be the first to hear the news.

She listened intently. As Foxe informed Gardiner, who followed at a slower pace, 'she seemed to take the same marvellously to heart, rejoice and comfort ... with promise of large recompense for your good acquittal.' Henry then arrived and Anne left. The king studied the documents, while Foxe assured him that they had requested them exactly as instructed. Clement, he said, had 'passed the same without alteration of any sentence or word'.

While this was strictly true, it overlooked the fact that the cardinal scrutinising the commission in the papal chancery before it was sealed had amended the wording, explicitly declaring it unprecedented. Clement had claimed this would not matter, because he was willing to satisfy Henry 'to the uttermost of his power'. But sure enough, when the small print was unpicked, it became clear that it did: the document did not completely prohibit an appeal.

Henry, calling Anne back in, 'caused [Foxe] to repeat the same thing again before her'. She questioned him forensically and 'at great length'. She was especially keen, Foxe said, to know 'what towardness and benevolence I perceived the pope's holiness to be of', that is, what his attitude to the case seemed to be in person. As to how far Katherine retained a right of appeal, Henry looked more dubious. He would put it, he said, to Wolsey's judgment. The audience ended with Foxe sent to see Wolsey at Durham House, the Bishop of Durham's town house, the largest property on the Strand with its gardens overlooking the Thames. In 1523, Wolsey had sequestered it, when the scale of his building works at York Place made the place uninhabitable.[42]

When Foxe arrived, Wolsey was in bed. By the next afternoon, he had read all the paperwork and decided it would suffice. To double check, he had Foxe read it aloud in the presence of Anne's father and Dr John Bell, an experienced church lawyer and archdeacon of Gloucester. Two days afterwards, he was still of the same opinion, but later in the week Dr Wolman and other experts raised a series of objections. They came to believe that the commission's wording required three distinct, but interlocking, judgments to be given on different aspects of the case, creating an uncertainty which Katherine's lawyers could exploit.[43]

The upshot was that Gardiner was sent back to Orvieto to begin again. It was agreed that Campeggi would bring with him a revised and final commission, but by June there was no word of it and no sign of Campeggi. In a fury, Henry told Foxe to tell Gardiner that, 'in case [Campeggi] never come, ye [are] never to return'. But try as he might, Gardiner could report nothing beyond 'great difficulties pretended and contrived delays'.[44]

Suddenly these concerns receded into the background as a deadly virus known as the 'sweat' hit London and the south-east. First experienced in 1495, 1507 and 1518, the symptoms were muscle pains and headaches, abdominal pain, vomiting, breathlessness, a raging temperature and unimaginable sweating. To this day, doctors and medical historians do not fully understand precisely what the sweating sickness was: its final outbreak was recorded in 1551.

The disease spread like wildfire as the wealthy shut up their town houses and fled with their servants to the countryside. The courts of law and most businesses closed, apart from notaries, who did a roaring trade in wills. When one of Anne's maids fell ill, Henry left for Waltham Abbey in Essex, taking her brother, while she hurried to the safety of Hever to join her parents. With George next contracting the virus, Henry – 'much troubled' – made off swiftly again, this time for Hertfordshire, since for him, death was for other people.[45]

Then Anne herself succumbed.

14

The Sweat

Anne's return to Hever and Henry's flight to Waltham Abbey triggered a fresh flurry of love letters. All are undated, but we can pinpoint the progress of the virus with some accuracy. Brian Tuke, the latest recruit to Henry's elite band of personal secretaries and the Master of the Posts, informed Cuthbert Tunstall that the infection had arrived in London on Friday 5 June 1528, when he took refuge in Stepney. He was right to be afraid: many died within the first four hours and only those able to make it through the first twenty-four tended to survive. Anne's maid became sick on the 16th, and within a week, over a hundred people in London would be dead, by which time the virus was rampaging through the suburbs and into Surrey. Soon, worryingly, it reached Kent.[1]

There was no proven cure. Anne's step-grandmother, Agnes Tylney, Dowager Duchess of Norfolk, assured Wolsey that 'treacle and water imperial' did the trick, or else 'little or no sustenance or drink until sixteen hours be past', coupled with 'vinegar, wormwood, rosewater and crumbs of brown bread' wrapped in a linen cloth 'to smell unto your nose'. Home remedies of this type were the bane of medical practitioners' lives: when Lady Lisle prescribed a 'powder' for Tylney's third son, Lord Edmund, he wrote to complain, 'Ye hath made me such a pisser that I dare not this day go abroad.'[2]

Keeping away for a week from those who had recently recovered from the virus was soon judged to be the wisest precaution.

Tuke was the first commentator systematically to advocate social distancing. 'The infection ... is highly to be feared and avoided and all occasions thereof to be eschewed, which cannot be, if men resort together in great companies in infect airs and places.' John Caius, a 'doctour in phisicke' who wrote extensively on the sickness, advised this as well and prescribed a posset of milk, vinegar and herbs to stimulate sweating.[3]

Besides Anne's brother, Henry had taken only Katherine, Tuke, Thomas Heneage, Henry Norris, William Carey and a handful of privy chamber staff to Waltham. His fear of disease was well known: if travelling to Calais, he always insisted on having the town checked for contagion first.[4] Well practised in establishing his own form of lockdown, he was ready to move at a moment's notice should anyone in his vicinity fall ill. He retained up to four physicians and three apothecaries at any one time and offered medical tips at every opportunity. Worrying about Wolsey, who stayed close to London, he urged him 'to keep out of all air where any of that infection is ... to use small suppers, and to drink little wine' and once a week 'use the pills of Rasis' as a prophylactic.* Should the cardinal be unlucky enough to catch the virus, he should take care 'to sweat moderately without suffering it to run in' to the lungs or kidneys. If unable to sweat, he was to ask his doctors for a posset.[5]

Henry had an additional weapon in his armoury: God, with whom he always thought he had a special relationship. Just to be sure, he began hearing three Masses daily.[6] But not everyone, including Anne, he supposed, was so fortunate. Writing to her before she succumbed, he confessed (in French) to his 'uneasy qualms' about her health. Barely a week had passed since he reached Waltham and thus far, as he was informed, she had experienced no symptoms. 'As you have not yet felt anything,' he continues, 'I

---

*'Pills of Rasis', one of Henry's favourite medications along with rhubarb pills, camomile oil and 'liquorice sticks', were made up by blending Socotrine aloes, saffron and myrrh and were taken in a syrup made with honey and fumitory water.

hope and take it for granted that it will pass you by as I trust it has with us.' By 'us', he largely meant the royal 'we' – as he had swiftly abandoned Waltham for the 'wholesome air' of Hunsdon, because, he informed her casually, 'two ushers, two grooms of the chamber, and your brother ... fell ill and are receiving every care.'[7]

George Boleyn made a full recovery after a shaky start and was soon back at court. So far, it seemed, there was no cause for his sister to worry too much. She should feel comforted, writes Henry, 'that few women or none have this malady, and none of our court, and few elsewhere have died of it.' Perhaps anxious that his sudden flight and their separation had unnerved her, but more likely that she deeply resented him taking Katherine with him, and not her, he seeks to reassure her. She should not fret over his absence: 'wherever I may be, I am yours.' She should not have 'unreasonable thoughts' of his fidelity; he would 'rid' her of these if she was 'between [his] arms'. She should 'be brave, and avoid the evil as much as you can, and I hope shortly to make you sing for joy of your return.' And he signs himself 'H Rex' enclosed within the letters of the French word 'immuable', meaning 'Henry the Steadfast – the Constant, the Immovable.'[8]

Scarcely had the ink dried on this letter than Henry received 'the most grievous news that could arrive': Anne had the sweat, and so did her father. He was given the message 'suddenly in the night', which means it was felt to be of sufficient importance to wake him. His anguish is plain to see. Writing in French, he 'laments the news ... of my mistress's sickness, whom I esteem more than all the world, and whose health I desire as my own'. If only she could be made well again, he tells her, he would 'willingly bear the half of your illness'. Coming from a man who hardly thought it fit to visit or console the sick at any other point in his whole life, this was quite a pledge: except, of course, that it was safe to make a grand gesture when he knew it to be impossible. What he could, and did do, was to send Anne one of his own doctors, although not the one who would normally have been his first choice: 'The physician in whom I most trust is absent.' He had hoped, 'through him, and his methods, to obtain one of my chief joys in this world, that is to say, that my mistress should be cured'. In his place, Henry was sending his 'second' doctor. Should he cure her, the king vows to 'love him more than ever'. He signs the letter 'HR', placing her initials, 'AB', once more inside a heart he drew himself.[9]

The absent favourite physician was John Chambre (or Chambers), a graduate of Oxford and Padua and the first President of the Royal College of Physicians. He soon arrived and could be found taking supper with Henry in a turret room.[10] Off to Hever in the meantime, however, went Dr William Butts, a Norfolk man of a strong evangelical persuasion. He had treated both the Duke of Norfolk and Princess Mary successfully for other illnesses, but with Anne it was touch and go. As Tuke informed Wolsey, with her, the sweat 'turned in before the time', which put her in 'jeopardy'. Tuke, who self-isolated in the privy chamber and whose report is dated 23 June, received this information from Heneage, but learned also that although Anne and her father had been seriously ill, each were now safely 'past the danger thereof'. They both went on to make 'their perfect recovery'.[11]

Henry would reward Butts with a salary of £100 a year. But first, he celebrated by going out shooting. In fact, his conduct in Hunsdon suggests his fears for Anne did not trouble him quite so much as he claimed to her. As Heneage noted, the king was 'very merry' in Hunsdon, 'for there was none fell sick of the sweat since he came hither'. This was about to change. In a scribbled postscript written that evening, Heneage says how 'this night as the king went to bed, word came to his grace that Master William Carey was departed out of this present world.' He had made the mistake, just four days before, of paying a visit to one of his properties in Essex and caught the sweat.[12]

While in Hunsdon, Henry resumed work on the 'King's Book'. Tuke told Wolsey how late at night the king 'commeth by my chamber door, and doth for the most part, going and coming, turn in, for devising with me upon his book and other things occurrent.'[13] Shortly afterwards, Heneage remarked how the king was troubled by pains 'in his head', the result of his efforts at authorship.[14]

Henry left on the 26th, moving on to one of Wolsey's houses, Tyttenhanger, near Shenley in Hertfordshire.[15] All the while, the sweat continued to rage. Among those recovering were Tuke (he came close to death despite his precautions), Norris, Sir Thomas Cheyne and Urian Brereton, a groom of the privy chamber. Anne liked Urian, and in 1530 went out hunting with him, although an oft-repeated story that she named a lapdog after him is unsupported by proof. When their greyhounds killed a cow, Henry had to pay the owner 10s in compensation. Urian had an elder brother, William, a fellow groom, who escaped the virus.[16]

Even before the victims of the sweat lay cold in their graves, covetous eyes focused on what could be rich pickings. Francis Bryan was an early beneficiary of Carey's death. Possibly at Anne's request, he was readmitted to the privy chamber in Carey's place and became her most vociferous champion besides the king and her own family. George Boleyn got the keepership of Beaulieu and the office of Master of the Buckhounds.[17] In seeking favours, no one was quicker than Anne herself. Within days, she had Henry shifting his mind to what could be done for the widowed Mary Boleyn. In another letter to his 'good sweetheart', this time in English, he says:

> As touching your sister's matter, I have caused Walter Walsh
> [another groom of the privy chamber] to write to my lord [Sir
> Thomas Boleyn?] mine mind therein, whereby I trust that Eve
> shall not have power to deceive Adam. For surely, whatsoever
> is said, it cannot so stand with his honour but that he must
> needs take her his natural daughter now in her extreme
> necessity.[18]

Henry's meaning is obscure. Most likely the passage relates to Mary's desire to secure the wardship and associated revenues of her young son Henry, now that her husband was dead. As the heir to feudal lands in Essex, Hampshire, Wiltshire and Buckinghamshire, several of which were held 'in chief of the crown' (as it was said), the boy counted as a royal ward. Why Mary's father would not bid for the grant himself is hard to explain beyond the fact that he was notoriously mean.

It did not matter, because Anne stepped in. Using her hold over the king, she obtained in her own right 'custody of the lands of William Carey, deceased, during the minority of Henry Carey, his son and heir, with the wardship and marriage of the said heir'.[19] For a single woman and a commoner to win such a wardship even of her own nephew was unprecedented. She could get her way because Henry was missing her terribly. He had begun his letter by praying God 'to send us shortly together, for I promise you I long for it'. He thinks, he says, constantly of her: 'and seeing my darling is absent, I cannot less do than to send her some flesh representing my name, which is hart flesh for Henry; prognosticating that hereafter God willing, you must enjoy some of mine.' Another of his playful love conceits, his thought is more overtly sexual than it was the first time he sent her venison, for now he longs to penetrate her.[20]

Over her next patronage suit, Anne got into a fight with Wolsey. William Carey's sister Eleanor, a nun of Wilton Abbey in Wiltshire, wished to fill the vacancy for the next abbess, an appointment made by the Church. Before he died, William had lobbied Wolsey repeatedly on her behalf. When Anne took up the cause, Henry stood by to assist, until he discovered Eleanor's murky history. She 'hath confessed herself', he tells his 'good sweetheart', his 'own darling' in another letter a few days later, genuinely shocked, guilty of having 'two children by two different priests, and further since hath been kept by a servant of the Lord Broke that was, and that not long ago'. 'I would not for all the gold in the world cloak your conscience nor mine to make her ruler of a house which is of so ungodly demeanour.'[21]

But if Henry thought Anne would abandon the suit, he had to think again. She had lost out to Wolsey earlier in the year when she failed to get her candidate for abbot of Peterborough elected. This time, she would have her way. Two candidates were in contention for the post: Eleanor and the existing prioress, Isobel Jordan, and Wolsey backed the prioress, a reputable candidate favoured by most of the nuns. Henry, trapped between Anne and the cardinal, decided that a compromise candidate should be found: 'some good and well-disposed woman'.[22] Three times he wrote to Wolsey through Dr Bell, vetoing Jordan's appointment. Any deviation from this would mean that 'divers [some, i.e. Anne] will find themselves aggrieved'.

Without appreciating the full extent of Anne's influence in the matter, Wolsey went ahead and appointed Jordan. Little did he know that Henry was not simply discussing the nomination at Wilton with Anne; by now he was relaying state papers to Hever by courier for her to vet.[23]

Hardly was Wolsey's decision made when he received a stark warning from Heneage. In a masterly understatement, his court intelligencer informed him that 'the king's Highness was not best content with the election of the abbess of Wilton ... for of all women he would not have had her.'[24] For Wolsey to ignore Henry's wishes (and therefore Anne's) so blatantly, and over such a trivial matter, seems at first sight unfathomable. Was it a lapse in concentration – more than possible because the sweat had now reached his household and he feared for his own life? Or could he simply have overlooked Dr Bell's directives?[25]

Neither was the reason. Wolsey defied Henry because news had arrived from Gardiner that Pope Clement, now in Viterbo, had at last issued the revised papal commission to consider Henry's divorce. Campeggi would be bringing it shortly to London.[26] Suddenly, the cardinal's position was strengthened again, so he decided to do what he considered to be right and appoint the worthier candidate. He might be damned by Henry for it, but he would not be damned by God.

Henry retaliated furiously. This was a very different man from the one who so sensitively drew Anne's initials within a heart: this was the one who could send Empson and Dudley to their deaths without a qualm; who could summarily execute Edmund de la Pole before going off on his French war because he deemed it prudent; who condemned the Duke of Buckingham not just to death but to the butchery of an inexperienced headsman. His letter to Wolsey, written in his own hand on 14 July 1528, is excoriating, even more so as it was cloaked in the form of a gentle 'admonition' from his 'loving sovereign, lord and friend'. The cardinal was to 'think it spoken of no displeasure, but of him that would [do] you as much good, both of body and soul, as you would yourself'.[27]

Pleasantries, if such they were, aside, Henry went on the attack:

> Methink it is not the right trayne [duty] of a trusty loving friend and servant, when the matter is put by the master's consent into his arbitrament and judgment (specially in a matter wherein his master hath both royalty and interest) to elect and choose a person which was by him defended [forbidden]. And yet another thing which much displeaseth me more: that is, to cloak your offence made by [claiming] ignorance of my pleasure, saying that you expressly know not my determinate mind in that behalf.

Henry then quotes his original instruction to Wolsey word for word. And he continues: 'My Lord, it is a double offence both to do ill, and colour it too ... wherefore good my Lord, use no more that way with me, for there is no man living that more hateth it.'[28]

Having made his views clear, Henry magnanimously declared himself satisfied with Wolsey's abject apology.[29] But from this point onwards, he became yet more difficult to advise. He would still take a steer from Wolsey, but if he issued instructions or made a decisive comment, he expected obedience. He had only to begin a sentence with a characteristic 'Well' for all around him to know that his mind was fixed and it was safer not to argue. When getting impatient or if he believed his decisions were being questioned, he developed a verbal trick of iteration, asking if the person speaking was sure of something 'once, twice or thrice'.[30]

Anxious to cover his back, Wolsey wrote to Anne, and sent her a gift. His letter does not survive, but her reply does. Partly charred to a cinder in a catastrophic fire in 1731 in Ashburnham House, Westminster, where some of these documents were stored, Anne's hastily scribbled note was fortunately transcribed in full by Richard Fiddes for his *Life of Cardinal Wolsey* in 1724, and enough of the burned manuscript survives for us to check the accuracy of his copy. Her tone was once more that of a supplicant. 'In my most humblest wise that my poor heart can think,' she begins, 'I do thank your grace for your kind letter, and for your rich and goodly present, the which I shall never be able to deserve without your great help.' Was the 'present' a gift, or was it the news that Gardiner had obtained the revised commission? Whichever, it drew Anne to claim, somewhat extravagantly, 'that all the days of my life I am most bound of all creatures, next the king's grace, to love and serve your grace, of the which I beseech you never to doubt, that ever I shall vary from this thought as long as any breath is in my body.'

And as before, she ends with a promise of rewards, but only on the basis of performance, turning the offer into a veiled threat:

> And as for the coming of the legate, I desire that much, and
> if it be God's pleasure, I pray him to send this matter shortly
> to a good end; and then I trust, my Lord, to recompense part
> of your great pains, for the which I must require you in the
> meantime to accept my goodwill in the stead of the power, the
> which must proceed partly from you, as our Lord knoweth.[31]

Anne wrote this letter while still in quarantine. But as July ended, the virus was in retreat, and she and Henry could be reunited. Her arrival was predicted on the 30th by the resident French ambassador, Jean du Bellay, Bishop of Bayonne. Henry was then in Ampthill, where he had gone after leaving Tyttenhanger. As Anne would soon return, he was preparing to pack up and leave for Windsor Castle, intending to hunt red deer along the way.[32]

The same day, du Bellay, a moderate evangelical whose opinions resembled those of Marguerite of Angoulême and whom Anne treated as a confidant, sent his more conservative patron, the Duke de Montmorency, Grand Master of France and Francis's childhood friend, his opinion as to how things stood. In his judgment, Henry was far more committed to marrying Anne than Wolsey appreciated. 'I do not believe', says du Bellay, 'he knows the situation as well as he thinks, however much he pretends to.'[33]

Once back at court, Anne sent Wolsey another letter. Undated and with no indication of where she and Henry were at the time,

and another casualty of the fire of 1731 with burn marks all around
the sides, it must all the same have followed on closely from its
predecessor. The difference, and it is a remarkable one, is that she
persuaded Henry to co-author it. Here, for the first time, they
wrote jointly as a couple.

What prompted the letter was the lack of information on
Campeggi's progress. All they knew had come from Gregorio Casali
in a message brought by John Barlow, who reported that the legate,
who was constantly afflicted by gout, making travel difficult, aimed
to set out by sea on a Genoese ship from Corneto (now Tarquinia),
near Viterbo, intending to land in Marseille and from there travel
overland via Lyon to Paris, and onwards via Calais to London.[34]
Anne writes: 'In my most humblest wise that my heart can think,
I desire you to pardon me that I am so bold to trouble you with my
simple and rude writing.' After enquiries into Wolsey's health, she
says, 'I do know the great pains and trouble that you have taken for
me, both day and night, is never to be recompensed on my part, but
only in loving you, next unto the king's grace, above all creatures
living.' This brings her to the point. 'My Lord, I do assure you, I do
long to hear from you news of the legate; for I do hope, and they
come from you, they shall be very good; and I am sure you desire it
as much as I, and more, and [if] it were possible, as I know it is not.'

Henry then adds his postscript. 'The writer of this letter would
not cease till she had caused me likewise to set to my hand; desiring
you, though it be short, to take it in good part.' And, like Anne,
he presses for information, but more ominously. 'The not hearing
of the legate's arrival in France causeth us somewhat to muse;
notwithstanding, we trust by your diligence and vigilancy ... shortly
to be eased out of that trouble.'

Henry and Anne jointly signed the letter. First, he writes, 'By
your loving sovereign and friend, Henry R', and she adds, 'Your
humble servant, Anne Boleyn'. Part of his cipher and all of Anne's
signature, other than the first letter, were destroyed in the fire of
1731, but fortunately the whole document was transcribed in 1714
by Gilbert Burnet in preparation for a revised edition of his *History
of the Reformation of the Church of England*.[35]

To reward Barlow, Anne's father, writing from Penshurst, asked Wolsey to appoint him to the rectory of Sundridge in Kent, where his friends the Isleys owned the manor house. On the death of Thomas Isley in 1519, his son, Sir Henry, had taken over the estate, but he lacked the right to make appointments to the church there. Boleyn wanted the rectory for Barlow to hold alongside his existing position in Hever. Alas, the cardinal instead licensed Barlow to receive Tonbridge by mistake. His error brought him a scornful rebuke from Anne. 'I thank your grace', she writes, 'for the gift [of] this benefice for Master Barlow, howbeit this standeth to none effect, for it is made for Tonbridge and I would have it, if your pleasure were so, for Sundridge; for Tonbridge is in my lord my father's gift ... and it is not yet void.'[36]

It is commonly believed that to offset the rebuke, Anne offered the cardinal a rare plaudit: 'I reckon myself much bound to your grace', she is supposed to have written, 'for all that hath taken pain in the king's matter; it shall be my daily study to imagine all the ways that I can devise to do them service and pleasure.'[37] This rendering has a word missing. Anne's manuscript actually says, 'I reckon myself much bound to your grace for all *these* that hath taken pain in the king's matter.' In other words, her thanks go to Barlow and the others who had successfully obtained the revised commission that Campeggi would bring, rather than to Wolsey himself. She would be 'much bound to your grace' for ensuring they received their just rewards.[38]

And that was not all. Anne's note had a postscript. 'My Lord, I beseech your Grace with all my heart to remember the parson of Honey Lane for my sake shortly.' This was explosive. The 'parson' (or rector) in question was none other than Dr Robert Forman, whose curate, Thomas Garrett, had supplied Luther's books to Oxford students. With her memories of Queen Claude and Louise of Savoy's impromptu seminars with Denys Briçonnet and Jacques Lefèvre d'Étaples still fresh in her mind, Anne found shocking Wolsey's pursuit of men who, to her mind, had done nothing wrong beyond encouraging those who believed that faith is found in Scripture. Such men, with royal indulgence, would have been safe in France. She could not help Garrett, who had already been forced to abjure, but she could help Forman, and she did: despite being caught in possession of Luther's books, some with his handwritten comments in the margins, he was let off with a 'secret penance' that saved him from public exposure and a criminal record.[39]

On 21 August, Henry sent Francis Bryan to Paris to await Campeggi's arrival. Not just Anne's cousin, he too was a religious reformer and critic of the papacy. Du Bellay described him as 'a relation of [Anne] and one of those she likes best'. Of his journey across the Channel in a fierce gale which left him horribly seasick and forced to wade ashore near Calais at ten o'clock at night, Bryan wrote, 'I had never a worse passage.' He hurried on to Paris as fast as he could, only to find Campeggi had not arrived and did not do so until three weeks later: his gout was so painful, he had to be carried for most of the way from Lyon by horse litter.[40]

Campeggi entered Paris on Monday 14 September, six weeks after first beginning his journey.[41] The stage from Paris to Calais took another fortnight instead of the usual three days, and it was only on the 29th that, for the second time in his life, he set foot on English soil. Shortly before the 8th, as de Mendoza informed Margaret of Austria, Henry had sent Anne away again to stay with her parents in Hever, believing it to be impolitic for Campeggi to find her at his side. Confident, however, that the delays would soon be over, the king began writing to her once again.[42]

The first of these new letters was sent on about 17 or 18 September, with Henry still awaiting Campeggi's arrival. Replying to another of Anne's (now lost), Henry wrote (in English), 'to send you now these news: the legate which we most desired arrived at Paris on Sunday or Monday last past, so that I trust by the next Monday [21st] to hear of his arrival at Calais.' And with Campeggi at last within reach, he continues: 'I trust ... to enjoy that which I have so long longed for to God's pleasure and both our comfort; no more to you at this present mine own darling for lack of time, but that I would you were in my arms or I in yours, for I think it long since I kissed you.' He closes on the by now familiar hunting theme. 'Written after the killing of a hart at 11 of the clock, minding with

God's grace tomorrow timely to kill another; by the hand of him which I trust shortly shall be yours.'[43]

The king's second letter followed two more notes from Anne, one of which had expressed sharp impatience over the continuing delays.[44] Still tormented by gout, Campeggi did not arrive in London until 9 October, by which time he was too ill to attend the lavish reception arranged for him. Wolsey paid him three visits but another fortnight elapsed before he could travel by barge to meet Henry at Bridewell Palace. He did bring the crucial revised commission with him, but his orders were to show it only to Henry and Wolsey, and it was not to be used in court nor to leave his possession. Clement had promised that the legates could proceed to a final sentence, but not in writing.[45]

With Campeggi finally present, and now convalescent, Henry was euphoric, utterly convinced that his marriage to Katherine would soon be judged in contravention of Leviticus. After an audience with him on 22 October, Campeggi exclaimed that so convinced was the king that a divorce was his by right, 'an angel descending from heaven would be unable to persuade him otherwise.'[46]

In his letter Henry told Anne 'what joy' it was to him 'to understand your conformableness to reason, and of the suppressing of your inutile [useless] and vain thoughts and fantasies with the bridle of reason'. Clearly, she had anticipated either continuing delays or the outright failure of Campeggi's mission. Some who saw him carried into London said that because he looked so ill, he was on the point of death. Perhaps these stories had reached Hever? If so, she could cast her doubts aside, since from Campeggi 'shall come both to you and me the greatest quietness that may be in this world'.

Perhaps Anne was cross that she was sent away to Hever and could not question Campeggi for herself? She should think again. 'The unfeigned sickness of this well willing legate doth somewhat retard his access to your presence, but I trust verily when God shall send him health, he will with diligence recompense his demur.' If she worried over Campeggi's potential bias towards Charles, she should forget those concerns too. 'For I know well where he hath

said (lamenting the saying and bruit [rumour] that he should be
imperial) that it should be well known in this matter that he is not
imperial.'

One other matter Anne should know was: 'The cause why this
bearer [messenger] tarrieth so long is the business that I have
had to dress up gear* for you, which I trust ere long to see you
occupy.' Does this mean, as one historian has suggested, that the
king's preparations for the wedding were already in train?[47] If so,
no evidence of them can be found in the royal wardrobe accounts,
although these are patchy and incomplete. What Henry meant
by the 'gear' that Anne was to 'occupy' is uncertain, but he then
adds punningly, 'and then I trust to occupy yours, which shall be
recompense enough to me for all my pains and labours.'[48]

What Henry did not know was that Clement, communicating
through his secretary on 16 September from Viterbo, had sent
Campeggi a warning:

> If in satisfying [Henry] the pope would incur merely personal
> danger, his love and obligations to the King are so great that he
> would content him unhesitatingly; but as this, because of the
> peril of recent events, involves the certain ruin of the Apostolic
> See and the whole of the Church (*la certa ruina delle Sede
> Apostolica e di tutto lo stato Ecclesiastico*), the pope must beware
> of kindling an inextinguishable conflagration in Christendom.
> The Emperor declares himself well satisfied with the pope's
> neutrality and is willing to agree to a peace through his
> intercession. But, if so great an injury be done to the Emperor,
> all hope of peace is lost, and the Church cannot escape utter
> ruin.[49]

Anne, not Henry, had been right. A *renversement* in papal policy
was imminent. The pressure was mounting, and soon events would
bring it to a head.

---

*The word 'gear' can refer to apparel or to household stuff, including, perhaps, a bed.

15

Wolsey's Nemesis

The *renversement* in Pope Clement's policy is easily explained. Despite the French pledge to force the Habsburgs into peace talks if Henry and Wolsey signed the Treaty of Amiens, Charles retained the upper hand. When Henry agreed to the treaty, he never meant to fight a war, only to assist Francis indirectly. On 22 January 1528, French and English heralds formally defied Charles, but Henry considered this to be no more than a threat, not a genuine declaration of war. He got a nasty surprise when Charles, in retaliation, had all English ships in Flemish ports arrested. Faced with ruin, English merchants and clothiers engaged in the Low Countries trade laid off their workers, who took to the streets in mass protests. The very idea of warfare in alliance with France, the traditional enemy, itself aroused huge popular unrest. By June, Henry and Wolsey had no option but to make a temporary truce with Margaret of Austria, so that the English cloth fleet could sail and trade resume with the 'mart' towns of Antwerp and Bergen-op-Zoom.[1]

After Henry's heralds had defied Charles, Francis sent an army across the Alps under Marshal Lautrec, brother of his mistress Françoise de Foix, coupled with a naval attack to recover Genoa led by Andrea Doria, a Genoese admiral who had defected to France. Once Lombardy was recaptured, Lautrec was to march on Naples. Over some eighteen or so months, Henry laid out £112,437 (worth over £112 million in modern values) in subsidies for these campaigns. His chief aim was to intimidate Clement, clearing the path for Wolsey and Campeggi to allow him to marry Anne.[2]

Lombardy was indeed recaptured, and soon a large French army was besieging Naples, which was blockaded by a Genoese fleet under Filippino Doria, Andrea's nephew. But from his refuge in Viterbo, the pope refused to budge. And as the summer heat took hold, a cholera epidemic crippled the French forces, after which Andrea Doria and his nephew withdrew to La Spezia and then defected back to Charles, taking the fleet with them and lifting the blockade. When Lautrec died on 17 August among the rotting corpses in his camp, it was the beginning of the end.[3]

On 12 September, just two days before Campeggi entered Paris on his way to London, Genoa recovered its independence and the whole of the Ligurian coast fell into Charles's hands, the French project collapsing completely. In trepidation of what might be shortly to come, Clement made the choice that wrecked Henry and Anne's hopes of a speedy settlement of 'our matter'. He ordered his secretary to send the gout-smitten legate strict instructions: 'You are not to proceed to sentence, under any pretext, without express commission; but [must] protract the matter as long as possible.'[4]

Campeggi played a masterly hand. He began by holding lengthy meetings with Henry and Wolsey, and with Katherine, whom he tried in vain to persuade to enter a nunnery.[5] Then, in a bolt from the blue, Katherine showed Campeggi a Spanish copy of the precursor to Pope Julius II's bull of dispensation, the so-called 'Brief' sent to the dying Isabella of Castile.[6] Its reappearance raised the stakes for Henry and Anne. Partly this was because of the discrepancy over whether Prince Arthur's marriage was definitely consummated or only 'perhaps', but mainly because Clement's commission empowered the legates to consider the validity of the king's marriage in the light of Julius's final bull of dispensation, and no other document.[7]

Armed with the 'Brief', Katherine began a war of attrition. She got a message to Charles, asking Clement to halt the divorce proceedings. And in a masterly move, she appeared before Campeggi to deny in the confessional that her marriage to Arthur had been consummated. Normally, we should not know what is said between confessor and penitent, but in this case, we do, because Katherine urged Campeggi to tell the world:

> That she in her conscience affirms that from 14 November [1501], when she was espoused to the deceased Arthur, to 2 April following, when he died, she did not sleep with him more than seven nights, and from this she stayed intact and undefiled, just as she had come from her mother's womb.[8]

With matters going sour for Henry and Anne, Wolsey began to panic. 'He alleged', Campeggi advised Clement, 'if the king's desire is not complied with ... the speedy and total ruin will follow of the kingdom, of his Lordship, and of the Church's influence.' 'I have constantly debated this matter', he adds, 'in order that things might continue as they were, [but] I have no more moved him [Wolsey] than if I had spoken to a rock.'[9]

On Sunday 8 November, the king summoned his nobles and councillors to Bridewell. Repeating his familiar claim that Gabriel de Gramont had first alerted him to the potentially incestuous state of his marriage, he had, he said, 'asked counsel of the greatest clerks in Christendom' and sent for Campeggi 'only to know the truth and to settle my conscience and for none other cause as God can judge'. A sullen silence ensued, which the king broke by apparently inviting candid opinions, save that 'if any man should speak of it otherwise than he ought to his prince, he would show them who was master'. Jean du Bellay, who reports the scene, claims he even added, 'No head was so pretty [*si belle*] that he would not make it fly.' When told of this, Anne immediately knew issuing such threats so early in the proceedings was a bad mistake. She insisted on returning to court to help oversee the divorce policy. Henry was missing her terribly, and so, to minimise the scandal of their meeting while Campeggi was nearby, he arranged a clandestine reunion rather than a full return to court.[10]

Two days later, he sent Katherine to Greenwich and rode to meet Anne. His itinerary shows he lodged for two or three nights in Nicholas Carew's house in Beddington, Surrey.[11] One of his undated love letters relates to the rendezvous. It begins:

> These shall be to advertise you of the great elengenesse
> [loneliness, misery][12] that I find here since your departing ...
> I think your kindness and my fervencies of love causeth it, for
> otherwise I would not have thought it possible that for so little
> a while it should have grieved me.

Henry complains that time stood still while he and Anne were apart. A short time could seem to last 'a whole fortnight', and he goes on to say, 'but now that I am coming toward you, me thinketh my pains have been half relieved.'[13]

The present tense of that remark, 'now that I *am* coming' can only refer to his Beddington visit. So, what follows belongs to that time too:

> Also, I am right well comforted insomuch that my book
> maketh substantially for my matter, in writing whereof I have
> spent above four hours this day, which caused me now to write
> the shorter letter to you at this time because of some pain in
> my head. Wishing myself, [e]specially an [i.e. in the] evenings,
> in my sweetheart's arms, whose pretty duckies I trust shortly to
> kiss.[14]

Contrary to what is often supposed, then, Henry was still putting the finishing touches to the 'King's Book' *after* Campeggi arrived in London.

Back in Bridewell, Henry wrote to Anne again:

> Darling, though I have scant leisure, yet remembering my
> promise, I thought it convenient to certify you briefly in what
> case our affairs stand. As touching a lodging for you, we have
> gotten one by my lord cardinal's means, the like whereof could
> not have been found here about for all causes, as this bearer
> shall more show you. As touching our other affairs, I assure

you, there can be no more done, nor more diligence used, nor all manner of dangers better both foreseen and provided for.[15]

Katherine was ordered back to Bridewell, then banished to Richmond and Hampton Court. Anne was now to occupy apartments at Greenwich, and her father was to oversee the transfer. On 9 December, du Bellay informed the Duke de Montmorency that she had arrived. Anne 'is at last come here', he writes, 'and the king has lodged her in a very fine lodging, which he has prepared for her close by his own. Greater court is now paid to her every day than has been to the Queen for a long time.' The king 'goes and comes', du Bellay continues, 'shuttling between Bridewell and Greenwich' to see Anne, with excursions to Richmond and Hampton Court to see Katherine, 'who will not return here for some time (*elle ne retournera ici de longtemps*)'.[16]

In fact, the arrangement only lasted until Christmas, when it was no longer possible for Henry and Anne to keep Katherine away. She duly reappeared in Greenwich, where all three spent the festival in what was almost, if not quite, a *ménage à trois*. Du Bellay, writing on Christmas Day, explains:

> The whole court has retired to Greenwich, where open house is kept both by the King and Queen, as it used to be in former years. Mademoiselle de Boulan is there also, having her establishment apart (*ayant son cas à part*), as I should think she does not like to meet with the Queen.[17]

But as soon as the holidays were over, Henry sent Katherine back to Richmond, staying with Anne in Greenwich.

Their reunion had rapid effects. Within days of Anne's leaving Hever, her cousin Francis Bryan departed for Rome as a special ambassador, from where he conducted parallel correspondences with her, the king and Wolsey.[18] (His independent reports to Anne are lost, but he twice refers to them in his letters to Henry.) Braving another Channel crossing, his task was first to visit Francis and Louise of Savoy in Paris and exhort them to step up the pressure on the pope. He was then to cross the Alps, find Clement, and persuade him to wrap up the divorce suit quickly, and with no appeal: Henry had evidently decided to try and circumvent the slow-moving Campeggi entirely. No effort was to be spared to recover and discredit the Vatican's original copy of the 'Brief'. Since Bryan's Italian was rudimentary, Pietro Vannes, formerly Wolsey's and now Henry's Lucchese-born Latin secretary, was to accompany him.[19]

From Paris, Bryan sent Henry a warning from Francis that there were fifth columnists among his councillors who opposed the divorce.[20] Arriving in Rome in mid-January, he found Clement dangerously ill and had to wait weeks to gain an audience.[21] Once admitted, he filed regular reports to Henry and Anne and, it was said after his return, began sleeping with a papal courtesan to gain intelligence.[22] The claim is entirely credible: when in Paris a year later, Bryan wrote to another of Henry's diplomats, William Benet, then in Rome, asking him 'to recommend me most heartily to Signora Angela, and desire her to send me a pair of sweet, perfumed gloves'.[23]

Bryan strained every nerve on his cousin's behalf, 'first', as he said, 'by fair means and afterwards by foul'.[24] Anne wanted nothing left to chance. A fortnight after Christmas, as Bryan was arriving in Rome, she persuaded Henry to send Stephen Gardiner to reinforce him. He too departed at once and, like Bryan, he was to correspond with Anne independently of Henry.[25] Acknowledging this in a handwritten note from Greenwich on Sunday 4 April, she writes: 'Master Stephens, I thank you for my letter, wherein I perceive the willing and faithful mind that you have to do me pleasure.'

> I pray God to send you well to speed in all your matters, so that you would send me to the study how to reward your high service. I do trust in God you shall not repent it, and that the end of this journey shall be more pleasant to me than your first, for that was but a rejoicing hope, which causing the like of it, does put me to the more pain and they that are partakers with

me, as you do know. And therefore, I do trust that this hard
beginning shall make the better ending.[26]

Anne enclosed cramp rings with her note, 'praying you to
distribute them as you think best' and to 'assure them [I] will be glad
to do them any pleasure which shall be in my power'. A prophylactic
against cramp and epilepsy, these rings were supplied by Cornelius
Hayes and blessed by the king on Maundy Thursday. The process
involved the king placing the rings at the foot of the crucifix for
a moment and touching them. By tradition, the royal touch gave
them the power to heal. It was the queen's role to give them out,
and by usurping Katherine's function in this manner, Anne was
making a point.

Bryan's mission failed. As he wailed, 'the pope ... will do nothing
for your Grace.' And with an unmistakable dig at Wolsey, he
added, 'Nothing will serve. And whosoever hath made your Grace
believe that he [Clement] would do for you in this cause, hath not,
as I think, done your Grace the best service.' All he felt he had
achieved was to set Vannes and Gregorio Casali on a search for
the 'Brief' in the papal registers, where they found no trace of it,
enabling Henry to claim it was a forgery.[27]

By the beginning of May, Bryan had given up hope: 'We be like
men that hope to gather fruit on a rotten stock.' Gardiner too had
done all he could.[28] Most telling is Bryan's unwillingness to deliver
the bad news to Anne, delegating the task to Henry:

> Sir, I write a letter to my cousin Anne, but I dare not write
> to her the truth of this, because I do not know whether your
> Grace will be contented that she should know it so shortly,
> or no; but I have said to her in my letter that I am sure your
> Grace will make her privy to all our news.[29]

Gardiner's final report, sent on 4 May, brought more bad news.
'Applying all my poor wit and learning to attain at the pope's hands
some part of the accomplishment of your Highness's desires', he
says, 'now [we] see it called in question whether the authority given

to the legates ... should be revoked or no.'[30] This last-minute talk
of revoking the powers already issued to hear the king's case rang
alarm bells. Henry and Anne decided they could wait no longer,
instructing Wolsey to summon Campeggi and rule on the king's
marriage without delay, using the commission they had already
received.

On 22 May, du Bellay briefed Montmorency. Wolsey, he says, 'is
in the greatest pain he ever was'. The Dukes of Suffolk and Norfolk
had turned on him, believing that 'he had not done as much to
advance the king's marriage [to Anne] as he would have done had
he really wanted it.' Or as Cavendish puts it, the dukes supped
with the devil, lying 'in a wait with my Lady Anne Boleyn to espy
a convenient time and occasion to take the Cardinal in a brake
[snare]'.[31]

At Anne's request, Henry recalled Wolsey's agents John Taylor
and Sir John Russell from France. In their places, Suffolk and Sir
William Fitzwilliam crossed the Channel. The king ordered them
to seek out Francis and his mother and offer them every assistance
in ransoming the French king's sons, who were still held in Spain –
this in exchange for nudging Clement into 'a final determination'
of the divorce. And in a separate briefing he gave his brother-in-
law secret instructions to identify the fifth columnists about whom
Bryan had warned. It was a golden opportunity for Suffolk to
denounce Wolsey.[32]

Henry then gave final approval to the 6,500-word submission
he planned to deliver in the legatine court. Based substantially on
the 'King's Book', it took the form of a handwritten *libellus* (legal
pleading) designed to be read out in court. The finished manuscript
was later given to the library of Trinity College, Cambridge, where
it lay unrecognised until 1984. Sixteen folios long with twenty-six
lines to a page, written in a fine italic hand by a professional scribe
on vellum, it addressed itself almost exclusively to the Levitical
prohibition, which Henry claimed was absolute.[33]

On 31 May, Wolsey and Campeggi opened the legatine court
in the Parliament Chamber in Blackfriars, where they summoned
Henry and Katherine to appear on 18 June. By then, Henry had

sent Anne to her father's London house for the sake of appearances. The couple had been so close recently that du Bellay declared he would not have been surprised if she was pregnant. Unable to leave her for long, Henry stopped by to see her when travelling by barge along the Thames, claiming he was waiting for the tide to change to make it safe to pass under London Bridge.[34]

On the eve of the opening session of the court, Katherine appealed to the pope to set aside the entire proceeding, but the judges overruled her.[35] When the proceedings began, Henry sat under a canopy of cloth of gold to the right of the legates. Katherine sat on their left, and the moment she was called, she crossed the courtroom, and in a theatrical performance graphically described by Cavendish, threw herself at the king's feet.

'Sir,' she began, speaking in broken English, 'I beseech you for all the loves that hath been between us, and for the love of God, let me have justice and right.'

> I take God and all the world to witness that I have been to
> you a true, humble and obedient wife, ever conformable to
> your will and pleasure, that never said or did anything to the
> contrary thereof, being always well pleased and contented with
> all things wherein ye had any delight or dalliance, whether it
> were in little or much I never grudged in word or countenance
> or showed a visage or spark of discontentation.[36]

She urged her husband to spare her 'the extremity of this new court until I may be advertised what way and order my friends in Spain would advise me to take'. Finally, kneeling humbly before him, she entreated him to consider her honour, her daughter's and his own. 'And to God I commit my case', she said, after which she rose, curtseyed low and marched out of the courtroom, her head held high.[37]

Three times the court crier summoned her back, but she ignored him. When it was Henry's chance to speak, he repeated his claim that he acted not from 'any carnal concupiscence nor for any displeasure or mislike of the queen's person and age', but because of genuine doubts and 'scruples of conscience' about his marriage. He then launched into his *libellus* and handed over the finished manuscript to the legates.[38]

In her absence it was left to Katherine's legal team, notably John Fisher, to seek to dismantle Henry's case. Delivering an eloquent speech at the court's fifth session on 28 June and taking his cue from the church calendar (it was the eve of the Nativity of St John the Baptist), Fisher enraged Henry by comparing him to the biblical King Herod, who had beheaded the Baptist after he rebuked him for divorcing his wife. He then lodged a doorstopper of some 16,000 words with the legates, contesting the king's submission.[39]

The next stage was the examination of witnesses. Given the importance to Henry and Anne of proving Katherine's first marriage had been consummated, William Thomas, once Arthur's privy chamber groom, who had moved to Henry's service and was knighted at Tournai before retiring to Wales, was one of the first. Now 'aged 50 years of age or thereabouts', he remembered escorting Arthur after his marriage

> clad in his nightgown unto the princess's bedchamber during often and sundry times, whereunto he [Arthur] entered and there continued all nights and that at the mornings he received him at the said doors in semblable fashion.

Altogether in London and Ludlow, Katherine and Arthur 'of his knowledge continued together as man and wife, prince and princess of Wales, by the space of five months or thereabouts'.[40]

Another courtier, Sir Anthony Willoughby, then told how Arthur had called for ale as he emerged to breakfast on the morning after his wedding night, saying 'Willoughby, bring me a cup of ale, for I have been this night in the midst of Spain.' The Duke of Suffolk, who hastened back from France to testify, corroborated this. Anne's father, unsurprisingly, swore to the same effect. The possibility that the teenage Arthur might want to swagger and boast of his bedroom prowess in the company of sniggering male courtiers was quietly ignored. Only the Earl of Shrewsbury, Harry Percy's father-in-law and one of the queen's most loyal supporters, hedged his bets.[41]

International events intruded again when Louise of Savoy and Margaret of Austria began discussing terms for a Franco-Habsburg peace behind Henry's back. Suffolk, while in France, had done his utmost to scupper the talks, but abjectly failed. Wolsey wanted to travel with all speed to Cambrai where formal negotiations were due to begin, but could only do so by suspending the legatine court, so Henry sent Bishop Tunstall and Thomas More instead. Recognising the threat, Wolsey appealed to Francis, through du Bellay, to press Clement again to grant the divorce at once.[42]

All was to no effect. On 21 June, a week before William Thomas gave his evidence, the Comte de Saint-Pol, the new French commander in Italy, was routed and captured at Landriano, twelve miles south-east of Milan, while on his way to retake Genoa. On top of his earlier losses, Francis lacked the commanders and the cash to continue fighting, whereas, with silver bullion starting to arrive in quantity from the Americas, Charles had both. The French collapse convinced Clement that he had nothing to gain by staying neutral. Only Charles could offer the protection he needed. 'I have quite made up my mind', he announced, 'to become an imperialist, and to live and die as such.' On 29 June, he signed the Treaty of Barcelona with Charles, promising to crown him in Bologna and to absolve all those responsible for the sack of Rome.[43]

Now Charles sent a new resident ambassador to London, carrying letters and a message for his aunt. 'You may be sure', he was to tell her, 'that I have greatly at heart this affair of yours, and that as much care shall be bestowed upon it as if it were my own.'[44] The ambassador was Eustace Chapuys, a dapper Savoyard born in Annecy, a man blessed with a cheeky smile, a sharp ear for gossip, a fertile imagination and a brilliant turn of phrase. Able to wear many masks and speak in a variety of voices, seen by Anne as a scourge, he learned to play the parts of a courtier to Henry, a friend to Katherine and a spy to Charles. But his main tasks were to reconstruct an Anglo-Habsburg alliance against the French and to protect Katherine and Princess Mary from Henry's reprisals.[45]

Events now moved at speed. On 5 July the haggling between Louise and Margaret began in Cambrai. Informed of the peace talks, du Bellay said that Suffolk had a face of marble and Henry one of alabaster: they knew what was coming. On the 16th, Clement revoked Henry's case to Rome: on the 23rd, Campeggi torpedoed the legatine court, declaring it adjourned until October. Hearing this, Suffolk rose in disgust, thumped the table with his fist and uttered the one remark of his that everyone remembers, 'By the Mass, now I see that the old said saw is true, that it was never merry in England whilst we had cardinals amongst us.'[46]

Terms in Cambrai were settled within a month. Known as the 'Ladies' Peace' ('*Paix des dames*'), the treaty obliged Francis to renounce his conquests in Italy and the Low Countries. He also agreed to marry Charles's sister, Eleanor, and to pay 2 million gold crowns of the sun to ransom his two sons. Tunstall and Thomas More arrived in time to add clauses ending the economic war with the Low Countries, but the treaty destroyed what was left of Wolsey's credibility.[47]

On 31 July, Henry and Anne left Greenwich on the king's summer progress. With Katherine seemingly excluded, they mainly spent the days hunting, before settling for two weeks at Grafton in Northamptonshire, a small but beautifully situated manor house which Henry had purchased in 1526. While there, Anne exercised more authority than she had ever done. After dinner on the day Chapuys arrived in Grafton to present his credentials, he found everything suddenly stopped because Anne was ready to begin the afternoon's hunt.[48]

Once informed of the peace settlement, Henry summoned Parliament to meet on 3 November with the intention of impeaching Wolsey.[49] But then, to Anne's dismay, he backtracked. By 14 September, he had allowed Katherine to join the royal progress, and on the 19th, Wolsey and Campeggi were granted an audience before the latter departed for Rome.[50] Henry, paralysed by indecision, first graciously received them, after which everyone went to Chapel. And 'after dinner', Henry and Wolsey spoke privately 'at the least for the space of two hours'. Next morning, they spoke again for almost as long, then sat together in the Council until dinner time, after which the cardinals took their leave.[51]

Despite this show of amiability, if such it was, Wolsey never saw Henry again. On 9 October, the first day of the Michaelmas legal term, Christopher Hales, the attorney-general, indicted him in the Court of King's Bench for *praemunire* (the ancient criminal offence of procuring papal bulls from Rome to the detriment of the crown). According to du Bellay, his choice was this or impeachment in Parliament. Wolsey begged the king to pity him, describing himself as 'your poor, heavy and wretched priest' and 'your Grace's most prostrate poor chaplain, creature and bedesman', but to no avail. On the 17th, he was stripped of the Great Seal, the emblem of his office as Lord Chancellor. On the 22nd, he pleaded guilty to *praemunire*, surrendered all his property to Henry and threw himself on the king's mercy. 'The Duke of Norfolk is made chief of the Council,' du Bellay continues, 'and in his absence Suffolk, and above all [*par dessus tout*], Mademoiselle Anne.' Thomas More replaced Wolsey as Lord Chancellor, but with most of his predecessor's responsibilities stripped out.[52]

Once more, though, Henry faltered, sending Wolsey 'a ring of gold ... [one] he knew very well for it was always the privy token between the king and him', and a message bidding him 'to be of good cheer, for he was as much in his highness's favour as ever he was'. By the 27th, du Bellay wondered if the cardinal might stage a comeback. Almost endearingly, Henry had found he had a deep emotional bond with Wolsey which was difficult to break. The two had worked in concert for almost twenty years. Often, they strolled arm-in-arm together in conversation around the king's privy gardens. And like all narcissists, Henry was unwilling to admit he had been wrong in trusting Wolsey for so long.[53]

At this, Anne smouldered. Now back with Henry in Windsor Castle while Wolsey was at Esher in Surrey, she worked with her father and the two dukes to topple him. Visiting the cardinal in Esher, du Bellay found him reduced to tears. He implored Francis and his mother to rescue him, beseeching them to remind Henry how useful he could be. Of his enemies, he feared Anne the most, who, he said, 'had made [the king] promise that he will never allow him another audience, because she really thinks he could not help feeling sorry for him'. According to Cavendish, Wolsey called Anne 'the night crow' – the woman who sat up late with Henry and filled his head with subversive ideas.[54]

Shortly after Christmas, Wolsey fell sick with dropsy and a fever. He pleaded for Dr Butts, whom Henry sent to him with yet another ring, while Anne – if only at the king's insistence – threw in a tablet of gold. Butts delivered the gifts, he said, 'with the most comfortablest words he could devise' and Wolsey recovered.[55]

Clutching at straws, Wolsey showered the few church revenues he could still control on friends and enemies alike. George Boleyn bagged a munificent annuity of £200 for life (over £200,000 a year in modern values).[56] It did not work. Despite a barrage of fresh entreaties to Henry made throughout 1530, the most he could obtain was a conditional pardon. His trusted agent Richard Page took a letter to Anne, asking her to intercede, but it went unanswered. 'She gave kind words but will not promise to speak to the king for you.' This understated her response. The truth was that 'None dares speak to the king on his part for fear of Madam Anne's displeasure.'[57]

Forbidden to come within seven miles of the court, Wolsey renewed his appeals to Francis and Louise to help him, then left for Richmond. There he stayed until early April, when he was licensed to travel north to perform his spiritual duties as Archbishop of York, taking a lump sum in cash, a pension of 1,000 marks and just enough tapestry and silver plate to furnish five rooms.[58] This was, in effect, banishment.

By the end of November, he would be dead. The *coup de grâce* came from Norfolk and Anne, who forced Wolsey's Italian physician, Agostino Agostini, into testifying that Wolsey was plotting with the pope, the French and possibly Charles to secure his reinstatement. On the evening of the 4th, Walter Walsh, who with Anne's brother carried confidential messages for her, and, ironically, Harry Percy rode into the courtyard of Cawood Castle, the principal palace of the archbishops of York, during supper.

Percy arrested Wolsey, while Walsh, wearing a hood to conceal his identity, seized Agostini and branded him a traitor. Sick and weak, Wolsey was taken to the Earl of Shrewsbury's house at Sheffield Park, where he was allowed to rest until Sir William Kingston arrived to bring him south. Agostini was locked in the Tower, then dragged to Norfolk's house, where he stayed until 'he was singing the tune as they wished him'.[59]

Wolsey made it no further than Leicester Abbey, dying after suffering extreme bouts of vomiting and diarrhoea. No longer could he stand between the Boleyns and power. They believed the future to be theirs and meant to exploit it to the full.[60]

16

The Durham House Group

Anne knew that her tactic of frustrating Henry's sexual desire could not last indefinitely. So far, it had worked because they were both hunting the same quarry: marriage. But the months immediately after the failure of the Blackfriars court and Wolsey's dismissal were a challenge. Henry seemed to be further away from a divorce than ever. He and Katherine were still married; Anne was still plain 'Mistress Boleyn' or 'Mistress Anne'. He had promised to make her his wife, and she to give him a legitimate son. With their relationship in stasis, his desire can only have increased because of the obstacle to acting on it: later in life, during a similar period of enforced celibacy, he would speak of his wet dreams. But he dared not have a fling while courting Anne.[1] There was so little privacy at court, even in the 'privy' recesses of his side of the royal household. Courtiers and flunkeys were everywhere, eyes and ears open. Nor was a fling what he truly wanted: despite the time Anne made him wait, he really did believe that he would always be faithful to her as his father was to his mother. He loved her so much, court watchers said, that he could barely be apart from her for more than an hour.[2] For him, it seems, the sweetest embrace was the one yet to be tasted.

It was not so for Anne. Could she really depend on him to begin all over again on the divorce after two years of failure? From her perspective, his indecision over Wolsey's disgrace was preying on her mind. She had committed herself to Henry, but he was still shuttling between her and Katherine and seemed caught in a vice between his wife and the woman he longed to marry. This was not the first time Anne had harboured doubts. When Henry distanced himself from her during the sweat and withdrew to Hunsdon, he felt obliged to dismiss her 'unreasonable thoughts' of his fidelity, grandly declaring 'wherever I may be, I am yours' and signing himself 'Henry the Steadfast'. But grandiose words alone were not enough. She knew, to move things forward, she had to steel his nerves. If she could not yet marry Henry and become his co-sovereign, she and her family would at the very least help him govern in the way she had seen Francis's mother and sister do in France. That Anne wanted to be queen did not mean she lacked ideals and principles: indeed, she was hungry to put them into practice.

On 12 October 1529, just three days after Wolsey was indicted for *praemunire*, Jean du Bellay, in his final weeks as the French ambassador, sent a candid dispatch in cipher to the Duke de Montmorency. Anne and her father (*Monsieur Boullan et la Demoiselle*), he says, had set out to monopolise power. Her father assured him, he continues, that the other councillors, even the Dukes of Norfolk and Suffolk, 'have no credit except what it pleases [Anne] to give them, which is as true as the Gospel'. He might have added that Suffolk was already being written out of the script: by the year's end, he would rarely attend council meetings, not so much because he was lazy as is so often claimed, but because of his enmity to Anne. His antagonism was reciprocated. Fully aware of his and, especially, of his wife's true feelings about her, she would retaliate venomously over the coming months to any perceived slight. Their exchanges became so heated that, during one, she accused Suffolk of sexually molesting his daughter. Others who provoked her to lash out were Gertrude Blount and two more of Katherine's ladies.[3]

Du Bellay's advice was that 'for the total expedition of French affairs', Montmorency should cultivate Anne's brother George, the family's 'little prince' (*petit prince*), who was to be made a special ambassador to Paris.[4] George's selection for this plum diplomatic post could only have resulted from his sister's intervention. As he was barely twenty-five and had no diplomatic experience, his selection was a brave choice. Aware of this disadvantage, Anne asked her father to warn du Bellay to make sure George was received with more than ordinary honour. Not only should he be wined and dined by leading courtiers whom she individually named, but he was to enjoy the same level of respect that would be accorded to her father, the experienced diplomat of the family, even if, as du Bellay quipped sardonically, to everyone else, the whole exercise seemed likely to end in farce.[5]

It was not just in politics that Anne demanded a fresh architecture. She also did so literally. Just two days after Wolsey surrendered to Henry, she and her mother went secretly with the king in the royal barge to York Place in Westminster to inspect the site, accompanied by Henry Norris. There, they watched as the king's officers made a detailed inventory of the fallen cardinal's possessions. Some weeks later, Henry and Anne laid before James Nedeham, the royal architect, their plans for a new palace, to be named Whitehall. In a gargantuan expansion even of Wolsey's scheme of works, they called for new lodgings, vastly extended gardens, a tiltyard, tennis courts, bowling alleys, a cockpit and a hunting park. The cockpit was to be encrusted with stone animals and gilded vanes and to come complete with seats for Henry and Anne as she loved to see the birds fight. She would make Henry build a similar cockpit at Greenwich Palace. She then demanded timber coops be made there 'for the peacock and the pelican that were brought to the king out of the New Found land [i.e. North America: what Anne called a peacock was probably a turkey]', so they could be shut up at night because she 'could not take her rest in [the] mornings for the noise of the same'. The new hunting park at Whitehall, stocked chiefly with game birds and rabbits bred in adjacent yards, was to be enclosed by a moat and inner wall some two miles long, wrapped around the south, west and north sides of the palace. All of this, once the construction and landscaping works were sufficiently advanced, was to be crowned by the addition of a satellite palace, St James's, across the park, which was to become the home of Henry and Anne's future son and heir.[6]

This was Henry's most ambitious building project so far. The construction works cost prodigious sums and required the demolition of hundreds of neighbouring houses, most of them owned by former members of Wolsey's household – all this combined with land exchanges, purchases and further sequestrations. The largest of the land swaps required the abbot and monks of Westminster Abbey to surrender around 100 acres for the new park. In return they received lands in Berkshire. For the works at St James's, a medieval hospital for the care of women lepers was flattened and the sisters pensioned off.[7]

The finest of the apartments at the new Whitehall site, those Wolsey had meant to occupy himself when he had finished building them, were to be reserved for Anne, where the interior decorations, as in the extensive remodelling she and Henry ordered at Hampton Court, were to include examples of 'antique work', imitating the Renaissance styles she had seen taking shape in Cardinal Georges d'Amboise's château of Gaillon. Whitehall would become her favourite palace, partly for these reasons, but chiefly for another: the layout she devised meant there were no rooms for Katherine. The orders to commence work would be issued in the first months of 1530.[8]

Further to empower her family, Anne secured promotions for her father and brother. On 8 December, Henry raised Sir Thomas Boleyn, Viscount Rochford, to the earldoms of Wiltshire and Ormond and a month later appointed him Lord Privy Seal, giving him oversight of much government business. Next, Henry gave the new Earl of Wiltshire the use of Durham House on the Strand, another property vacated by Wolsey, with all its valuable contents, along with a raft of generous annuities and pensions. George became Viscount Rochford, his wife, therefore, Viscountess, and known as 'Lady Rochford'. Anne, from now on, would be known by the courtesy title of 'Lady Anne Rochford'.[9]

The grant of the Ormond title, which came complete with a formal grant of many of the English estates to which Anne's father had laid claim for over a decade, was made possible by a final settlement with the Butlers. By deeds sealed in February 1528, Piers Butler surrendered his disputed claims, and in exchange received the earldom of Ossory and a long lease of many former Ormond lands in Ireland. No longer did Anne need to be kept single to marry Piers's son, Sir James.[10]

The day after the promotions, Henry threw a banquet at Whitehall for the Boleyns and other carefully chosen guests, during which Anne sat beside the king as if already a crowned queen. '[It] is a thing which was never before done in this country', exclaimed a scandalised Eustace Chapuys. After the meal followed dancing and entertainments, 'so that it seemed as if nothing were wanting but the priest to give away the nuptial ring and pronounce the blessing'. To avoid a scene, Henry had sent Katherine away 'to hold her own fête of sorrow and weeping'.[11]

Anne wanted Katherine banished permanently from court, her servants dismissed and access to her beloved daughter, Princess Mary, soon to be fourteen, restricted or denied so that the two women could not easily collude against her. But it was never so simple. Nine days before the banquet, on St Andrew's Day, Katherine had upbraided Henry over his refusal to eat with her or visit her apartments, leading to a spectacular quarrel. Weary of her reproaches, he lectured her on his interpretation of the texts from Leviticus. For such arguments, she retorted, 'I care not a straw.' It was for the pope to decide, and 'for each doctor or lawyer who might decide in your favour and against me, I shall find a thousand to declare that the marriage is good and indissoluble.'

This triggered a confrontation with Anne, who understood well enough that Henry would come off worse in a slanging match with his wife. 'Did I not tell you', she scolded him, 'that when you disputed with the queen, she was sure to have the upper hand? I see that some fine morning, you will succumb to her reasoning, and that you will cast me off.' And more revealingly, she complained about her wasted youth. Thanks to his vacillation, she said: 'I have been waiting long and might in the meanwhile have contracted some advantageous marriage, out of which I might have had issue, which is the greatest consolation in this world – but alas, farewell to my time and youth.' Despite outward bravado, she was never quite so sure of herself as she could appear.[12]

The upshot was that Anne refused to spend Christmas with
Henry. It greatly unsettled her that, to get his own back, he then
spent the festival with Katherine in Greenwich.[13] The lovers' first
quarrel, it ended almost as soon as it began, with Henry climbing
down. On New Year's Eve, he sent Walter Walsh to Anne with
a peace offering of £110 in cash (worth over £110,000 today),
marking the onset of an almost obscene flood of grants and rewards
over the next twenty or so months. A consignment of purple velvet
and 'certain stuff' cost £219 11s 4d. William Locke, an evangelical
mercer originally from Norfolk, one of Anne's regular suppliers of
luxury fabrics, charged the king £232 10s 3d 'for silks and divers
other things' for her. A single purchase of crimson satin cost £16.
Regular sums were disbursed for Anne's day gowns, nightgowns,
cloaks and fashionable sleeves, several made by John Scut, one of
Henry's personal tailors whom he later assigned specially to her, and
for furs, budge-skins (lamb's skin with the wool turned outwards)
and linen cloth.[14]

To indulge her love of outdoor sports and perhaps to remind her
that she had 'pierced him to the heart', Henry sent her crossbows,
arrows, shafts, shooting gloves and a bracer to guard her wrist.
Riding equipment for her included saddles, one specially to be
'of the French fashion, with a pillow of down covered with black
velvet' and 'a head of copper and gilt graven with letters and with
antique work'. Matching saddle hose, a mounting stool, harnesses
'fringed with silk and gold with tassels and buttons of silk and
gold', horse-bits, reins and girths came too. Two more saddles, to
be made from the finest Spanish leather, were to be 'pillion saddles'
for Anne and Henry to ride out together. Henry even ordered two
saddles of black leather with a special double harness and collars for
the mules carrying her litter.

Another gift may have been a pistol-shaped gold whistle, now in
the Victoria and Albert Museum, engraved in relief with scrolling
foliage on the stock and traditionally called 'Anne Boleyn's whistle'.
Besides being a whistle used for luring a falcon or hawk back to its
owner's glove, it contains a straight toothpick, another toothpick
with a sickle-shaped end, and a spoon for removing earwax. Whistles

of this type were often decorative – worn as jewellery or sewn onto masking costumes – but they were also eminently practical.[15]

Henry paid regular fees and annuities to Anne's receiver-general, George Taylor, who moved from her father's service and was 'employed about my Lady Anne Rochford's business' full-time, and to servants who came into contact with Anne.[16] The king rewarded one of her servants for finding her a hare, and her father's servants for bringing hawks, a peregrine falcon and a goshawk as gifts to the king. Lady Russell's servant in turn had a reward of £2 for 'bringing a stag and a greyhound to my lady Anne'. The mayor of London's servant received 6s 8d for bringing her cherries. Henry also paid Anne's not inconsiderable gambling debts and gave her £20 to redeem a jewel belonging to her sister Mary from a pawnbroker. In February 1531, George Taylor was paid £66 13s 4d for purchasing a farm in Greenwich for her enjoyment. A few weeks later, Henry's armourer received £2 4s 7d 'for garnishing of a desk with latten [an alloy of copper, zinc, lead and tin] and gold for my Lady Anne Rochford', and her embroiderer got £18 14s 9½d for yet more work for her.[17]

So besotted was Henry, he gave Anne chests full of the most exquisite jewels – it was as if he was a puppy seeking her approval. He paid his goldsmith, Cornelius Hayes, £7 18s 8d for nineteen diamonds set in a truelove of crown gold [i.e. a decoration or design symbolising true love, such as a true-love knot],* perhaps to wear on Valentine's Day. He then paid £9 0s 3d for nineteen larger stones to embellish her French hoods. A catherine wheel of solid gold, set with thirteen diamonds, cost £3 19s. 4d. Twenty-one rubies set in roses of crown gold cost £4 4s. Other gifts included twenty-one diamonds 'set upon rose hearts', a golden girdle, two bracelets set with diamonds and pearls, tablets of crown gold, 'borders of gold for her sleeves set with diamonds and pearls', gold buttons, a 'borasse flower of diamonds', a ring with a large 'table' (or flat)

---

*The term crown gold refers to 22-carat gold alloy, which Henry introduced into England for use in the coinage.

diamond and a brooch of Our Lady of Boulogne, a popular saint for
English travellers crossing the Channel.[18] Possibly a New Year's gift
for Anne in 1531, the brooch shows that a distinctive and traditional
depiction of the Virgin Mary was not thought inappropriate either
to the donor or to its Lefèvrist recipient.[19]

But even when Henry showered countless gifts on Anne, she
refused to be bought. She was still his sweetheart, not his wife. For
the remedy, she looked to her relatives, now settled in Durham
House. More than ever, the Boleyns functioned as a family firm,
and they believed they had a secret weapon. While in Essex
during the king's summer progress in early August 1529, Henry
and Anne, along with courtiers including Stephen Gardiner and
Edward Foxe, had lodged at Waltham Abbey, and it was there that
Gardiner and Foxe were reunited with a forty-year-old theologian
they knew in Cambridge. This was Thomas Cranmer, who was
staying nearby with relatives called Cressy, whose two sons he was
tutoring. Gardiner and Foxe were billeted with the Cressys, where
over dinner they told Cranmer about the divorce. It was Cranmer
who first suggested widening the focus away from the annulment
suit in Rome towards a more general approach by canvassing
learned opinions in the king's favour from the leading European
universities. That way, Henry would gain moral authority for his
cause which could be deployed in the Vatican.[20]

Once the royal progress was over, Foxe brought Cranmer to
Henry, who sent him off to join the team of co-authors who had
helped him compile the *libellus* he submitted to the legatine court
at Blackfriars.[21] Still comprising Foxe himself, John Stokesley and
Niccolò de Burgo, this group had already moved into Durham
House, where they worked under Thomas Boleyn's supervision.
Their latest assignment was to identify fresher, bolder arguments
for the divorce.[22]

When Henry started sending relays of agents and ambassadors
to Europe, Anne's brother was the first to leave. Armed with an
advance payment of £240 towards his expenses and with his letters
of accreditation signed by Henry, in which he described him as 'a
gentleman of our privy chamber', George left for Paris just as soon

as Wolsey pleaded guilty to the *praemunire* charge, taking John Barlow as his courier.[23] Stokesley was to shadow him to compensate for his inexperience. Their instructions were to explain to Francis the key elements of the king's argument as laid out in the *libellus*; to persuade him to lobby for Henry in Rome; and most importantly to go to the left bank of the Seine and urge the luminaries of the Faculty of Theology in the Sorbonne to deliver a favourable opinion on the divorce.[24]

Next to depart was Anne's father, who left for Bologna at the head of a handpicked delegation, including Cranmer, charged with tackling Charles and the pope.[25] Charles, whom the pope finally crowned as Holy Roman Emperor and King of Lombardy during their extended stay, was more powerful than ever. On 14 October 1529, during the Turkish siege of Vienna, his Spanish marksmen had used their arquebuses to shoot down Sultan Suleiman's forces, just as they had done with the French at Pavia four years before, leaving him free again to concentrate on Italy and Germany.

On 5 November, Charles entered Bologna in triumph, greeted with cries of 'Charles, Charles, Empire, Empire, victory, victory!' On meeting Clement, with whom he lodged in the Palazzo Pubblico (now the Palazzo d'Accursio) where they occupied adjoining rooms, he dismounted and fell to his knees. So confident was he, he refused to release Francis's two young sons from their long captivity in Spain until every penny of their ransom was paid. This, at least, gave the Boleyns some bargaining space with Francis and his mother, who were desperate to recover the boys.[26]

Reaching Bologna in the second week of March, Anne's father found Charles deaf to any of Henry's arguments, saying Boleyn 'was not to be believed ... as he was a party' and that 'I intend the affair to be determined by justice.' As Sir Thomas explained afterwards to Henry, Charles delivered his opinions passionately. 'He is set in the contrary part of your Grace's great matter', not just 'by the fashion of his speech' or what he said, but 'by often repeating of the same'.[27]

The king's delegation fared no better with Clement, who raised the stakes by demanding Henry come to Rome and prohibiting his remarriage until Katherine's appeal had been heard. At an audience on 23 March, the pope stood resolute. As Boleyn ruefully complained, 'The pope is led by the Emperor, so that he neither will, nor dare displease him.'[28]

In Paris, meanwhile, the French found the younger Boleyn diplomat, George, to be courteous, charming and where necessary a plain speaker. He made some progress with the Faculty of Theology, but before they could deliver their verdict, Francis left for Dijon and when George obtained an audience near Troyes on or about 10 January, he found him evasive. The French king gave George a chain of gold costing a staggering 2,445 *livres*, a munificent prize, but one of less use to him than the Sorbonne's verdict, which he was unable to secure. In mid-February, he returned empty-handed to Durham House.[29]

To redeem George's failure, Thomas Boleyn diverted to Angoulême on his way home from Italy to call on Francis and Louise of Savoy, and met with more success. In exchange for a pledge of more than 100,000 crowns of the sun towards the ransom of his two sons, Francis ordered Pierre Lizet, the President of the University of Paris, to silence the Sorbonne's dissenters. When a favourable verdict was finally secured by fifty-three votes against forty-seven, John Barlow took it to Rome at once. So delighted was Henry, he had it proclaimed through the streets of London by a crier.[30]

While Thomas and George were abroad, Gardiner and Foxe went to Oxford and Cambridge to secure more ammunition for use in Rome. Nimbly realigning himself after Wolsey's disgrace, Gardiner was now Henry's secretary. Other agents, working mainly but not exclusively under Stokesley's direction, lobbied academics in universities across Europe: Angers, Orléans, Bourges, Poitiers and Toulouse in France; Venice, Padua, Pavia and Ferrara in Italy; Salamanca and Alcalá in Spain; and more in Germany. Those sent to Italy, in consultation with Gregorio Casali, ransacked libraries chiefly in Rome, Venice and Padua for Latin, Greek and Hebrew sources concerning matrimony and papal powers. At first their efforts were hampered by the unwillingness of librarians to open their doors. In Venice, one of Stokesley's agents complained of the treachery of Casali's brother Giambattista, who had lied to him about the whereabouts of a letter in Greek, then fobbed him off for weeks with a fake catalogue of books in the library of St Mark's. Anne would pay particular attention to claims that Giambattista was a papal spy.[31]

By the summer of 1530, Stokesley had amassed judgments in the king's favour from nine European faculties. Sleight of hand was used with the equivocal verdict from Angers, which was said to be favourable to Henry even though the theologians there insisted that marriage to a dead brother's widow was not forbidden, and that the pope could dispense the impediment for a reasonable cause.[32]

But what were Henry and Anne to do with these newfound weapons? It would take many months for the work of the Durham House group to reach fruition, but when it finally did, Foxe would delight Henry by showing him a 110-page Latin dossier explaining the 'true difference between royal and ecclesiastical power'. A momentous document whose scruffy, uninviting appearance belies its significance, it is headed 'Ex sacris scripturis et authoribus Catholicis' ('Compiled from Holy Scriptures and Catholic Authors') and known today as the 'Collectanea satis copiosa' ('Sufficiently plentiful collections'). Evolving from the 'King's Book' and then marshalling new sources culled from biblical texts, the Church Fathers, the decrees of Church Councils, Roman law, Anglo-Saxon laws and national histories and chronicles, it made the bold argument that the pope was merely the Bishop of Rome. As such, his jurisdiction did not extend beyond his own diocese, whereas the King of England was the 'Vicar of Christ' in his kingdom.[33]

According to the dossier, Henry's 'lawful' powers were just as 'imperial' as those of the early Byzantine emperors, notably Constantine the Great and Justinian, or the Old Testament rulers David and Solomon (Henry's favourite kings were David and Solomon, and he could quote verbatim from the Old Testament and the *Code* and *Institutes* of Justinian). Should he choose to reappropriate his regal powers, he might appoint his own bishops instead of merely nominating candidates to the pope, and he

could reform the monasteries. He might then also empower the
Archbishop of Canterbury, or else a panel of bishops, to investigate
and reach a verdict on his 'scruples of conscience', with no appeal
allowed. None of this, Foxe argued, would make Henry schismatic
like Luther. He would merely be 'restoring' to himself legitimate
royal rights which, historically, Anglo-Saxon and Norman kings
had exercised, and which the papacy had usurped. (Some of the
dossier's claims were true, although their historical contexts could
be misunderstood; others were twisted to prove what its compilers
wanted the king to believe.) Only Henry II in late 1169 at the height
of his quarrel with Archbishop Thomas Becket had dared to make
claims like these, and he had been forced to make amends after the
appalling scandal of Becket's murder.

When finally shown the dossier, Henry loved it, annotating it
approvingly in forty-six places with comments such as 'ubi hic?'
('whence does this come?'), 'de illicitis matrimoniis' ('concerning
illicit marriages') and 'bene nota' ('note well'). His mind ran
riot as he saw how, on this evidence, he had been right to claim
that Wolsey should have dealt with his suit for annulment of his
marriage promptly, and in England.[34]

By then, the session of Parliament Henry had originally
summoned to impeach Wolsey was over. The only business the king
had laid before it was a brazen bill to cancel repayment of his debts.
With that done, individual members of the House of Commons
took their opportunity to demand Church reform in return. Laws
were enacted to curtail fees for proving wills and burying the dead,
and to punish clergy who neglected their duties. Clerics were
from now on to be resident in their parishes and heavily fined for
activities not considered to be spiritual.[35]

Henry then prorogued Parliament until 1 October 1530, while
awaiting news from Europe. In the interim, he urged his new
Lord Chancellor, Thomas More, to revisit the 'great matter'.
Acutely aware that the ground was shifting and that the king's
favour came at a price, More had little choice but to agree. Sent to
Durham House to be shown some of Foxe's material, he found his
opinion was unchanged. As he later recalled, Henry, hearing this

unwelcome news, replied that he 'never was willing to put any man in ruffle or trouble of his conscience' and that he would use only those councillors in his suit for divorce 'whose conscience his Grace perceived well and fully persuaded upon that part'. In return, More offered to serve Henry faithfully 'in other things'. It was a Faustian bargain with a degree of tolerance on the king's side which More knew to be paper-thin, but which for the moment he appreciated.[36]

More – famed for his masterly *Utopia*, which had envisaged a New World in which kings were philosophers and philosophers kings – was prudently biding his time. Katherine's other advocates, though, were far from silent. Chief among them were John Fisher, who had spoken so eloquently at the Blackfriars court, and Thomas Abel, one of her chaplains. Fisher appealed to Clement to declare the recently enacted clerical reform laws 'null and void' on the grounds that Parliament had lacked the power to make them, then wrote a book defending Katherine entitled *De Causa Matrimonii* ('Concerning the Cause of Marriage'), which Chapuys smuggled to Spain to be printed. In the eyes of the Boleyns, both More and Fisher were now marked men, whom they meant to exclude from Henry's counsels and, if possible, from attending Parliament when it reassembled. When a humble cook, whether as a prank, a mistake or perhaps deliberately, almost killed Fisher and several of his servants by putting laxatives in their food, fingers pointed at Anne and her father. So popular was Katherine in London that many of the ordinary citizens believed the Boleyns to be capable of anything, even poisoning a bishop.[37]

By the spring of 1530, Henry and Anne were fully reconciled and out riding pillion through the countryside, trying out her expensive new saddles to the astonishment of gawping villagers. As she had always planned, she rode out without female attendants, so they could be alone together.[38] It was coincidental but perhaps unfortunate that, almost at this very moment, a marriage between a Jew and his dead brother's wife took place in a synagogue in Rome, right under Clement's nose.[39] Henry, too, would shortly need to appoint a proctor or *excusator* to represent him in the papal Consistory, should he wish to avoid a judgment in Katherine's

favour being issued by default.[40] Another thing the couple still had
to overcome was Katherine's refusal to move out of Henry's palaces.
While Thomas Boleyn had been abroad, Katherine had occupied
the best lodgings in the royal palaces, leaving Anne to battle for
space.[41] For all Henry's apparent commitment to her, the struggle
to displace Katherine from his life had barely begun.

17

A Breakthrough at Last?

Perhaps as early as 1527 or 1528, Anne and her brother were purchasing a series of books published by three trailblazing printers. In 1525 and again in 1526, the Sorbonne and the Parlement of Paris condemned translations of the scriptures, or parts of them, into French, along with several evangelical works. Despite this, Jacques Lefèvre d'Étaples and his friends, whose impromptu seminars at the court in Paris Anne still well recalled, sought to popularise their reforming ideas in slim, inexpensive manuals written in homely, everyday French. Once these books became available, Anne and her brother George began to read them avidly.[1]

Among the 910 books listed in an inventory of the Upper Library at Whitehall Palace after Henry's death were at least fifteen by Lefèvre and his followers, which Simon du Bois published in Paris and latterly Alençon where the members of Guillaume Briçonnet's preaching team known as the Cercle de Meaux could safely operate under Marguerite of Angoulême's protection. Another three du Bois books, now lost, were also once in the library since their titles appear in the inventory. Such books are exceptionally rare: at least four of Anne or George's copies are unique survivals: no one else in the English court is known to have purchased them, and certainly not Henry.[2]

Books published by the next most prolific of the Lefèvrist printers, Martin L'Empereur (*alias* Martin de Keyser) and Johann

Prüss the Younger, follow the same pattern. Based in Antwerp, where he also printed books for William Tyndale, L'Empereur put out some thirty theological titles in French between 1525 and 1534, of which thirteen were in the Upper Library. Prüss, who worked in Strassburg, is only known to have printed five reformist books in French, but Anne or George owned three of them. Books which Anne acquired before her marriage were 'garnished with "A" crowned', and those afterwards with the cipher 'HA' for Henry and Anne.[3]

Overall, Anne and George owned perhaps forty evangelical books in French or by French printers, several by Lefèvre himself.[4] One of their earliest acquisitions was the *Sentence de frère Jehan Guibert*, which du Bois printed in 1527. It chronicles the pardon of a Lefèvrist hermit who had been condemned to be burned at the stake after saying that the Mass should be replaced by Gospel readings, but who was exonerated on appeal after four years in prison: a personal victory for him and for the whole Cercle de Meaux.[5] Another early purchase was *Le livre de vraye et parfaicte oraison* ('The Book of True and Perfect Prayer'), first printed in 1528, a work interspersing the Lord's Prayer, Creed and Ten Commandments with helpful meditations and prayers. It was one of many evangelical books proclaiming the truth and sufficiency of Scripture as God's word.[6]

With Henry's money behind her, Anne began acquiring deluxe copies of more traditional devotional books, proving it was not these basic aids to worship that she wished to reform. She began with two Books of Hours, both now in the collections of Hever Castle. The first, a manuscript produced in Bruges around 1450, has twenty-three glorious full-page miniatures including the Adoration of the Magi, eight large-topped miniatures with full-page borders and twenty-three smaller miniatures, all framed by gilded sprays of fruit and flowers interlaced with grotesques and curling acanthus leaves. Beneath a full-page miniature of the Last Judgment is a holograph inscription, 'Le temps viendra / Je anne boleyn' ('The time will come / I Anne Boleyn'), with a drawing of an armillary sphere, one of Queen Claude's badges, inserted between 'Je' and 'anne'.[7]

Next, Anne acquired a Book of Hours printed in Paris in about 1528 by Germain and Gilles Hardouyn. The brothers specialised in works on vellum in small editions, leaving clients free to order hand-coloured decorations if they wished.[8] Anne had her copy lavishly illuminated. At the foot of a page facing a depiction of the Presentation of Christ in the Temple, she wrote: 'Remember me when you do pray / That hope doth lead from day to day / Anne Boleyn.'[9] A commonly repeated view that her inscription faces an image of the Coronation of the Virgin, referencing her desire to be Queen of England, is not accurate: the image of the Virgin's Coronation is on a different page.

In an extraordinary twist of fate, Katherine had purchased the very same book. Bequeathed to one of her gentlewomen, it was acquired in about 1906 for the Morgan Library in New York. Was this a coincidence or a gesture of one-upmanship? If the latter, Anne was the victor. Her copy is illuminated to a higher standard and with more full-length, gilded architectural borders. All copies came with intercessions to saints and Katherine had two manuscript leaves added to hers, the first with a prayer to be used in worship before a Corpus Christi image,* the other with an invocation to St Roch, a popular saint whose aid was sought against pestilence. It seems likely that the two women read their books very differently, as the Lefèvrists questioned the value of the veneration of images and of intercessions to saints.[10]

Sometime in late 1529 or early 1530, Anne went one stage further, personally commissioning an exquisite handwritten French psalter in which her Rochford heraldic arms appear on several pages in a lozenge, intertwined with a cipher that links her initials to Henry's. Now in the Getty Library at Wormsley, this was an aspirational work: teeming with brilliantly coloured rubrication and elaborate borders including interlaced acanthus leaves and flowers,

---

*In Catholic iconography, a Corpus Christi image depicts the dead Christ held in the arms of the Father, and resembles that of Our Lady of Pity in which Mary, rather than the Father, displays his wounds.

strawberries, jewels, pearls, dolphin's heads and so on, it proclaims to the world her imminent arrival in the royal family.[11]

How did she obtain these books? In the case of the psalter, Anne sought the assistance of Jean du Bellay, who wanted a similar book for himself. The printed books from the presses of du Bois and others George could well have purchased during his missions to France in and after 1529. Before then, John Barlow, whom Anne had rewarded with the rectory of Sundridge, was very likely gathering up books on his journeys back and forth between London, Paris and Italy.[12]

Later, Anne used scouts to source French biblical texts. One was William Locke, her chief supplier of silks, who fetched her books from Antwerp.[13] Another was William Latymer, the fiery rector of the London parish of St Laurence Pountney, whom she made one of her chaplains. In 'A Brief Treatise or Chronicle of the Most Virtuous Lady Anne Boleyn', which he wrote in the 1550s, Latymer tells us she was 'very expert in the French tongue, exercising herself continually in reading the French Bible and other French books of like effect and conceived great pleasure in the same'.[14] A Parisian scholar, Louis de Brun, who presented a treatise on letter writing to her as a New Year's gift in 1530, says she could never be found

> without some French book in [her] hand which is useful and
> necessary for teaching and discovering the true and straight
> path of all virtues ... And chiefly I have seen [her] this last Lent
> and the one before ... constantly reading the salutary epistles of
> St Paul.[15]

But it was not only Lefèvrist books that Anne and George were reading. George would shortly acquire a copy of a French translation of the Catalan polymath Ramón Lull's *Libre de l'Ordre de Cavalleria* ('Book of the Order of Chivalry'), written between 1274 and 1276. What caught his eye was the fact that Lull sought to reconceptualise the knightly office as a cosmic struggle between good and evil on the road to eternal salvation.[16] More famously, Anne acquired a copy of Tyndale's *The Obedience of a Christian*

Man, published in October 1528, which made exalted claims for princely power.[17] Determined to shape Henry's way of thinking, she marked such passages with her fingernail for his attention. One of her gentlewomen, Anne Gaynesford, a kinswoman of her receiver, George Taylor, and Thomas Wyatt's cousin, then saw the book and showed it to her suitor, George Zouche, from whom Dr Richard Sampson, Dean of Henry's Chapel and one of Wolsey's stalwarts, snatched it on suspicion of heresy.

George Wyatt would incorporate this story into his *Life of Anne Boleyn*. He describes how, informed of the book's loss, Anne vowed: 'Well, it shall be the dearest book that ever the dean or cardinal took away', and asked Henry to order its return. On recovering it, she 'besought his grace most tenderly' to read it, prudently not telling him the name of its author.[18] Delighted with its vindication of the powers of kings as the agents of change, Henry memorably declared, 'this book is for me and all kings to read.'

Anne also had a copy of Simon Fish's *A Supplication for the Beggars*, an Antwerp imprint from 1528, which denied the existence of purgatory and vilified the clergy as 'ravenous wolves'. Wolsey twice drove its author into exile, but when George Boleyn showed Fish's book to Henry at his sister's suggestion, all was forgiven.[19] Anne cannot be linked directly to Fish, rather to the circle around him. When Fish sold copies of Tyndale's *New Testament* from his house by the Whitefriars, between Fleet Street and the Thames, one of his customers was a Norwich book pedlar, Robert Necton, a man close to Geoffrey Lome, servant of Dr Robert Forman, the 'parson' of Honey Lane for whom Anne had already intervened.[20]

On Sunday 12 June 1530, while Wolsey was still alive and lodged in Southwell, Nottinghamshire, on his journey to his diocese of York, Henry convened a Great Council of nobles and councillors in Windsor Castle. The idea came from George Boleyn, inspired by the French 'Assembly of Notables', a consultative body through which the king could persuade the country's elites to support his policies and take strong measures for 'the good and repose of the realm'.[21] Henry called on all those attending the Council to add their names and seals to a final petition to Pope Clement, demanding

a speedy divorce as the wish of the whole kingdom. If the pope
declined, the king would take matters into his own hands. When
a majority bridled at this threatening language, a watered-down
petition was agreed on. The document, an impressive three-foot-
wide parchment, was then carried round the country in a chest
for some eighty-three signatories to sign and affix their wax seals.
Thomas More excused himself from signing, about which Henry
later complained.[22]

Clement, however, dismissed the petition, blaming Henry
for the delays to his case by his refusal to engage with the legal
process in Rome. In September, the king forbade the reception
into England of papal decrees prejudicial to his prerogative. This
followed appeals to Rome by several English bishops against the
Church reform laws passed in Parliament in 1529. Henry then
ordered Christopher Hales to file *praemunire* indictments in the
King's Bench against fourteen (soon to be sixteen) of these clerics
or their notaries, accusing them of illegally assisting Wolsey in his
use of papal jurisdiction. The indictments were the opening salvo
in what was about to become a central Boleyn strategy: a campaign
to tighten a ligature around the Church and clergy in England to
force movement on the divorce.[23]

On 5 October, Francis Bryan left for France: his remit was to
urge Francis to campaign for Henry in Rome. By then, the ransom
for Francis's sons had been paid and, as Henry had contributed
generously, it was time to call in the favour. The moment was
doubly opportune as the question of the French king's marriage
to Charles's sister, Eleanor, had been resolved. A proxy wedding
had taken place, and Eleanor crossed the frontier near to Bayonne
on the same day as the king's sons, closely watched by Bryan. This
dynastic alliance turned out to alter none of the fundamentals of
Franco-Habsburg relations, so Henry and Anne had less to fear on
that score than they had once imagined.[24]

Francis sent Gabriel de Gramont to lobby the Vatican, but also,
which Anne found more worrying, to seek a betrothal of his second
son, the Duke of Orléans, to the pope's niece, Catherine de' Medici.
He made little progress on either count at first, while the usual

seeming breakthroughs in Rome that invariably came to nothing took a toll on Anne's nerves, made worse by the arrival of a papal nuncio with a decree in his pocket ordering the king to return to Katherine. When the nuncio went to court, Anne's father told him bluntly that people cared 'neither for pope nor popes in England, not even if St Peter should come alive again'.[25] For Anne personally, however, everything seemed to be in jeopardy. When Henry's old habits of visiting and sometimes dining with the queen suddenly resumed, her doubts over his commitment were rekindled. It was as if his wife had cast a magic spell over him. When it really came to it, could he ever escape her? Was his brave talk of taking matters into his own hands no more than bluster?

So uneasy by mid-November was Anne over what she saw as Henry's backsliding that she attempted to eavesdrop on an audience he gave to Eustace Chapuys: the meeting was in the gallery of the privy chamber, and she was spotted peering through an adjacent window, straining to hear what was said. Seeing her, Henry led the envoy down into the middle of the room, where they could not be overheard. For once, he did not share his confidences with her, although it proved to be an isolated instance.[26]

In truth, Henry was jittery himself. One day in late November, he suddenly turned on his councillors and exclaimed that Wolsey had been a better statesman than any of them. This triggered a scene in which, once again, Anne bewailed her lost youth and threatened to leave him until, reputedly with watery eyes, he begged her 'not to forsake him'. She agreed to stay but, if Chapuys is to be believed, struck out at her critics by ordering the defiant motto *Ainsi sera, groigne qui groigne* ('This is how it's going to be, grudge if you like') to be embroidered on the liveries of her servants.

It was a deliberately combative adaptation of one of the mottos of her first patron, Margaret of Austria, who had recently died in Mechelen at the age of fifty. In response, Katherine's friends seized on the original version: *Groigne qui groigne et vive Burgoigne.* 'Vive Burgoigne', they called out to Anne behind her back as she walked through the court, which was code for 'vive Charles' and by inference 'vive Katherine'. All this rattled her, and by Christmas

Day her servants were back in their old liveries. Margaret would be succeeded as regent of the Low Countries by Charles's sister, Marie, the widowed Queen of Hungary, whom Anne knew from her days in the Mechelen schoolroom: she was no friend of the Boleyns.[27]

Over Christmas, though, Anne was said to be 'as brave as a lion', a remark doubtless linked to her decision to commission heraldic arms which included the black lion of Rochford on a silver background with the letter 'A' in gold above along with the cipher 'HEN REX SL', which stands for 'Henricus Rex, souverain liege' ('King Henry, sovereign lord').[28] Now that her father was Earl of Wiltshire and her brother Viscount Rochford, the right to display arms came to her automatically and to show that the bearer was a woman, she had them encased in a lozenge. More questionable was the manufacture by her or her father of a fake genealogical pedigree, declaring the Boleyns descended from a noble French knight, a move greeted with derision as the family's modest origins in the textile trade were so well known.[29]

When Katherine arrived in Greenwich to preside over the Christmas festivities, Anne defiantly told one of her ladies that she 'wished all the Spaniards were at the bottom of the sea', that she 'cared not for the queen or any of her family' and that she 'would rather see her hanged than have to confess that she was her mistress'.[30] To mollify her, Henry sent a surreptitious £100 in cash from his privy purse 'towards her New Year's gift'. No gift list for courtiers survives for this year, but those whose servants received handsome rewards from the king included Anne's father, mother, brother, sister and sister-in-law Jane Parker, so the Boleyns were clearly in high favour. The trouble, for Anne, was that Katherine took centre stage at the ceremony when gifts were exchanged and Henry dined with her afterwards, inviting talk that he would send Anne away. He could not expect either of the women in his life to tolerate this humiliating limbo much longer: even if Katherine was temperamentally equipped to playing a waiting game, Anne was not.[31]

More disagreements followed, not helped by a scurrilous farce put on by Anne's father to entertain the new French ambassador,

Gabriel de la Guiche, Jean du Bellay's replacement, who reached London a day or so after Christmas Day. Pulling none of its punches, the play depicted Wolsey going down to hell. Ordered by the Duke of Norfolk to be printed, the piece does not survive, but if it was meant to amuse the ambassador, it backfired as de la Guiche found it tasteless and volubly reprimanded (*blâme fort*) the Duke. Wolsey, he reminded him, had once been a very good friend to France. It was unwise to upset de la Guiche in this way, and Anne found that when she and Henry feasted him on Shrove Tuesday, their reception was cool.[32]

By then Anne and Henry were back in her comfort zone on the new Whitehall site, where Katherine had no space. All the Boleyns had apartments there, and in hours of relaxation George and his father played cards, shovelboard, bowls or tennis with Henry or each other, or with Anne and Sir Thomas Cheyne, or with a new young recruit to the king's privy chamber, Francis Weston.[33]

Parliament reconvened on 16 January 1531, just as the evidence against the churchmen accused of *praemunire* in the King's Bench was due to be heard. While entertaining Chapuys, Norfolk hinted at a coming storm when he treated the ambassador to a garbled precis of extracts from the Durham House dossier. Henry, he said, had 'a right of empire in his kingdom and recognised no superior'. He would allow no appeals to Rome and Clement had no authority over him or his subjects, except possibly in matters of heresy. To clinch his point, the Duke showed Chapuys a transcript of an inscription taken from a reputed seal of King Arthur hanging in Westminster Abbey. This claimed that Arthur had been the 'emperor' of 'Britain', France and much of western Europe, as set forth in chronicles and Malory's *Morte D'Arthur*. In reply, the bemused envoy could only burst out laughing and say he was surprised Henry did not also claim to be emperor of Asia.[34]

On 21 January, Henry dropped his King's Bench prosecutions but ordered the clergy to purchase a parliamentary pardon by paying him an astronomical fine of £118,000 (worth over £120 million today). On 7 February, he called on them to recognise him as the 'Sole Protector and Supreme Head of the English Church and clergy'. They reluctantly complied, with the qualifying proviso 'as far as the law of Christ allows' added.[35]

The proviso was agreed after a new royal servant entered Convocation (the churchmen's synod which met concurrently with Parliament), looking for Archbishop Warham. Thomas Cromwell, making his first public appearance on Henry's behalf, was a forty-five-year-old self-made legal counsel, son of a Putney yeoman. Lithe as the leopard which he later kept as a pet, he was fluent in Italian, French and Latin and had served Wolsey faithfully almost to the end, until further persistence meant career suicide. Before that, he had fought in Italy as a mercenary, was present at the battle of Garigliano just north of Naples in 1503 and had worked for the Frescobaldi mercantile family in Florence and London. Simply being in Florence around the time when Niccolò Machiavelli stalked the halls of the Palazzo della Signoria would have been an education. In the late 1530s, Lord Morley could rightly assume that Cromwell would be pleased by a gift of Machiavelli's *Istorie fiorentine* ('History of Florence') and *Il principe* ('The Prince'). But Cromwell did not need *Il principe* to reach many of the same conclusions about ambition, princely courts and the art of mastering fortune, as in Florence they were inscribed in the world around him.[36]

Sometime about 1513–14, Cromwell worked in Antwerp for London's Company of Merchant Adventurers before undertaking missions to Rome for private clients and finally serving Wolsey on special projects. Now gaining attention as Henry's parliamentary manager, he was never one of Anne's favoured protégés: his loyalty was to the king alone and he would climb the ladder thanks to his legal and administrative skills. He never looked to Anne or her family for advancement, other than in 1529, when he sought her uncle Norfolk's patronage to help him find a parliamentary seat. Not a single letter exists between Anne and Cromwell between 1531 and 1534 and favours from her to him are almost impossible to find. He would cooperate with the Boleyns when ordered by Henry to do so or when it suited him, but not otherwise: he shared her family's view of the pope and Catholic clergy, but they did not formally align their efforts at religious reform. Cromwell was a man for Henry and Anne to use, but also one to watch. He had his own intelligence networks acquired while working for Wolsey and the Frescobaldi. The danger for Anne was that he might one day come to have his own agenda, different from hers.[37]

What Cromwell told Warham was never disclosed, but as soon as he returned to Henry, the king sent in George Boleyn. He arrived in the synod clutching a handful of papers he had written himself, two of which can still be traced.[38] Docketed as 'matters touching the king's prerogative', the longer, more impressive of them was on the theme of Christian obedience, arguing that kings rightly wielded 'the sword of correction'. They alone could restore the Church to how it had been before the popes corrupted it. Only 'a Christian prince of godly zeal' would have 'the power effectually to subdue and repress all falsehoods'. His 'supreme authority, grounded on God's Word, ought in no case to be restrained by any frustrate decrees of popish laws or void prescripts of human traditions.' This was Tyndale writ large and shows the effects of *The Obedience* on George's consciousness.[39]

Henry's divorce campaign now took on a fresh twist. With Anne urging him on, he sounded out evangelical leaders on the Continent. So taken was he by the arguments of *The Obedience* that he spent several months on a futile effort to tempt its author back to England. It was only later that, in a reversion to character, he raged at Tyndale for his views on the sacraments, calling him a heretic and his writings 'rude' and 'unclerkly' – his abrupt change of mind sprang from Thomas More's uncovering of what Tyndale's religious beliefs really involved.[40]

The first reformer to meet Henry and Anne in person, travelling under a safe-conduct, was one Simon Grynée from Basel, already a stronghold of reformist thought. He arrived in late March 1531 and left in July, around the time Robert Barnes, whom Wolsey had forced to abjure, reappeared. Each was offered money in exchange for canvassing Protestant opinions on the divorce, but if the Swiss theologians were divided, the Germans were hostile. The most that Luther would concede was that, so long as Henry treated Katherine decently, he was entitled to marry Anne bigamously. It had been a false trail.[41]

By the onset of March, the clergy had granted both Henry's new title and the fine, after which Parliament passed a bill pardoning them. On the 30th, More, on Henry's instructions and showing visible discomfort, then laid the university opinions before both Houses of Parliament. The opinions and the *libellus* which Henry had presented to the Blackfriars court in 1529 were subsequently published together in a volume that would carry in its slightly expanded English translation the mouthful of a title *The Determinations of the Most Famous and Most Excellent Universities of Italy and France, that it is so unlawful for a man to marry his brother's wife that the pope hath no power to dispense therewith*. Parliament was then prorogued until the end of the year.[42]

On 31 May, Henry sent a thirty-strong deputation to Katherine late at night. Their task was to impress on her Henry's rights as an 'imperial' sovereign and urge her to withdraw her appeal to Rome to make way for a hearing by English judges. Such arguments again utterly failed to move her. The king, her husband, she retorted, 'is sovereign in his realm as far as regards temporal jurisdiction; but as to the spiritual, it is not pleasing to God either that the king should so intend or that she should consent, for the pope was the only true sovereign and Vicar of God, who has power to judge of spiritual matters, of which marriage was one.' And that was that, as she would never give way.[43]

So impressive was Katherine's performance that Stephen Gardiner began to distance himself from Anne. Suffolk and his duchess, meanwhile, entirely blamed her for Katherine's predicament. So did Norfolk under a mounting assault from his estranged wife, whom Anne dismissed from court. For a time, even Henry wobbled, complaining that Anne chivvied him about something almost every day in ways Katherine had never contemplated. From Anne's perspective, one can see why. She feared he was about to leave her high and dry. Even though he had promised faithfully to stop visiting or dining with his wife, he had done it twice more, at both the Easter and Whitsun festivals. Faced with that, he could hardly expect Anne not to feel vulnerable.[44]

The fullest reported clash concerned Sir Henry Guildford of Leeds Castle in Kent, since 1522 the comptroller of the king's household. Devoted to Katherine, he declared that 'it would be the best deed in the world to tie all the doctors who had invented and supported this affair in a cart, and send them to Rome to maintain their opinion, or meet with the confusion they deserve.' On hearing this, Anne threatened to sack him once she was queen, to which Guildford replied that 'she should have no trouble', because when that day came, he would resign. He went to Henry, who told him only, 'You should not trouble yourself with what women say.'[45]

And then there was a truly momentous change, and Anne at last achieved the breakthrough she sought. On 14 July, Henry set out with her from Windsor Castle on his usual summer progress, leaving Katherine behind.[46] They would go alone. Not just that, almost the entire court was to be discharged for the rest of the summer. A month later, Katherine received a message that Henry wished to return to Windsor overnight and that she was to remove herself to The More in Hertfordshire, Wolsey's former house. From there she was sent away again, this time with fewer servants, to Easthampstead in Berkshire, a much smaller property where no major repairs had been carried out for many years, before returning to The More. There she was left in isolation, while her rival assumed the trappings of royalty. Now Anne talked confidently of being married in three or four months and began to appoint her own household officers, beginning with an almoner. This was almost certainly Dr Nicholas Shaxton, an evangelical preacher well known to her uncle, Sir James Boleyn, and to Dr William Butts.[47]

Henry had at last decided that he would never see Katherine again. He was on the cusp of putting the Durham House group's ideas into practice – to obtain the divorce regardless of Clement's strictures and Katherine's appeal.[48] But he had to be realistic. To do that, with all the danger implicit in such a move should Charles decide to attack him, he needed a dependable ally and brother in arms, and that, he knew, had to be Francis. If ever the Anglo-French alliance was needed, it was now.

18

The Falcon Ascendant

Now that Anne presided at court in Katherine's place – the place of a queen – she could once again hope to take command and direct the divorce strategy as an equal partner. Never did she come closer to replicating Wolsey's level of power and influence than over the next eighteen months. She was ready to propel Henry onwards towards a complete rupture with the pope. She had to – her future depended on it.

To do that, they needed to cultivate Francis. Anne played her part before the summer progress of 1531 was over. On or about 23 September, while she and Henry were hawking on the Essex and Hertfordshire border, she invited Louise of Savoy's agent, Giovanni Gioacchino di Passano, to dine with her at Hunsdon. There they discussed a proposal for a new, more ambitious Anglo-French alliance even than Wolsey had attempted in Amiens. Offering mutual aid, it was not to be directed specifically against Charles but more designed to achieve Henry's jurisdictional independence from the pope and supremacy over the English Church as laid down in the Durham House dossier.[1]

On 8 October, Francis sent Anne's confidant, Jean du Bellay, to England for exploratory talks and on the evening of the 21st, she and Henry entertained him and di Passano to supper in Brian Tuke's house at Pyrgo in Essex. Du Bellay sat with Anne and Henry at the upper end of the table, and di Passano at the lower end with

Anne's parents, her uncle Norfolk, Stephen Gardiner, Sir William
Fitzwilliam and two unnamed ladies. Amid the conviviality, the
serious business of the new treaty was considered, and du Bellay
hurried home to France to discuss it.[2]

When du Bellay sent back instead the unexpected word of
Louise's death at the age of fifty-five, Henry put his whole court
into mourning. Francis Bryan and Edward Foxe heard the news
in Compiègne, where they saw Marguerite of Angoulême to be
especially distressed. In consultation with Marguerite, who succeeded
her mother as a prime source of information for English diplomats,
Foxe was instructed to keep a close watch on Eleanor, Charles's sister
and now Francis's wife, to see if a rumour of a clandestine meeting
between the emperor and the French king had substance to it. It
proved false, and he and Bryan were ordered home.[3]

The result of du Bellay's mission was the dispatch to London
of Gilles de la Pommeraye, an experienced, ingratiating diplomat,
to relieve di Passano. He spoke seven languages and was another
moderate evangelical reformer. Arriving on Christmas Eve, he was
escorted by barge to Greenwich, where Anne and Henry fêted him
for four days. As part of their charm offensive, they lodged him
in Bridewell Palace, where, as he informed his fellow diplomat
François de Dinteville, Bishop of Auxerre, a former almoner to
Louise of Savoy and de Gramont's replacement in Rome, he was
royally entertained.[4]

Anne was jubilant, as this was the first year that she and Henry
had spent the holidays together as if they were already married,
and she meant to enjoy it – although they did not sleep together.
Anne and her growing retinue of servants and attendants now
commandeered the whole of the vacated queen's apartments,
allowing the couple – and by this time nobody could doubt they
were a couple – to signal her future role.[5]

Much though many courtiers might privately grumble that
Christmas was not the same without Katherine, they could only
watch as the Boleyns and their coterie paraded their intimacy
with Henry, playing cards, dice and shovelboard with him.[6] When
exchanging New Year's gifts, the king's presents showed just how

much he favoured them. Anne received a set of magnificent tapestries interwoven with gold and silver thread, together with richly embroidered crimson satin bed hangings, fringed with cloth of gold and silver. Doubtless Henry looked forward to the day when he would be able to enjoy them with her.* In return, she gave him a stunning set of Pyrenean boar spears studded with jewels to proclaim his sporting but also sexual abilities. George gave him two gilt 'hyngers' or hunting daggers on velvet girdles which he could hang around his already thickening waist and in return received a large gilt cup with a cover. Thomas Boleyn gave a black velvet box holding an expensive looking-glass set in gold. Anne's mother offered cloth of gold and silver shirt collars, neatly packaged in a needlework coffer. They too received handsome gilt cups. Katherine, although forbidden to write or come within twenty miles of the court, sent a gold cup, which Henry refused. He gave her no gift and forbade his courtiers to do so.[7]

With Bryan and Foxe recalled, Stephen Gardiner, recently elevated to the bishopric of Winchester, was sent to Francis to lobby anew for an enhanced alliance. Shown a report from Gregorio Casali in Rome that Henry could no longer delay appearing before the Consistory or naming his proctor, Francis urged Clement to remit the divorce suit to English judges, but dragged his heels over the alliance. This was because the 'straight' and 'perfect amity' Anne and Henry had in mind was to be backed by military and financial aid should Charles retaliate. War on his terms or in his interests was one thing, war merely for their sake quite another.[8]

When in January 1532 Parliament reassembled, Henry was still awaiting news of Gardiner's embassy. The session began with bad-tempered arguments over taxes and feudal dues, after which individual members of the House of Commons turned again to Church reform.[9] On 18 March, Thomas Cromwell, after a series of highly charged debates, incited MPs, possibly on his own initiative, possibly under orders, to petition the king to intervene. Seizing the

---

*Should the king want sex or to see his wife privately, he would visit her, never the reverse.

opportunity, Henry sent Edward Foxe to the bishops after Easter with a series of demands amounting to a frontal assault on the Church. No longer were the clergy to hold their synods without first obtaining a royal writ. When they did assemble, no new church law should be enacted without prior royal assent. Existing laws judged to be agreeable to God's word and the king's prerogative could remain in force, but only after scrutiny by a panel of royal commissioners. The bishops valiantly resisted, assisted in the House of Lords by Thomas More, but to no avail. Parliament was abruptly prorogued while Anne's father, brother, uncle and several other councillors demanded the churchmen's immediate surrender.

On 15 May, it reluctantly came. Next day, the bishops' representatives signed the necessary documents. Within hours, More resigned as Lord Chancellor, handing back the Great Seal and claiming he was 'not equal to the work'. With his departure, Katherine lost one of her most reliable sources of information, as did Chapuys. His successor in the post would be Sir Thomas Audley, an efficient, compliant lawyer already employed as Cromwell's assistant.[10]

In Brussels, Paris, Lyon, Antwerp, Valladolid, Seville, Venice and Rome, churchmen, merchants and ordinary citizens waited to see whether Henry would dare to defy the pope to divorce Katherine and marry Anne, and if so, how Charles and Clement would respond. It was at this moment that the talks with de la Pommeraye burst back into life. The diplomacy revived not because of Gardiner's embassy, from which he had returned empty-handed on 6 March, but because in Germany a confederation of Protestant and Catholic princes conveniently came together at this moment to defend their collective interests against Charles and the Habsburgs. Francis, with his eye on one day returning to Italy, refused to ally with them, but offered to help them bankroll a future war against Charles, provided Henry would also contribute.[11]

Beginning on 30 April, proposals for an Anglo-French 'convention' were drafted and, on 18 May, Francis ordered de la Pommeraye to reopen the negotiations. These, on Henry's side, were conducted by Anne's father and Edward Foxe, recently made the king's almoner. To be sure of his ground, de la Pommeraye made a flying visit to see Francis in Châteaubriant in Brittany, returning to London on 9 June. The terms of the new Treaty of Mutual Aid were agreed in principle two weeks later, to be fully finalised and ratified in September. Henry's copy is lost, but Francis's is safely tucked away in the Archives Nationales in Paris, with copies of the subsidiary documents in the archives of the French Ministry of Foreign Affairs. The treaty would commit Francis, if Henry was attacked, to providing a crack force of 500 troops within a maximum of three months and up to 5,000 more in case of more extensive hostilities, with ships made available if the need arose, complete with all victuals and weaponry. Henry would reciprocate if Francis was threatened, and if Charles placed a trade embargo on English merchants, Francis would do the same to Flemish merchants. With such relatively small forces, the treaty was a largely symbolic commitment on Francis's side, but a major victory for Henry and Anne: no previous French king had ever promised to send troops or munitions to defend England itself from attack.[12]

Henry next ordered Katherine to leave the comforts of The More and seclude herself.[13] Anne had good reasons for demanding this. She believed the churchmen's capitulation made Henry's divorce straightforward and they could marry almost immediately. Now approaching thirty-two and having waited five years, she had niggling concerns about her fertility. According to Chapuys, de la Pommeraye approved of the wedding plan, saying 'If this king wishes to marry again, he'd be well advised not to listen to those who counsel him to waste time and money, but just follow King Louis [XII]'s example and marry the woman he wants.'[14]

Henry at first agreed, commissioning and writing the preface to a short, pithy propaganda pamphlet, *A Glasse of the Truthe*, to be printed in English and French and distributed ahead of the wedding. Highlighting the dangers of female succession and the need for a legitimate male heir, the work drew on the 'King's Book' and the Durham House dossier, then went beyond both, asserting that if Clement attempted to retaliate, he had exceeded his powers and could be lawfully disobeyed.[15]

Unfortunately for Anne, many of Henry's councillors, including even her own father, found this a step too far too fast, at least until the new open-ended alliance with Francis was officially ratified. Archbishop Warham still refused to pronounce the divorce, and Charles, successfully holding the Turks at bay in Hungary, was just too powerful. Having come this far, Thomas Boleyn was not going to hazard everything his family had gained for the sake of a few extra weeks.[16]

Norfolk too quarrelled with his niece over her wish for haste, later telling Chapuys in a rare moment of candour that 'without his and [Anne's] father's protests, the secret wedding plan would have gone ahead.' Their relations had soured earlier in the year, when Anne accused him of dynastic ambition in seeking to marry his son and her cousin, the fifteen-year-old Henry Howard, the new Earl of Surrey, to Princess Mary. It was a potentially lethal charge, the more offensive to Norfolk since, until they quarrelled, Anne had encouraged the match. To deflect the attack, the duke quickly betrothed his son instead to Lady Frances de Vere, the Earl of Oxford's daughter, although neither party was yet old enough to cohabit.[17]

Tensions ran high in these months. On Easter Day in Greenwich, the court preacher, William Peto, Minister-Provincial of the Franciscan Observants and one of Katherine's supporters, delivered an inflammatory sermon telling Henry it was an affliction of princes to be misled daily by flatterers and false councillors. Summoned to explain himself, he dared to tell Henry he risked losing his crown if he married Anne. Put under house arrest, then allowed to flee abroad, Friar Peto continued his attacks from the Low Countries, and a rival preacher charged with refuting his sermon found himself heckled by Peto's friends. Disgusted by the turn of events, the Duchess of Suffolk publicly confronted Anne, using what the Venetian ambassador in London described as such 'offensive language' it did not bear repeating.[18]

A further blip occurred when Mary Talbot, whom Harry Percy had been forced to marry, tried to discredit Anne. She had her reasons: her father had never paid her dowry, and Percy, who succeeded as Earl of Northumberland in 1527, still refused to provide adequately for her. That, he said, was because they were never lawfully married, since he had pledged himself to Anne. Talbot complained to her father, who sent her letter to the Duke of Norfolk, who confronted his niece.

Sensing danger, Anne wisely insisted the allegations be investigated to head them off. In July, Percy was examined on oath by Warham, when he swore on the Mass in front of Norfolk and Henry's lawyers that there had been no precontract with Anne. Whether he committed perjury is a question that cannot be answered. Given that the penalty at the time was understood to be damnation in hell, it seems unlikely, but rumours persisted all the same.[19]

With Anne fretting once more, Henry reassured her of his enduring love with the gift of Hanworth in Middlesex, an idyllic moated manor house convenient for Hampton Court and the Thames, complete with a deer park, an aviary for singing birds and a kitchen garden famous for its strawberries. Henry, two years before, had granted the manor to Gardiner as a reward for his efforts towards the divorce but now stripped him of it since, as the new Bishop of Winchester, he had led the churchmen's resistance to the king's demands concerning church law. Anne, whose growing suspicion of Gardiner was reinforced by his hostility to the evangelical reformers, quickly took possession of the house, and within months the royal craftsmen were refurbishing it at Henry's expense. Boxes, cupboards, desks, chairs, tables, doors and other joinery were specially fitted and she had a Florentine painter, Antonio Toto, redecorate the rooms using a range of colours such as white and red lead, blue bice or azurite, spruce ochre and green verdigris.[20]

With ratification of the new alliance imminent, Henry and Anne invited de la Pommeraye to accompany them for parts of their summer progress, which slowly wended its way from Greenwich towards Woodstock in Oxfordshire and ended up in Hampton Court. To add to their luggage, Henry placed another large order for 'stuff' with his suppliers, notably 'two saddles of the French fashion with seats of down' for Anne, fitted with 'two deep coverings of velvet fringed with silk and gold' and 'heads of copper and gilt and [en]graven'. They were to come with matching harnesses, girths, mounting stools and other riding accoutrements.[21]

De la Pommeraye joined the royal progress at Ampthill in July, at Grafton in August and at Windsor in early September, the hospitality concluding with a dinner given by Anne at Hanworth. As he reported to his patron, the Duke de Montmorency:

> All day long I have time alone with [the king] while out hunting, and there he talks to me about all his private affairs and takes as much trouble to show me good sport as if I were a great personage. Sometimes he leaves me with Madame Anne, for each of us to use our crossbows to shoot the deer as they pass, as is their custom here. Sometimes she and I are left entirely alone in a different place to chase the deer, and whenever we arrive at any of their houses, it is never too much trouble to show me around and tell me what she plans to do there. She has presented me with hunting clothes, a hat, a horn and a greyhound.[22]

All this had to have a purpose. Plans were afoot with de la Pommeraye for a new summit between Henry and Francis where their friendship could be fully realised. Anne was to accompany Henry as if she was already his wife, which in turn would allow Francis to thank her personally 'for the many good services she has rendered and is daily rendering him'. To further sweeten relations, Marguerite of Angoulême sent Henry a portrait: the sitter is unknown, but it was almost certainly Francis.[23]

According to de la Pommeraye, Anne's interventions on behalf of France 'are more than his master, the king, could ever sufficiently acknowledge or repay'. Seeing a new world closer in prospect, courtiers scrambled to defer to Anne and win her favour. As the royal progress set out, Lady Lisle sent her a present of peewits and a bow from Calais which Anne 'did greatly esteem and commanded a string to be set on it ... but it was somewhat too big'. In return, Lisle asked for special licences to export beer and to import tapestries and other luxury goods, to which Anne 'made no answer ... [but] she do trust to do you good some other ways, which she saith she would gladly do.'[24] Next, Lady Russell, who had lost the wardship of both her own daughters after Anne's interventions, did her best to win her favour, sending her a stag and a greyhound. While she accepted them, Anne sidestepped any reciprocal obligation by passing the gifts to Henry, who ordered 40s to be paid to the servant bringing them.[25]

The appearance of Halley's Comet, first observed streaking across the sky in August, was the occasion for much muttering and comment. For Anne the omen seemed favourable, as on the morning of Sunday 1 September in Windsor Castle and with de la Pommeraye as the guest of honour, Henry ennobled her as Marquis of Pembroke in her own right, with an annual income accruing from a grant of estates worth over £1,000 a year.[26] As she knelt before him, flanked by the officers of arms, he placed a coronet on her head and a mantle of crimson velvet furred with ermine around her shoulders, then handed her the patent of nobility. She wore her hair 'sparsi', as the Venetian ambassador described it, meaning 'hanging loose'.[27] Anne's grant followed the same format as for the creation of male peers and closely resembled the one Francis made to his sister Marguerite in 1517, which Anne had witnessed. As Duke of Berry, Marguerite had become male in terms of status, entitled to the traditional rights and privileges ascribed to the male siblings of the king. Henry gave Anne something strikingly similar, and to make sure no one missed the point, de la Pommeraye was guest of honour at the ceremony.[28]

As a marquis, Anne could sit in the House of Lords, and the title would automatically descend to her offspring even if illegitimately conceived.* For her heraldic insignia, she chose a white falcon, crowned and holding a sceptre in one foot, perched on a tapering

---

*Whether the omission of the customary words 'lawfully begotten' in the Latin text of the patent was a drafting error will never be known. Nobody noticed at the time.

stump of 'woodstock' (rootstock or tree-stump) out of which sprouted offshoots of white and red roses with the motto 'Mihi et Meae' ('For me and for mine'). The rootstock is a centuries-old royal badge; the falcon became Anne's personal badge, and by picturing it sceptred and bearing an imperial crown, she could have sent out no stronger signal of her belief that Henry would share his crown with her. The white falcon ultimately derived from the heraldic crest of the Butlers, Earls of Ormond, her grandmother's ancestors. She had already had it added – uncrowned but with wings fully displayed – to the music manuscript she had acquired in France, where it decorates one of the Latin motets by Jean Mouton.[29]

With Anne now a marquis, Henry escorted his guests down the hill from the Castle to St George's Chapel, where after Mass he ratified the Treaty of Mutual Aid. De la Pommeraye then did the same on behalf of Francis, after which Edward Foxe delivered 'an eloquent oration in Latin in praise of peace, love and amity'.[30] When he had finished, Henry led his guests back to the Castle, where he laid on a solemn feast. Within days, the earliest proof copies of *A Glasse of the Truthe* were rolling off the presses, only to be delayed for a fortnight by misprints and other 'certain errors' which Henry insisted be corrected before the pamphlet was distributed.[31]

Next came the summit, to take place half in Calais, half in Boulogne, and to last eight days in all.[32] Throughout August and September, Anne busily stocked up on clothes, while Henry commissioned new jewellery from Cornelius Hayes. Several of the finest stones are marked in the inventory as 'reserved' for Anne, who also now insisted that Katherine surrender her jewels to her.[33] At first, she refused to comply, telling Chapuys she considered it 'a sin and a load upon my conscience ... to give up my jewels for such a wicked purpose as that of ornamenting a person who is the scandal of Christendom'. But when Henry sent Richard Page, now a gentleman of his privy chamber, to her with written orders, she felt impelled to yield.[34]

By taking Anne to the summit as if she was his queen, Henry earned the lasting enmity of his sister, the Duchess of Suffolk, who loathed and resented Anne as much as before and refused to accompany him to Calais, using her declining health as an excuse. An awkward point of protocol arose: who was to receive Anne? Francis had the good sense not even to suggest that his wife Eleanor, Charles's sister, attend. Henry and Anne proposed Marguerite of Angoulême, by now married to Henry d'Albret, the titular King of Navarre, after the Duke of Alençon's untimely death. She, however, was with her new husband in the south of France, where they were trying for children. In the end, Anne's retinue numbered only between twenty and thirty women and she was formally greeted on arrival in Calais by Sir Richard Whethill, the mayor, and other local dignitaries.[35]

Several hours before dawn on Friday 11 October, Henry and Anne boarded the *Swallow* at Dover. Diplomatic chatter had suggested they would be married during the summit, but it was now too late for that to be arranged. After an uneventful crossing, they reached Calais by 10 a.m., where they relaxed in the royal lodgings in the Exchequer for ten days. On Saturday, Montmorency sent Anne a gift of grapes and pears. She 'lives like a queen', remarked the Venetian ambassador, 'and the king accompanies her to Mass and everywhere as if she was such.'[36]

The rendezvous between Francis and Henry was on the 21st, midway between Calais and Boulogne, when each arrived with a retinue of 600. It was a far less lavish occasion than the Field of Cloth of Gold, but both kings still dressed as showily as possible. Henry wore a red velvet surcoat covered with gold braid and studded with pearls, Francis a slashed coat of crimson velvet lined with cloth of gold, with the lining plucked out through the cuts. They embraced five or six times on horseback, then rode off towards Boulogne, all the while hawking together. Francis's sons greeted them on the outskirts of the town. As a token of high honour, Henry at once dismounted and kissed all three on the mouth. To a loud artillery salute, they proceeded to the shrine of Our Lady of Boulogne, where they each made offerings of alms. For the next four days, Francis entertained Henry royally in the abbey, presenting him with white velvet and satin clothes matching his own, along with a bed and a superlatively embroidered set of crimson bed-hangings, dripping with pearls, costing 13,500 *livres* (around £1,500, worth £1.5 million today), which he had ordered from Odinet Turquet, a leading Paris supplier.[37]

On Friday the 25th, Francis left Boulogne with Henry for Calais, bringing with him 300 pack mules laden with his luggage. As they approached, 3,000 cannons fired a volley from the battlements. Francis lodged in Staple Hall on the main square. Next day, both kings went to Mass together, and in the afternoon sat with their councils. On Sunday, they heard Mass privately in their lodgings, then attended a bull- and bearbaiting. Anne made no appearance. Francis had sent her an enormous diamond valued at 15,000 gold crowns (around £3,500, or £3½ million today) – but she was choosing her moment to greet him. So far, all she had chosen to do was to give a dressing-down to Gregorio Casali, who had travelled from Rome for the summit, for not handling Henry's business better, since 'she had hoped to be married in the middle of September'.[38]

The climax followed on Sunday evening. Henry laid on a sumptuous banquet for Francis in the great hall of the Exchequer with over 170 different dishes. Tapestries interwoven with gold and silver thread shimmered from the walls, reflecting the light from the thousands of candles which illuminated the tables. A buffet, fifteen or so feet high, was laden with solid gold and silver plate. Anne was still not at Henry's side during the banquet. Instead, with her sister Mary, her brother George's wife Jane, Lady Lisle and three other women, she was preparing for the masque that was to follow: as the guests finished their last dish, served on gold plates, the seven masked ladies suddenly entered the hall to the gentle strains of Henry's minstrels. Clad in cloth of gold, cloth of silver and crimson satin fringed with gold thread, and with all eyes upon them, the maskers turned towards the spectators and then selected dancing partners.[39]

Now Anne took centre stage for – as she and Henry had planned – her choice was Francis himself. After a couple of dances, a beaming Henry began to remove the 'visors' from the ladies' faces 'so that there their beauties were showed'. When he removed Anne's visor and announced who she was, Francis was genuinely impressed. He had not had even so much as a glimpse of her for ten years, but soon he was talking animatedly to her, almost as entranced as Henry. Her perfect French and those years serving Queen Claude meant that she knew exactly what to say. Francis found her captivating. As Henry watched proudly, the couple talked and danced for over an hour before Francis bade them adieu.[40]

This was perhaps the greatest of all the turning points in Henry and Anne's story. With the ratification of the Treaty of Mutual Aid and the fact that Francis had acknowledged her with his gift of the diamond – not to forget the gift of the bed which could surely have only one meaning – she felt her position might finally be secure. Her dance and talk with Francis as if she were already queen at the closing of the summit gave her the international recognition she needed, the fulfilment of many months, indeed years of planning.

Flushed with a sense of optimism, triumph and, crucially, acceptance, the couple now began sleeping together. The decision must have been Anne's. Henry had waited for almost six full years: she had fully tested his commitment. It was now or never. We can assume he was ecstatic from the fact that, after re-crossing the Channel, the couple took almost a fortnight to travel fewer than seventy miles on their journey home through Kent. To satisfy their own sense of propriety, they exchanged wedding vows 'privily' (meaning without witnesses and probably without a priest, a move of highly dubious validity) in Dover on St Erkenwald's Day (14 November). According to Edward Hall, this happened shortly after their ship had landed and Henry had offered alms of 4s 8d at the travellers' shrine of Our Lady in the Rock.[41]

On returning to London, the king threw himself into action. No longer did he intend to wait for a verdict from Rome: he would use Parliament to block Katherine's appeal to the pope and his own church courts to get his divorce. To Anne's delight, Archbishop Warham had just died, and Henry's choice to succeed him was Cranmer. For his consecration to be valid, Cranmer needed papal bulls from Clement. After that, all surely could proceed smoothly.[42]

19

The Marriage

On 20 November 1532, Henry and Anne played cards with Francis Bryan and the young Francis Weston of the privy chamber while lodged at Stone Castle in Kent. Their game, known as Pope Julius's game, involved cards, cash and counters: the nine of diamonds was the 'Pope' and a winning card. Usually Henry lost, and this day was no exception, costing him £9 6s 8d.[1] Stone, the ancestral home of Bridget Wilshire, was the penultimate stop on the couple's leisurely journey home. Bridget and Anne had always been close. When Bridget gave birth to a child after taking Sir Nicholas Harvey of Ickworth in Suffolk as her second husband, the king – doubtless at Anne's request – sent the nurse and midwife a purse containing £3 6s 8d.[2] But something untoward happened and Bridget left court. Shortly before her elevation as Marquis of Pembroke, Anne had sent her a note, apologising for any slight she might have given and pleading for her return. Unusually for Anne, the letter is conciliatory to the point of obsequiousness.

> Madam, I pray you as you love me to give credence to my servant, this bearer, touching your removing and anything else that he shall tell you of my behalf, for I will desire you to do nothing but that shall be for your wealth. And Madam, though at all times I have not showed the love that I bear you as much as it was indeed, yet may I trust that you shall well

prove that I loved you a great deal more than I made fair for, and assuredly, next mine own mother, I know no woman alive that I love better; and at length, with God's grace, you shall prove that it is unfeigned, and I trust you do know me for such a one that I will write nothing to comfort you in your trouble but I will abide by it as long as I live. And therefore, I pray you leave your indiscreet trouble, both for displeasing of God and also for displeasing of me, that doth love you so entirely. And trusting in God that you will thus do, I make an end. With the ill hand of

> Your own assured friend during my life,
> Anne Rochford[3]

Anne's letter, curiously, ended up not in Bridget's family papers, but in Cromwell's, from where in the 1590s it was pillaged by Sir Robert Cotton for his collections, now in the British Library.[4]

Precisely what Bridget's 'indiscreet trouble' was is perplexing. More intriguing is why Anne so badly wanted to keep on the right side of her, since as a rule, she was unfazed about making enemies. Whatever the reason, once Anne sent her letter, she appears to have thought no more about it. She had every reason to forget, because all eyes after the summit were focused on Rome, where Francis had sent Gabriel de Gramont and François de Tournon to invite Clement to Nice for a conference. There, among other business, Francis hoped to persuade him to grant Henry's divorce.[5] To help the French envoys win over the Italian cardinals to his cause, Henry had Cromwell, now made Master of the Jewels, remit them 9,000 marks (£6,000, worth over £6 million today) to distribute as bribes.[6]

Four days after arriving back in Greenwich, Henry took Anne to the Tower to show her his secret treasury in the Jewel House and to inspect the queen's apartments, which she would occupy on the night before her coronation. She decided changes were needed: the Presence Chamber was to have a new roof and floor and be fitted with a 'great carrel window' on the west side and two smaller windows opposite, overlooking the Thames. All these windows were to have 'leaning places' so she could admire the panoramic views. She also ordered extensive improvements to the privy chamber, where a splendid new gallery was constructed for her to walk in.[7]

The year's Christmas celebrations were marked by a symbolic change. When the royal carpenters made ready to display New Year's gifts, they built 'trestles and boards for the Lady Marquis of Pembroke's New Year gifts to stand upon'. The trestles needed to be strong as over the Christmas period, Henry transferred almost three hundredweight of gilt plate – around 140 separate pieces, worth £1,200 (over £1.2 million in modern values) – to Anne, with New Year's gifts of silver or gilt flagons, standing salts, candlesticks, bowls, pots and spoons. Some of this plate had once belonged to Wolsey, some to William Compton, who had died of the sweating sickness in debt to Henry. Cornelius Hayes received instructions to remove all previous ownership marks and to 'strike' or 'burnish' Anne's heraldic arms as Marquis of Pembroke in their place. New pieces were to be 'gilded, engraved, or enamelled' with her falcon badge.[8]

Henry was rewarded when, in the third week of January, Anne learned that she was pregnant. Her news thrilled him: the child, he was convinced, would be a boy – the future Prince of Wales for whom he had so long yearned. But if his son was to be legitimate, he would at the very least need to be born in lawful wedlock: the law regarded a baby conceived out of wedlock, but born within it, to be a rightful heir, even if some lawyers quibbled. Now timing became crucial.

De Gramont and de Tournon found the pope in Bologna on 3 January 1533 still smarting from a bruising rendezvous with Charles, and so made excellent progress. Clement agreed both to come to Nice, where Charles would be safely at a distance, and to handle Henry's case 'so dexterously that no harm will be done to him'. Henry and Anne took this as a vindication of their Francophile policy. What they never fully appreciated was that Francis had a different motive: he had revived in earnest his plan of 1529, which then so worried Anne, to marry his second son, Henry, Duke of

Orléans, to Clement's niece. All this was part of his wider game to detach Clement from Charles, so paving the way for a French return to Italy. In Calais before the end of the summit, Francis had aired the idea of the betrothal, but only vaguely and incidentally, allowing Henry to believe that such a match would be pursued only after his divorce was secured.[9]

Awkwardly, the papal bulls needed for Cranmer's consecration were not expected to emerge from the Consistory in Rome for at least three months. A tricky situation required an unconventional response and it was quick to come. Henry, in his own eyes, was free to marry. He had long regarded his marriage to Katherine as invalid, and he knew enough church law to realise that a second marriage during annulment proceedings was retroactively considered valid once the first was annulled. He would have his divorce as soon as Cranmer's bulls arrived, so any taint of bigamy could be dispelled at that point.[10]

Shortly before dawn, then, on 24 or 25 January, Henry and Anne stepped into a newly matted barge and were rowed from Greenwich to Whitehall with a few attendants. On disembarking, they made their way to the gatehouse and were secretly married in an upstairs chamber. Just three witnesses are thought to have attended: Henry Norris, Thomas Heneage and Anne Savage, one of Anne's gentlewomen and a kinswoman of William Brereton, said to be 'a lady of masculine spirit'. Chroniclers said she carried the bride's train, before leaving Anne's service to marry Thomas, Lord Berkeley.[11] Writing in the 1550s, Nicholas Harpsfield said the officiating priest was Dr Rowland Lee. One of Henry's chaplains, he would soon be made Bishop of Coventry and Lichfield. Chapuys, however, who investigated the facts, says George Browne, a man well acquainted with Cromwell whom the king made Prior of the Austin Friars in London, was the officiant.[12]

Henry had recalled Parliament to meet on 4 February. In readiness, he and Anne moved from Greenwich to Whitehall, where they occupied as many of the newly remodelled royal apartments there as the workmen had completed. Cromwell, whose main task was to manage the Commons, had prepared multiple drafts of legislation to block judicial appeals to Rome for Henry to vet and approve. The law would prohibit all appeals on whatever grounds from the English courts to the pope, stopping Katherine in her tracks. Cromwell's dependable assistant Thomas Audley, the recently appointed Lord Chancellor, would preside in the House of Lords instead of Thomas More. In the wings stood Cranmer, who took over lodgings usually occupied by one of the canons of St Stephen's Chapel close to Whitehall, a location perfectly situated for consultations on the next legal and theological moves on the divorce.[13]

Next, one of Cromwell's clerks drew up a document for a dozen or so carefully selected churchmen to endorse. It does not survive, but as reported by Chapuys it called on them to agree that the king's marriage was invalid, because God's law forbade marriage with a deceased brother's widow. Cranmer, already (somewhat prematurely) listed as 'My lord of Canterbury', and Edward Foxe were among those who willingly signed, but Stephen Gardiner and others refused.[14]

Anne's father, meanwhile, worked on Katherine's supporters in the House of Lords. On 13 February, he sounded out Thomas Manners, Earl of Rutland, as to whether he would support a marriage between Henry and Anne should the question come before Parliament. When Rutland said that such 'spiritual matters' could not be settled that way, he was brusquely told to conform to Henry's wishes or face the consequences. The encounter followed a deliberately staged scene in Anne's apartments, when – to keep everyone guessing as to what had already happened in the room above the Whitehall gatehouse – she had declared that 'I am as sure of my own death that I shall very soon be married to the king.'[15]

Anne now became unstoppable, brazenly joking about the situation. On the 15th, she boasted to her uncle Norfolk that if she did not find herself with child by Easter (which, of course, she already knew herself to be), she would go on a pilgrimage to pray to the Virgin Mary – since she was a Lefèvrist, who questioned the value of such intercessions, her remark was sardonic. On the 22nd, she talked loudly in front of a group of courtiers that appears to have included her former suitor Thomas Wyatt, saying that she had a sudden craving for apples. Overhearing her, Henry declared it was a sign she had to be pregnant, a suggestion she mischievously tossed aside. She then turned on her heel and walked back to her apartments, laughing excitedly.[16]

Two days later, on St Matthias' Day, Anne entertained Henry to dinner. On the walls of her Presence Chamber were the finest of the gold and silver tapestries he had given her. To the side stood a large buffet, its high shelves groaning with the best of her newly acquired gilt plate. She sat on Henry's right at the top table, with the Duke of Suffolk, Audley and other specially chosen lords and ladies on a cross-table lower down the room. So preoccupied were the couple with each other during the meal that Henry scarcely talked to other guests, other than when he called down to bait the Duke of Norfolk's estranged wife, Elizabeth Stafford, for her loyalty to Katherine: 'Has not the Lady Marquis got a grand dowry and a rich marriage', he cried in triumph, 'because all that we see, and more besides, belongs to her?'[17]

The next day was Shrove Tuesday, when Anne and Henry feasted the new resident French ambassador, who had arrived on the 5th or 6th. This was the remarkable Jean de Dinteville, Bailly of Troyes and Seigneur de Polisy in Champagne, the younger brother of de la Pommeraye's friend François. Born in 1504, he was approaching twenty-nine when he arrived in London. Stocky and of middling height, he had broad shoulders, a full face, a large nose, a full head of dark brown hair, a thick beard and moustache and big wide-set brown eyes. A confident man with a natty dress style, he loved to wear his velvet cap at a jaunty angle if his surviving portraits are anything to judge by. His instructions, issued by the Duke de Montmorency, were to advise Henry to place his hopes on the outcome of the meeting in Nice.[18]

The Shrove Tuesday feast was a purely social occasion, but the next day de Dinteville had a second, longer audience in which Henry spoke excitedly of the forthcoming Franco-papal conference and promised to send Anne's father or uncle Norfolk to Nice, with plenary powers to join the negotiations as they thought fit. At this point, Henry was blithely unaware that Francis held his second son's betrothal to be the main reason for the conference.[19] Henry did have a favour to ask of de Dinteville: he wanted Francis to instruct de Gramont and de Tournon to persuade Clement to hold Katherine's appeal in abeyance and not to 'innovate' (meaning impose sanctions) against him until after the conference. Francis agreed on condition that Henry, on his side, made no further moves on the divorce or attacks on the Church until the talks were over.[20]

At this stage, of course, neither de Dinteville nor Francis knew that Anne and Henry were already married. By not disclosing this crucial fact, Henry had sorely deceived his key ally. So deep did this deception go that as late as 16 March, Montmorency enclosed a letter for Anne inside a packet for de Dinteville which addressed her only as 'Madame la Marquise' and not as Henry's wife.[21] Ten days or so before that letter arrived, de Dinteville at last picked up rumours. He was unsure what they meant, but Henry knew it was no longer wise to keep Francis in the dark. On the 11th, he named Anne's brother, George, as a special ambassador to France, instructing Cromwell to pay him £106 13s 4d in advance for his expenses, to last for forty days.[22]

George's instructions, which Henry dictated in perfect French, run to sixteen pages of closely written text. Directed to 'our most loyal councillor, Lord Rochford, gentleman of our privy chamber', they show their author to have become as overbearingly condescending as can be imagined in one ruler addressing another. George was first to present Francis with letters which Henry, as a matter of courtesy, would write in his own hand, and then express the 'great joy, comfort and pleasure' he felt in the personal friendship and 'perfect and unbreakable amity and perpetual alliance' the two monarchs shared. Only then was George, choosing his moment, to drop his bombshell by informing Francis that Henry had married Anne, justifying it in terms of the country's need for 'a masculine succession and posterity'. Henry, he was to say, acted purely from necessity: Clement's obstinacy and Charles's interference made further delay impossible. George was then to instruct Francis, on his honour, to behave as Henry's 'true friend and brother' by keeping the news of his marriage completely secret from everyone, especially in Rome, until after Easter, when he would announce it himself.

Henry wished Francis to order de Gramont and de Tournon to comply with detailed instructions that he would himself issue for their talks with the pope.[23] And on the question of the planned betrothal itself, Henry felt obliged to offer his fellow monarch some 'fraternal advice'. The idea of forging a Franco-papal dynastic alliance in Nice, George was to say, was all very well: it would be invaluable if it hastened Clement's grant of Henry's annulment, but Francis should be wary. The fourteen-year-old Catherine de' Medici, the pope's niece, was a far from ideal match. 'I must be plain with you', Henry concluded, 'that, in view of the low blood and poor family from which she comes, and the very noble and most illustrious progeny of the royal house of France, a marriage to our very dear and much beloved cousin and godson, the Duke of Orléans, would be gravely unequal and unfit.'[24]

George left London on the 13th and, on reaching Calais, rode post-haste to find Francis, who was then in Fère-en-Tardenois on the borders of Champagne. Two eyewitness reports, one by Francis, the other by Jean du Bellay, describe his frosty reception.[25] When he first arrived, he spoke too forcibly and brashly. He was too eager for a quick answer, winging his diplomacy as he went along. Francis may not have been sorry that Henry and Anne had finally married, but he bridled at Henry's presumption in asking him to keep the fact secret. He was being asked to dupe Clement, just as Henry had duped him. Francis had his own interests to serve, and he had no intention of allowing his ambassadors in Rome to take their instructions from Henry.[26]

Du Bellay, drawing on his experiences in London, suspected a growing rift between Norfolk and the Boleyns behind the scenes. Anne, George and their father saw great danger in the upcoming conference if it meant Francis marrying his son to the pope's niece. Norfolk disagreed, and he it was, not Thomas Boleyn, whom Henry would choose as his representative in Nice. The Boleyns, du Bellay believed, did not regard Norfolk as entirely reliable where their interests were at stake: he was too close to the Duke de Montmorency.[27]

Francis, unable to oblige George but unwilling to make an enemy of Anne's beloved brother, gave him a munificent gift of 2,250 *livres* (worth over £281,000 today) in cash.[28] George left France on or shortly after 5 April, returning home to find that, three weeks earlier, Cromwell had introduced the final draft of a bill in Restraint of Appeals into the House of Commons. It declared England to be 'an empire' (i.e. a fully sovereign jurisdiction) 'governed by one Supreme Head and king'. This, the bill insisted, was fully proved 'by divers sundry old authentic histories and chronicles', which, of course, meant those rediscovered in the Durham House dossier.[29] Not just Katherine's appeal to Rome, but all appeals to jurisdictions beyond the realm were outlawed.

For weeks, the opposition held firm: it came to comprise a coalition of Katherine's supporters and those with commercial interests who feared Charles would retaliate with another trade embargo or other economic sanctions. A damaged list of some thirty-five names of MPs compiled by Cromwell lies buried in the archives, identifying the most vocal critics of the bill. Two of Thomas More's sons-in-law, William Roper and William Dauntesey, were among them, as was Robert Fisher, Bishop John's brother. No longer in Parliament himself, More urged the Warwickshire member George Throckmorton, who had connections to the exiled Friar Peto, to vote against the legislation. He told him that, by speaking his mind in support of the Catholic cause, he would 'deserve great reward of God and thanks of the king's grace at length' – once, that is, Henry came to his senses and recalled Katherine. It was during these debates that Cromwell honed his skills at browbeating opponents.[30]

Cranmer's bulls had by this time arrived from Rome. Thanks to de Gramont and de Tournon's skilful lobbying, Clement issued them with remarkable speed and even waived the usual fee of 1,500 florins, not guessing where this might lead. The new archbishop was consecrated in St Stephen's Chapel on Passion Sunday, 30 March. As Parliament was in session, several of its members may well have heard him demonstratively protest while taking his oath that such loyalty as he owed to the pope could not override his duty to the king. In the Commons during the first week in April, the bill in Restraint of Appeals underwent minor amendments: the Lords made no traceable alterations and the Act had received the royal assent by the weekend.[31]

Cranmer took the chair in the churchmen's Convocation on 1 April. Within a few days, most of those still prepared to attend had been coerced into supporting motions arguing, first that marriage with a deceased brother's widow was forbidden by God's law without exceptions, and secondly that the consummation of Katherine's marriage to Arthur was sufficiently proved. John Fisher, who led the opposition to the first, was briefly jailed, and then put under house arrest until after the vote. Dr Richard Wolman, despite representing Henry in Wolsey's secret tribunal in 1527, asked to resign as Prolocutor of the synod before the second, ostensibly on grounds of ill-health. Edward Foxe, who sat in the synod as Archdeacon of Leicester, was named in his place. When Henry demanded that these verdicts in his favour be certified in a public legal instrument, the synod obeyed.[32]

Now Henry and Anne's dream was possible and he began talking openly of his plans for her coronation. All that remained was for Cranmer to open a formal trial of Henry's case after Easter. On the Wednesday of Holy Week (9 April), he sent a delegation led by the Dukes of Norfolk and Suffolk to Ampthill to persuade Katherine to accept Cranmer's judgment, offering her all favour if she would give way. When she refused, Norfolk informed her bluntly for the first time that Anne and Henry were already married. After their departure Lord Mountjoy, Katherine's chamberlain, brought more bad news. No longer would Henry allow her to call herself queen. From now on, she was to be known only as the 'Lady Katherine, Princess Dowager of England'. A month after Easter, the king would slash her income and the size of her household. She defiantly replied that so long as she lived, she would call herself queen.

Katherine was not being obstinate purely to punish Henry: to her mind, her marriage was still valid, allowed by papal dispensation and blessed by God, a holy sacrament which no man, not even a king, could overrule. She could never bow to threats from the king's ministers or even Henry himself because that would be to deny God. She would draw her strength from her religion – and Charles. She still hoped that her husband would return to her but, in the meantime, she would fight, no matter how unhappy or rejected she felt. In any case, there was her daughter Mary to consider. Katherine's anxiety when Henry had ennobled Fitzroy was as nothing compared to the danger posed to Mary's chances of becoming queen should Anne give birth to a son. Katherine would fight for her daughter too. But another cruel blow came on the same day as the visit from Norfolk and Suffolk: Henry callously forbade Mary either to write or send messages to her mother, and even when, in great distress, she offered to show him all that passed between them, he continued to refuse. Like Anne, Henry feared the pressure that might come if mother and daughter combined against him.[33]

Anne's great moment came at last on Holy Saturday (the 12th) in Greenwich Palace, to which she and Henry had returned after Parliament was prorogued. On her way to the Vigil Mass of Easter, she processed in state along the royal gallery from the queen's apartments – glaziers were already fixing her heraldic arms and falcon badges into the windows – to the Chapel at the far end of the building. On arrival, she spotted Wolsey's arms painted on the 'great organs in the Chapel' and ordered them to be replaced by hers. As the outraged Chapuys wrote to tell Charles, she 'was loaded with jewels and clothed in a robe of cloth of gold tissue', the most expensive type, as it was delicately woven with raised loops of the finest metal thread in several heights and thicknesses. With her cousin, Lady Mary Howard, Norfolk's daughter, carrying her train and as many as sixty women in attendance, she received 'the solemnities' previously given to Katherine. Once in the Chapel, she sat in the queen's elevated pew, leaving it only to offer alms until it was time to return to her Presence Chamber.[34]

The same day, Anne changed her title from 'Lady Marquis' to queen and Henry ordered preachers to make public prayers for her by name – something reserved for established royalty. But when, on Easter Day, George Browne urged his congregation to pray for 'Queen Anne' in his packed friary church, thereby becoming the first person to acknowledge to Londoners beyond the court that she and Henry were married, over half walked out. 'All the world is astonished at it', wrote Chapuys to Charles, 'for it looks like a dream, and even those who take her part know not whether to laugh or to cry.' In a rage, Henry summoned the Lord Mayor, Sir Stephen Peacock, and ordered him to ensure nothing like that happened again. Nobody, he said, 'should dare to murmur at his marriage'. The citizens' wives were said to be particularly vehement in their abuse of Anne.[35]

On Good Friday, Cranmer had humbly sought Henry's licence to open an archiepiscopal court 'to proceed to the examination, final determination and judgment' of the king's first marriage. Once granted, Henry and Katherine received a formal summons to appear before him in Dunstable Priory in Bedfordshire, well out of the public eye. The first session was on 10 May, when Henry was represented by Dr Bell. Katherine made things easier by failing to appear. The trial itself began on the 12th, when the evidence, much of it recycled from the Blackfriars court, began to be heard, and ended on the 23rd when Cranmer pronounced the marriage null and void. All that was needed to complete the process was a definitive verdict that Anne and Henry's marriage was valid.[36]

In London, de Dinteville listened for news, eager to know (as he reported to Francis) 'if the other queen is [Henry's] wife or not', but more concerned to know whether an archiepiscopal divorce, coupled with the Act in Restraint of Appeals, might provoke Clement into cancelling the conference in Nice. To prevent this, de Dinteville urged Henry to consider delaying publication of the Act of Appeals, but he refused. The same applied to an announcement of Cranmer's sentence once it was given. 'That's impossible', Henry retorted, 'because it must be published and generally known before [Anne's] coronation, which must take place on Whitsunday.' The reason, he said, was simple. Anne was visibly pregnant. 'The child is to become the sole heir of the kingdom': 'I will not allow the pope to give an earlier judgment or do anything to throw doubt on its legitimacy.'[37]

On 28 May Cranmer, from a gallery in the archbishop's palace in Lambeth across the Thames from Westminster and with Cromwell and four others as witnesses, gave sentence that Anne and Henry's marriage was valid. Shortly afterwards, a certified copy of the decree on parchment was enrolled in the records of the royal Chancery to follow on from the earlier decree of divorce. Now the path ahead was clear.[38]

Henry had given considerable thought to the form of Anne's coronation in Westminster Abbey during the four months since their secret marriage. On 28 April, he started sending out invitations to the women Anne insisted should join her coronation procession.[39] He also began revising the king's coronation oath to reflect his newly 'rediscovered' imperial power as set out in the Durham House dossier and the preamble to the Act in Restraint of Appeals. Only the first page of his draft has survived, but the changes were drastic, reflecting his repudiation of papal authority and his assertion of royal supremacy over the English Church.[40]

But if Henry was revising the king's coronation oath, he must also, at least at first, have envisaged a second coronation of his own jointly with Anne's, just as he had insisted that Katherine be crowned alongside him at the beginning of his reign. A second coronation would be a way in which he could see himself anew. If this was briefly considered, it did not happen. Insufficient time was left to allow such a radical upending of tradition. Anne's first appearance as queen, over the Easter weekend, had been no random scheduling. Easter was the holiest festival of the Christian year. The second holiest was Whitsunday, the Feast of Pentecost, the day on which the Holy Spirit in the shape of a dove descended upon the Apostles on the fiftieth day after Easter, marking the founding of the Church. As Henry had already explained to de Dinteville, he was adamant that Anne be crowned then. In any case, she needed to be crowned before her pregnancy became even more embarrassingly obvious.

She would be crowned alone, but this did not mean scaling back anything of the ritual, the panoply or the public celebrations.

The climactic event of their six-year courtship and their shared endeavour, Anne's coronation would mark a rite of passage to their future and their love. But it was also a bargain. Henry was fulfilling his promise, giving Anne all that she wanted, and in return she would give him not just the love he wanted and the love he felt he needed, but also the legitimate son and heir who would assure the succession. In that critical respect, their relationship would turn out to be deeply transactional.

20

Anne's Triumph

While Cranmer's court in Dunstable was still deliberating, letters arrived from Greenwich for Sir Stephen Peacock proclaiming that Henry wished his 'most dear and well-beloved wife Queen Anne' to be crowned in Westminster Abbey on 'the Whitsunday next ensuing' (1 June). With barely more than a fortnight to go, the Londoners were to organise a spectacular river pageant for her as she travelled along the Thames to the refurbished royal lodgings in the Tower, then 'order and garnish' the city streets with pageants or tableaux for her triumphal procession on her way towards the Abbey. A committee, including the chronicler Edward Hall, quickly offered to provide at least three of these shows. Hoping to share the burden, they resolved to ask Anne's uncle, the Duke of Norfolk, whether the German Hanseatic merchants or other foreign guilds might contribute some of the rest, and 'Mr Cromwell' whether the City could borrow 'some workmen out of the king's works ... because the time is very short as painters and other', and if Henry himself would lend them his minstrels for the day.[1]

Anne was determined that everyone who mattered should attend. Families found themselves divided. Thomas More's conscience would not allow him to attend the coronation of a queen he believed to be living in adultery, nor – like his friend John Fisher – did he believe that Henry could be Supreme Head of the English Church or that Parliament had the power to block appeals to Rome. His wife Alice did not share his opinions, fully aware that moral principles did not pay the bills or feed the family; nor did his brother-in-law, John Rastell, who joined the reformers and entered Cromwell's service. One of More's sons-in-law, Giles Allington, a friend of Sir Thomas Cheyne, went so far as to accept the role of cupbearer at Anne's coronation banquet.[2]

Anne would have all the traditional pomp and circumstance stipulated by the *Liber Regalis* (the manuscript textbook for the coronation service, compiled in 1308 and kept at Westminster Abbey) and the so-called 'Royal Book' (a collection of precedents, ordinances and notes compiled over many years) which laid down protocol for all manner of royal occasions, such as coronations, funerals, the birth and christening of children and ceremonial parades. In interpreting these rituals, no detail was too small. Her costume was meticulously prescribed. For the procession through London's streets, she needed a 'kirtle' (bodice and skirt), surcoat and mantle of white cloth of gold or tissue furred with ermine, with silk and gold fringes and tassels for the mantle. She should wear a gold coif 'garnished with precious stones' on her head. For the coronation, she needed robes of purple velvet furred with ermine. A 'rich crown and a sceptre of gold' were obligatory. She was to process to and from Westminster Hall to the high altar of the Abbey and back on a 'ray cloth' (an expensive blue velvet fabric on which the king or queen walked barefoot). Her coronation chair was to be dressed in cloth of gold and cushions. She was to be 'houselled' (receive the sacrament) during the ceremony, and afterwards 'to have a secret refection [private meal] of such meat as she likes best'. A hidden 'stage' (alcove or closet) was to be 'made, latticed and covered with rich cloths', for Henry to watch unobserved if he wished, with a similar arrangement in Westminster Hall for the banquet.[3]

Anne, however, would enjoy more than the Royal Book prescribed. Her celebrations were to last for five days rather than the customary three for a queen crowned alone. They were to begin with the glittering river flotilla, followed by the creation of new Knights of the Bath, the entry into London, the coronation and banquet, culminating with jousting in the tiltyard. According to unverified Milanese costings, the total expenditure ran to 300,000 gold ducats (£65,000, or over £65 million in modern values) of which the Londoners had to fund two-thirds. Just two payments made 'for stuff' delivered to the Great Wardrobe included £203 for silk and £1,131 (worth over £1.2 million today) to John Malt, another of Henry's tailors, who was put to work making Anne's robes.[4]

Almost invariably, Anne's biographers claim that it was she who had demanded the more elaborate and costly festivities, but more likely this was a doting Henry. To begin with, the arrangements for the river procession closely replicated those arranged for Elizabeth of York.[5] Far more than just a public recognition of Anne's new status, they marked a tangible link between Henry's beloved wife and his adored mother.[6]

Henry commissioned a new crown for Anne, almost certainly the unspecified item in the royal accounts for which he paid Cornelius Hayes £300.[7] Amongst the surviving Milanese state papers is a much-cited account of Henry sending a messenger for Katherine's crown: its keeper, one 'Master Sadocho', bravely refused to hand it over. Summoned by an angry Henry, Sadocho is reported to have thrown his hat upon the ground, vowing that 'he would suffer his head to lay where his cap did' rather than surrender the crown. Colourful though it is, this story is more likely to be apocryphal and Henry had a new crown made to reflect a new beginning.[8]

Anne did not wear Katherine's crown but she did commandeer her barge. Chapuys, incredulous at such effrontery, exploded to Charles that the queen's arms 'had been removed ... and rather ignominiously torn off and cut to pieces', so that Anne's could replace them. 'God grant that she may be satisfied with the barge, the jewels and the queen's husband without attempting anything ... against the persons of the queen and princess,' he continued dryly. Rather like Henry VII's name and badges overwriting Richard III's after the Battle of Bosworth, Anne's coronation would overwrite Katherine's.[9]

With all these preparations complete, the river flotilla began in glorious weather at 1 p.m. on Thursday 29 May, when Peacock and his aldermen, dressed in scarlet and with their golden chains of office gleaming on their breasts, gathered at St Mary's Hill in the ward of Billingsgate ready to embark. The city's contingent of fifty or so barges were ablaze with colour, strewn with flowers and richly decorated with bells, pennants, flags, escutcheons and Henry and Anne's heraldic arms. One vessel, the famous *Bachelor's Barge*, made its reappearance. It had stolen the show in Elizabeth of York's river procession, when it carried on its deck a great red mechanical dragon which, primed with gunpowder, 'spouted flames of fire into [the] Thames'. Now it did so again, except this time it was surrounded by 'terrible monsters and wild men casting fire and making hideous noises'. Well out of range of the gunpowder, the Lord Mayor's barge, rowing against the tide, kept abreast of a musicians' barge and another bearing a 'mount' with a golden stump of rootstock from which red and white roses grew, capped by Anne's white falcon device wearing a closed or 'imperial' crown. This element of the heraldry, the use of a crown with enclosing arches rather than a simple circlet, was an important piece of symbolism as such crowns were emblems of imperial status and hence the kind of political independence from the papacy that Henry was asserting with this coronation.[10]

Once the barges reached Greenwich, they turned around skilfully and cast anchor so that they could leave in reverse order, joined by dozens of other vessels decked out just as brightly. Altogether, there were about 320, so many that the Thames became alive with colour, noise and 'minstrels continually playing'. At about 3 p.m., Anne, shimmering from head to toe in white cloth of gold, stepped onto what was now her barge. It was her first big state occasion. She revelled in the attention, and never once showed signs of nerves: her stage presence was obvious to all. Other barges carried her ladies and the most important nobles and bishops, notably her father and the Duke of Suffolk. Henry sailed in his own barge but stayed deliberately low-key, letting the focus stay on Anne. According to Cranmer, he 'came always before her secretly in a barge, as well from Greenwich to the Tower, as from the Tower to Westminster'. Anne's brother George was nowhere to be seen: he had already left for Calais with her uncle Norfolk and cousin, Sir Francis Bryan, on a fresh embassy to observe the Franco-papal conference planned for Nice. He would be away for almost two months.[11]

As the oarsmen now rowed with the tide, the return journey took only half an hour. Cannon thundered out a salute as they passed Wapping and approached Tower Wharf. Sir William Kingston, the Constable of the Tower and the recipient of strict instructions to keep a vacant landing space for Anne's barge, assisted her ashore. Henry, who had hurried on ahead so that he could greet his wife with a kiss, then formally received her, after which she entered the hallowed precincts by a freshly constructed timber bridge over the moat at the eastern end of the wharf, leading to her privy garden in the innermost ward, where she was lost to view.[12]

On Friday came the investiture of eighteen new Knights of the Bath. The ceremony, which by tradition the queen did not attend, began after dinner, when those chosen – among them Francis Weston and Henry Parker, George Boleyn's brother-in-law – observed the age-old rituals. These began with a ceremonial bath, followed by an all-night vigil, confession and attendance at Mass, after which the knights were dubbed by the king early on Saturday morning.[13]

Anne's triumphal procession on Saturday afternoon was the first since Charles and Henry's in 1522; it promised to be a wonderful day out.[14] Just in case anyone became over-excited, velvet-clad constables with staves were enlisted to keep order, and the artisans and apprentices were confined to one side of the freshly gravelled streets to allow the scarlet-clad aldermen and members of the livery companies to occupy the other. Few would be disappointed, even if Chapuys described the day sneeringly as a 'cold, meagre and uncomfortable thing, to the great dissatisfaction not only of common people, but also of the rest'. But then he had described the previous day's river parade similarly: 'the said triumph', he said, 'consisted entirely in the multitude of those who took part in it, but all the people showed themselves as sorry as though it had been a funeral.'[15]

The procession left the Tower at about 5 p.m., as soon as Peacock was certain that all was ready. It was to end some three hours later at Westminster Hall, where wine and a light supper would be served to the queen.[16] Significantly, the long cavalcade was led by twelve Frenchmen in the service of Jean de Dinteville. Each man wore a livery of dark blue velvet with yellow and blue sleeves, with white ostrich plumes in their hats. On this most English of days, Anne was determined to proclaim herself a Francophile. To ensure these specially tailored liveries were the best that money could buy, Francis sent de Dinteville 500 gold crowns of the sun to pay for them.[17]

Next came the judges in their scarlet robes, who had arrived late but were squeezed into the line just before the new Knights of the Bath. Close behind were nobles and leading churchmen, including Cranmer, followed by de Dinteville himself and Carlo Capelli, the Venetian ambassador, splendidly robed. Chapuys, predictably, did not attend. A phalanx of councillors and lesser courtiers came next. It was like a 'Who's Who' of Henry's England. Suffolk, appointed as Lord High Constable solely for the day and willing to play a supervisory role in the proceedings whatever his private feelings, was in his element. In one respect, the pressure he felt to avoid contact with Anne was reduced, as his own wife, Henry's sister, who loathed Anne more than he did, was mortally ill and would die before the month's end after appealing, in vain, for her brother to see her one last time.

Finally came the woman the Londoners itched to see close-up for themselves. Her cushioned open litter was covered in white cloth of tissue, her mules were trapped in white damask. While she chose to dress as far as possible in the French fashion, much of what she should wear and how she should appear was already laid down in the Royal Book. Beneath her gold coif her dark brown hair, left loose and virginal, cascaded down her back. Again, as the Royal Book instructed, a canopy of cloth of gold was held over her head, carried by the four barons of the Cinque Ports, the four golden staves supporting it garnished with little silver bells.[18]

By loaning the city a small army of royal carpenters, painters and musicians and by conscripting the support of the Hanseatic merchants, Norfolk and Cromwell had ensured a full programme of six tableaux and fully developed pageants.[19] For the pageants, Peacock had recruited two notable scriptwriters, John Leland and Nicholas Udall. Their brief was to maintain tradition, but also, for the first time in a Tudor coronation event, to exploit the classical tropes of the Italian and French Renaissance to reshape the image of a queen to fit Anne's personal taste.[20]

Not all the pageants would be classical in their imagery: there had simply not been sufficient time to prepare more than three of those. The rest had to be largely recycled versions of traditional displays for which the scenery and costumes already existed. The first of these, beside Leadenhall, featured a mechanical device like the one used during Queen Claude's coronation festivities. Starring an actor playing St Anne, the Virgin's mother, the setting was a castle with a heavenly ceiling. Within it sat St Anne with her children and grandchildren, and the underlying message was that by emulating her, Anne would assure the succession and nurture the true Christian faith. As her litter passed by, a replica of a white falcon swooped down on a wire and alighted on a rootstock 'whereout sprang a multitude of white and red roses curiously wrought'. A clockwork angel then descended on another wire, clutching a crown which it placed on the falcon's head.[21]

At St Paul's Gate, chorister-actors representing three holy virgins, 'rich clothed', sat beneath 'a fair round throne' clutching 'tablets' (or placards), one of which bore a closed crown held by angels and the legend 'Veni amica coronaberis' ('Come my love, thou shalt be crowned'), a line borrowed from the ancient mystery play of *The Coronation of the Virgin*, annually performed as part of the Londoners' usual Corpus Christi cycle of plays. What was new was that Leland and Udall substantially rewrote the fifteenth-century script to link Anne to the classical Greek goddess Astraea – the 'Just Virgin' – as well as to Mariology. It was Astraea's return to earth, as the Roman poets Virgil had predicted in his fourth Eclogue and Ovid in his *Metamorphoses*, that would lead to the birth of a child and herald the start of a new Golden Age.[22]

The three newly devised classical displays would be very much a contrast, although their ultimate meaning was similar. The first, and most spectacular, staged by the Hanseatic merchants at the corner of Gracechurch Street, was a depiction of Mount Parnassus with the fountain of Helicon in its midst. Fashioned of white marble, the fountain gushed from midday to dusk with free wine for the citizens to enjoy. On each side of the stage stood a tall, baroque column, surmounted by heraldic arms and an imperial crown. Apollo with his lyre presided on the Mount, seated in an arched arbour on top of which a white falcon perched.[23] Around him the nine Muses played sweet music and displayed verses written in golden letters praising the new queen. Once more, the central motif would be Anne's future role as a mother. Already six months pregnant, she would be the citizens' security since her child would be a son. All this became clear when each of the Muses addressed verses to Anne.[24] Described by Hall as 'costly' and 'marvellous cunning', the set was designed by Holbein, who had already painted or drawn several of the German merchants' portraits.[25]

Other classically inspired pageants were in Cornhill and at the west end of Cheapside. In the first, Leland and Udall recast the daughters of Zeus – Aglaia (beauty), Thalia (abundance) and Euphrosyne (mirth), worshipped in ancient Greece as the 'Three Graces' – in the roles of 'Hearty Gladness', 'Stable Honour' and 'Continual Success'. Sitting together on a gilded throne behind a fountain described as a 'spring of grace' which also flowed with wine, they vowed to bestow on Anne their talents and qualities.[26]

In Cheapside, Anne watched a pageant which Hall described as 'full of melody and song' on the theme of the Judgment of Paris, history's first recorded beauty contest. Udall wrote the script, which required Paris, at Jupiter's command, to adjudicate between the conflicting claims of the goddesses Juno, Pallas and Venus. Seeking to give an honest verdict, Paris concludes that Venus deserves the prize of a golden apple, until – in a startling deviation from the usual story – he suddenly sees Anne. Addressing her directly, he declares she is 'as peerless in riches, wit and beauty' as the others, but comes with a 'worthiness' too, rooted in her fertility.[27] For her awaits a far greater prize. As a child narrator explains:

> For you is ready a Crown Imperial,
> To your joy, honour, and glory immortal.

As Anne's procession left the City of London, they passed the last of the displays, another of those which recycled existing material. At the Conduit (public water fountain) in Fleet Street, a troupe of actors reused a script first performed in 1377 for Richard II's coronation. Masons had transformed the site into a celestial castle with four turrets. Each turret contained an actor representing one of the four cardinal Virtues (prudence, justice, fortitude and temperance), whose message was that with Anne as Henry's queen, London – indeed all England – had become the New Jerusalem, or Paradise on earth.[28]

By the time they trudged home, the Londoners had plenty to talk about. Not everything had quite gone according to plan: some of the onlookers burst out laughing when they caught sight of the couple's new cipher 'HA' emblazoned everywhere – crying 'Ha, ha, ha!' as Anne passed by. Others refused to cry 'God save the Queen' or take off their caps, provoking Anne's woman fool to retort that they 'must all have scurvy heads and dare not show them'. Anne's Francophilia was a significant factor as well as popular support for Katherine: it was said the crowds greeted Jean de Dinteville and his liveried Frenchmen at the head of the procession with a volley of insults, such as 'Whoreson knave' and 'French dog'.[29]

Shortly before 7 a.m. the following day, Whitsunday itself, Peacock and his colleagues left the City by barge and were rowed to the narrow wharf at Westminster Stairs with another full day ahead of them. Between eight and nine o'clock, Anne made her entrance into the upper end of the Hall, where she sat on a marble throne while final preparations were made for her walk to the Abbey.[30] Clad in her purple coronation robes and wearing her gold coif and jewelled circlet on her head, she seemed like a vision. Never had she loved life so much.

Arrayed in the centre of the Hall were the abbey's Benedictine monks in their golden copes, with everyone of importance at Henry's court, in Parliament, the Church or the City (except those dissenters like More, Fisher and the Duke of Norfolk's estranged wife, Elizabeth Stafford, who refused to appear). Anyone whom Henry had personally invited knew their attendance that weekend was obligatory despite the daunting cost – Anne Brooke, Lady Cobham, the wife of the Boleyns' Kentish neighbour George, now 9th Lord Cobham, for example, was ordered to source white or grey palfreys for herself and her ladies and to purchase their robes. Only her own apparel was provided by the Great Wardrobe.[31] Among the few to dare to send written apologies was Sir William Courtenay of Powderham, the Marquis of Exeter's cousin. In a letter to Cromwell, he asked to be excused, claiming he was unable to ride 'without great pain' following a fall from his horse.[32]

As Anne began her walk from the Hall along the uneven path towards the west door of the Abbey, she was preceded by servants stepping backwards to unroll the ray cloth in front of her. They continued to do so as she proceeded up the nave and into the sanctuary until she reached St Edward the Confessor's shrine and the high altar. Over her head, the barons of the Cinque Ports held their golden canopy, as on the previous day. Before her in the procession were the monks, followed by the mitred bishops and archbishops in their pontifical vestments, the nobles in their Parliament robes, and behind them the Earl of Oxford carrying St Edward's crown, the Marquis of Dorset with the golden sceptre and the Earl of Arundel holding the ivory rod. The Duke of Suffolk, today acting as High Steward and bearing his long white staff of office in his hand, took care to make himself especially visible to the watching crowds, as did a proud Thomas Boleyn, who took his place with the other earls.[33]

In a letter to a friend, Cranmer says how he 'received the queen apparelled in a robe of purple velvet, and all the ladies and gentlewomen in robes and gowns of scarlet according to the manner used before time in such business' and how he 'did set the crown on her head ... upon a scaffold [stage] which was made between the high altar and the choir'.[34] De Dinteville amplifies this. From his place near the front, he saw that, when Anne was to be crowned, she mounted a platform covered with red cloth set up on the famous Cosmati pavement in front of the high altar and sat in a chair which was further raised by two steps.[35] Notes by heralds from the College of Arms add that

> she was sat in a rich chair, and after that she had rested a while she descended down to the high altar and there prostrated herself while [Cranmer] said certain collects over her; then she rose and the [arch]bishop anointed her on the head and on the breast, and then she was led up again to her chair where, after divers orisons [prayers] said, the archbishop set the crown of St Edward on her head and then delivered her the sceptre of gold in her right hand and the rod of ivory with the dove in the left hand.[36]

Crowned and twice anointed with holy oil and chrism, Anne was now every inch a queen. No longer was she a commoner. The dramatic novelty was that she was crowned in St Edward's chair with St Edward's crown. A recently discovered manuscript compiled by one of Henry's chamber officials, later owned by John Anstis, an early eighteenth-century bibliophile, records that St Edward's chair – the sovereign's special coronation chair – was indeed one of two fetched from the Abbey's treasury for Anne's coronation, for which a covering of 'cloth of gold baudekin' (the finest of all silks embroidered with solid gold thread) was to be provided.[37] This was the chair reserved for kings, just as St Edward's crown was reserved for the crowning of kings, not consorts. It is true that while choristers sang a glorious *Te Deum*, Cranmer 'took off the crown of St Edward being heavy' from Anne's head 'and set on her head the crown made for her'. But that was a purely practical arrangement on account of its weight. In no way did it diminish the significance of the use of St Edward's crown for the actual moment of coronation.[38]

The coronation Mass then began, during which Anne made her offering and afterwards knelt to receive the sacrament. When the Mass was finished, she made a second offering at St Edward's shrine, then slipped inside a 'traverse' (partitioned space behind a curtain) in a side-aisle for refreshments.[39] When she emerged to process back to Westminster Hall, she seems to have been briefly overcome by the flood of emotions she must have felt during the four-hour ceremony, since 'her right hand was sustained by her father, the Earl of Wiltshire.' On reaching the Hall, a fanfare of sackbuts and trumpets burst out 'marvellous freshly', and she retired to her withdrawing chamber to prepare herself for the banquet.[40]

After a short respite, she was out on show again. For this most special event the windows of the Hall had been freshly glazed and the walls hung with 'rich cloth of Arras' (tapestries interwoven with gold or silver thread). There, beneath the magnificent fourteenth-century oak hammerbeam roof and carved angels, Anne presided at her own table on a dais, a golden cloth of estate above her head, the platform twelve steps high and railed off from the four long tables in the main body of the Hall where everyone else would eat. At one of these tables sat the women of the court, at another were the nobles with the bishops and Lord Chancellor Audley, at the third the barons of the Cinque Ports with the judges and legal officials, and at the fourth Peacock and the London aldermen, all grouped by rank and office.

Anne ate alone apart from Cranmer, who was seated at the same table but kept at a respectful distance. The Earl of Oxford directed the servers and other leading nobles played their part: the Earl of Essex was named as carver, the newly created Earl of Sussex as sewer (royal taster), the Earl of Arundel as chief butler, and so on. Two evangelical Londoners, Robert Packington and George Tadlowe, assisted Arundel. On standby closest to Anne's chair stood her friend Elizabeth Browne holding a fine cloth, ready to shield her face 'when she list to spit or do otherwise at her pleasure'. Maybe sweetest of all for Anne, her old suitor, Thomas Wyatt, was obliged to deputise for his sick father as her chief ewerer for the day, holding up a large golden dish of clean water for her to wash her fingers and dab her face with a linen napkin.[41]

The food was more than plentiful: course followed course, trumpets sounding as each was brought in. Sir Stephen Peacock was offered thirty-three dishes: Anne had twenty-four to choose from for her second course and thirty for her third. From a gallery above the Hall, Henry's minstrels played gentle serenades while the Duke of Suffolk, still in his supervisory role, rode around the Hall on his horse, 'gorgeously accoutred' in crimson velvet with a doublet glistening with pearls, to check that all was as it should be.[42]

The climax came when Garter King of Arms led his fellow heralds into the Hall. Crying out 'Largesse, largesse', they threw coins towards the guests, just as Anne remembered from Queen Claude's coronation banquet in the Palais-Royal. Unseen by anyone, Henry kept a close eye on everything from a hidden alcove cut through into the Hall from the upper level of the adjacent cloisters high up on the right-hand side of where Anne sat under her cloth of estate. With him were de Dinteville and Carlo Capelli.[43]

Finally, as dusk fell and the banquet drew to its close, spices, marzipan and other delicacies were served with sweet white wine. Anne drank no more than a sip from a golden cup handed to her by Peacock – his final duty, but one very much worth his while, since after lowering the cup from her lips, she presented it to him as a gift. She then withdrew to change her clothes, leaving shortly afterwards by barge for nearby Whitehall to spend the night with Henry.[44]

After the day of the coronation itself, Monday's jousts were hardly exciting, arousing little other than polite comment. De Dinteville paid them slightly more attention. As he informed the Duke de Montmorency, they were between teams of eight against eight, the challengers led by Lord William Howard, the answerers by Nicholas Carew. Notes compiled by the heralds say, 'there were very few spears broken.'[45] It hardly mattered: no one now could deny that Anne was queen, and in Henry's eyes and hers, likely to remain so for the rest of their lives.

Except that once they were king and queen, Henry and Anne had to perform their lives on the public stage in a way she at least may not have fully imagined. No longer living in the twilight world of an illicit courtship, they had embarked on a drama of their own making, gambling on success in what would fast develop into an international poker game. Each had their own expectations, but the greatest for both was the one signalled by Leland and Udall in their pageant scripts. No longer was it Henry who was to be England's 'deliverer': it was to be Anne in the shape of the son whom she must now safely bear. His birth would mark the beginning of the new Golden Age: it was as if Henry was an eighteen-year-old again.

21

The Ambassadors

The three months after the coronation were the high-water mark of Henry and Anne's marriage. Returning in the royal barge to Greenwich, they loitered there until early July, before beginning a leisurely honeymoon tour of Surrey.[1] In these halcyon weeks, Henry believed nothing was too good for his wife. When she demanded a cloth of estate for her throne-room as large and costly as his, he instantly ordered it. If she needed more furniture for her privy chamber, he sent her chairs upholstered in cloth of gold, with gilt and enamel pommels. When she asked him for fine small Turkish carpets to line the shelves of her cupboards and for velvet to reupholster her elevated pew in the Chapel Royal, he swiftly provided them. He had her initials and arms engraved alongside his upon the royal plate and the deluxe bindings of books in the royal library.[2] She wore Katherine's jewels at every opportunity. And although Henry had already made her wealthy as Marquis of Pembroke in her own right, he began stripping Katherine of her lands and granting them to Anne, so that she came to possess houses, manors, castles, deer parks, hunting grounds and woodlands scattered all around the country.[3]

Katherine was now the past, a position bluntly spelt out to her when a second delegation of Henry's councillors visited her in Ampthill. Coughing, ill, suffering acute pain in her foot caused when she had accidentally stepped on a pin, Katherine received them lying on a low pallet bed. She listened intently as they informed her that she must never more call herself queen. Henceforth, as officially nothing more than Arthur's widow, she was to be known only as 'the Princess Dowager' just as Henry had previously demanded.

If the councillors thought Katherine too weak to respond, they underestimated her. Gathering her strength, she demanded to read the king's instructions. After perusing them, she defiantly scored out every reference to 'Princess Dowager'. She was not that, she snapped: she would be Henry's wife until she drew her last breath. Indeed, she had already ordered new liveries for all her servants bearing the letters 'H' and 'K'. All the same, Henry had her evicted from Ampthill and taken to Buckden Place in Huntingdonshire, bordering the flood plain of the Great Ouse, which she loathed. After a year, she would move, voluntarily, to Kimbolton Castle, seven miles away, a property Henry had granted to Sir Richard Wingfield and which his widow, Bridget Wilshire, had vacated on marrying Sir Nicholas Harvey. There, guarded by two gentlemen on whose loyalty the king could rely, she spoke mainly Spanish, would acknowledge nobody who did not call her queen and shut herself away, only venturing out to stroll in her private garden.[4]

Anne was supremely confident that her and Henry's pro-French diplomacy would triumph and was thrilled to receive congratulations on her marriage and pregnancy from Marguerite of Angoulême. Relayed by Jean de Dinteville, they arrived in a letter sent from Paris on 22 June. 'Please take pains', Marguerite urged the ambassador, 'to give my humble good wishes to the good grace of the Queen of England. I was wonderfully glad to hear of her good news from the lords of Norfolk and Rochford.'[5] Marguerite wanted to write because she was, she explained, in the later stages of pregnancy herself, which would prevent her attending the forthcoming conference in Nice.[6] To boost Anne's morale further, Francis sent her a fresh clutch of expensive gifts. They included copious supplies of velvet, silk sheets and fine embroidered coverlets, and a magnificent litter of a bespoke design used for pregnant women in France, borne by three mules, which he also supplied. Chapuys watched it arrive in the last week of June, along with saddles, bridles and accoutrements for the mules. Thrilled with the gift, Anne immediately tried it out, taking it for a three-mile ride.[7]

With the Anglo-French alliance seeming so strong, Anne believed it would not be long before Clement would cease all talk of Henry's 'great matter', which could be quietly forgotten. Through de Dinteville, Francis was sharing with her and Henry the latest dispatches Gabriel de Gramont and François de Tournon sent him from Rome. Charles's agents, however, were now demanding Henry's excommunication.[8] At first, it looked as if the French would triumph. As a Mantuan diplomat reported, 'Neither his Holiness nor the Sacred College assent [to the excommunication], so as not to multiply the scandal,' but by the end of June things had changed and it seemed there was no way for Henry to avoid censure. Hearing this, Anne accused Gregorio Casali of treachery, and Henry – never able to resist punishing those who refused to give his new wife what she wanted – dismissed him. Before doing so, he ordered him to warn Clement that, should he dare to sanction him, Henry would appeal to a future General Council of the Church.

As Anne read the international scene, the Anglo-French alliance was unstoppable. But what she and Henry had still not grasped was how far Francis was playing them to win English support – and cash subsidies – for another round of Italian adventures. Francis would do his best to help them in Rome – he genuinely believed Clement had treated Henry shabbily – but his prime ambition was to recover the Duchy of Milan where Charles was about to install Francesco Sforza as a Habsburg puppet. He also meant to marry, and not simply betroth, the Duke of Orléans to the pope's niece during the forthcoming Franco-papal conference – without warning Henry.[9]

Back in London, de Dinteville sympathised with Henry and Anne, but his approach was more guarded than they believed it to be. The ambassador had strong evangelical instincts: critical of the bureaucracy and corruption of the Roman Church, he was a Lefèvrist at heart, but like his diplomatic predecessors Jean du

Bellay and Gilles de la Pommeraye, his patron was the morally conservative Duke de Montmorency, Grand Master of France. The Duke, who was de Dinteville's kinsman and addressed him consistently as 'mon cousin', was not prepared to jeopardise France's relations with Rome by accommodating Anne any more than was strictly necessary. Both he and de Dinteville feared an onslaught of the Lutheran heresy in England, and potentially in France, if the Boleyns had their way. De Dinteville's latest instructions, issued by Montmorency, were to urge Henry to rest his hopes on the interview in Nice while himself liaising closely on all matters with the Duke of Norfolk, with whom he was to share intelligence and seek advice. Both Montmorency and de Dinteville feared that, under the spell of the Boleyns, Henry would ask Francis to join him in breaking with Rome.[10]

De Dinteville shared his apprehensions with his brother and fellow Lefèvrist, François, the resident French ambassador to the Vatican. Both believed that by taking steps which increasingly threatened schism, Henry disqualified himself as a credible, constructive critic of the papacy and advocate of the kind of Church reform that the French evangelical party favoured. 'Did you not tell me', de Dinteville asked François, clutching at straws, 'that some time ago you said to the ambassadors of this king [Henry] that you had heard the pope say that, where this king's "great matter" is concerned, it would be better for everyone if he just went ahead and married her?' 'If this was so', he continued, 'it is a thing which would serve [Henry] splendidly.' He might claim that in marrying Anne he had acted on Clement's own advice, privately tendered beforehand.[11]

More indirectly, de Dinteville voiced his concerns by commissioning Holbein to paint what is one of the sixteenth century's most famous and enigmatic masterpieces. *The Ambassadors* is ostensibly no more than a sumptuous snapshot of a brief reunion between de Dinteville and his good friend Georges de Selve, Bishop of Lavaur and another Lefèvrist, after Francis sent de Selve to London on an errand. However, powerful evidence exists to suggest it is, in considerable part, a visceral political commentary on the catastrophe de Dinteville (and by association Montmorency) envisaged for Christendom and France if the Boleyns were to be successful in persuading Francis to join Henry in repudiating the pope.

Letters in the Bibliothèque Nationale in Paris explain that de Selve, who had reached London sometime between late February and Easter and who left shortly before Anne's coronation in June, only came because Francis asked him to convey a secret message to de Dinteville, one Montmorency should not know about.[12] Usually, the message (of which no copy survives) is said to concern Anne's public recognition. More likely, however, is that the message renewed, but more emphatically, an urgent request Francis had made some weeks earlier, that Henry should personally attend the talks in Nice, so that the two kings together 'may conclude all these great affairs'. The last thing Francis wanted was a rupture between his English ally and Rome, but unlike Montmorency, he believed the best way to avert that was by face-to-face talks with Clement with Henry present. Montmorency, for his part, wanted only his ally the Duke of Norfolk to attend.[13]

The painting relates to Anne in several singular respects. One is signalled by the floor on which de Dinteville and de Selve stand. This turns out to be an almost exact replication of the very spot on the unique Cosmati pavement in front of the high altar at Westminster Abbey where she was to be crowned. On the shelves of the buffet between the two men, meanwhile, are numerous objects with symbolic value. The cylindrical pillar dial (a portable form of solar clock), positioned beside the celestial globe towards the left of the upper shelf on which the two friends rest their arms, is set to a date between 10 and 15 April 1533, the Easter festival during which Anne first processed to Chapel with full royal honours.[14] The celestial globe is set to indicate the terrestrial latitude of 42°N, which, according to contemporary computations, was the latitude of Rome, where at the time of the painting Clement anxiously awaited news of the verdict of the Dunstable court.[15]

On the lower shelf, a partially open book, bound in red leather and placed in front of a terrestrial globe which is ingeniously customised to show de Dinteville's home of Polisy, reproduces a page from the second printing of a popular German arithmetic manual known for short as *Kauffmans Rechnung* ('A Merchant's Calculator' or 'Book of Reckoning'). When viewed using high-resolution photography, the image of the page, which in the book follows sections on addition, subtraction and multiplication, is selected from one dealing with division and begins with the word 'Dividirt' ('Divide').[16]

To the right is a lute, which cannot be played because it has a broken string. It represents some sort of harmony which has been disrupted: almost everyone who has written on *The Ambassadors* refers to the Italian Andrea Alciati's *Emblemata*, published in 1531, which compares the maintaining of an alliance to the keeping in tune of a lute, where the author remarks how easy it is to break a string. Lying diagonally beside the lute at the extreme right of the shelf is a set of wooden flutes of differing diameters and pitches in a leather case. Very few people have noticed that one is missing from the set, so if handed to players, the consort would be broken too.[17]

In front of the lute, another book shows pages from Johann Walther's *Geystliche Gesangk buchleyn* ('Holy Hymnbook'), first published in 1524. Luther was its co-author, choosing the words set to the music. Two hymns, taken from the first edition of the tenor part-book, are depicted on facing pages, clearly selected and paired for very specific reasons as they are not consecutive in this or any of the later editions, nor are they numbered as illustrated.[18] On the left is the *Veni Sancte Spiritus* ('Come Holy Ghost'), the invocation for the Feast of Pentecost, the day on which Anne was crowned; on the right is Luther's shortened version of the 'Ten Commandments'. As works common to both Catholic and Protestant faiths, they form the starting point for a debate whereby religious divisions might be healed and a schism in Christendom perhaps averted.[19]

Although some commentators credit *The Ambassadors* with being one of the first secular paintings of Henry VIII's England, this is belied by the distorted, anamorphic skull towards the bottom and a silver crucifix hidden in the extreme top-left. Badges linked to this iconography were commonly worn as warnings against vanity and pride, and in the painting de Dinteville has a small silver badge bearing a skull pinned to his hat. The form of distortion used to conceal the larger skull, known as slant anamorphosis, was familiar to artists from Leonardo da Vinci's time onwards: the images are restored to normal proportions when viewed sideways, or in some cases through a telescopic device attached to one side of the frame.[20] In combination with the skull, the crucifix – which peeps out at a right angle from the side of the green backcloth – interrogates sin and worldly ambition and offers true faith as the remedy. Taking everything together, this iconography surely suggests how far de Dinteville considered Henry and Anne's threat to break with Rome (and involve France if they could) to be a monumental blunder from which the peace and security of a united Christendom might never recover: only the ambassadors themselves offered a chance of holding everything together.

With high summer fast approaching, the date for Francis's conference with the pope was postponed to September, and then again to October. Clement intended to travel by sea, but first Montmorency, in whose galleys he would sail, had to drive away Turkish pirates from the Italian coast. The venue was changed to Marseille after the Duke of Savoy, in fear of Charles, issued exaggerated reports of plague in Nice.

With Anne's *accouchement* expected for early September, Henry's anxieties sharply focused his mind. On 14 June, he gave Norfolk, then kicking his heels in Amiens, revised instructions: he was to lead his delegation to Paris and from there to the French court, where he was to dissuade Francis 'shortly and briefly' from meeting the pope at all. If Francis persisted, Norfolk was to ask him not to make any terms with Clement before Henry's divorce had been settled. Should Norfolk, on arrival in Marseille, find that Clement tried to speak to him directly, he should explain that he had only been sent to France to visit Francis 'as a testimony of the perfect amity and friendship between us', and leave the negotiating to Francis, who was to be forcibly reminded of his treaty obligations to Henry.[21]

In Paris, Norfolk had two meetings with Marguerite of Angoulême, both lasting for 'at least five hours'. The letter in which he reported home these conversations has been horribly damaged by water and the hearty appetites of rodents. What can still be read is electric. Marguerite, he said:

> is one of the most wisest frank women, and best setter forth of her purpose that I have spoken with, and as affectionate to Your Majesty as an [if] she were your own sister, and she likewise unto the queen [Anne]. Sir, in communing with me, she said that she had divers matters of importance that she would open unto me, so that [if] I would promise her upon my truth not to disclose no part of the same, save only to Your Highness or the queen, which I promised her.

In the first instance, she warned him to beware of the Duke de Montmorency, who was leading him on. Wholly unreliable where Anne was concerned, Montmorency was pro-Habsburg and a secret adherent of Charles's sister Eleanor, now Queen of France. 'There is no nobleman in France so much imperial as the said Duke is ... she assured me I should find [him] more friendly in words than deeds, if the cause touched anything against the Emperor.' Francis was an entirely different matter and Norfolk should confide only in him. He understood Henry's predicament: his own marriage to Eleanor had proved to be a grave disappointment. According to Marguerite, the couple were temperamentally and sexually incompatible. Eleanor was 'very hot in bed'. She 'desireth to be too much embraced', greatly annoying Francis who just wanted sex.[22]

Norfolk finally caught up with Francis in Riom, the capital of the Auvergne, and afterwards in Lyon, where he and George Boleyn first heard the news that Henry and Anne most dreaded. After taking a vote in the Consistory on 11 July, Clement had censured Henry, declared his marriage to Anne invalid and ordered him to return to Katherine. Under heavy French pressure, the pope agreed to a temporary suspension of the sentence to give Henry time to comply. If the English king refused, he would be excommunicated and the country placed under an interdict. The pope's decree endorsed the use of military force and, privately, Clement talked of incentivising Francis to join Charles in a papal crusade against Henry by promising to restore Calais to France.[23]

So shocked was Norfolk that he almost fainted and the news came as a severe jolt to Francis too. Recovering his composure, the duke sent Anne's brother post-haste back home to seek fresh instructions. Completing the 600-mile journey in under a week, George saw Henry in Windsor on 28 July, and from there rode to Guildford, where the king summoned a crisis meeting of councillors for the next day. Anne's honeymoon was rudely interrupted. Henry – not yet daring to tell her the true reason – peremptorily left to join her brother on the pretext of hunting, telling his courtiers (as Chapuys heard from his spies) that he wished 'to spare her any sorrow or disappointment likely to endanger the life of her child'.[24]

No sooner was the council meeting over than Henry sent George back to France, where he and Norfolk were to try once again to persuade Francis to cancel the conference: if they failed, he and his colleagues were to boycott the event and return home. Such was Henry's anxiety, his desire to assert absolute control, that he would torpedo the diplomacy if he could, rather than risk an uncertain outcome. With that choice made, he sent envoys to Rome with orders to appeal against the papal sanctions to a General Council of the Church, which from Clement's point of view would be the ultimate insult and a point of no return.[25]

Norfolk met Francis privately in mid-August in Montpellier, where the French king refused to change his mind about meeting the pope and urged the duke to break ranks and still attend the conference, claiming that if he did, Clement would soften his tone. It was an impossible ask: Norfolk wavered for two days, but then replied that he had received express orders to return and dared not disobey them.[26]

When, on 30 August, Norfolk returned to London empty-handed, it ought to have been clear to Anne that her keystone Francophile policy needed a fundamental rethink. And yet, she saw no reason to panic or doubt the strength of her relationship with

Henry – if anything, she appeared steelier than before. According to George Taylor, now receiver-general of the jointure lands she had taken over from Katherine, the couple were 'in good health and as merry as ever I saw them in my life'.[27] Sir John Russell and Richard Page, both watching closely from the privy chamber, said the same: 'The king's highness is merry and in good health, and I never saw him merrier of a great while than he is now.'[28] Having decided to shun the conference, Henry was in denial about the threat posed by Clement's decree of excommunication, and was already saying of the pope: 'To revoke or put back anything that is done here, either in marriage, statute, sentence or proclamation ... we have, will and shall by all ways and means say "Nay" and declare our "Nay" in such sort as the world shall hear and the pope feel it.'[29]

Such was his devotion to Anne, Henry was prepared to defy Francis, Charles, the pope and the world for her. He also felt sufficiently experienced in international affairs to know that as soon as Francis felt threatened again by Charles, he would see the error of his ways and seek Henry's support. Henry still believed that he and Anne could shape events to their own advantage. And at least one good thing might come out of the meeting at Marseille, if, and when, it took place: no longer did it appear that Clement was resolved to 'live and die' an imperialist. From now on, he and Francis seemed set on collaborating to build up an anti-Habsburg alliance that would expel Charles from Italy.

But there was no time for thinking through the implications of that now. Anne found the final weeks of her pregnancy difficult, and Henry insisted that everything be made as comfortable as possible for her.[30] The *accouchement* was to be in Greenwich, where he had been born and where he and his mother had once been so happy. He wanted everything to be perfect, so he sent Anne one of his most magnificent sets of embroidered bed-hangings for her lying-in chamber, one which had once formed part of the ransom of Jean II, Duke of Alençon, who was captured in 1424 during the Hundred Years' War. In the queen's signet office, meanwhile, clerks penned dozens of circular letters, headed 'By the Queen', ready to proclaim the glad tidings 'of the deliverance and bringing forth of a prince'. So confident were the royal couple after consulting physicians and astrologers that their child would be male, the word 'prince' had already been filled in.[31]

Anne thought of one further thing herself. When Katherine had come to England, she had brought a beautifully embroidered Spanish christening robe which she had used for Princess Mary's baptism. Now Anne demanded that Henry obtain it for her child. Katherine, repelled that this even be suggested by the woman she saw as nothing more than a whore, instantly refused. Caught in the middle, Henry chose not to pursue the matter, a small but sweet victory for Katherine against the woman she believed had ruined her life.[32]

In response, Anne turned on Henry. She never cared for anyone more than for the child she was about to have, and it was logical to her that Katherine's christening robe should pass to her as the king's new wife. It was at moments like this that the jealousy, vulnerability and frustration she felt at the opposition she faced had the potential to boil over into intemperate words or petty or spiteful actions.

Just a few days after the christening robe incident, Chapuys gleefully reported a different quarrel in a dispatch to Charles. Anne, he said, had berated her husband because he looked at another woman. Resenting being taken to task, Henry rounded on her, telling her that she must shut her eyes and 'endure' as 'those who were better than herself had done' before her, reminding her that he could cast her down as quickly as he had raised her up. They then did not speak to each other for two or three days.

The dating of this episode has been questioned: supposedly, a modern editor mistakenly antedated the dispatch by a year, but since, towards its close, the recently widowed Duke of Suffolk's over-hasty marriage to his young ward, the fourteen-year-old heiress Lady Katherine Willoughby, is discussed, a misdating is unlikely. We know for sure the wedding took place in September 1533. More credible is the ambassador's final remark: 'No doubt these things are lovers' quarrels, to which we must not attach too great importance.' Certainly, the tiff did not last: one of Anne's maids would soon be reassuring Chapuys that in a much-vaunted boast, Henry had claimed that he would rather 'beg alms from door to door' than be parted from his wife, he loved her so much.[33]

By the time Anne made ready to go into labour, the tiff was forgotten. In accordance with the Royal Book and ordinances which Henry's grandmother, Margaret Beaufort, had laid down, female servants blacked out all but one of the windows of Anne's lying-in chamber, hung the walls and ceiling with blue cloth of arras (fine silk tapestry woven with gold thread) and called for the midwife. Male servants would leave food and other goods at the outermost door, but not enter, for childbirth was considered a female affair. Warm, thickly carpeted and supplied with down pillows and 'a rich altar', Anne's rooms were luxurious. They were kept dark as draughts and daylight were considered dangerous. A false roof was made and carefully lined 'for to seal' it, and carpenters were paid for 'the stapling [blocking, fastening] of divers creves [cracks and crevices] to doors and windows for keeping forth the wind'.

There were two beds for Anne, one for use during the day and as such half-throne, half-bed, surmounted by a crimson satin canopy, and the 'royal' or Alençon bed. There was even a specially erected buffet with deep shelves where Anne's gold and silver plate would be displayed. A French royal doctor later noted that 'all women are not delivered after one fashion; for some are delivered in their bed; others sitting in a chair; some standing being supported and held up by the standers by; or else leaning upon the side of a bed, table or chair; others kneeling being held up by the arms.' But the 'best and safest way' was 'in their bed', which was how Anne planned the birth.[34]

Henry waited anxiously as the days passed. Finally, after a relatively easy delivery, the longed-for child was born between 12 noon and 1 p.m. on Sunday 7 September. But, after everything that had gone into making this moment a dream, the child was a girl. Anne's circular letters had to be hastily doctored so that instead of a 'prince', a princess was proclaimed. The letters still managed to go out on the day of the birth as Anne intended. But because of lack of space between the words, the spelling had to be 'princes'. No more could be done – there was insufficient room for more than one 's'. Chapuys found it all hilarious.[35]

Henry shrugged off the disappointment. For someone who had waited so many years for a living son in wedlock after the death of Katherine's son in 1511, he was remarkably composed. Like his earlier reaction after Katherine gave birth to Princess Mary, or Francis's over Queen Claude's first two children, he took encouragement from the fact that his wife had proved she could bear a healthy baby. To him, he said, that was what mattered. He felt sure she would be pregnant again within months. He had *Te Deum* sung in St Paul's, with Sir Stephen Peacock once more on duty, and arranged a lavish christening. It is true he cancelled the two-day celebratory tournament he had originally planned – but in doing so, he merely followed royal protocol as daughters were never honoured in that way. All the same, Anne knew she needed to be vigilant. Henry might continue to protest his undying devotion, but she would need to tread carefully. That is, until she had a son.[36]

Henry personally choreographed his daughter's christening as a great show of unity, forcing Katherine's supporters to share duties with the Boleyns. The ceremony took place on Wednesday 10 September, at four o'clock in the afternoon in the Franciscan friary church in Greenwich, where Henry had himself been christened. Since tradition prevented kings from attending their children's baptisms and a newly delivered woman was forbidden by church law from entering a church until she had been ritually purified, the Duke of Norfolk presided. Jean de Dinteville was an honoured guest. The christening was performed by the new Bishop of London, John Stokesley, who named the child Elizabeth after Henry's beloved mother. Gertrude Blount, Katherine's close friend, was forced to be a godmother.[37]

Once the ceremony was over, the yeomen of the guard who lined the side-aisles lit their torches. The sudden blaze of light was the cue for a herald to cry out, 'God of his infinite goodness send prosperous life and long to the high and mighty Princess of England, Elizabeth.' The trumpets blew, after which Cranmer, another of the baby's godparents, carried her to the high altar to confirm her. Afterwards, the child was taken to her nursery where two cradles awaited her – a smaller one for everyday use and a 'cradle of estate' for when she would be shown to visitors – and the costly gifts which Anne had received were taken to the door of her lying-in chamber to be inventoried. Finally, a message arrived from Henry ordering sweet wine and comfits to be served.[38]

Meanwhile, the Franco-papal conference went ahead in October despite Henry's protests. News from Anne's cousin, Francis Bryan, whom Henry sent to Marseille with Stephen Gardiner on condition 'they never present themselves to the pope', only served to enrage him. The proceedings began, Bryan's letter solemnly recounted between copious laments over the 'evil wines' he found in the city, when Francis kissed Clement's foot and grovelled before him, after which the Duke of Orléans married Catherine de' Medici with the pope officiating, and without any resolution of Henry's affairs. After reading Bryan's dispatch, Henry crumpled it up and threw it on the floor. Stomping back and forth, he called Francis a traitor, a villain and the pope's gull. During the acrimonious exchanges that followed, he railed at Francis, who complained of Henry's ingratitude, reminding him that it was solely thanks to French lobbying in Rome that Cranmer was Archbishop of Canterbury. De Dinteville attempted to pacify Henry, turning in vain to Anne's family for support. When his health buckled under the strain, he retired to France.[39]

Henry took satisfaction only from reports of a comedy of errors in which, before Clement left Marseille in November, a young Edmund Bonner, a protégé of Cromwell who had been in Rome and had then followed the pope to France, took matters into his own hands. Barging into the pope's lodgings as Clement was starting breakfast, he harangued him while at the same time apologising in a backhanded way for his discourtesy. An hour or two later, he managed to serve the pope with notice of Henry's appeal to a General Council. Scandalised by the insult to his honoured guest, Francis had Bonner deported.[40]

Seeking to rebuild his relations with Henry once Clement had departed, Francis sent Anne's favourite diplomat, Jean du Bellay, now Bishop of Paris, back to London on a special mission. He arrived a week before Christmas and in her delight Anne greeted him in the French manner with a kiss on the cheek. With du Bellay adamant that last-minute diplomacy in Rome could still achieve a reconciliation with Clement, the festival was celebrated 'with great solemnity'. The royal couple were sleeping regularly together and Anne believed it would not be long before she was pregnant again. Henry would have a son and their dynasty would be secure. There had been many setbacks along the way, but this time she was determined everything would turn out right.[41]

22

Anne the Queen

When Henry wrote his love letters to Anne and she turned the tables on him by demanding marriage, she envisaged a mould-breaking role for herself. Unlike Katherine, she never intended to sit quietly in her own apartments sewing her husband's shirts. As early as December 1530, she hired a shirt maker.[1] She was not prepared to while away her time in her privy chamber, to be paraded on state occasions or to be a gentle feminine presence, a foil to her husband's masculinity. She it was who, with the help of her family, had destroyed Wolsey and propelled Henry into breaking with the pope. Now she wanted to set herself apart from her predecessors, to associate herself with everything new and to exercise power on her own account. Passionate about religion, education and poor relief,* she wanted to change England.

Given her addiction to all things French, Anne harboured revolutionary ideas about courtly protocol. Unlike Katherine, who had excluded men from her privy chamber apart from her own officers or relatives, she allowed the sexes to intermingle relatively freely. The risk was that mixed-sex gatherings were prey to accusations of misconduct: Anne would need to keep a strict eye to restrain gossiping or flirting.[2]

*See also below, pp. 319–24, 345–9.

We can identify most of Anne's women. No official rosters survive, but the original, handwritten version of the New Year's gift roll for 1534 lists not only the gifts, the names of the donors and their relative values, but also blocks together groups of donors and recipients. And it does so in formats which enable us to go part of the way to separating out those serving Anne, some as ladies-in-waiting, some as gentlewomen, some in wages, some not, from those attending court largely in a ceremonial capacity.[3]

After his honeymoon tour of Surrey, Henry transferred his niece, the eighteen-year-old Lady Margaret Douglas, from Princess Mary's household to Anne's. She was the daughter of his sister, Margaret, by her second husband, Archibald Douglas, Earl of Angus, whom she had married after being widowed by the death of James IV of Scotland at the Battle of Flodden.[4] As Francis heard in March 1534, the king treated his niece like a daughter: 'He holds her in the highest esteem and keeps her in the care of the queen, his wife.'[5] Margaret loved clothes, shoes and parties, and Henry provided her with the costliest gowns and vast quantities of shoes, gloves and stockings. That Anne favoured her is proved by her own gifts: 'a fringe of Venice gold made to garnish a saddle' with silk and 'half a dozen of round points made of silk and gold' for the same saddle and 'two round buttons of silk and gold made for the reins of the bridle'. Possibly they went out riding together, as Anne ordered similar items around the same time for herself.[6]

In shaping her side of the court, Anne's strongest allies were her family: her mother, her sister Mary, her sister-in-law Jane Parker, her cousin Lady Mary Howard and her favourite aunt, Lady Anne Shelton.[7] Howard, whom Holbein sketched for a now lost portrait during these years, was Anne's strongest, most vocal champion, an independent woman with evangelical sympathies and cultural tastes close to her own.[8]

Next came Anne's longstanding friends Bridget Wilshire, who had returned to court, and Elizabeth Browne. After the tragic early death of Sir Nicholas Harvey, Bridget took as her third husband Robert Tyrwhitt, a wealthy landowner and courtier ten years younger than herself. She is last heard of alive in the gift roll for 1534, when she gave Henry 'a shirt of cambric, the collar wrought with gold'. Possibly she died in childbirth.[9]

Browne had starred with Anne and Jane Parker in the Château Vert masque and taken a prominent place in Anne's coronation procession. Now a countess and married to the thirty-eight-year-old Henry Somerset, 2nd Earl of Worcester, she was on warm enough terms with Anne to be given a surreptitious loan of £100 (worth over £100,000 today) which – it later transpired – had no fixed repayment date and lacked even a note of obligation. It was a debt the two women privately agreed would never be disclosed to Browne's husband.[10]

Of Anne's gentlewomen, Mary Shelton, a confidante of Bess Holland, was closest to her.[11] Sir John and Lady Shelton had six daughters of whom only two, Mary and Margaret, came to court. Anne's biographers tend to conflate them, but the sources identify two separate women.[12] Mary became a dominant presence in Anne's privy chamber, and when Holbein drew her, he picked out her snub nose, delicately curled lips, deep soulful eyes, and, more suggestively, the outline of her décolletage.[13] No definite record exists of Margaret before January 1536, although it is more than likely she was there with her sister for the New Year celebrations in 1535 when an episode damaging to Anne would take place.[14]

Other favoured gentlewomen include Elizabeth Hill, Thomas Isley of Sundridge's daughter, who married Henry's serjeant of the cellar. Anne had known her since their fathers sat together as magistrates in Kent.[15] Margaret Gamage, the daughter of a Welsh knight, was Jane Parker's cousin.[16] The affectionately named 'Nan' Cobham cannot be George, Lord Cobham's wife, Anne, as is often assumed, since nobody would have referred to a peer's wife as Nan except as an insult. Maybe she was a daughter of George's uncle, Sir Edward Cobham?[17] Whether Anne Gaynesford kept faith with Anne after marrying George Zouche is harder to establish. A golden-haired young woman named 'Mistress Zouche' whom Holbein depicts wearing a fashionable French hood and holding a carnation, a symbol of betrothal, might be her; or the sitter could be Lord Zouche's daughter, Mary, to whom Henry later gave a pension.[18]

But Anne could not just choose friends and allies as her 'ladies of presence', because Henry allowed several career courtiers to transfer from Katherine's service. Lady Elizabeth Boleyn, Sir James's wife, had always gravitated towards Katherine, as did Lady Mary Kingston, the Constable of the Tower's wife, and Margaret Coffyn, the wife of Anne's Master of the Horse. Lady Jane Calthorpe, although also linked by kinship ties to Anne, had done a five-year stint as Princess Mary's governess.[19] Jane Ashley, one of Katherine's maids, served Anne and Jane Seymour before marrying Sir Peter Mewtas.[20] Another, Margery Horsman, whom Holbein represents as slim and demure, stayed at court until 1537, when Sir Michael Lyster took her as his second wife.[21]

The dark horse would prove to be Jane Seymour, the twenty-five-year-old daughter of Sir John Seymour of Wolf Hall, who had served Katherine as a maid of honour and was promoted to gentlewoman. According to the gift roll, Henry gave her a gilt cruce (a small drinking vessel with two handles and a cover) weighing 8 oz, as well as giving one to Mary Shelton.[22] Chapuys described her as 'of middle height and nobody thinks that she has much beauty. Her complexion is so whitish that she may be called rather pale ... [She] is not very intelligent and said to be very haughty.' Her brothers, Edward, outstandingly able, and Thomas, egregiously ambitious, were both rising stars.[23]

These women came to know Anne intimately. They were able to see and hear all that occurred. They knew to whom she talked, could eavesdrop on her conversations and observe her studying the evangelical books which so moulded her opinions. They could detect the ebbs and flows of her marriage by spying on her and take stock of how male courtiers approached and spoke to her. They saw her at her best, and at her worst; when she was happy, angry, frustrated or vulnerable. Those closest to her bedchamber would also know when another monthly period came and went and whether she was pregnant. The danger lay in their capacity to tell their tales to their fathers or brothers, lovers or friends and supporters in Henry's household.

Anne's regal status demanded pomp and magnificence, and on the Continent she had been surrounded by some of the most famous artworks of the Italian and northern European Renaissance. The intensity of that cultural exposure had given her sophisticated tastes, which she could now afford to indulge. She commissioned Holbein to design the first New Year's gift she presented to Henry after their marriage – a large silver-gilt basin and table fountain to provide a jet or spray of water for cleaning the royal fingers during a banquet. With its rubies, pearls and diamonds, and its supporting satyrs and nymphs (the nymphs at the base appeared to be squeezing their breasts to make the water flow), the fountain made a 'goodly' centrepiece for the table. The piece was melted down for scrap in 1620, but two of the artist's preliminary drawings have survived. The larger, more finished one includes a depiction of Anne's crowned white falcon holding a sceptre, perched above a rootstock sprouting roses, prominently positioned between the satyrs who support the lid, which is capped by an imperial crown.[24]

Holbein then designed jewellery for Anne bearing floriated interlaced letters. One such piece has an intertwined 'HA' monogram for Henry and Anne; another has an 'HI' cipher ('Henry Immuable' – 'Henry the Steadfast') set with an emerald and three suspended pearls. A third has the 'HISA' cipher, most likely for 'Henry Immuable Serviteur Anne'. While these echo phrases in the king's early love letters, the meaning of three more designs featuring a floriated interlaced 'ABCE' cipher is still unresolved.[25]

Holbein's drawings extol the value Anne placed on the visual arts as queen. However, no authenticated depiction by Holbein of Anne herself has survived. Whether the two most famous panel portraits of her, wearing a French hood and two pearl necklaces from which hangs a letter 'B' with three pearls pendant, both dating from the 1590s, are based on a lost original by him is impossible to judge. That one of his drawings bears the legend 'Anna Bollein Queen' is meaningless, because the inscription, like several others, was added a century or more later and is based upon identifications made in the late 1540s, several of which got mixed up. That drawing depicts a solid-looking woman, thick-necked and double-chinned, wearing a loose informal robe which no fashion-conscious queen would choose for a portrait. Since Holbein drew a Wyatt coat of arms on the back of the sheet, most likely the sitter is Jane Haute, who in 1536 was preparing to marry Thomas Wyatt's son.[26]

Another Holbein drawing, later the basis of a Wenceslas Holler engraving, also purports to be of Anne. It depicts an attractive woman with dark eyes and a composed expression, chicly dressed and wearing a necklace and bodice with a square neckline. But the sitter lacks Anne's long slender neck and the inscription is in a seventeenth-century hand.[27]

If, however, Anne did not ask Holbein to draw or paint her, she commissioned a second New Year's gift for Henry from him to memorialise the king's position as Supreme Head of the Church. A tablet miniature painting on vellum (22.9 x 18.3 cm) on the theme of 'King Solomon and the Queen of Sheba', still in the Royal Collection, the work is in grisaille, but with extensive touches of gold and a plentiful use of silver (now turned black), and an ultramarine background. The only additional colour comes from the single, evocative detail of the red and green of the strawberries offered to Solomon.

The piece is not just a simple reconstruction of a biblical story. The key figure is Solomon, who sits on a marble throne, wearing his crown and holding a sceptre. With his elbows out, his hands on his hips and his legs astride, he dominates the composition. On either side of him stand his priests and nobles. To the left on the steps below the throne, the Queen of Sheba, seen in profile with outstretched hands, salutes Solomon, her ladies walking in a crescent-shaped procession behind her, followed by her male servants offering gifts to the king.[28]

Since Holbein's depiction of Solomon is a vivid likeness of Henry and the Queen of Sheba was a traditional emblem of the Church, the painting depicts him as Supreme Head receiving the homage of the Church of England. Inscribed in Latin on either side of the throne and on the cloth of estate behind it is Sheba's salutation, based on verses from the Old Testament, announcing that Henry is appointed directly by and is accountable only to God. On the steps of the throne is written: 'By your virtues you have exceeded your reputation.' The original biblical texts of Sheba's address begin: 'Happy are your wives, happy are these your servants, who continually stand before you and hear your wisdom', echoed in the motto, 'The Most Happy', which Anne adopted after her marriage. In Holbein's rendition, however, 'wives' is changed to 'men' – it seems that, when commissioning the work, Anne had no intention of encouraging Henry to imitate Solomon's notorious polygamy.[29]

Before pursuing her more radical ideas, Anne had routine duties to perform. One concerned her lands. It was conventional for queens to have their jointures, the income from which could be used for patronage, gifts, luxuries and day-to-day expenses, but what made Anne unique, once Henry had finished transferring further vast quantities of property to her, was the sheer scale of her possessions. In 1535 alone, she gained an income of £5,056 16s 11d from these estates (worth over £5 million today), considerably more than Katherine had received.[30]

In administering her lands and finances, Anne followed precedent. Since at least 1403, queens had a council for this purpose with an office close to Westminster Hall.[31] Hers was overseen by her uncle Sir James Boleyn, assisted by Sir Edward Baynton, her vice-chamberlain, and with Sir William Coffyn, her Master of the Horse, and her trusted receiver George Taylor as regular working members. But while much of Anne's fiscal and estate business was managed entirely by the council, her personal approval was required before certain leases could be sealed or books of survey and valuation approved. Her auditors and their assistants would tour her estates to inspect the rent-rolls and compile a valuation of her property each year. In areas where her lands lay, she paid fees to some eighty-two local rent collectors, stewards, bailiffs and keepers of parks, and had six lawyers and three other legal professionals kept on retainer.[32]

One of the council's functions was to arbitrate in disputes amongst her tenants or lessees. In this way Anne would learn of infringements on her estates, such as the occasion when Robert Rolf of Hadleigh in Suffolk complained of an intrusion on a mill.

Intriguingly, Anne involved herself in another 'cause longstanding in the court of Chancery', requesting the Lord Chancellor, Sir Thomas Audley, 'to use such expedition as he may conveniently with his lawful favours'. The case was between 'one Broke and A.B.': the only known case matching the description and date is John and Alice Broke of Manningtree in Essex *versus* Alice Banham, a widow, concerning lands near Ipswich in Suffolk. The litigation arose because Banham wished to retain lands she had been given by a certain John Cardinal, to whom she was betrothed but who had died before the wedding, and the Brokes contested the gift. If this is indeed the issue which Anne took up, the likely explanation is that one of the parties was her tenant or a former servant.[33]

The worldly-wise Lady Lisle showered Anne with gifts in the hope of favours. In January 1533, she gave her a little dog called 'Purquoy', perhaps after the French 'pourquoi' meaning 'why?' (although the dog had originally been given to Francis Bryan).[34] She followed up with a dozen freshly killed dotterels – small, edible, plover-like birds – delivered to the queen by George Boleyn. Anne ate six for dinner and six for supper as, she said, they were 'a special good dish'. Lisle then sent a linnet in a cage which once hung in her own chamber. It was 'a pleasant singing bird, which doth not cease at no time to give her Grace rejoicing with her pleasant song'.[35]

Anne adored Purquoy. As Francis Bryan reported back to the Lisles about the dog he very briefly owned, the pet was 'so well liked by the Queen that it remained not above an hour in my hands but that her Grace took it from me'.[36] Purquoy scampered happily about Anne's side of the court for almost two years before dying after falling out of a window. Lady Lisle heard the news from Margery Horsman. When the accident happened, everyone knew that Anne 'setteth so much store' by her beloved Purquoy that 'there durst nobody tell her Grace of it, till it pleased the King's highness to tell her Grace of it.' (Henry loved his own dogs, paying substantial rewards to those returning his spaniels, Cut and Ball, when they got lost, so would have understood his wife's distress.) Horsman advised that, should Lady Lisle be considering sending

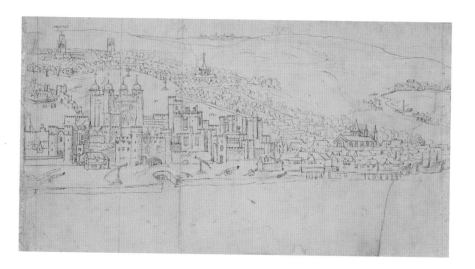

Above: View of the Tower of London from the south bank of the Thames, c.1544, by Anthonis van den Wyngaerde. *Below left:* Henry aged about eighteen shortly before he married Katherine of Aragon, by an unknown artist. *Below right:* While the identity of the sitter is unproven, the fact that she wears a collar depicting the letter 'K' and Tudor roses, and a 'C' for 'Catalina' (her Spanish name) on her dress, suggests that she is the young Katherine of Aragon, by Michel Sittow.

Above: Hever Castle, the Boleyn seat in Kent where Anne spent her childhood after 1505. *Below left:* Margaret of Austria, after Bernard van Orley. *Below right:* Claude, Queen of France, by an unknown artist.

LA·ROYNE·CLAVDE
femme de françois 1.er

Top left: Louise of Savoy, mother of Francis I, by Jean Clouet. *Top right:* Francis I, King of France, aged about 32, by Jean Clouet. *Above left:* Marguerite of Angoulême, sister of Francis I, aged about 35, by Jean Clouet. *Right:* Anne de Graville presenting a copy of her French adaptation of Boccaccio's *Teseida* to Claude, watched by the queen's *demoiselles*.

Above: Letter from Anne to her father from Tervuren, 1513. *Below:* Henry's younger sister Mary, briefly Queen of France, and Charles Brandon, Duke of Suffolk, by an unknown artist.

Above left: Charles of Ghent (later King of Spain, and Holy Roman Emperor as Charles V), by Bernard van Orley. *Above right:* Princess Mary aged about six, when betrothed to Charles V, c.1522, by Lucas Horenbout. *Below:* The challenge at the 'Castle of Loyalty', organised by Thomas Wyatt and his friends for the celebrations at Christmas 1524.

Top left: Thomas Wyatt, by Hans Holbein the Younger. *Top right:* Henry's suit of armour, 1527, made in the royal workshops in Greenwich and presented to François de la Tour, Viscount de Turenne. *Left:* Mary Boleyn, Hever Castle version, by an unknown artist. *Above right:* Katherine of Aragon aged about forty-one, by Lucas Horenbout.

Above: Henry VIII aged about thirty-five, by Lucas Horenbout.
Below: Anne Boleyn, Hever Castle version, by an unknown artist.

Above: Henry's love note in French to Anne, scribbled beneath a miniature of Christ as the 'Man of Sorrows': 'If you remember my love in your prayers as strongly as I adore you, I shall hardly be forgotten, for I am yours, Henry R always'. *Right:* Anne's response to Henry's love note, written beneath a miniature of the Annunciation: 'By daily proof you shall me find / To be to you both loving and kind'.

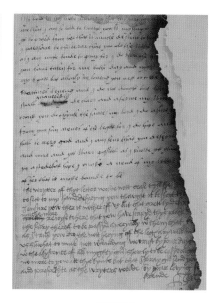

Top left: One of Henry's seventeen love letters to Anne, written in French after learning that she had the sweating sickness. He signed 'HR', interspersing the literals with Anne's interlaced initials 'AB' inside a heart he drew himself. *Top right:* Joint letter of Henry and Anne (partially charred in a fire of 1731) to Wolsey, early August 1528, expressing concern at the slow progress of Cardinal Lorenzo Campeggi on his journey from Italy to London. *Above left:* Pope Clement VII, c.1531, by Sebastiano del Piombo. *Above right:* Cardinal Wolsey, by an unknown artist.

Above: Anne's specially commissioned psalter, c.1529–30, showing her monograms and the black lion of Rochford.
Right: Anne's illuminated Book of Hours produced in Bruges, c.1450, with her message: 'Le temps viendra / Je anne boleyn' ('The time will come / I Anne Boleyn'). A drawing of an armillary sphere, one of Queen Claude's badges, is inserted between 'Je' and 'anne'.

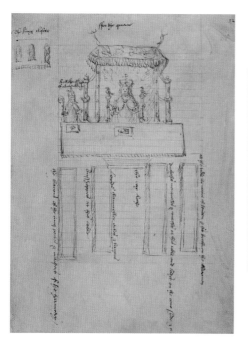

Above left: The seating plan for Anne's coronation banquet in Westminster Hall. *Above right:* Anne's falcon badge, sceptred and bearing an imperial crown, set within an illuminated initial letter T from *The Ecclesiaste*. The falcon perches on a rootstock out of which sprout offshoots of white and red roses. *Below:* Hans Holbein the Younger's design for a pageant on the theme of Mount Parnassus staged for Anne's coronation celebrations.

The Ambassadors, Jean de Dinteville and Georges de Selve, by Hans Holbein the Younger.

Top left: A badly defaced proof version of Anne's portrait medal of 1534, struck (but apparently not issued) to celebrate the son she believed she was expecting. It bears the cipher 'AR' and her motto 'The Most Happy'. *Top right:* A design for jewellery for Anne by Hans Holbein the Younger. The interlaced letters of the 'HISA' cipher within a circle most likely stand for 'Henry Immuable Serviteur Anne' ('Henry the Steadfast, servant of Anne'). *Above left:* The front cover of Volume II of Anne's copy of the French translation of the Bible by Jacques Lefèvre d'Étaples. The embossed letters of the 'HA' cipher flank a Tudor rose above and below a quotation from St John's Gospel split between the front and back covers. *Above right:* Hans Holbein the Younger's design for a table fountain which Anne commissioned as a New Year's gift for Henry after their marriage. Anne's falcon badge, sceptred and crowned, appears between the left and central satyrs.

Top left: Lady Mary Howard, Duchess of Richmond: Anne's cousin, lady-in-waiting and leading champion, a woman with evangelical sympathies close to her own, by Hans Holbein the Younger. *Top right:* Mary Shelton, one of Anne's gentlewomen and a dominant presence in her privy chamber, later married to Sir Anthony Heveningham, by Hans Holbein the Younger. *Above left:* Margery Horsman, one of Katherine's maids, later Anne's gentlewoman; in 1537, she married Sir Michael Lyster, by Hans Holbein the Younger. *Above right:* 'Mistress Zouche', a gentlewoman wearing Anne's trademark French hood; she may well be Anne Gaynesford, who served Anne before she was queen and went on to marry George Zouche, or she could be Lord Zouche's daughter, Mary, to whom Henry later gave a pension, by Hans Holbein the Younger.

Anna Bollein Queen.

Above left: Unknown woman, by Hans Holbein the Younger, later inscribed 'Anna Bollein Queen'. A Wyatt coat of arms on the back of the sheet suggests the real sitter is Jane Haute, who in 1536 was preparing to marry Thomas Wyatt's son. *Above right:* Three gentlewomen performing the chanson 'Jouyssance vous donneray' for their private entertainment, c.1520. The chanson also appears near the end of the music manuscript Anne acquired in France. By the Master of the Female Half-Lengths. *Right:* Hans Holbein the Younger's tablet miniature on the theme of 'King Solomon and the Queen of Sheba', commissioned by Anne for Henry as a New Year's gift to memorialise his role as Supreme Head of the Church.

Top left: Thomas Cromwell, by Hans Holbein the Younger. *Above:* The 'Chequers' ring which opens to reveal a full-face likeness of Anne and a profile of her daughter Elizabeth as Queen of England. *Left:* Jane Seymour, one of Katherine's maids, later Anne's gentlewoman, depicted as Henry's third wife, by Hans Holbein the Younger.

Anne another dog, she should know that 'her Grace setteth more store by a dog than by a bitch.'[37]

Often Anne was approached by those whose real target was the king or the increasingly ubiquitous Thomas Cromwell, whom Henry appointed to be his principal secretary in April 1534. Lady Lisle tried this method when she and her husband fought to save a weir in Umberleigh in Devon which had fallen foul of legislation designed to protect the passage of river traffic. As local bureaucrats failed to respond to assurances that the offending weir did not impede navigation, and some weirs belonging to Anne and Henry had already been pulled down, a direct appeal to the queen to 'move the King's Grace, the Lord Chancellor or Mr Secretary' was rather a lost cause. 'Mr Secretary', as John Husee, their court agent, warned Viscount and Lady Lisle, 'is very earnest in the same and will show no favour.'[38]

More successful was John Crayford, Master of Clare College and Vice-Chancellor of Cambridge University. In July 1535, he humbly petitioned Henry to redress a legal anomaly which had seen newly assessed tax demands, intended for wealthier clergy, imposed on academics holding poorly paid college fellowships. He wrote to Anne on the same matter. Sympathetic to his pleas, she broached what was clearly a blatant injustice with Henry, who at first did nothing, prompting Crayford to write again. The second time, her interventions succeeded: in the session of Parliament beginning on 4 February 1536, Henry rectified the anomaly.[39]

Before her coronation, Anne had successfully lobbied Wolsey to protect Dr Robert Forman from charges of heresy. According to the 1583 edition of John Foxe's *Acts and Monuments* (or 'Book of Martyrs'), she secured the release from prison of Thomas Patmore, the evangelical parson of Much Hadham, Hertfordshire.[40] William Latymer tells of a French gentlewoman named 'Mistress Mary' who fled to London 'for religion' and was so well received by Anne that she declared she had gained more in exile than from staying at home. Another reformer to whom she offered sanctuary was the German educator Jean Sturm, a man said to be very wise and 'of a great modesty', but he declined.[41] In May 1534, she would take up the cudgels on behalf of Richard Harman, an exiled evangelical expelled by Wolsey from the Company of Merchant Adventurers for supplying copies of Tyndale's *New Testament* to Simon Fish. In letters issued under her signet seal, she ordered Cromwell to restore Harman to his place in the Company and allow him home 'with all speed and favour convenient'.[42]

In March 1534, she rescued Nicholas Bourbon, another evangelical and a poet whom Marguerite of Angoulême had recruited as a tutor to her daughter, Jeanne. His pithy attacks on the inquisitors of the Sorbonne had got him imprisoned and his possessions, including his pet nightingale, seized. Bourbon credited his release to Francis's intervention, but elsewhere his writings show it was at Anne's instigation.[43] Once freed, he travelled to London, where Anne arranged for him to lodge with William Butts and later with Cornelius Hayes and his wife. So grateful was he that his poetry includes a eulogy to Anne, and others to Holbein, who both drew and painted him, and who shared a friendship with Butts and Hayes. 'Hans painted me better than Apelles', he exclaimed in another of his verses.[44]

To keep Bourbon busy, Anne appointed him as tutor to her nephew and ward Henry Carey, to Henry Norris's son, and to Bridget Wilshire's son, Thomas, by her marriage to Sir Nicholas Harvey. The boys were aged between six and ten and were taught on Anne's side of the household. Specially for them, Bourbon wrote his second book, the *Paedagogion* (or 'School for Young Pages'), published in Lyon after he returned to France towards the end of 1535.[45]

Like her father, her brother George and her sister-in-law Jane Parker, Anne was a patron of individual scholars, including Nicholas Heath and Thomas Thirlby, both later made bishops, and William Bill, later Dean of Westminster. In September 1535, the celebrated Cambridge scholar John Cheke, who later married one of the daughters of Anne's gentlewoman Elizabeth Hill, praised her munificence, saying students only had to be recommended to her by one of her chaplains to win her support. She endowed scholarships at Oxford and Cambridge, giving £40 to each university in the first year of her reign and £80 annually thereafter. She tracked the careers of her beneficiaries, notably that of John Aylmer, a novice monk whom she understood to be of 'good learning, and demeanour, and virtuous governance' and who was studying at Cambridge. She wrote on his behalf to William Thornton, Abbot of St Mary's, York, who had interrupted Aylmer's studies, recalling him to the monastery to undertake mundane tasks 'to no little disturbance and inquisition of his mind'. Much irked by Thornton's obduracy, Anne ordered him to return Aylmer to the university and give him 'sufficient exhibition to the maintenance of his study there'. If this was unacceptable to Thornton, he was to explain 'in writing, by this bearer, a cause reasonable why you defer to accomplish our said request'.[46]

Such was Anne's concern for reform, she retained an entire cohort of evangelical chaplains.[47] Besides Latymer and Nicholas Shaxton, for whom she secured the bishopric of Salisbury, they included the combative Cambridge evangelical Hugh Latimer (whom Anne first recruited as a Lenten court preacher in 1530), John Skip (Shaxton's replacement as queen's almoner), Robert Singleton and Matthew Parker. Singleton, described as a 'lantern and light' of Anne's household, doubled as one of Cromwell's informants denouncing seditious papists. Anne poached Parker in 1535 from Corpus Christi College, Cambridge: his mother, Alice Monins or Monings, came from Kent and may have been known to her. Such was her trust in him, Anne wanted him to have a special care for the spiritual wellbeing of her daughter, a charge he would remember in 1559, shortly before Elizabeth made him her first Archbishop of Canterbury.[48]

Anne pushed hard for her people. In January 1534, she wrote to the Corporation of Bristol successfully securing their cooperation in a rigged selection process in favour of her preferred candidate as Master of the Hospital of St John Redcliffe. Later the same year, she appointed William Barlow, John's brother, as prior of Haverfordwest, Pembrokeshire, where (as he said) he battled the forces of Antichrist and strove 'sincerely to preach the Gospel of Christ'. Afterwards, Anne nominated him as Bishop of St Asaph, and when his opponents blocked his path, she found him the bishopric of St David's instead.[49]

Being nominated by Anne for a post was never the end of the story. When in 1534 the evangelical Edward Crome failed to take up the benefice of St Mary Aldermary, one of London's wealthiest parishes, she hauled him to account. She marvelled 'not a little', she explained, 'that, albeit heretofore we have signified unto you at sundry times our pleasure concerning your promotion unto the parsonage of Aldermary ... yet you hitherto have deferred the taking on you of the same'. She would not allow this: 'Our express mind and pleasure is that you shall use no farther delays in this matter but take on you the cure and charge of the said benefice ... as you tender our pleasure in any behalf.' What especially riled her was that, when Crome had been accused of heresy in 1531, she had prevailed upon Henry to have him released. Suitably chastened, Crome did indeed take up his post and went on to preach a series of highly popular, if often inflammatory sermons.[50]

In October 1535, Anne helped Cromwell to sponsor the Southwark printer James Nicolson's reissue of the exiled Miles Coverdale's banned translation of the Bible, the first complete version in English. On this they could work clandestinely together as it was a subject dear to both their hearts.[51] Unlike Coverdale's original text, which had been printed in Cologne or Antwerp and smuggled into London, Nicolson's reissue came with a stirring dedication in which Coverdale eulogised Anne as the king's 'dearest, just wife and most virtuous princess'. An introductory prayer and verses chosen from the psalms to be said after the reading of every chapter were the work of Nicholas Shaxton.[52]

Anne's role in the project was most likely limited to offering her protection and perhaps a gift of money. Given her husband's views at the time, even that was risky – it was only in 1537 that Cromwell finally obtained the king's licence for an English Bible. In 1535, Henry's priority was for a revised version of the old Latin Vulgate text, for which he wrote the preface and chose a special typeface suitable for his own now ageing eyes.[53] To mollify Henry, Anne (or perhaps Cromwell) arranged for Nicolson's printing to include a magnificent title-page border, designed by Holbein, depicting the king as Supreme Head of the Church, sitting on his throne and handing a copy to his bishops.[54]

Prudence meant that Anne had to be selective in choosing whom to assist. It is no surprise that when, early in 1536, Tristram Revell, a former Cambridge scholar who needed funding for his studies, tried to present her with an English translation of François Lambert's *Somme Chrestienne*, a snappy digest of Lutheran theology printed for the French market in 1529, she replied that she 'would not trouble herself about the work'. This was despite a fulsome preface, comparing her to John the Baptist and rejoicing in 'the fellowship which your Grace hath in the Gospel'.[55]

Just as Queen Claude and the Lefèvrists had taken a keen interest in monastic reform, so did Anne. She never impugned or disparaged the religious life as a general ideal but would order Cromwell to investigate individual foundations where she felt her influence was needed, such as in the Cistercian house at Vale Royal in Cheshire and the Augustinian priory at Thetford in Norfolk.[56] Latymer, with some hyperbole, recounts her inspecting the Bridgettine nunnery at Syon while staying in Richmond for Easter in 1535. When the abbess refused her entry, avowing that a married woman was not permitted within the walls, she persisted and, with 'fair and sweet words', had her way. Once inside, she found the nuns, dressed all in white, prostrate on the floor of their chapel, 'grovelling with their faces downwards to the ground'. Seeing through this show of 'dissimulated holiness', she berated them for their 'ignorant praying' and for using Latin prayer books rather than English ones.[57]

Anne also put social responsibility high on her list of priorities. She wished to see the assets of a modest number of the less effective religious houses redeployed to more socially useful purposes, a policy which should not have been unduly controversial, given that Wolsey had done the same to found colleges in Oxford and Ipswich. In this way, the original founders' intentions might be better fulfilled by offering educational opportunities, hospitality and charity to the poor. Matthew Parker was in the vanguard of what she hoped to create. After recruiting him, she made him dean of the college of Stoke-by-Clare in Suffolk, a small but unusually wealthy

institution under her patronage, where he founded a grammar
school and song school supported by bursaries and scholarships to
Cambridge. In his revised statutes for the college, Parker omitted
any requirement that the Bible scholar say the Mass, appointing a
Scripture reader and preacher instead. In place of prayers for the
dead as in the past, the college offered a free education to the local
poor with Anne as its patron.[58]

Eager to clamp down on superstitions and outright shams,
Anne instructed her chaplains during the summer of 1535 to
investigate the famous relic of the Holy Blood at Hailes Abbey
in Gloucestershire, a vastly profitable pilgrimage site second only
to that of the murdered Thomas Becket's in Canterbury which in
1538 Henry would have demolished and its rich treasures despoiled.
Supposedly a quantity of Christ's blood preserved in a crystal phial,
the Hailes Abbey relic was displayed for veneration – and cash
donations. Possibly seeing it herself while she and Henry lodged in
nearby Winchcombe, Anne thought it was a fraud, which it was.
Mistakenly, Latymer claims that the relic was swiftly removed, but
that took another three years, since Henry was persuaded only with
the greatest difficulty that it was spurious.[59]

Anne would reign for only 1,083 days before disaster engulfed
her, and yet in that short time she would enlarge the role of queen.
Her formative years had impressed upon her what forthright and
determined women could achieve. She stood her ground for what
she believed in, and her devotion to ideas, especially religious ones,
meant she was bound to prove divisive in the aggressively masculine
environment of Henry's court. She was a keen judge of men,
appreciating the impetus for change which eager young evangelicals
could exert, and was protective and encouraging towards them. She
took her responsibilities in financial affairs very seriously, understood
the value of landed wealth and how in the case of monastic assets
their partial reallocation could benefit society. She knew when to
persist, and when to pause or step back, fully aware of the hackles a
woman could raise when exercising authority in a deeply patriarchal
world. In these qualities, she stands proudly in the pantheon of
history alongside her daughter, Elizabeth.

23

Dangerous Times

On 15 January 1534, Henry reconvened Parliament, where in early February Thomas Cromwell, in his capacity as the king's parliamentary manager, introduced bills to abolish payments to Rome and to confirm the reduction of Katherine's title to that of 'Princess Dowager'. On 20 March, there followed a bill declaring Katherine's marriage null and void and settling the succession on Anne's children. The crown was to descend by primogeniture, first to Henry and Anne's sons, and then to their heirs. In default of male progeny, Anne's daughter, Elizabeth, was to succeed. As finally enacted and enforced, the Act of Succession would require the king's male subjects over the age of fourteen to swear an oath affirming the 'whole effects and contents' of the measure. The Act created several new forms of treason: deeds or writings threatening the king or 'derogating' or slandering his marriage to Anne were to be adjudged high treason. And in a draconian extension of the law, the definition of treason was widened to include opposition, or incitement to opposition, by words alone, punishable with life imprisonment and loss of property.[1]

On 23 March, the Monday of Passion Week, the bill settling the succession on Anne's children cleared its passage in the House of Lords. On the same day in Rome, the cardinals voted unanimously in the Consistory in favour of Katherine, and Clement declared her marriage to Henry to be valid and Anne's null and void. Jean du Bellay's last-minute diplomacy in Rome had conspicuously failed. The one glimmer of light was that the question of the king's excommunication was left ambiguous, as Clement, despite his earlier bluster, was anxious not to provoke war at a moment when Charles was preoccupied with a Lutheran uprising in Germany and with fresh incursions of the Turks in the western Mediterranean and north Africa, where they had captured Tunis. Still, the threat of papal sanctions loomed large over Henry.[2]

From now on, however, Henry intended to make his break with Rome irrevocable and give legislative status to his claim to be Supreme Head of the Church. His commitment to Anne was as strong as on the day of their marriage. She was his lawful wife and rightful queen, the woman he loved and wanted by his side for the rest of his life and reign. If Clement resisted, he would defy him. If his subjects objected, then he would teach them their duties of obedience to sovereign rulers. Dissidents must suppress or cloak their opinions, or else be prepared to suffer the penalties. Papal jurisdiction, he maintained, had been exercised in England 'but only by negligence or usurpation as we take it and esteem'. He recognised no superior on earth, 'but only God'.[3]

After Anne's coronation, opposition to Henry's second marriage had ceased to be confined to backstairs gossip or murmurings in London. And whenever they encountered it, Henry and Anne acted as one. People had to choose which side they were on, theirs or Katherine's. Much of what was said by Katherine's supporters would be collated in 1585 by Nicholas Sander in his *De origine ac progressu schismatis Anglicani* ('Concerning the Origin and Progress of the English Schism'), a scabrous attack on Henry's break with Rome told from a Catholic recusant perspective. According to Sander, Anne was a femme fatale, a sex siren shipped off to France to complete her education after being caught in bed with a Boleyn butler and a chaplain. A calculating vixen, she was disconcertingly tall and sallow in complexion, much disfigured by 'a projecting tooth under the upper lip, and on her right hand six fingers'. Her neck was scrofulous with 'a large wen' or goitre, so to hide its ugliness, she wore a ruff or dress with a high neckline covering her

throat. Rumours were rife, continues Sander, that Henry had slept
with Anne's mother as well as with Mary Boleyn – some said Anne
was the king's illegitimate daughter. On the circulation of such
gossip, Sander hit closer to home. A report survives of a daring Sir
George Throckmorton making the claim during an audience with
the king, provoking Henry to retort, 'Never with the mother' and
Cromwell to add untruthfully, 'Nor never with the sister neither.'[4]

In its more focused form, opposition was co-ordinated by
Chapuys, who pumped courtiers such as Gertrude Blount and
Elizabeth Stafford for news and acted as a point of contact for
Katherine's friends and other dissidents. After Thomas More
resigned as Lord Chancellor, Chapuys got much of his inside
information from Cromwell, with whom he conversed in
French: although the two could never fully trust each other, each
enjoyed the other's company and respected the other's diplomatic
skills. While Henry and Anne were on their honeymoon, Chapuys
compared Cromwell's talents favourably to Wolsey's, saying that
the king should be grateful for so loyal a servant and insinuating
how high he might rise if only Anne could be got out of the
way. Chapuys, who had served the Duke of Bourbon during his
campaigns in Provence and northern Italy, well understood the value
of Cromwell's worldly experience. He saw too how far Cromwell
had developed a particular understanding of the value of an Anglo-
Habsburg alliance while working in Antwerp for the Company of
Merchant Adventurers: there, Cromwell had come to appreciate
the English economy's reliance on the Low Countries trade and
the commercial and political advantages of a rapprochement with
Charles. So far, Cromwell was in no position to advocate this, but
it would not be long before Chapuys would drop hints that only
the Boleyns were the obstacle to such a move.[5]

The crackdown began when Cromwell first contemplated using
torture against dissident friars and Henry instructed Cranmer to
silence Elizabeth Barton, a Benedictine nun at the Priory of St
Sepulchre, Canterbury.[6] Better known as the 'Nun of Kent', Barton
had been a maidservant in a Kent gentry household in 1525 when
she won fame by experiencing visions after falling ill and being

miraculously cured. Her reputation as a mystic continued to grow
after she became a nun, and her revelations were widely shared.
Her influence was dangerously extensive: Wolsey, Thomas More
and Bishop Fisher were among those who interviewed her, and
even Henry met her at least once.[7]

The trouble began in 1527 when she was politicised by her spiritual
director and confessor, Dr Edward Bocking. Soon Barton stirred up
a flurry, praising Katherine and vilifying Anne. Claiming prophetic
powers, she predicted God's vengeance on Henry in a deadly plague
and said she had seen the place reserved for him in hell. She called
Anne a heretic whore, a Jezebel whom the dogs would devour. If
the king married her, 'he should not live six months after'. His
divorce from Katherine, she said, was a root with three branches,
and England 'should never be merry again until the root were
plucked up'. Her supporters copied out and distributed 'miraculous
letters' alleged to have been written in heaven and handed to her
by an angel. Some were printed in a series of incendiary pamphlets
that drew on the prophecies of Merlin, including the so-called
'Mouldwarp' prophecy, which predicted that rebels would drive
Henry away to an island in the sea where he would be cursed with
God's own mouth. These, along with the writings of Katherine's
former chaplains against her divorce and all 700 copies of a work
called *The Nun's Book*, were seized and destroyed.[8]

Throughout the autumn of 1533, Barton and her supporters
were rounded up, arrested and questioned in the Star Chamber
at Westminster, where the king's councillors sat judicially to try
special cases. Cromwell prepared the interrogatories, as he would
with so many more suspected traitors over the next seven years.
Cranmer and Hugh Latimer joined him as principal interrogators.
Henry, who blamed Barton for all his and Anne's disappointments,
demanded treason charges, but the judges sent word that she could
be indicted only for inciting sedition. The alternative was for
Parliament to pass an Act of Attainder, an extreme, highly dubious
measure left over from the Wars of the Roses, which would condemn
Barton as a traitor without trial. Chapuys informed Charles that
'although some of the principal judges would sooner die' than twist

the law as Henry wished, yet no one dared contradict him, 'so that it seems as if he had made a total divorce not only from his wife but from good conscience, humanity and gentleness which he used to have'.[9]

Cromwell had no compunction about using an Act of Attainder, quickly reassuring Henry that he could summon up the necessary votes, provided he arranged for certain key figures to stay away from Parliament or abstain from voting. The king was delighted and relieved, considering himself absolved from all responsibility for what was about to happen. Using this underhand technique, Cromwell got Parliament to convict Barton and five of her supporters, mainly monks, of high treason, and on 20 April, they were dragged on a hurdle from the Tower to the gallows at Tyburn, where they were hanged.[10]

Beginning with More and Fisher the week before, Henry had begun to order the Londoners to swear to the Act of Succession, with the rest of the country to follow. Fisher refused and was sent to the Tower. When More also refused, Cromwell personally tried to persuade him to change his mind. Refusing again, he was remitted overnight to Westminster Abbey, then taken to join Fisher. Others sent to the Tower in May and June included the Carthusian priors of London and Sheen, John Houghton and Richard Reynolds, along with several cartloads of friars. More noted that the process had been illegal: the oath he was required to swear included words beyond those legally prescribed. He had spotted this at once, the first of several such tricks that Cromwell would employ. It would do him no good. Henry believed he had promised at his accession to give England stability, and that was what he meant to do. Such exemplary punishments as those imposed on More and Fisher were a clear warning to those who opposed the policies for which he had parliamentary sanction.[11]

No sooner were More and Fisher safely in the Tower than Henry, sensing danger everywhere, came to suspect a group of regional nobles of plotting to overthrow him. He especially questioned the loyalty of William, Lord Dacre of Gilsland, one of the landowners who policed the northern border with Scotland. At the same time, he chose a new governor for Ireland to replace Gerald Fitzgerald, Earl of Kildare, whom he summoned peremptorily to court.[12]

In May, Henry pounced on Dacre while he lingered in London after attending Parliament. Chapuys heard that Anne had turned against him for defending Katherine and Princess Mary: until she gave birth to a son, she would always fear the former queen and her daughter and anyone who supported them. But when the king had Dacre put on trial accused of treasonable collusion with the Scots and produced witnesses to testify to the truth of the charge, he was spectacularly freed after defending himself unaided for seven hours, the only nobleman to be acquitted by his peers during Henry's reign. Undeterred, the king had him rearrested and returned to the Tower as soon as he left court. Only after he accepted an astronomical fine of £10,000 and undertook not to go more than ten miles from London without the king's written permission was he left alone.[13]

In Dublin in June Kildare's son and deputy, Lord Offaly, defied Henry and raised a rebellion, forcing the inhabitants of towns to swear loyalty to Charles and the pope, and claiming he would get the assistance of 12,000 Spaniards. He ordered those born in England to leave Ireland without delay on pain of death. Soon the country was convulsed: Dublin Castle was besieged and the rebels went on an orgy of looting and burning, firing artillery in the streets and terrifying the citizens. One of Cromwell's spies wrote of how Offaly and his adherents 'do make their vaunt and boast that they be of the pope's sect and band, and him will they serve against the king and all his partakers'. It took a massive English army fourteen months to suppress the revolt, costing thousands of lives. In retaliation for his son's actions, Henry sent Kildare to the Tower, where he died.[14]

Once Offaly's revolt raised the threat level, opposition to Henry and Anne would be ruthlessly sought out and crushed. In Henley-on-Thames, one Marjorie Cowpland was hauled before the magistrates for calling Henry a traitor and extortioner 'and as for Queen Anne, she is but a strong harlot'. When a local officer warned her that he was the king's servant, she replied, 'the king's servant, the devil's turd'. In Oxfordshire, a woman was questioned for calling Anne 'a

whore and a harlot of her living'. In Suffolk, Margaret Chancellor
was arrested for calling Anne 'a naughty whore' and 'a goggle-eyed
whore'. 'God save Queen Katherine,' she had continued. In Essex,
a Colchester monk said that the king and his councillors were
schismatics, and when Henry was last in Calais, Anne 'followed
him like a dog its master'. In a tavern in Cambridge, Henry Kylbie,
on an overnight stopover between London and Leicester, called
Henry a heretic, adding that 'this business had never been if the
king had not married Anne Boleyn'. In Buckinghamshire, George
Baburney, a tailor of Newport Pagnell, was indicted at the assizes
for saying, 'The king is but a heretic, a thief, a harlot and a traitor
to God and his laws, and before Midsummer Day next coming,
I trust to play football with his head.' In Warwickshire, a priest
called out, 'The queen is a whore and a harlot.' He would later
be burned at the stake at Smithfield on conviction of heresy. In
Hertfordshire, a man called Anne 'a churl's daughter and a whore'.
In Lancashire, priests were accused of saying, 'I will take none for
queen but Queen Katherine.'[15]

Several of these accused pleaded drunkenness, but this did
not always work. Hearing of Baburney's words, Francis Bryan
recommended the man go on trial, drunk or not, on the grounds
that 'the due execution of justice in this case shall be a very great
example and the safeguard of many.' Within days, Baburney was
hanging from the gallows.[16]

Most damning were whispers among those still within courtly
circles. Elizabeth Amadas, the widow of Cromwell's predecessor
as Master of the Jewels, said: 'My Lady Anne should be burned
for she is a harlot.' Henry Norris, she insisted, 'was bawd between
the king and her'. The king 'hath kept both the mother and the
daughter', and Anne's father 'was bawd to both to his wife and his
two daughters'.[17]

Three weeks after Epiphany in 1534, Anne told her husband
that she was pregnant again. This time, it simply had to be a boy.[18]
Ready for his son, Henry commissioned a brand new 'cradle of
estate' in solid silver from Cornelius Hayes, to be garnished with
roses and studded with gemstones. The next payment in the

accounts is one to Holbein for painting figures of Adam and Eve for the royal nursery. Richly embroidered bedding and cloth of gold bespoke baby clothes were added to the king's order. Other preparations at Eltham 'against the coming of the prince' included putting up an iron canopy over the cradle and repainting the room with yellow ochre. Anne, meanwhile, decided that she would need suitable reading matter to pass the time while awaiting the birth, and besides the new cradle, Hayes was paid £4 for supplying and binding two books for her (their titles are unknown) and 6s 0d for 'garnishing' them with silver-gilt, while William Locke received 43s 9d for the fine velvet covering them.[19]

So confident was Anne of a son that she had a portrait medal designed, ready for the celebration of the birth. A single proof copy, cast in lead, survives, badly defaced as if later attacked with a hammer. In it, she is depicted three-quarter face, untypically wearing a gable headdress and a bodice with a square neckline. She has tight-fitting upper sleeves and no collar, and from the upper of her two rows of pearls hangs a pectoral cross. Her choice of costume was deliberate: she wished to present herself to the world as an Englishwoman with English taste, not as the Francophile she really was.[20] The proof bears the cipher 'AR' ('Anna Regina') and her motto, 'The Most Happy', and is dated 'Anno 1534'. The damage means that the nose is now flattened and the left cheek and eye largely obliterated. Enough is still visible to see an oval-shaped face, a long assertive neck, a strong chin and high cheek bones.[21]

News of the pregnancy was suppressed until Maundy Thursday, when it was time for Henry and Anne to distribute the traditional cramp rings. As George Taylor reported to Lady Lisle, 'The King's grace and the Queen is [sic] merry and in good health, thanks to our Lord; and the Queen hath a goodly belly – praying our Lord to send us a prince.' Gloomily, Chapuys informed Charles that Anne was 'in a state of health and of an age to have many more children'. The Boleyns, and Henry, could only hope that his forebodings proved true.[22]

On Good Friday, Gilles de la Pommeraye, now Francis's maître d'hôtel, returned to London for five days on a special mission. His great asset to Henry and Anne was that his sole patron was Francis himself, not the Duke de Montmorency. To mark a break with the failures of the past, Henry ordered Cromwell to send him 300 gold crowns of the sun as a gift.[23] Nothing was too much trouble for Anne in her desire to please him. On Easter Tuesday, she took him to Eltham to see Elizabeth. He saw the child first in her 'cradle of estate' dressed in cloth of gold, covered by a quilt of ermine and underneath a canopy of crimson cloth of gold blazoned with the royal arms. Then he saw her 'quite naked' (*toute nue*).

Anne made clear her intent: she sought to betroth her daughter to a French prince as soon as she was twelve. This was her opening bid in a fresh campaign to rekindle the Anglo-French alliance after the setbacks of the past year. It was to this end that she drew up a plan for a new Anglo-French summit to be held in Calais in the summer – one between the two kings, but in which she would fully participate. In readiness, Henry commissioned eye-wateringly expensive renovations at the royal lodgings in the Exchequer in Calais where he, Anne and Francis would stay. Both the king's and queen's apartments were to be remodelled. An entirely new wing was to be constructed for Francis leading off an inner courtyard, complete with a great chamber, dining chamber, privy chamber, bedchamber, gallery, 'arraying chamber', privy closet to hear Mass and private kitchens with gardens adjacent. And to ensure his comfort, an en suite 'stool chamber' was to be built at the side of his bedchamber, with additional 'jakes' (or lavatories) outside for his attendants and servants.[24]

Henry sent George Boleyn on a fourth mission to France to finalise the arrangements, accompanied by Sir William Fitzwilliam.[25] Francis quickly agreed to Anne's new summit, but beyond that said little. A huge shockwave had swept through Paris and much of France some months before when a leading evangelical, the newly elected rector of the Sorbonne, Nicolas Cop, fled into exile in the reforming city of Basel after delivering an inflammatory sermon in Paris. Marguerite of Angoulême, who fêted George and Fitzwilliam and gave each of them a solid gold cup with a lid, found herself caught in the crossfire. Her protégé and almoner, Gérard Roussel, a prominent Lefèvrist and member of the Cercle de Meaux, stood accused of preaching heresy in a series of Lenten sermons. Cop's flight was the prelude to some 300 arrests, culminating in October 1534 in the so-called 'Affair of the Placards', when Protestant broadsheets attacking the Mass would be posted up throughout Paris and five provincial towns, and even in Amboise where Francis was staying. In Paris, fears exploded that the reformers were about to sack the Louvre, burn down the churches and massacre the faithful.[26]

With Francis keen to reassert his Catholic orthodoxy, the Boleyns' Francophile policy stalled. Now questioning the value of the summit Anne had proposed, Henry decided to postpone it, first from July to August, and then to September. Finally, he sent George back to France with instructions further to defer it to the following April. To smooth things over, George was to pretend that any delay had been expressly at his sister's request, on the grounds that she was now 'so far gone with child' that she would be unable to travel. And because Marguerite was 'a princess whom [Anne] had ever entirely loved and never doubted of correspondence on her behalf again', George was to 'open unto her the very bottom of the queen's stomach and to declare what causes hath especially moved her Grace to be so earnest a suitor in this matter'. For Anne's part, Henry explained, 'there was no one thing which her Grace so much desired ... as the want of [Marguerite's] company with whom to have conference, for more causes than were mete [fitting] to be expressed.'[27]

After personally checking and signing George's instructions, the king warned him to temper his speech with Francis so that he would 'smell not' Henry to be the true cause of the delay, but 'all in the queen's name'.[28]

It was not, however, just about the summit that Henry had doubts. Whether he or Dr Butts was in touch with Anne's physician, Dr Richard Berthelet (or Bartlot), about her pregnancy is unknown. Either way, the king's concerns would prove justified.[29] In late July or early August after George returned from France and while Anne and Henry were on a reduced summer progress in Surrey, she had a sudden stillbirth.* Her lying-in chamber was never occupied and as soon as she could stand again, she shut herself away in her privy chamber.[30] One daughter, one stillbirth: no amount of spin could convert such blatant failure into success. For Henry, it was both emotionally devastating and achingly familiar; he had been here before.

To add to his uncertainty, news had come that Clement was on his deathbed with stomach cancer: a conclave would shortly be summoned to elect a new pope. What would happen when his successor took office? Perhaps the Franco-papal alliance would collapse? But if it did, would the new pope ally with Charles, which from Henry's point of view would be worse?

With so many personal and political worries, Henry's devotion to Anne briefly but visibly wavered. The couple now rarely appeared together in public and Henry's eye started to rove. In September, he began flirting with another woman – her identity is not disclosed, but whoever it was, she was one of Anne's women and religiously conservative. There is no evidence that Henry slept with her.[31]

Things moved beyond a lover's tiff only when this mystery woman sent the eighteen-year-old Princess Mary a message of comfort, 'telling her to take good heart', since 'her tribulations will come to an end much sooner than she expected'. What especially rankled with Anne was that the woman assured Mary that 'should the opportunity occur, she would show herself her true friend and devoted servant.' Still feeling exposed after the stillbirth, Anne declared this to be an insult to her as queen and insisted the woman be sent away. Previous demands of this sort had always been met. This time, her protest backfired: all she achieved was to anger Henry. Not prepared to be taken to task by his wife or to squabble with her over his daughter, whom he greatly loved as his own flesh and blood despite her allegiance to her mother, he walked away

---

*This episode is often called a miscarriage, but it occurred in the third trimester of the pregnancy.

'in a great passion, complaining loudly of her importunity and vexatiousness'.[32]

Hoping to break the impasse, Anne asked her brother's wife, Jane Parker, to help her get the mystery woman banished from court. Jane, she believed, could be trusted. Together they plotted how best to deal with the interloper: Jane would pick a quarrel 'or otherwise' with her so that Henry, finding it all too tiresome and preferring a quiet life, would dismiss the girl. Chapuys spoke of Jane 'joining in a conspiracy' to that effect, perhaps suggesting more of the Boleyn family was involved. However, it all went awry and the one who would be rusticated for the Christmas season was Jane, not Anne's rival.[33]

Too much should not be made of the incident: Anne's rival, if such she really was, quickly sank into oblivion, her name unknown to us. 'The young lady who was lately in the king's favour is so no longer', Chapuys informed Charles in the New Year. This, he gleefully suggested, was because one of Anne's cousins, one of the daughters of Sir John and Lady Anne Shelton, had 'succeeded to her place'. This could have been Mary Shelton but is more likely to have been her sister Margaret. And yet, barely was the ink dry than Chapuys, fully attuned to the ways in which gossip exploded and then disintegrated, in the echo-chamber of Henry's court, began to think such reports greatly exaggerated. Anne and Henry's relationship was volatile, but still strong. Its volatility, the ambassador mused on reflection, was what gave it its spice.[34]

Whether or not Henry dallied with one of the Shelton sisters, the rumour mill believed he had, and courtiers could think this way because, unlike Elizabeth Woodville after her marriage to Edward IV, Anne failed quickly to produce living sons. Woodville's fecundity gave her absolute security: she could endure her husband's flirtations and affairs without obvious complaint, whereas it became apparent Anne dared not tolerate even a single potential rival without feeling threatened. Gossiping courtiers had set loose the soaring falcon of Anne's jealousy and turned her into prey. These were not just becoming dangerous times for Henry and Anne's opponents; they were becoming dangerous for Anne too.

24

Family Matters

While Henry and Anne sought to define a daily routine, she struggled to reconcile her maternal feelings with her public role as queen. As a younger son, Henry had spent his earliest years in the care of his mother, but Elizabeth was, in her father's eyes and Parliament's, the heir to the throne until he and Anne had a son. That meant Henry insisted on the rules laid down by royal protocol according to which he controlled everything. Anne would not have expected to breastfeed Elizabeth herself, since this was considered likely to delay future pregnancies.[1] By tradition, a wet-nurse was employed, usually the wife of one of the queen's trusted servants. Elizabeth Woodville's daughter, Cecily, had been nursed by Isabel Stidolf, the wife of Thomas Stidolf, her receiver of fee-farms, and now Anne's child would be nursed and weaned by Agnes Penred (or Pendred), the first wife of Thomas Penred, lately one of Lady Lisle's partners at cards.[2]

The question of her longer-term upbringing was decided when Elizabeth was three months old. She was to have a governess known as a 'Lady Mistress' and be sent in a horse litter with her nurse to the Old Palace of Hatfield in Hertfordshire, twenty-five miles north of London, which Henry sequestered from the Bishop of Ely. To break the journey, she would lodge overnight at Elsings in Enfield, Middlesex. Later, she would move to Eltham, where Henry had spent much of his own childhood. As a council minute recorded:

The Lady Princess shall be conveyed from hence towards
Hatfield upon Wednesday the next week, and that Wednesday
night to repose and lie at the house of the Earl of Rutland in
Enfield, and the next day to be conveyed to Hatfield, and there
to remain with such family in household as the King's Highness
hath assigned and established for the same.[3]

The woman Henry chose to oversee his daughter was Lady Margaret
Bryan, Sir Francis's mother, who had performed these same tasks
for Princess Mary and Henry Fitzroy.[4]

From now on, Anne's role was limited to visiting Elizabeth in
her nursery, seeing her when she was brought to court, writing to
Lady Bryan and buying her gifts and clothes. She made sure her
daughter had the best of everything. Thus, she sent her tailor John
Scut to take Elizabeth's measurements for caps and bonnets in the
latest styles, such as a purple satin one overlaid with a rich golden
caul, a white satin one which also had a golden caul, and a crimson
one, each costing between £3 and £4 (between £3,000 and £4,000
in modern values). She had 'a pair of periwigs'* made for the child
and sent crimson satin and crimson fringe to pad the headboard
of her cradle. If Anne was not satisfied with the bonnets, or if the
child grew out of them, they were to be 'amended according to her
grace's pleasure'.[5]

Anne visited Elizabeth whenever she could, twice in mid-
February 1534 and again in March. In April, she and Henry rode
the five miles from Greenwich to visit her while she was at Eltham.
As Sir William Kingston, who accompanied them, informed a
curious Viscount Lisle: Elizabeth was 'as goodly a child as hath
been seen, and her grace is much in the king's favour'. Anne saw
her daughter again that October, travelling in the royal barge from
Hampton Court to Richmond. Other opportunities came when
Henry had the little princess brought to court 'with divers of her

---

*This is only the second known usage of the term for hair extensions in the English
language.

servants', which could be for as long as five weeks at a time as in the early months of 1535.[6]

Anne also began to plan her daughter's education.[7] To her dismay, she discovered as other queens had before her that her influence would be restricted as the king insisted on his sole control for as long as Elizabeth was his heir. When, for instance, Lady Bryan approached Cromwell asking for permission to have the child weaned at the age of twenty-five months, he forwarded her request straight to Henry, who instructed Sir William Paulet, the new comptroller of the king's household, to approve it. Paulet filled a vacancy created by Sir Henry Guildford's death and quickly made himself useful. In a letter to Cromwell, with whom he was on the best of terms, he tactfully observed that permission to have Elizabeth weaned had been granted by 'his Grace, with the assent of the queen's Grace'. But this was fiction: Anne was simply told to confirm what Henry had already decided. Only then could she write to Lady Bryan to discuss further details.[8]

What Anne could and did do, however, was to strike at any rivals her daughter might have. There were two: her stepchildren Princess Mary and Henry Fitzroy. Very quickly, she found that dealing with Mary was more problematic than she had supposed. Although frequently ill, especially when menstruating, Mary nevertheless possessed an inner strength almost as deep as her mother's. Initially stunned psychologically when her father decided to strip her of her royal title, she kept her composure. When in one classic exchange Anne's uncle, the Duke of Norfolk, carelessly referred to Elizabeth as 'Princess of Wales', Mary silenced him by retorting, 'That is a title which belongs to me by right, and to no one else.' She would never accept that she was anything other than a true princess, so when coldly informed by Anne's father that she was now to be known as merely the 'Lady Mary', she rebelled. She wrote directly to Henry, saying that as a king and queen's daughter, she knew she was a princess, and while she would obey him in all things as 'an obedient daughter', she could not renounce what was hers by right. This was despite Anne's instructions that Mary should be handled as 'the accursed bastard that she was'.[9]

When, in January 1534, Henry visited Mary on his own to persuade her to resign her title, Anne was greatly put out. Concerned that he might relent when confronted with his daughter, she ordered messengers to chase after him, making it clear that he was not to see or speak directly with her. Afraid to upset his new wife, the king appealed to Cromwell, Paulet and Sir William Kingston to intercede with Mary – with predictable failure. His daughter's position was strengthened by the fact that she was not yet legally made illegitimate, even if Anne called her that. The Act of Succession, passed in March 1534, had merely declared Katherine's marriage invalid, confirmed that she 'shall be from henceforth called and reputed only Dowager to Prince Arthur and not queen of this realm', and settled the crown on Anne's children. Nothing was said explicitly about Mary.[10]

Despite Anne's badgering, Henry still loved and respected his daughter. All he wanted was for her to accept his second marriage for the reality it was, and the strongest inducement he could offer her by way of persuasion was the continuation of her independent household. By October 1533, this still numbered around 162 staff and was based at Beaulieu, the fairy-tale palace Henry had created on the site of New Hall. If Mary accepted her demotion, he would let her keep most of her staff.[11] When she refused, Henry ordered the privy council to devise a plan for reducing her household, but so sensitive was the issue – not least because Norfolk was himself half-opposed to it – that the councillors became deadlocked.

The Boleyns eventually triumphed, and a scheme for the 'diminishing of the house and ordering of the Lady Mary' was agreed. In parallel, the council arranged 'for the diminishing' of Katherine's entourage, which would gradually be reduced to a core largely made up of her loyal Spanish gentlewomen, her confessor, her physician and apothecary, two grooms of the chamber, three maids of honour and six to eight other women.[12]

A delegation of councillors, led by Norfolk, was sent to Mary to deliver the bad news. She was also losing her independent living: she was to be evicted from Beaulieu and transferred to Elizabeth's nursery, where she was to be treated as an inferior to the new princess.[13] Henry put Anne's favourite aunt, Lady Anne Shelton, and her husband Sir John in charge. How far Lady Shelton was comfortable with the assignment may be questioned. Several times, she found herself caught between Mary, who was meant to be a subordinate but had no official governess appointed, and Lady Bryan, Elizabeth's governess. Sent with the Duke of Norfolk to interpose, George Boleyn reproved Lady Shelton for treating Mary too leniently but, to her credit, Anne's aunt replied that no matter what rank the girl possessed, she deserved to be treated with kindness. On one matter Shelton followed Anne's wishes to the letter. Instructed never to allow Mary to use the title of princess and, if she did, to 'box her ears as a cursed bastard', she informed the teenager – quite contrary to the truth – that 'her father did not care in the least that she should renounce her title, since by statute she was declared a bastard and incapable.' When, during the ensuing feud, Mary went on hunger strike, Henry ordered her best clothes to be given away as a punishment. She then had a breakdown so disturbing that he relented and sent Dr Butts to attend her. He might be angry with her but she was still his child. Predictably, however, all Katherine's requests to nurse her daughter were rejected.[14]

Unlike Henry, who had no real wish to ill-treat or harm his daughter, Anne saw in her a dynastic threat. Mary was popular, Anne was not; Mary's father was a king, her own was not; Mary's supporters, considering her Henry's rightful heir, would forever contest and repudiate Anne's issue. Driven beyond endurance by Mary's unshakable resolve, Anne tried every trick she knew to subdue her. What really rankled was Mary's refusal to walk beside Elizabeth when she began to toddle, to share a horse litter with her, to defer to her and occupy the less prominent seat in the royal barge, and to eat with her, expecting instead to be served separately in her own room.[15]

Switching briefly from the stick to the carrot, Anne told Mary that if she would acknowledge her as queen, she could come to court and she would intercede for her with the king, only to find that Mary treated her offer with contempt. 'Should the king's mistress ... do her the favour she spoke of', she retorted, 'she would certainly be most grateful to her.' But the only queen she recognised was her mother. The riposte left Anne seething, threatening 'to put down that proud Spanish blood ... and do her worst'. Small wonder, then, that a rumour spread that Anne was thinking of having both Katherine and her daughter poisoned. She was later reputed, probably maliciously, to have said that either Mary would be her death or she Mary's, and that should she ever be left as regent of England as Katherine had been when the king was in France, she would have the girl executed.[16]

Anne was almost as harsh towards her stepson Henry Fitzroy, even though he did nothing to earn her displeasure. Her concern arose purely because he was male. Just as Katherine had feared in 1525 when Henry raised Fitzroy to the Dukedoms of Richmond and Somerset, Anne knew that illegitimacy was not an insuperable obstacle to kingship. Henry had acknowledged Fitzroy as his son, had educated him as if he was a contender for the succession and supported him in regal style. Since Fitzroy needed someone new to oversee his household after Wolsey was displaced, Norfolk persuaded Henry to make his own son, Henry Howard, the young Earl of Surrey, the boy's companion and mentor 'that he may attain both knowledge and virtue'. Three years older than Fitzroy, the young earl was a brilliant linguist and poet second only to Thomas Wyatt in his mastery of language. Going on to pioneer blank verse and the verse paragraph, for which he is hailed as Shakespeare's precursor, he was also a superlative horseman and champion of the ideals of chivalry. The king considered him to be a perfect role model for his son, and in November 1532, following the Anglo-French summit at which Anne danced with Francis, he sent the two teenagers off to France for a year, to join the Dauphin's household. There they could improve their French and demonstrate Henry's commitment to the Treaty of Mutual Aid. It was an arrangement that greatly boosted Henry's ego, making Fitzroy visible to the European powers as the living proof of his ability to father a healthy son.[17]

Warmly received by Francis and the Duke de Montmorency on his arrival at the French court, Fitzroy was quartered in the

Dauphin's lodgings and took his meals with the prince. During the winter months, Fitzroy and Surrey stayed in Paris, but in the spring of 1533, they travelled with Francis to Fontainebleau and onwards to Lyon, and then to Toulouse and Montpellier. They were there in mid-August, just as Norfolk's delegation arrived bearing Henry's instructions to persuade Francis to cancel the Franco-papal conference planned for Marseille. When Francis refused, the two teenagers were recalled in haste, the excuse being that it was time for Fitzroy to marry and for Surrey to begin to cohabit with his young wife.[18]

Anne's hostility towards Fitzroy crystallised after his return. Should he make an advantageous marriage, perhaps with a European princess, his prospects could soar. Such plans had been mooted before. One candidate had been Catherine de' Medici, now married to the Duke of Orléans, another the Infanta Maria of Portugal, Charles's niece.[19] In October 1528, the recently arrived Cardinal Campeggi had tentatively, if scandalously, proposed Fitzroy's betrothal to his own now-demoted half-sister. Clutching at straws to divert Henry from his plans to divorce Katherine, he had advised Clement's secretary that, providing a suitable dispensation was granted, this might prove 'a means of establishing the succession' before rejecting the plan as too fantastical.[20]

From Anne's perspective, the fastest, safest option was to marry Fitzroy off to one of her own trusted relatives. Despite her rift with her uncle, she believed her best choice to be her cousin Mary Howard, Surrey's sister. Neither Norfolk nor his estranged duchess, if left to their own devices, would have chosen Fitzroy as a son-in-law: they already had more suitable, safer candidates in mind. But Anne won Henry over, and his decision was final.[21]

On 26 November 1533, Fitzroy and Mary Howard exchanged their wedding vows in a low-key ceremony in the Chapel Royal at Hampton Court. Henry appropriated for their use the magnificent riverside house adjacent to Whitehall belonging to the Bishop of Norwich, but since both were still just fourteen, they would not immediately cohabit and appear not to have done so later with any enthusiasm, so it could hardly have been a love match. This was a far cry from the nuptials of de' Medici and the Duke of Orléans in Marseille, who by coincidence were also both fourteen and who, after their wedding feast, were led to a sumptuously decorated bridal chamber, where they enjoyed uninhibited sex watched over by Francis, who declared 'each had shown valour in the joust'.[22]

Once Fitzroy was married, Anne left him alone. She had less reason now to fear him. Her attention moved to her own sister, the widowed Mary Boleyn, who around the spring of 1534 was banished from court for secretly marrying the lowly, impecunious William Stafford. A member of the Calais garrison who had attended Anne's coronation banquet as a humble servitor, Stafford was the younger son of a minor Midlands gentry family and had no relationship to the late Duke of Buckingham.

Anne was furious, castigating her sister. As a matter of protocol, no one could marry into the royal family without the king's permission and the sanctions normally imposed on those who flaunted aristocratic and royal conventions must be upheld, otherwise Anne's own standing might be questioned. From the Boleyn family's vantage-point, furthermore, far from marrying up, this was marrying down. Henry too was angry, although much less so, it seems, than his wife.[23]

Mary believed her only hope for herself and her husband was to appeal to Cromwell. It indicates the newly promoted principal secretary's subtle arrogation of power, a view John Husee confirmed when he advised Viscount Lisle: 'I perceive Mr Secretary's mind is that your lordship should not write to any man to make mediation in your causes, but only to him.'[24]

In a remarkable letter to Cromwell, Mary poured out her heart. She and Stafford, she confessed, 'did not well to be so hasty nor so bold' in marrying without royal consent, but 'he was young and love overcame reason'. Such was their love, 'I had rather beg my bread with him than to be the greatest queen christened,' almost an eerie echo of Henry's own much-vaunted boast that, rather than be parted from Anne, he 'would beg alms from door to door'.[25]

Her father and brother, she said, had violently rejected her, but so had her sister, the woman who had replaced her in Henry's bed.

The only way forward would be for Cromwell to intervene with the king and persuade *him* to intercede with Anne for her and her husband: 'for, as far as I can perceive, her Grace is so highly displeased with us both that, without the king be so good lord to us as to withdraw his rigour and sue for us, we are never like to recover her Grace's favour.'[26] We will never be privy to Cromwell's reply, if there was one, as it is lost, but the appeal failed and Mary had to wait until Anne was dead to recover her position and inheritance.[27]

In Rome, Pope Clement died in September 1534 just days after commissioning Michelangelo to paint *The Last Judgement* above the altar in the Sistine Chapel. In a conclave lasting only a single day, Cardinal Alessandro Farnese was elected Pope Paul III after duping Francis into believing he would be pro-French. Once enthroned in St Peter's chair, however, he declared himself an imperialist who was committed to working with Charles. We can only imagine Henry's consternation on hearing the news. His only mild consolation was Francis's discomfort at discovering that, by marrying his second son to a de' Medici, he had turned a diplomatic coup into a potentially damaging *mésalliance*.[28]

On 3 November, with no more illusions about the attitude of the papacy, Henry ordered Cromwell to enshrine the king's position as Supreme Head of the English Church in statute, and to devise a fresh oath of supremacy and allegiance for his subjects to swear. The Act swiftly passed, followed at a slower pace by a much-contested Treason Act, making it a capital offence to traduce or threaten the royal family, or to deny their titles (especially Henry's as Supreme Head), or to call the king a heretic, schismatic, tyrant, infidel or usurper.[29]

Adjunct to the Act of Supremacy, Henry gave Cromwell plenary powers as his 'Vicar-general' to oversee a national visitation (or census) of the religious houses. In the story of Cromwell's rise, this would become a major inflexion point. As the year drew towards its close, he began experimenting with drafts of special commissions addressed to people he trusted to visit and inspect the monasteries, seeking out abuses.[30] The fact that he was able to choose his own nominees, ghost-write their instructions and sign them in Henry's name using an inked stamp of the king's signature tells us everything about the shifting realities of power. Within six months or so, such letters would be sent out in large quantities and without reference to the king. And it would not be long before the visitation reports (known as *comperta*) were returned to London, filled with scandalous stories of sexually active monks and nuns, involving whoring, sodomy and a great deal more, giving Cromwell exactly what Henry wanted.[31]

Shortly before the draft Supremacy legislation was laid before Parliament, Francis sent the tall, proud Philippe Chabot, Seigneur de Brion, the new Admiral of France, to London at the head of a large retinue. A man shortly to oust the Duke de Montmorency from his dominant position in the French court, Chabot was handsomely entertained in Calais by Viscount and Lady Lisle, and then met in Dover by George Boleyn, whom Henry had recently made Warden of the Cinque Ports and Constable of Dover Castle. Anne personally greeted him by the riverside Stairs at Whitehall Palace where he disembarked from the king's great barge called *The Lyon*, which was specially adapted for the visit.[32]

Henry did his best to entertain Chabot magnificently, but the Admiral was cool. He stayed for only fifteen days, during which he skipped all but one of the tennis matches which Henry laid on for him and all but two of the banquets and masques. He largely avoided Anne, and she and George were numbed by his proposals. He had come, not to replace the Treaty of Mutual Aid with a dynastic alliance offering the prospect of a future closer tie between the two kingdoms, but because Charles was offering the French king generous concessions concerning his claim to the Duchy of Milan if he successfully arranged a marriage between the Dauphin and Katherine's daughter Mary. Chabot's instructions required him to base his negotiations on the subsidiary treaties between England and France in 1518 at the time of Wolsey's Treaty of Universal Peace. He was nonplussed when Anne insisted that it must be Elizabeth – not her stepdaughter – who should marry one of Francis's sons. Henry too said that the Admiral must be joking in proposing Mary as the bride.

Much affronted, Chabot showed them his instructions under the Great Seal of France, which also called on Anne to stop referring to Mary as a bastard and urged Henry to resume his obedience to Rome. Henry was being asked – and by the very same ally whose friendship Anne had made central to his policy and was central to their own *raison d'être* as a married couple – to repudiate almost all the Acts of the last two or three years and to annul the oaths and declarations he had demanded from his subjects.[33]

Henry saw instantly what lay behind Chabot's mission: Francis was considering whether it might be worth his while to switch from the English alliance to a pro-Habsburg one, and wanted to see what England might offer in return for maintaining the status quo. He artfully retorted that he would consider giving Mary's hand in marriage provided she and the Dauphin renounce all claims to the English throne: alternatively, he would give Elizabeth to the Dauphin and without that restriction. Chabot was blindsided by this response. He sat on his hands while awaiting new instructions, and when none arrived, he decided to return to France.

The eve of his departure was not without incident. In Chabot's honour, Henry arranged a final banquet and masque at which he seated the Admiral with himself and Anne. Shortly after the dancing began, Henry went to find Palamèdes Gontier, Francis's secretary who assisted Chabot, to ask him to join them. Left alone with the Admiral and with a wall of silence between them, Anne burst into a fit of uncontrollable laughter. 'Why, Madam, do you laugh at me?' demanded Chabot. Her answer, that she had spotted Henry flirting in the body of the hall instead of fetching Gontier, did not reassure him. When Chabot left next day, he had no parting gift to present, which must have irked her – whereas to Lady Lisle in Calais, he sent two pet marmosets and a long-tailed monkey from Brazil with advice on how best to feed them. Had Anne known of the monkeys, she would have resented the slight, even though, as John Husee advised Lisle, 'the queen loveth no such beasts nor can scant abide the sight of them'.[34]

Chabot's mission opened Henry's mind to the unwelcome probability that Francis would never join him in breaking with

Rome. Once the Admiral's retinue reached Dover on their way home, the English king began seriously to question Anne's Francophile approach to international affairs. Early in the New Year, in a scene that delighted Chapuys, she was thrown onto the defensive: allegedly she turned on her uncle Norfolk during a quarrel in her privy chamber, angrily rebuking him for not doing more for her in the privy council. Momentarily disarmed, the duke dropped his mask sufficiently on reaching the outer hall of the palace to be overheard calling Anne 'a great whore' (*grande putain*).[35]

Some relief came in late January 1535 with the return of Gontier, bearing an answer to Henry's counterproposal. The revised French offer was straightforward: if Henry would take definitive steps to exclude his elder daughter from the succession, valid under international law, and treat Elizabeth as his sole heir, then Anne's daughter could be betrothed to Charles, Duke of Angoulême, the French king's third son. By way of a dowry, Francis wanted large cash subsidies to fund an invasion of Piedmont and Lombardy. He also wished Henry to renounce his own existing claim to the French throne. To such open-ended commitments, Henry took exception. After thinking it over, he answered that the best way to secure recognition of Elizabeth's legitimacy and rights of succession was for Pope Paul to revoke his predecessor's censures – all doubts then would cease.[36]

After Mass on the afternoon of the Day of the Purification of the Virgin Mary (2 February), Cromwell took Gontier into a bay window in the queen's Presence Chamber to speak privately to Anne. As the envoy reported back to Chabot, she complained bitterly of Francis's delays and equivocations, which had caused her husband many doubts and unwelcome thoughts. Fighting back her tears, she said Chabot should understand that he must find some remedy as a matter of extreme urgency 'so that she may not be hung out to dry and cast away' (*qu'elle ne demeure assolée et perdue*). 'Already she sees herself very close to both these fates and in more grief and trouble than before her marriage.' Her dark, flashing eyes darting anxiously around the room as she spoke, she warned, 'I cannot speak as fully as I wish for the fear of where

I am and the eyes all around which are watching my face, both those of my husband and the courtiers who are here.' She said she could not write, nor see him again, nor stay longer. She then rejoined Henry as he left for the great hall, where a masque was just beginning. But she did not go to the masque herself: she slipped away and retreated to her bedchamber. Gontier concluded his dispatch to Chabot by saying, 'Sir, as far as I can tell, she is not at her ease. In my small judgment, this is because of the king's doubts and suspicions.'[37]

When Henry agreed to one last diplomatic push, French and English delegates were summoned to meet in Calais for late May. Sensing failure from the outset, Cromwell, whom Henry originally wished to accompany the Duke of Norfolk, made his excuses, pleading a recent bout of fever. In his stead went Anne's brother George on this, his sixth and final mission to France, assisted by Sir William Fitzwilliam and Edward Foxe. Possibly because of Cromwell's influence, Henry was even more specific than usual in his instructions. The envoys were to meet Chabot in Calais, where Norfolk was to do most of the talking – no longer was George to wing things. Elizabeth, it was now proposed, would be betrothed to the Duke of Angoulême when she was seven. The Duke was to finish his education in England, or if Henry and Anne had a son, then Elizabeth was to be educated in France. Francis was to make no more marriage alliances or leagues with Charles without English consent. Finally, Francis must bind himself and his three sons to help revoke the papal censures against Henry. He must also use his influence to block any future General Councils of the Church summoned by Pope Paul. If a Council was to meet, it was to be only at such a time and place as Henry agreed to. Once he had wanted a General Council to intervene on his behalf, but now he was less sure. It was a sign of things to come that, after the envoys had been given their instructions, Cromwell ordered Fitzwilliam to spy on George and report back to him. With his sister as queen, George, Cromwell believed, was becoming too much of a nuisance. Cromwell, by now, had oceanic ambitions, to which George was almost as much of a threat as Anne.[38]

Wary of Fitzwilliam, whom he rightfully suspected, George urged him to stay behind in Dover while he, Norfolk and Foxe travelled alone to Calais. Fitzwilliam refused. In France, George met Chabot several times, but made no progress. Seeing the danger, he hastened back to London on 14 June, leaving Norfolk and Fitzwilliam behind, ostensibly to secure fresh instructions from Henry. Instead, he headed straight for Anne's apartments where he stayed closeted alone with her for several hours. As Chapuys vividly remembered, she was in a foul temper afterwards. Meanwhile, Cromwell openly snubbed the new French ambassador, Antoine de Castelnau, Gabriel de Gramont's nephew and successor as Bishop of Tarbes. Hoping to present his credentials to Henry at court and hear the news from Calais, he was left kicking his heels in an anteroom of Cromwell's house in the Austin Friars until 10 p.m., at which point the principal secretary brusquely dismissed him. Later lodged by Henry in Bridewell Palace like his immediate predecessors, he was then asked to leave by Cromwell, although the request was later withdrawn.[39]

The balance of power was visibly shifting when, after two days of fierce debates in the privy council, Cromwell found it possible to reassure Chapuys that Anne's plans for an Anglo-French dynastic league were on hold; that he would persuade Henry never to allow George to return to France on diplomatic missions; and that he would work towards the re-establishment of an amity with Charles. He added that if Anne were ever 'to know the familiar terms on which you and I are, she would surely try to cause us both some trouble'. Only three days before, he claimed, he and she had quarrelled, with Anne telling him 'that she would like to see his head off his shoulders'. How much credence should be given to that alleged threat is hard to judge. Chapuys, who was no fool, believed Cromwell simply threw it in to inflate his own importance.[40]

One thing is certain. With Henry increasingly unable to command the honour he expected from his fellow monarchs and with his nobles and privy councillors coming to question the wisdom of his international policy, Anne had everything to lose. She retained just one trump card, the one she had always possessed: if she could produce a living son, she would be invincible, and her critics silenced. To do that, she had to sustain, but not satiate, Henry's sexual interest in her.

25

Piety and Pastime

For Anne, expressing her religious beliefs was like walking a tightrope. Whereas she was a reformer by conviction, her husband's zeal focused exclusively on the papacy and opponents of his break with Rome. To the despair of the Lutheran princes of Germany, who longed to ally with him, he continued to regard their central doctrine of justification by faith alone as outright heresy. And, given the Catholics' hatred of Anne as the whore of Babylon who had ousted Katherine as queen, her position had to be delicately pitched. Her critics, notably Chapuys, impugned her for her alleged Lutheranism even though – like Henry – she denied Luther's central doctrine. Her religion has been debated endlessly, but in her own mind, she was a Lefèvrist who, like Queen Claude or Marguerite of Angoulême, did not want to dismantle the Catholic faith or the Church itself, but to see it reformed from within. That she was devout was never in question: among her treasured possessions were 'two little candlesticks of ivory trimmed with silver and gilt' for the altar in her private oratory.[1]

Judging by the reports of her chaplain William Latymer, her apartments were hives of evangelical piety with her ladies studying the English Bible and sewing clothes for the poor. Not long after her coronation, she gave her chaplains and officials what amounted to a pep talk. 'You know', she began, 'that princes be the very fountains and wellsprings of whom all other inferior magistrates receive their authority.'

> Who, as in a theatre or open stage, play the chief parts, to
> the admiration of the inferior subjects and multitude. And
> we ourselves are not altogether ignorant of the necessary
> charge required in so high a personage; not found wantons,
> not pampered pleasures, not licentious liberty or trifling
> idleness, but virtuous demeanour, godly conversation, sober
> communication and integrity of life.[2]

That her regal status required displays of luxury and magnificence, she insisted, did not mean they should tolerate waste, superfluity or vainglory. Her surplus resources she wanted given over in alms:

> the distributing whereof I have committed to you that be
> mine almoners, and in your absence to you my chaplains, my
> pleasure is: that you all take especial regard in the choice of
> such poor people as shall be found most needy; not vagrants
> and lazy beggars ... but poor, needy and impotent householders
> over charged with children, not having any sustenance, comfort
> or relief otherwise; and to such I command mine alms liberally.[3]

We can take this to be a true reflection of Anne's beliefs: as an eye- and earwitness Latymer was able to report accurately the basic elements of what Anne said, even if his language is idealised.[4]

When in 1533, Richard Lyst, a lay brother amongst the Franciscan Observants in Greenwich, wrote to Anne complaining about his bullying superior, John Forrest, he included thanks for her 'good and beneficial' charity to his mother.[5] According to Latymer's narrative, besides washing and kissing the feet of 'simple poor women' on Maundy Thursday, Anne substantially increased her alms for that special day. Hearing that an honest recipient confessed she had inadvertently received too much, Anne had her share doubled in reward. She gave out 'shirts and smocks and sheets' sewn by her gentlewomen 'to the use of the poor'. When, during an extended

royal progress with Henry towards Bristol during the summer of
1535, she encountered 'an earnest and eager embracer of God's
Word' and his wife who had fallen on hard times, she told them to
accept God's providence but sweetened the pill with the gift of a
purse of £20 in gold.[6]

Latymer's account is corroborated by passages in the 1563 and
1570 editions of John Foxe's *Acts and Monuments*. Following a brief
report of Thomas More's resignation as Lord Chancellor in May 1532,
Foxe interpolated a section on Anne's charity based on information
indirectly obtained from her silkwoman (a needlewoman who
sews and embroiders clothing made of silk), the fervent evangelical
Jane Wilkinson; and more directly from Mary Howard and Simon
Fish's widow. According to Foxe, every week during the year
before her coronation, Anne handed out clothing and £100 in
alms to the poor. As queen, she gave generously to widows and
poor householders, giving £3 and £4 at a time for the purchase of
livestock. She sent her sub-almoner to the towns surrounding her
properties to compile lists of the poorest householders and then
allocate funds. Every day she carried a little purse with her from
which she offered alms to the needy.[7]

Anne's ethos was underpinned by the example of the charitable
deeds of her great-grandfather, Sir Geoffrey Boleyn, and by her
religious convictions. The books she cherished most, Latymer tells
us, were her French and English vernacular Bibles, especially the
Gospels. An English text was always made available on a lectern
for members of her household 'to read upon when they would'.
'Neither', he continues, 'did her Majesty disdain in her own person
sundry times to repair to the common desk where the said bible was
placed, yielding herein example to others to the like endeavour.'
At the same time, she 'charged her chaplains to be furnished of
all kind[s] of French books that reverently treated of the whole
scriptures; wonderfully lamenting her ignorance in the Latin
tongue, for want whereof she acknowledge[d] herself marvellously
embased [i.e. humbled, impaired].'[8]

After her creation as Marquis of Pembroke, Anne required all
her religious texts to be deluxe editions, or if such versions did not

exist, to be copied out by hand onto vellum by Flemish-trained craftsmen, so as to be fit for a queen. In 1534, she would acquire a copy on vellum of Martin L'Empereur's Antwerp edition of Tyndale's illicit *New Testament* with her heraldic arms emblazoned on the second title page and the words 'Anna Regina Angliae' ('Anne, Queen of England') painted on the gilt edges of the leaves. She purchased from the same printer a handsome two-volume set of the revised edition of Lefèvre's complete Bible translation into French, *La saincte Bible en Francoys*. Once in her possession, she had the books magnificently bound with gold letters of the 'HA' cipher flanking a crowned Tudor rose at the top and bottom of each side of the covers.[9]

Chapuys tells us how Anne's brother George supported her religious ideals and would insist on discussing what the weary ambassador misleadingly called the 'Lutheran principles in which he takes such pride' at every opportunity.[10] At her request, George had books printed by Simon du Bois used as the copy-texts for deluxe manuscripts. The first, with a full-page image of the Crucifixion and illuminations of Anne's coat-of-arms as Marquis, was *The Pistellis and Gospelles for the LII Sondayes in the Yere*. Based on the *Epistres et evangiles des cinquante et deux dimanches de l'an* by Lefèvre from an edition issued in Alençon in 1531 or 1532 and condemned by the Sorbonne, the finished manuscript has the Epistle and Gospel readings for every Sunday of the year in French, followed by commentaries translated into English by George. In a preface to his sister, he explains:

> I have been so bold to send unto you, not Jewels or gold, whereof you have plenty ... but a rude translation of a well-willer, a good matter meanly handled, most humbly desiring you with favour to weigh the weakness of my dull wit and patiently to pardon where any fault is, always considering that by your commandment I have adventured to do this.[11]

A second work written by the same scribe was *The Ecclesiaste* with text from an edition prepared by Lefèvre and printed by du

Bois in about 1531, and with commentary from the *Ecclesiastes Salomonis* of Johann Brenz, a German evangelical. Brilliantly decorated with small illuminated initial letters and eight larger ones by Gerard Horenbout, and replete with Anne and Henry's badges and heraldic arms, the manuscript, purchased for the library at Alnwick Castle in Northumberland in about 1899, still retains its original (now faded) black velvet binding on wooden boards. Anne's motto 'The Most Happy' is included, as is her falcon badge and an elaborate device with an anchor hanging from an armillary sphere.[12]

Another fine manuscript presented to Anne as queen is a 490-line French evangelical poem, *Le pasteur évangélique* ('The Evangelical Pastor'), a variant of a slightly shorter version later published under the title *Le sermon du bon pasteur et du mauvais* ('The Sermon of the Good and Bad Shepherd'). In its later format, the poem was included in the 1541 edition of Clément Marot's *Psaumes* (or 'Psalms'), which appeared in Antwerp. Marot, the doyen of French poetry during Francis's reign, was a prominent evangelical, famously rescued from prison by Marguerite of Angoulême.[13]

The frontispiece of Anne's copy prominently displays her heraldic arms within a wreath of oak leaves sprouting acorns and with a crowned silver falcon on its stump at the base. The last fifty lines, which extol the 'amity' between England and France, flatteringly pair Anne with Marguerite and Henry with Francis, and end with a prophecy that Christ the Good Shepherd will give Anne a son in Henry's image, whom they will live to see grow into adulthood. The donor is yet to be identified, but a plausible candidate is Jean de Dinteville.[14]

Latymer tells us that Anne 'seldom or never' ate with Henry on her side of the court

> without some argument of Scripture thoroughly debated. And in like manner the lord chamberlain and vice-chamberlain of her side for the time being gave themselves wholly in all their dinners and suppers to the discussing of some doubt or other in Scripture.

Henry, 'divers and sundry times', would join in these discussions. On one occasion, he and Anne's uncle, Sir James Boleyn, argued against Hugh Latimer and Nicholas Shaxton, and afterwards continued their exchanges by correspondence.[15]

One day, Latymer continues, Anne found 'certain idle poesies' inscribed in a prayer book – something he seems to forget Anne had once done herself during her early courtship with Henry, and evidently something Anne too might have forgotten – and was determined to find the culprit. 'She would not be satisfied by any means before she understood certainly to whom the book pertained.' When at length she discovered her cousin Mary Shelton to be the offender, she 'wonderfully rebuked her that [she] would permit such wanton toys in her book of prayers, which she termed a mirror or glass wherein she might learn to address her wandering thoughts'.[16]

But there is a completely different side to the story. Scripture and 'pastime' (i.e. recreation, amusement) blended uneasily in Anne's household. Both Anne's privy purse accounts and the Revels Accounts are missing for the years when she was queen, so that much of the glitter, the sparkle, the opulence of her side of the court is lost to us. But enough survives to show us that a striking transformation began almost at once. Just over a week after Anne's coronation, her vice-chamberlain, Sir Edward Baynton, penned a chatty letter to her brother George who had gone to observe the Franco-papal conference in Marseille. 'And as for pastime in the Queen's chamber', he wrote, '[it] was never more. If any of you that be now departed have any ladies that ye thought favoured you, and somewhat would mourn at [the de]parting of their servants, I can no whit perceive the same by their dancing and pastime they do use here.'[17]

The use of the word 'servants' in this context is illuminating. By 'servants', he, of course, meant *serviteurs* according to the code governing games of courtly love: the men who, as Marguerite of Angoulême had so presciently warned, wanted sex without strings, whether a woman was married or not.

Latymer's description bears little relation to Baynton's, and it is more the latter's view which Lancelot de Carle confirmed when he depicted Anne presiding over a French-style court of pleasure and courtly love. Around her, he said, there were

> Dances, games and multiple pastimes,
> Hunts and pleasures beyond compare
> To occupy lords and *demoiselles*.
> Many tournaments were undertaken for the ladies:
> Each man put his lance on his thigh,
> Or fought vigorously with the sword,
> Finally, all pleasures, disports,
> And all dalliances ended congenially.[18]

And there was always Anne's woman fool to provide jokes and more ribald entertainment. For her, the queen purchased gowns and a 'green satin cap' bedecked with 'fringing and garnishing'. We do not know the fool's name, but she spoke several languages and had been on a pilgrimage to Jerusalem. She may have been the same 'Jane the fool' who went on to serve both Queen Katherine Parr and Henry's daughter Mary.[19]

Poetry, in particular its lyric form, was the art form through which much of the game of courtly love was played. Circles of friends not only recited but sang (and in one case) danced poetic texts.[20] We can see how this culture thrived in Anne's circle through the extraordinary Devonshire Manuscript, so-called because it was borrowed from the Duke of Devonshire's library at Chatsworth early in the nineteenth century by G. F. Nott. He failed to return it: instead it was sold in January 1842 and is now in the British Library.[21] A pocket-sized volume of 114 folios together with ten somewhat fragmentary endpapers, the book circulated amongst a coterie of friends and lovers for private use; in it they wrote poems and inserted notes and signatures as though in a scrap book. Perhaps beginning as an amusing way for them to while away the hours, it contains poems and verses, some original, many copied, and extracts taken from literature which tell of lovers separated by the politics of their world, together with cryptic messages, jottings, ciphers, anagrams, marginalia and references to love and loss.

Many elements are culled from Chaucer's *Troilus and Criseyde*, now conveniently to hand in William Thynne's 1532 collected edition of the poet's *Works*.[22] In a biting satire of his own, printed in 1533 and entitled *Pasquil the Playne*, Sir Thomas Elyot, who supported Katherine, quipped that fashionable courtiers were never to be seen without a copy of *Troilus*.[23]

Compiled over a decade or so, the Devonshire Manuscript's contents suggest that the most intense period of writing and circulation was during the mid- to late 1530s and early 1540s. The volume seems to have belonged initially to Mary Howard (Fitzroy's wife), as the initials 'M.F.' are stamped in gold on the front cover, but Mary Shelton's signature is on the first of the endpapers and she acted as a kind of overseer.[24] There are between twelve and twenty contributors, with some entries little more than a word or two, filled in haphazardly over the years and often with wide spaces left between them. Crossings-out, interlineations, smudges, blots and marginal notes abound. Overall, the manuscript shares many of the characteristics of a notepad.[25]

The Devonshire Manuscript boasts three recurring themes. Secrecy in love is essential, as ears are always listening and eyes watching. Love is never untouched by politics, power or treachery, especially for women. Counterfeiting feelings is essential because ill-advised love affairs can have catastrophic consequences. The opening poem gives the flavour:

> Take hede be tyme leste ye be spyede [spied],
> Yo[r] lovyng Iyes [eyes] can not hide;
> At last the trwthe [truth] will sure be tryde [tried];
> Therefore, take hed [heed].
> For Som ther be of crafite [crafty] Kynde,
> Thowe [though] yow shew no parte of yo[r] mynde,
> Sewrlye there Ies [surely their eyes] ye can not blynde;
> Therefore, take hed [heed].[26]

Although some 129 out of a total of 185 poems in the manuscript have been attributed to Thomas Wyatt, including this one, nowhere does his handwriting appear in the folios and no evidence exists that he ever handled them. His compositions were either copied from elsewhere or, more likely, the contributors knew them off by heart.[27]

The book ended up as Margaret Douglas's property in or about 1537. Of the identifiable hands, Mary Shelton's is relatively prolific. She signed her name in two different places apart from the flyleaf and included verses of her own, in the margin of one of which she wrote 'r[h]yme dogrel'. Beside one poem she scrawled 'lerne but to syng yt'. In the margins of another in which a lovesick suitor describes himself as 'suffryng in sorow', someone (probably Margaret Douglas) scribbled the waspish retort: 'fforget thys'. In reply, Mary countered: 'yt ys worthy'. It seems she and the king's niece kept close company, as her entries often follow Margaret's. Then, below the final stanza, Mary added 'ondesyerd sarwes / reqwer no hyar / mary shelton [undesired service / require[s] no hire]'. The poem must have been written for her as the initial letters of its seven stanzas form the acrostic 'SHELTUN'. Acrostics and riddles, full of double hinges and hidden meanings, were all part of the courtly syntax which Mary, and Anne herself, knew so well.[28]

'Songes' or 'balettes' ('ballets' or ballads) were the terms contemporaries, including Anne, used to describe poems of this kind, and after his death, George Boleyn was remembered as an accomplished 'makar' (maker) of 'divers songs and sonnets', albeit not in Wyatt's league.[29] Possible poems by George have been much discussed by literary experts, but no firm candidates for a canon of his work can be identified.[30] Some of his verses, however, are said to have been printed in the mysterious *Courte of Venus*, published in 1538, of which no complete copy survives.[31] Queen Elizabeth's godson, John Harington, whose father was one of Henry's musicians and personally knew Wyatt, named George as the author of a celebrated poem in the *Courte of Venus* which appears as a variant in the Devonshire Manuscript, where it is claimed for Wyatt. Headlined by Harington as 'The lover complaineth of the unkindness of his love', it begins:

My lute awake; performe the last
Labour that thou and I shal wast[e],
and end that I have new begone [begun];
For when this song is gon[e] and past,
My lute be stil[l] for I have done.[32]

Another major contributor to the Devonshire Manuscript was the twenty-three-year-old Lord Thomas Howard, whose elder brother William led the challengers at Anne's coronation jousts. Twenty-eight poems are in his handwriting, chiefly by, or else adapted from Wyatt, but eight are his own work.[33] Of the remaining entries, two are verses by a kinsman of Mary Shelton, the twenty-seven-year-old Edmund Knyvet, although neither is in his handwriting.[34]

Did Anne also contribute? Some scholars maintain that a cryptic anagram refers to her:

am el men
anem e
as I haue dese
I ama yowrs an

The answer is said to be 'ANNA'.[35]

This is wishful thinking. The anagram has no obvious solution, and the handwriting bears no relation to Anne's. On the page, the lines are randomly scattered. The 'an' in the last line is not a signature. The final 'e' in the second line is out of alignment and looks more like a superscript. Someone could even have been testing their pen.[36]

Fully realised in the court masque, poetry and art were closely tied to dancing and music. Dancing was central to social and political engagement at Henry's court, and Anne danced in masques, disguisings and at festivals from the Château Vert entertainment onwards. Describing her years with Queen Claude, de Carle said, 'She knew how to sing and dance well / ... to play the lute and other instruments.' Whether chansons by Jean Mouton and Claudin de Sermisy were performed in her privy chamber as Henry's queen, we cannot know for sure. The tantalising clue is that the music book she brought home from France contains cues for performers of a uniquely English type.[37] On the minus side, the doubts and fears of having a woman in power could lead to accusations that she was a dancing whore.[38]

One song near the end of Anne's music manuscript may help us glimpse a little more. Entitled 'Jouyssance vous donneray' by de Sermisy, it was a setting of a lyric poem by Marot. His texts concern love in all its aspects, courtly, comic and serious, and the nature of the 'jouissance' promised here seems unambiguous: 'I will give you pleasure, my love / And I will lead you where your lively hope pretends / I will not leave you again when dead.' An imaginary performance of this very song dating from about the year 1520 can be seen in a remarkable painting by the so-called 'Master of the Female Half-lengths'. There, the piece is performed by three women for their private entertainment. With the score on a table before them, one plays the flute, another the lute, while the third sings.[39]

Anne's private apartments had a vibrant buzz of life about them, which invites discussion of the biggest conundrum of all: with the new ease with which men could visit the queen's side of the court, which male courtiers other than Lord Thomas Howard made their way there while attention was focused elsewhere? Initially, Henry's privy chamber intimates came to 'pay court' to Anne largely (as they thought) to flatter him for marrying his trophy wife and as a matter of self-interest. Soon, however, they realised that the games, the banter, the interaction with the women made it an enjoyable way to spend time. Of the male courtiers flitting in and out – other than Anne's uncle, Sir James Boleyn, and other principal officers – her brother George was chief. They had always been close and Anne's rise to power was very much a Boleyn family enterprise.

The logistics of court communications dictated that Henry Norris, as the king's chief gentleman, would also regularly appear carrying messages. One of Henry's most favoured servants since at least 1517, he shared Anne's evangelical sympathies and was happy to have his son educated in her household by Nicholas Bourbon.

In his early thirties and recently widowed, he was regarded by Anne's gentlewomen as a potential catch. His heraldic coat-of-arms featured a merlin and Baynton, in his chatty letter to George, directly following on from his mention of *serviteurs*, says, 'there is a hawk that is called a merlyon [merlin] that I do think is not yet ready to fly at the larks in this country.' If Baynton meant Norris, as surely he must, it suggests that although he was not yet ready to wed again, he could still be considered fair game for Anne's unmarried women.[40]

Francis Weston, one of the Knights of the Bath created at Anne's coronation and a nephew of William Weston, the head of the Order of the Knights Hospitaller of St John, was another visitor: we know this since Anne would make no secret of it.[41] Henry liked him too, paying for his apparel and giving him money on his marriage. Born in 1511 and a gentleman of the privy chamber when he was twenty-one, he was renowned as a dancer, horseman and tennis-player and for his skill at cards, bowls and dice, at which he sometimes partnered Anne and regularly beat Henry. His marriage to Anne Pickering, the daughter and heir of Sir Christopher Pickering of Killington in Cumbria, did not stop him from playing games of courtly love. George Cavendish described him as one who 'wantonly lived without fear or dread' who, not fearing God, followed 'his fantasy and his wanton lust'.[42]

Mark Smeaton was a musician and groom of the privy chamber sometimes summoned by Anne to play the virginals. He may have begun his career in service to her brother, who gave his copy of a fifteenth-century French translation of *The Lamentations of Matheolus* to Smeaton, who inscribed in it: 'À moi, M. Marc S'. A Latin verse satire on women and the miseries of marriage by the thirteenth-century cleric Mathieu of Boulogne, the manuscript, now in the British Library, includes both the satire and the translator's rebuttal.[43] Otherwise, Smeaton is a shadowy figure about whom little is known. One scholar claims that several of the annotations in Anne's music book are Smeaton's, but there is no proof. Generally agreed is that he came of humble stock: Cavendish claimed his father was a carpenter and his mother eked out a living by spinning.[44]

William Brereton, who in June 1530 had been given a reward of
£40 for carrying Henry's petition to the pope around the country
for signature, is often said to have spent much time in the queen's
apartments but is unlikely to have done so.[45] The unreliable *Spanish
Chronicle* claims he was among those to whom Anne showed
greatest favour, while citing no evidence.[46] Whatever the truth,
Brereton, already in his late forties, was no gallant youth fluttering
about Anne. Succeeding his father as the chamberlain of Chester
before Anne became queen, he was increasingly absent from court.
Baynton's letter to George begins by saying, 'Master William
Brereton hath not been here since your lordship's departure for to
have communication in the matter your lordship put me in trust
in.' The probability is that his younger brother, Urian, with whom
Anne had gone out hunting, had more to do with her.[47]

The most notable absentee is Wyatt: no evidence exists that
he frequented Anne's side of the court while she was queen. The
chances are that after deputising for his father as chief ewerer at her
coronation banquet he spent much of the next three years helping
to consolidate the status of his family in Kent and Yorkshire. In 1535,
the year he was knighted, he secured the lucrative high stewardship
of the abbey of West Malling in Kent and an eighty-year lease on
Arygden Park in Yorkshire. Surviving correspondence proves that
he owed the grant of the high stewardship to Henry, not to Anne.[48]

The Devonshire Manuscript aside, we lack specific examples of
dalliance to back up Baynton's disclosure that with Anne as queen,
'pastime in the Queen's chamber ... was never more'. The code of
silence attached to the subject is understandable: both honour and
discretion required it. But there is one sensational exception which
proves how discipline in Anne's apartments became laxer than
under Katherine with the relatively free mingling of the sexes.

In the sultry summer of 1535 while the court was on its progress
towards Bristol, Margaret Douglas, now nearly twenty, found it
possible not just to exchange poems with Lord Thomas Howard, but
also to embark upon a steamy sexual relationship. The Devonshire
Manuscript contains seventeen poems in her handwriting (and she
marked or annotated another forty-three), and at least one leading

scholar confidently believes that she used them to chronicle the earlier stages of the relationship, as well as the more calamitous conclusion.[49] Courtly love with its exhilarating language and repartee, its music, poetry and sexual frisson, had finally got out of hand. Eight or nine months into the relationship, around Easter 1536, her lover secretly proposed, and shortly afterwards, he and Douglas contracted a clandestine marriage, exchanging pledges to marry *per verba de praesenti* ('by vows made in the present time'), and not *de futuro*, which, if so, meant they were legally married.[50]

The couple took great care that Anne did not suspect them, and they were successful – it was not until six weeks after her execution that the truth seeped out. Sent by Cromwell to handle the interrogations was a young, ambitious clerk in the king's signet office, Thomas Wriothesley, who had copied out portions of early drafts of the 'King's Book' on the divorce and helped William Brereton collect signatures for the petition to the pope.[51] A terrified Thomas Smith, one of Lord Thomas's servants, testified how his lovesick master would loiter in the corridors close to Anne's privy chamber, waiting to see when the coast was clear. 'He would watch', he said, 'till my Lady Boleyn* was gone and then steal into her chamber' to make love to Douglas. What made it worse, Mary Howard was often present, aiding and abetting the delinquents.[52] When questioned himself, Lord Thomas confessed the affair had begun 'about a twelve months' previously, and that the couple had exchanged tokens. He had given Douglas cramp rings, and she gave him a diamond and a miniature portrait of herself. Another accessory to their affair was Anne's gentlewoman, Margaret Gamage, who went on to marry Lord William Howard as his second wife.[53]

The couple had ignored Marguerite of Angoulême's wisdom that in royal courts, a woman should avoid the love that becomes too powerful to be concealed. The result was that a full-blown illicit affair, and involving no less a person than Henry's niece, began

---

*This refers to Lady Elizabeth Boleyn, who it seems policed the queen's apartments.

in Anne's household under her very nose. Did she know about it and tolerate it, which, given the strict protocol on marriages to members of the royal family or indeed her own stubborn rejection of her sister Mary for a similar offence, seems unlikely? Or did she lose control of what was happening within her immediate circle? Whichever was the case, it exposed a damaging vulnerability.

26

Court Conspiracy

By June 1535, Anne's attempts to betroth her daughter Elizabeth to the Duke of Angoulême had come to nothing. Her brother George's mission to Calais had miserably failed, but a fresh twist meant all was far from lost: Charles was preparing again for war in Italy and Francis might need England yet. After recapturing Tunis from the Turks, Charles shipped a large field army from Barcelona to Sicily. From there, he set out towards Naples, heading for Rome at the start of what he envisaged as a triumphal march through Italy. In Paris, the Duke de Montmorency retired to his estates in Chantilly, clearing the way for Admiral Chabot, who led the war party. Francis was not quite ready yet to cross the Alps. He needed more time to secure his alliances and muster his troops. Further delays ensued when he fell sick in Dijon with suspected dysentery and needed three months to convalesce.[1]

Before leaving with Anne on their summer progress towards Bristol, Henry struck at the Carthusian priors John Houghton and Richard Reynolds, then at Thomas More and John Fisher, the four most celebrated opponents of his break with Rome. He had so far hesitated, aware of the danger of making martyrs out of such eminent men. He picked off the priors first, commissioning a special court in Westminster Hall to 'hear and determine' their 'damnable treasons', packing the bench by appointing to it Cromwell, the Duke of Norfolk and Anne's brother George and her father,

among others, so that the professional judges were outnumbered
by courtiers eleven to ten. When the jurors refused to convict,
Cromwell, in a rage, stormed into the jury room, threatening them
so that, terrified, they brought in a guilty verdict.[2]

Henry had More and Fisher indicted after Pope Paul made the
latter a cardinal and sent him his red hat. Indignant at the news,
the king placed an embargo on the hat when it arrived in Calais.
Then, laughing uproariously, he promised Anne that he would
teach Fisher a lesson. 'Let the Pope send him a hat when he will,'
he exclaimed, 'but I will so provide that whensoever it commeth,
he shall wear it on his shoulders; for head shall he have none to set
it on.'[3]

Faced with the newly devised oath of supremacy, Fisher, who
had pastoral responsibilities, resolutely denied it and was convicted
of treason. More's situation was different, as was his approach. As
a layman, he was content to be a private citizen and so refused
to answer, which under the Treason Act was not an offence. In
hounding these men through the courts, Henry delighted Anne,
who agreed with him that anyone who opposed them must face the
consequences. When on Thursday 1 July, More entered a packed
Westminster Hall, he would have visibly paled on seeing whom
Cromwell had placed in the jury box: among them were Sir Thomas
Palmer, one of the king's favourite dicing partners; Sir Thomas
Spert, the Clerk Comptroller of the Royal Navy; Geoffrey Chamber,
one of Cromwell's lesser minions; and most disconcertingly, John
Parnell, a fast-talking Lutheran and vintner to the Boleyns who had
tried to have More impeached for a judgment he had given against
him as Lord Chancellor.[4]

To guarantee a conviction, Richard Rich, the Solicitor-General
and only witness for the prosecution, selectively reported what
More had said to him in the Tower. Once the jury had returned
and declared a guilty verdict, but before sentence was handed
down, More availed himself of a technical procedure known as
'motion in arrest of judgment'. Its purpose was to allow the accused
to address the court in mitigation. We know what More said
thanks to a detailed report in French, made by a secretary to the

recently arrived Antoine de Castelnau, almost certainly Lancelot de Carle, who independently informs us of his knowledge of the trial. Speaking his true mind now, More defied Henry, saying that the Act of Supremacy was invalid because Parliament lacked the authority to make it. Cuttingly, he mocked George Boleyn's failed efforts to persuade Francis to break with Rome.[5]

For the Duke of Norfolk, who had been on two of these missions and was More's longstanding friend, this rankled. It was not so much whether the Boleyns' policy of attempting to persuade Francis to break with the pope had been credible; the sting was in More's innuendo that everyone knew it had failed and that Henry was being misled by his wife.

Still, the verdict was unavoidable. The priors, Fisher and More were all executed on Tower Hill, their severed heads set upon poles on London Bridge as a warning to others. To stifle the last prayers of the priors, who had suffered the full horrors of hanging, disembowelling and quartering, the hangman stuffed their severed genitals into their mouths to choke them. Thomas and George Boleyn joined those courtiers who went along to watch.[6]

On 26 July, Pope Paul issued a decree in the Consistory condemning Henry as a heretic and schismatic, and depriving him of his kingdom.[7] Christian princes were ordered to shun him but the king and Anne, then out daily hunting and hawking, were unperturbed. With Charles keeping everybody in Italy fully occupied, Rome had no chance of enforcing the decree. Throughout July, August and September Henry and Anne were happy together, feasting, making love, entertaining guests, honouring those who had voted for the royal supremacy and Treason Act in Parliament by paying them visits.[8] When on the road towards Bristol, Will Somer, the king's inexperienced new fool, attempted 'ribald jests' at Anne's and her daughter's expense, Henry physically attacked him. Somer fled for his life, taking refuge with Nicholas Carew at his house in Beddington until the king calmed down.[9]

For six days in the first week of September, Henry and Anne were guests of Sir John Seymour and his wife at Wolf Hall in Wiltshire, closely watched by Cromwell, who on 23 July had joined the royal progress in Winchcombe and shadowed it for the next two months.[10] As we know, their daughter Jane was one of Anne's gentlewomen. Whether she was at home that summer we do not know, but the chances are she was. Henry had so far barely noticed her – but before long would be thinking wistfully of her.[11]

In Winchester, Anne attended the consecrations of Edward Foxe as Bishop of Hereford and Hugh Latimer as Bishop of Worcester. They received their staffs and mitres on the same day as John Hilsey, a protégé of Cromwell who replaced Fisher.[12] While in the city, Anne tried to renew contact with Marguerite of Angoulême, begging de Castelnau to relay to her a message stating, 'What I most desire other than having a son is for God to give me the grace to see you again'.[13]

By now Francis had sent Jean de Dinteville on a special mission to London, where Pope Paul's decree had caused uproar. Italian merchants fled the city and the Londoners feared for their livelihoods, believing Charles was poised to impose fresh trade embargoes on English goods just at the time when Anglo-Flemish trade was booming. De Dinteville was to inform Henry that Francis would be happy to stand by him, but if mutual assistance was needed against Charles, or if Francis chose for any reason to reassert his claim to Milan, then England must bear at least one-third of the costs. Henry granted de Dinteville an audience near Winchester, but declined to answer his proposals, instead offering to send one of his councillors to France to continue talks.[14]

Before returning to France, de Dinteville asked to visit Henry's daughters, and was escorted to the royal nursery in Eltham. On arrival, he was allowed to see Elizabeth, but not Mary. According to Chapuys, Mary wanted to meet him, but on Anne's instructions, Lady Shelton shut her up in her room and had the windows sealed. De Dinteville's version was that his escort, a gentleman of Henry's privy chamber, had surreptitiously warned him that he had secret instructions from Anne to spy on him, so there would have been no point in visiting Mary anyway.[15]

The trusted councillor Henry sent to France as resident ambassador was Stephen Gardiner, a man no longer palatable to

Anne. His instructions were to negotiate the best possible terms for a fresh anti-Habsburg alliance. He was not to rule out subsidies for Francis's international ambitions but must ensure that Henry's contributions to any future French campaigns were kept to a minimum.[16]

Scarcely had Gardiner located Francis when news arrived from Italy of the death on 1 November of Francesco Sforza, Duke of Milan. Jean du Bellay, still languishing in Rome, predicted that Sforza's death 'will bring to a head all of Christendom's affairs, and not just those of Italy'.[17] In 1534, Charles had married Sforza to his twelve-year-old niece, Christina of Denmark. (She was the daughter of Christian II of Denmark and Charles's sister Isabella, whom Anne would have remembered from the Mechelen schoolroom.) Since the bride had been too young for children, the duchy was claimed by Charles. Francis was determined to block that.

Henry sent Anne's cousin, Francis Bryan, to France, to update Gardiner and seek an audience with Marguerite of Angoulême. Since war had become likelier, Bryan was to seek her advice on how best to revive the Treaty of Mutual Aid. He was also to raise a variety of commercial disputes involving the detention of English ships and their cargoes in the harbour in Bordeaux, clashes which were beginning to cloud Anglo-French relations.[18]

Determined to monopolise the flow of information, Cromwell instructed Bryan, who found Marguerite near Seurre in Burgundy, to report to him and Henry alone, and not, as in the past, to Anne as well. If Anne's message to Marguerite relayed by de Castelnau marked an attempt to reopen an independent diplomacy, Cromwell firmly nipped it in the bud. What's more, Cromwell, not Anne, drafted Bryan's terms of reference for the mission, even though one of its main objectives was to win over Marguerite.[19]

Now Anne and her brother's power struggle with Cromwell had begun. In 1534, she had made Cromwell high steward of her jointure lands, but that grant was a sinecure, a sweetener rather than a real role. So far, their sparring had been intermittent, beginning a month or so after Anne's coronation, when she had vetoed the marriage of Cromwell's favourite nephew, Richard Williams, to the widowed daughter-in-law of Sir William Courtenay of Powderham, as she felt Courtenay had snubbed her when he excused himself from her coronation. In that skirmish, Anne was the victor.[20] Shortly afterwards, Anne refused to take the wife of Stephen Vaughan, one of Cromwell's most trusted servants, as her silkwoman in place of Jane Wilkinson. This was despite the woman submitting examples of her handiwork for Anne to inspect.[21]

George first quarrelled with Cromwell in November 1534 after he was overruled in his capacity as Warden of the Cinque Ports and Constable of Dover Castle. When George gave orders to the Mayor of Rye, Cromwell countermanded them without informing him, so he learned of the reversal through third parties. It seemed to George, who laid out his grievances in a courteous but transparently pained letter, that Cromwell had encouraged complaints against him, since he had intervened in another matter which 'I never heard of before'. When the circumstances were investigated, George maintained, he believed Cromwell would find he had dealt 'both in right and justice' and 'ye will find no fault therewith'.[22]

The gap between Anne and Cromwell widened once Pope Paul began to back his sanctions with a credible enforcement plan. In an unsettling move, Charles's sisters – Eleanor, Francis's wife, and Marie of Hungary, the new regent of the Low Countries – held secret talks on the Flemish border with Admiral Chabot in attendance. The upshot was that Francis, while reserving his position, agreed to assist the pope in carrying out his sentences if Charles did too.

Fully aware of such developments, Chapuys inveigled Cromwell into closer, more intimate confidences. A consensus emerged between them that Anne was the main obstacle to an Anglo-Habsburg rapprochement which, from Cromwell's perspective, had all along been the way to circumvent papal sanctions and guarantee free trade for English merchants in their most important markets. It was also, he believed, consistent with the king's true principles and beliefs, for he knew Henry still harboured doubts about his break with the pope. On 13 December, from Naples, Charles wrote secretly to Cromwell, thanking him for his signals of support and offering 'to gratify him in anything that may occur, so that he may know that he has not ill-employed his pains'. It was a letter we can be confident Cromwell did not share with Henry.[23]

Although Anne and Henry celebrated Christmas at Eltham with a reduced court, they were exultant. Anne was pregnant again. Writing shortly afterwards to Lady Shelton about her many failed attempts to force Henry's daughter Mary to acknowledge or defer to her, she remarked, 'What I have done has been more for charity than for anything the king or I care what road she takes, or whether she will change her purpose, for if I have a son, as I hope shortly, I know what will happen to her.'[24]

It was from Eltham on the 27th that Henry summoned Chapuys to visit him, but two days later letters arrived from Katherine's Spanish physician in Kimbolton warning that she was likely to die, and the ambassador rushed to see her for one final time. The final crisis of what may well have been stomach cancer began on Christmas Day. Katherine died peacefully at about 2 p.m. on 7 January 1536 and would be interred three weeks later as Dowager Princess of Wales in the north transept of Peterborough Abbey. Swiftly inventoried by Sir Edward Baynton, most of her possessions, notably two ivory chessboards, went to Henry, but others came to Anne.[25]

On the day after Katherine's death, which was the first Sunday after Epiphany, Anne and Henry dressed in yellow satin. Although the fact is sometimes questioned, Edward Hall is emphatic that Anne at least 'wore yellow for the mourning'. Henry, who sported a white feather in his hat, led Elizabeth to Mass, holding her hand in the grand procession to Chapel to the sound of 'trumpets and other great triumphs'. After dinner, he danced with her in his arms, showing her off 'first to one and then to another' of his courtiers while her pregnant mother looked on in delight. For the Boleyns, this was a time for happy families. Henry had already told Chapuys that with Katherine out of the way, Charles would 'no longer have cause to trouble himself about the affairs of this kingdom'.[26]

Calamity then struck in two stages. While jousting in the lists at Greenwich on the 24th, Henry had a serious riding accident. Knocked off his horse by an opponent, he fell to the ground while fully armed, with his horse on top of him. The court came to a standstill: would he survive, and if he did, would he be paralysed? For two hours he lay concussed and immobile before returning to consciousness. Five days later, the very day on which Katherine was buried, Anne miscarried a male foetus, said to be about three and a half months old. She claimed it was fright and worry for her husband that caused her to miscarry, blaming her uncle Norfolk for delivering the news insensitively. Henry at first kept his own counsel: although severely shaken by his accident, he was determined never to show it. In a state of denial, he went onto the attack, declaring how he had invested all his hopes in Anne's giving him a living son and she had let him down. 'I see', he said grimly, 'that God will not give me male children.'²⁷

In response, Anne turned on him for looking at Jane Seymour and the unnamed woman with whom he had flirted at the time he rusticated George's wife from court. Her tongue-lashing did her no good. Henry's thoughts were now running riot: if the intelligence slipped to Chapuys by Henry Courtenay and his wife was accurate, he had already told his privy chamber intimates that Anne had used sorcery to win his affections. After all, it simply had to be her fault, not his, that her promises to give him a healthy son had come to nothing. Jane Seymour was waiting in the wings, backed by her brothers and their allies. Or at least, this is the conventional explanation of what was shortly to unfold.²⁸

But there is more to it. Coming to the fore was Henry's own innate sense of insecurity. It did not take much imagination for him to discern that the mood in France was fast turning against him. With Katherine dead, a rapprochement with Charles was entirely feasible. And where Anne was concerned, betrayal was the order of the day. While shadowing Francis's court as the English ambassador, Gardiner, the man to whom she had once sent cramp rings, rubbed shoulders with the papal nuncio to France, Rodolfo Pio da Carpi, who had embarked on a vitriolic smear campaign to blacken her name. After news of her miscarriage reached him, he started a rumour that Anne – whom he called 'that woman' ('quella fem[m]ina') – had never actually been pregnant and only pretended to miscarry to play for time, with her sister Mary abetting her. It was in this context that di Carpi quoted Francis's purported remark that Anne's sister had 'done service' to him and his courtiers while in France.[29]

According to Alexander Ales (*alias* Alan), a young Scots evangelical in Cromwell's entourage, Gardiner fed back hostile reports about Anne to Thomas Wriothesley, who passed them on to Cromwell. Ales is not a disinterested party: he wrote his memoir a quarter of a century later for Anne's daughter on her accession as queen. All the same, his detail is graphic. Writing in Latin, Ales maintained that Gardiner's reports to Wriothesley included copies of 'certain letters' accusing Anne of adultery. Cromwell then briefed the king, who ordered surveillance. 'Spies' watched Anne's apartments and suborned her servants, on the strength of which Cromwell informed Henry that his wife had been observed dancing and disporting herself ('ducentem choreas') with certain gentlemen of the king's privy chamber, and he could produce witnesses who would say they saw her kissing her own brother. 'And they have in their possession letters in which she informs him [George] that she is pregnant.'[30]

The only authentic detail in Ales's account is likely to be that Gardiner was supplying Cromwell with ammunition designed to discredit Anne. Cromwell's exceptional praise for Gardiner, a man he intensely disliked, conveyed to Chapuys around this time reinforces these suspicions.[31] On 24 February, Cromwell secretly met Chapuys early in the morning at his house in the Austin Friars. In what soon developed into an audacious conspiracy, they discussed terms for an Anglo-Habsburg 'amity', although Cromwell made it clear that, so far, he was acting on his own initiative.[32]

Chapuys immediately wrote to Charles for fresh instructions. A second rendezvous with Cromwell was then unexpectedly cancelled after news arrived that Admiral Chabot had occupied Savoy. The French armies did not cross the frontier to attack Milan yet as if there was to be war, Francis wanted Charles to be the one to start it. When de Castelnau briefed Henry and Cromwell about the French plans and the advantages of a joint enterprise, he was roundly rebuffed. Instead of receiving the support Francis might have expected, all de Castelnau got was bickering over the commercial disputes between the two countries.[33]

On 27 March, the letter Chapuys sent Charles seeking new instructions reached him in Gaeta, just south of Rome. Things were moving fast: by then, Henry's court was buzzing with talk of Jane Seymour. Just like Anne before her, Jane refused to become the king's mistress but, unlike her, did so sweetly and self-effacingly. Probably even the Boleyns did not know exactly when Henry became besotted with the woman who was such a contrast to the spirited Anne, but Jane was on the scene by the end of February, when the king made her brother, Edward, a gentleman of the privy chamber. In mid-March, while Jane was attending Anne in Greenwich, Henry sent her a letter and a purse full of sovereigns, which gifted her an opportunity for which she had been well coached by Nicholas Carew. After kissing the missive, she returned it unopened, 'then throwing herself on her knees', begged the messenger humbly to inform the king that 'she was a gentlewoman of good and honourable parents'. She 'had no greater riches in the world than her honour', she said, 'which she would not injure for a thousand deaths'. If Henry 'wished to make her some present in money, she begged it might be when God enabled her to make some honourable match'.[34]

It was a performance worthy of Katherine in her youth. On hearing of it, Henry declared how Jane 'had behaved most virtuously', and from now on he would visit her only in the presence of her relatives. Naturally, the carefully tutored Jane declined this too. And, equally naturally, Henry admired her virtue even more.

At a dinner Chapuys hosted for the Courtenays in late March, all the talk was of a feud between Anne and Cromwell and of Henry's plans for a new marriage, conceivably to Jane. Speaking later to Cromwell in a bay window out of earshot at the ambassador's house, Chapuys ventured to suggest (as he informed Charles) that a new marriage 'would be the way to avoid much evil'. Everyone knew, he said, that whatever was said or preached from the pulpit, Henry and Anne's relationship 'will never be held as lawful', but if a fight was coming, Cromwell should prepare himself for it better than Wolsey had done.

To this, Cromwell replied that he was fully conscious of the perils of royal courts. He defended his conduct, saying he had never promoted the Boleyn marriage, but 'had merely smoothed the way'. Then, leaning against the window and putting his hand to his mouth to suppress a pretence of laughter, he assured Chapuys that 'despite Henry's natural inclination to entertain and serve ladies (*à festoyer et servir dames*), he still believed he would continue to live honestly and chastely in his present marriage ... but should he happen to choose another wife, she would certainly not be French.' It was a response, it seems, that Charles anticipated in his instructions to Chapuys, where he added: 'And if perhaps the king of England should wish to marry again, you are not to discourage it.'[35]

At Mass on Passion Sunday, 2 April, Anne gave Cromwell the chance he needed. It was the day of the final Lenten sermon, and she arranged for John Skip, her new almoner, to deliver it before Henry and the entire court in the Chapel Royal in Whitehall. Skip began by reminding his audience how in the Old Testament, the children of Israel had been grievously punished 'for that they would not give firm confidence and belief unto the Word of God'. It all seemed uncontroversial, until Skip began to call upon those in authority, not just clergy, but the nobility and higher powers, to ensure that when 'looking upon other men's faults', they did so charitably, or else 'they may be damned for their labour'.

As Skip warmed to his theme, his sermon turned into a biting critique of Henry and Cromwell's policy for which, afterwards, he was repeatedly interrogated. Charges levelled against him included malice, slander, presumption, lack of charity, sedition, treason, deviation from the Gospels and attacking 'the great posts, pillars and columns sustaining up and holding up the commonwealth as principally the king, secondly his council, thirdly his nobles, fourthly the whole Parliament'. Contempt of Parliament was an especially threatening accusation.[36]

Skip preached this sermon a fortnight after Parliament, now reconvened, had approved a bill Henry personally laid before it to seize for the royal coffers the wealth of some 200 of the smaller monasteries. The legislation left Henry free to spend the proceeds at his discretion: no provision was made for education, welfare or the relief of the poor, provoking a clash of wills with Anne. Twelve days still had to elapse before Parliament's closing session at which the king would give the royal assent to the bill, making it law. Skip's sermon was thus not just a trenchant exhortation for Lent, but specifically triggered by the decision to secularise monastic endowments. Anne was weaponising Skip in a final appeal from the pulpit to her husband's conscience to get him to rethink his plans.

During the last summer progress, Anne had been presented with a book, *The Forme and Man[n]er of Subvention or Helpyng for Po[or] People*, which its author, William Marshall, a talented London lawyer and evangelical, dedicated to her. (She already knew of Marshall from a reforming 'Prymer' modelled on Books of Hours, printed with the 'HA' cipher on the title page above the royal arms.) The book described how the civic authorities of Ypres in Flanders had pioneered a trailblazing welfare system, and in his preface, Marshall praised Anne as 'the flower of all queens', appealing to her to be 'a mediatrix and mean[s]', so that 'under the shield, protection and defence of our most dread sovereign lord and your most dear husband', similar ideas might prevail in England.[37]

After reading Marshall's book, Anne became the eager patron of a sixty-six-page poor law draft which he prepared. The draft is often attributed to Cromwell's patronage, but it was never filed among his papers, did not originate from his office and was not written on the paper stock used by his clerks and assistants. Marshall's ideas were ambitious, aiming to remedy the problems of poverty and unemployment by instituting a national programme of engineering works on roads, harbours, public buildings, rivers and watercourses. In overall charge was to be a 'Council to avoid vagabonds'. Able-bodied persons employed on the scheme were to receive 'reasonable wages' funded by a graduated tax on wealthier clergy and property-owners, besides food and free medical care. Vagabonds failing to report for work were to be arrested and forced into labour. The sick, disabled and others genuinely incapacitated were to receive relief funded through taxes and parish collections. Overseers of the poor were to punish the idle or recalcitrant.[38]

An eyewitness vividly reported how, in Parliament in the second week of March 1536, Cromwell, acting on Henry's instructions (or just possibly a House of Commons' committee acting autonomously), bowdlerised the reform bill. Under watered-down proposals, it became the responsibility of local mayors and other municipal and parish officials to find work for the unemployed. Vagrants and lazy beggars were to be forced into handicrafts, but the 'deserving' poor were to be relieved as were lepers and the bedridden. Poor children were to be found training or apprenticeships. The flaw in these modified arrangements was that funding now relied on voluntary acts of charity.[39]

In a deliberate leak from Cromwell's office two days before the dissolution bill was presented to the House of Lords, the claim was that the smaller religious houses would be suppressed 'to the king's use for the maintenance of certain notable persons in learning and good qualities about his Highness'. This persuaded well-informed eyewitnesses to believe that the dissolution bill and Marshall's poor relief bill were directly connected. The one would generate the funds necessary for the other.[40]

The truth is that even as Cromwell peddled this disinformation, Henry was selling lands belonging to Sawley and Coverham abbeys in Yorkshire.[41] So strongly did Anne feel about such pillaging, she tried to reprieve at least two nunneries. 'The queen's Grace hath moved the king's Majesty for me, and hath offered his Highness two thousand marks [worth over £1.3 million today] in recompense of that house of Catesby', wrote Joyce Bekeley, the ousted Cistercian prioress to Cromwell some weeks later, 'and hath as yet no perfect answer.' Anne next tried to save the Benedictine nunnery at Nun Monkton in Yorkshire, but it was still suppressed. William Latymer tells of a delegation of abbots and priors calling on Anne once her opposition to suppression was known, seeking her protection. Shaken by the findings of Cromwell's visitation commissioners, she lectured them on their failings, but hinted that she might change her mind if they reformed and considered putting part of their wealth towards supporting 'poor students in the universities, of whom there may be hope of profiting the congregation of Christ and our native country'.[42]

During his sermon – something he would never have dared to do unless incited by Anne – Skip revisited the biblical story of King Ahasuerus. According to the biblical text, the king's chief minister, Haman, offered to pay 10,000 talents to cover the costs of killing the Jews, but Ahasuerus said he could keep his money as he was only interested in Jewish disregard for his laws.[43] Skip, however, rescripted the narrative so that in his version, Haman promised to *raise* 10,000 talents for the royal coffers. He then embellishes his story by adding that, once Haman is told by Ahasuerus that he could keep for himself any money raised from the pogrom, he was 'much more crueller against them [the Jews] than he was before, because he perceived that he should have the 10,000 talents'.

With this adaption of the story, Skip fed a suspicion, already sweeping across the country, that Cromwell and his apparatchiks saw the confiscation of monastic assets as a chance to line their own pockets.[44] 'But', as Skip continued, 'there was a good woman which this gentle King Ahasuerus loved very well and put his trust in because he knew that she was ever his friend.' She gave the king the opposite advice, 'declaring unto him the innocence of the said [Jewish] people and the malicious intent of his said councillor Haman'. The Jews were saved and Haman hanged.[45]

No one in Skip's audience could have missed the allusion. Ahasuerus was Henry, Haman was Cromwell and the good woman, whom Skip tactfully did not identify, was the queen, Ahasuerus's wife Esther – for whom read Anne. Skip was announcing in barely coded language that Anne wished to reverse the decision to suppress these monasteries for purely financial gain. The analogy with Esther came naturally to her: the same biblical heroine had been Queen Claude's role model.

By encouraging Skip to depict Henry as a misguided ruler and Cromwell as the king's evil genius, Anne infuriated her husband. The last time similar sentiments had been invoked was in London at the time of the arrests of Empson and Dudley.[46] We can

understand her motive: she meant to shock him into remembering
that he had once promised her that he would trust her; that they
would work together in a partnership with shared values, allowing
her to exercise power on her own account and take the lead in such
matters as educational and welfare reform. What she overlooked
was how far her husband cared about his reputation – she would
not be allowed to humiliate him before his entire court like this.
Her actions put his masculinity on the line.

Anne was still presiding at court on 15 April when a fast courier
arrived from Gaeta bearing Charles's instructions to Chapuys. As
they were lengthy and in cipher, he had to work through the night
to read them. Finally, he knew their contents. He was authorised
to negotiate a full offensive and defensive alliance with England,
provided Henry settled with the pope and restored his daughter
Mary to her title and rightful place in the succession. Always a
pragmatist, Charles softened these conditions by promising to do
all he could to reconcile Henry to the pope, which could be done
through mediators. Restoring Mary, he knew, would be almost
impossible with Anne around, but he left the door ajar. If she
abandoned France and embraced the new alliance, she could stay
as queen, since with Katherine dead, Charles no longer felt tied
on that point. If she resisted the proposed terms, he told Chapuys:

> you should not break off the talks but try to find out exactly
> what it is she wants ('ne faut pourtant enfin rompre la pratique,
> mais assentir du tout en tout ce aussi à quoi elle s'arrêtera');
> and, after making such representations to her as you think fit,
> say you will refer to us. If you find her demands too excessive
> you may use Cromwell's help if he can and will do what he has
> promised.[47]

But from where Cromwell sat, if Henry was to switch sides, both
Anne and her brother – who had championed the Anglo-French
alliance from the outset – had to go. He knew Anne would never
take advantage of the terms offered by Charles. She might perhaps
agree to cloak her Lefèvrist sympathies: Marguerite of Angoulême

did the same after the Affair of the Placards. What Anne would never agree to was restoring Mary. She would fight for Elizabeth, her own daughter, as Katherine had fought for hers. Cromwell knew the score. All he needed was a pretext to propel Henry into action.

27

Into the Abyss

The fast courier's arrival from Gaeta was the prelude to what Henry hoped to turn into a bidding war between Charles and Francis's ambassadors for his support.[1] On Easter Day, 16 April, Chapuys requested an audience and was put off until Tuesday. Antoine de Castelnau asked for, and was granted, one for Wednesday. Over the festival, the king made a show of continuing commitment to Anne. He resumed dining and sleeping with her and was making plans to take her to Dover to inspect the defences, and afterwards to Calais where he had established a gun foundry. The Boleyns were still receiving valuable grants of land or leases. Throughout Lent, it had been Anne's protégés who preached the officially approved sermons at Paul's Cross in London. Although he might be considering it, Henry was not easily to be nudged into switching alliances after the indignities that Charles had heaped upon him.[2]

On reaching Greenwich early on Tuesday, Chapuys was greeted by George Boleyn. When Henry was ready to process along the gallery to Mass in the Chapel Royal, Cromwell arrived and asked Chapuys if he would first pay his respects to Anne, explaining, as the flustered envoy later told Charles, that after dinner 'I should speak with the king at leisure, and that on leaving him, according to their custom, I should go into the council chamber and explain my charge.' Out of loyalty to Katherine (and to reflect his master's official position), Chapuys, so far, had scrupulously avoided acknowledging Anne as Henry's wife, speaking of her in the third person only as 'the Lady' or 'the Concubine'. He made his excuses, but on being escorted inside the Chapel by George, found himself placed near the door where Anne would descend from her elevated pew during the offertory. Knowing he would be there, she deliberately turned to him as she passed, forcing him to bow, before sweeping to her place at Henry's side. For her it was a victory and one she particularly prized; for the ambassador, a humiliation.

After Mass, Henry dined with Anne, leaving George to take Chapuys to dinner with the principal noblemen in Henry's own Dining Chamber. This very much disappointed Anne, who was fully aware of, and concerned by, the diplomatic see-saw playing out around her. After dinner, she put on a show of abandoning her commitment to the French alliance. 'It is a great shame', she said using weasel words, 'for the king of France to treat his own uncle, the Duke of Savoy, as he was doing, and make preparations for the invasion of Milan ... It is as if the king of France, weary of life on account of his illnesses, wishes by war to shorten his days.'[3]

Chapuys got his audience with Henry after dinner. Led into the recesses of a bay window in the king's privy chamber, he made his pitch for an Anglo-Habsburg alliance, after which Henry summoned Cromwell, to whom everything was repeated. Chapuys was then sent to make small talk with Edward Seymour, Jane's brother, in another corner of the room, while Henry and Cromwell engaged in a vehement altercation in the window. Henry was not ready to commit quite yet. He insisted on waiting to hear what the French had to offer. Finally, Cromwell, 'at breaking point' (*rompant et grandissant*), claimed to be 'so thirsty he could continue no longer', sending for something to drink and recovering his composure by sitting out of Henry's sightline on a coffer.

Henry recalled Chapuys to the window, telling him that the proposed terms must be set down in writing before he could respond. To Cromwell's barely concealed irritation, he added that his quarrel with the pope, of which Anne was the chief symbol, was his personal affair, and so was the way he treated his elder daughter. It seemed as if he had already rejected Charles's offer out of hand.

Only if Anne were to be removed, a dramatic step, would these obstacles fade away.[4]

The following day, it was de Castelnau's turn. This time it was the Duke of Norfolk who was sent to greet him, glibly assuring him he need not worry as whatever terms Charles had offered, 'things would stay exactly as they were before'. George and other privy councillors then joined them as they made ready for Henry to process once more to Mass. Talking with de Castelnau as they walked along the gallery, the king briefly outlined the terms Charles had offered. Broadly hinting that he would prefer to continue with the existing Anglo-French alliance, Henry added sententiously, 'I do not wish to make myself a judge between princes, and I have heard that Francis has a good and just cause for making war in Savoy.' His intelligence, he said, was that Charles was assembling a massive army, but could not afford to pay it for very long. Francis, he advised, should fortify his garrisons and wait for Charles to attack, using the intervening time to muster his own forces. The longer the delay, the more Charles's funds would be depleted. Many men would desert for lack of pay, which would force him to abandon Italy to Francis.[5]

In his audience, de Castelnau proposed a new Anglo-French league. Francis would agree to make no peace with Charles without consulting Henry. Should it be proposed by mutual consent to attack the Low Countries, the costs of war would be equally divided. If war broke out in Italy, Henry would provide Francis with monthly 'contributions' of 50,000 crowns of the sun.

Henry politely but firmly hedged. Since de Castelnau had said nothing about Pope Paul's sanctions, he demanded to know where he stood should Francis and Charles make peace. Would Francis continue to support him? He also worried about the costs of commitments to wars in Savoy or northern Italy from which he could expect no obvious benefits. Francis, he suddenly interjected, had promised to send Jean de Dinteville back to London as a special ambassador with less onerous terms. He was 'much offended and greatly astonished (*fort fâché et ébahi*)' that the promised envoy had yet to arrive.[6]

Once de Castelnau departed, the privy council sat with Henry for upwards of three or four hours.[7] Three days later, Henry summoned the ambassador again and asked him to ride post-haste to France and return with Francis's final offer. He was to depart on Tuesday, after first collecting written counterproposals from Cromwell. But by then, the council, despite sitting daily until nine or ten o'clock at night, still could not agree on a strategy, and so his departure was delayed.[8]

The weight of opinion, though, had swung against France. Of those supporting Cromwell in his bid to restore the Anglo-Habsburg alliance, Fitzwilliam, his stepbrother Sir Anthony Browne, Sir William Paulet, Sir William Kingston and Sir John Russell took the lead. Linked variously by ties of kinship, land dealings and friendship, they had a firm grip on senior positions at court. Browne, Fitzwilliam and Paulet shared a conservative outlook on faith and life. Always uneasy about Henry's divorce and the rise of the Boleyns, they favoured the restoration of Katherine's daughter Mary to her title and position. They made common cause with Nicholas Carew and with the Courtenays, all of whom were busily coaching Jane Seymour on her lines. The Dukes of Norfolk and Suffolk were equally open to a switch of alliances. Both had quarrelled with Anne but were waiting for Henry to make up his mind.[9]

Even Anne's cousin, Sir Francis Bryan, and her protégé Sir Thomas Cheyne had turned against her. Bryan, Carew's brother-in-law, signalled his change of allegiance in a theatrically staged quarrel with George Boleyn as early as December 1534, and Cheyne began looking to Cromwell for patronage shortly afterwards. Was it also a coincidence that Browne, Fitzwilliam and Paulet had all been with George on diplomatic missions to Francis: did they share a grievance arising from their experiences there?[10]

Conventional wisdom has it that Henry turned against both France and his second wife on St George's Day (23 April), when he preferred Carew over George Boleyn for election to a vacancy as a Knight of the Garter. Anne 'has not had sufficient credit to get her own brother knighted', gloated Chapuys in triumph until he realised his mistake. In fact, Henry had already promised Francis that Carew would be selected at the first opportunity. A snub to Carew would have been one to Francis, and on the 23rd, Henry was not ready for that.[11]

But by Tuesday the 25th, Henry was slowly veering towards the terms offered by Chapuys. What he would not accept was a reconciliation with Rome, whether by Charles's mediation or anyone else's. Why would he, he asked, when he had already rejected overtures directly from the pope? He did, however, offer to meet Charles halfway over the question of Mary's restoration, providing she 'would humbly submit herself to our grace without reluctation [sic], contention or wrestling against the determination of our laws'. But he would not be dictated to on the matter; rather he must be trusted to act honourably 'without search of foreign advice'.[12]

Change was now in the wind. On Thursday the 27th, when de Castelnau was ready to depart for France, Cromwell handed him a radically different document to the one he was expecting, one containing more stringent terms, with the result that he refused to make the journey. Considering the mission to be a lost cause, he merely sent the counterproposals to Francis by his regular courier.[13]

Later the same day, Henry ordered the recall of Parliament. It was to reconvene on 8 June, the earliest possible date allowing for the time needed for fresh elections to the House of Commons. Why? There was nothing, ostensibly, for it to do – the king had sent its members home on Good Friday, just thirteen days earlier, after giving the royal assent to the Act for the Suppression of the Smaller Monasteries. Perhaps significantly, the very same day, an unnamed courtier sounded out John Stokesley, who had baptised Anne's daughter Elizabeth, about the feasibility of a second royal divorce. The grounds, according to Chapuys, were to be that Anne had been precontracted, and perhaps even legally married, to Harry Percy, despite his later denial on oath. When asked outright if a divorce was feasible, Stokesley wisely refused to answer unless Henry asked him the question in person.[14]

No changes had been made to Henry and Anne's itinerary: the plan was still for them to inspect the defences at Dover. They were to leave Greenwich the day after the May Day jousts, spend the first night in Rochester and arrive in Dover on 5 May. However, John Husee, Viscount Lisle's court agent, heard whispers of 'a matter which is of no small weight, which I reserve to my coming', although all was well in the privy chamber, he added reassuringly, where Henry Norris and Richard Page continued to prefer letters and suits to the king on the Lisles' behalf. On 28 April, plans for the Dover trip were still in place. In fact, this was the very day on which Thomas Warley, another of Lady Lisle's servants, sent her a message from Anne 'that my lady should meet her at Dover, as Mistress Margery Horsman showed me yesterday'.[15]

On Saturday the 29th, Henry first began seriously to consider whether it might, after all, be necessary to divest himself of Anne.[16] He arrived at this conclusion after reading fully ciphered dispatches from Rome sent by his ambassador to Charles, Richard Pate. Written respectively on 12 and 14 April and already made redundant in part by fresh instructions from Henry, they chiefly reported on an audience Pate had secured with Charles in late March, when the latter first made it clear that – with Katherine dead – he was eager to renew his 'amity' with Henry. Much of Pate's information was out of date, but one aspect of his commentary brought Henry up short. For as Pate reported, Charles was actively considering enforcing Paul's decree depriving Henry of his kingdom should the English king reject his terms, a move to which Francis's agents in Rome were raising no objection. Musing upon all that had happened over the past twenty or so years, Henry strongly suspected that Francis would abandon him should Charles decide to attack. Equally, the Habsburgs would never allow French influence to reach the point where Francis controlled both sides of the English Channel and blocked the sea route from Spain to the Low Countries.[17]

Here was food for thought. Far from being courted by both sides in a bidding war, Henry faced a choice between the Scylla of Francis or the Charybdis of Charles. He decided to choose Charles, but to stall indefinitely on meeting his conditions.

International affairs were finally taking precedence over Henry's feelings for Anne, and his behaviour was showing it. For the last four days, Nicholas Carew had stationed Jane Seymour at his house in Beddington where Henry paid her night-time visits, an arrangement resonant of events after Campeggi's arrival during the king's courtship of Anne.[18] Carew even risked writing to Mary, urging her to 'take courage', because the king was 'sick and tired' of his current wife.[19]

And yet, when it really came to it, was it so certain that Henry would repudiate Anne? Was the threat of papal sanctions to be enforced by Charles enough on its own to push him into making such a momentous decision? Or would there need to be something else?

The pretext for which Cromwell had been waiting came on the afternoon of the 29th, when Anne was overheard conversing with the young musician and groom of the privy chamber, Mark Smeaton. According to Anne's own later recollection of the incident, she had found Smeaton standing in the bay window of her Presence Chamber, staring longingly at her. When she asked him why he was so sad, he said mournfully, 'It is no matter.' To which she answered haughtily, 'You may not look to have me speak to you as I should do to a nobleman, because you be an inferior person.' 'No, no, madam,' Smeaton replied, 'a look sufficed me, and thus fare you well.'[20]

When one of Cromwell's spies reported the encounter, the principal secretary moved in for the kill. To him, the episode smacked of a dangerous over-familiarity and perhaps he could find more, even worse incidents.

When, early the next day, Sunday the 30th, Smeaton left Greenwich on his way to London, he was arrested in Stepney and held at a house Cromwell owned there. He was closely questioned, then led to the Tower early in the morning on May Day, where he was said to have been 'well lodged', but according to one of Henry Norris's servants, George Constantine, a schoolfellow of William Brereton, 'the saying was that he was first grievously racked'. Once in his cell, Smeaton was clapped in irons. Later informed of this, Anne said, 'that was because he was no gentleman'. She insisted that, until the incident of the 29th in her Presence Chamber, she had only been alone once with him. That was in Winchester during the summer progress of 1535, when she 'sent for him to play on the virginals'. Her version of events, now in the British Library, is contained in one of a series of letters from Kingston, the Constable of the Tower, to Cromwell. Although again badly charred at the edges in the Ashburnham House fire of 1731, enough of these letters can be read with the help of notes and transcripts made by the early eighteenth-century antiquary John Strype, who had access to them before the fire.[21]

The unreliable *Spanish Chronicle* has a more lurid description of Smeaton's arrest, claiming Cromwell inveigled the unfortunate musician to his house with promises of favours, whereupon two thugs tied a knotted rope around his head and forced him to confess to sleeping with Anne.[22]

No one knows for sure what Smeaton really confessed, but a strong probability is that, at least at first, he deflected the charge that he lusted after Anne himself by reporting a potentially scandalous encounter in her privy chamber between her and Norris. Another badly charred letter records Anne's version of events. While bantering with Norris, their talk got completely out of hand after she teased him over his sexual pursuit of her cousin 'Madge', more likely Margaret than Mary Shelton.* Why had he not married her? He was a widower, so there was no reason to hold back.

When Norris replied that he 'would tarry a time', she had unwisely retorted: 'You look for dead men's shoes; for if aught came to the king but good, you would look to have me.' Startled by the folly of her reckless remark, Norris angrily countered: 'If he should have any such thought, he would his head were off.' He understood at once that such badinage could be construed as a plot to murder Henry. To this, Anne replied that she 'could undo him if she would'. At which point, 'they fell out'.

---

*Although 'Madge' is more commonly a diminutive of Margaret than Mary, we cannot be sure and the jury is still out.

Their exchange, like that with Smeaton, had taken place near the end of the week beginning Monday the 24th, probably on Friday the 28th or Saturday the 29th. Realising she had crossed a line as news of the encounter rippled through the court, Anne rushed Norris off on Sunday morning to John Skip, her almoner, where he swore an oath that she was 'a good woman'. But it was too late, the damage was done. Henry's life appeared to have been threatened. And that was how he would see it.[23]

At eleven o'clock at night on Sunday, the king changed his plans to visit Dover with Anne. At that point, his intention was to postpone their departure, and 'to set forward to Dover the next week'. Later, the visit was cancelled. Viscount and Lady Lisle heard the news in a letter dated Monday 1 May.[24] We cannot know for sure whether Henry confronted Anne late on the Sunday evening, as many of Anne's biographers suspect. But by then, he clearly knew the outline, if not the full details, of what Cromwell was claiming to uncover. If Alexander Ales is to be believed, such a confrontation did take place. The Scottish evangelical was at court on that day, hoping to receive from Cromwell the payment of a stipend the king had promised him. As he informed Anne's daughter Elizabeth after her accession, years later:

Never shall I forget the sorrow which I felt when I saw the most serene queen, your most religious mother, carrying you, still a little baby, in her arms and entreating the most serene king, your father, in Greenwich Palace, from the open window of which he was looking into the courtyard, when she brought you to him. I did not perfectly understand what had been going on, but the faces and gestures of the speakers plainly showed that the king was angry, although he could conceal his anger wonderfully well. Yet from the protracted conference of the council (for whom the crowd was waiting until it was quite dark, expecting that they would return to London), it was most obvious to everyone that some deep and difficult question was being discussed.[25]

Without feeling any need for a more thorough examination of the facts, Henry saw himself as dishonoured, betrayed, cuckolded, made a laughing stock. The unstuffy, more casual approach to discipline on Anne's side of the court and the pastimes enjoyed there were about to be her undoing, because as soon as Henry received Cromwell's information, it looked to him as if the world would think he was failing (and might even be thought *unable*) to keep order in his own family and household.

Only briefly did Henry dither before deciding to be rid of Anne. As originally planned, the couple attended the May Day jousts at Greenwich, where Anne's brother George faced Henry Norris on the field. It was all ostensibly good-humoured and quite normal. If Lancelot de Carle, de Castelnau's secretary, is to be believed, Henry even lent Norris his horse when Norris's own refused to enter the lists.[26] What was not normal was the king's subsequent behaviour. As an astonished Edward Hall reported, 'On May Day were a solemn jousts [sic] kept at Greenwich, and suddenly from the jousts the king departed, having not above six persons with him ... Of this sudden departing, many men mused, but most chiefly the queen.'

Spurning his barge, Henry rode back to Whitehall, having ordered Norris and a mere five or so others to accompany him. 'And all the way, as I heard say', claimed Constantine, he 'had Master Norris in examination and promised him his pardon in case he would utter the truth.' Norris, however, 'would confess nothing to the king, whereupon he was committed to the Tower in the morning'. Anne and George were left behind in Greenwich, but, after a hurried conference between them, George rushed to London in a desperate pursuit to find out what was happening.[27]

As Anne passed her last night of relative freedom in Greenwich, it was impossible for her to make sense of what had just occurred. The jousts had begun as expected: George had performed well, showing great prowess with his lance and turning his horse skilfully.[28] With no warning at all, it had turned sour. Why had Henry left so abruptly? Why had he ridden back to Whitehall rather than wait for the tide and go by barge? Why had he made Norris accompany him?

Why had she heard nothing since? Had George learned anything? She knew about Henry's infatuation with Jane Seymour, she knew about the possible rapprochement with Charles, she knew how her last miscarriage had undermined her. But she knew nothing yet of Mark Smeaton's arrest at Stepney. Nor did she perhaps know that a new Parliament had been summoned.

After what can at best have been a very unsettled night, she was to learn more the following morning, when her uncle Norfolk, together with Cromwell, Lord Chancellor Audley, Fitzwilliam and Paulet, were ushered into her presence for what became a highly disturbing interview as she faced a barrage of questions. She complained that Norfolk kept saying 'Tut, tut, tut' and shaking his head; she complained that she was 'cruelly handled'; she said that Fitzwilliam was 'in the Forest of Windsor' (presumably meaning staring into space and not looking at her), although she acknowledged that Paulet behaved like a 'very gentleman'.[29]

The aftermath of their questioning was swift and terrifying: Anne was led to a waiting barge and rowed along the Thames to the Tower escorted by the same group of councillors, where she was charged with adultery. Since the barge was open, she was in full view of any startled citizens who gazed in disbelief from the riverbanks. The irony of the situation would not have escaped her. As the thick walls of the fortress grew ever closer with each stroke of the oars, she was engulfed in a parody of the joyous time almost three years before when she had taken the same route from Greenwich on the way to her coronation. Again, she was met by Kingston, but now there were no welcoming gun salutes, there was no accompanying flotilla, and there was no Henry impatient to enfold her in his arms. Kingston received her just as courteously, but as his prisoner.[30]

She arrived between five and six o'clock in the evening, unaware that George had been brought there earlier in the day. Norris, she knew, had preceded her at dawn. When she crossed the narrow bridge leading from Tower Wharf across the moat on her way to the queen's lodgings where she was to be held, she 'fell on her knees before the said lords, beseeching God to help her as she was not guilty of that whereof she was accused'.[31]

News travelled fast: the very same evening in his rooms in Gray's Inn in Holborn, the Welsh lawyer Roland Bulkeley wrote a letter to his brother in Anglesey, telling him that Anne was in the Tower with her father, brother, Norris and Smeaton, and with 'divers other sundry ladies' to attend her. 'The causes of their coming there', he continued, 'is [sic] for certain high treason, committed concerning their prince: that is to say, that Master Norris should have ado with the queen, and Mark [Smeaton] and the other[s] accessories to the same. They are like to suffer; all the more is the pity.' Only on the matter of Anne's father, who was neither arrested nor accused, was Bulkeley substantially mistaken.[32]

Chapuys sent Charles an urgent dispatch the same night. Despite everything, the ambassador was genuinely astounded at 'the sudden change from yesterday to this day'. Chapuys knew by then that the charge against Anne was adultery, although he believed it to have been with Smeaton rather than Norris, whom he thought had only been an accessory. He knew that Norris and George had been put in the Tower, and some hours before Anne, but had no idea why.[33]

And it did not stop there: Cromwell still lacked enough potentially damning information. On Wednesday 3 May, Sir Edward Baynton, Anne's vice-chamberlain, wrote to warn Fitzwilliam that no one would confess 'any actual thing' against Anne, 'but only Mark'. 'Wherefore in my foolish conceit it should much touch the king's honour if it should no farther appear. And I cannot believe but that the other two be as fully culpable as ever was he. And I think assuredly, the one keepeth the other's counsel.' Keen to die in his bed when his time came and eager to prove his loyalty to Henry, Baynton for his cooperation would soon profit from unusually generous grants of ex-monastic land.

Baynton felt sure that the 'other two', presumably Norris and George, were guilty and were somehow colluding. What can still be read of the end of his letter, another unfortunate casualty of the fire of 1731, appears to suggest that Anne was relying on their silence.[34]

Now the interrogations began, with Fitzwilliam and Anthony Browne in charge. If Constantine is to be believed, it would be

Fitzwilliam who tricked Norris into a confession – if so, he retracted it before his trial.[35] As Cromwell himself explained, 'in most secret sort, certain persons of the privy chamber and others of her [the queen's] side were examined.' On Thursday the 4th, Francis Weston and William Brereton joined the prisoners in the Tower. On Saturday the 8th, Richard Page and Thomas Wyatt were arrested. Briefly under suspicion, but soon released, was another of Mary Shelton's kinsmen, Henry Knyvet, whose letters to 'Mr Weston' (possibly Francis's father) and 'young Weston's wife' were seized. Chapuys felt sure that Wyatt and Page had been detained on Anne's account. Wyatt later claimed that his imprisonment was the result of the 'old, undeserved evil will' of the Duke of Suffolk.[36]

Weston's interrogation was the direct result of Anne's own anxious musings after her arrest. She first brought his name up on Wednesday 3 May, when she unwisely disclosed in the Tower that she feared him the most. What she revealed was an encounter that may have taken place at any point over the previous twelve months. She herself dated it to 'Whitsun Monday', later corrected to 'Whitsun Tuesday last' (i.e. 18 May 1535). She had, she said, taken Weston to task for neglecting his wife and flirting with one of the Shelton sisters. Weston insinuated in reply that Norris came more to the queen's chamber for Anne than for 'Madge', then topped this by saying that he himself loved someone in her household better than either this Shelton sister or his wife. When Anne asked him 'Who is that?', he answered, 'It is yourself.' Shocked by so audacious a reply, she had promptly 'defied him' (meaning silenced him), but the damage was already done.[37]

Cromwell then questioned Anne's cousin Sir Francis Bryan. He had left court for Buckinghamshire but was urgently recalled. As he reported: 'I was suddenly sent for, marvelling thereof, and debated the matter in my mind why this should be. At the last, I considered and knew myself true and clear in conscience unto my prince.' 'With all speed without fear' he returned and appeared before Cromwell, 'and after that to the king's grace and nothing found in me, nor never shall be found, but just and true to my master, the king's grace'. Bryan now discovered how valuable his quarrel with

George Boleyn had been to him. He was swiftly exonerated and by 13 May had replaced Norris as chief gentleman of Henry's privy chamber.[38]

Wyatt and Page were still in the Tower on 12 May, 'as it is said', or so Husee informed Viscount Lisle, 'without danger of death, but Mr Page is banished the king's presence and court for ever'. The picture was more confused the following day, when Husee continued, 'Some other say that Wyatt and Mr Page are as like to suffer as the others; and the saying now is that those which shall suffer shall die when the queen and her brother goeth to execution.'[39]

Husee's news was premature. On the 19th, Wyatt and Page were still in the Tower, but were soon freed, in Wyatt's case more or less immediately.[40] Wyatt was discharged at Cromwell's instigation; Page at Henry's with support from Edward Seymour. On 10 May, Wyatt's father, the aged Sir Henry, received a letter from Cromwell 'to his great comfort', reassuring him of his son's safety. And on 18 July, Page told Lady Lisle, 'I am long ago at liberty, and the king [is] my good and gracious lord.' 'Hitherto', he continued, 'I have not greatly assayed to be a daily courtier again, and the king, being so much my good lord as to give me liberty, I am more mete for the country than the court.' (He ate his words in 1544, returning to be chamberlain to Prince Edward, Jane Seymour's son.)[41]

Why William Brereton was arrested is more of a puzzle, as the sources are silent. Maybe he was too closely attached to George Boleyn, or maybe he was a casualty of a longstanding feud with Cromwell arising from his misdemeanours as chamberlain of Chester? In that role he had stood in the way of Cromwell's plans to realign the government of the Welsh borderlands. His most notorious offence was the judicial murder of John ap Gryffith Eyton, his former deputy, whom he hanged in defiance of Cromwell's orders. His younger brother Urian's career was unaffected by his arrest. Urian continued to thrive at court and would prove especially useful to William's widow.[42]

On 3 May, Baynton had advised that the women of the court be questioned. He had, he said, 'mused much' of Margery Horsman.

She 'hath used her[self] strangely toward me of late, being her friend as I have been'.[43] Little did he know that Horsman had been cosying up to Cromwell for the past six months. When she needed a favour for one of her cousins who sought a lease from the priory of Dereham in Norfolk, she knew the person to ask was him and not Anne.[44]

As Cromwell later claimed, 'the queen's abomination, both in incontinent living and other offences towards the king's highness was so rank and common, that her ladies of the privy chamber and her chamberers could not contain it within their breasts.'[45] Elizabeth Browne, Countess of Worcester, Sir Anthony's sister and by now some twenty weeks pregnant, was said to have been the first to arouse suspicions. When her brother rebuked her for her flirtations on the queen's side of the court, she unthinkingly blurted out hints of similar misdeeds by Anne. De Carle flags up Browne's role as an accuser. According to his verse history, one woman, 'the sister of one of the most straightlaced of the councillors', was the source of the most damning testimony. This matches an admittedly garbled French prose account in the Lansdowne Manuscripts in the British Library, where the accusation is attributed to the sister of one 'Antoine Brun', who was wrongly said to be Henry's physician.[46]

Revisiting the story once the executions were over, Husee informed the Lisles, 'The first accusers [were] the Lady Worcester and Nan Cobham, with one maid more. But the Lady Worcester was the first ground, as God knoweth.' And in a postscript to a letter dated 25 May, he reiterated, 'Touching the queen's accusers, my Lady Worcester beareth name to be the principal.' How Nan Cobham got sucked into the drama is unknown, but under pressure from Cromwell she is likely to have crumbled.[47]

With the accusations coming in thick and fast, fear and terror paralysed the court and spread outwards into the country. As earlier with the treason charges against the Duke of Buckingham in 1521 what shocked everyone was the speed and vindictiveness with which the king decided to strike. No sooner had Roland Bulkeley's letter reached Shrewsbury on its way to his brother than his messenger was arrested and thrown into the town gaol. What most alarmed the members of the Council in Wales, to whom the civic authorities referred the matter, was the news of Anne's arrest, which at first, they could not believe and were afraid to discuss in case it was false. 'Forasmuch', they wrote in all haste (and all innocence) to Cromwell, 'as the said news be to this Council and all and singular the true and faithful liege people of this realm much dolorous and doleful ... God forbid that ever it should so chance.'[48]

Even a nonentity with connections to Anne's court could be caught in the purge. After the arrests of Wyatt and Page, it was said that Harry Webb, a sewer of Anne's privy chamber, 'should be taken in the West Country and put in hold for the same cause'. First seen at court in 1514 at the betrothal of Henry's younger sister, Mary, to Louis XII, Webb had carried out various errands for Henry and Anne between 1530 and 1531 for which the king paid him on her behalf. By September 1535, he was firmly ensconced in Anne's household, where he was assessed for tax payments. He went on to serve Jane Seymour after Anne's death.[49]

But then, court life under Henry had never been tranquil: already by 1534, Husee had warned Viscount Lisle, 'I perceive a man had need take heed what he write[s].'[50] Anne's principal officers, Sir James Boleyn, Baynton, Coffyn and George Taylor, protected themselves by defecting to Cromwell, while several of her women, notably Jane Parker, Margery Horsman, Bess Holland and Nan Cobham, transitioned into Jane Seymour's service.[51] On the very day of Anne's execution, Husee could inform Lady Lisle that 'George Taylor is merry.' This was because Cromwell had already given him a valuable grant as 'general-receiver of the possessions of the late queen'. As Taylor himself explained, 'I trust the King's Highness will be good and gracious lord unto me, and so I have a special trust in his Grace.'[52]

Anne's father escaped the cull by the simple expedients of consenting to condemn her and her brother's alleged crimes, agreeing to sit with the royal justices at the trials of Norris, Brereton, Weston and Smeaton when they took place, and humbly deferring thereafter in all things to Cromwell. From now on, whenever he approached the principal secretary, Thomas Boleyn's language would be that of an inferior to a superior, and very shortly Henry would strip him of his office of Lord Privy Seal and confer it on Cromwell. Here brought low with his children was the father of the woman to whom the king had once denied nothing. In a matter of weeks, the Boleyn family firm had simply disintegrated.[53]

28

The Trials Begin

Anne's arrest was the beginning of the end for her. Her pact with Henry had been that she would give him the son that Katherine could not. In that she had abjectly failed, and the king's response to her recent miscarriage indicated just how much he blamed her, and how little hope he now held out of another successful male pregnancy. Nothing with Henry would ever be his fault: if he believed he had been wronged by his wife, her days as his queen were numbered. Here was a ruler, now in mid-life and with a binary view of the world, who saw only obedient subordinates or enemies to be defeated. Wolsey, on his way south after his arrest, had cautioned Sir William Kingston, who was to escort him, that if he ever joined the king's council, he should be 'well advised and assured what matter ye put in his head, for ye will never pull it out again'. Anne may not have heard of the incident, but she would have understood the concept.[1]

On Friday 5 May, the day after Francis Weston and William Brereton were arrested, Henry shut himself away in Whitehall. 'His Grace came not abroad', John Husee informed Viscount Lisle, 'except it were in the garden, and in his boat at night, at which times it may become no man to prevent him, these fourteen days.'[2] He meant to control every aspect of the forthcoming trials, just as he had done with the Duke of Buckingham's fifteen years earlier. Among his advisers, only Cromwell would be fully in the picture.

A few days before the hearings were to begin, the king moved from Whitehall to Hampton Court. Otherwise, he stayed largely in seclusion. An information blackout was imposed, even for leading councillors. Late on Thursday the 11th, Sir William Paulet urgently warned Cromwell that the Duke of Norfolk, despite being selected to preside over the proceedings, was unsure if he was to go ahead. He could take no further action in the matter, he said, 'till he knew the king's pleasure, and so he willed me to advertise you'. Shortly afterwards the duke received the news that he was expected to open the first of the trials early the very next morning.[3]

Cromwell, eager to glean any possible scraps of usable evidence from the already doomed queen, ordered Kingston faithfully to report her every word straight back to him, a task which the loyal Constable assiduously fulfilled. He watched, listened and recorded everything Anne said, readily assisted by the four carefully chosen ladies whom Henry had deputed to attend her and to spy on her. They all heartily disapproved of Anne, and one was also secretly leaking information about her to Chapuys.[4] She could expect no sympathy from her aunt, Lady Elizabeth Boleyn, or Kingston's wife, Lady Mary. The other two were Mrs Coffyn and, according to the antiquary John Strype's transcript, a 'Mistress Stonor'. Besides watching Anne's every movement during the day, Lady Boleyn and Mrs Coffyn slept on pallet beds by the door to her bedchamber, to be sure that anything she said, even in her sleep, reached Cromwell's ears.[5]

Margaret Coffyn we have already met as the wife of Anne's Master of the Horse. Now busily saving his own skin in what was rapidly becoming a witch hunt of Anne's inner circle, Sir William was happy to avail the use of his wife as one of Cromwell's spies. The identity of the elusive 'Stonor' can for the first time be narrowed down to two women. One is Elizabeth Stonor, the wife of Walter Walsh from the king's privy chamber and William Compton's widow. In about 1540, she remarried Sir Philip Hoby and was drawn by Holbein. The other is her mother, another Elizabeth, the second wife of Sir Walter Stonor of Stonor Park, Oxfordshire, with whom the Boleyns were engaged in a bitter quarrel. More likely it is the older woman, as the younger would have been known as 'Mistress Walsh' while Anne was queen. The records place neither in Anne's household, but one of them rode in Jane Seymour's funeral procession beside Margery Horsman. The Boleyns made the fatal mistake of backing a flamboyant kinsman, Adrian Fortescue, in an acrimonious property dispute at a time when Cromwell supported the Stonors. That Sir Walter was another of the principal secretary's informers helped to fuel the flames.[6]

Anne recoiled from all four women. She twice complained about them, volubly, to Kingston. 'I think', she said cuttingly on the second of these occasions, it showed 'much unkindness in the king to put such about me as I never loved'. Kingston answered, 'I showed her that the king took them to be honest and good women', to which Anne retorted, 'I would have had [those] of mine own privy chamber which I favour most.'[7]

The first of Kingston's letters described how Anne behaved from the moment her barge arrived at the Tower. She was at first close to panic. 'Shall I go into a dungeon?' she asked him fearfully. On that the Constable was able to reassure her. 'No, madam', he replied, 'you shall go into your lodging that you lay in at your coronation.' Overwhelmed by sheer relief, she broke down. 'It is too good for me', she said, falling to her knees in a paroxysm of tears. But then, to Kingston's bewilderment, she 'fell to a great laughing', which she 'hath done so many times since', a sign of the intense psychological pressure she faced.[8]

Arriving in her apartments, she regained some composure, requesting that Kingston should 'move' Henry to allow her to have the holy sacrament 'in the closet by her chamber, [so] that she might pray for mercy'. She repeated the request a day or two later, when she also asked for her almoner, John Skip, now released after interrogation about his inflammatory sermon. When she went on to inquire whether Kingston knew why she was imprisoned, she let slip that she had some idea of the potential charges, presumably from her uncle Norfolk's questioning that morning. She was, she vowed, 'clear from the company of man'. She was Henry's 'true wedded wife'; but had heard that she would be accused of adultery with three men. Her problem was that she had no way of proving her innocence 'without I should open my body'. Upon which, in a perfectly timed theatrical display, 'she opened her gown'. In so doing, she exposed her pure white linen smock as an expression of her blamelessness.[9]

She had a good idea who two of the men might be. Norris, whom she thought might have accused her, was in the Tower with her, she said, and so was Mark Smeaton. In response to her fears for her brother's whereabouts, Kingston told her that he had seen him in the morning 'afore dinner in the court' and had left him at Whitehall, although this was misleading as George and Norris had been brought to the Tower earlier that day.[10] But she also worried about her mother who, she thought, would die 'for sorrow' and for Elizabeth Browne, whose child, she had heard, did not 'stir in her body' for anxiety about her, which strongly suggests she was unaware that Browne too had accused her.[11]

Anne next asked Kingston whether she would die without justice and the Constable sanctimoniously rebuked her. That was impossible, he said, because 'the poorest subject the king hath had justice'. This time the peals of laughter she gave in reply were entirely derisive; she had been at Henry's side long enough to realise how her husband operated. A day or so later, she returned to the theme, saying, 'I shall have justice.' When Kingston answered, 'Have no doubt therein', she confidently replied, 'If any man accuse[s] me, I can say but "nay", and they can bring no witness.' Little did she know what Cromwell had in store for her.[12]

What Cromwell most wanted from Anne was information on anyone else he could implicate, fresh examples of her reckless speech, and confirmation that incidents which he knew about from hearsay reports had really taken place, so that he could make them seem incriminating while widening the circle of the accused. She could not have been more obliging. Terrified by her predicament and its sheer suddenness, she could not think straight, talking and talking, 'babbling' as it was said, sometimes almost incoherently. By even conceding that Smeaton and Norris might have been arrested, she appeared to admit that discipline within her privy chamber was too lax and her own conduct indiscreet. She even joked about it, by asking Mary Kingston whether anyone made the prisoners' beds and when told that it was unlikely, she punned on the word 'pallets', meaning beds, and 'ballets', meaning poetry of the type that had been rife in her privy chamber and in the Devonshire Manuscript, and for which her brother George, besides Wyatt, was renowned. They 'might make ballets well now', she quipped.[13]

Unable to stop herself, she went on to provide details to prove just how slack things had been. On Wednesday 3 May, she described to Mrs Coffyn the very incidents with Norris and Weston which had triggered the crisis, and which so far can only have been known to Cromwell from his spies. To have Anne confirm the existence of those encounters in her own words from her own lips was even more than Cromwell might have hoped for. She did the same with the incident with Mark Smeaton. Of William Brereton, she said nothing at all. Maybe she was not told he had been arrested? Or maybe there was nothing to say?[14]

Very few dared to speak up openly for Anne or for any of the other prisoners: those who did included Weston's wife and mother and George Boleyn's wife, Jane Parker, along with Jean de Dinteville and Archbishop Cranmer. Always a divisive figure, Anne had never had the ability or more likely the will to cultivate long-term supporters, relying largely on her family and its networks. As the realisation of defeat sunk in, she hoped for help from other quarters. Her belief that the 'most part of England prays for me' was close to delusional, and she looked in vain for her friends to intercede. As Kingston informed Cromwell, she had exclaimed, 'I would [to] God I had my bishops for they would all go to the king for me.' In fact, apart from Cranmer and Skip, they were nowhere to be seen. Nicholas Shaxton, her first almoner, even denounced her to Cromwell as a woman 'who hath exceedingly deceived me'.[15]

Weston's mother, 'suffering in great pain', according to Lancelot de Carle, came in person to petition Henry. Weston's wife Anne, an heiress in her own right, offered all her income and goods for his deliverance. Jane Parker, using Francis Bryan and Nicholas Carew as her intermediaries, sent a gentleman-usher to the Tower to see how George was, and to say that 'she would humbly sue unto the king's highness for her husband'. George professed himself grateful for his wife's efforts but, by now weeping himself, asked Kingston when he would be questioned by the council as he thought he would be before his trial, not realising that Cromwell was already moving ahead to the trial itself.[16]

Jean de Dinteville, belatedly arriving from Boulogne on 17 May, also pleaded fruitlessly for Weston, whose father he knew.[17] The only one of 'her' bishops actively to speak up for Anne was Cranmer, and he did so ambivalently. Fearing his intervention, Cromwell, on the day of her and her brother's arrest, had sent him an urgent summons to Lambeth which also forbade him from attempting to see the king. Since all Cranmer knew came from gossip on the streets, he resolved on Wednesday 3 May to pen a carefully worded defence of Anne to Henry. 'I am in such a perplexity', he began, 'that my mind is clean amazed; for I never had better opinion in woman than I had in her, which making me to think that she should not be culpable.' But the archbishop, who had known Henry long enough, was sufficiently canny to protect his own back: 'And again, I think your Highness would not have gone so far, except she had surely been culpable.'[18]

In a letter clouded by double negatives, ambiguity and weasel words, Cranmer salved his conscience without too much personal risk. Whether Henry read his letter, assuming it ever reached him, is a moot point. If he did, he is likely to have given it no more than a cursory glance, as his mind was made up. All he could focus on – other than his demure Jane Seymour – was that he had been cruelly deceived.

Henry wanted justice done his own way. His pride had been sorely injured, and as part of this mental shift, he set to work and began writing a 'tragedy' of his own devising, castigating Anne's alleged sexual crimes, a manuscript he was seen to carry around with him and show to Chapuys and others in moments of blind rage. He began insisting that over a hundred men had enjoyed illicit sex with Anne. Venturing out late one night for supper with John Kite, Bishop of Carlisle, a former protégé of Wolsey who partnered

Kingston at cards, he declared how he had 'long expected' this turn of events. He showed his 'tragedy' to Kite, who briefly scanned it and remembered it contained a passage in which Anne and her brother had mocked the king's poetry. That rings true, and a similar allegation would resurface during Anne and George's trials.[19]

Kingston, meanwhile, continued to send reports to Cromwell. Increasingly, Anne's wayward, changeable behaviour under pressure mystified even an old hand like him. At one moment, she declared she was as 'cruelly handled as was never seen', but 'I think the king does it to prove me.' At this, she 'did laugh withal, and was very merry'.[20] At another, she said she wanted to die, only to insist almost at once that she wanted to live. She prophesised wildly that there would be no rain until she was freed; she went on and on so much that an exasperated Lady Elizabeth Boleyn rounded on her, tartly reminding her that her love of 'tales has brought you to this'. Prisoner or not, however, she could happily eat a 'great dinner'. The cost of her 'diets' (food and other necessaries) for her seventeen days in the Tower was £25 4s 6d (over £25,000 in modern values). In these, her final days, at least she could still live like a queen.[21]

She could still behave as if it were she, rather than Kingston, who was in control. She would command his attendance whenever she wished for news and expect him to come. 'Where have you been all day?' she snapped at one point. Anxious for her brother, she 'sent' for the Constable to demand he tell her where George was. When Kingston obliged, she replied that she was glad that she and George were near to each other. And she 'desired' Kingston to take a letter to Cromwell, a task the Constable refused to undertake, although he agreed to convey a verbal message instead.[22]

Kingston's refusal to deliver a letter for her suggests that she was not allowed to send letters at all. Yet, in the British Library are six copies of a famous one, dated 'from [the] Tower the 6th of May', which is signed 'Your most loyal and ever faithful wife', and purports to have been penned by Anne to Henry from 'my doleful prison in the Tower'. The writer begins by saying that she has received his message, delivered to her by one who was her 'ancient professed enemy' (Cromwell?), telling her that, if she confesses 'a truth', she will regain Henry's favour.

> I no sooner received this message by him, than I rightly
> conceived your meaning. And if, as you say, confessing a truth
> indeed may procure my safety, I shall with all willingness
> and duty perform your command. But let not your Grace
> ever imagine that your poor wife will ever be brought to
> acknowledge a fault, where not so much as a thought thereof
> proceeded. And to speak a truth, never Prince had wife more
> loyal in all duty and in all true affection, than you have ever
> found in Anne Boleyn, with which name and place I could
> willingly have contented myself, if God and your Grace's
> pleasure had so been pleased. Neither did I at any time so far
> forget myself in my exaltation, or received Queenship, but that
> I always looked for such an alteration as now I find, for the
> ground of my preferment being on no surer foundation than
> your Grace's fancy, the least alteration was fit and sufficient (I
> knew) to draw that fancy to some other subject.

She begged him not to allow any 'light fancy or bad counsel' to influence him against her so that there was a 'blot' on her reputation, and on their daughter. She entreated him for a lawful trial, not one masterminded by her 'sworn enemies' for, she says, 'my truth shall fear no open shame.'

> But if you have already determined of me, and that not
> only my death, but an infamous slander must bring you the
> enjoying of your desired happiness, then I desire of God
> that he will pardon your great sin therein, and likewise mine
> enemies, the instruments thereof, and that he will not call
> you to a strict account for your unprincely and cruel usage of
> me at his general Judgment seat, where both you and myself
> must shortly appear, and in whose just judgment I doubt not,
> whatsoever the world may think of me, my innocence shall be
> openly known and sufficiently cleared.

Here, it seems, is the old Anne back again, the self-assured, articulate, defiant Anne. It is just what we would love her to have said. And we would also have expected her to plead for the lives of those likely to die with her, and so she does:

My last and only request shall be, that myself may only bear the burden of your Grace's displeasure, and that it may not touch the innocent souls of those poor gentlemen whom I understand are likewise in straight imprisonment for my sake. If I have ever found favour in your sight, if ever the name of Anne Boleyn hath been pleasing in your ears, let me obtain this last request.[23]

It is wonderful stuff, but there is no holograph original. So is the letter genuine or faked?[24] The first certain reference to it comes a century after Anne's death when it was printed in Lord Herbert of Cherbury's *The Life and Reign of King Henry the Eighth*, which was begun in 1632 and first published in 1649.[25] 'I thought fit to transcribe [it] here', Herbert tells us, 'without other Credit yet than it is said to be found among the papers of Cromwell then Secretary, and for the rest seems ancient and consonant to the matter in question.' Herbert was, by the standards of his time, an absolute professional: the first serious historian of the reign of Henry VIII, one of the very best until the twentieth century. He could see very quickly, as we can today, by comparing this document with the genuine letters Anne wrote, among others, to Wolsey, that what here purports to be the 'original' is not in her handwriting, nor does it match her distinctive orthography, use of language or spelling habits. But while Herbert is reluctant to pronounce it a forgery, neither does he declare it genuine: 'But whether this letter were elegantly written by her, or any else heretofore, I know as little as [to] what answer might be made thereunto.'[26]

So, did she write it? If so, she was able to compose a powerfully argued valedictory just four days after she had succumbed to the fits of uncontrollable laughter and mood swings that so alarmed Kingston. The letter is dated, but Anne did not date any of her genuine letters. Is the tone too defiant? Would she have dared to mention Cromwell or Jane in these relatively explicit terms? Would she have presumed to remind Henry that he was accountable to God for his actions? Perhaps, for Anne was always bold; but would she really have gone this far when she knew her life was hanging by a thread? It seems unlikely.

Strangely, nobody until now appears to have examined the space below the end of the letter on the verso (back) of the folio, where there is a badly charred 10-line annotation or commentary, another legacy of the 1731 fire. Burnet, the last person to see the document before it was damaged, neglected to transcribe this, but from what can still be read, 'a messenger' is being sent to the 'Queen ... willing her to confess', telling her 'she must conceal nothing'. It appears that she owes this as a final duty to Henry for raising her so high.[27] Can this be genuine? The one certainty is that the author of the annotation was also the author or copyist of the letter beginning on the recto (front) of the folio: the handwriting and orthography are identical.

Preparations for the trials now began. As early as Monday 24 April, Cromwell, on his own initiative, had drawn up letters authorising special commissions of *oyer et terminer* ('to hear and determine') for Kent and Middlesex, outside of the usual twice-yearly general commissions in which two of the king's judges, assisted by the most senior local magistrates, would hear serious criminal matters, notably treasons and felonies, in proceedings begun by indictment. So unusual were these two commissions that Ralph Pexall, the Clerk of the Crown in Chancery, copied them down in his precedent book.[28]

Their purpose became clear on Tuesday 9 May, when writs based on them were issued to the sheriffs of Kent and Middlesex to summon grand juries to indict prisoners suspected of heinous crimes.* Cromwell's preparations were meticulous. The foreman

---

*Before the reforms to the legal system in England and Wales in 1933, accused persons were first indicted by grand juries in their local jurisdictions, and then committed for trial, when a verdict on their guilt would be assessed by trial jurors. The Tudor system resembles present-day procedures in the USA, where the right to grand-jury indictment in Federal courts for serious crimes is protected by the Fifth Amendment.

of the grand jury in Middlesex was Giles Heron, one of Thomas More's more staunchly Catholic sons-in-law, who thirsted for revenge on the Boleyns. In Kent, one of the selected grand jurors was Richard Fisher, brother of John Fisher, the executed Bishop of Rochester. The Middlesex panel, which took the lead, assembled at Westminster next day; the Kent panel met in Deptford on the 11th. Both levelled largely identical charges against each of the six accused that were lewd and sensational. Expertly crafted to shock and disgust, they were ingenious because they were so wide in scope and all-encompassing. Some were linked to specific dates and places, others were generalised, and they ranged over the whole of the three years since Anne's coronation.[29]

For example, 'bearing malice against the king, and following her own frail and carnal lust', Anne did 'falsely and traitorously procure and corrupt several of the king's close body servants to become her sexual partners by means of obscene language, touching, gifts, vile provocation and licentious seduction'. In turn, she 'procured and incited' Norris, Brereton, Weston and Smeaton 'to carnal copulation' and 'her own natural brother' George to incest, 'alluring him with her tongue in his mouth and the said George's tongue in hers, and also with kisses, gifts and jewels'. Anne and George, the charges said, 'despising the commands of God, and all human laws', frequently had sex together, 'sometimes by his own procurement and sometimes by hers'. Norris, Brereton, Weston and Smeaton she tempted into bed by 'sweet words, kisses, touches and otherwise'. As a result, these men, 'being thus inflamed by carnal love of the queen', became jealous of one another. And 'to satisfy her inordinate desires ... she would not allow them to converse with any other woman without her great displeasure and indignation.'

At various places and dates, Anne gave them 'great gifts and rewards' to inveigle them into sex. What's more, she and they, on several occasions, 'compassed and imagined Henry's death', and Anne several times promised each of these traitors that she would marry one of them whenever the king departed this life, affirming that she 'would never love him in her heart'. Finally, Henry, gaining intelligence of these vices, crimes and despicable treasons, had become so afflicted that 'certain harms and dangers had physically accrued to his royal body'. Hence Anne and these abominable traitors had acted in contempt of him and 'to the danger of his royal person and body, and to the scandal, danger, detriment and derogation of the issue and heirs of the said king and queen'.

Of some twenty specimen charges, those involving Norris and Brereton were said to have taken place mainly in 1533, Weston in 1534, Smeaton in 1534 and 1535, and George in 1535. Cromwell had adopted a scattergun approach, daringly believing no one was going to check, since the given dates and locations rarely matched Anne's itinerary. Several times the offences were said to have occurred at Whitehall when in fact she was in Greenwich. Norris, for example, was alleged to have slept with her at Whitehall on 12 October 1533, when she was still convalescing in Greenwich after Elizabeth was born. Even from the records which are still available, it can be shown that, at most, barely six or seven of the twenty charges are theoretically possible. On thirteen occasions, it is an incontestable fact that Henry and Anne were not in the places where the alleged offences took place. Those and other details were outright fabrications. Careless though this may seem, the devil was not in such details, but in the generalised charges, which in the case of each prisoner were said to have taken place on 'divers', 'various' or 'several' occasions before or after the particular dates specified, so it would be pointless for Anne or her presumed paramours to attempt to explain away any one of those dates or times because there were so many other unspecified, and therefore unanswerable, allegations. Subsequent events showed that the indictments may well have been defective in law. In the first place, sex with a consenting queen was not yet made treason in its own right. Secondly, legal counsel held in 1579 in a case involving Norris's property, which had reverted to the crown on his conviction, that his forfeiture was invalid because it was not shown precisely in every instance when and where his treasons were committed.[30]

The key charge, legally, was that by offering to marry one of her 'lovers' once Henry was no more, Anne and her co-defendants had both imagined and constructively planned for the king's death, and that, if true, was treason. And yet it was the incest charge, graphically narrated, which most horrified the judges and trial jurors. Incest was taboo, and especially abhorrent and sensitive to Henry, who from the very beginning of his campaign to divorce Katherine had claimed that sexual intercourse with a brother's widow was incest pure and simple, and 'in such high degree against the law of nature'. All the same, he had married Anne despite his earlier, well-publicised affair with her sister Mary. In the eyes of many church lawyers, that too was incestuous, views which perhaps helped to fuel his genuine sense of revulsion.

Writing to Lady Lisle on Sunday 13 May, John Husee thought that the charges were almost too heinous for a virtuous woman like herself to hear.

> Madam, I think verily, if all the books and chronicles were
> totally revolved [studied, contemplated], and to the uttermost
> prosecuted and tried, which against women hath been penned,
> contrived and written since Adam and Eve, those same were,
> I think, verily nothing in comparison of that which hath been
> done and committed by Anne the Queen.[31]

For Husee, their sheer magnitude, and their appalling nature, had to make them true. For this, astonishingly, there was legal precedent. Contrary to modern constitutional beliefs, 'conviction by notoriety' was an old and established, if rarely used, concept known to Tudor lawyers. Writing in 1533, Thomas More acknowledged that by English law, judges might sometimes imprison and convict suspects without indictment based on 'the fame and behaviour [that] the man is in his country'.[32]

The first of the trials began on Friday 12 May, in Westminster Hall, the scene of Anne's coronation banquet a mere three years before. What most impressed de Carle was the chilling sight of the 'great axe' displayed at the side of the courtroom, the blade at first turned away from the prisoners, but ready to swing towards them to show that they were doomed if judgment was given against them. (The detail surely suggests that de Castelnau's secretary was among the dozens of spectators crammed into the main body of the Hall or in the gallery.)[33]

It was decided to hear the cases of the commoners – Norris, Brereton, Weston and Smeaton – first. For this, there was an obvious reason. By declaring those four to be principals to the crimes and not accessories, they could be separately tried and condemned. As peers of the realm, Anne (as Marquis of Pembroke) and George (as Viscount Rochford) had the right to be tried instead in the Court of the Lord Steward, in which the jurors would be the rest of the nobility assisted by the Lord Chancellor and the royal justices. By hearing their cases only after the guilt of the commoners had been established, the less easily manipulated peers would be presented with what was tantamount to a fait accompli. If the commoners were guilty of treasonable adultery, then so was Anne. The additional matter of incest was Cromwell's way of ensuring that her brother could be trapped in the snare and brought down with her. He was taking no chances that George would survive to rival or obstruct him.

Named as judges for the commoners were Anne's father, her uncle Norfolk, the Duke of Suffolk and four other nobles (who were legally able to sit in judgment on commoners, although the reverse did not apply), along with Audley, Cromwell, Fitzwilliam, Paulet and the royal justices. As with the jury selections earlier, Cromwell took no chances with the trial jurors. Every single one who made it onto the panel was a royal servant or someone with a grudge against one of the prisoners, or an opponent of Anne or the break with Rome, or else within Cromwell's sphere of influence. Henry's cronies Sir Thomas Palmer, Sir Thomas Spert, Geoffrey Chamber and Gregory Lovell, all on the trial jury that condemned Thomas More, made their reappearance. Christopher Morris, the king's Master of the Ordnance, now joined them. Among jurors bearing personal grudges was More's son-in-law William Dauntesey.[34]

Led by Kingston's officers into the Hall, the four accused had little chance of acquittal. Never in treason trials, unless witnesses were called, were the accused able to discover the sources of the prosecution's evidence or to produce witnesses of their own. They had no right to legal representation: indeed this was expressly forbidden. If necessary, the court might assign legal counsel to a prisoner wishing to raise a point of law against his indictment. Otherwise, the royal justices were expected to advise the accused on how to plead their case and to ensure that the law was strictly followed. All of this was entirely normal. If the sources we have are to be believed, no witnesses would appear during the trial. Such evidence as would be given would be submitted only by report or in legal argument. Although a longstanding convention held that two witnesses were usually required to convict, the law in cases of treason allowed the testimony of just one, as Thomas More's case had shown. But in the trials of the four commoners, and of Anne and George too, all the evidence given on the day would be hearsay.[35]

Mark Smeaton, probably hoping for mercy, or for a less painful death than the barbaric agonies of hanging, disembowelling and quartering reserved for traitors, pleaded guilty to committing adultery with the queen three times, but denied the rest of the charges. The others, protesting their innocence, pleaded not guilty on all counts, but to no avail. Guilty verdicts were inevitable. In the margins of the court's records, now in the National Archives in Kew, the ominous cipher 'T&S' was written four times, once for each prisoner. This was the Latin abbreviation for '*Trahendum et suspendendum*': 'to be dragged [on a hurdle to the gallows at Tyburn], and then hanged.'[36]

Chapuys, who may have been watching from the gallery, declared it to be a miscarriage of justice. The prisoners, he informed Charles, had been 'sentenced on mere presumption or on very slight grounds, without legal proof or valid confession' (*par presumption et aucuns indices, sans preuve ne confession valide*). Manifestly, Smeaton's confession had been extracted under torture.[37]

Returned to Kingston's custody, the condemned men were rowed back to the Tower. On reaching the inner ward, they were told to prepare themselves for death. Always among the first to discover what was going on, Husee thought it might come on Monday the

15th. On the 13th, he revised his opinion. 'Here are so many tales I cannot well tell which to write', he wryly observed. All the same, he shrewdly foretold what was likely to come. 'I think verily they shall all suffer.'[38]

29

The Falcon at Bay

Anne and George's trials took place in the Lord Steward's Court, before a jury of their peers. Henry appointed Anne's uncle Norfolk to preside (as with the High Constableship, the king otherwise kept the Lord Steward's office vacant), and the duke summoned twenty-six peers. Most of the lords who had officiated at her coronation banquet were there. George's father-in-law, Lord Morley, a man happier in his library than at court, but who could be counted on to bend with the wind, was included, but Thomas Boleyn was excused, despite having expressed willingness to serve as part of his efforts to distance himself from the collapse of his family's fortunes. Not forgotten was Harry Percy, whom Anne had once hoped to marry. Quietly hiding himself away in his house in Newington Green, near Hackney, where he was seriously ill, he was ordered to attend, more fearful than ever that his earlier entanglement with her would bring him down. A notable absentee was Anne's stepson Henry Fitzroy, although we do not know why.[1]

For reasons of security, Henry held the trials in the so-called 'King's Hall' at the Tower, almost certainly the great hall in the White Tower. There, a timber scaffold was erected to create the courtroom, with places for the peers and for the royal justices, who in this court attended not as judges but purely to give legal advice. Norfolk, holding a long white 'wand' (staff) of office in his hand, sat on a dais beneath a cloth of estate, with Lord Chancellor Audley on his right and the Duke of Suffolk to the left. Specially constructed stands for spectators, among whom the king took care to include Antoine de Castelnau, overlooked the courtroom. If Henry wanted security, he had no concerns about confidentiality. Some 2,000 people attended, says Chapuys (possibly with exaggeration).[2]

The court's procedure was well established. The Constable of the Tower led the accused into court, after which the Clerk of the Crown read the indictment, the prisoner pleaded and the prosecuting counsel (normally the attorney-general) gave his evidence. The prisoner could then respond, after which he or she was escorted from the courtroom while the peers deliberated on their verdict, which did not have to be unanimous. They announced their decisions individually, beginning with the nobleman of the lowest rank and progressing to that of the highest. A simple majority of the twenty-six was enough to convict. Once the verdict was given, the prisoner had another opportunity to speak. (Thomas More had availed himself of this to make his resounding attack on Henry's royal supremacy.) Finally, the Lord Steward pronounced sentence.[3]

Several of Anne's biographers claim that documents are missing from the court records, and go on to consider whether Cromwell, or even Anne's daughter Elizabeth, might have purged them. The records in treason trials, all without exception written on parchment, were filed with the proceedings of the Crown side of the Court of King's Bench and stored in the so-called *Baga de Secretis* ('Bag of Secrets'). This was the name, in Anglo-Norman French, given in the fourteenth century to the large leather bag used to protect this special class of documents from prying eyes. Later they were kept inside a 'press' (or cupboard) to which access required the attendance of three separate keyholders. The great 'Bag' itself had disappeared by the early eighteenth century, but many of the smaller bags or 'pouches' in which individual cases were filed survive and their contents, although crumpled, are in good condition. The crucial point is that the records of Anne and George's cases as once stored in the Bag are intact. When closely compared with those for all the other state trials in Henry's reign, nothing is missing from them.

What are lost are preparatory witness statements and pre-trial examinations that it now seems certain *did* once exist (see Appendix 3) but which were never kept in the Bag. In a letter to Stephen Gardiner in France, Cromwell claimed that what he called 'the very confessions' were 'so abominable that a great part of them were never given in evidence, but clearly kept secret'.[4] In their absence, third-party sources help us to reconstruct the trials and their aftermath. Chapuys gives the fullest account, to which John Husee's letters to Viscount and Lady Lisle and the observations of Norris's servant, George Constantine, add circumstantial details. The most valuable contribution comes from Sir John Spelman, who had attended the preliminary hearings in Westminster Hall and Deptford in his capacity as a Justice of the King's Bench, helped to convict the four commoners and then sat as an adviser to the peers. The original of his private notebook is now missing, but much of its contents were faithfully transcribed by Gilbert Burnet in 1679.[5]

The London chroniclers also played their parts. Edward Hall moves straight from Anne's arrest to her execution, omitting the trials, but Charles Wriothesley, Thomas's cousin and one of the heralds, left a closely observed account.[6] So did Anthony Anthony, a groom of the king's chamber and Surveyor of the Ordnance in the Tower. While the original is lost, a copy was later owned by the Elizabethan antiquary, John Stow, and afterwards consulted by Burnet and by one Thomas Turner.[7] In the Bodleian Library are Turner's notes, many of which, he says, came 'out of an old original diary or Journal wrot with ye proper hand of one Mr Anthony Anthony ... the said Anthony being a contemporary to ye Action, and (as he saith himself) an eye- and earwitness.'[8]

Last come the notes chiefly of Anne and George's scaffold speeches, now in the Bibliothèque Nationale in Paris and almost certainly compiled by Lancelot de Carle, who used them when composing the poem 'La histoire de la royne Anne Boullant d'Angleterre', which he dated 2 June 1536.[9] They inspired spin-offs in various formats and languages.[10] Versions developed as newsletters can be found in French, Italian and Portuguese. The best known, slightly expanded, of these takes the form of a letter by a so-called 'Portuguese gentleman': there was of course no such person. To write an open letter to a fictitious 'friend in the country' (or another country) as a way of circulating a newsletter had been a literary commonplace since the age of Cicero.[11] A second newsletter cluster derives from a pro-Habsburg account sent either by or for Chapuys to the regent Marie of Hungary in Brussels.[12] None of these sources is definitive on their own: they must all be studied, then collated with the records in the Bag of Secrets.

Anne's day in court was Monday 15 May. Henry had decided this over the weekend when he ordered the Clerk of the Crown to issue a writ commanding the royal justices to make themselves available to assist the peers that day by ensuring all was done 'by the laws and customs of England'.[13] She was to be tried early in the morning: then it would be George's turn. But the Boleyn siblings were mentally and verbally agile. In what they knew to be a fight to the death, both showed their mettle. The panic-stricken 'babbling' Anne was no more. This was Anne at her finest; this was the confident, highly articulate woman with the dark, flashing eyes whom Henry had once worshipped. She was fearless.

When the peers and justices were in their places, Sir William Kingston brought in his prisoner, who was attended by Lady Elizabeth Boleyn and Lady Kingston. He led her to the bar of the court, where a chair was prepared for her. After the indictment was read, Anne raised her right hand and pleaded not guilty.[14] Only then did she hear the full extent of the prosecution's evidence against her from the attorney-general, Christopher Hales. Besides the indictment, there was, says Chapuys, an added charge that certain tokens had been exchanged between her and Norris, and that these amounted to a promise that she would marry him after Henry's death.[15] The threat to Henry's family was invoked: Hales alleged that Anne had poisoned Katherine and plotted to do the same to her stepdaughter, Mary. Just for good measure, the court was told that she and George had laughed at the king and ridiculed his manner of dress 'and that she showed in certain ways that she did not love the king and was tired of him'.[16]

Spelman adds that it was averred in evidence that Anne and George had 'conspired the king's death, for she said that the king should never have her heart, and she said to each of the four [commoners] by himself that she loved him more than the others'. This, he says, 'slandered the issue [Elizabeth] which was begotten between her and the king', itself treason by a clause in the Act of Succession passed in 1534.[17] More substantially, he continues:

And all the evidence was of bawdry and lechery, so that there was no such whore in the realm. Note that this matter was disclosed by a woman called the Lady Wingfield, who had been a servant to the said queen and of the same qualities; and suddenly the said Wingfield became sick and a short time before her death showed this matter to one of her etc.[18]

The final 'etc.' may not signal that anything is missing as lawyers routinely used this abbreviation to indicate self-evident matter. When transcribing Spelman's notebook, Burnet observed 'and here unluckily the rest of the page is torn off', but he did not think it called for a sinister explanation.[19]

When she died in 1534, Bridget Wilshire (widow of Sir Richard Wingfield and Sir Nicholas Harvey) was still the wife of Robert Tyrwhitt. On learning of the charges against Anne in advance of the trials, which as a seasoned courtier he could hardly have failed to do, it is likely that Tyrwhitt supplied Cromwell with a report of Bridget's disclosures, leading to a search of her papers. Of old Lincolnshire stock, Tyrwhitt and his brother Philip had close connections through their mother, Maud Tailboys, to Katherine and her daughter. That might fully explain why Anne's letter to Bridget, written shortly before she was created Marquis of Pembroke, ended up in the principal secretary's archives.[20]

If we could only know what, if anything, Bridget had gleaned of Anne's dealings with Harry Percy and Thomas Wyatt, all might be clearer. Had Anne needed to keep something her friend knew hidden from Henry, possibly originating from her early years in Kent or when she had first returned from France? And when

Spelman described Bridget as 'a servant to the said queen and of the same qualities', what did he mean?

Whatever the precise circumstances, Bridget's evidence was both hearsay and at least two years old. As Burnet disdainfully observes, 'the safest sort of forgery ... is to lay a thing on a dead person's name, where there is no fear of discovery.'[21]

No other witness statement was produced. Perhaps the most remarkable aspect of Anne's trial was that she was never confronted with Mark Smeaton, the one person who had undisputedly confessed to adultery with her – but then Cromwell could hardly trust him not to retract his statement. Would the young musician really have had the confidence, or the need, given he was already a condemned man, to repeat it to Anne's face? Perhaps this, above all other reasons, is why the only significant proof of her guilt laid before the peers was the testimony of a woman who was dead.[22]

Anne's response was to deny everything. As she had told Kingston in the Tower, 'If any man accuse[s] me, I can say but "nay", and they can bring no witness.' And 'nay' is what she proceeded to say. She denied she had been unfaithful to Henry; that she had imagined or plotted his death; that she had committed incest with her brother; that she had exchanged secret tokens with Norris or promised to marry him; that she had poisoned Katherine or planned to poison Mary. She admitted only that she had given money to Francis Weston, but added that she had done the same for several impecunious young courtiers, and always without criminal intent.[23]

Many were impressed by her performance. From Turner's notes it might seem Anthony Anthony merely wrote that 'she would not confess', but in his *Chronicles of England* towards the end of the 1570s, with the benefit of a copy of Anthony's journal before him, John Stow adds that 'she seemed fully to clear herself of all matters laid to her charge.'[24] Wriothesley's *Chronicle* agrees, saying that 'she made so wise and discreet answers to all things laid against her, excusing herself with her words so clearly, as though she had never been faulty to the same.' Both Chapuys and de Carle were mightily impressed.[25] She defended herself robustly, says Chapuys, 'giving more than sufficiently convincing replies to each and every charge'.[26] That he had been her stalwart enemy adds weight to his words. 'She held herself more constant than a tree-stump / That does not fear hail or the impetuous wind', declares de Carle.

> She defended her honour soberly,
> Without becoming flustered, but constantly
> Her face guaranteed her words
> Were not just oratory.[27]

And yet, the guilty verdict was never in doubt. When it came, it was unanimous. Rightly is it said that 'the question which presented itself to the minds of the lords, was not whether she was guilty of the charges contained in the indictments, but whether she was to die or not.'[28] As Wriothesley reports, 'After they had communed together, the youngest lord of the said inquest was called first to give [a] verdict, who said "Guilty", and so every lord and earl after their degrees said "Guilty" to the last, and so condemned her.'[29]

The Duke of Norfolk then gave judgment.[30] The chilling Latin of the documents in the Bag of Secrets reports the sentence, which Wriothesley translates word for word:

> Because thou hast offended our sovereign the king's grace in
> committing treason against his person, and here attainted of the
> same, the law of the realm is this, that thou hast deserved death,
> and thy judgment is this: That thou shalt be burned here within
> the Tower of London on the Green, else to have thy head smitten
> off as the king's pleasure shall be further known of the same.[31]

A sentence in the alternative, Spelman says, was 'because she was a queen', although the real reason was because neither Norfolk nor anyone else at this point knew what Henry's pleasure would be. Only he would decide the method of execution. It caused, Spelman added, the royal justices to murmur 'for such judgment

... had not been seen'.* As Anthony Anthony independently noted, 'the old customs of the land' were that a woman traitor should be burned. But then, never had an English queen been condemned for treasonable adultery before, except in the romantic fiction of Malory's *Morte d'Arthur*.[32]

Anne should now have been taken back to the Tower, but if Chapuys and de Carle are correct, she was allowed to speak in mitigation. (Properly, this should have been done after the verdict of the peers, but before the sentence.) Did she do so? Chapuys reports that she did. She was ready to die, she said, but extremely sorry to hear that others who were innocent and the king's loyal subjects 'were to die purely on her account'. She then requested a short time for 'shrift' (confession) to prepare for death (*pour disposer sa conscience*).[33]

As she was led from the courtroom, a commotion arose on the bench. Harry Percy, white as a sheet, had collapsed and had to be carried out.[34] George then followed his sister into the King's Hall for his own reckoning. Anne had been taken away before he was brought in, so there was no final meeting between them. Other than the now absent Percy, he faced the same group of peers as had his sister and largely the same charges. Like her, he pleaded not guilty as he too prepared to argue for his life. Like her, he had to defend himself unassisted.[35]

Once Hales began to present his evidence, a murmur spread through the courtroom as it became clear that a conviction might be more difficult to secure. The central charge, that George had committed incest with his sister, was not easy to prove. As Chapuys explained, it rested on no more than 'presumption'. It was said only that he had 'once passed many hours in her company' and that there had been 'other little follies' which were unspecified.[36] The alleged offences were said to have taken place in November and December 1535, but no details were given. It was inevitable that

---

*What most offended the justices was a sentence which lacked the certainty lawyers so prized.

since the Boleyns worked as one almost from the outset of Henry's courtship of Anne, she and George would have often been together, but in truth a substantive charge could only have been linked to one specific incident: the episode in June 1535 when George had suddenly left the Anglo-French conference with Admiral Chabot in Calais to update his sister after failing to secure Princess Elizabeth's betrothal to Charles, Duke of Angoulême, when he was alone with her in her bedchamber for several hours.[37]

In reply to Hales's submission, says Chapuys, George answered to such powerful effect that 'many who were present at the trial and heard what he said had no difficulty in waging two to one that he would be acquitted, the more so since no witnesses were called to give evidence against him' – and this was despite Anne's conviction an hour or so before for the same offence. Wriothesley writes to similar effect: George 'made answer so prudently and wisely to all articles laid against him, that marvel it was to hear, and never would confess anything, but made himself as clear as though he had never offended'.[38]

De Carle too commented on his calm rebuttal of the evidence:

To everything he responded persuasively,
Point by point, without confusing the order,
So much that one never saw a man respond better.
No, not even More, who had such an abundance
Of eloquence and knowledge.[39]

George's tour de force is surely proof that he was more of a potential threat to Cromwell than is believed by those biographers who have dismissed him as little more than a cipher or a glorified messenger boy, carrying love notes between Henry and Anne.[40] He rose to further heights when, in a fresh twist to a riveting trial, Hales handed him a piece of paper containing an accusation which he was instructed to read silently, not aloud, and answer with a 'yes' or a 'no'. In a blatant act of defiance which infuriated Cromwell, who wished the question kept secret, George read it out clearly, and in full, so that it was audible to everyone in the stands. The question asked whether his wife, Jane Parker, had ever told him that Anne had confided to her that Henry 'was no good at sex with women, and that he had neither prowess nor force (*ne vertu ne puissance*)'.[41]

Because she trusted her implicitly, Anne might easily have shared such a secret with her sister-in-law, who could have passed it on to George. Most likely she did, since George refused to answer. 'I will', he said in a good lawyerly fashion, 'not in this point arouse any suspicion which might prejudice the king's issue.'

Unwilling to drop his line of questioning, Hales next claimed that George had spread malicious reports which called into question the paternity of Anne's child Elizabeth. George did not dignify this with an answer. He knew his own sister.

His continuing defiance was his undoing: every peer delivered a guilty verdict. Norfolk then pronounced sentence and the ominous cipher 'T&S' was written in the court records. Like the four commoners, George was to suffer a felon's death on the gallows, a sentence he accepted with equanimity, asking only that his debts should be paid since his property was now forfeited to the king.[42]

Much speculation followed of how his alleged crimes were uncovered. De Carle has him telling his judges:

And on the advice of only one woman
You want to cast on such a great blame
That, because of her supposition,
You decide to condemn me.[43]

Constantine believed George would have been acquitted 'had it not been for a letter'.[44] The so-called Portuguese gentleman talks of 'that person, who more out of envy and jealousy than out of love towards the king, did betray this accursed secret, and together with it, the names of those who had joined in the evil doings of the unchaste queen'.[45] No names are disclosed, but in the Portuguese original the gender of the first of the personal pronouns is female. If John Husee's reports to Lady Lisle are to be believed the reference is to Elizabeth Browne (see Appendix 4).

On Tuesday the 16th, Cranmer arrived at the Tower. Well might he have had qualms about his visit since he had not come out of pastoral care or goodwill. Henry had sent him, because he wanted to discover from Anne before she died the grounds on which their marriage could lawfully be annulled. As with Katherine, it was important to him to believe that his marriage was invalid, and always had been. When he married Jane Seymour, psychologically he needed to feel he was a bachelor.[46]

The easiest way would have been to revive the idea of a precontract with Harry Percy, but Anne's former suitor failed to oblige. On the 13th, two days before he was called to sit with the peers in judgment on her, Percy had written to Cromwell repeating his denial that a precontract had existed between them. Politely, but firmly, he reminded the principal secretary that he had been questioned about this before, and under oath. What transpired between Cranmer and Anne at their meeting we can only imagine, but from what would shortly follow, it appears that she defended the lawfulness of her marriage (and thus the certainty of her daughter's legitimacy) to the last.[47]

Later in the day, Kingston was summoned to Whitehall for an audience with Henry. His instructions were that George and the commoners were 'to die tomorrow'. During the interview, the harassed Constable verbally delivered 'petitions' from George, which the king received coldly. Regarding Anne, Henry informed him that Cranmer 'should be her confessor'. When reporting this an hour or so later to Cromwell, Kingston noted that the archbishop had already been to see her that day, 'and not in that matter'.[48]

Returning to the Tower, Kingston informed Anne's brother of his fate 'and so he accepted it very well and will do his best to be ready'. George, meanwhile, wished Cromwell to act on his petitions as to his debts, as they 'toucheth his conscience much, as he saith'. What most troubled him related to a payment of £100 with a promise of a second at Whitsuntide, received from a Cistercian monk. In return, the monk was to be made abbot of Valle Crucis in north-east Wales. George had heard that Cromwell was in the process of suppressing Valle Crucis, but he was unable to reimburse the monk, since Henry had his goods and papers. If nothing was arranged, the monk would 'be undone'.[49]

Over dinner in the Tower that day, Anne spoke of retiring to a nunnery and was still 'in hope of life'. When feeding the information back to Cromwell, Kingston urged him to establish Henry's wishes 'touching the queen, as well for her comfort as for the preparations of scaffolds and other necessaries'. Unlike on Tower Hill, where a permanent scaffold stood, none yet stood on the Green within the Tower and if one was needed, carpenters must be summoned. Another of the Constable's worries was that George and the commoners had been condemned to die at Tyburn. Was that still the case, he wondered?[50]

To his credit, Cromwell answered swiftly. No death warrant was yet prepared for George and the commoners, he said, but it would come. In Anne's case, Henry had decided that she would be beheaded, not burned, by an executioner sent from Calais.[51]

Replying by return, Kingston expressed his thanks. 'I am very glad', he said, 'to hear of the executioner of Calais, for he can handle that matter.' George and the commoners 'be all ready and I trust clean to God'. He would warn them, he said, in the morning. He would send for the carpenters to begin constructing on the Green within the Tower a scaffold of 'some reasonable height so that all men present may see it'.[52]

One issue which greatly troubled Anne was still unresolved. 'As yet', Kingston explained, 'I hear nothing of my lord of Canterbury, and the queen desireth much to be shriven.' Whether the archbishop ever reappeared to hear her final confession, we do not know for certain, but since he was ordered to do so by Henry, we can only assume he obeyed.

Early next day, Wednesday the 17th, Kingston received the warrant directing him to take George and the four commoners to Tower Hill for execution. The recently discovered document, copied into Ralph Pexall's precedent book, disproves an old tradition that Mark Smeaton was dragged to Tyburn and hanged.[53] Kingston was probably correct in saying they were resigned to their fate. A romantic tradition has it that one of them used his final moments to scratch Anne's falcon badge, lacking its crown, on the wall of the Beauchamp Tower.[54] A farewell letter from Weston has survived, neatly appended to a list of his debts amounting to about £900. 'Father and mother and wife', it poignantly begins:

> I shall humbly desire you for the salvation of my soul to
> discharge me of this bill, and to forgive me of all the offences
> that I have done to you, and in especial to my wife, which
> I desire for the love of God to forgive me and to pray for me.[55]

An hour or so later, at nine o'clock, as the condemned men made ready to die, Cranmer opened a special church court in Lambeth to hear Henry's case for annulment of his marriage to Anne.[56] After a session lasting less than two hours, Cranmer certified that the marriage had always been invalid, declaring that this was so 'for divers true, just and legitimate causes' but not saying what any of those were. In his notebook, Spelman gave the reason as 'a precontract made by the queen with another [meaning Harry Percy] before the marriage between her and the king'.[57]

Husee, an eyewitness at Tower Hill, assured Lady Lisle that all five prisoners 'died very charitably'. Norris, reports George Constantine, 'said almost nothing at all'. Brereton merely said, 'I have deserved to die if it were a thousand deaths, but the cause whereof I die, judge not. But if ye judge, judge the best,' perhaps as far as he dared to go in asserting his innocence. Weston said, 'I had thought to have lived in abomination yet these twenty or thirty years, and then to have made amends.' Smeaton combined convention with brevity, declaring, 'Masters, I pray you all pray for me, for I have deserved the death.'[58]

George was more audacious. Multiple versions exist of his speech, all broadly similar in theme and format. At first, he followed convention:

> Masters all, I am not come hither for to preach, but for to
> die, for I have deserved for to die if I had twenty lives more
> shamefully than can be devised, for I am a wretched sinner

and I have sinned shamefully ... I pray you, take heed by me,
and especially my lords and gentlemen of the court, the which
I have been among, take heed by me, and beware of such a fall,
and I pray to God the Father, the Son and the Holy Ghost,
three persons and one God, that my death may be an example
unto you all, and beware: trust not in the vanity of the world,
and especially in the flattering of the court.[59]

Normally, this is where a scaffold speech would end, but not
George's. Chapuys thought he would recant his evangelical beliefs,
but he was wrong. On the contrary, George extolled them:

It is commonly said that I was a professor of the Holy Gospel
of Jesus Christ. In order that the Word of God is not to be
brought into scandal because of me, I say to you all, that if
I had followed the Word of God in fact ... I would not have
fallen into the case I am now in. I read the Gospel of Jesus
Christ, but I did not follow it. If I had done so, I would still
have lived among you. For this, Sirs, for the love of God, hold
tight to the truth and follow it, because one follower is worth
more than three readers.[60]

As George's head was severed from his body, Anne remained
confined. Chapuys claims Henry insisted that she witness her
brother's end 'from the windows of her prison'. Mercifully this was
impossible: no view of Tower Hill was available from the queen's
apartments.[61] But if she was spared the anguish of watching her
'sweet brother' and the others die, her own ordeal continued.
Attended by women she loathed and from whom she could expect
neither sympathy nor comfort, she faced the cruel uncertainty of
waiting for Kingston's return.

Waiting just as impatiently were Henry and his new love.

Epilogue

With Anne and George dead, Henry was free to marry Jane Seymour, free to abandon the French alliance and free to make a full rapprochement with Charles. In the process, Cromwell rid himself of his rivals, consolidated his power and became Henry's unchallenged chief minister. Thomas Wyatt, cauterised by his own narrow escape, deftly wove poignant epitaphs for each of the king's male victims into the central verses of a poem:

Some say, 'Rochford, hadst thou been not so proud,
For thy great wit each man would thee bemoan.'
Since as it is so, many cry aloud,
'It is great loss that thou art dead and gone.'

Ah, Norris, Norris, my tears begin to run
To think what hap did thee so lead or guide,
Whereby thou hast both thee and thine undone,
That is bewailed in court of every side ...

Ah, Weston, Weston, that pleasant was and young,
In active things who might with thee compare? ...
And we that now in court doth lead our life,
Most part in mind doth thee lament and moan ...

Brereton, farewell, as one that least I knew.
Great was thy love with divers [i.e. many], as I hear,

But common voice doth not so sore thee rue
As other twain that doth before appear.
But yet no doubt but thy friends thee lament
And other hear their piteous cry and moan ...

Ah, Mark, what moan should I for thee make more
Since that thy death thou hast deserved best,
Save only that mine eye is forced sore
With piteous plaint to moan thee with the rest? ...[1]

On 30 May 1536, a mere eleven days after his 'own sweetheart' took her last breath, Henry and Jane were quietly married in the queen's closet at Whitehall.[2] He believed he had finally found a wife who would offer him the love he wanted and the love he needed, but without attempting to oversee his policies or tell him what to do. Sir John Russell quipped in a letter to Viscount Lisle how Henry 'hath come out of hell and into heaven', for Jane 'is as gentle a lady as ever I knew, and as fair a queen as any in Christendom'. Henry could now enjoy the 'gentleness' of his new queen and forget the 'cursedness and the unhappiness in the other'. But this famous observation is not quite what it seems. The rest of it comprised advice for Lisle. 'Wherefore, my lord', he wrote, 'me think it were very well done, when you do write to the king again, that you do rejoice that he is so well matched with so gracious a woman as she is, and you hear reported.' Henry may have found the woman of his dreams, but he still craved reassurance and approval.[3]

There were strange loose ends to be addressed. On 1 June, any children Anne might have by her marriage to Henry were inadvertently declared the king's legitimate heirs by the Irish Parliament. In a bizarre twist, the parliament had begun its work on 1 May, and on the 17th, William Brabazon, Cromwell's agent, wrote from Dublin to tell him the names of those Acts which had already passed in the Lower House: the agreement of the Lords would follow shortly. All that was needed was the king's assent, to be given by proxy by two royal justices arriving from London. Among the English legislation which the session was meant to extend to Ireland was the 1534 Act of Succession. Caught unawares by this embarrassing oversight, Cromwell ordered the Irish privy council to 'stay' the proceedings without delay. His letter failed to arrive until 3 June, two days too late. All had to be unscrambled afterwards.[4]

On 8 June, the English Parliament reconvened. In his opening address to members of both Houses, Lord Chancellor Audley compared Henry to King Solomon, whose mantra (or so he said) was 'Remember the past, consider the present, provide for the future.' Anne, he insisted, was a wicked woman, justly convicted of treason. Once made aware of her depravity, Henry had done his duty in sending her for trial, the welfare and stability of his subjects uppermost in his mind. The reason Parliament had been summoned, he continued, was because those Acts favouring Anne and her progeny must be replaced.[5]

Henry's replacement for the 1534 Act of Succession laid down the orthodoxy about the Boleyns that prevailed for the rest of his reign. He had thought his marriage to Anne to be 'pure, sincere, perfect and good' until 'God of his infinite goodness, from whom no secret things can be hid, hath caused to be brought to light ... certain just, true and lawful impediments.' Anne had proved to be false, endangering not just the king's honour, but his life 'to the utter loss, disinheritance and desolation of this realm'.[6]

The revised Act stripped Elizabeth of her title as princess and declared her illegitimate, then left the throne to the king's heirs by Jane, or if there were none, to whoever Henry chose to designate in his will. Perhaps he was considering restoring Mary as he had hinted to Charles he might, except that the Act, explicitly for the first time, declared her illegitimate as well. Only in 1544, when Henry at last returned to France as Charles's ally to lead an army against Francis did he reinstate his daughters in the line of succession, although neither was legitimised.[7] More likely, he had his eye on Henry Fitzroy, whom he moved into the newly completed St James's Palace, which Anne had earmarked for her and the king's future son and heir.[8] If that indeed was in his mind, it came to nothing. The question of Fitzroy's accession became moot when, on or about 8 July, the teenager succumbed to bronchial pneumonia. Two weeks later he was dead.[9]

Jane, whose motto was 'Bound to obey and serve', proved to be Henry's ideal wife and queen.[10] She did not argue with her husband – only briefly did she question his decision to suppress the smaller monasteries, and quickly backtracked when he reminded her of Anne's fate. 'Remember', he warned her menacingly, 'that the last queen died in consequence of meddling too much.'[11] Jane could be mean and blinkered, but she had her own style – distinctively and purposefully English in contrast to Anne's. No French gowns or hoods for Jane: the old-fashioned English gable headdress was her livery badge of loyalty.[12]

On 12 October 1537, barely sixteen months after her wedding, Jane gave birth to a healthy son at Hampton Court. An uneventful pregnancy was followed by a difficult labour that lasted two days and three nights. Henry named his son Edward, after Edward III, his royal ancestor through the Beaufort line. Jane, who never recovered from the labour, received the last rites twelve days later. She died of a post-natal haemorrhage, aged just twenty-eight. Henry was bereft, writing to Francis: 'It has seemed good to divine providence, whose will is most sacred, to mingle my joy with the bitterness of the striking down of the woman who brought me this good fortune.' He had 1,200 Masses said for her in London alone, and she was buried in state in St George's Chapel in Windsor in a grave that he would later choose to share with her.[13]

With the passing of the new Act of Succession, history was rewritten and the verdicts of Anne and George's trials enshrined in statute. How could so many intelligent people have apparently given credence to the charges levelled against them in court? That it was politic to do so is obvious, but there is more. On Anne's side, she never fully understood how far the courtly 'pastimes' she had condoned in her apartments had given rise to a sex scandal. Games and flirtations of this risqué, French-inspired sort would never again be seen in England, not even in Charles I's reign after he married the French princess, Henrietta Maria. Their only other appearance in the British Isles was at the court of Mary Queen of Scots, where they helped to destroy another queen.[14]

On Henry's side, nothing mattered more to him than honour, reputation and a sense of being in control. What drove him to topple Anne were accusations he felt could not safely be ignored, swiftly followed by an investigation that seemingly uncovered compelling evidence and took on its own tragic momentum. Steered relentlessly by Cromwell, this advanced to the point where any suggestion that Anne might be innocent seemed to be evidence of the speaker's own guilt. Throughout, Henry's actions seemed to himself to be utterly justifiable, responsible and reasonable. Whether he compared Norris's encounter with Anne to that between Sir Lancelot and Guinevere in the *Morte d'Arthur*, with himself playing the part of the cuckolded Arthur, is pure speculation. But when he decided to put Anne on trial for treasonable adultery, one conceptual basis for doing so lay in Malory's work.[15]

Quite why Henry felt so strongly that her death was necessary is an intriguing question. Why did he not stay her execution at the last moment, as he occasionally did in other cases and as Anne had half-believed he would? If he was to marry Jane, the most important thing was for his marriage to Anne to be annulled. Given her willingness to retreat to a nunnery, it seems unlikely she would have caused him further problems, although her brother George undoubtedly would have. Partly it was because of the scandalous nature of the pretext for her arrest: once a charge of treasonable adultery was decided upon, he felt obliged to go through with an execution. Partly it was because he was just so enraged by the talk that he was unable to keep order in his own family and household, which suggested he was unfit to rule.

Mainly, though, it was because he came to think Anne was genuinely guilty. So acute was his sense of betrayal that he slid into 'victim' mode, self-indulgently persuading himself that he was the target of a dark conspiracy masterminded by Anne to kill him and marry one of her lovers, probably Norris. His mood of mawkish self-pity meant that all he could focus on was the lucky escape he and his children had evidently had. On the evening after Anne's arrest, when Fitzroy came to say goodnight to him, he told him with tears in his eyes that he and his sister – meaning Mary, not

Elizabeth – 'ought to thank God for having escaped from the hands of that woman who had planned their death by poison'.[16]

Only for a moment had Henry dithered. And with the decision made, he lacked all sense of conflict or guilt about Anne's execution. This is proved by his extreme reaction in June 1537 after Sir Francis Bryan warned him that Lancelot de Carle's poem 'La histoire de la royne Anne Boullant d'Angleterre' had been printed and was openly circulating in France. In a fury, Henry ordered Stephen Gardiner to seek an immediate audience with Francis and demand all copies be destroyed. Surprisingly, Francis obliged: the printed text disappeared, and did not reappear until 1545, when it was republished in Lyon.[17]

Not everyone in Parliament or beyond believed that Anne was a whore. Charles's sister, Marie of Hungary, was reporting news received from England when she informed her brother a mere ten days after Anne and George's trial that since none but Smeaton had confessed, people think that Henry invented 'this manner of pleading' (ce stil) to get rid of her.[18] In London, and especially among evangelical members of the Mercers' Company, there were signs of discontent. Sir John Allen, the Lord Mayor, who had witnessed both Anne's and the commoners' trials and executions, a man well known to Henry and Cromwell and who sat regularly with the privy council, always suspected that Anne was innocent. George Constantine claimed that 'there was much muttering of Queen Anne's death'. Chapuys, no friend of Anne but fundamentally an honest man, best captured the mood when he observed that 'although everybody rejoices at the execution of the *putain* [whore], there are some who murmur at the mode of procedure [used] against her and the others, and people speak variously of the king.'[19]

A generation later, George Wyatt, reflecting on the evidence at his disposal in his *Life of Anne Boleyn*, considered her alleged acts of incest and adultery to be 'by the circumstances impossible to commit'. Impossible 'for the necessary and no small attendance of ladies ever about her, whereof some, as after appeared, even aspired unto her place and right in the king's love'. Impossible also 'because neither she could remove so great ladies, by office appointed to attend upon her continually, from being witnesses to her doings'.[20]

When, just seven weeks after Anne's execution, news of Margaret Douglas's clandestine marriage trickled out, she and her lover were arrested. Henry sent them to the Tower, but when her mother, the king's elder sister, strongly protested, Henry confined his niece to the nunnery at Syon for almost a year.[21] Parliament attainted Lord Thomas Howard of high treason and made it treason to marry into the royal family without the king's permission. Although the death sentence was suspended, Lord Thomas fell sick and died in the Tower fifteen months later.[22] Douglas, meanwhile, was allowed to return to court, where she would be known as 'Lady Margaret Howard' – surely proof that Henry could destroy her secret marriage but could not dissolve it.[23]

Other than the Duke of Suffolk, whose instinct for self-preservation was honed to perfection, few of those left standing, or even who profited most after Anne's fall, would survive long. Grovel as they might to recover Henry's trust and their position at court, her parents never really did. Shunted sideways, Thomas Boleyn died in his bed in 1539 at Hever, and still lies in St Peter's church, memorialised by a life-sized brass effigy. Anne's mother died the previous year in the family's London house and was carried by barge to Lambeth parish church beside the Thames to be interred there 'with torches burning and four banners set out of all quarters of the barge'.[24] Thomas reached a financial settlement with George's widow, Jane Parker, who became a career courtier, serving Jane Seymour and Anne of Cleves, before becoming fatally embroiled in Katherine Howard's dalliance with Thomas Culpepper. In 1542, she too was beheaded on a scaffold erected on Tower Green before the 'House of Ordnance'.[25]

Within weeks of Anne's death, Cromwell gained the position he had always coveted as the king's chief minister. Granted sweeping fresh powers as 'Vicar-general' over the Church, as well as being Lord Privy Seal and eventually Lord Great Chamberlain, he continued to work as an evangelical reformer, often behind the king's back, strangely echoing Anne's values even after he had destroyed her.[26]

Not for nothing did John Foxe call Anne and Cromwell the twin, if decidedly ill-matched, architects of the English Reformation. When Cromwell too crossed the line and was executed in 1540, Henry reverted to more traditionally Catholic theological opinions, but held firm to his political repudiation of Rome and the papacy.

Of Anne's suitors, Harry Percy died in the summer of 1537, aged no more than thirty-five. By then he had lost his speech and was losing his sight; his stomach was distended and 'all his body as yellow as saffron'. Thomas Wyatt resumed his diplomatic career after his release from the Tower, although he found himself increasingly ill-matched to the role. By a cruel twist of fate, a malicious accusation of treachery made by Edmund Bonner led to his return to the Tower in 1541. Almost as cruel was the fact that, once Wyatt established his innocence, Henry – in a biting act of hypocrisy – dictated that the price of his freedom was to take back the wife he had so long ago repudiated and live with her as a good husband, which he appears grudgingly to have done, although only up to a point and not for long, dying peacefully the next year.[27]

Anne's cousin, Francis Bryan, enjoyed his moment of glory as the new chief gentleman of Henry's privy chamber, but his influence waned after he was suspected of advocating a reconciliation with Rome. By the end of 1538, he had been replaced: he died in 1550 in Ireland. His brother-in-law, Nicholas Carew, and Henry Courtenay, Marquis of Exeter, both lost their heads on charges, levelled by Cromwell, that they were plotting to restore Mary to her rightful place. Far luckier was Anne's uncle Norfolk. Although attainted in Parliament of treason in the twilight weeks of Henry's reign, he survived because the king died in the early hours of the very morning on which he was due to face the axe. His son, Henry Howard, Earl of Surrey, tried and sentenced a fortnight earlier, was less fortunate.

Mary Howard, Surrey's sister and Fitzroy's widow, fell under a cloud for her role in concealing Margaret Douglas's affair. She struggled to obtain her jointure and was forced to sell her jewels. She narrowly survived Norfolk's and Surrey's arrests and brought up her dead brother's children herself, employing John Foxe as their tutor. She never remarried, even though her father tried to betroth her to Thomas Seymour, the younger of Jane's brothers.[28]

Anne's cousin, Mary Shelton, also refused to marry at first and went on to have a longstanding affair with Thomas Clere, Surrey's servant and lifelong friend. When making his will in 1544, Clere bequeathed her a half-share in a dozen Norfolk manors, and when he died, Surrey wrote an epitaph, which included the lines:

Shelton for love, Surrey for lord thou chose;
Ay me, while life did last that league was tender.

Only then, did Mary marry as the second wife of Sir Anthony Heveningham, a wealthy Norfolk landowner, and when he died, the much younger Philip Appleyard, stepbrother of Amy Robsart, the ill-fated first wife of Elizabeth's favourite and suitor, Robert Dudley.[29]

The young Prince Edward became king on his father's death in 1547, at the age of nine, but died before his sixteenth birthday, also of bronchial pneumonia. Under Cranmer's tutelage, he steered the country in a straightforwardly Protestant direction. When his fervently Catholic half-sister Mary succeeded him, she married Charles's son, Philip, then regent and heir to the throne of Spain, and brought about a reunion with Rome. The marriage was childless and she died a sad and lonely woman in 1558, leaving the way open to Anne's daughter, who in the end was the only real winner.

Once Elizabeth was queen, she swiftly restored the break with Rome. Without Anne and her daughter, England would never have ended up a Protestant country. In *An Harborowe* [Harbour] *for Faithfull and Trewe Subiectes*, published in 1559, John Aylmer, the novice monk whose Cambridge education Anne had supported, hailed her as 'the chief, first and only cause of the banishing the beast of Rome with all his beggarly baggage'. She was the 'crop and root' of the Reformation. 'Was there ever in England', he asked, 'a greater feat wrought by any man than this was by a woman?'[30]

During her long reign, Elizabeth chose to let sleeping queens lie. There are clues, however, as to her feelings. One is the so-called

'Chequers Ring', a stunning piece of goldsmith's work which was later bequeathed to the nation and is now kept at the Prime Minister's official country house in Buckinghamshire. With her cipher on the bezel, the 'E' made of six table-cut diamonds and the 'R' etched in blue enamel, the mother-of-pearl ring opens to show the enamelled busts and miniature portraits of two women. One is a profile of herself, the other a full-face depiction of Anne, the likeness closest to the portrait medal struck in 1534. Elizabeth never criticised her father but it is surely significant that the portraits are of herself and her mother, and not him.[31]

As queen, Elizabeth relied on her mother's relatives closely. In practice, this usually meant Mary Boleyn's son, Henry Carey, and his daughter, Katherine (or 'Kate'). Within weeks of her accession, she created him Lord Hunsdon, settled her mother's manor of Hunsdon on him, and granted him other estates in Hertfordshire, Kent and Essex worth £4,000 a year. Whenever she needed someone whom she could completely trust, she sent for him immediately. She made Kate one of her maids at the age of twelve and a gentlewoman of the privy chamber when barely fifteen. The nearest thing Elizabeth ever had to a friend, Kate went on to marry Lord William Howard and Margaret Gamage's son, Charles, whom the queen put in charge of the fleet that defeated the Spanish Armada.

William Stafford's second wife, Dorothy, whom he married after Mary Boleyn's death, was one of Elizabeth's favourite sleeping companions. For more than thirty years she was one of three or four gentlewomen whom the queen chose to sleep in turn beside her on a pallet bed.

Anne had been the love of Henry's life. Despite later becoming infatuated with the young Katherine Howard, never again would he feel the intensity of the passion he had felt for Anne. Her chief offence, having won the king's heart, was her jealousy of anyone who threatened to come between them, a fault she may have acknowledged. In Lancelot de Carle's poem is a fuller version of the speech she supposedly made after sentence at her trial. In it, she confesses: 'I have not always shown [the king] the humility that I should have ... because of some jealousy. I know that in this, virtue failed me, but for the rest, God is my witness that I committed no other wrongs against him.'[32]

That she had felt that way was the result of the vulnerability she sensed at points of crisis. When she and Henry worked as a team for his divorce, they were as one. They shared the same goal; they strove to achieve it with the same tenacity and resolve. Once they were married, they were no longer hunting the same quarry. Then, as time passed, what Henry had found so captivating about her ran the risk of gradually paling, especially when she failed to produce the promised son. What was so enchanting in a mistress would prove less appealing in a wife. However, the Anne who had the examples of Louise of Savoy and Marguerite of Angoulême before her could never settle for the self-abnegation expected from a subservient, obedient wife. She had too much zest, too much audacity, too many unfulfilled ambitions of her own for that.

Anne was an extraordinarily modern woman, a supremely talented, captivating spirit comfortable in her own skin and confident in her destiny. Even her nemesis Cromwell was prepared to praise her wit, intelligence and courage.[33] Very much a product of her family's experiences and traditions, she had unique qualities of charm and resilience. A voice determined to be heard in the cacophony of sound in Henry's court, she read her own books, framed her own opinions and was ready to defend them against all comers. She was the first queen of England to champion a reforming agenda certainly where religion was concerned. Her major character flaw was succumbing to the dizzying effects of power and hubris. De Carle was not far wrong when he depicted her as basically good and virtuous, until ambition turned her head:

Perhaps it was for the common reason
Of inconstant and changing fortune,
Or that God wants to show us more often
That great honours and worldly goods are only wind ...[34]

Energised by Henry's devotion, she thought she could have everything she wanted, and that what she wanted was right;

somehow, she was able to ignore the fallout that this could cause. When battling for something, whether it was her family's profits and positions, or those of her protégés, or for a cause she believed in such as religion, education and poor relief, and especially for her daughter's dynastic status, she was the epitome of discipline and determination. But as with her weaponising of Skip's sermon, although her motives were honourable, she often could not comprehend how far she had crossed a boundary and would infuriate her husband. Arguably her greatest weakness sprang from her unwillingness to ask herself before their marriage what Henry would really be like to live with. What would be the quality of their relationship? Could they confide unreservedly in each other? A solid marriage, even at the highest social level, is one with an emotional cornerstone.

Whether she truly loved Henry is the hardest question to answer. Her searing experience with Harry Percy had taught her never to expect too much from romance, and when her sister found true love with the lowly William Stafford, the violence of her response may have masked an element of sexual jealousy, perhaps mirrored in her private admission that Henry was no good in bed because 'he had neither prowess nor force'. The best clue to her feelings is the message she slipped during Mass to Henry in reply to his at the time of their courtship. When she wrote, 'By daily proof you shall me find / To be to you both loving and kind,' did she say this from the heart, or was it what she felt she needed to say at that moment? If unpacked, her words are gentle, not passionate, more like the sort of affection women who found themselves in arranged marriages were expected to give to their spouse when they promised to 'love, cherish and obey'. Henry spoke in a different register: 'If you remember my love in your prayers as strongly as I adore you, I shall hardly be forgotten, for I am yours, Henry R always.'

When Anne fell, Henry tried to airbrush her out of his life, ordering as many of her portraits, clothes, artworks, personal possessions and letters to be destroyed as he could, creating a challenge for biographers to see who she really was. If she ever did sit for Holbein, this is when her portrait would have disappeared.

The only significant possessions to escape the cull were some fifty or so of her and her brother's books and manuscripts. Many were taken for Henry's collections where their provenance was obscured by the insertion of his own inventory numbers, and a few were given away or taken as souvenirs at the time of her arrest. Most would later come to the collections of the British Library, but others such as Lefèvre's *The Ecclesiaste* at Alnwick Castle, Anne's French psalter bought by J. Paul Getty and the two Books of Hours now at Hever would eventually be sold at auction or passed to dealers.

We have already seen that the Book of Hours in which Henry and Anne had exchanged love notes came into Bess Holland's possession. Of the books at Hever, the Book of Hours on vellum with Anne's inscription, 'Remember me when you do pray / That hope doth lead from day to day / Anne Boleyn', ended up with her gentlewoman Elizabeth Hill. Ultraviolet light has revealed partially erased inscriptions by Hill's mother, aunt and a female cousin among others. No solid evidence supports the romantic traditions that Anne gave Holland and Hill these books on the scaffold – Kingston's reports make clear that neither woman was with her in the Tower.[35]

Anne was not responsible for the wholesale destruction associated with Henry's suppression of the monasteries, even if her plan to redeploy some of their wealth to more profitable uses encouraged his ideas. The king's plunder of the Church – not long after Anne's death he seized the property of all 600 or so religious houses – purely for the royal coffers, rather than to found schools, universities and hospitals or fund scholarships and apprenticeships, sparked mass revolts in Lincolnshire, Yorkshire and most of the North. The rebels came perilously close to success before being brutally suppressed, with many hanged from trees.

Henry had begun his reign as an 'affable' prince. He took the throne in a blaze of adulation and yet within him lay deep-seated insecurities. A fortnight before his coronation, he impulsively married Katherine and listened to her for a while, and then once he tired of her, he transferred his affections elsewhere. When he fell for Anne and married her, his passion was real. In the halcyon days of their six-year courtship, when he found her mere presence beside him intoxicating, he may have thought that he could share the responsibilities of ruling with her, but this was an illusion. Would a man who sent out his ambassadors and diplomats with ventriloquised instructions, who scripted in advance their answers to multiple hypothetical questions, really surrender a significant portion of his authority to his wife?

Over-indulged by a doting mother and over-protected by an autocratic father, Henry grew into a narcissist who saw exercising control as his birthright, a man who never accepted blame for his own actions and always looked for scapegoats. A stickler for obedience and a stranger to remorse or guilt, he confronted any challenge to his authority with a wall of anger, his fear and insecurity so effectively buried that he did not even acknowledge they existed. By first undermining and then destroying Anne's more influential critics, notably Thomas More and John Fisher, and finally turning against her and her brother, Henry gradually metamorphosed from the supremely gifted teenager he had once been, into the brooding, awesome presence Holbein came to immortalise. Bad diet, drinking and lack of exercise after his near-fatal accident while jousting in 1536 made things worse. According to measurements taken for a new suit of armour, his chest circumference ballooned to fifty-seven inches and his waistline to fifty-four: he became the only king of England to be instantly recognisable by his shape.[36]

His marriage to Anne left an indelible mark on him psychologically. If his female-dominated childhood had made him more inclined to trust the advice of a woman than was the norm for a sixteenth-century ruler, his rejection of Anne obliterated that tendency. Never again, he said, would he make that mistake. In his quest for dynastic security, he was constantly guarding against plots and conspiracies. Bullying and hectoring everyone around him until he got his way, he became infinitely suspicious. His ambition was unchanged. Far from detaching England from Europe after the break with Rome, he planned to re-engage with the Continent on a far grander scale than before by calling the pope and the rulers of Christendom to order under his prophetic vision. For all that, he never felt totally safe. His rapprochement with Charles soon hit several bouts of turbulence. Henry and Francis still needed each other, but endlessly bickered over border disputes around Calais and over French influence in Scotland until war broke out and Henry captured Boulogne at massive cost, only to be betrayed by Charles.

Wyatt did not dare to write Anne's epitaph. And yet he managed to create in just a few lines of poetry one of the most compelling verdicts on her catastrophe and on Henry's reign. A presence throughout her life, sometimes in the foreground, more often in the shadows, but always looking and listening, Wyatt never forgot his encounters with her. Vivid stanzas in a poem he wrote at the time of his imprisonment in 1536 fathom the depths of his emotion:

These bloody days have broken my heart.
My lust, my youth did them depart,
And blind desire of estate.
Who hastes to climb seeks to revert,
Of truth, *circa Regna tonat.**

The Bell Tower showed me such sight
That in my head sticks day and night.
There did I learn out of a grate,
For all favour, glory, or might,
That yet *circa Regna tonat.*[37]

Whether Wyatt glimpsed Anne's execution from an upper slit window of the Bell Tower in fact or only in his imagination makes little difference. Depicting Henry's court as a gilded cage, a world of fear and uncertainty full of trapdoors and sliding panels where tragic events can be precipitated by Chinese whispers, he proved far more incisively than the Devonshire Manuscript how lyric poetry with its subversive possibilities could function as an ideal medium for saying what could never otherwise be said.

*'about the throne the thunder roars'.

For all Henry's protestations to the contrary, the atmosphere at his court in his final years was almost as unsettled and claustrophobic as during the Wars of the Roses. John Husee answered the charge that he no longer sent reports of state affairs to the Lisles by explaining, 'I thereby might put myself in danger of my life ... for there is divers here that hath been punished for reading and copying with publishing abroad of news; yea, some of them are at this hour in the Tower.'[38] Civil order was maintained, but only because Henry sold the bulk of the confiscated monastic lands at rock-bottom prices to willing purchasers to create a whole new class of property-owners with a vested interest in the status quo. Spies and informers stalked the country, safe-conducts were needed to travel abroad and the posts were intercepted – no one felt completely safe.

The tumultuous events of Henry and Anne's courtship and marriage had made them the cynosure of all eyes for the best part of a decade and changed England for ever. But Anne did not change Henry. He changed himself.

Appendix I
Anne Boleyn's Date of Birth

For over 400 years the respective dates of birth of the Boleyn siblings have vexed historians, beginning with William Camden in 1615. The Blickling parish registers recording dates of births, marriages and deaths do not begin until 1559. Camden created much of the confusion by giving a date of 1507 for Anne's birth in a marginal annotation to his *Annals of Queen Elizabeth*, while the rest of his text contains a mixture of accurate, inaccurate and bowdlerised information about Anne's early life.[1] Inconsistent evidence comes from Mary Boleyn's descendants: her grandson George said emphatically in 1597, on his father Lord Hunsdon's assurance, that Mary was the elder sister and sketched out a pedigree to prove it.[2] The inscription on a funeral monument in Cranford, Middlesex, to Lady Berkeley, Hunsdon's granddaughter, still legible in 1890 when it was recorded, contradicts this by giving Mary as the second daughter. A pedigree in the Harleian Manuscripts in the British Library follows this.[3] The conundrum may finally be resolved by a newly discovered manuscript tucked away in the library of The Queen's College, Oxford, never seen before by Anne's biographers. A collection of pedigrees in the hand of Nicholas Charles, Lancaster Herald at the College of Arms (d. 1613), this gives Anne as the younger sister.[4]

The modern consensus, established by Professor E. W. Ives by 2004 and supported by this new document, is that birth dates of around 1499 for Mary, 1500 or 1501 for Anne and 1503 or 1504 for George are likely to be correct, although all these dates could just possibly be a year or so later.[5] What is undeniable is that these Boleyn siblings followed on from each other quite swiftly. Not only did Thomas Boleyn tell us he had 'but fifty pounds' for him and his wife to live on in these years, he added that, in those years, 'she brought me forth every year a child'.[6] Of course, infant mortality was high in the sixteenth century and not all children survived. In subsequent years, while living in Kent, Thomas and Elizabeth Boleyn would lose two more children in infancy.[7]

Appendix 2
Sources for Anne's Movements in France

Until now, the sources used by Anne's biographers to track her movements in France have largely been chance references and the so-called 'Journal de Louise de Savoye', first printed in 1838 as an appendix to an early edition of Florange's chronicle.[1] However, the 'Journal', unlike the chronicle, is a sixteenth-century fake: or rather, as Louise did not keep a diary, it was ghost-written, not entirely reliably, probably by her chaplain, François du Moulin de Rochefort.[2] Claude's itinerary as published in the ten-volume *Catalogue des Actes de François Ier* relies chiefly on du Moulin's work. Beyond this, Anne's whereabouts have been a subject of endless speculation.[3]

Much of the solution has in fact been in plain sight, and in print, since 1897. The source from which du Moulin selected his more accurate information was the almost daily journal kept by Jean Barrillon, the secretary to Cardinal Antoine Duprat, the Chancellor of France. Wherever Duprat went, Barrillon followed, and he carefully noted those occasions when Claude's itinerary differed from her husband's. Combining his testimony with discoveries in French municipal archives and in local historical and archaeological publications, a richer account is available of Anne's experiences.[4]

Appendix 3
Sources for the Trials of Anne and George Boleyn

For Anne and George's trials, as with the trials of the four commoners in Westminster Hall, we have clear accounts of the charges, the names of the judges, the order of proceedings, the verdicts of the court and the sentences, but no first-hand verbatim record of exactly what was said by the accused or by counsel for the prosecution. We know from Chapuys and other sources that no witnesses were called, but we have no official record of what, and how much, or how little, evidence was produced.[1]

The confusion lies in the fate of any preparatory witness statements and pre-trial examinations that once existed but have now disappeared. In cases of high treason, the accused were subject to repeated examinations before the king's councillors. Lengthy questionnaires, called 'interrogatories', were prepared to steer the questioning, and verbatim transcripts, almost exclusively on paper, were made of the answers. Such interrogatories and depositions partially survive for similar trials of the period, including the trial of the Duke of Buckingham in 1521 and More's and Bishop Fisher's trials, and in greater quantities for the charges brought against Queen Katherine Howard in 1542.[2]

None of these documents was ever filed in the Bag of Secrets. They were kept in bundles alongside large quantities of the more important State Papers, correspondence and diplomatic documents stacked in Henry's study near his 'old bedchamber' in his 'secret lodging' at Whitehall. Sir Robert Cotton's predations excepted, the papers were left untouched until 1618, when all were moved into the tower over the gateway linking the eastern and western parts of the palace, colloquially known as the 'Holbein Gate'. In 1619 they narrowly escaped a serious fire, only to suffer more losses during the Civil War. Many had been 'hastily and confusedly thrown into blankets' at the time of the fire, while damp and vermin also wreaked their inevitable havoc.

Not until 1825 was a serious effort begun to catalogue, preserve and publish them, by which time many had disintegrated.[3] What was entirely unknown, until now, is the survival of an inventory made in 1544 of the most important documents, which William Paget instructed William Honnyngs to sort, bag up and re-stack in cupboards, coffers, chests and cabinets, and which lies hidden in an obscure class of rarely produced documents in the National Archives in Kew.[4] That was when Paget replaced Ralph Sadler, Cromwell's successor as the king's principal secretary. Always a methodical man, Paget ordered Honnyngs, one of the privy council's clerks, to make an inventory of these documents as he sorted them.

Until now never used by biographers writing on Henry and Anne, the inventory shows that papers relating to suspected traitors or their associates between around 1531 and 1544 included 'a little coffer of Mr Norris's writings', 'a little coffer of the Lord Rochford's [i.e. George Boleyn's] writings', and 'a bag of the Lady Rochford's [i.e. Jane Parker's] letters'. Plainly, Parker's letters were seized at the time of Katherine Howard's fall, as is proved by an adjacent entry in the inventory concerning 'a bag of letters [and] confessions etc touching the matter of the last Queen attainted'.[5] The confiscation of Norris and George's writings, however, can only have arisen at the time of the trials of 1536. They were not destroyed by Cromwell; otherwise, Paget and Honnyngs could not have been bagging them up in 1544, when Anne's nemesis was already four years dead. Sadly, they were not individually listed at the time they were bagged up and re-stacked so we cannot now know the extent of what is lost.

Appendix 4
The Identity of the Woman Giving Evidence Against George Boleyn

John Husee in his letters to Lady Lisle is emphatic that Elizabeth Browne, Countess of Worcester, was the main source of Cromwell's evidence against the Boleyn siblings. On 24 May 1536, he wrote: 'The first accusers [were] the Lady Worcester, and Nan Cobham, with one maid more. But the Lady Worcester was the first ground, as God knoweth.' On the 25th, he continued, 'Touching the Queen's accusers, my Lady Worcester beareth name to be the principal.'[1]

Sir John Spelman in his notes on Anne and George's trials says, 'And all the evidence was of bawdry and lechery, so that there was no such whore in the realm. Note that this matter was disclosed by a woman called the Lady Wingfield, who had been a servant to the said queen and of the same qualities ...'[2] By 'Lady Wingfield', Spelman clearly means not the Countess of Worcester, but Anne's childhood friend Bridget Wilshire (widow of Sir Richard Wingfield and Sir Nicholas Harvey), a statement not incompatible with Husee's remarks, as it is perfectly possible that Wingfield's posthumous testimony was given *during* the trials, but that the original indictments were founded on the pre-trial interrogations of Browne and Nan Cobham.

Despite this, several historians claim that, concerning the main charge, that of treasonable incest, the prosecution's case may have rested on the deposition of Jane Parker, which would mean George was betrayed by his wife.[3] To believe this requires a substantial leap of faith: Wriothesley, Spelman, Chapuys, Husee, de Carle, the unreliable *Spanish Chronicle*, George Constantine and the so-called Portuguese gentleman all fail to name Jane in this connection despite some robust but mistaken assertions to the contrary.[4] A related claim that Jane confessed on the scaffold at the time of Katherine Howard's fall to falsely accusing George is based on a shameless forgery by Gregorio Leti, who also forged letters he claimed were Anne's.[5]

An allegation that Jane had a motive as her marriage was childless and unhappy, linked to a related claim that George had an illegitimate son, lacks evidence and is inconclusive.[6] In 1593, one George Boleyn, Dean of Lichfield, wrote a letter to the Earl of Shrewsbury in which he refers to Mary Scudamore, the daughter of Sir John Shelton junior and Margaret Parker, as 'my good friend and cousin whom I love well'.[7] But 'cousin' was a slippery term in the sixteenth century, and this younger George could have been an illegitimate son of any of the Boleyn tribe. In his will, the dean names Mary Boleyn's grandson, George, 2nd Lord Hunsdon, as one of his benefactors, and another grandson, Sir William Knollys, as his executor, 'because he is my kinsman'.[8] Once again, this is inconclusive. Although Sir Thomas Boleyn left a will on his death in 1539, it has not survived and its contents are only partially known from a subsequent Chancery case.[9] But what emerged as his family land settlement, drawn up on his deathbed and afterwards approved by Henry, makes Mary Boleyn his principal beneficiary, with no mention of, or provision for, a grandson by George, legitimate or otherwise.[10]

Other recent assertions that a note of Thomas Turner's alleging Jane to be 'a particular instrument in the death of Queen Anne' comes from Anthony Anthony's journal are mistaken. When checked in the Bodleian Library, the source reference Turner cites correlates precisely to the 1649 printed edition of Lord Herbert of

Cherbury's *The Life and Reign of King Henry the Eighth*, rather than to the journal, a fact established in 2007 by Julia Fox.[11] And as Fox discovered, Herbert's source was John Foxe's *Acts and Monuments*, not Anthony Anthony. Jane did not appear in the 1563 edition of Foxe's work but became a marginal note in that of 1576. 'It is reported of some', this reads, citing no source, 'that this Lady Rochford forged a false letter against her husband and Queen Anne her sister[-in-law], by the which they were both cast away.'[12]

George Wyatt, writing his *Life of Anne Boleyn* between 1595 and 1605, called Jane a 'wicked wife, accuser of her own husband, even to the seeking of his own blood'.[13] He did not elaborate as to his sources, but elsewhere in his text claims among his informants 'a lady that first attended on her [Anne] ... with whose house and mine there was then kindred', and 'a lady of noble birth, living in those times, and well acquainted with the persons that most this concerneth, from whom I am myself descended'.[14]

The first of Wyatt's sources might perhaps have been Anne Gaynesford, his grandfather's cousin, who served Anne Boleyn from around 1528 and went on to marry her suitor George Zouche. The caveat must be that, if she was indeed Wyatt's source, her information came to him through hearsay at best, since she was dead before he was born. In his will, made in 1548, Zouche mentions Ellen, not Anne, as 'now' his 'well-beloved wife'. Since George Wyatt was not born until 1553, he could neither have known nor spoken to Gaynesford.[15]

As for the mysterious second lady, she might have been Margaret Lee, Thomas Wyatt's sister and mother of Elizabeth I's Queen's Champion, Sir Henry Lee, to whom in romantic fiction Anne is said to have given a girdle book shortly before her execution. Married to Anthony Lee of Quarrendon in Buckinghamshire, she would be painted by Holbein in the early 1540s. But she too was dead by the time George Wyatt was born – Lee had remarried by the end of 1548 – so such information as she was able to provide must have come down second- or third-hand through her family.[16]

However, no sooner had Wyatt levelled his accusation than he went on to question whether what Jane had purportedly said was true. Maybe she had said it 'more to be rid of [her husband] than of true ground against him?' Wyatt then compounded his doubts, adding that when it came to the hour of judgment: 'the young nobleman, the Lord Rochford, by the common opinion of men of best understanding in those days, was ... condemned only upon some point of a statute of words then in force.'[17] It should be noted that, writing in the 1550s, George Cavendish accused Jane only for her later treasonable association with Katherine Howard, and not for any alleged offences relating to Anne or George.[18]

Championed a generation later by Burnet, the innuendo spun by Foxe's note and Wyatt's speculation created a fictional narrative in which Jane, 'a spiteful wife', 'a woman of no sort of virtue' and 'jealous' of her husband, 'carried many stories to the king ... to persuade [him] that there was a familiarity between the queen and her brother'.[19] What seems more likely is that Jane, under Cromwell's relentless questioning, repeated Anne's indiscretion about Henry's erectile dysfunction, the basis of the paper handed to George in court. In later retellings, that became 'a letter', the same one George Constantine and Foxe mention in their different ways. It was, of course, enough.[20]

Abbreviations

The Harvard system is used in citing references to printed sources. Abbreviated citations of primary and secondary materials identify the works listed in the Bibliography, where full references are given. For example, Carley (2000) refers to J. P. Carley, *The Libraries of King Henry VIII* (London, 2000); Carley (1989) refers to J. P. Carley, 'John Leland and the Foundations of the Royal Library: The Westminster Inventory of 1542', *Bulletin of the Society for Renaissance Studies*, 7 (1989), pp. 13–22.

Manuscripts are cited by the reference numbers used to request the documents in the various archives and libraries. Most items are foliated and are cited in that way. A minority, however, are paginated, and a few are neither foliated nor paginated. In identifying locations, the following abbreviations are used:

AAV	Archivio Apostolico Vaticano, Rome
AGR	Archives générales du Royaume, Brussels
AGS	Archivo General de Simancas
AHM	Archivo Histórico Nacional, Madrid
AJ	*Antiquaries Journal*
AMB	Archives municipales de Besançon
ANF	Archives Nationales de France, Paris
BAV	Biblioteca Apostolica Vaticana, Rome
BIHR	*Bulletin of the Institute of Historical Research*
BL	British Library, London

BM	British Museum, London
BMA	Bibliothèque municipale d'Angers
BMB	Bibliothèque municipale de Bordeaux
BMS	Bibliothèque municipale de Soissons
BMV	Bibliothèque municipale de Valenciennes
BNF	Bibliothèque Nationale de France, Paris
Bodleian	Bodleian Library, Oxford
CADMA	Centre des Archives diplomatiques du Ministère des Affaires étrangères, La Courneuve, Paris
CAF	*Catalogue des actes de François Ier*, 10 vols (Paris, 1887–1908)
Camusat	*Meslanges historiques, ou recueil de plusieurs actes, traictez, lettres missives, et autres mémoires qui peuvent servir en la déduction de l'histoire, depuis l'an 1390 jusques à l'an 1580*, ed. N. Camusat, 3rd edn, 3 vols in 1, plus Appendices (Troyes, 1644)
CCA	Canterbury Cathedral Archives and Library
CCC	Corpus Christi College, Cambridge
CCR	*Calendar of Close Rolls*, ed. H. C. Maxwell-Lyte, A. E. Stamp et al., 61 vols (London, 1902–1963)
CPE	*The Complete Peerage of England, Scotland, Ireland, Great Britain and the United Kingdom*, ed. G. E. C[okayne], 13 vols in 6 (Gloucester, 1987)
CPR	*Calendar of Patent Rolls*, ed. H. C. Maxwell-Lyte, R. C. Fowler, C. T. Flower, J. H. Collingridge et al., 71 vols (London, 1891–1974)
CSPF	*Calendar of State Papers, Foreign*, ed. W. B. Turnbull, J. Stevenson and A. J. Crosby, 25 vols in 28 parts (London, 1861–1950)
CSPM	*Calendar of State Papers and Manuscripts Existing in the Archives Collection of Milan, 1359–1618*, 1 vol. [series not completed] (London, 1912)
CSPSp	*Calendar of Letters, Despatches, and State Papers Relating to the Negotiations between England and Spain, Preserved in the Archives at Vienna,*

	Brussels, Simancas and Elsewhere, 13 vols in 19 parts, with Supplements (London, 1862–1954)
CSPV	*Calendar of State Papers and Manuscripts relating to English Affairs in the Archives and Collections of Venice and in other Libraries of Northern Italy*, 38 vols (London, 1864–1947)
CUL	Cambridge University Library
CW	*Yale Edition of the Complete Works of St Thomas More*, ed. R.S. Sylvester, C. H. Miller et al., 15 vols in 21 parts (New Haven, 1963–97)
CWE	*Collected Works of Erasmus*, ed. R. A. B. Mynors et al., 76 vols (Toronto, 1974–2021)
DIB	*Irish Dictionary of Biography*, available at https://www.dib.ie/
DKR	*Annual Reports of the Deputy Keeper of the Public Record Office*, 120 vols (London, 1840–1960)
Du Bellay	*Correspondance du Cardinal Jean du Bellay*, ed. R. Scheurer, 2 vols (Paris, 1969–73)
EETS	Early English Text Society
EHR	*English Historical Review*
Ellis	*Original Letters, Illustrative of British History*, ed. H. Ellis, 1st–3rd Series, 11 vols (London, 1842–46)
FF	Ancien Fonds Français
Fitzroy Inventory	*Inventories of the Wardrobes, Plate, Chapel Stuff etc. of Henry Fitzroy, Duke of Richmond, and of the Wardrobe Stuff at Baynard's Castle of Katherine, Princess Dowager*, ed. J. G. Nichols, Camden Society, Old Series, 61 (1855), pp. 1–55
Fitzwilliam	Fitzwilliam Museum, Cambridge
Folger	Folger Shakespeare Library, Washington D.C.
GMO	*Grove Music Online*, available at https://www.oxfordmusiconline.com/grovemusic/
HC, 1509–1558	*The House of Commons, 1509–1558*, ed. S. T. Bindoff, 3 vols (London, 1982)

HC, 1558–1603	*The House of Commons, 1558–1603*, ed. P. Hasler, 3 vols (London, 1981)
HEH	Henry E. Huntington Library, San Marino, California
HHStA	Haus-, Hof- und Staatsarchiv, Vienna
HJ	*Historical Journal*
HLRO	House of Lords Record Office, London
HMC	Reports of the Historical Manuscripts Commission
HR	*Historical Research*
JBS	*Journal of British Studies*
JEH	*Journal of Ecclesiastical History*
KHLC	Kent History and Library Centre
Lisle Letters	*The Lisle Letters*, ed. M. St. Clare Byrne, 6 vols (Chicago and London, 1981)
LJ	*Journals of the House of Lords*, 12 vols (London, 1676–1891)
LMA	London Metropolitan Archives
LP	*Letters and Papers, Foreign and Domestic, of the Reign of Henry VIII*, ed. J. S. Brewer, J. Gairdner and R. H. Brodie, 21 vols in 32 parts, and Addenda (London, 1862–1932)
LPL	Lambeth Palace Library
MMA	Metropolitan Museum of Art, New York
MS	Manuscript
NA	National Archives, Kew
NAF	Nouvelles Acquisitions Françaises
NECA	Northumberland Estates, Collections and Archives, Alnwick Castle MSS
Nichols	*John Nichols's The Progresses and Public Processions of Queen Elizabeth I: A New Edition*, ed. E. Goldring, J. E. Archer et al., 5 vols (Oxford, 2014)
NLS	National Library of Scotland
NLW	National Library of Wales
NPG	National Portrait Gallery, London

NQ	*Notes and Queries*
ODNB	*The New Oxford Dictionary of National Biography*, available at http://www.oxforddnb.com/
OED	*The Oxford English Dictionary*, available at https://www.oed.com/
PML	Morgan Library and Museum, New York
PP	*Past and Present*
PPE, Henry	*Privy Purse Expenses of King Henry VIII from November MDXXIX to December MDXXXII*, ed. N. H. Nicolas (London, 1827)
PPE, Mary	*Privy Purse Expenses of the Princess Mary, Daughter of King Henry the Eighth, afterwards Queen Mary*, ed. F. Madden (London, 1831)
RCIN	Royal Collection, Inventory number
RO	Record Office
RQ	*Renaissance Quarterly*
SCJ	*Sixteenth Century Journal*
SHDM	'A Social History of the Devonshire Manuscript', available at https://en.wikibooks.org/wiki/The_Devonshire_Manuscript
SHR	*Scottish Historical Review*
SR	*Statutes of the Realm*, ed. A. Luders, T. E. Tomlins, J. Raithby et al., 11 vols (London, 1810–28)
SRO	Suffolk Record Office, Ipswich branch
St. Pap.	*State Papers during the Reign of Henry VIII*, 11 vols, Record Commission (London, 1830–52)
STC	*A Short-Title Catalogue of Books Printed in England, Scotland and Ireland, and of English Books Printed Abroad*, ed. W. A. Jackson, F. S. Ferguson and K. F. Pantzer, 2nd edn, 3 vols (London, 1976–91)
TCC	Trinity College, Cambridge, Wren Library
TRHS	*Transactions of the Royal Historical Society*

TRP	*Tudor Royal Proclamations*, ed. P. L. Hughes and J. F. Larkin, 3 vols (New Haven and London, 1964–69)
V&A	Victoria and Albert Museum, London
VCH	Victoria County History
WRO	Worcester Record Office

Folio citations in State Paper classes at the NA refer to the stamped numbers at the top right of each manuscript leaf, which collate to the digitised images available in *State Papers Online*. Folio citations to MSS in the BL are to the numbers currently in use in the Department of Manuscripts, and not to those marked up in the pre-1900 period and listed in the older printed catalogues. Manuscripts preserved at the NA are cited as follows:

C 1	Chancery, Early Chancery Proceedings
C 3	Court of Chancery, Six Clerks' Office, Pleadings, Series II
C 4	Chancery, Six Clerks' Office, Answers etc.
C 24	Court of Chancery, Examiners' Office: Town Depositions
C 47	Chancery, Files, Miscellanea
C 54	Chancery, Close Rolls
C 66	Chancery, Patent Rolls
C 78	Chancery, Decree Rolls
C 82	Chancery, Warrants for the Great Seal, Series II
C 131	Chancery, Extents for Debts, Series I
C 140	Chancery, *Inquisitiones Post Mortem*, Series I
C 142	Chancery, *Inquisitiones Post Mortem*, Series II
C 146	Chancery, Ancient Deeds, Series C
C 147	Chancery, Ancient Deeds, Series CC
C 193	Chancery, Miscellaneous Books
C 241	Chancery, Certificates of Statute Merchant and Statute Staple

CP 40	Court of Common Pleas, Plea Rolls
E 36	Exchequer, Treasury of the Receipt, Miscellaneous Books
E 40	Exchequer, Treasury of the Receipt, Ancient Deeds, Series A
E 41	Exchequer, Treasury of the Receipt, Ancient Deeds, Series AA
E 101	Exchequer, King's Remembrancer, Various Accounts
E 117	Exchequer, Church Goods Inventories and Miscellanea
E 133	Exchequer, King's Remembrancer, Barons' Depositions
E 150	Exchequer, King's Remembrancer, Escheators' Files, *Inquisitiones Post Mortem*, Series II
E 159	Exchequer, King's Remembrancer, Memoranda Rolls
E 163	Exchequer, King's Remembrancer, Miscellanea
E 179	Exchequer, King's Remembrancer, Subsidy Rolls
E 298	Exchequer, Augmentation Office, Queens' Councils
E 315	Exchequer, Augmentation Office, Miscellaneous Books
E 371	Exchequer, Lord Treasurer's Remembrancer, Originalia Rolls
E 404	Exchequer of Receipt, Warrants and Issues
E 405	Exchequer of Receipt, Rolls of Receipts and Issues
E 407	Exchequer of Receipt, Miscellanea
HCA 3	High Court of Admiralty, Act Books and Minutes
IND 1	Public Record Office, Indexes to Various Series
KB 8	Court of King's Bench, Crown Side, Bag of Secrets
KB 9	Court of King's Bench, Ancient Indictments
KB 27	Court of King's Bench, *Coram Rege* Rolls
KB 29	Court of King's Bench, Controlment Rolls
LC 2	Lord Chamberlain's Department, Special Events
LC 9	Lord Chamberlain's Department, Accounts and Miscellanea
OBS	Obsolete Lists and Indexes
PRO 31/3	Public Record Office, Transcripts from French Archives

PRO 31/9   Public Record Office, Transcripts from Rome Archives, Series I

PROB 11   Prerogative Court of Canterbury, Registered Copy Wills

PROB 51   Prerogative Court of Canterbury, Administration Bonds

PSO 2   Warrants for the Privy Seal, Series 2

REQ 2   Court of Requests, Proceedings

SC 1   Ancient Correspondence of the Chancery and Exchequer

SP 1   State Papers, Henry VIII, General Series

SP 2   State Papers, Henry VIII, Folio Volumes

SP 6   State Papers, Henry VIII, Theological Tracts

SP 9   State Papers, Miscellaneous

SP 12   State Papers, Domestic, Elizabeth I

SP 45   State Papers, Various

SP 46   State Papers, Supplementary

SP 60   State Papers, Ireland, Henry VIII

SP 70   State Papers, Foreign, General Series, Elizabeth I

STAC 2   Star Chamber Proceedings, Henry VIII

STAC 10   Star Chamber Proceedings, Miscellaneous

WARD 7   Court of Wards and Liveries, *Inquisitiones Post Mortem*

Notes

1 All details of Tower topography are from Colvin, Brown and Cook (1963–82), II, pp. 706–29; ibid., III, pp. 262–77; Keay (2001), pp. 28–49.

2 BL, Cotton MS, Otho C.X, fo. 227; Singer (1847), pp. 460–1; *CSPSp*, V, ii, no. 55 (p. 131).

3 The imperial ambassador, Eustace Chapuys, made the same mistake: *LP*, X, no. 908 (p. 380).

4 NA, C 193/3, fo. 80 is the Clerk of the Crown's copy of the writ. It is dated 18 May. Almost invariably, such warrants were delivered to the Tower authorities on the evening before the execution. The original parchment version of the document does not survive.

5 BL, Cotton MS, Otho C.X, fo. 227; Singer (1847), pp. 460–1; Bodleian, Folio.Δ.624, facing p. 385; *LP*, X, no. 910; *CSPSp*, V, ii, no. 55 (p. 131); Ellis, 1st Series, II, pp. 64–5. Proof of the king's advance planning lies in the fact that the Calais headsman needed to be commissioned, cross the Channel and make his way to London, which would take between one and two weeks.

6 BL, Cotton MS, Otho C.X, fo. 227; Singer (1847), p. 461.

7 *LP*, XI, no. 381.

8 BNF, MS Dupuy 373, fo. 112; Gachard (1885), I, p. 17, n. 1; *LP*, X, no. 911 (1); Hayward (2016), p. 231.

9 *Lisle Letters*, III, no. 698; Bodleian, Folio.Δ.624, facing p. 385; Wriothesley (1875–77), I, p. 41.

10 BNF, MS Dupuy 373, fo. 112.

11 Some ten accounts of Anne's execution survive, several based on the same copy-text or closely related to each other. English accounts are Hall (1809), p. 819; Bodleian, Folio.Δ.624, facing pp. 384, 385; Wriothesley (1875–77), I, pp. 41–2; Spelman (1976–77), I, p. 59; Stow (1631), p. 573 (not in the 1580 edition). French accounts are BNF, MS Dupuy 373, fo. 112 (partially and inaccurately printed in Hamy [1898], pp. ccccxxxvii–ccccxxxviii); Schmid (2009), pp. 170–4; Ascoli (1927), pp. 269–72 (ll. 1203–1292). A Portuguese account is [Bentley] (1831), pp. 264–65. Imperial accounts in French or Spanish are Gachard (1885), I, p. 17, n.1; *LP*, X, no. 911 (1, 2); Froude (1861), pp. 116–17. See also *LP*, X, no. 908 (p. 130); *CSPSp*, V, ii, no. 55 (pp. 130–1). For the putative authorship of the primary French account and the links between it and other versions, see above, pp. 387–8. Modern accounts of the execution are Friedmann (1884), II, pp. 294–6; Ives (2004), pp. 357–9.

12 Bodleian, Folio.Δ.624, facing p. 384.

13 *Lisle Letters*, III, no. 697.

14 Walker (2002), pp. 8–9.

15 Hall (1809), p. 819. Similar renderings can be found in Wriothesley (1875–77), I, pp. 41–2; Bodleian, Folio.Δ.624, facing p. 385; Stow (1631), p. 573; Singer (1827), p. 448; Foxe (1843–49), V, p. 135; Wyatt (1968), p. 189.

16 Bodleian, Folio.Δ.624, facing p. 385. The French rendering is similarly explicit. According to this, Anne declared only: 'I blame not my judges, nor any other group of people, because it is the law of the country that has condemned me. For this I accept death willingly, asking pardon from everyone.' See BNF, Dupuy MS 373, fo. 112.

17 BNF, MS Dupuy 373, fo. 112; Gachard (1885), I, p. 17, n. 1; *LP*, X, no. 911 (1, 2); Bodleian, Folio.Δ.624, facing p. 385; Wriothesley (1875–77), I, p. 42; Hayward (2016), pp. 236, 239.

18 BL, Cotton MS, Otho C.X, fo. 228v; Singer (1827), pp. 456–7.

19 Hall (1809), pp. 588–90; Brown (1854), II, pp. 74–5; *Lisle Letters*, III, nos. 704, 716. For other examples see ibid., III, pp. 385–6.

20 Spelman (1976–77), I, p. 59; NA, SP 1/103, fo. 30.

21 *LP*, XI, no. 381. The reports of Marie of Hungary and the *Spanish Chronicle* that the headsman was from St Omer, not Calais, seem to be inaccurate: *LP*, X, no. 965; *Spanish Chronicle* (1889), p. 70.

22 Spelman (1976–77), I, p. 59; Hall (1809), p. 819; Wriothesley (1875–77), I, p. 42; BNF, MS Dupuy 373, fo. 112.

23 Spelman (1976–77), I, p. 59; BNF, MS Dupuy 373, fo. 112; Hamy (1898), p. ccccxxxvii. No evidence exists that Spelman made the remark about the paternoster. And despite constant repetition, the claim that the headsman picked up the head and held it aloft, crying 'So perish all the king's enemies', is pure invention.

24 *Lisle Letters*, III, no. 698; ibid., IV, no. 846.

25 Gachard (1885), I, p. 17, n. 1; BNF, MS Dupuy 373, fo. 112; *LP*, X, no. 911 (1); Hamy (1898), p. ccccxxxvii.

26 Bodleian, Folio.Δ.624, facing p. 384.

27 Ibid.; Wriothesley (1875–77), I, p. 42.

28 Bell (1877), pp. 26–8. Whether these bones were really Anne's or those of another female victim of Tudor justice is still a mystery.

1 HENRY: CHILDHOOD AND ADOLESCENCE

1 Hayward (2007), pp. 1, 6; Sanuto (1824–84), VIII, cols 281–2.

2 Pronay and Cox (1986), p. 185.

3 Pollnitz (2015), pp. 29–34, 42–9.

4 *LP*, XVII, no. 251.

5 Folger, PA6295.A3.1502 Cage.

6 Neville (1990), pp. 128–30.

7 Malory (1978), I, pp. 1–451; ibid., II, pp. 455–1098; ibid., III, pp. 1099–260; Starkey (1998), pp. 171–96; Starkey (2008), pp. 118–35; Carley (2000), pp. 3–29; Carley (2004b), p. 36 and plate 29.

8 Roper (1935), p. 11; Pollnitz (2015), pp. 42–55; Orme (1996), pp. 283–305; Starkey (2008), pp. 172–83.

9 NA, LC 2/1/1, fo. 73v; NA, E 101/420/1, no. 56; NA, E 36/214, fos. 51, 72v; NA, E 36/215, fos. 45, 132, 210, 214, 218, 226, 358; NA, E 36/216, fo. 78v; BL, Additional MS 21,481, fos. 23, 102v, 113v, 137v; BL, Additional MS 59,899, fos. 37, 55v, 68v, 82v; Ellis, 2nd Series, I, pp. 272–3; Stevens (1961), pp. 275–6; Blezzard and Palmer (2000), pp. 259–72; Siemens (1997), pp. 41–74; Kaufmann (2017), pp. 8–31; Brown (1854), I, p. 86.

10 *Memorials of Henry VII* (1858), pp. 116, 120, 124; Pollnitz (2015), p. 48; Starkey (2008), pp. 221–33; Jones and Underwood (1992), p. 79.

11 *LP*, IV, i, nos. 1901, 1939 (p. 863); Starkey (2008), pp. 175–80; Pollnitz (2015), p. 55; Miller (1986), p. 85; *ODNB*, s.v. 'Fitzwilliam, Sir

William', 'Browne, Sir Anthony', 'Courtenay, Henry'; *HC, 1509–1558*, I, pp. 518–19; ibid., II, pp. 142–3.

12 *CWE*, I, pp. 195–7; Pollnitz (2015), pp. 47–8, 60; Starkey (2008), pp. 129–33.

13 Thomas and Thornley (1938), p. 254; Pollnitz (2015), p. 43; Starkey (2008), pp. 114–15.

14 Kipling (1990), pp. xiii–xxix.

15 *LP*, IV, iii, no. 5791.

16 Kipling (1990), pp. 12–35; Rogers (1961), pp. 2–3.

17 *LP*, IV, iii, no. 5791; Starkey (2008), pp. 144–5.

18 Kipling (1990), pp. 39–42.

19 *LP*, IV, iii, no. 5859; Gunn (1988), pp. 28–31.

20 Kipling (1990), pp. 52–8; Gunn (1988), pp. 28–9.

21 *CSPSp, Supplement to Vols. I and II*, no. 1; *LP*, IV, iii, no. 5791 (p. 2588); Fox (2011), pp. 86–7; Brandi (1965), p. 488.

22 Kipling (1990), p. 91; Guy (2013), pp. 1–3; Starkey (2004), pp. 76–7.

23 Kipling (1990), pp. 80–1.

24 Thomas and Thornley (1938), p. 321.

25 Allen (Oxford, 1906–58), I, p. 436; mistranslated in *CWE*, II, p. 129.

26 Cunningham (2009), pp. 459–81; Berwick y de Alba (1907), p. 449; Thurley (2017), p. 95.

27 *LP Richard III and Henry VII* (1861–3), I, p. 233.

28 Harrison (1972), pp. 88–99; Horowitz (2018), pp. 37–188.

29 *CSPSp*, I, no. 364.

30 *CSPSp*, I, no. 396; AGS, PTR/LEG. 53/92; Swinburne (1686), pp. 47–8.

31 AGS, PTR/LEG. 53/90, 93; AGS, PTR/LEG. 61/116; Rymer (1704–35), XIII, pp. 89–90; *CSPSp*, I, no. 389; Kelly (1976), p. 105. A crucial issue usually forgotten is that the final version of the papal dispensation was backdated to match the date of the 'Brief'.

32 *LP Richard III and Henry VII* (1861–3), I, pp. 167, 247–8; II, pp. 342–3, 346–7.

33 *LP*, IV, iii, no. 5791; *CSPSp*, I, no. 435.

34 *CSPSp*, I, nos. 526, 532, 541, 543; *CSPSp, Supplement to Vols. 1 and II*, no. 21.

35 *LP*, I, ii, no. 2072; Starkey (2008), pp. 206–19.

36 Biddle (2000), pp. 422–4, 432–45.

37 *CSPSp*, IV, i, no. 224 (p. 348), where the original French appears in a note; NA, SP 1/288, fo. 143v.

38 Aram (1998), pp. 348–51; Parker (2019), pp. 51–6.

39 Guy (2019), pp. 19–36.

40 NA, E 36/214, fos. 79v, 158; BL, Additional MS 7099, fos. 76, 92, 96; BL, Additional MS 59,899, fos. 85, 101, 188, 107v. See also Dietz (1921), p. 85.

41 Jones and Underwood (1992), pp. 91–2, 235–6.

2 HENRY: APPRENTICE KING

1 Allen (1906–58), I, no. 215.

2 BL, C.33.g.7; Rawdon Brown (1854), I, pp. 85–6.

3 *LP*, I, i, nos. 1, 11 (1, 10), 54 (3, 43), 131, 132 (18, 26, 34, 50, 65), 357 (41); McGlynn (2004), pp. 161–2; Rawcliffe (1978), p. 36; Miller (1986), pp. 50–1, 166–7.

4 *LP*, I, i, no. 84. For further discussion on why Henry chose Katherine, see Starkey (2004), pp. 111–13; Starkey (2008), pp. 277–92.

5 *LP*, IV, iii, no. 5774 (6); Scarisbrick (1968), pp. 12–13.

6 Halliwell (1848), I, p. 198; *LP*, I, i, no. 119.

7 *CSPSp*, II, nos. 27, 28, 32; *LP*, I, i, no 127; Wood (1846) I, pp. 157–61.

8 Sylvester (1959), pp. 11–12; Starkey (2008), pp. 363–6.

9 Vergil (1950), p. 247; Sylvester (1959), p. 13; Pollnitz (2015), p. 70.

10 For a detailed examination of the song and its provenance, see Siemens (1997), pp. 121–30.

11 AGS, PTR/LEG. 54/100; *CSPSp*, II, no. 19; *LP*, I, i, no. 112.

12 NA, KB 8/4.

13 AGS, PTR/LEG. 54/51; AGS, EST/LEG. 1365/35. On first arriving in England, Katherine signed as 'la Princesa de Gales': AGS, PTR/LEG. 54/27–33.

14 *CSPSp*, I, nos. 541, 551; *CSPSp, Supplement to Vols. 1 and II*, no. 21.

15 *CSPSp*, I, no. 603; *CSPSp, Supplement to Vols. I and II*, nos. 2, 3, 5, 8 (pp. 36–44), 9 (pp. 44–6); *CSPSp*, II, no. 238; AGS, PTR/LEG. 54/121; Ellis, 1st Series, I, pp. 80–1; Starkey (2004), pp. 104, 148–9, 155–6.

16 Rex (2014), pp. 7–8.

17 *LP*, I, i, nos. 670, 698; Anglo (1969), pp. 111–13; Hall (1809), pp. 517–19.

18 Prescott (1854), p. 342.

19 Hall (1809), p. 519; NA, LC 2/1, fos. 159–73 (*LP*, I, i, no. 707).

20 *CSPV*, II, nos. 329, 555, 942, 1103, 1123; *LP*, I, ii, nos. 3333, 3440, 3500, 3581; Chamberlin (1932), pp. 262–3.

21 *CSPV*, II, nos. 329, 555, 942, 1103, 1123.

22 Whiteley and Kramer (2010), pp. 827–48. One of Katherine's sisters, Maria, Queen of Portugal, gave birth to seventeen children: another sister, Juana, had two sons as well as four daughters.

23 *CSPV*, II, no. 691.

24 Sanuto (1824–84), VIII, col. 213; Sanuto (1824–84), IX, col. 149; *LP*, I, i, nos. 5, 156; Scarisbrick (1968), pp. 25–6.

25 *CSPV*, II, nos. 28, 33, 45.

26 *LP*, II, i, nos. 887, 894; *CSPV*, II, no. 53; *LP*, I, i, no. 842.

27 For the Italian context, see Shaw and Mallett (2019), pp. 109–41.

28 *LP*, I, i, nos. 939, 945, 969 (40); *CSPSp*, II, nos. 58, 59; Hall (1809), pp. 527–32; Scarisbrick (1968), pp. 29–34; Dietz (1921), pp. 91–2; Murphy (2015), pp. 25–56.

29 Sanuto (1824–84), XXVIII, col. 76; *ODNB*, s.v. 'Pace, Richard'; Brown (1854), I, p. 155; Pollard (1929), pp. 16–25.

30 Hall (1809), pp. 536–45, 549–52; Cruickshank (1969), pp. 82–93, 114–18.

31 Gachard (1874), II, p. 16; Hall (1809), pp. 552–3, where the dates are wrong by a few days; *LP*, I, ii, no. 2391 (pp. 1060–1); *CSPM*, I, nos. 654, 657; *CSPV*, II, no. 328; NA, SP 1/230, fo. 213; [Académie des Sciences, Belles Lettres et Arts de Besançon] (1806–1975), III, p. 408; Le Roux (1715), p. 108.

32 BL, Cotton MS, Vespasian F.III, fo. 33; Hall (1809), pp. 545–8; *LP*, I, ii, no. 2268; *CSPV*, II, nos. 316 (p. 134), 340 (p. 146); *The Times*, 27 May 2020, p. 20. Earlier letters from Katherine to Wolsey are BL, Cotton MS, Caligula D.VI, fos. 92–4, but these are not holograph, and merely signed by Katherine. She still spoke in broken English in 1529: Sylvester (1959), p. 80.

33 Macquéreau (1838), p. 40.

34 Hall (1809), pp. 554–5; *LP*, I, ii, no. 2391; Cruickshank (1969), pp. 137–50.

35 Hall (1809), p. 566; *LP*, I, ii, nos. 2347, 2375, 2380, 2391; Parker (2019), p. 42.

3 ANNE: CHILDHOOD AND ADOLESCENCE

1 Venn (1897–1901), I, p. 9; Robinson (1915), pp. 1–10; Biggs (2016), II, pp. 260–1.
2 Blomefield (1739–75), II, pp. 511–12; ibid., III, pp. 626–7; ibid., IV, p. 425; Lyell and Watney (1936), p. 42; Sutton (2005), pp. 209–34; Wedgwood and Holt (1936), pp. 90–1; Dean (1987), pp. 2–12; Mackay (2018b), pp. 18–22. For invaluable background, see Thurley (2020), at https://www.gresham.ac.uk/lectures-and-events/boleyn-houses.
3 Smith (1982), pp. 7, 10, 17, 21–2, 29, 32, 92; NA, C 1/18/67.
4 Since Fastolf had his own brick kilns at Caister, and as Caister tiles and a brick impressed with the heraldic arms of Fastolf were found at Blickling, it is possible he did more work there than surviving records suggest. The brick was later reinstalled at Mannington Hall. See Purdy (1901), p. 325.
5 Davis (2004), II, no. 619; NA, C 146/137; C 146/862; C 146/1784; C 146/5972; C 140/10/21.
6 NA, PROB 11/6/33; Rye (1891), p. 52.
7 NA, PROB 11/5/12.
8 NA, PROB 11/14/790; Blomefield (1739–75), II, pp. 511–12; ibid., III, pp. 626–7, 719; Venn, (1897–1901), I, p. 21.
9 If Anne Hoo foresaw the potential of a union with the Butlers, she did not live long enough to see it come fully to fruition. *CPE*, X, pp. 131–3; Blomefield (1739–75), II, pp. 511–12; Morant (1768), I, pp. 270–1, 281; NA, SC 1/51/189; NA, E 41/420.
10 NA, C 146/1990; C 146/1955; C 146/4769; C 146/4804; C 146/6086; NA, E 40/7701; Wedgwood and Holt (1936), pp. 466–7; Page (1904–12), II, pp. 348–75; Austin and Blundell (1928), I, p. 211. Thomas Hoo was in debt: NA, C 131/80/8–9.
11 Baker (2012), I, p. 333; *LP Richard III and Henry VII* (1861–3), I, Appendix A, pp. 403, 410; Dean (1987), pp. 12–20; Mackay (2018b), pp. 22–3.
12 Baker (2012), I, p. 332; Dean (1987), pp. 21–5; Mackay (2018b), pp. 24–5. The marriage settlement was finalised in 1501. See *CCR, 1500–1509*, pp. 63–4.
13 [Bentley] (1831), p. 119.
14 NA, C 241/275/256; Thurley (2020), at https://www.gresham.ac.uk/lectures-and-events/boleyn-houses.
15 NA, SP 1/105, fos. 5–6; Ellis, 3rd Series, III, pp. 22–3.

16 HMC, *Twelfth Report [Rutland MSS]*, Appendix, IV, i, p. 18.

17 *LP*, I, i, nos. 20, 81–2; NA, LC 9/50, fos. 125, 204.

18 Hall (1809), p. 519; NA, LC 2/1, fos. 159–73; *LP*, I, i, nos. 697, 707.

19 The main body of the house was modernised and partially rebuilt in the reign of James I by Sir Henry Hobart, a successful lawyer, who retained much of the older building. Before embarking on his renovations, Hobart leased the west range to a certain William Cardynall of Eaton in the City of Norwich, together with outbuildings. The range, fully described in the lease, remained as it had been in Anne's time. See Stanley-Millson and Newman (1986), p. 5. It was not until the remodelling begun by the 2nd Earl of Buckinghamshire in 1765 that all visible trace of the house as Anne would have known it disappeared. See Blomefield (1739–75), III, pp. 625–6; Smith (1982), pp. 36–8; Stanley-Millson and Newman (1986), pp. 1–15; [Maddison and Newman] (1987), pp. 4–15.

20 NA, PROB 11/14/790.

21 NA, SP 1/132, fos. 34–5. Boleyn's letter is addressed to Thomas Cromwell.

22 BL, Royal MS, 7 C.XVI, fos. 104–5; Thirsk (2006), pp. 115–16.

23 'Country' used this way always means 'county': William Dalling, for example, had complained to Parliament in 1433 that William Paston 'taketh divers fees and rewards of divers persons within the shire[s] of Norfolk and Suffolk, and is withhold with every matter in the said countries'. See Davis (2004), II, no. 869.

24 Hasted (1797), III, pp. 190–8; Astor (1975), pp. 14–17; Thurley (2020), at https://www.gresham.ac.uk/lectures-and-events/boleyn-houses.

25 Something of Sir Thomas Boleyn's social reach in Kent can be glimpsed from Zell (1974), pp. 15–73, and from the lists of those with whom he served on local commissions of the peace. Thomas Boleyn served as a JP in Kent in 1509, 1510, 1514, 1515, 1517, 1524, 1526, 1528, 1531, 1532, 1533, 1537 and 1538 (information from John Guy's database compiled from *LP* and NA, E 371). For his role as sheriff of Kent, see NA, C 131/97/14, C 131/98/4, C 131/102/10–11, C 131/262/6; *List of Sheriffs* (1963), p. 69.

26 Isley served on commissions of the peace in Kent in 1509, 1510, 1512, 1514 and 1515.

27 BL, Cotton MS, Vespasian F.XIII, fo. 198; NA, PROB 11/22/71; *LP*, I, i, nos. 1576, 1694, 1768; *LP*, II, ii, nos. 2593, 2854, 2875; *LP* II, i,

nos. 424, 425. Wilshire served on commissions of the peace in Kent in 1509, 1510, 1512, 1514, 1515, 1521, 1524 and 1526.

28 NA, PROB 11/22/71.

29 Isabel died in 1485, after which William, by then an esquire of the body to Henry VII, swiftly remarried. He and his much younger second wife had a son, Thomas, whom Anne's father got to know well and both families were friends of the Wilshires of Stone. See Madden (1834–43), I, p. 314; Stephenson (1926), p. 324; *HC, 1509–1558*, I, pp. 634–8; Weaver (1631), p. 700; Rye (1891), p. 52; André (1901), p. 249; *LP*, I, i, no. 158 (85); *ODNB*, s.v. 'Cheyne, Thomas'.

30 Since Heydon did not die until 1510 and owned property in Kent as well as East Anglia, the young Anne Boleyn might conceivably have met her. Thomas Brooke married Heydon's daughter, Dorothy, as his first wife, and the couple had seven sons and six daughters. See Blomefield (1739–75), III, pp. 709–10; NA, PROB 11/16/733; *CPE*, III, p. 347.

31 PROB 11/14/336; Ellis, 3rd Series, II, pp. 274–5.

32 Gunn (2016), pp. 232–3.

33 Ibid., p. 131; *LP,* I, i, no. 1083 (26); *ODNB*, s.v. 'Wyatt, Sir Henry'.

34 NA, C 54/379; WRO, Microfilm 705:349/12946/508642. Ormond died in 1515, see NA, PROB 11/18/184. Thomas was also to pay his mother a second annuity of 200 marks, the money to be handed over in twice-yearly instalments in the parish church of Blickling between the hours of 8 a.m. and 11 a.m.

35 Rymer (1704–35), XIII, pp. 258–9; *LP* II, i, no. 257 (40); *LP*, II, ii, p. 1490; Thomas and Thornley (1938), pp. 371, 456; Hall (1809), p. 518.

36 *Du Bellay*, I, no. 30; NA, SP 1/59, fo. 99, a rent instalment of £5 6s. 8d. For the likely location, see NA, SP 3/12, fo. 42; *Lisle Letters*, V, nos. 1137, 1139.

4 ANNE: APPRENTICE COURTIER

1 *LP*, I, i, no. 1213. Useful background to the mission can be found in Dean (1987), pp. 36–45.

2 MacDonald (2002), pp. 112–18.

3 *LP*, I, i, nos. 1213, 1226.

4 *LP*, I, i, nos. 1245, 1252, 1258. The episode was likely staged for Boleyn's benefit since the longbow was England's national weapon. Charles,

who was passionate about hunting, chiefly falconry or shooting game, preferred crossbows.

5 *LP*, I, i, no. 1750; *CSPSp*, II, no. 97. Boleyn's instructions are not extant, but Henry's letter to Maximilian laying out the ground for the mission can be found in BL, Cotton MS, Galba B.III, fo. 17.

6 *LP*, I, ii, nos. 1871, 2053 (1, 5).

7 Attreed (2012), pp. 18, 20; Marvin (1977), p. 24; Siemens (2009), p. 148; Friedmann (1884), I, p. 128.

8 *LP*, I, i, nos. 1338, 1350, 1362.

9 Le Glay (1839), II, p. 461, n. 2; Paget (1981), pp. 164–5.

10 Eichberger (2002), pp. 185–94; Smith (2011), pp. 16, 37; Paget (1981), p. 165; Urkevich (1997), pp. 106–11; Sadlack (2011), p. 164.

11 MMA, Robert Lehman Collection, 1975; Eichberger (2018), p. 83.

12 Eichberger (1996), pp. 259–79; Eichberger (2002), pp. 189–92; Eichberger (2018), pp. 83–7; BL, Additional MS 7970, fo. IV.

13 Reiffenberg (1836), p. 154; [Académie des Sciences, Belles Lettres et Arts de Besançon] (1806–1975), III, pp. 408–9, 449 (where 'Bullan' is erroneously rendered as 'Bulleux').

14 [Académie des Sciences, Belles Lettres et Arts de Besançon] (1806–1975), III, pp. 408–9.

15 *ODNB*, s.v. 'Howard [*née* Stafford], Elizabeth'; Le Glay (1839), II, pp. 81–2; Paget (1981), p. 166; Eichberger (1996), p. 268; Eichberger (2002), p. 190.

16 Eichberger (1996), pp. 261–7; Eichberger (2002), pp. 188–9.

17 Reiffenberg (1836), pp. 152–7; [Académie des Sciences, Belles Lettres et Arts de Besançon] (1806–1975), III, pp. 417–22.

18 De Jongh (1953), pp. 161–8; MacDonald (2002), pp. 118–20; De Jonge (1989–90), pp. 253–82.

19 Henne (1858–60), V, pp. 13–14, has the cleanest version of the French original. See also [Académie Royale des Sciences, des Lettres et des Beaux-Arts de Belgique], 5th Series, 14 (1928), p. 98; De Boom (1935), p. 123; Ives (2004), pp. 21, 370.

20 Her phrase, 'scripte à Veure', has been variously misinterpreted to mean that the letter was written at Hever, or at Briare (in the Upper Loire), or even written at five o'clock ('à V heures').

21 Paget (1981), pp. 164–6.

22 CCC, MS 119, fo. 21; Ellis, 2nd Series, II, pp. 10–11; Sergeant (1923), Appendix D. A Latin translation of Anne's letter, possibly by her later

chaplain Matthew Parker, at fo. 25, is more obtuse in crucial parts than the original French.

23 Le Glay (1839), I, pp. 273–4.

24 See above, pp. 26–8.

25 BL, Cotton MS, Titus B.I, fos. 146–54; *Calais Chronicle* (1846), pp. 71–6; *LP*, I, ii, no. 2941.

26 Starkey (2004), p. 280.

27 BL, Cotton MS, Titus B.I, fos. 146–54.

28 Hall (1809), p. 568; *Calais Chronicle* (1846), p. 75.

29 *LP*, I, ii, nos. 2656, 2741.

30 *LP*, I, ii, no. 3061; Parker (2019), p. 39.

31 *LP*, I, ii., nos. 3139, 3142, 3146, 3171; *CSPV*, II, no. 505; Ellis, 2nd Series, I, pp. 244–5.

32 Richardson (1995), p. 42.

33 J. E. Hodgkin in *NQ*, 8th Series, VIII (Aug. 24, 1895), pp. 141–2; Sergeant (1923), Appendix D.

34 Bonnardot (1833), I, p. 217.

35 See, for instance, Dean (1987), pp. 50–1.

36 *Rutland Papers* (1842), p. 26.

37 For a succinct summary of the difficulties, see Ives (2004), pp. 27–8, 371 n. 27. The 2004 discovery was made by R. J. Knecht in BNF, MS FF 7853, fo. 305v.

5 FOCUS ON FRANCE

1 *LP*, I, ii, nos. 3153, 3174; Le Glay (1839), II, pp. 579, 580.

2 See also Paget (1981), p. 168; Ives (2004), pp. 27–8.

3 Hall (1809), p. 570; Leland (1774), II, p. 702; *LP*, I, ii, no. 3348 (3).

4 For the title, see BNF, MS FF 1742. Other manuscripts include BNF, MS FF 2370; BNF, MS FF 10,194; BNF, MS FF 12,795; BMB, MS 313; BMS, MS 201, fos. 18v–26v; BMS, MS 202, fos. 141–63; BL, Additional MS 40,662. Modern editions of the poem are Schmid (2009), pp. 110–75; Ascoli (1927), pp. 231–71.

5 Schmid (2009), pp. 111–12; Ascoli (1927), p. 233 (ll. 39–48). Here and elsewhere, our translation of the French text is amended better to reflect the sense of the original.

6 BL, Cotton MS, Vitellius C. XI, fos. 155r–v; *LP*, I, ii, no. 3357.

7 For such erroneous claims, see *Rutland Papers* (1842), p. 26; Friedmann (1884), II, pp. 315–18: Brown (1911), p. 110.

8 BNF, MS FF 7856, p. 825; BNF, MS NAF 9175, fo. 365. A suggestion that Anne travelled to France incognito as a servant to her elder sibling does not bear serious consideration. Aside from the lack of evidence, it was not done for a young gentlewoman to become a servant to anyone except a social superior.

9 *LP*, I, ii, no. 3435.

10 Parker (2019), p. 14.

11 NA, SP 70/22, fo. 39v. See also Masson (1868), p. 545.

12 *LP*, II, i, pp. ix–xxxiii; Gunn (1988), pp. 32–8; Brown (1911), pp. 148–72. Judging by Mary's expressions of disgust at what she calls the new French king's 'fantasies and suits', Francis may well have made some sort of sexual proposition himself, which can only have added to her attraction to the dashing Suffolk.

13 BNF, MS Clairambault 316, fo. 40; BL, Cotton MS, Vespasian F. XIII, fo. 153; BL, Cotton MS Caligula D. VI, fo. 213v; NA, SP 1/10, fos. 82, 84–5; *LP*, II, i, nos. 222–31; Sadlack (2011), pp. 102–3, 182–4.

14 Barrillon (1897–99), I, pp. 12–17; Gunn (1988), pp. 36–8. See also Lincolnshire Archives Office, MS 2ANC3/B.

15 Hall (1809), p. 580; *LP*, II, ii, p. 1501.

16 Florange (1913), I, pp. 168–9; BNF, MS Clairambault 316, fos. 3v, 44.

17 Florange (1913), I, pp. 168–9; BNF, MS Clairambault 316, fo. 44; Barrillon (1897–99), I, pp. 54–6. Boleyn's embassy was also motivated by Henry's desire to recover more of his sister Mary's jewels and to discuss an offer from Francis to buy back Tournai. See *LP*, II, i, nos. 140, 175, 178, 184, 224, 231, 304.

18 Ives (2004), p. 29; Mackay (2018b), p. 78.

19 Dallington (1604), sig. D3.

20 *CAF*, I, no. 595; *CAF*, V, nos. 16,291, 17,194; *CAF*, VII, no. 25,446; *CAF*, VIII, no. 381.

21 Knecht (1994), p. 17; *Procédures politiques* (1885), p. cvii; Castelain (1996), p. 42; La Saussaye (1886), pp. 21–2; Wilson-Chevalier (2018), p. 144; Wilson-Chevalier (2010), pp. 129, 142–4; Cholakian and Cholakian (2005), p. 51.

22 Butterworth (2018), pp. 350–63; Skemp and Cholakian (2008), pp. 371–4.

23 Cholakian and Cholakian (2005), pp. 40–1; Wilson-Chevalier (2018), pp. 139–72; Ferguson and McKinley (2013), p. 4.

24 For Katherine's women, see Beer (2018b), pp. 83–95; Laynesmith
   (2004), pp. 244–8; Hayward (2007), p. III.
25 *CAF*, I, nos. 576, 1802, 2345, 2617; *CAF*, III, no. 10349; *CAF*, V,
   no. 18541; *CAF*, VI, no. 19458; *CAF*, VII, no. 27301; BNF, MS NAF
   9175, fos. 367–9; BNF, MS FF 7856, pp. 1001–6; Castelain (1986),
   p. 85; Kolk (2009), pp. 3–22; Potter (2003), pp. 138–9; Jollet (1997),
   pp. 170–1. The *première dame* kept a check on expenditure and
   supervised the procurement of clothing, cosmetics, medicine and
   other personal requirements. When the queen entertained visitors, it
   was she who introduced them and showed them to their place. Male
   servants included the *chevalier d'honneur, gentilshommes d'honneur*
   and the noblemen who served the queen and her guests at table,
   along with a secretary, almoner, confessor, valets of the wardrobe,
   equerries of the stables and others.
26 Chatenet (2002), pp. 187–98, 206–7; Chatenet (1992), pp. 72–5;
   Chatenet and Whiteley (1992), pp. 60–71. In the Louvre, where
   space was restricted before Francis's building renovations, the queen's
   bed was placed against the wall at the far end of her *chambre de
   retrait*, with a *dressoir* to set gold and silver plate on and a writing
   desk nearby.
27 Brown (2010), pp. 144–66; Szkilnik (2010), pp. 65–80; L'Estrange
   (2016), pp. 708–28; Bouchard (2018), pp. 241–59; Wilson-Chevalier
   (2010), pp. 125–6, 141; Broomhall (2018), pp. 22–3.
28 BNF, MS Arsenal 5116, fo. iv; Wilson-Chevalier (2010), pp. 124–8;
   Wilson-Chevalier (2015), pp. 109–10; Wilson-Chevalier (2018),
   pp. 143–4, 160–1.
29 Wilson-Chevalier (2018), p. 153; Knecht (1994), pp. 427–31.
30 Schmid (2009), p. 112; Ascoli (1927), p. 234 (ll. 52–8).
31 Born in the Pas-de-Calais, Mouton had been enticed away from a
   post in Grenoble by Anne of Brittany, who retained him until her
   death. He was re-employed by Louis XII and then by Claude and
   Francis as their chief composer, writing chansons and dance music
   for secular festivals and motets and Masses for use in the royal
   chapels.
32 Anne knew of Sermisy. He had joined the Sainte-Chapelle as a
   singer at a young age and was a member of the Chapelle Royale. See
   Lowinsky (1969–70), pp. 1–28; Urkevich (1997), pp. 37–8; Urkevich
   (2009), pp. 176–7; Dumitrescu (2017), pp. 150–1; Christoffersen

(1994), I, p. 97; *GMO*, s.v. 'Jean Mouton', 'Josquin des Prez', 'Claudin de Sermisy'.

33 *CSPSp, Supplement to Vols. 1 and II*, no. 8 (pp. 39–40); Hall (1809), p. 580; *LP*, I, i, no. 20 (p. 17); NA, E 36/215, fo. 225 (*LP*, II, ii, p. 1471); BNF, MS NAF 9175, fos. 491, 495; BNF, MS FF 7856, pp. 1033, 1047; Murphy (2003), pp. 19–20; Samman (1988), p. 148; Hayward (2007), pp. 309–10.

34 Her husband, the much older Jean de Laval, Seigneur de Châteaubriant, knew to turn a blind eye. He and their sons, and most importantly Odet de Foix, Seigneur de Lautrec, the Marshal of France, Françoise's brother, were in the highest of favour. See BNF, MS NAF 9175, fo. 367v; Knecht (1994), pp. 116–17; Crawford (2010), pp. 119–20; Richardson (2014a), pp. 199–200.

35 Musée Dobrée, Nantes, MS 17, fo. 33v. See Hochner (2010), pp. 764–74, and fig. 3.

6 THE QUEEN'S *DEMOISELLE*

1 Dreux du Radier (1808), IV, p. 95; Friedmann (1884), II, p. 320; Gairdner (1893), p. 56. See also Warnicke (1989), pp. 246–7.

2 Barrillon (1897–99), I, pp. 60–4; Desjardins (1861–72), II, p. 692.

3 Barrillon (1897–99), I, p. 86.

4 *LP*, II, i, no. 1113.

5 Barrillon (1897–99), I, pp. 176–86; Baux, Bourrilly and Mabilly (1904), pp. 31–5.

6 Baux, Bourrilly and Mabilly (1904), pp. 35–48.

7 Porrer (2009), pp. 17–50, 75, 120–2, 135–6; Holban (1935), pp. 26–43; Orth (1982), pp. 57–8; Castelain (1986), pp. 44–7; Wilson-Chevalier (2015), pp. 95–118; Wilson-Chevalier (2018), pp. 155–64; Rex (1991), pp. 65–77; Reid (2001), pp. 31–8, 88–168, 184–90, 253–4.

8 BNF, MS Clairambault 316, fo. 125; ANF, X/1a/9322, nos. 78, 79, 91; Renaudet (1916), pp. 586–7; Doucet (1921), I, pp. 328–30; Wilson-Chevalier (2015), pp. 95–118. The prayer book for Renée is Biblioteca Estense Universitaria, Modena, MS Lat. 614 (unfortunately stolen in 1994: for a facsimile, see *Libro d'Ore di Renata di Francia*, [Modena, 1998]). For Chantereau as the translator of the *Vita* of St Veronica, dedicated to Claude, see BMA, MS 823, front flyleaf.

9 Reid (2013), pp. 29–58; Reid (2018), pp. 88–168, 263–83; Knecht (1972), pp. 159–64; Cholakian and Cholakian (2005), pp. 66–103.

10 Heller (1972), pp. 42–77; Reid (2001), pp. 97, 100, 450, 526–7; Reid (2013), pp. 97–8, 272–6.

11 Baux, Bourrilly and Mabilly (1904), pp. 37–64, where some of the dates are incorrect, e.g. Claude and Louise made their entry on 'Thursday' 23 January, not 3rd; Castelain (1986), pp. 46–9; Barrillon (1897–99), I, pp. 186–200; [Académie des Sciences, Lettres et Arts de Marseille] (1803–1925), vol. for 1884–5 [unnumbered], pp. 217–24, where the dates are correct.

12 *CSPSp*, II, nos. 244, 253, 254.

13 BNF, MS Clairambault 316, fos. 91–2; Barrillon (1897–99), I, pp. 204–49; Castelain (1986), pp. 49–50; *CAF*, V, no. 16,216; Richardson (1995), p. 74.

14 BNF, MS FF 5750, fos. 19–37; Barillon (1897–99), I, p. 308; Castelain (1986), pp. 53–5; Gringore (2005), pp. 43–58.

15 BNF, MS FF 5750, fos. 37v–9; Castelain (1986), pp. 53–8; Gringore (2005), pp. 43–58; Brown (2010), pp. 54–6.

16 BNF, MS FF 5750, fo. 37v; BL, MS Stowe 582, fo. 32v; Castelain (1986), pp. 56–8; Gringore (2005), p. 46; Brown (2010), pp. 56–62.

17 Anon (1517), fos. 14–15 (only copy at BNF, Rés. Lb30 [29]); Castelain (1986), pp. 57–8.

18 The most important places Claude and her women visited were Amiens, where they arrived on 17 June; Abbeville, where they stopped for two days; Boulogne, Montreuil and Dieppe, and then Rouen, where Claude made an *entrée royale* and stayed almost a month.

19 BNF, MS Clairambault 316, fos. 115v–17, 118v; Barrillon (1897–99), I, pp. 311–23; Castelain (1986), pp. 56–61.

20 BNF, MS Clairambault 316, fo. 123v.

21 Cholakian (1991), pp. 9–10, 16–18, 20–33, 50, 117–28, 165, 230–1; Skemp and Cholakian (2008), pp. 21–35. Marguerite's *Heptaméron*, composed in the last six years of her life, is crammed full of scandalous stories of male adultery, treachery and hypocrisy. The work, partly, was crafted as a response to the 1537 French translation of Baldassare Castiglione's *Il Libro del Cortegiano* ('The Book of the Courtier'), first published in Venice in 1528. The overall model was Giovanni Boccaccio's *Decameron*.

22 Marguerite of Angoulême (1984), *Nouvelles* 4, 10, 14, 16, 22, 26; Ferguson and McKinley (2013), pp. 336–60; Skemp and Cholakian

(2008), pp. 1–37; Atance (1969), pp. 278–317; Butterworth (2016), pp. 80–100.

23 *Ordonnances* (1902–40), II, no. 139; *CAF*, I, nos. 742, 1396; Stephenson (2004), p. 4; Stephenson (2000), pp. 108–13; Cholakian and Cholakian (2005), pp. 51–2.

24 Castelain (1986), pp. 59–61; Barrillon (1897–99), I, pp. 324–5; Lebey (1904), pp. 90–1.

25 *CAF*, V, no. 16,740; Knecht (1994), p. 116; Wilson-Chevalier (2007), p. 81. In the belief that holy relics could assist in the delivery, Francis ordered the abbey of Bassac, near Cognac, to lend his wife the cord with which Christ had supposedly been tied to the Cross, while Claude asked the cathedral of Dol-de-Bretagne, near Saint-Malo, to allow her to borrow the famous silk belt of St Margaret, long loaned to noble Breton ladies in childbirth.

26 BNF, MS Clairambault 316, fos. 129, 149v; Barrillon (1897–99), II, p. 86. The commonly cited date of 13 June for the wedding is incorrect.

27 BNF, MS Clairambault 316, fos. 150–2; Barrillon (1897–9), II, p. 78; Florange (1913), I, pp. 222–6; Castelain (1986), pp. 62–7; Néret (1942), pp. 146–8; Knecht (1994), p. 116; Knecht (1998), pp. 7–8.

28 Barrillon (1897–99), II, p. 87; Hall (1809), pp. 592–3; Knecht (1994), p. 170; Richardson (1995), pp. 79–85.

29 Knecht (1994), pp. 154–64; Cameron (1970), pp. 119–49.

30 Arnaud (1987), pp. 140–4; Bourdigné (1842), pp. 316–25; Sanuto (1824–84), XXV, cols 528, 529, 530, 533, 537; Castelain (1986), p. 69.

31 Warner (1996), pp. 87–105; Sanuto (1824–84), XXV, cols 598, 610, 692; Jones (2003), pp. 293–8; Travers (1836–41), II, pp. 278–9; Guépin (1839), p. 213; Castelain (1986), pp. 69–70.

32 Warner (1996), pp. 87–105, citing Bibliothèque Municipale, Nantes, MS 2,280.

33 Hall (1809), pp. 594–5; *Ordonnances* (1902–40), II, nos. 165–9; Rymer (1704–35), XIII, pp. 619–54; BNF, MS Clairambault 316, fos. 173–4; Barrillon (1897–99), II, pp. 108–13; BL, Cotton MS, Vitellius B.XX, fos. 101–11v; *LP*, II, ii, nos. 4480, 4481, 4491, 4669–71, and p. 1479; Richardson (1995), p. 88.

34 BNF, MS Clairambault 316, fos. 199–200; Hall (1809), p. 596; Richardson (1995), pp. 99–104.

35 Barrillon (1897–99), II, pp. 108–13; Castelain (1986), p. 70; Richardson (2014b), pp. 28–9.

36 Hall (1809), p. 596; *LP*, II, ii, nos. 4674–5; Barrillon (1897–99), II, pp. 112–15; Sanuto (1824–84), XXVI, cols 349–52.

37 BL, Cotton MS, Caligula D.VII, fo. 98; Hall (1809), p. 597; Sanuto (1824–84), XXVI, cols 352–5.

38 Bryan (1548), sigs. c5–d2, [f7]–g2v, [h8v]–i6.

39 Anne's grandmother, Elizabeth Howard (*née* Tylney), was by her first husband the mother of Margaret Bryan (*née* Bourchier), mother of Sir Francis.

40 *LP*, III, i, nos. 246, 273; *CSPV*, II, nos. 1230, 1235; Walker (1989), pp. 6–16; Richardson (1995), p. 97; Richardson (1999), pp. 131–7.

41 BL, Cotton MS, Caligula D.VII, fo. 98; Ellis, 1st Series, I, p. 151; *LP*, III, i, nos. 118, 121, 122, 129, 131, 142, 145, 170, 189, 210, 212, 223, 246, 273, 289, 311, 320, 348, 352, 416, 446, 447, 454, 468, 514, 530, 549.

42 *LP*, III, i, no. 70; Mackay (2018b), pp. 82–91.

43 Parker (2019), pp. 87–94; Nitti (1892), pp. 168–214.

7 LOOKING TO THE FUTURE

1 BL, Cotton MS, Caligula D.VII, fos. 101–2; Wilson-Chevalier (2018), p. 151.

2 Ellis, 1st Series, I, pp. 159–62; BL, Cotton MS, Caligula D.VII, fo. 106r–v; Barrillon (1897–99), II, pp. 122–3; ANF, Angleterre J//920/31; *LP*, III, i, nos. 129, 145, 170, 289, 306, 311.

3 Barrillon (1897–99), II, pp. 147–8; *LP*, III, i, nos. 118, 122, 131, 170, 246, 397, 415, 416, 446, 488.

4 Barrillon (1897–99), II, pp. 149–63; Sanuto (1824–84), XXVIII, cols 342–8; Wilson-Chevalier (2018), pp. 151–2; Castelain (1986), pp. 73–6.

5 *LP*, III, i, nos. 549, 629, 662, 663, 666.

6 Hayward (2007), pp. 226–7; Gutch (1781), II, p. 290; NA, E 101/418/18. For Page's early career, see NA, E 179/69/9; NA, E 41/58–9, 527; NA, SP 46/186, fos. 99–100.

7 *LP*, III, ii, p. 1539.

8 *Calais Chronicle* (1846), pp. 19–27; *Rutland Papers* (1842), pp. 28–39; Richardson (2014b), pp. 79–90, and Appendices A and B.

9 Richardson (2014b), pp. 38–72.

10 Hall (1809), p. 604.

11 *CSPV*, III, p. 15.

12 Hall (1809), p. 605; Sanuto (1824–84), XXIX, cols 225–32; *CSPV*, III, no. 50; *LP*, III, i, nos. 728, 835, 843.

13 Barrillon (1897–99), II, p. 168; Richardson (2014b), pp. 107–20.

14 *CSPV*, III, no. 69.

15 Ibid., no. 60.

16 Florange (1913), I, p. 272; Richardson (2014b), pp. 120–40; *LP*, III, i, nos. 491, 577.

17 Sanuto (1824–84), XXIX, cols 22–4; Hall (1809), pp. 611–19; *CSPV*, III, nos. 69, 84, 95; Richardson (2014b), pp. 120–40.

18 BNF, MS Clairambault 316, fo. 257r–v.

19 Sanuto (1824–84), XXIX, cols 21, 23, 26–8, 30–1; Hall (1809), pp. 515–16; Barrillon (1897–99), II, p. 170; *CSPV*, III, nos. 73, 80, 84, 85; Castelain (1986), pp. 76–7; Hayward (2007), pp. 171–3.

20 Barrillon (1897–99), II, pp. 172–3; Hall (1809), pp. 620–1.

21 Hall (1809), pp. 621–2; *Rutland Papers* (1842), pp. 49–59; Sanuto (1824–84), XXIX, cols 250–4; *CSPV*, III, no. 50; Anglo (1969), pp. 168–9.

22 For the thinking behind this, see Parker (2019), p. 155.

23 Barrillon (1897–99), II, pp. 176–84; Raymond (1859), pp. 369–80; Castelain (1986), pp. 79–82; Knecht (1994), pp. 175–7.

24 BL, Cotton MS, Vitellius B.XX, fos. 239–42v; *LP*, III, i, no. 1213.

25 Le Glay (1845), II, pp. 507–9; Barrillon (1897–99), II, pp. 184–7; Florange (1913), I, pp. 280–7; *LP*, III, ii, nos. 1513, 1555; Gwyn (1980), pp. 755–72; Knecht (1994), pp. 177–9.

26 *LP*, IV, i, no. 1901.

27 *LP*, III, ii, no. 1581.

28 Barrillon (1897–99), II, pp. 188–90; *LP*, III, ii, nos. 1705–6, 1708, 1714–15, 1729, 1732–3, 1736, 1742–3, 1753, 1762, 1764–5, 1768–9; Knecht (1994), pp. 179–82.

29 *LP*, III, ii, nos. 1994, 2012–13, 2052.

30 BL, Cotton MS, Caligula D.VIII, fos. 182v–3.

31 *LP*, III, ii, no. 1994.

32 *LP*, III, ii, no. 1899; Hall (1809), p. 628.

33 *LP*, II, ii, p. 1501.

34 HMC, *Twelfth Report [Rutland MSS]*, Appendix, IV, i, p. 22.

35 *LP*, III, ii, nos. 1547, 1555, 1557, 1610, 1693–4, 1705–6, 1714–15, 1753; Clark (2018), p. 48.

8 FIRST ENCOUNTERS

1 Sylvester (1959), pp. xxxvi–viii, 28–9.

2 Sanuto (1824–84), XLVII, col. 11.

3 'S'elle estoit belle et de taille elegante, / Estoit des yeulx encor[es] plus attirante, / Lesquelz savoit bien conduyre a propos, / En les tenant quelquefoys en repos, / Aucunesfoys envoyant en message / Porter du cueur le secret tesmongaige.' Schmid (2009), p. 113; Ascoli (1927), p. 234 (ll. 61–6).

4 *LP*, X, no. 1182; BL, Additional MS 28,585, fos. 43–5; *CSPSp*, IV, ii, no. 967. For Barlow's career and attachments to the Boleyns, see BL, Cotton MS, Vespasian F.III, fo. 34; *LP*, IV, nos. 3749, 4647; *LP*, V, no. 533, and p. 317 (unnumbered); *ODNB*, s.v. 'Barlow, William [subsumes entry on John]'. It was said of him that he 'always belonged to [Anne], had his promotion by her, and had been ambassador for her in divers places beyond sea before she was queen.' Information on his appointment as rector from St Peter's church, Hever.

5 Robinson (1846–47), II, p. 553.

6 See above, pp. 114, 115.

7 Sanuto (1824–84), LVII, col. 316. 'Madama Anna non è delle più belle del mondo. La statura è commune, le carne tengono del negro, il collo lungo, la bocha grande, il petto non molto relevato, in effeto non ha altro che Io appetito grande de quello re et li occhi che sono neri et belli, et ha più grande modo de intertenimento de servitori che avesse la regina quando era in flore.'

8 Sanuto (1824–84), LVII, col. 23.

9 NA, SP 1/18, fos. 171–2; NA, E 36/215, p. 430; NA, E 101/622/31; NA, E 40/3955; NA, E 41/190; *LP*, II, ii, p. 1470. For Ormond's death, see NA, PROB 11/18/184. Henry's two visits in June 1515 are recorded in NA, OBS 1419.

10 NA, C 146/9376, C 146/9378, C 146/9379–84; Northants R.O., F(M) Charter/2302; Lysons (1806–22), I, p. 108; Page (1904–12), II, pp. 348–75, and n. 135; Davis (1855), p. 18. Although there is no doubt that Boleyn sold Luton Hoo to Fermour probably early in 1523, the indenture for sale was never enrolled. Doubtless this was to keep the sale confidential, as Margaret Butler did not die until 1540, outliving her son by a year. Fermour continued to own Luton Hoo until his death in 1551: NA, PROB 11/35/40.

11 NA, E 101/419/5; NA, SP 1/19, fo. 19; *LP*, III, ii, no. 2214 (24). Boleyn
    surrendered the comptrollership of the household on 30 September
    1521. He took up the treasurer's post soon afterwards.

12 NA, E 101/419/5; HEH, Ellesmere MS 2655, fos. 10–11, 16v, 17v.

13 A second letter from Boleyn, sent from Blois, completes the story.
    During an audience given to Boleyn's chaplain, then ferrying letters
    to and from the French court, Wolsey gave a reassurance that Anne's
    father would indeed be the next treasurer. For this, Sir Thomas
    declared, 'I think myself more bounded to your grace than I can
    desire', adding tellingly 'I know his highness and your grace to be
    of one will.' See NA, SP 1/18, fos. 171–2; NA, SP 1/19, fo. 19; Gunn
    (2016), pp. 291–2. For the legend, see Pollard (1929), p. 222, n. 1;
    Sylvester (1959), pp. 204–5; Woods (1974), p. 91.

14 NA, SP 60/1, fo. 51; *St. Pap.*, II, pp. 50–1, 57; Round (1886), pp. 25–37;
    ODNB, s.v. 'Butler, James'.

15 *ODNB*, s.v. 'Butler, James'; *DIB*, s.v. 'Butler, James'.

16 *CSPV*, III, nos. 210, 213; Ellis, 2nd Series, I, pp. 286–8; *LP*, III, i, nos.
    1273, 1274; Rex (1989), pp. 85–106.

17 Villasancta (1523), sig. A1v.

18 *LP*, III, i, no. 1237; Cameron (1991), pp. 102–3.

19 The scene could have been adapted by William Cornish out of any
    of the familiar tales of romance and chivalry such as the *Romaunt of
    the Rose*, the best-known didactic poem of courtly love in the canon,
    translated into Middle English by several hands, notably Chaucer's,
    from the original French text.

20 Hall (1809), pp. 631–2; Anglo (1969), pp. 120–1.

21 Richardson (2014b), Appendix A (p. 217); *Calais Chronicle* (1846),
    p. 25; *Rutland Papers* (1842), p. 38.

22 *LP*, I, i, no 20 (p. 15); *LP*, III, ii, no. 2305, and pp. 1545, 1559; Anglo
    (1969), pp. 120–1.

23 AAV, Archivum Arcis, Arm. I–XVIII, 6529, fos. 172, 173, 176–8; BL,
    Additional MS 8715, fo. 222v; Baroni (1962), no. 152. The summary
    in *LP*, X, no. 450 obliterates the context.

24 Sanuto (1824–84), XXVI, col. 278; *CSPV*, II, nos. 1103, 1123; Murphy
    (2003), pp. 20–6.

25 *CSPSp, Supplement to Vols. I and II*, no. 8 (pp. 39–40); Murphy
    (2003), pp. 7–8; Samman (1988), p. 175; Bernard (1981), p. 757.

26 Murphy (2003), pp. 24–5.

27 Bessie was married off to Gilbert Tailboys, the young heir of George, Lord Tailboys of Kyme and his wife Elizabeth Gascoigne, the sister of one of Wolsey's most trustworthy retainers; Murphy (2003), pp. 27–35.

28 Primitive forms of contraception were well understood at Henry's court. See Murphy (2003), pp. 22–3.

29 BL, Royal MS, 14 B.XXXII (unfoliated); NA, SP 1/40, fo. 159.

30 *LP*, III, ii, nos. 2074 (5), 2214 (29), 2297 (12); *LP*, III, ii, p. 1539; *LP*, IV, ii, no. 2972.

31 BL, Additional MS 1938, fo. 44.

32 NA, KB 9/53; NA, KB 8/5; BL, Harleian MS 283, fo. 72; *LP*, III, i, nos. 1284 (1–5), 1285 (pp. 495–505), 1356; *CSPV*, III, no. 213; Hall (1809), pp. 623–4; Harris (1986), pp. 180–202.

33 LMA, COL/CA/01/01/005 (MS Repertory 5), fos. 199v, 204.

34 NA, C 66/640 [21]; NA, C 147/196; *LJ* (1767–1846), I, p. cxiii; *LP*, III, ii, nos. 2214 (24, 29); KHLC, MSS U908/T51/7, 8.

35 For reimbursement to Sir Thomas Boleyn of the costs of building repairs at Penshurst and Tonbridge, see NA, SP 1/40, fo. 160; *LP*, IV, i, no. 1550.

36 Stephenson (1926), pp. 236, 251.

37 The exact date when George was admitted to the privy chamber is unclear, but he had risen to the rank of groom at least by August 1525, when Wolsey began drafting the Eltham Ordinances, later striking out his name. See NA, SP 1/37, fos. 53, 58, 90.

38 *LP*, III, ii, no. 2214 (29); *LP*, IV, i, no. 546 (2).

39 NA, SP 1/37, fo. 53.

40 Sylvester (1959), p. 29.

41 Vergil (1950), p. 331.

42 Camden (1915), p. 2.

43 Loades (1968), p. 143; Singer (1827), p. 423.

9 ANNE IN LOVE

1 Hall (1809), pp. 634–5.

2 *CSPSp, Further Supplement*, pp. xviii–xxxiv, 24, 36, 47–56, 62–112, 130–49; *LP*, III, ii, no. 2333 (3, 12).

3 *CSPSp, Further Supplement*, p. 71; Campbell and Foister (1986), pp. 721–5; NPG, no. 6453.

4 Hall (1809), p. 635.

5 *LP*, III, ii, nos. 2288, 2289, 2305, 2306, 2333, 2360; Hall (1809), pp. 635–7; *CSPV*, II, nos. 466–7; *Rutland Papers* (1842), pp. 59–100; Anglo (1969), pp. 170–206.

6 Thurley (1993), pp. 40–2. See also the so-called 'Agas' map of early-modern London produced between 1561 and 1570, at https://mapoflondon.uvic.ca/agas.htm.

7 Hall (1809), pp. 638–40; Anglo (1969), p. 197.

8 *CSPSp*, II, no. 437; Anglo (1969), pp. 202–5.

9 *LP*, III, ii, no. 2292 (1, 2); Hall (1809), pp. 636–7.

10 AGS, PTR/LEG. 55/12.

11 *CSPSp*, II, nos. 427, 430–4; *CSPSp, Further Supplement*, pp. 194–6; *LP*, III, ii, nos. 2322, 2333 (3, 6); Biddle (2000), pp. 425–32.

12 Sylvester (1959), p. 30.

13 With their stronghold around Alnwick Castle in Northumberland and estates spilling over into Cumberland, Yorkshire and beyond, the Percys could muster more than 8,000 troops for the royal army from their tenants, whereas the Boleyns could barely raise 300. See *LP*, I, ii, no. 2053 (1–3); *ODNB*, s.v. 'Percy, Henry Algernon, 5th Earl of Northumberland'.

14 Sylvester (1959), p. 30.

15 Ibid., pp. 30–1.

16 *LP*, IV, ii, nos. 3379–80; *LP*, V, no. 395. On the debts of the 5th Earl, there is much confusion. See Fonblanque (1887), II, pp. 381–3, where the debt is multiplied tenfold in error.

17 Sylvester (1959), p. 32.

18 Swinburne (1686), pp. 12–13, 40–1, 71–2, 203–12.

19 For the backstory, see Lodge (1838), I, pp. 20–1; *LP*, II, i, nos. 1893, 1935, 1969–70; *LP*, II, ii, nos. 3819, 3820.

20 Sylvester (1959), pp. 32–4.

21 *LP*, III, ii, nos. 3321–2, 3648; NA, SP 1/34, fos. 71–80; NA, SP 1/44, fos. 17–19.

22 NA, SP 1/44, fos. 17–19; *LP*, IV, ii, no. 3380 (p. 1534); *LP*, IV, iii, no. 5920. Starkey believes 1526 to be the wedding year, but this is too late. See Starkey (2004), pp. 276–7.

23 Sylvester (1959), p. 31.

24 *St. Pap.*, I, pp. 91–2.

25 *LP*, III, ii, nos. 1709, 1718–19; Quinn (1961), pp. 324–34; Round (1886), pp. 36–7, 44–5.

26 Sylvester (1959), p. 34.

27 *LP*, III, ii, nos. 2481, 2567 (3, 5), 2591. The dowry offer was later raised to 1 million ducats.

28 *LP*, III, ii, nos. 2650, 2663, 2697, 2764, 2772–3, 2879–80, 2898, 2952; Mackay (2018b), pp. 105–7.

29 Doucet (1921), I, pp. 203–54.

30 *LP*, III, ii, nos. 3030, 3055, 3154, 3225, 3307, 3346.

31 Gunn (1986), pp. 596–634.

32 *St. Pap.*, VI, pp. 221–31, 233–9; *LP*, IV, i, nos. 420–2; Parker (2019), pp. 144–8; Knecht (1994), pp. 205–18.

33 Sylvester (1959), pp. 34–5. The exact timing of Anne's return is uncertain, but this date makes the most sense of the conflicting evidence.

34 On 19 November, Percy asked to borrow £150 to equip himself, believing he was to participate in the event. See NA, SP 1/32, fos. 256–61; Hall (1809), pp. 688–9; Hoyle (1992), pp. 95–6; Brigden (2012), pp. 39–44; Starkey (2004), pp. 271–2; Anglo (1969), pp. 115–17.

35 George had received a valuable grant just weeks before. See *LP*, IV, i, no. 546 (2); Brigden (2012), p. 45.

36 Hall (1809), pp. 674, 688–90.

37 Ibid., pp. 689–91; Starkey (2004), p. 273.

38 NA, SP 1/32, fos. 260–1; Starkey (2004), p. 271; Brigden (2012), p. 49.

39 WRO, Microfilm 705:349/12946/498729; HLRO, MS PO/1/1539.

40 Brigden (2012), p. 49. For Elizabeth Darrell, see *LP*, III, ii, no. 2305; *LP*, V, p. 319.

41 Muir (1963), I, pp. 40–1, 206, 264; Brigden (2012), pp. 92–6; Starkey (2004), pp. 268–71; *ODNB*, s.v. 'Wyatt, Sir Thomas'.

42 Several claims are made that Wyatt was a knight of the body in 1518, but the first documentary evidence relates to 1529. See *LP*, IV, iii, nos. 5978 (26), 6490 (23). His alleged appointment in 1518 as 'a sewer extraordinary', sworn to the king to attend his table in his dining chamber and taste his food, is a fiction. Although *LP*, II, i, no. 2735 lists him as such, the entry is based on the list of Henry's household in BL, Royal MS, 7 F.XIV, fos. 100–8, which the editors of *LP* have misdated. It can be dated precisely to between 18 March and 1 May 1536. Wyatt's name appears on fo. 101v.

43 *LP*, IV, i, no. 214.

44 *LP*, VI, no. 278 (10), which recites Wyatt's earlier grant of the clerkship.

10 AN ANXIOUS YEAR

1 Parker (2019), pp. 149–53; Knecht (1994), pp. 218–27.

2 *CSPSp*, III, i, no. 33.

3 Knecht (1994), pp. 208–18; Parker (2019), p. 151.

4 BL, Cotton MS, Vespasian C.III, fo. 176v.

5 *St. Pap.*, I, pp. 153–6, 317–18.

6 BL, Cotton MS, Vespasian C.III, fos. 29–48v; *St. Pap.*, VI, pp. 412–36; Powell (2005), pp. 421–43.

7 BL, Cotton MS, Vespasian C.III, fos. 135–43v; *LP*, IV, i, nos. 1389, 1421, 1710; *CAF*, IX, p. 21; Parker (2019), pp. 159–60.

8 Singer (1827), pp. 424–5. For Wyatt's situation, see Brigden (2019), pp. 1406–39.

9 BL, Egerton MS 2711, fo. 66v; Rebholz (1978), no. 28, and p. 357.

10 Brigden (2012), pp. 188–90, 548–9. Retha Warnicke has suggested that not enough attention is given to the possibility that by 'country', Wyatt may have meant Kent rather than England. Except he did not use the phrase 'my country', the commonest usage where the county alone is concerned, but 'our country'. See Warnicke (1986), p. 572.

11 Rebholz (1978), no. 11.

12 Lerer (1997), pp. 103–6; Siemens (1997), pp. 188–92.

13 Brigden (2012), pp. 155–63; Rossiter (2009), pp. 69–88; Grant (2019), pp. 63–91; Powell (2005), pp. 428–30.

14 Grant (2019), pp. 86–8.

15 A possible irony is that Henry often hunted using nets, unlike Francis I, who stoutly maintained that the practice was cruel as the animals should be given a sporting chance to escape. See Richardson (2013), pp. 127–41.

16 Grant (2019), pp. 86–8; Ives (2004), p. 75.

17 Harpsfield (1878), p. 253.

18 *Spanish Chronicle* (1889), pp. 68–9.

19 BL, Harleian MS 282, fo. 123v; Muir (1963), p. 148.

20 Singer (1827), pp. 426–7.

21 *PPE, Henry*, p. 211.

22 *LP*, IV, iii, nos. 5978 (26), 6490 (23), 6751 (24); HHStA, England, Korrespondenz, Karton 4, fo. 313; *CSPSp*, IV, i, no. 302; Brigden

(2012), pp. 163–4, and p. 605, n. 36; Friedmann (1884), I, p. 121 and n. 1; Harrier (1954), pp. 581–4.

23 HHStA, England, Korrespondenz, Karton 4, fo. 313; Brigden (2012), p. 605, n. 36; Friedmann (1884), I, p. 121 and n. 1; *CSPSp*, IV, i, no. 302. Chapuys believed the two incidents referred to the same man but may have become confused by the flood of gossip, not least as he did not speak English.

24 Wyatt (1528), [sig.] A2–3; Brigden and Woolfson (2005), pp. 464–511; Brigden (2012), pp. 60–4, 103–28, 164–5; Muir (1963), pp. 6–12.

25 See also Ives (2004), pp. 72–80.

26 Singer (1827), pp. 432–3; Singer (1825), I, p. 41.

27 *CAF*, IX, p. 21; Pocock (1870), II, p. 386; Rex (2003), pp. 16–27.

28 Fitzroy Inventory, pp. lxxx–lxxxiv; Hall (1809), p. 703; *LP*, IV, i, no. 1431; Murphy (2003), pp. 36–65.

29 *CSPV*, III, no. 1053; Starkey (2004), pp. 198–9.

30 Hall (1809), p. 703; *LP*, IV, i, no. 1431; *LP*, IV, ii, nos. 2541, 3142 (29).

31 Ellis, 1st Series, II, pp. 67–8; *LP*, X, no. 1010; NA, SP 1/37, fos. 53, 58. For the date of the marriage settlement, see WRO, Microfilm 705:349/12946/498729.

32 Starkey, Ward and Hawkyard (1998), nos. 1865–6.

33 *LP*, IV, i, no. 1525; Samman (1988), p. 73; Ellis, 1st Series, II, pp. 19–20.

34 *Ordonnances* (1902–40), IV, nos. 394–5, 398–400; *LP*, IV, i, nos. 1516, 1525, 1531, 1570, 1573, 1578–9, 1595, 1600–3, 1606, 1609, 1617, 1663, 1669; Colvin, Brown and Cook (1963–82), IV, pp. 164–5.

35 BNF, MS FF 4996, fos. 143–62; *LP*, IV, i, nos. 1559, 1739, 1770, 1783, 1788, 1799, 1801, 1818; *St. Pap.*, VI, pp. 490–521; *CSPV*, III, no. 1062.

36 *LP*, IV, i, no. 1888; Hall (1809), p. 707.

37 *CSPV*, III, no. 1193; NA, OBS 1419.

38 NA, E150/981/7; NA, C 142/48/107; NA, C 142/48/70.

39 The first recorded suggestion that the child was the king's came in the treason trial of the Middlesex priest John Hale in 1535, but he and his colleague Robert Feron were virulent critics of Henry and made a series of wild allegations. Historians generally agree that William Carey was the father, but the case is not completely closed. See NA, KB 8/7, Pt 1; *LP*, VIII, nos. 567, 609; Varlow (2007), pp. 320–2; Ives (2004), pp. 16–17, 190.

40 *LP*, IV, i, no. 1899; Sharkey (2008), pp. 129–30; Parker (2019), pp. 164–5.

41 *Ordonnances* (1902–40), IV, no. 411; Knecht (1994), pp. 244–8, 257; Parker (2019), pp. 153–8.
42 Ellis, 2nd Series, I, pp. 333–7.

11 HENRY IN LOVE

1 Hall (1809), pp. 707–8.
2 BAV, MS Vat.Lat.3731.pt.A; Savage (1949), pp. 27–48. The letters are now digitised at https://digi.vatlib.it/view/MSS_Vat.lat.3731.pt.A.
3 Savage (1949), pp. 7–12.
4 Savage (1949), pp. 27–8, 30, 32, 34, 36–7, 39–40, 40–41, 43–4, 45–8; Lerer (1997), pp. 93–5.
5 In these paragraphs, we are indebted to the masterly discussion of the letters from this point of view by Starkey (2004), pp. 278–84. We have not always agreed with Starkey's ordering, especially of the earlier letters, but his reconstruction is also entirely credible.
6 *LP*, IV, ii, nos. 2407, 2439; NA, OBS 1419; Starkey (2004), p. 279.
7 Savage (1949), pp. 27–8. In quotations from the French letters in this edition, we have corrected a small number of mistranslations and smoothed out some awkward phrases.
8 Savage (1949), pp. 40–1.
9 Lerer (1997), pp. 103–6.
10 Savage (1949), p. 41.
11 Starkey (1987), pp. 105–7.
12 NA, SP 1/37, fo. 90 (formerly 102).
13 Savage (1949), pp. 33–4.
14 Ibid., pp. 29–30.
15 Ibid., pp. 38–9. The king's reply (and therefore Anne's terms as expressed in her lost letter) is prone to misunderstanding because his mild protest – that in real life it was unbecoming for him to visit his lady 'au lieu de servante' – tends to be mistranslated. In the sixteenth century, the primary meaning of *au lieu* relates to a person's role, rank, calling or function, and only secondarily to a house, lodging or dwelling place. Here the primary meaning is the obvious one. To assume that 'au lieu de servante' means Katherine's apartments, Anne's father's house in London, or some other secret hideaway, is mistaken. See Cotgrave (1611), s.v. 'lieu'; Starkey (2004), p. 281.
16 BAV, MS Vat.Lat.3731.pt.A, fo. 7; Starkey (2004), p. 281.
17 Starkey (2004), p. 281.

18 Hall (1809), p. 719.

19 Buettner (2001), pp. 598–625; Hayward (2005), p. 127.

20 Savage (1949), pp. 34–6.

21 Ibid., pp. 35–6.

22 This suggests that, in fact, Henry first became enamoured of Anne a month or two before he showed his hand at the Shrovetide masque.

23 NA, SP 1/59, fo. 100r–v.

24 Savage (1949), pp. 42–3.

25 Accession no: Loan:Met Anon.2:3–1998.

12 THE 'SECRET MATTER'

1 Charlotte (b. 1516), Francis (b. 1518), Henry (b. 1519), Madeleine (b. 1520), Charles (b. 1522), Marguerite (b. 1523).

2 *LP*, IV, ii, nos. 2606, 2651.

3 *CSPSp*, III, ii, no. 8; Cameron (1991), pp. 340–1.

4 NA, SP 1/39, fo. 5.

5 Sharkey (2008), pp. 118–48.

6 BL, Cotton MS, Caligula D.IX, fos. 272–8; 301v–9; *LP*, IV, ii, nos. 2651, 2728, 2742, 2771, 2772; Richardson (1995), pp. 159–69.

7 BL, Cotton MS, Caligula D.X, fos. 39–40v; *LP*, IV, ii, nos. 2974, 2981.

8 Rymer (1704–35), XIV, pp. 218–27; *LP*, IV, ii, nos. 2974, 3080, 3105.

9 Sylvester (1959), p. 35.

10 NA, E 36/227, fos. 11–57v; NA, SP 2/C, fos. 328v–48.

11 Guy (2008), pp. 170–1.

12 Hall (1809), pp. 722–4; Anglo (1969), pp. 212–4; *CSPV*, IV, no. 105; Starkey (2004), pp. 284–5.

13 BNF, MS NAF 7004, fo. 80v.

14 NA, SP 1/42, fo. 72r–v; *LP*, IV, ii, no. 3193; Richardson (1995), pp. 173–4.

15 Sylvester (1959), p. 83; Richardson (1995), pp. 168–9. See also *Ambassades* (1905), no. 163.

16 No mention of the objection can be found in the minutes of the French embassy, but it is more likely to have been a topic reserved for private discussion, or before de Gramont's embassy arrived during the talks in Poissy. See *LP*, IV, ii, nos. 2728, 2772, 2790, 3009, 3010, 3105; BNF, MS NAF 7004, fos. 3–87.

17 Flannigan (2020), pp. 92, 199–200.

18 Starkey (2008), pp. 279–80; *LP*, IV, iii, no. 5791 (pp. 2588–9).

19 NA, SP 2/C, fos. 9–20; Scarisbrick (1968), pp. 154–5.
20 Surtz and Murphy (1988), pp. ii–iii; Harpsfield (1878), pp. 37–231.
21 *St. Pap.*, I, pp. 189–90.
22 Hook (1969), pp. 167–90.
23 *CSPSp*, III, ii, no. 113 (p. 276).
24 *St. Pap.*, I, p. 197.
25 Ibid., pp. 215–16; Scarisbrick (1968), pp. 156–7.
26 *CSPSp*, III, ii, nos. 113 (p. 277), 166, 674; *LP*, IV, ii, nos. 3312, 3265, 3278, 3283.
27 *St. Pap.*, I, pp. 194–5.
28 Forrest (1875), pp. 1–148.
29 *St. Pap.*, I, pp. 194–5.
30 Sylvester (1959), pp. 44–6; *CSPV*, IV, no. 129.
31 BL, Cotton MS, Vitellius B.IX, fos. 194–6v, 232–7v; *LP*, IV, ii, no. 3186; *St. Pap.*, I, pp. 191–3; Richardson (1995), pp. 174–9; Sharkey (2008), pp. 166–7; Gunn and Lindley (1991), pp. 151–2.
32 *St. Pap.*, I, pp. 212–13; Sylvester (1959), pp. 45–54.
33 NA, E 30/1111–14; *LP*, IV, ii, no. 3356 (1–7); CADMA, MS 8CP/002, fos. 6–34v; Rymer (1704–35), XIV, pp. 203–27.
34 *St. Pap.*, I, p. 260.
35 BL, Cotton MS, Vitellius B.IX, fos. 194–6v, 232–7v; Le Grand (1688), III, pp. 4–13; Sharkey (2008), p. 166; Sylvester (1959), pp. 54–62; Sharkey (2011), p. 240.
36 *LP*, IV, ii, nos. 3363, 3400.
37 NA, SP 1/42, fo. 244.
38 Colvin, Brown and Cook (1963–82), IV, pp. 172–5.
39 NA, SP 1/66, fo. 26; NA, OBS, 1419; Savage (1949), pp. 31–2; *SR*, III, pp. 479–81; Pocock (1870), I, p. 11; Colvin, Brown and Crook (1963–82), IV, pp. 154–6.
40 *Lisle Letters*, I, p. 550; Nott (1816), I, p. lxxi.
41 *LP*, IV, iii, no. 6738; *LP*, VI, no. 1164; *LP*, VIII, no. 263 (p. 104); Wood (1846), II, p. 371; Clark (2018), pp. 48, 49, 80, 84. Bess's father was Norfolk's secretary. Slanderous claims by the duchess that Holland was 'but a churl's daughter and of no gentle blood' and fit only to be 'washer of my nursery' were fake news. When she died, she was found to have been a substantial heiress owning property in her own right in Lincolnshire and Suffolk. See NA, C 142/87/13, 92; NA, E 150/582/15; NA, WARD 7/4/44, 58; NA, REQ 2/5/25; NA, PROB

51/128; Wood (1846), II, pp. 224, 370–1; *CPR, Edward VI*, II, p. 140; Blomefield (1739–75), IV, pp. 336, 734.

42 Sanuto (1824–84), LVI, cols 287–8; NA, SP 1/37, fo. 53; *CSPV*, IV, no. 761; *LP*, V, no. 287; Gunn (1988), pp. 85–7. One might speculate that Anne had picked up raunchy gossip in France about Mary and Suffolk's pre-marital relationship, or maybe the Boleyns knew embarrassing details about Suffolk's unwelcome advances to Margaret of Austria?

43 *LP*, VI, no. 1125; *LP*, IX, no. 776; *LP*, X, no. 199; *CSPSp*, IV, ii, no. 1127 (p. 800); Starkey (2004), p. 551.

44 Hall (1809), pp. 721, 729, 732; Gunn and Lindley (1991), pp. 160–77.

45 *St. Pap.*, I, pp. 264–6.

46 *St. Pap.*, I, p. 267.

47 *St. Pap.*, I, pp. 267–8.

13 ANNE MAKES HER MARK

1 *St. Pap.*, I, pp. 267–78; ibid., VII, pp. 1–2; NA, SP 6/13, fos. 102–10.

2 Gairdner (1896), pp. 685–6; *St. Pap.*, VII, pp. 1–3; Sharkey (2011), p. 242.

3 *LP*, IV, ii, no. 3802; Fletcher (2012), pp. 1–32.

4 *St. Pap.*, VII, pp. 23–6, 29–35; *LP*, IV, ii, nos. 3662, 3693.

5 Gairdner (1896), pp. 686–7.

6 *St. Pap.*, VII, pp. 13–14.

7 *ODNB*, s.v. 'Barlow, William [subsumes entry on John]'.

8 *CSPSp*, III, ii, nos. 152, 224.

9 Rogers (1961), p. 207.

10 'When brethren dwell together, and one of them dieth without children, the wife of the deceased shall not marry to another; but his brother shall take her and raise up seed for his brother': Deuteronomy 25:5. See Rogers (1961), pp. 207–8; Murphy (1995), pp. 135–58.

11 Wakefield (c.1534a), sigs. O4v–P1; Surtz and Murphy (1988), pp. xii–xiii; Rex (1991), pp. 58–9, 165–70; Trapp (1992), p. 25.

12 Wakefield (c.1534a), sig. P3v; Wakefield (c.1534b), sigs. D4–E1.

13 Rogers (1961), p. 208.

14 NA, SP 1/104A, fos. 1–140; printed in 1539 and 1555. See also Duffy (2013), pp. 204–7.

15 Pole (1555), Bk. 3, p. lxxvi (*verso*); Starkey (2004), p. 287.

16 Hall (1809), pp. 735–6; *Hansische Geschichtsblätter* (1871–2006), III, pp. 160–72; *LP*, IV, i, nos. 995, 1962; Marshall (2017), pp. 135–45.

17 Foxe (1843–9), V, pp. 414–20 and Appendix 6; Strype (1822), I, ii, p. 55; Brigden (1989), pp. 112–16, 126–8, 158–61; Dowling (1984), pp. 30–46.

18 BL, Cotton MS, Vitellius B.X, fo. 34; *St. Pap.*, VII, pp. 18–21, 23–6, 29–35, 37–44; *LP*, IV, ii, nos. 3693–4, 3784–5, 3787–8, 3821; Pocock (1870), I, pp. 22–7; Gairdner (1896), pp. 692–3.

19 BL, Cotton MS, Vespasian F.XIII, fo. 141; Savage (1949), pp. 49–50.

20 Pocock (1870), I, p. 74.

21 Ibid., pp. 116, 120, 156, 158.

22 *LP*, IV, ii, no. 3913; HMC, *Manuscripts of the Marquis of Salisbury*, I, p. 6; Pocock (1870), I, pp. 95–159.

23 BAV, MS Vat.Lat.373, fo. 13; Savage (1949), p. 46, where the transcription is in error.

24 Savage (1949), pp. 46–7.

25 Ibid., p. 46.

26 Browne had attended the fête at the Bastille in 1518 and stayed on in France. Francis showed him great favour, taking him hunting and making him an honorary *gentilhomme de la chambre*, but it would not take long for Browne to nurture a sharp antipathy to everything French. See BNF, MS Dupuy 33, fo. 65; Richardson (1999), p. 131; Brigden (2012), p. 128; *ODNB*, s.v. 'Browne, Sir Anthony'.

27 *LP*, IV, i, no. 1939 (p. 863); *LP*, IV, ii. no. 3691; NA, SP 1/37, fo. 53; *Household Ordinances* (1790), pp. 154–5. A powerful influence on Carew was his wife Elizabeth (*née* Bryan), the daughter of Margaret Bryan (*née* Bourchier), governess in turn to Princess Mary and Henry Fitzroy.

28 Ellis, 3rd Series, II, pp. 131–4.

29 Sylvester (1959), p. 35.

30 Sotheby's sale, London, 13 April 2022, lot 72.

31 For these interests, see CCA, CCA-DCc-ChAnt/F/37; CCA, CCA-DCc-ChAnt/F/40; NA, C 1/770/38; NA, C 24/3, no. 12. One presumes the £400 was to purchase the salt marshes outright, but this is an inference.

32 NA, SP 1/47, fo. 111; Sotheby's sale, London, 13 April 2022, lot 72; *ODNB*, s.v. 'Chambers, John'.

33 NA, SP 1/49, fo. 63.

34 NA, SP 1/47, fo. III; NA, SP 1/49, fos. 63, 167; *LP*, IV, ii, no. 4007; *HC, 1509–1558*, I, pp. 634–7; Ives (2004), pp. 106–7. Henry claimed Cheyne 'was proud and full of opprobrious words, little esteeming his friends that did most for him', although he later relented.

35 *Ambassades* (1905), no. 188 (p. 543); *HC, 1509–1558*, I, p. 635.

36 BL, Kings MS 9. In or about 1546, Holland married Henry Reppes of Mendham, Suffolk, and died in a gruesome childbirth scene in 1548. Shortly before or just after she breathed her last (the witness statements vary), a botched Caesarian section was performed, when 'the child was ripped out of her belly' – a boy, who lived for only half an hour. See BL, Egerton MS 2713, fos. 16–17; NA, REQ 2/5/25; Zupanec (2017), pp. 3–4.

37 BL, Kings MS 9, fo. 231v. A sixteenth-century ownership inscription at the front of the manuscript (fo. Ir) identifies Henry and Elizabeth Reppes.

38 BL, Kings MS 9, fo. 66v.

39 Overtaking Gambara near Paris, they had travelled via Lyon and from there across the frozen Mont Cenis pass and on to Genoa and then Lucca. See *LP*, IV, ii, nos. 4007, 4076, 4078; NA, SP 1/47, fo. 109.

40 NA SP 1/63, fos. 244–64, 265–86v, 287–302v, 303, 304–13v, 314, 315–58, 360–84v, 385. See Surtz and Murphy (1988), pp. iv–xxi.

41 *LP*, IV, ii, nos. 4090, 4103, 4118–20, 4167, 4171; Pocock (1870), I, pp. 95–140; Scarisbrick (1968), pp. 207–9.

42 Pocock (1870), I, pp. 141–5.

43 Ibid., pp. 145–55.

44 Ibid., pp. 156–9, 163–5; *LP*, IV, ii, nos. 4288, 4289.

45 *LP* IV, ii, nos. 4332–3, 4391, 4398, 4408–9, 4417–18, 4422, 4428–9, 4439–40, 4450, 4452–3, 4542; Savage (1949), pp. 30–2, 39–40, 43–5; Flood (2003), pp. 147–76.

14 THE SWEAT

1 *LP*, IV, ii, nos. 4332, 4391, 4409, 4542, 4633; Flood (2003), p. 151.

2 Wood (1846), II, p. 29; *Lisle Letters*, II, no. 399.

3 Caius (1552), pp. 12–13, 32–5. For modern medical analysis, see Thwaites, Taviner and Gant (1997), pp. 580–2; Thwaites, Taviner and Gant (1998), pp. 96–8.

4 *Lisle Letters*, II, no. 206.

5 *St. Pap.*, I, p. 299; NA, SP 1/228, fos. 143–60. 'Pills of Rasis' took their name from the early-medieval Arab scholar Abu Bakr Muhammad ibn Zakariya al-Razi, known as 'Rhazes' or 'Rasis' in the west, and popularised by the eleventh-century physician Ibn Sina – better known by his Latin name, Avicenna.

6 *LP*, IV, ii, no. 4542.

7 Savage (1949), pp. 30–2; *LP*, IV, ii, no. 4404. Dates are collated with the king's itinerary: NA, OBS 1419.

8 Savage (1949), pp. 30–2 (with minor amendments based on the French text). See also Starkey (2004), p. 331.

9 Savage (1949), pp. 43–4; *St. Pap.*, I, pp. 298–9; *LP*, IV, ii, nos. 4409, 4542.

10 *St. Pap.*, I, p. 296.

11 NA, SP 1/48, fo. 199; *St. Pap.*, I, pp. 289–90.

12 NA, SP 1/48, fo. 199. See also *St. Pap.*, I, p. 300 for Tuke's report.

13 *St. Pap.*, I, p. 300.

14 NA, SP 1/49, fos. 128, 132v.

15 NA, SP 1/48, fo. 216; *LP*, IV, ii, nos. 4422, 4428, 4438, 4486, 4497; NA OBS 1419.

16 *St. Pap.*, I, pp. 302, 303; *LP*, IV, ii, nos. 4429, 4438, 4440, 4510; Savage (1949), p. 44. For the Breretons, see NA, E 101/419/20; NA, E 101/420/1, no. 8; E 101/420/11, fo. 13v; NA, C 1/952/65–8; NA, C 78/2/65; *PPE, Henry*, p. 74; Sylvester (1959), pp. 139–40; Thornton (2000), pp. 160–1; Ives (1976), pp. 1–55.

17 NA, E 101/420/11, fo. 27v; *LP*, IV, ii, nos. 4422, 4779, 4993 (15).

18 BAV, MS Vat.lat.3731.pt.A, fo. 8; Savage (1949), pp. 39–40.

19 *LP*, V, no. 11 (wrongly dated in *LP*); NA, E150/981/7; NA, C 142/48/107; NA, C 142/48/70.

20 Savage (1949), pp. 39–40.

21 Knowles (1958), pp. 92–6; NA, SP 1/48, fo. 199; Savage (1949), p. 45.

22 Knowles (1958), pp. 94–5.

23 *St. Pap.*, I, p. 300.

24 Ibid., pp. 313–16, and p. 314, n. 1; *LP*, IV, ii, nos. 4476, 4488, 4497, 4549.

25 *St. Pap.*, I, p. 307; Fiddes (1724), p. 399.

26 *St. Pap.*, VII, pp. 77–9; *LP*, IV, ii, no. 4440; Gairdner (1897), pp. 7–8.

27 Fiddes (1724), Appendix, pp. 174, 176.

28 Ibid., pp. 175–6; *St. Pap.*, I, pp. 316–17. To make matters worse for Wolsey, Henry humiliated him by reading aloud his blistering reprimand to Russell and Heneage before sending it.

29 Fiddes (1724), p. 399.

30 *Lisle Letters*, III, no. 719; ibid., V, no. 1466; *LP*, VI, no. 351 (p. 164); Starkey (1991a), pp. 44–5, 83.

31 Fiddes (1724), Appendix, p. 255. The original is BL, Cotton MS, Otho C.X, fo. 220.

32 *Ambassades* (1905), no. 132 (p. 363); *St. Pap.*, I, pp. 323–5; *LP*, IV, ii, no. 4649 (wrongly dated).

33 *Ambassades* (1905), no. 132 (pp. 363–5).

34 *LP*, IV, ii, nos. 4379, 4401, 4533.

35 BL, Cotton MS, Vitellius B.XII, fo. 4; Burnet (1820), I, i, pp. 86–7; Savage (1949), pp. 50–1.

36 NA, SP 1/50, fo. 1; BL, Cotton MS, Vespasian F.III, fo. 34 (formerly fo. 32); NA, E/41/121.

37 See, for instance, Fletcher (2012), p. 43.

38 BL, Cotton MS, Vespasian F.III, fo. 34 (formerly fo. 32).

39 *CW*, VI. i, pp. 269–70, 379–99; *LP*, IV, ii, no. 4073; Brigden (1989), pp. 115–16, 128, 161.

40 *LP*, IV, ii, no. 4656 (2); *Ambassades* (1905), no. 140 (pp. 381–2, 386–7); *St. Pap.*, VII, pp. 93–4; *LP*, IV, ii, no. 4735.

41 *LP*, IV, ii, nos. 4735, 4736.

42 *Ambassades* (1905), no. 151; *CSPSp*, III, ii, no. 541.

43 Savage (1949), pp. 36–7.

44 Since both of Anne's letters have disappeared, their contents must be inferred from the king's replies.

45 *Ambassades* (1905), no. 152; *LP*, IV, ii, no. 4857; Ehses (1893) nos. 23, 29; Gairdner (1897), pp. 7–8; Scarisbrick (1968), pp. 212–13.

46 Ehses (1892), no. 29; *LP*, IV, ii, nos. 4857–8.

47 Starkey (2004), p. 338.

48 Savage (1949), p. 48.

49 Porcacchi (1571), fos. 20v–1v; *LP*, IV, ii, no. 4737.

15 WOLSEY'S NEMESIS

1 Knecht (1994), pp. 273–4, 278–9; Hall (1809), pp. 741–8; *Ambassades* (1905), no. 109; *LP*, IV, ii, nos. 3453, 3455, 3597, 3827, 3844, 4376–8, 4386–7; Gunn and Lindley (1991), pp. 160–77; Guy (2019), pp. 19–31.

2 *Ambassades* (1905), nos. 95–100, 105, 109; *LP*, IV, iii, no. 5515.

3 *LP*, IV, ii, nos. 4228, 4255, 4325, 4644, 4663, 4679, 4705, 4714.

4 Porcacchi (1571), fos. 20v–1v; *LP*, IV, ii, no. 4737.

5 *LP*, IV, ii, no. 4856; *CSPSp*, III, ii, no. 586 (pp. 840–1). The legality of this solution, without linked annulment proceedings, was dubious, and Campeggi knew it, but it wasted time.

6 *CSPSp*, III, ii, no. 644 (p. 973); *LP*, IV, iii, nos. 5154, 5177, 5301, 5376, 5468, 5469 and Appendix no. 211; Pocock (1870), II, p. 431; Kelly (1976), pp. 62–7.

7 *CSPSp*, IV, i, no. 571.

8 Theiner (1864), no. 1010 (pp. 573–4); *LP*, IV, ii, no. 4875; *CSPV*, IV, no. 860; *CSPSp*, III, ii, no. 586 (pp. 842–3).

9 *LP*, IV, ii, no. 4881.

10 *Ambassades* (1905), no. 163 (pp. 463–4); Hall (1809), pp. 754–5; *CSPSp*, III, ii, no. 586.

11 NA, OBS 1419; *CSPSp*, III, ii, no. 586 (p. 846). Whether Henry travelled the 20 miles or so to Hever and back each day from Beddington, or whether Anne moved closer to him, is uncertain. De Mendoza believed Anne moved to a location within 5 miles of Beddington. See *CSPSp*, III, ii, no. 586 (p. 846).

12 *OED*, s.v. 'elengenesse'. See also Starkey (2004), pp. 339–40.

13 Savage wrongly transcribes 'am coming' as 'was coming'.

14 Savage (1949), p. 47; BAV, MS Vat.Lat.3731.pt.A, fo. 15; Starkey (2004), pp. 339–40. The original manuscript also shows that the word 'evenings' is definitely plural, and not singular as rendered in printed editions.

15 Savage (1949), p. 37.

16 *Ambassades* (1905), no. 171; *LP*, IV, ii, no. 5016.

17 *Ambassades* (1905), no. 178; *LP*, IV, ii, no. 5063.

18 *LP*, IV, ii, nos. 5008, 5013, 5042, 5061, 5073; *LP*, IV, iii, nos. 5151–2, 5123, 5230, 5315, 5370, 5481, 5519; *St. Pap.*, VII, pp. 148–51, 166–70.

19 *LP*, IV, ii, nos. 4977–79, 5014. Although also appointed to assist Bryan, William Benet and William Knight were ordered to remain in France and did not advance beyond Lyon.

20 Bryan's warning is later referenced by the Duke of Suffolk and was probably in a lost letter to Henry from Chambéry: *St. Pap.*, VII, pp. 143, 182.

21 *St. Pap.*, VII, pp. 148–51.

22 Brigden (2012), p. 118.

23 *St. Pap.*, VII, p. 272; Brigden (2012), pp. 118–19. According to George Wyatt, courtesans were on tap in the Vatican. When his grandfather and Sir John Russell had been in Rome, 'a chief favourite of his Holiness' had come to greet them and offered them 'two of the most choice of courtesans ... to refresh them withal after their long journey and absence from their wives, with a plenary dispensation verbal for that should be done by them.' See Wyatt (1968), p. 27.

24 *St. Pap.*, VII, p. 169.

25 Ibid., pp. 145–7; *Ambassades* (1905), no. 188 (p. 543).

26 NA, SP 1/53, fos. 149–50.

27 *St. Pap.*, VII, p. 167; *LP*, IV, iii, no. 5179.

28 *St. Pap.*, VII, p. 169.

29 Ibid., p. 167.

30 NA, SP 1/53, fo. 243.

31 *Du Bellay*, I, no. 7 *bis* (p. 22); Sylvester (1959), pp. 43–4.

32 *Du Bellay*, I, nos. 4, 7, 15, 17 (p. 58), 22; *St. Pap.*, VII, pp. 182–4; *LP*, IV, iii, nos. 5582, 5597, 5675, 5701.

33 TCC, MS B.15.19, now digitised at https://mss-cat.trin.cam.ac.uk/Manuscript/B.15.19; Surtz and Murphy (1988), pp. x–xv.

34 *Du Bellay*, I, no. 11; *LP*, IV, iii, no. 5679. Henry did have a point. So hazardous was it to pass between the twenty stone pillars of the bridge when the tide was at its height that passengers routinely disembarked, many walking to the other side of the bridge before resuming their journey.

35 Pocock (1870), II, pp. 609–13; *LP*, IV, iii, no. 5694; Kelly (1976), pp. 77–9. Lists of the documents filed can be found in *LP*, IV, iii, no. 5768 (1–2).

36 Sylvester (1959), pp. 80–2.

37 Ibid., p. 82; *LP*, IV, iii, no. 5702.

38 *LP*, IV, iii, nos. 5695, 5702, 5713, 5716, 5733; Sylvester (1959), pp. 82–5.

39 *LP*, IV, iii, no. 5732; Rex (1991), pp. 170–9.

40 BL, Cotton MS, Vitellius B. XII, fos. 109–24.

41 BL, Cotton MS, Vitellius B. XII, fos. 73–7; 83–8; BL, Cotton MS, Appendix XXVII, fos. 58–82v; *LP*, IV iii, nos. 5774 (1–17), 5778; Herbert of Cherbury (1649), pp. 242–5.

42 BL, Cotton MS, Vitellius B.XII, fo. 197v; *LP*, IV, iii, nos. 5581–2, 5700, 5704, 5710–11, 5744; *St. Pap.*, VII, pp. 188–90; Richardson

(1995), pp. 192–3. In a moment of desperation, Wolsey scribbled a note to the pope's secretary, boasting that he could mediate in the talks to Clement's advantage, but only if the pope did not revoke Henry's case. To Casali he was more direct, admitting that he was finished if the pope did revoke it.

43 *CSPSp*, IV, nos. 36, 56; Knecht (1994), pp. 279–82; Parker (2019), pp. 184–7.

44 *CSPSp*, IV, nos. 54, 57.

45 *LP*, VIII, no. 48 (p. 15).

46 *LP*, IV, iii, no. 5791; Sylvester (1959), p. 90; Hall (1809), p. 758.

47 *LP*, IV, iii, nos. 5741, 5733, 5829–30, 5832–3, 5840; *Du Bellay*, I, no. 16; *St. Pap.*, I, pp. 342–3.

48 BL, Lansdowne MS 1, fo. 210; Sylvester (1959), p. 92; Fiddes (1724), p. 493; *CSPSp*, IV, i, no. 160 (p. 234).

49 Guy (1980), pp. 106–8, 206–7.

50 *CSPSp*, IV, i, no. 160 (pp. 222–34).

51 Sylvester (1959), pp. 92–7; Hall (1809), p. 759; Ellis, 1st Series, I, pp. 307–10. George Boleyn escorted Campeggi to Dover and perhaps was responsible for the order for his luggage to be searched. See NA, E 101/420/11, fo. 81; *LP*, IV, iii, no. 6016.

52 *LP*, IV, iii, nos. 6017, 6025, 6030, 6035; *St. Pap.*, I, pp. 347–8; NA, C 54/398; *Du Bellay*, I, nos. 44, 46; Guy (1980), pp. 31–2, 97–104. There is confusion as to the date Wolsey lost the Chancellorship. The Close Roll gives it as the 17th.

53 Sylvester (1959), pp. 101–2; *Du Bellay*, I, no. 46; *St. Pap.*, I, pp. 348–9.

54 *Du Bellay*, I, no. 43; *CSPSp*, IV, i, no. 135; Sylvester (1959), p. 137.

55 *LP*, IV, iii, no. 6151; Sylvester (1959), pp. 120–1; Fiddes (1724), Appendix, p. 258.

56 NA, SP 1/55, fo. 21; *LP*, IV, iii, nos. 5815 (27, 28), 5906 (4), 6088, 6115; *LJ* (1767–1846), I, p. clxxxviii; *St. Pap.*, I, p. 355.

57 Fiddes (1724), p. 509, and Appendix, pp. 259–60; *LP*, IV, iii, nos. 6213–14.

58 BNF, MS FF 3014, fos. 78–81v; Sylvester (1959), pp. 127, 132–44; *LP*, IV, iii, nos. 6199, 6214, 6220, 6273, 6294–5, 6344.

59 Sylvester (1959), pp. 152–7; Hall (1809), pp. 773–4; *LP*, IV, iii, no. 6738; Hammond (1975), pp. 215–35.

60 Sylvester (1959), pp. 168–82; Gardiner (1984), pp. 99–107; *LP*, IV, iii, no. 6738; *CSPV*, IV, nos. 631–2, 637; *CSPSp*, IV, i, no. 492 (pp. 804–5); *CSPM*, I, no. 838.

16 THE DURHAM HOUSE GROUP

1 Strype (1822), I, ii, pp. 461–2.
2 *CSPSp*, IV, ii, no. 995 (p. 512); *LP*, V, no. 1316.
3 BNF, MS Clairambault 329, fo. 10; *Du Bellay*, I, no. 41 *bis*, *CSPSp*, IV, i, nos. 354 (p. 600), 422 (p. 710); *CSPSp*, IV, ii, nos. 765 (p. 214), 739 (p. 177); Gunn (1988), pp. 116–19.
4 *Du Bellay*, I, no. 41 *bis*.
5 Ibid.
6 Ibid., no. 46; *LP*, IV, iii, nos. 6026, 6199; *CSPSp*, IV, i, nos. 194 (pp. 303–4), 257; *LP*, V, no. 238; *CSPV*, IV, no. 664; Hall (1809), p. 786; Green and Thurley (1987), pp. 66–98; Colvin, Brown and Cooke (1963–82), IV, pp. 105, 241.
7 *LP*, X, no. 775 (1–4); Green and Thurley (1987), pp. 66–8, 73–6.
8 *CSPSp*, IV, ii, no. 720 (p. 154); *LP*, V, no. 238; NA, E 101/425/14; Green and Thurley (1987), pp. 66–7.
9 *LP*, IV, iii, nos. 6083, 6085, 6163 (1); *CSPSp*, IV, i, no. 232 (p. 366).
10 *LP*, IV, ii, no. 3937; Round (1886), p. 46; Ives (2004), pp. 35–6.
11 *CSPSp*, IV, i, no. 232 (p. 366).
12 Ibid., no. 224 (pp. 351–2).
13 Ibid., no. 241 (pp. 385–6); Hall (1809), p. 768.
14 NA, E 101/418/1 (unfoliated); *PPE, Henry*, pp. 4, 13, 14, 44, 45, 47, 50, 72, 88, 90, 97, 101, 108, 179, 183, 222, 223, 261. For the allocation of Scut to Anne, see NA, SP 1/103, fo. 321v.
15 V&A, LOAN:MET ANON.1–1984. Another example was sold at Dix Noonan Webb auctioneers on 17 March 2020.
16 *Lisle Letters*, I, pp. 332–3.
17 *PPE, Henry*, pp. 10, 48, 61, 88, 97, 98, 111, 113, 123, 128, 131, 179, 216, 221, 245, 254.
18 NA, SP 1/66, fos. 26v, 27v–32; *LP*, V, no. 276.
19 NA, SP 1/58, fo. 215; Hall (1809), p. 791; Waterton (1879), pp. 269–72. The brooch may have been recycled from a similar piece with a ruby, three diamonds and three pearls seized from Wolsey and recorded in the inventory of his jewel chest.

20 *Narratives* (1859), pp. 240–2; MacCulloch (1996), pp. 44–7. Cranmer may well have been prompted by Robert Wakefield, whom he almost certainly knew and who had already written to Henry offering to 'defend your cause or question in all the universities in Christendom'. See Wakefield (c.1534a), sig. P4.

21 *Narratives* (1859), pp. 242–3.

22 The supervisory role of Thomas Boleyn can be seen from NA, SP 1/57, fo. 253, a letter in his unmistakable scribbling hand sent to one of the team members in Rome. Unfortunately, most of it is written in a code which has so far defied decipherment. The letter is misattributed to George Boleyn, whose hand is much neater and more Francophile. See *LP*, IV, iii, no. 6539. A genuine example of George's hand is SP 3/7, fo. 9.

23 NA, E 101/420/11, fos. 60v, 75; BNF, MS FF 3005, fo. 23; *LP*, IV, iii, no. 6147.

24 *St. Pap.*, VII, pp. 219–24.

25 For Cranmer's role, see *Narratives* (1859), p. 243; NA, SP 1/56, fo. 137; NA, E 101/420/11, fos. 76v, 133. Unlike the others, he did not return until 23 October 1530, the date his expenses payments ceased, since he carried on to Rome, where he was granted the title of Penitentiary-General of England by the pope and assisted Stokesley's team of agents rounding up university opinions.

26 Parker (2019), pp. 188–91.

27 NA, SP 1/56, fos. 125–137v; *LP*, IV, iii, nos. 6111, 6254, 6285, 6290, 6293, 6307; *St. Pap.*, VII, pp. 234–5.

28 *St. Pap.*, VII, pp. 234–5; *LP*, IV, iii, nos. 6256, 6293. For the preparations, see *LP*, IV, iii, nos. 6227, 6253–4; *CSPSp*, IV, i, no. 250 (p. 422); NA, E 101/420/11, fos. 76v, 131.

29 *St. Pap.*, VII, pp. 227–9; *CAF*, I, no. 3594; *CAF*, VIII, p. 467 (itinerary, not numbered).

30 *St. Pap.*, VII, pp. 235–8; *LP*, IV, iii, nos. 6321, 6411, 6449, 6455, 6562–5, 6592, 6755; NA, E 101/420/11, fo. 101v; Knecht (1994), pp. 293–4; MacCulloch (1996), p. 50.

31 *LP*, IV, iii, nos. 6149–50, 6153, 6156, 6165, 6170, 6173–4, 6192–4, 6209, 6229, 6235, 6238, 6250–1, 6280, 6354, 6375, 6406, 6423, 6425, 6445, 6569, 6607, 6758; Fletcher (2012), pp. 126–7, 142–3.

32 Le Grand (1688), III, pp. 507–8; *LP*, IV, iii, nos. 5426, 6370–1, 6400, 6448, 6481, 6491, 6493–4, 6497, 6625, 6628–9, 6631–2, 6633, 6636,

6639, 6641; *CSPSp.*, IV, i, nos. 430, 432; Surtz and Murphy (1988), pp. xxi–xxv. Verdicts from Pavia and Ferrara supported Henry's case, even though for some unknown reason he chose not to publish those decisions, when the other eight were printed in 1531.

33 BL, Cotton MS, Cleopatra E.VI, fos. 16–135; Nicholson (1988), pp. 19–30.

34 BL, Cotton MS, Cleopatra E.VI, fos. 20, 21v, 23, 28v, 29, 31v, 32, 33v, 34, 37v, 38, 39v, 41, 45, 45v, 49v, 53v, 64v, 97v, 98v, 102v, 105, 105v, 106v, 107; *St. Pap.*, VII, p. 271.

35 Guy (1980), pp. 113–29; Brigden (1989), pp. 174–8, 182; Palmer (2002), pp. 173–208. George Robinson and Robert Packington led the secret cell: NA, C 1/772/57, C 1/565/74–81, C 1/669/4–5, C 1/673/50, C 1/880/51–2, C 1/830/23, C 1/1153/42–3; NA, PROB 11/27/46; Hall (1809), pp. 764–8; Lehmberg (1970), pp. 76–104.

36 Rogers (1961), p. 210.

37 AGS, PTR/LEG. 53/109; Bradford (1850), pp. 299–300; *LP*, IV, iii, no. 6199; *LP*, V, no. 120; *CSPV*, IV, no. 668; Guy (1980), p. 139; Rex (1991), pp. 176–80.

38 *CSPSp*, IV, i, no. 302; *CSPSp*, IV, ii, no. 765.

39 *LP*, IV, iii, no. 6661; *CSPSp*, IV, i, no. 446. Although dated 2 October 1530, the report refers to a wedding much earlier in the year.

40 *LP*, IV, iii, no. 6638; Scarisbrick (1968), pp. 260–2.

41 NA, SP 1/57, fo. 130; *CSPV*, IV, no. 584.

17 A BREAKTHROUGH AT LAST?

1 Higman (1983), pp. 91–111; Higman (1984), pp. 11–56; Higman (2016), pp. 17–67.

2 The combined total represents almost du Bois's entire theological output in French: Carley (2004a), pp. 131–46; Carley (2004b), pp. 124–33; Carley (2000), pp. lvii–lviii.

3 Carley (2004a), pp. 131–46; Carley (2000), p. 266. Other books once belonging to Anne were brought from Windsor to the Jewel House in the Tower after Henry's death. Some were elaborately bound in crimson velvet or cloth of silver, which fits perfectly with the accounts of Cornelius Hayes, who fulfilled orders for her, either bookbinding or making gold clasps for books and 'garnishing' them with silver and gilt or crown gold. See NA, SP 1/66, fos. 27v–8.

4 In France, such books were relatively easy to come by despite the
   efforts of the Sorbonne. Besides Louise of Savoy and Marguerite of
   Angoulême, Francis protected Lefèvre and appointed him as a tutor
   to the younger royal children after Queen Claude's death. See Heller
   (1972), pp. 42–77.

5 BL, C.37.a.22(6); Reid (2001), pp. 283, 445–7.

6 Carley (2004a), p. 141.

7 Christie's sale, London, 26 November 1997, lot. 3. The inscription
   appears on fo. 99v. The format of Anne's name makes it certain that
   her signature preceded December 1529, when her father would be
   ennobled as an earl and she became the 'Lady Anne Rochford'.

8 A sales technique first employed by Johann Fust and Johann Gutenberg
   in Mainz for Bibles intended for monastic use, printing on vellum
   offered clients seeking a fine manuscript the opportunity to acquire
   works at more modest expense. Cheap copies were printed on paper.

9 Hever Castle, *Hore beate Marie virginis ad usum ... Sarum*, facing
   sig. [E iv]. See McCaffrey (2021a), at https://www.the-tls.co.uk/
   articles/inscriptions-discovered-in-a-book-owned-by-anne-bol
   eyn-essay-kate-e-mccaffrey. As with her earlier inscription, the form
   of Anne's name and of the lettering makes clear that her verse was
   added before 1529. The Presentation in the Temple may have been
   one of her favourite images, as a full-page depiction of this same
   scene, gloriously gilded, is in her Bruges manuscript.

10 PML, Accession no. 1034, sold at Sotheby's in 1897 for £50.
   The attribution to Katherine comes from the partially legible
   inscription: 'Thys boke was good quen[–] kat[–]in boke / and she
   gave yt to [–]g Coke hir woman / And [–] gave yt Betryce Ogle
   hyr dowghter / [and] she gave yt to Ri[–] Ogle hyr husband ...'
   The first of the added leaves is at the front, the second at the back.
   A comparable copy, lacking added leaves, is TCC, C.30.9. See also
   McCaffrey (2021b), at https://www.historyextra.com/period/tudor/
   team-catherine-team-anne-why-choose.

11 J. Paul Getty Collection, Wormsley; previously Sotheby's sale,
   London, 7 December 1982, lot 62; on public display in 2000 in the
   Morgan Library.

12 *Du Bellay*, I, no. 65 (p. 142).

13 Locke's daughter Rose later recounted: 'I remember that I have heard
   my father say that when he was a young merchant and used to go

beyond sea, Queen Anne Boleyn ... caused him to get her the Gospels and Epistles written in parchment in French together with the psalms.' BL, Additional MS 43,827, fo. 2; Dowling and Shakespeare (1982), p. 97; Dowling (1984), pp. 32–3, 40; Dowling (1990), p. 28; Sutton (2005), p. 390.

14 Latymer is not to be confused with the more famous Hugh Latimer. Dowling (1990), pp. 23–65, 501–3; *LP*, IV, iii, no. 6162. The general assumption is the chronicle was meant as a gift for Elizabeth I. We cannot be sure that she ever received or read it. If aiming for preferment, he succeeded, becoming Dean of Peterborough, a canon of Westminster and eventually Elizabeth's own chaplain and clerk of her closet; equally he may have wanted to revive Anne's name and counter Catholic propaganda.

15 BL, Royal MS, 20 B.XVII, fo. 1; Carley (1998), p. 271; Taylor (2012), p. 17 and n. 10; Dowling (1990), p. 63; Dowling (1984), p. 33.

16 So impressed by Lull's book was George, he commissioned Thomas Wall, one of the heralds, to make an English translation for Henry. A rough draft can still be read in the National Archives in Kew. See NA, SP 9/31/2, fos. 1–33; NLS, MS Adv.31.1.9; Lull (2015), pp. 8–13; Carley (2000), p. 208; Carley (2004b), p. 133; Pugh (2005), pp. 380–6.

17 Walter (1848), pp. 174–8.

18 *Narratives* (1859), pp. 52–7; Singer (1827), pp. 438–41: Dowling (1984), pp. 36–7; *Lisle Letters*, I, pp. 518–19. The story was first reported by John Louth, a graduate of Corpus Christi College, Cambridge, who spent the earlier part of his career in the Zouche household. In 1579, he gave a written report to the Protestant martyrologist, John Foxe.

19 Foxe (1843–9), IV, pp. 656–8.

20 Strype (1822), I, ii, pp. 63–5; NA, STAC 2/31/fragments; BL, Cotton MS, Cleopatra E.V, fo. 350v; Brigden (1989), pp. 115, 128; Guy (1980), p. 108; Dowling (1984), p. 43; *ODNB*, s.v. 'Fish, Simon'. Another account claims it was two London merchants, George Elyot and George Robinson, not Anne, who showed their copy of the *Supplication* to the king, see Foxe (1843–9), IV, p. 658.

21 *CSPSp*, IV, i, nos. 354, 366; Sylvester (1959), pp. 139–40; Richardson (2008), pp. 99–102.

22 Originally kept in a coffer covered with green velvet and secured with silver and gilt bands and a padlock, the petition, complete with 81 of the original 83 seals, was rediscovered in 1926 in the Vatican

archives, stored under a chair. See AAV, Archivum Arcis, Arm. I–
XVIII, 4098A; NA, SP 1–57, fos. 194–204; *LP*, IV, iii, nos. 6489,
6513; *CSPSp*, IV, i, nos. 354, 366, 460 (p. 762); Pocock (1870), I,
pp. 429–33; *PPE, Henry*, p. 51; Sylvester (1959), pp. 139–40.

23 Pocock (1870), I, pp. 434–7; *TRP* (1964–69), I, no. 130; Hall (1809),
pp. 772–3; *CSPSp*, IV, i, no. 433; Guy (1982), pp. 482–8.

24 *St. Pap.*, VII, pp. 211–15, 288–92; *LP*, IV, iii, nos. 6665, 6675, 6733;
Hall (1809), p. 772; Richardson (2008), pp. 100–1.

25 For the ebbs and flows of policy and the battle of words around this
time, see *St. Pap.*, VII, pp. 261–6, 269–71; *LP*, IV, iii, nos. 6667,
6705, 6739, 6759 and Appendix no. 262; *CSPSp*, IV, i, nos. 429, 433,
445, 460; Theiner (1864), no. 1022.

26 *CSPSp*, IV, i, nos. 433, 492.

27 Ibid., nos. 509 (p. 819), 547 (p. 852); *CSPSp*, IV, ii, no. 586; Friedmann
(1884), I, p. 128, nn. 2–3.

28 *LP*, V, no. 24; J. Paul Getty Collection, Wormsley, previously
Sotheby's sale, London, 7 December 1982, lot 62. For another
example, see BL, Harleian MS 6561, fo. 2r.

29 Dreux du Radier (1808), IV, pp. 93–5; Friedmann (1884), I, pp. 37–8.

30 *CSPSp*, IV, i, no. 509; *CSPSp*, IV, ii, no. 584; *LP*, V, no. 24.

31 *PPE, Henry*, p. 101; NA, E 101/420/11, fos. 145–9; *CSPSp*, IV, ii, nos.
589 (p. 12), 683, 720 (p. 153); *LP*, V, no. 70.

32 *LP*, V, nos. 61, 64, 120, 216; *CSPSp*, IV, ii, nos. 608, 610, 612; 615;
CAF, IX, p. 25; Friedmann (1884), I, p. 127 and n. 1.

33 *PPE, Henry*, pp. 17, 36, 72, 98, 131, 144; *LP*, V, no. 238; *CSPSp*, IV, ii,
no. 720 (p. 154).

34 *LP*, V, no. 45; Nicholson (1988), pp. 23–5.

35 Guy (1982), pp. 488–500.

36 NA, E 36/256, fos. 155, 161; MacCulloch (2018), pp. 22–35. My thanks
to Alexander Lee for discussing the kinds of experiences Cromwell
would have enjoyed in Florence.

37 Lehmberg (1970), pp. 114–15; MacCulloch (2018), pp. 9–128.

38 NA, SP 6/2, fos. 81–3; Pocock (1870), II, pp. 100–3; Haas (1980),
pp. 317–25. A fragment of a third tract is NA, SP 1/105, fos. 53–6.

39 NA, SP 6/2, fos. 82, 83.

40 *LP*, V, nos. 65, 153, 201, 246, 248, 303; MacCulloch (2018), pp. 139–41.

41 *LP*, IV, iii, no. 6627; *LP*, V, no. 287 (p. 138); *CSPSp*, IV, ii, no. 888
(p. 367); Robinson (1846–47), II, pp. 554–7; McEntegart (2002),
pp. 38–41; MacCulloch (1996), pp. 60–6.

42 *LP*, V, no. 171; Hall (1809), pp. 775–80; BL, C.37.f.2; Surtz and
Murphy (1988), pp. iii–xxxvi, 2–277; Guy (1980), pp. 150–65.

43 *LP*, V, no. 287.

44 Ibid., nos. 216, 238, 287; *CSPSp*, IV, ii, no. 720.

45 *LP*, V, no. 287. Chapuys claims that Guildford resigned there and
then. In fact, he withdrew from court for a while to cool his temper
but would return by November. When he died in May 1532, Henry
gave most of his plate to Anne.

46 Hall (1809), p. 781; *LP*, V, no. 308; *CSPSp*, IV, ii, no. 753; NA,
OBS 1419.

47 *LP*, V, nos. 340, 375, 401; BL, Additional MS 71,009, fo. 58v; *CSPSp*,
IV, ii, nos. 765, 778, 786; Cox (1846), p. 309.

48 Hall (1809), p. 781; *LP*, V, no. 361.

18 THE FALCON ASCENDANT

1 *CSPSp*, IV, ii, no. 802 (p. 254); *LP*, V, no. 488; Richardson (1995),
pp. 208–16; Richardson (2008), pp. 102–3.

2 *CAF*, II, no. 4266; *CAF*, VII, no. 29132; *CAF*, IX, p. 25; *CSPSp*, IV,
ii, no. 814 (p. 272); *CSPV*, IV, no. 701.

3 *CSPV*, IV, no. 701; *LP*, V, no. 548.

4 BNF, MS Dupuy 547, fo. 220; Camusat, II, fos. 78v–9; *LP*, V, nos.
614, 883.

5 BNF, MS FF 7856, p. 925; *CAF*, IX, p. 25; *CSPSp*, IV, i, no. 555
(p. 862), calendared in the wrong year; *LP*, V, nos. 614, 696.

6 Hall (1809), p. 784; *PPE, Henry*, pp. 189, 195, 209, 210–11.

7 NA, E 101/420/15; *CSPSp*, IV, ii, no. 880 (p. 354); *LP*, V, no. 696.

8 BNF, MS Dupuy 547, fo. 50; NA, SP 2/N, fos. 148–54, 155–7; Pocock
(1870), II, pp. 155–73, 184–9, 190–206; *LP*, V, nos. 706, 805, 807;
Richardson (2008), pp. 102–3.

9 Hall (1809), p. 784; Lehmberg (1970), pp. 131–60; Guy (1980),
pp. 164–74, 180–5; MacCulloch (2018), pp. 157–71.

10 NA, SP 6/1, fos. 86–95; Pocock (1870), II, pp. 257–8; Hall (1809),
pp. 784–5; *LP*, V, nos. 1013, 1016 (1–5), 1017–21, 1023 (1), 1025, 1046,
1075; Guy (1980), pp. 189–201.

11 Pocock (1870), II, pp. 169–73, 184–9, 190–206; Richardson (2008), pp. 102–3.

12 BNF, MS Dupuy 547, fos. 75–8; ANF, AE/III/31; Camusat, II, fos. 84–8, 93; CADMA, MS 8CP/002, fos. 92–103, with subsidiary treaties at fos. 92–103, 104–18, 119–20; *CAF*, II, nos. 4565, 4573, 4670; Du Bellay and Du Bellay (1908–19), II, p. 144; *CSPV*, IV, nos. 765, 778; Richardson (2008), pp. 103–4.

13 *LP*, V, nos. 1046, 1127, 1520, 1536; *LP*, VI, no. 1253, 1522; Mattingly (1950), pp. 269–70.

14 *CSPSp*, IV, ii, no. 934; *LP*, V, no. 941; for the original French, see Friedmann (1884), I, p. 157, n. 2.

15 Bodleian, Tanner 186; Pocock (1870), II, pp. 385–421; Rex (2003), pp. 16–27; Elton (1972), pp. 177–80; Surtz and Murphy (1988), pp. xxxiii–xxxvi; Nicholson (1988), pp. 20–1.

16 *CSPSp*, IV, ii, no. 1077 (original French on p. 699); Friedmann (1884), I, p. 157, n. 3; Parker (2019), pp. 226–30.

17 *LP*, V, no. 941 (p. 442); Nott (1816), I, p. xxiii; *CSPSp*, IV, ii, no. 1077 (original French on p. 699); *LP*, VI, no. 556 (p. 243).

18 *LP*, V, no. 941; Sanuto (1824–84), LVI, cols 287–8.

19 *LP*, IV, iii, no. 5920; BL, Cotton MS, Otho C.X, fo. 224; LPL, MS 695, fo. 73; Friedmann (1884), I, pp. 159–61; Burnet (1820), III, ii, p. 152; *CPR, Edward VI*, IV, p. 407; Ives (2004), p. 166.

20 *LP*, IV, iii, no. 6542 (23); *LP*, V, nos. 1139 (32), 1207 (7); Colvin, Brown and Cook (1963–82), IV, pp. 147–9; Foister (2012), pp. 291–3. One of Toto's specialisms was decorative 'antique work', which at Anne's request he applied to the 'outer wall' and 'certain chimneys', as he did later at Hampton Court and Whitehall. He was also paid for 'new painting and gilding certain antique heads' at Hanworth, possibly including terracotta roundels with classical busts as their centrepiece.

21 NA, E 101/418/1 (unfoliated).

22 BNF, MS Dupuy 547, fo. 131; BNF, MS Dupuy 726, fo. 58; Le Grand (1688), III, pp. 556–7, misleadingly calendared in *LP*, V, no. 1187, where the wrong du Bellay is also named; *CSPV*, IV, no. 808; *CSPSp*, IV, ii, no. 1003 (p. 525).

23 BNF, MS Dupuy 726, fo. 60; *Du Bellay*, I, no. 136; Du Bellay and Du Bellay (1908–19), II, pp. 144–6; *CAF*, IX, p. 26; *CSPSp*, IV, ii,

nos. 993, 995; *CSPV*, V, no. 1032; *PPE, Henry*, p. 221; Richardson (2008), p. 105.

24 *CSPSp*, IV, ii, no. 995; *Lisle Letters*, I, no. xxxii (p. 332). As the letter is dated 'from Waltham this Monday', it must have been written on 8 July 1532. The alternative is 9 August 1529, which is too early. Ives's suggestion of 8 August 1532 is mistaken. It is neither a Monday, nor were Henry and Anne in Waltham then: they had already reached Woodstock. See NA, OBS 1419; *PPE, Henry*, pp. 241–5; Ives (2004), p. 389, n. 35.

25 *PPE, Henry*, p. 245.

26 Hall (1809), p. 790; BL, Harleian MS 303, fos. 1–3; *LP*, V, no. 1370 (1–3).

27 Sanuto (1824–84), LVII, cols 23–4.

28 Hall (1809), p. 790; Sanuto (1824–84), LVII, cols 23–4; *CSPV*, IV, no. 802; *CSPSp*, IV, ii, no. 993 (p. 508); *LP*, V, nos. 1274 (3, 6), 1292.

29 BL, Harleian MS 303, fo. 1; Camden (1870), pp. 372–3. Another example, carved in oak, and believed to be a stray from Hampton Court was offered in Bonham's sale, Oxford, 18 September 2019, lot 408, where it is fully described in the catalogue. After a somewhat regrettable restoration, it is on display in Hampton Court. For the music manuscript, see Urkevich (1997), pp. 220–1, which supersedes Lowinski (1969–70), p. 15.

30 Hall (1809), p. 790; *CSPSp*, IV, ii, no. 993; *CSPV*, IV, no. 802.

31 Hall (1809), p. 790; Ellis, 3rd Series, II, pp. 196–9; Rex (2003), pp. 23–5.

32 BNF, MS Dupuy 547, fos. 131–2; Hamy (1898), pp. xxvi–xxix, xxxi–xxxviii, xlv–lix; *LP*, V, nos. 1256, 1308, 1373; Camusat, II, fos. 105–6; Richardson (1995), pp. 218–19.

33 NA, E 101/421/5 (unfoliated); BL, Royal MS, 7 C.XVI, fos. 41–6, especially fos. 41r–v; *LP*, V, nos. 1298–9, 1376, 1377, 1485; Camusat, II, fo. 108v.

34 *CSPSp*, IV, ii, nos. 802 (p. 254, where calendared in the wrong year), 1003 (pp. 524–5); *LP*, IV, iii, no. 6072 (18); *LP*, V, no. 1377; NA, E 101/421/3; NA, E 101/421/7.

35 Le Grand (1688), III, pp. 556–7 (wrongly attributed to Jean du Bellay in *LP*, V, no. 1187); Hamy (1898), pp. ix–xii, 143–4; *LP*, V, no. 1377 (p. 592); *CSPSp*, IV, ii, nos. 993, 995, 1003 (p. 528); Sanuto (1824–84), 57, cols 293–6; *CSPV*, IV, nos. 802, 822 (wrongly numbered 823).

36 Hall (1809), p. 790; *Tudor Tracts* (1903), p. 4; *CSPV*, IV, pp. xvi–xvii, and no. 824; *PPE, Henry*, p. 267.

37 Hall (1809), pp. 791–2; *Tudor Tracts* (1903), pp. 5–6; Sanuto (1824–84), 57, cols 294–5; Hamy (1898), p. clxxvi; Camusat, II, fos. 106–7; *CSPV*, IV, nos. 822, 824; Richardson (1995), p. 221. For Turquet, see ANF, MC/ET/XIX/167; *CAF*, II, nos. 5252, 7255; *CAF*, VI, no. 21,085; *CAF*, VII, no. 28,852.

38 Hall (1809), pp. 792–3; *Tudor Tracts* (1903), pp. 6–7; Camusat, II, fos. 107–8; *LP*, V, no. 1538; NA, SP 1/77, fo. 50.

39 Hall (1809), pp. 793–4; *Tudor Tracts* (1903), p. 7; Hamy (1898), pp. clxxvii–clxxxviii.

40 Hall (1809), p. 794; *Tudor Tracts* (1903), p. 7.

41 Hall (1809), p. 794; *PPE, Henry*, p. 273.

42 MacCulloch (1996), pp. 76–8.

19 THE MARRIAGE

1 *PPE, Henry*, pp. 274, 275, 276, 277.

2 NA, E 101/420/15; *HC, 1509–1558*, II, p. 310; *PPE, Henry*, p. 197. A minor courtier, said to be 'a strong partisan' of Anne, Sir Nicholas Harvey had ridden in the lists at the Field of Cloth of Gold and was one of Henry's ambassadors to Germany and Brussels. See *LP*, IV, iii, no. 6511.

3 BL, Cotton MS, Vespasian F.XIII, fo. 198.

4 See above, p. 389.

5 BNF, MS Dupuy 547, fo. 182; Camusat, II, fos. 111v–15v; *LP*, VI, nos. 38, 64.

6 *CSPSp*, IV, ii, nos. 1033 (p. 566); *LP*, V, no. 1633.

7 *LP*, V, no. 1633; *LP*, VI, no. 5; Thurley (1993), pp. 33, 51; Colvin, Brown and Cook (1963–82), III, pp. 266–7; Keay (2001), pp. 28–49.

8 NA, SP 1/73, fos. 8–9; NA, SP 2/N, fos. 1–5; NA, E 101/421/9 (unfoliated); *LP*, V, no. 1685; *LP*, VI, no. 32 (not always accurately calendared); Hayward (2005), p. 127. Boleyn family members or retainers given generous gifts of plate by Henry at New Year included her father, her brother George, her uncle James Boleyn, and her favourite aunt Lady Anne Shelton.

9 Camusat, II, fo. 8; *LP*, VI, no. 92; Hamy (1898), pp. cclxxx–cclxxxi, cclxxxv–ccxcvi; Richardson (2008), pp. 105–6.

10 MacCulloch (1996), Appendix 2.

11 Savage returned briefly to court to ride on a palfrey in Anne's coronation procession, but as an independent noblewoman. See BL, Additional MS 71,009, fo. 58v; Smyth (1883), II, pp. 252–3; Harris (2002), p. 226.

12 Harpsfield (1878), pp. 234–5; *LP*, VI, nos. 142 (p. 65), 391; *LP*, VIII, no. 121; Stow (1631), p. 562 (entry not found in the 1580 edition); Harris (1997), pp. 215–17; Nichols (2014), V, p. 3 and n. 2; Ives (1976), pp. 54, 243; Murray (2009), pp. 91–3; Holder (2011), pp. 160–9, 232. For Savage's first appearance as Anne's gentlewoman, see NA, E 101/420/15.

13 *LP*, VI, no. 73; Lehmberg (1970), pp. 161–71; Elton (1974–92), II, pp. 82–106; MacCulloch (2018), pp. 209–17.

14 *LP*, VI, nos. 142, 150, 180; *CSPSp*, IV, ii, no. 1047 (p. 599); Elton (1974–92), II, pp. 98–100; Friedmann (1884), I, pp. 188–9.

15 *CSPSp*, IV, ii, no. 1048; *LP*, VI, no. 160.

16 Friedmann (1884), I, p. 189, n. 2; ibid., p. 190, n.1. In both cases, the full French texts of Chapuys' dispatches are given. See also Brigden (2012), pp. 185, 610, n. 9.

17 *CSPSp*, IV, ii, no. 1055 (p. 617, n. 1 for the original French); *LP*, VI, no. 212.

18 Camusat, II, fos. 121v–2v; BNF, MS Dupuy 547, fo. 214; *LP*, VI, nos. 111, 160, 212; *CSPV*, IV, ii, no. 858; Hervey (1900), pp. 36–71; Hervey (1904), p. 413. Like de la Pommeraye, Henry gave de Dinteville apartments in Bridewell Palace and when he was invited to court, the royal bargemen were ordered to find him a boat, with eight or ten oarsmen, at the king's expense.

19 BNF, MS FF 23,515, fos. 85v–6; *LP*, VI, no. 1426 (p. 570).

20 BNF, MS Dupuy 547, fos. 205–8, 291–2; Camusat, II, fos. 123v–4v; Friedmann (1884), I, pp. 191–2.

21 BNF, MS Dupuy 547, fo. 214; Camusat, II, fos. 82v–3.

22 NA, E 101/421/9 (unfoliated).

23 NA, SP 1/75, fos. 21–2; *St. Pap.*, VII, p. 435, n. 1.

24 NA, SP 1/75, fos. 13–20v; *St. Pap.*, VII, pp. 427–37.

25 BNF, MS Dupuy 547, fos. 218–19, 221–2; Camusat, II, fos. 78, 79–80v.

26 BNF, MS Dupuy 547, fos. 221–2. See also Friedmann (1884), pp. 192–3.

27 BNF, MS Dupuy 547, fos. 218–19; BNF, MS FF 3005, fos. 42, 44.

28 *CAF*, II, no. 5628. Mackay (2018a), p. 181, posits a meeting between George and Marguerite d'Angoulême before he left France, but cites no evidence.

29 NA, SP 2/N, fos. 39–46 (part of the top of fo. 39 is torn off, missing words supplied from other copies); Nicholson (1988), pp. 19–30; Guy (1997), pp. 213–30.

30 *LP*, VI, nos. 235, 296; *CSPSp*, IV, ii, nos. 1056 (p. 624), 1057; *HC, 1509–1558*, I, pp. 10–11; Guy (1980), pp. 210–11; Hawkyard (2016), pp. 299–306.

31 Cox (1846), p. 460; Elton (1974–82), II, pp. 101–6; Lehmberg (1970), pp. 174–6; MacCulloch (1996), pp. 88–9.

32 Pocock (1870), II, pp. 446–59; *LP*, VI, nos. 317, 324; *CSPSp*, IV, ii, no. 1058; *CSPV*, IV, no. 870; Lehmberg (1970), pp. 176–8; MacCulloch (1996), p. 89.

33 *LP*, VI, nos. 324, 351, 391; *CSPSp*, IV, ii, nos. 1058, 1061–2; *CSPV*, IV, no. 870; Wriothesley (1875–77), I, p. 18. See also *LP*, VI, nos. 759, 760, 765.

34 *CSPSp*, IV, ii, no. 1061 (pp. 643–4); *LP*, VI, no. 351; *CSPV*, IV, no. 870; Wriothesley (1875–77), I, p. 17; Colvin, Brown and Crook (1963–82), IV, pp. 104–5.

35 *CSPSp*, IV, ii, no. 1062; *LP*, VI, no. 391; *CSPV*, IV, no. 878.

36 *St. Pap.*, I, pp. 390–7; Ellis, 1st Series, II, pp. 35–6; Cox (1846), pp. 243–4; MacCulloch (1996), pp. 90–4.

37 BNF, MS Dupuy 547, fos. 237–8; Camusat, II, fos. 128–9.

38 NA, C 66/663 [8]; *LP*, VI, no. 737 (7).

39 Ellis, 3rd Series, II, pp. 274–5.

40 BL, Cotton MS, Tiberius E.VIII, fo. 100 (formerly 89); Wickham Legg (1901), pp. xxviii–xxxi, 166, 240–1; Hunt (2008), pp. 47–50; Ullmann (1979), p. 183. Since Edward II's reign, the coronation oath had bound the king to uphold 'the laws and customs of the realm and to his power keep them' which 'the people have made and chosen'. Henry, however, inserted the word 'approved' before 'customs' and added that only those laws that are 'lawful and not prejudicial to his crown or imperial jurisdiction' and which 'the nobles and people have made and chosen with his consent' would be upheld.

20 ANNE'S TRIUMPH

1 LMA, COL/CA/01/01/009 (MS Repertory 9), fos. 1–7; Hall (1809), p. 798.
2 *LP*, VI, nos. 701, 1176, 1457; *LP*, VII, nos. 955, 1151; Roper (1935), pp. 58–9; Guy (2008), pp. 244–5. Allington was the second husband of Thomas More's stepdaughter Alice Elryngton, *née* Middleton. He later changed his mind about Anne and sat on the trial jury that found the four commoners accused with her guilty of all charges. See Wriothesley (1875–77), I, p. 204.
3 *LP*, VI, no. 396; *Antiquarian Repertory* (1807–9), I, pp. 296–341, especially pp. 302–4; BL, Additional MS 71,009, fo. 57v. For the order of a queen's coronation without the king, see Wickham Legg (1901), pp. 128–30.
4 Hall (1809), p. 798; *CSPM*, I, no. 911 (p. 557); NA, E 101/421/6 (unfoliated); LMA, COL/CA/01/01/009, fos. 7–8; Kipling (1997), pp. 45–50. See also *LP*, VI, nos. 396, 583 (4–5).
5 Anglo (1969), pp. 49–50, 247–8.
6 Laynesmith (2004), pp. 89–90.
7 NA, E 101/421/6 (unfoliated).
8 *CSPM*, I, no. 911 (p. 558); Hunt (2008), p. 53.
9 *LP*, VI, no. 556 (pp. 240–1, 244); *CSPSp*, IV, no. 1077 (pp. 693, 700).
10 Hall (1809), pp. 799–800; *LP*, VI, nos. 563, 601; Camusat, II, fo. 17; Nichols, V, pp. 5–8; Spelman (1976–7), I, p. 69; Anglo (1969), pp. 49–50, 247–8. A discrepancy exists between Hall's account and that of the heralds in the College of Arms as to the position and role of the *Bachelor's Barge*. The heralds' account is likely to be preferable and is followed here.
11 *CSPSp*, IV, ii, no. 1077 (p. 700); Ellis, 1st Series, II, p. 38.
12 Hall (1809), pp. 799–800; *LP*, VI, nos. 5, 563, 601; Colvin, Brown and Cook (1963–82), III, pp. 266–7.
13 Hall (1809), p. 800; Nichols, V, pp. 8–9; Keay (2001), p. 41.
14 *LP*, VI, no. 601; Hall (1809), p. 800.
15 *LP*, VI, nos. 556 (p. 244), 653; Nichols, V, p. 9.
16 *LP*, VI, nos. 583, 584; Camusat, II, fo. 17.
17 Hall (1809), pp. 800–1; Camusat, II, fo. 17v; Nichols, V, pp. 9–12; Spelman (1976–7), I, p. 69; Ellis, 1st Series, I, pp. 304–5; Ellis, 1st Series, II, pp. 37–8; *CAF*, II, no. 6639; *CSPV*, IV, no. 927.

18 BL, Additional MS 71,009, fos. 57v–8; Hall (1809), pp. 800–1; Camusat, II, fo. 17; *LP*, VI, nos. 583, 684; Laynesmith (2004), p. 93.

19 Pageants were staged at the corner of Gracechurch Street, beside Leadenhall where Midsummer pageants were held, in Cornhill, in Cheapside, at St Paul's Gate and in Fleet Street. Tableaux – static, unscripted displays – were laid on in Fenchurch Street, other parts of Cheapside, at the east end of St Paul's churchyard, in Ludgate and at Temple Bar.

20 Hall (1809), pp. 801–2; *Tudor Tracts* (1903), pp. 11–28; Nichols, V, pp. 24–60; Kipling (1997), pp. 39–72; Anglo (1969), pp. 243–61; Hunt (2008), pp. 56–76; Ives (2004), pp. 218–30.

21 *Tudor Tracts* (1903), pp. 15–16, 20–1; Nichols, V, pp. 12–14, 32–7.

22 Virgil, *Eclogue* IV, ll. 6–10; Yates (1947), pp. 30–7.

23 In a deliberate misreading of the emblem, the disgruntled Chapuys states that the arbour was surmounted by the double-headed eagle associated with the Habsburgs, claiming this was an insult to Anne and that it had angered her. See *CSPSp*, IV, ii, no. 1107 (p. 755).

24 Nichols, V, pp. 49, 50, 53.

25 Hall (1809), p. 801; *Tudor Tracts* (1903), p. 15; Nichols, V, p. 12; Kipling (1997), pp. 60–3; Anglo (1969), pp. 249–52; Foister (2004), pp. 128–37. A preparatory drawing for the pageant, reliably attributed to Holbein, can still be seen in the Kupferstichkabinett, part of the Staatliche Museen zu Berlin.

26 *Tudor Tracts* (1903), p. 16; Nichols, V, pp. 14, 37–9.

27 Hall (1809), pp. 801–2; *Tudor Tracts* (1903), pp. 16, 25–7; Nichols, V, pp. 14, 39–41; Anglo (1969), p. 256.

28 Hall (1809), p. 802; *Tudor Tracts* (1903), p. 17; Nichols, V, pp. 15–16, 59–60; Kipling (1997), pp. 52–3, 60.

29 NA, PRO 31/9/145; *LP*, VI, no. 585; Anglo (1969), pp. 259–60.

30 BL, Additional MS 71,009, fo. 57v; Hall (1809), p. 802; Nichols, V, pp. 16–17; Spelman (1976–7), I, p. 70.

31 Ellis, 3rd Series, II, p. 275.

32 *LP*, VI, no. 521; Nichols, V, pp. 16–18.

33 BL, Additional MS 71,009, fo. 59; Hall (1809), pp. 802–3; Camusat, II, fo. 18; Nichols, V, pp. 16–19; *LP*, VI, nos. 584, 601, 661; *Tudor Tracts* (1903), pp. 18–19; Wriothesley (1875–77), I, pp. 19–20.

34 Ellis, 1st Series, II, pp. 38–9.

35 Camusat, II, fo. 18.

36 Nichols, V, p. 18.

37 BL, Additional MS 71,009, fo. 59. See also Wriothesley (1875–77), I, p. 20.

38 Nichols, V, p. 18; Hunt (2008), p. 52.

39 Nichols, V, pp. 18–19.

40 Hall (1809), p. 803.

41 Ibid., pp. 804–5; Camusat, II, fo. 18; Nichols, V, pp. 19–20; LMA, COL/CA/01/01/009, fo. 2; Spelman (1976–7), I, p. 70.

42 Hall (1809), pp. 804–05; Camusat, II, fo. 18; Nichols, V, p. 21.

43 BL, Harleian MS 41, fo. 12; Camusat, II, fo. 18v; Wriothesley (1875–77), I, pp. 20–1; Nichols, V, p. 21; Biggs (2016), I, p. 82.

44 Hall (1809), p. 805; Nichols, V, pp. 21–2; Wriothesley (1875–77), I, pp. 21–2.

45 *CSPV*, IV, no. 912; Camusat, II, fo. 18v; Nichols, V, p. 22. A pamphlet printed by Wynkyn de Worde describing these events says, 'many spears' were broken 'valiantly', but this was for propaganda purposes. Wriothesley repeats this but concedes several horses refused to enter the lists, 'which was great displeasure to some of them that ran'. See *Tudor Tracts* (1903), p. 19; Wriothesley (1875–77), I, p. 22.

21 THE AMBASSADORS

1 *Lisle Letters*, I, no. 22; NA, OBS 1419; Hall (1809), p. 805.

2 NA, E 101/421/16 (unfoliated); *LP*, VI, no. 602.

3 *SR*, III, pp. 479–81; NA, SP 2/O, fos. 75–6 (incomplete); BL, Cotton MS, Vespasian C.XIV, fo. 28; *LP*, I, i, no. 94 (35); *LP*, VII, nos. 249, 352, 419 (25, 26), 1204.

4 *CSPSp*, IV, ii, no. 1164; *CSPSp*, V, i, nos. 1 (p. 4), 75, 134, 148, 210–11, 237; *CSPV*, IV, no. 923; *LP*, III, ii, no. 3376 (1); *LP*, VI, nos. 759, 760, 765; NA, C 142/44/105; NA, PROB 11/22/51; Montagu (1864), I, pp. 186–8; Mattingly (1950), pp. 280–2.

5 BNF, MS Dupuy 726, fo. 98.

6 The outcome of the pregnancy is unknown. Her letter is the first known and only evidence of it. Her daughter, Jeanne, was born in 1528. A son, Jean, born in 1530, died at six months.

7 *CAF*, II, nos. 5721, 5829; *CSPV*, IV, no. 893; *CSPSp*, IV, ii, no. 1091; *LP*, VI, no. 720.

8 Camusat, II, fo. 133.

9 *LP*, VI, no. 541; Richardson (2008), pp. 105–6.

10 BNF, MS Dupuy 547, fos. 214, 229–30, 236; Camusat, II, fos. 82v–3,
    124v–5, 127v; Decrue (1885), I, p. 204; Richardson (1995), p. 225.

11 BNF, MS Dupuy 726, fo. 46; Hervey (1900), pp. 78–81; Richardson
    (2008), p. 109.

12 BNF, MS Dupuy 726, fo. 46; BNF, MS FF 15,971, fo. 4; Hervey
    (1900), pp. 76–80.

13 BNF, MS Dupuy 547, fo. 226; BNF, MS Dupuy 726, fo. 46; Camusat,
    II, fos. 83v–4, 124v–5, 127v; Richardson (2008), pp. 108–9; Foister,
    Roy and Wyld (1997), pp. 14–18.

14 A metal pointer fitted to the top of the cylinder was turned to the
    approximate date by lining it up with the relevant sign of the zodiac
    etched around the circumference for that time of year, allowing the
    sun's rays to cast a shadow indicating the time of day. See Hervey
    (1990), pp. 225–7; Ives (1994b), pp. 39–40; Foister, Roy and Wyld
    (1997), pp. 33–4, 43; Dekker and Lippincott (1999), pp. 107–9.

15 Likewise, the equinoctial dial at the centre of the upper shelf, the
    horary quadrant behind it, and the polyhedral dial to its right,
    instruments normally used for calculating the time, would in the
    form depicted in the painting have been unable 'to tell the time'
    in any recognisable scientific sense, since all three are purposefully
    disassembled, disabled or deliberately mis-set to suggest that the
    times are 'out of joint'. See Foister, Roy and Wyld (1997), pp. 30–9;
    Dekker and Lippincott (1999), pp. 105–6, 109–17.

16 Apian (1527), sig. Q8v; Buskirk (2013), pp. 64–70.

17 Hervey (1900), pp. 227–32; Rasmussen (1995), pp. 115–22; Foister,
    Roy and Wyld (1997), pp. 42–3. Often flutes were associated with
    the sounds of war. Since their leather case resembles those used in the
    field by military fifers, the flutes may perhaps have been placed next
    to the lute to emphasise the risks of conflict, should Henry's defiance
    of the pope lead to his excommunication.

18 The tenor part-book is the copy-text, because it is the only one to
    include the words of both hymns.

19 Hervey (1900), pp. 151–3, 221–5; Foister, Roy and Wyld (1997),
    pp. 40–1. De Selve may well have encountered this highly popular
    Protestant hymnbook during a diplomatic mission to Germany
    in 1529 on which Francis had sent him. A planned speech on that
    occasion called on the Lutheran princes to reconcile themselves to
    the Church.

20 Foister, Roy and Wyld (1997), pp. 44–57; Frangenberg (1992), pp. 15–16.

21 Camusat II, fos. 127v, 128v–9, 137–9, 139v–40v; *St. Pap.*, VII, pp. 473–9; *LP*, VI, nos. 555, 641, 1038, 1099, 1135.

22 NA, SP 1/77, fos. 70–3. Francis Bryan, some months before, claimed that 'being both in one house', Francis and Eleanor 'lie not together once in four nights'. The French king made up for it by sleeping regularly with his new mistress, Anne d'Heilly, who had succeeded Françoise de Foix and whom he made Duchess d'Étampes. See *St. Pap.*, VII, p. 291.

23 BNF, MS Dupuy 33, fos. 52–4; *LP*, VI, nos. 557, 635, 643, 721, 774, 809, 810, 811, 940, 953; Camusat, II, fos. 8, 11v, 133v–5; Pocock (1870), II, pp. 677–8; Fletcher (2012), pp. 188–9.

24 BNF, MS Dupuy 33, fo. 54r–v; Bapst (1891), pp. 66–9; *CSPSp*, IV, ii, no. 1107 (p. 755); *LP*, VI, no. 918.

25 BNF, MS Dupuy 547, fos. 258–9; *St. Pap.*, VII, pp. 493–8; Camusat, II, fos. 135–6v, 137–9; Rymer (1704–35), XIV, pp. 476–9; *CSPSp*, IV, ii, no. 1108 (p. 761); Bapst (1891), pp. 67–9; *LP*, VI, no. 998.

26 Camusat, II, fos. 8v–9, 137–9; *LP*, VI, no. 1038.

27 *Lisle Letters*, I, no. 35.

28 Ibid., nos. 34, 59.

29 *St. Pap.*, VII, pp. 495–6.

30 Lancelot de Carle tells us: 'Quant commença de sentir remuer / Les petitz piedz, et qu'elle se veit prise, / O! qu'elle estoit bien saigement apprise / De se bien plaindre, et faire la dolente, / En voix piteuse et parolle tremblante, / Pour demonstrer la doulleur qu'elle avoit.' Schmid (2009), p. 117; Ascoli (1927), p. 153 (ll. 148–53).

31 *LP*, VI, no. 1069; Starkey and Hawkyard (1998), no. 9035; BL, Harleian MS 283, fo. 75.

32 *CSPSp*, IV, ii, no. 1105 (p. 756).

33 Ibid., nos. 1123, 1144 (p. 842); *LP*, VI, nos. 1069, 1392; Gunn (1988), pp. 132–3. Cf. Ives (2004), pp. 192–3. The new duchess was not good news for Anne. The daughter of Maria de Salinas, one of Katherine's most devoted Spanish gentlewomen, who had married an Englishman, she was loyal to her and to Princess Mary. She appears frequently in Mary's privy purse accounts, sending her gifts such as *aqua composita* (a remedy for indigestion or a 'surfeit') and playing cards with her. Only after Suffolk's death did she become enmeshed

with the circle of religious evangelicals surrounding Queen Katherine Parr. See *PPE, Mary*, pp. 7, 50, 51, 55, 58, 68, 69, 82, 96, 102, 143.

34 *Antiquarian Repertory* (1807–9), I, pp. 304–5, 333–7; *Household Ordinances* (1790), pp. 125–6; Guillemeau (1612), p. 88; Laynesmith (2004), pp. 112–14; Thurley (1993), pp. 140–1; Hayward (1998), p. 156; Starkey (2004), p. 506.

35 Bodleian, Folio.Δ.624, facing p. 360; BL, Harleian MS 283, fo. 75; *St. Pap.*, I, p. 407; *LP*, VI, no. 1112.

36 Wriothesley (1875–77), I, p. 22; *LP*, VI, no. 1111 (1, 3).

37 Bodleian, Folio.Δ.624, facing p. 360; Hall (1809), pp. 805–6; Camusat, II, fo. 139.

38 Hall (1809), pp. 805–6; *LP*, VI, no. 1111 (1, 3); *Antiquarian Repertory* (1807–9), I, pp. 305–6; *Household Ordinances* (1790), pp. 126–7.

39 BNF, MS Dupuy 33, fos. 57v–61; Le Grand (1688), III, pp. 571–88; Camusat, II, fos. 12, 19–21, 141v–2v; *LP*, VI, nos. 1280, 1299, 1301, 1331, 1403, 1426, 1435, 1479, 1558, 1572; *St. Pap.*, VII, p. 498; *Lisle Letters*, I, nos. 66, 66a. Bryan's dispatches, recorded as sent by courier, do not survive, but their contents are easily worked out from Henry's reactions.

40 Burnet (1820), III, ii, pp. 49–61; *LP*, VI, no. 1425.

41 NA, SP 3/15, fo. 47; Hall (1809), p. 808; *CSPSp*, IV, ii, nos. 1164, 1165 (p. 900); *LP*, VI, nos. 1558, 1571 (pp. 633–4); BNF, MS FF 5499, fos. 189, 189v–91, 191v–3, 193v–5v, 195v–7, 197–8; *Du Bellay*, I, nos. 170–5.

22 ANNE THE QUEEN

1 *PPE, Henry*, p. 97; *CSPSp*, IV, i, no. 354 (p. 600); Hayward (2007), p. 111.

2 For Katherine's protocol, see Beer (2018b), pp. 83–95; Laynesmith (2004), pp. 244–8; Hayward (2007), p. 111.

3 NA, E 101/421/13; Hayward (2005), pp. 125–75.

4 *PPE, Mary*, pp. lv–lvi; McIntosh (2002), pp. 87–9.

5 BNF, MS FF 5499, fo. 197v; *LP*, VII, Appendix 13 (inaccurately calendared).

6 NA, SP 1/103, fo. 324; *LP*, X, no. 913 (wrongly calendared).

7 NA, E 101/421/13; Clark (2018), pp. 100–3.

8 A recent study of the watermark coupled with the artist's notes showed that Holbein drew Howard between Anne's coronation and Fitzroy's death, barely nine weeks after Anne's. Foister (1978),

pp. 69–70; Parker (1983), no. 16; Button (2013), pp. 243–57. See also Sessions (1999), pp. 64–5.

9 NA, E 101/421/13; *HC, 1509–1558*, III, pp. 500–2.

10 BL, Additional MS 71,009, fo. 58r–v; NA, SP 1/129, fo. 174; NA, SP 1/103, fo. 318; NA, SP1/104, fo. 262; *LP*, X, nos. 912, 1257 (ix); *LP*, XIII, i, no. 450. The uncertainty over the amount is shown by the fact it was initially thought to be no more than £10.

11 Clark (2018), pp. 48–9, 58.

12 Mary Shelton later married Sir Anthony Heveningham, while Margaret became Thomas Wodehouse of Kimberley's wife. See Rye (1891), pp. 247, 322; Blomefield (1739–75), I, pp. 760, 767; ibid., III, p. 177; *HC, 1558–1603*, III, p. 647.

13 Parker (1983), no. 26.

14 *LP*, X, no. 282 (p. 103); *LP*, VIII, no. 263 (p. 104); Remley (1994), pp. 42–7.

15 Widowed in 1539, Hill went on to marry Sir John Mason, secretary to Thomas Wyatt and acting clerk of the privy council.

16 Parker and Gamage were, respectively, daughters of Alice and Margaret, daughters of Sir John St John of Bletsoe. Gamage might be the brown-haired, unidentified sitter wearing a French hood drawn by Holbein, or the unknown woman sporting a gold ornament: Parker (1983), nos. 61, 62.

17 NA, E 101/421/13; NA, PROB 11/23/361; NA, C 1/621/1; BL, Additional MS 71,009, fo. 42; *Lisle Letters*, III, p. 381. Perhaps she held a more menial post within Anne's household as suggested by Warnicke (1989), p. 203.

18 NA, E 101/420/15; NA, E 101/421/13; *LP*, IV, ii, no. 3479; *LP*, XVII, no. 283 (28); NA, PROB 11/34/123; NA, PROB 11/57/448; Parker (1983), no. 72; Foister (2004), pp. 26–7. Mary Zouche married Robert Burbage of Hayes Park Hall in Middlesex in or after 1542.

19 NA, E 101/421/13; *LP*, III, ii, nos. 1437, 1439, 1533, 1673, 2585 (3); *LP*, IV, i, no. 1577 (10); *LP*, XVI, nos. 380 (p. 179), 1489 (p. 699); NA, PROB 11/28/542; *Calais Chronicle* (1846), p. 25; Richardson (2014b), Appendix A (pp. 215–17); *HC, 1509–1558*, I, pp. 666–7; Blomefield (1739–75), II, p. 628; ibid., III, p. 719; Rye (1891), p. 39; Guy (2013), pp. 30–2, 42. Mary Kingston, *née* Scrope, had first married Edward Jerningham, who died in 1515. Coffyn was the daughter of Robert Dymoke, Katherine's chancellor. Lady Jane (*née* Blennerhasset),

Sir Philip Calthorpe's second wife, was appointed Princess Mary's governess in 1521.

20 NA, E 101/420/15; *LP*, XII, i, no. 795 (41); *LP*, XIII, ii, no. 766; Parker (1983), no. 21, where wrongly identified as 'Joan'. Jane's marriage to Peter Mewtas was in 1537. Her mother Anne and Elizabeth Boleyn were the daughters and co-heirs of John Wood of East Barsham, Norfolk. Jane's brother, John, soon found employment at court, and went on to become Elizabeth I's chief gentleman of the privy chamber. See Collins (1955), p. 199.

21 NA, E 101/420/15; NA, E 101/421/13; *LP*, XII, ii, nos. 973 (1, 2, 4), 1060 (p. 374), 1150 (44); PROB 11/34/405; Parker (1983), no. 20, where on grounds of age the sitter is more likely to be Horsman than her mother-in-law, the judge Sir Richard Lyster's wife, Jane Shirley.

22 NA, E 101/421/13; Wriothesley (1875–77), I, p. 43; *LP*, IX, nos. 271, 278, 326, 504 (2, 3, 6, 10), 729 (6, 7, 8, 16, 17, 18).

23 NA, E 101/421/13; *LP*, X, no. 901. Of the remaining women in the gift roll, little is known about 'Mistress Heneage', 'Mistress Morris', 'Mistress Nurse', 'Mistress Toppes' and 'Mistress Marshall'. Heneage seems to have been Sir Thomas Heneage's daughter Elizabeth, who was later promoted to lady-in-waiting. Morris might be the wife or daughter of Sir Christopher Morris, Master of the Ordnance, and 'Toppes' the wife or daughter of Denis Toppes, another of the king's servants. A single reference confirms that 'Mistress Marshall' oversaw the queen's maids. See NA, E 101/421/13; NA, SP 1/86, fo. 53v; *LP*, VII, no. 1265; *LP*, X, nos. 766, 870, 878 (2); *LP*, XII, ii, no. 617 (10); *LP*, XIII, i, no. 1520 (p. 574); *LP*, XV, no. 282 (16); *LP*, XIX, i, no. 812 (5); *Lisle Letters*, III, no. 735, and p. 441; *HC, 1509–1558*, II, p. 582; *CPR, Edward VI*, V, p. 70; Hayward (2005), pp. 147, 156, 157, 172, n. 122; *ODNB*, s.v. 'Heneage, Thomas'.

24 Collins (1955), pp. 468–9; Ives (1994b), pp. 37–8; Foister (2004), pp. 138, 142; Foister (2006), no. 93. No design for the basin into which the fountain discharged water has survived, but a description appears in the 1534 New Year's gift list: NA, E 101/421/13. The so-called 'Boleyn Cup', the cover of which is capped by a crowned falcon bearing a sceptre and dated 1535–6, reputedly given to the church of St John the Baptist, Cirencester, by Elizabeth's physician, Richard Master, was not designed by Holbein.

25 BM, SL,5308.3; BM, SL,5308.6; BM, SL,5308.7; BM, SL,5308.11; BM, SL,5308.115; BM, SL,5308.116.

26 Parker (1983), pp. 22–4, and no. 63; Foister (2004), p. 199; Brigden (2012), pp. 290, 292; Ives (1994b), pp. 40–2. For a contrary view, see Rowlands and Starkey (1983), pp. 90–2.

27 BM, 1975,0621.22; Ives (1994b), pp. 40–1.

28 RCIN 912188.

29 I Kings 10: 8–9, II Chronicles 9: 7–8; Foister (2004), pp. 152–5; Ives (1994b), pp. 38–9; Ives (2004), pp. 235–6. In a place where Holbein's first inscription differs slightly from the usual text of the Vulgate, the word 'constitutus' (the meaning of which could be ambiguous) has been bracketed to remove any suggestion that Henry had been 'elected' king by popular consent rather than 'established' by God.

30 *SR*, III, pp. 479–81; NA, SP 2/O, fos. 75–6 (incomplete); BL, Cotton MS, Vespasian C.XIV, fo. 28; BL, Cotton MS, Appendix XXVIII, fos. 84–92; BL, Harleian MS 303, fos. 1–3; *LP*, I, i, no. 94 (35); *LP*, IV, iii, no. 6437; *LP*, V, nos. 74, 1370 (1–3), 1499 (23); *LP*, VI, nos. 74, 1188; *LP*, VII, nos. 352, 419 (25, 26), 1204; *LP*, IX, no. 477; Beer (2018a), pp. 426–45.

31 Laynesmith (2004), pp. 232–4.

32 BL, Cotton MS, Vespasian C.XIV, fo. 28; BL, Cotton MS, Appendix XXVIII, fos. 84–92; BL, Additional MS 71,009, fos. 58v–9; NA, E 298/32, 33; NA, E 179/69/28; *LP*, VI, no. 1188; *LP*, VII, no. 352; *Lisle Letters*, I, p. 347. Anne made Thomas, Lord Burgh of Gainsborough, her chamberlain (his role was chiefly ceremonial). Other members of her council included John Uvedale (her secretary) and John Smith (her principal surveyor). Latymer wrongly states that Nicholas Udall was Anne's secretary, see Dowling (1990), p. 49. For Uvedale, see *ODNB*, s.v. 'Uvedale, John'.

33 NA, E 298/32; NA, C 1/696/18; *LP*, VII, nos. 569, 570. For Rolf, see also NA, PROB 11/35/116.

34 *Lisle Letters*, II, no. 109.

35 Ibid., nos. 182, 193, 302, 307.

36 Ibid., no. 114.

37 Ibid., no. 299a; *LP*, IX, no. 991 (wrongly dated); *PPE, Henry*, pp. 43, 108.

38 *Lisle Letters*, II, nos. 482–3, 492, 495, 496–8, and pp. 622–3; *Lisle Letters*, IV, no. 841.

39 BL, Cotton MS, Faustina C.III, fos. 481–2, 493–4; NA, SP 1/94, fo. 99; *LP*, X, no. 345; *SR*, III, pp. 599–601; Lehmberg (1970), pp. 229–30.

40 But Patmore's servant sent near identical petitions to Henry, to Anne and to Cromwell, and it is unclear which of them really engineered his release. See Foxe (1583), II, p. 1044; BL, Harleian MS 425, fo. 15; NA, SP 1/70, fos. 2–3; *LP*, V, no. 982; *LP*, VII, no. 923 (20, 26); *LP*, VIII, no. 1063; Brigden (1988), p. 36; Brigden (1989), pp. 121–2, 125, 190, 197, 205–7, 222; Dowling (1984), p. 42.

41 Dowling (1990), p. 56, and n. 18; *LP*, IX, no. 765.

42 BL, Cotton MS, Cleopatra, E. VI, fo. 350v; *LP*, VII, no. 664, Ellis, 1st Series, II, pp. 45–6.

43 She had learned of Bourbon's arrest either from Jean de Dinteville, with whom Bourbon was at school, or from Dr Butts.

44 Bourbon (1536), pp. 28–30; Bourbon (1538), pp. 153, 338, 409, 411, 427, 450; Parker (1983), no. 37; Dowling (1984), p. 42; Dowling (1990), pp. 36, 56; Ives (1996), pp. 97–9; Ives (1998), pp. 21–6; Ives (2004), pp. 274–6. The drawing survives, but the oil portrait is lost. What may pass for it can be seen only in the reduced form of a woodcut engraving.

45 Bourbon (1536), pp. 28–30; Bourbon (1538), pp. 85, 285.

46 Foxe (1570), II, p. 1198; NA, SP 1/92, fo. 139; *LP*, VIII, no. 710; Bruce and Perowne (1853), pp. 2–3; Dowling (1984), pp. 40–1; Dowling (1990), p. 57; Wood (1846), II, pp. 191–2; Freeman (1995), p. 802; Fox (2007), pp. 120–1.

47 Several were from Gonville Hall in Cambridge, where her great-great uncle Thomas had risen to be Master. See Venn (1897–1901), I, pp. 17, 19, 20–1, 27, 29. In identifying suitable candidates, Anne used Dr Butts, a college alumnus, as her talent-spotter.

48 CCC, MS 108, fo. 73; *LP*, VIII, no. 600; *LP*, X, nos. 612, 640; *LP*, XIII, i, no. 819; Bruce and Perowne (1853), p. 59; Dowling (1990), pp. 28, 36, 52, n. 9; Brigden (1989), pp. 221, 259, 349–52; Brigden (2012), pp. 195, 197–8.

49 *LP*, VII, no. 89; *LP*, VIII, nos. 412, 466; *LP*, IX, nos. 189, 1091; *LP*, X, nos. 19, 1182; Wood (1846), II, pp. 186–8; Ives (2004), pp. 261–2. For the details of Barlow's battle in Haverfordwest, see BL, Cotton MS, Cleopatra E.IV, fos. 128–9.

50 Wood (1846), II, pp. 188–9; *LP*, VII, no. 693; Venn (1897–1901), I, pp. 17–18; Foxe (1843–9), V, Appendix 16; Brigden (1989), pp. 222, 330–2; *ODNB*, s.v. 'Crome, Edward'.

51 Known in Antwerp as 'Jacques Nicolai', Nicolson was a Flemish immigrant glazier turned printer. Between 1526 and 1528, he had worked with Galyon Hone, the king's glazier, on the windows of the recently completed King's College Chapel in Cambridge, where Edward Foxe was now Provost.

52 NA, SP 1/96, fo. 33; *LP*, IX, no. 226; Willoughby (1936), pp. 1–16; Paisey and Bartrum (2009), pp. 244–7. For the dedication to Henry and Anne, and for Shaxton's prayers, see *STC*, no. 2063.3 (formerly the Marquis of Northampton's copy).

53 NA, SP 1/96, fo. 33; Freeman (2007), pp. 13–14.

54 Foister (2004), pp. 159–64; Ives (1996), pp. 91–2.

55 Revell (1536), sigs. X3–5v; NA, SP 1/102, fos. 113–14; *LP*, X, no. 371; Dowling (1984), p. 44; Dowling (1990), p. 28. The Latin edition of Lambert's book went under the title *Farrago Rerum Theologicarum*. See Higman (2016), pp. 26, 286; Reid (2001), p. 394.

56 *LP*, VIII, nos. 834, 1056; Wood (1846), II, p. 190; Ives (1996), p. 86.

57 Dowling (1990), p. 62; Da Costa (2012), pp. 114–15. For Anne at Richmond for Easter, see CCC, MS 108, fo. 73. For a more critical reading of this episode, see Bernard (1993), p. 6.

58 CCC, MS 108, fos. 53–72, 74; Bruce and Perowne (1853), pp. 4–5; Strype (1821), I, pp. 15–19; Beer (2018a), pp. 439–40; Ives (1996), p. 86.

59 Dowling (1990), pp. 60–1; *Lisle Letters*, V, no. 1131; Corrie (1845), p. 231; Rex (2014), pp. 17–18.

23 DANGEROUS TIMES

1 NA, SP 2/P, fos. 33–127; *SR*, III, pp. 462–74, 479–81, 484–6; *CSPSp*, V, i, nos. 4, 7–10, 19, 22, 32; Lehmberg (1970), pp. 190–9; Elton (1972), pp. 276–8; Gray (2012), pp. 51–84.

2 Le Grand (1688), III, pp. 636–8; BNF, MS FF 5499, fos. 200–1; *Du Bellay*, I, no. 181; *LP*, VII, nos. 367–1.

3 BL, Cotton MS, Cleopatra, E.VI, fo. 180; *St. Pap.*, I, p. 413; *LP*, VI, no. 1487 (1); Elton (1974–92), III, p. 101.

4 Highley (2005), pp. 161–4; Warnicke (1989), pp. 244–5; Guy (1980), pp. 210–11.

5 *CSPSp*, IV, ii, nos. 1072, 1073, 1107, 1108, 1127, 1130, 1132, 1144, 1153; *CSPSp*, V, i, nos. 105, 139, 142.

6 MacCulloch (1996), pp. 103–9; MacCulloch (2018), pp. 233–9.

7 NA, SP 1/80, fos. 118–32; *LP*, VI, no. 1468 (1–8).

8 NA, SP 1/80, fo. 128; Marshall (2003), pp. 40–2; Watt (1997), pp. 136–63; Dodds (1916), pp. 276–84; Devereux (1966), pp. 91–106.

9 *LP*, VI, nos. 1419, 1445, 1460, 1464, 1465, 1466, 1468, 1470, 1519, 1546; Hall (1809), pp. 806–7; *PPE, Henry*, p. 30; MacCulloch (1996), pp. 103–5; Elton (1972), pp. 274–5; Bernard (2005), pp. 87–101.

10 *SR*, III, pp. 446–51; *Lisle Letters*, II, no. 171; Lehmberg (1970), pp. 194–6.

11 The offending words were not contained in the Act of Succession itself, only in the preamble. Rogers (1961), no. 54; *Lisle Letters*, II, nos. 168, 171, 183, 185, 195, 215; *LP*, VII, nos. 530, 841; Gray (2012), Appendix D (pp. 228–9); Guy (2008), pp. 229–34; MacCulloch (2018), pp. 248–51.

12 Ellis (1995), pp. 173–206, 233–49.

13 *LP*, VII, no. 1013 (p. 389); Spelman (1976–7), I, pp. 54–5.

14 *St. Pap.*, II, pp. 197–8; *CSPSp*, V, i, nos. 70, 86, 87; Ellis (1995), pp. 207–32; Ellis (1976), pp. 807–30; Ellis (2019), pp. 705–19. For lesser troubles in Wales, see *LP*, VII, nos. 650, 710, 1193, 1206, 1567; *CSPSp*, V, i, nos. 90, 257; *LP*, VIII, no. 1; Marshall (2008), pp. 681–704; Bernard (2005), pp. 202–4.

15 NA, SP 1/84, fos. 94–5, 178; NA, SP 1/88, fo. 20; NA, SP 1/89, fo. 136; NA, SP 1/90, fo. 173; *LP*, VI, nos. 733, 964, 1254; *LP*, VII, nos. 454, 754, 840 (2), 1609 (imperfectly calendared); *LP*, VIII, nos. 196, 278; Ellis, 1st Series, II, pp. 42–5; ibid., 3rd Series, II, pp. 332–4; Elton (1972), p. 100.

16 NA, SP 1/90, fo. 173, where Bryan calls the suspect 'George Taylor', while adding that this was not his real name. For the correct identification, see NA, KB 9/531, fos. 5–11.

17 BL, Cotton MS, Cleopatra E.IV, fos. 99–100; *LP*, VI, no. 923.

18 *CSPSp*, IV, ii, no. 1061 (p. 368); *CSPSp*, V, i, no. 7 (p. 21); *LP*, VI, no. 351 (p. 164); *LP*, VII, no. 114 (p. 44).

19 *CSPSp*, V, i, no. 7; NA, SP 1/88, fo. 101; *LP*, VII, no. 1668; Hayward (2007), p. 198. The cradle must have been ordered for the 1534 pregnancy, not for Elizabeth, as Hayes's bill is addressed to Cromwell as the king's new principal secretary. See also Ives (2004), p. 394, n. 13.

20 BM, M.9010; Hayward (2007), p. 48; Ives (1994b), pp. 36–7. The medal may have been designed under the supervision of John Copynger, keeper of the Tower Mint.

21 *LP*, VII, no. 262 (13). See https://www.britishmuseum.org/collection/object/C_M-9010.

22 *CSPSp*, V, i, no. 7; NA, SP 3/14, fo. 5; *Lisle Letters*, II, no. 175.

23 NA, E 101/21/6 (unfoliated); *LP*, VII, no. 469.

24 *LP*, VII, nos. 469, 490; *CSPSp*, V, i, no. 40; BL, Cotton MS, Augustus I, Supplement 7; *Lisle Letters*, II, nos. 168, 170, 206; Colvin, Brown and Cook (1963–82), III, pp. 349–51.

25 *LP*, VII, no. 470 (very incomplete). The full force of Henry's instructions must be inferred from Francis's reply, see BNF, MS FF 3005, fos. 129–30; Friedmann (1884), II, pp. 3–5.

26 *CAF*, II, nos. 6996, 7019, 7244; *CAF*, VII, nos. 29,106, 29,234; BNF, MS FF 3005, fos. 129–30; Knecht (1994), pp. 307–21; Reid (2001), pp. 34–5, 39–41.

27 NA, SP 1/85, fos. 37–41; *St. Pap.*, VII, pp. 559–62, 562–4, 565–9; *LP*, VII, nos. 469, 662, 783–5, 957–8, 980; *CSPV*, V, nos. 13, 19, 21.

28 NA, SP 1/85, fos. 37–41.

29 *LP*, IX, no. 729 (2); NA, E 179/69/28; Wood (1691), I, col. 647; https://history.rcplondon.ac.uk/inspiring-physicians/richard-bart lot. Berthelet graduated from Oxford and in 1531 became President of the Royal College of Physicians.

30 *CSPSp*, V, i, no. 90 (p. 264); *LP*, VII, nos. 1081, 1088, 1181, 1185, 1193, 1234; NA, OBS/1419. Cf. Ives (2004), pp. 191–2, who dates the miscarriage slightly earlier. The evidence for a stillbirth is supported by the charges against Margaret Chancellor, which alleged that, besides calling Anne Boleyn 'a goggle-eyed whore', she had said 'that the queen's grace had one child by our said sovereign lord the king which she said was dead born, and she prayed God that she might never have other'. NA, SP 1/89, fo. 136.

31 *CSPSp*, V, i, nos. 88, 90, 93, 97, 101, 102, 118; *LP*, VII, nos. 1174, 1193, 1257, 1279, 1297, 1554.

32 *CSPSp*, V, i, nos. 102, 118; *LP*, VII, nos. 1297, 1554.

33 *CSPSp*, V, i, no. 118; *LP*, VII, no. 1554; Bapst (1891), p. 89, n. 2.

34 *CSPSp*, V, i, nos. 88, 93, 97, 118; *LP*, VII, nos. 1174, 1228, 1257, 1554; *LP*, VIII, no. 263 (p. 104).

24 FAMILY MATTERS

1 Laynesmith (2004), pp. 146–7; Kolata (1987), pp. 745–7.

2 NA, E 405/204 (annuities); NA, PROB 11/33/156; *Lisle Letters*, II, no. 129; *LP*, XIV, i, no. 936.

3 *St. Pap.*, I, p. 415.

4 Guy (2013), pp. 19, 23–4, 45, 78, 80, 91.

5 NA, SP 1/103, fos. 321–2v; *LP*, X, no. 913.

6 *Lisle Letters*, II, no. 169; *LP*, VII, nos. 171, 1297 (p. 497); *CSPSp*, V, i, nos. 22, 102 (p. 299); *LP*, VIII, no. 440.

7 Dowling (1990), p. 63.

8 *St. Pap.*, I, p. 426 (wrongly dated); *LP*, VII, no. 1241; *LP*, IX, no. 568.

9 *CSPSp*, IV, ii, nos. 1123 (p. 819), 1127, 1133, 1137 (p. 830), 1144 (p. 839), 1161 (pp. 881–2); *CSPSp*, V, i, nos. 10, 22; *LP*, VI, nos. 1207, 1249.

10 *CSPSp*, V, i, nos. 4, 8, 22; *LP*, VII, nos. 83, 121, 296; *SR*, III, p. 472.

11 *CSPSp*, V, i, no. 102 (p. 299); *LP*, VII, no. 1297 (p. 497); *PPE, Mary*, pp. lv–lvi; McIntosh (2002), pp. 87–9; Loades (2008), pp. 27–8.

12 *LP*, VI, nos. 1186, 1249; *CSPSp*, IV, ii, nos. 1137, 1144; *St. Pap.*, I, pp. 414–15.

13 *CSPSp*, IV, ii, no. 1144.

14 *LP*, VI, no. 1558; *LP*, VII, nos. 171, 214, 530, 1129, 1171, 1172; *LP*, VIII, nos. 200, 263 (pp. 101, 104), 440 (misdated); *CSPSp*, IV, ii, no. 1144; *CSPSp*, V, i, nos. 10, 17, 22, 26, 68, 90, 134; *PPE, Mary*, pp. lviii–lxiv.

15 *CSPSp*, V, i, nos. 2, 10, 31, 32, 86, 102; *LP*, VI, no. 1558.

16 *CSPSp*, V, i, nos. 10, 22, 68, 231, 871; *LP*, VII, no. 296; *LP*, IX, no. 873.

17 *CSPSp*, IV, i, no. 228 (p. 360); Sessions (1999), pp. 260–5; Murphy (2003), pp. 119–32.

18 Sanuto (1824–84), LVIII, cols 671–2; Murphy (2003), pp. 132–9.

19 Murphy (2003), pp. 83–90.

20 *LP*, IV, ii, nos. 4881, 5072; Murphy (2003), pp. 105–6.

21 NA, SP 1/111, fo. 204; *CSPSp*, IV, i, nos. 228 (p. 360), 460 (p. 762); *LP*, XI, no. 1138; Murphy (2003), pp. 122–4.

22 Murphy (2003), pp. 142–3; Knecht (1994), p. 300. The assignment of the house is from a notarial instrument transcribed into NA, HCA 3/2.

23 *HC, 1509–1558*, III, pp. 364–6; Harris (1997), pp. 228–9, and n. 64. The wedding did not take place before 1 January 1534, when Mary Boleyn was at court. See NA, E 101/421/13.

24 *Lisle Letters*, II, no. 375.

25 Although the original document has not been seen since 1753, Mary's letter was transcribed and sensationally published by Leonard Howard, a former Post Office clerk who rose to be chaplain to Frederick, Prince of Wales, the eldest son of George II. Despite the transcriber's reputation as a literary magpie, he was no forger and every line in the letter rings true. See Howard (1753), pp. 525–7 [*recte* 493–5]. The

version in Wood (1846), II, pp. 193–7 has mistranscriptions. See also *LP*, VII, no. 1655; *ODNB*, s.v. 'Howard, Leonard'.

26 Howard (1753), pp. 525–6 [*recte* 493–4].

27 NA, C 54/418 (entry no. 18); *LP*, XVIII, i, no. 623 (66); *HC, 1509–1558*, III, pp. 364–6.

28 *LP*, VII, nos. 1255, 1262, 1263, 1298, 1397, 1405; Parker (2019), p. 237.

29 *SR*, III, pp. 492, 508–9; Lehmberg (1970), pp. 201–5; Elton (1972), pp. 263–92; Gray (2012), pp. 56–84, 116–42, and Appendix G.

30 NA, SP 1/R, fos. 2–5; BL, Cotton MS, Cleopatra F.II, fos. 131–5; Logan (1988), pp. 658–67.

31 *LP*, X, nos. 137, 364; Hoyle (1995), pp. 275–305; Bernard (2005), pp. 244–76; Knowles (1959), pp. 291–393. For examples of Cromwell's use of a stamp of Henry's signature, see NA, SP 1/III, fos. 146–9v; BL, Cotton MS, Cleopatra E.V, fos. 298–300; Elton (1953), pp. 261–86, and especially p. 284, n. 4. A stamp was not new. It first appeared in Court of Requests business and within warrants issued under the Great Seal, mostly applied to circulars issued to prepare for the king's campaign in France in the spring of 1512. This was a wooden stamp, which historians call the 'wet stamp', to distinguish it from the dry stamp, which was entrusted to Anthony Denny in 1545. See Flannigan (2021), pp. 267–81.

32 BL, Cotton MS, Vespasian F.XIII, fo. 197; Bodleian MS, Rawlinson D.777, fos. 50–2; Bapst (1891), pp. 90–4; *LP*, VII, nos. 922 (16), 1291, 1416, 1437, 1507; *CSPSp*, V, i, no. 112; *CAF*, III, no. 7837.

33 Chabot's instructions have yet to be traced, but their contents can be clearly inferred from Henry's replies and the surrounding documents. *St. Pap.*, VII, pp. 584–7; *CSPSp*, V, i, nos. 111–12, 114, 118, 127; *LP*, VII, nos. 1437, 1482, 1507, 1554; *LP*, VIII, no. 48; Le Laboureur (1731), I, pp. 405–13; Decrue (1885), I, pp. 230–2; Mackay (2018a), p. 199.

34 *CSPSp*, V, i, no. 127 (p. 376); *LP*, VIII, no. 48; *Lisle Letters*, II, nos. 290, 290a, 421.

35 *CSPSp*, V, i, no. 122; *LP*, VIII, no. 1.

36 BL, Cotton MS, Caligula E.II, fos. 208–9; Le Laboureur (1731), I, pp. 405–13; *St. Pap.*, VII, pp. 587–90, 592–5, 596–9, 602–3; *LP*, VIII, nos. 174, 182, 189, 263, 336–7, 338 (wrongly dated), 339, 340, 341; *CAF*, III, no. 7473; Bapts (1891), pp. 99–105.

37 Le Laboureur (1731), I, p. 412.

---

38 *St. Pap.*, VII, pp. 592–5, 596–9, 602–3, 608–15; *LP*, VIII, nos. 341, 501, 502, 543, 556, 557, 578, 666, 726, 750, 751, 760, 792, 793, 794, 826; *CSPSp*, V, i, nos. 156, 157, 170; *Lisle Letters*, II, no. 363; Mackay (2018a), pp. 200–2.

39 NA, SP 1/92, fos. 169A–70; *LP*, VIII, nos. 760, 792, 823, 826, 909, 910, 1018; *CSPSp*, V, i, no. 170; *Du Bellay*, I, no. 237; *CAF*, III, no. 7834; *Calais Chronicle* (1846), p. 45; Herbert (1649), pp. 382–4; Bapts (1891), pp. 110–18.

40 *LP*, VIII, no. 826; *CSPSp*, V, i, no. 170.

25 PIETY AND PASTIME

1 NA, SP 1/103, fo. 318.
2 Dowling (1990), p. 50.
3 Ibid., pp. 51–2.
4 Ibid., pp. 48–54.
5 Ellis, 3rd Series, II, pp. 246–9. See also ibid., II, pp. 249–70.
6 Dowling (1990), pp. 50–1, 53–5.
7 Foxe (1570), II, p. 1198; Freeman (1995), pp. 801–2.
8 Dowling (1990), p. 63.
9 BL, C.23.a.8; BL, C.18.c.9; Carley (1998), pp. 261–72. The following paragraphs are greatly indebted to Carley (1998), pp. 261–80; Carley (2000), pp. lvi–lviii; Carley (2004a), pp. 131–46; Carley (2004b), pp. 124–33. See also Ives (1996), pp. 239–45, 268–76. On the covers of Lefèvre's Bible translation, Anne had biblical texts stamped in gold lettering.
10 *CSPSp*, V, ii, no. 43A (p. 91); *LP*, X, no. 699 (p. 290).
11 BL, Harleian MS 6561, fo. 2r–v; Carley (1998), pp. 263, 272; Higman (2016), p. 157.
12 NECA, Percy MS 465; James (2021), pp. 26–8; Higman (2016), p. 47. The falcon appears in the initial letter at fo. 23r, and the anchor and armillary sphere at fo. 34r.
13 BL, Royal MS, 16 E.XIII; BNF, MS FF 12,795, fos. 166–76; Marot (1879), I, pp. 66–76; Higman (2016), pp. 93–8, 330; Mayer (1965), pp. 286–303; Mayer (1986), pp. 337–46. In the BNF manuscript, one of the variants of the poem ascribes it to Almanque Papillon, one of Marot's younger protégés.
14 Sadly for the theory that the poem was specially composed for Anne, other versions exist dedicated to Francis, Marguerite and the king's

'noble children', and even Charles V. Although Anne was the poem's first dedicatee, it seems it could be adapted as required. See BL, Royal MS, 16 E.XIII, fos. iv, 14v–15v; Mayer (1986), pp. 340–6; Ives (2004), pp. 273–4.

15 Dowling (1990), p. 62.

16 Ibid., pp. 62–3.

17 NA, SP 1/76, fo. 168; *LP*, VI, no. 613.

18 Schmid (2009), pp. 115–16; Ascoli (1927), pp. 235–6 (ll. 117–24).

19 NA, SP 1/103, fo. 321v; NA, PRO 31/9/145; *LP*, VI, no. 585.

20 Saunders (1951), p. 509; Sessions (1999), p. 175.

21 BL, Additional MS 17,492, digitised at https://www.bl.uk/manuscripts/Viewer.aspx?ref=add_ms_17492_fs001r#.

22 Lerer (1997), pp. 89–90.

23 Elyot (1533), p. 4.

24 Southall (1964), pp. 142–50; Irish (2011), pp. 83–107; Stamatakis (2012), pp. 151–92; Sessions (1999), pp. 175–7.

25 Southall (1964), pp. 142–50; Baron (1994), pp. 318–35; Remley (1994), pp. 48–55. Work in progress shows there is tantalising evidence of what once was drypoint writing by which inkless impressions are made on the paper using a sharp implement like a stylus or hairpin. Such impressions can simply be a way of marking passages or suggesting that some lines of poetry should be considered as separate stanzas or from a different work, but they were also a way of conveying secret, surreptitious messages. See Powell (2019), pp. 37–53.

26 BL, Additional MS 17,492, fo. 2.

27 SHDM/Biographies, and Appendix II; Ives (2004), pp. 72–3.

28 BL, Additional MS 17,492, fos. 1, 6v–7, 22v, 65r–v, 81; Remley (1994), pp. 48–51; Baron (1994), p. 328; SHDM/Biographies, and Appendix II. The poem addressed to Shelton is attributed by some to Thomas Clere, and by others to Wyatt.

29 Bapts (1891), pp. 138–44; Singer (1825), II, p. 20; Lerer (1997), p. 202; Warner (2013), pp. 160, 195–9.

30 Powell (2016), pp. 193–224; Rollins (1928), II, pp. 82–5, 7, 91, 93, 189; Byrom (1932), p. 128; Nott (1816), I, p. xix; Bell (1854), pp. 232–3, 235–6, 244–6; Warner (2013), pp. 16–17.

31 George's poems purportedly reappeared anonymously in Richard Tottel's *Miscellany* of 1557, justifiably called a repository 'for [the] letters, loves and lives that populated Henry's court'. Containing

many poems by Wyatt and the Earl of Surrey, the full title of the *Miscellany* is *Songs and Sonnets, written by the Right Honourable Lord Henry Howard late Earl [of] Surrey, and Other[s]*.

32 Anon (1538), fo. 4r–v; Harington (1792), III, pp. 286–7; BL, Additional MS 17,492, fos. 14v–15; Tottel (1557), fos. 33v–4. Modern editors claim the poem for Wyatt. See Rebholz (1978), no. 109.

33 NA, E 36/120, fos. 53–65; *LP*, XI, no. 48 (1, 2); BL, Additional MS 17,492; SHDM/Biographies, and Appendix II; Southall (1964), pp. 142–50; Irish (2011), pp. 83–107.

34 BL, Additional MS 17,492, fos. 59v, 63v. A third Shelton sister, Anne, married Edmund Knyvet, eldest son of Sir Thomas Knyvet and the 2nd Duke of Norfolk's daughter Muriel, who made his career as a Norfolk landowner and rarely left the county. See *HC, 1509–1558*, II, pp. 482–3.

35 The puzzle is supposedly Anne's reply to one of Wyatt's verses:

That tyme that myrthe dyd ste[e]re my shypp
whyche now ys frowght with he[a]vines[s],
and fortune boate [bit] not then the lypp
But was Defence off my Dystresse,
then in my boke wrote my maystresse
'I am yowres, yow may well be sure,
and shall be whyle my lyff Dothe [en]dure.'

See BL, Additional MS 17,492, fos. 17v, 67v.

36 BL, Additional MS 17,492, fo. 67v; SHDM/Biographies, and Appendix II; Ives (2004), p. 73.

37 Schmid (2009), p. 112; Ascoli (1927), p. 234 (ll. 52–8); Lowinsky (1969–70), pp. 3, 19, 28.

38 Mirabella (2012), pp. 73–4.

39 Parkinson (1958), pp. 118–22; Urkevich (2009), pp. 176, 182. The painting is in the Harrach Collection, now in Schloss Rohrau in Lower Austria.

40 NA, SP 1/76, fo. 168. Norris had been Master of the Hawks since at least 1529. See E 101/420/11, fo. 25.

41 BL, Cotton MS, Otho C.X, fo. 229r–v; Singer (1827), pp. 452–3.

42 *PPE, Henry*, pp. 15, 17, 18, 37, 38, 44, 46, 50, 78, 86, 98, 126, 150, 186, 227, 229, 232, 248, 265, 271, 272, 274, 275, 277, 278; Schmid (2009), p. 149; Ascoli (1927), pp. 256–7 (ll. 789–94); Singer (1825), II, p. 30.

43 BL, Royal MS, 20 B.XXI (unfoliated); Carley (2004b), pp. 130–3; Brigden (2012), pp. 99–100; Blumenfeld-Kosinski (1994), pp. 705–25. For Smeaton, see *PPE, Henry*, pp. 11, 14, 18, 44, 53, 61, 73, 75, 78, 84, 86, 98, 100, 121. Very likely Thomas Wyatt presented George with the manuscript around the time of his marriage to Jane Parker. On the verso of the second folio, the recipient wrote: 'This book is mine / George Boleyn 1526'. Wyatt's notes are on the back flyleaves. Beside the initials 'JP' (Jane Parker?) and the Spanish motto 'presto para servir' ('ready to serve'), he writes 'forse' ('perhaps') three times. In Italian again, he observes ironically, 'My listeners, note this well / that the new expunges the old way of thought.' In French, he quips, 'He that is an ass, and thinks himself a hart [male deer, especially a stag] / On leaping the ditch will discover the truth.' In Latin, he writes in bold capitals: 'LAUDA: FINEM' ('praise the end'). Beneath is a motto in French: 'Rien que d'être' ('only to be').

44 BL, Cotton MS, Otho C.X, fo. 225r–v; Singer (1827), pp. 454–5; Singer (1825), II, pp. 36–7; Lowinsky (1969–70), pp. 17, 28.

45 *LP*, IV, iii, no. 6489; Sylvester (1959), pp. 139–40.

46 *Spanish Chronicle*, pp. 55–61.

47 NA, SP 1/76, fo. 168 (wrongly calendared in *LP*, VI, no. 613, where the 'not' is missed out); Ives (1976), pp. 1–2; Thornton (2000), pp. 195–216; BL, Royal MS, 7 F.XIV, fo. 100. Besides acquiring or inheriting large estates on his own account, Brereton's local prestige was vastly increased when he married Elizabeth Savage, a widowed daughter of the 1st Earl of Worcester.

48 Brigden (2012), pp. 173–6, 225–7, 292–3; Zell (1974), pp. 213–15.

49 Irish (2011), pp. 88–91; SHDM/Biographies, and Appendix II. For Irish, the distinction is between BL, Additional MS 17,492, fos. 40–4 (eight earlier poems, no later than the summer of 1536) and the so-called 'prison lyrics' on fos. 26–30.

50 NA, E 36/120, fos. 53–5v; *LP*, XI, nos. 48 (1, 2), 147 (p. 64); Swinburne (1686), pp. 12–13, 74–108; Irish (2011), pp. 83–7.

51 *LP*, IV, iii, nos. 5729, 6489.

52 NA, E 36/120, fo. 53v.

53 NA, E 36/120, fo. 55; *Lisle Letters*, III, no. 735, and p. 441; Wriothesley (1875–77), I, p. 49.

26 COURT CONSPIRACY

1 *LP*, IX, nos. 15, 696, 919, 947; Parker (2019), pp. 237–45; Knecht (1994), pp. 330–1.

2 NA, KB 8/7, Pt 1 (incorrectly calendared in *LP*, VIII, no. 609); Spelman (1976–77), I, pp. 56–7; *LP*, VIII, nos. 565, 566, 609; Harpsfield (1932), pp. 229–30.

3 Van Ortroy (1893), p. 164; Harpsfield (1932), Appendix 1, p. 235.

4 KB 8/7, Pts 2–3; NA, SP 2/R, fos. 20–1; Harpsfield (1932), Appendix 3. Palmer, Spert, Lovell and Chamber are identified from *PPE, Henry*, pp. 17, 22, 32, 33, 171, 267, 270; *LP*, VI, nos. 554, 841; *LP*, VIII, nos. 12, 816, 1148; *LP*, XII, ii, nos. 490, 783, 835, 852, 857, 1060 (p. 373); *LP*, XIII, i, no. 231; *HC, 1509–1558* (1982), III, pp. 54–6; *ODNB* (s.v. Spert, Sir Thomas). For Parnell, see Guy (2008), pp. 194, 204–5, 224.

5 BNF, MS Dupuy 373, fos. 101–4; BNF, MS FF 1701, fos. 185–90; BNF, MS FF 2832, fos. 191–3; BNF, MS FF 2960, fos. 64–70; BNF, MS FF 2981, fos. 44–5; BNF, MS FF 3969, fos. 63–7; BNF, MS FF 12,795, fos. 29–32; BNF, MS FF 16,539, fos. 30–3; Harpsfield (1932), Appendix 2; Schmid (2009), p. 154; Ascoli (1927), pp. 259–60 (ll. 882–6).

6 Roper (1935), pp. 86–96; Bodleian, Folio.Δ.624, facing pp. 392, 394; *LP*, VIII, nos. 666 (p. 251), 856, 858–9, 867, 886, 974; Derrett (1960), pp. 214–23; Derrett (1964a), pp. 449–77; Derrett (1964b), pp. 5–19; Guy (2008), pp. 258–63.

7 Camusat, II, fos. 27v–8v; *LP*, VIII, nos. 876, 909, 1115, 1116, 1117; *LP*, IX, nos. 15, 939, 940, 941, 944, 947.

8 *CSPSp*, V, i, no. 174 (p. 493); *LP*, VIII, no. 1106 (1); *LP*, IX, nos. 525, 555, 571; Starkey (1991), p. 118.

9 *CSPSp*, V, i, no. 184. Somer made his first appearance in the records on 24 June 1534, when clothes were ordered for him from the king's Great Wardrobe. There he is named as 'John Somer', but this is likely to be a scribal error. See NA, E 101/417/3, which fully itemises clothes which almost perfectly match what Will Somer wears in the 1544 painting of 'The Family of Henry VIII' in the Royal Collection.

10 NA, E 101/421/13; Wriothesley (1875–77), I, p. 43; *LP*, IX, nos. 271, 278, 326, 504 (2, 3, 6, 10), 729 (6, 7, 8, 16, 17, 18).

11 *LP*, IX, nos. 619, 620; NA, OBS 1419; Friedmann (1884), II, pp. 200–1. It was perhaps no coincidence that when, on account of the plague, the royal progress continued its way deeper into rural Hampshire

after visiting Winchester, it was to Edward Seymour's manor house at Elvetham that Henry retreated on his journey back to Windsor.

12 *Lisle Letters*, II, no. 451.

13 BNF, MS FF 3014, fo. 98.

14 BNF, MS Dupuy 547, fo. 307; Camusat, II, fos. 21–3v; *CAF*, III, no. 8060; *LP*, IX, no. 437.

15 BNF, MS Dupuy 547, fos. 200–4; *CSPSp*, V, i, no. 213.

16 *LP*, IX, nos. 443, 594, 595, 696; *LP*, XIII, ii, no. 444.

17 *Du Bellay*, II, no. 290 (p. 140).

18 *LP*, IX, nos. 714, 812 (2), 836, 838, 848, 861, 875, 919, 969, 970, 980; *LP*, X, no. 282.

19 BL, Cotton MS, Vespasian F.XIII, fo. 244; *LP*, IX, nos. 836, 848, 875, 969, 980.

20 *LP*, VI, nos. 521, 837; MacCulloch (2018), p. 114. Cromwell held many similar stewardships in the Duchy of Lancaster, at the Savoy hospital on the Strand, and at numerous religious houses. See *LP*, IX, nos. 478, 842.

21 NA, SP 1/78, fo. 50v; *LP*, VI, nos. 559, 917.

22 NA, SP 1/87, fo. 45; *LP*, VII, no. 1478.

23 Perrenot (1841–52), II, pp. 387–94; BNF, MS FF 5499, fos. 207–15, 215v–19; *Du Bellay*, II, nos. 251, 259; *LP*, IX, no. 269; *CSPSp*, V, i, nos. 213, 229, 235, 238, 239, 240, 243.

24 *LP*, X, no. 307 (2).

25 *LP*, IX, nos. 964 (p. 323), 1036, 1037, 1040; *LP*, X, nos. 28, 59, 60, 141 (pp. 49–51); *CSPSp*, V, i, nos. 238 (pp. 585–6), 246; *CSPSp*, V, ii, nos. 3, 4, 9 (pp. 15–16); Fitzroy Inventory, pp. 23–41.

26 *LP*, IX, no. 1036 (p. 358); *LP*, X, no. 141 (pp. 51–2); *CSPSp*, V, ii, no. 9 (pp. 18–22); Hall (1809), p. 818.

27 *LP*, X, nos. 200, 282, 294, 351 (p. 134), 352; *CSPSp*, V, ii, nos. 21, 29, 35.

28 *LP*, X, nos. 199, 282, 351; *CSPSp*, V, ii, nos. 13, 29.

29 Baroni (1962), nos. 94, 97, 111, 113, 152, 161; Lestocquoy (1961), nos. 74, 77, 86, 89, 126, 134; *LP*, X, nos. 175, 187, 190, 228, 279, 315, 359, 443, 450, 697, 831.

30 NA, SP 70/7, fos. 3–13, especially fos. 4–5; *CSPF*, I, no. 1303; Brigden (2012), pp. 286–7.

31 *CSPSp*, V, ii, no. 29 (p. 56); *LP*, X, no. 351 (p. 133). For the animosity
    between Cromwell and Gardiner, see Merriman (1902), II, pp. 19–20;
    MacCulloch (2018), p. 314.

32 *LP*, X, no. 351; *CSPSp*, V, ii, no. 29.

33 *LP*, X, nos. 430, 494; *Du Bellay*, II, no. 350; Knecht (1994), pp. 330–2.

34 *LP*, X, nos. 495, 601 (p. 245); *CSPSp*, V, ii, no. 43 (pp. 84–5).

35 *LP*, X, no. 601; *CSPSp*, V, ii, no. 43. For the quotations in the original
    French, see *CSPSp*, V, ii, pp. 81–2; Friedmann (1884), II, notes to
    pp. 226–7.

36 NA, SP 1/103, fos. 75–81. Skip's drafts and a report on the sermon by
    Thomas Wriothesley are from NA, SP 6/1, fos. 7–14; NA, SP 6/2, fos.
    1–3, 4–21v; NA, SP 6/6, fos. 43–55v; *LP*, X, no. 615 (1–5). See also Ives
    (1994a), pp. 395–400; Bernard (1993), pp. 13–18.

37 Marshall (1535b), sigs. Aii–Av. For the 'HA' cipher, see Marshall
    (1535a), title page; *STC*, no. 15,988. See also Bernard (1993), p. 6.

38 BL, Royal MS, 18 C.VI, fos. 1–33; Elton (1974–92), II, pp. 137–54;
    Elton (1973), p. 76.

39 BL, Cotton MS, Cleopatra E.IV, fos. 131–2; *SR*, III, pp. 558–62, 575–
    8; Lehmberg (1970), pp. 231–2; Fideler (1974), pp. 283–4.

40 *Lisle Letters*, III, no. 650; BL, Cotton MS, Cleopatra E.IV, fos. 131–2;
    LP, X, no. 462 (p. 190); Ives (1994a), pp. 396–7; Ives (2004), p. 310.

41 Hoyle (2001), pp. 79–80.

42 Ellis, 3rd Series, III, pp. 50–2; *LP*, XII, i, no. 786 (pp. 342–3); Dowling
    (1990), pp. 57–8.

43 For the biblical story, see Esther 3: 1–7:10.

44 NA, SP 6/1, fo. 8v; *CSPSp*, V, i, no. 118 (p. 346); *LP*, XI, no. 1244
    (p. 505); Ives (1994a), pp. 399–400.

45 NA, SP 6/1, fos. 8v–9.

46 Thomas and Thornley (1938), pp. 350–1.

47 AGR, MS Audience 379, fos. 1–15 (quotation from fo. 8); *LP*, X, nos.
    575 (where the date of the arrival of Chapuys' dispatch is incorrect),
    688, 699; *CSPSp*, V, ii, nos. 40, 43A.

27 INTO THE ABYSS

1 Parker (2019), pp. 246–56.

2 BNF, MS Dupuy 547, fos. 299–302; Camusat, II, fos. 155–7; *Lisle
   Letters*, III, no. 677; *LP*, X, nos. 597 (3, 4); 688, 699; Wriothesley
   (1875–77), I, p. 35.

3 *CSPSp*, V, ii, no. 43A (pp. 91–3); *LP*, X, no. 699; Friedmann (1884), II, pp. 228–32 (where the original French is given in the notes).

4 *CSPSp*, V, ii, no. 43A (pp. 93–8, original French on p. 95); *LP*, X, no. 699; Friedmann (1884), II, pp. 232–4; Ives (1992), pp. 662–3.

5 BNF, MS Dupuy 547, fos. 299–300; Camusat, II, fos. 155–6.

6 Although no first-hand account of the audience now survives, the terms offered by de Castelnau, along with many of Henry's reactions, were fed back to Stephen Gardiner and Sir John Wallop in their revised instructions. See *LP*, X, nos. 725, 760. It was in fact just bad luck that de Dinteville did not leave Paris for another three days and was then laid low for almost a fortnight in Boulogne by illness. See BNF, MS Dupuy 547, fos. 301v–2; Camusat, II, fo. 156v; *CAF*, III, no. 8421; *CSPSp*, V, ii, no. 55 (pp. 128, 129); *LP*, X, no. 759 (p. 318).

7 *CSPSp*, V, ii, no. 43A (p. 98); *LP*, X, no. 699 (p. 293).

8 *LP*, X, no. 752; *CSPSp*, V, ii, no. 47; *Lisle Letters*, III, no. 686.

9 BL, Cotton MS, Otho C.X, fos. 172–3v, 174–5, 229; BL, Cotton MS, Titus B.I, fos. 451–2v; BL, Cotton MS, Cleopatra E.IV, fo. 110; *Lisle Letters*, III, no. 703a, and pp. 378–84; *Lisle Letters*, IV, no. 847; *LP*, VII, no. 1036 (where misdated); *LP*, X, nos. 871, 1134 (1–4), 1150; Ives (1972), pp. 175–6; Ives (1992), pp. 659–61; Clark (2018), pp. 126–7.

10 NA, SP 1/91, fo. 65; *LP*, VII, no. 1554 (later corrected in *LP*, VIII, p. 570); *LP*, VIII, no. 356. The quarrel between Francis Bryan and George Boleyn appears to have had its origins in a dispute over a valuable wardship which Bryan sold to Sir Andrew Windsor and the wider affairs of the Fortescues of Ponsbourne, Hertfordshire. The Boleyns were distant cousins of the Fortescues, whereas in about 1522, Bryan had married Philippa, daughter and heir of Humphrey Spice of Black Notley in Essex, the widow of John Fortescue of Ponsbourne. See NA, C1/917/57–9; *LP*, III, ii, no. 2145 (8); *SR*, III, p. 264; Fortescue (1869), II, pp. 152, 156, 165, 170, 254; *ODNB*, s.v. 'Bryan, Sir Francis'.

11 *LP*, VIII, no. 174 (p. 61); *LP*, X, nos. 715, 752, 753; *CSPSp*, V, ii, no. 47 (p. 106); Le Laboureur (1731), I, p. 412.

12 *LP*, X, no. 725; *St. Pap*, VII, pp. 684–6.

13 *LP*, X, no. 752; *CSPSp*, V, ii, no. 47.

14 *CSPSp*, V, ii, nos. 47, 48; *LP*, X, nos. 736, 752, 782; Lehmberg (1977), p. 1.

15 *Lisle Letters*, III, nos. 680, 683, 684, 685, 686, 687.

16 BNF, MS Dupuy 547, fos. 303–6; Camusat, II, fos. 14v–17; *LP*, X, no. 759.

17 BL, Cotton MS, Vitellius B.XIV, fos. 162–72v; *LP*, X, nos. 666, 670; Friedmann (1884), II, pp. 210–11.

18 *CSPSp*, V, ii, no. 55 (p. 125).

19 *CSPSp*, V, ii, no. 47; *LP*, X, no. 752.

20 BL, Cotton MS, Otho C.X, fo. 225v; Singer (1827), pp. 454–5.

21 BL, Cotton MS, Otho C.X, fos. 225v, 228v; Singer (1827), pp. 454–5, 457; Amyot (1831), p. 64. For Strype's notes and transcripts, see Strype (1822), I, i, pp. 431–6. Ives's statement that Smeaton was not taken to the Tower until Monday at 6 p.m. is incorrect. His source is said to be Bodleian, Folio.Δ.624, facing p. 385, but this entry refers to Anne. See Ives (2004), pp. 326, 416, n. 35. For Constantine's backstory, see Guy (2008), pp. 197–8. His account of Anne's fall should be read with caution. The original document (Amyot [1831], pp. 56–78) has never been seen; all that was ever produced was a transcript, which Amyot received from John Payne Collier, a journalist, theatre critic and pseudo-Shakespearean scholar with a mixed reputation.

22 *Spanish Chronicle* (1889), pp. 60–1.

23 BL, Cotton MS, Otho C.X, fo. 229; Singer (1827), p. 452.

24 *Lisle Letters*, III, nos. 689, 690.

25 NA, SP 70/7, fo. 7r–v; *CSPF*, I, no. 1303 (p. 527).

26 Wriothesley (1875–77), I, p. 35; Schmid (2009), p. 135; Ascoli (1927), p. 247 (ll. 504–6).

27 Hall (1809), p. 819; Stow (1580), p. 1006; Amyot (1831), p. 64.

28 Schmid (2009), p. 134; Ascoli (1927), p. 247 (ll. 490–6).

29 BL, Cotton MS, Otho C.X, fo. 228v; Singer (1827), p. 456.

30 Stow (1580), p. 1006; Wriothesley (1875–77), I, p. 36; *CSPSp*, V, ii, no. 48; *LP*, X, no. 782.

31 Bodleian, Folio.Δ.624, facing p. 385; Stow (1580), p. 1006; Wriothesley (1875–77), I, p. 36.

32 NA, SP 1/103, fo. 215; *LP*, X, no. 785. Bulkeley's aim was to enable his brother to claim a cut of the spoils, for the vultures were already circling.

33 *CSPSp*, V, ii, no. 48; *LP*, X, no. 782.

34 Baynton's letter ends: 'the que[en] standeth stiffly in her opinion that she wo[uld] [illegible] which I think is in the trust that she [illegible] other two.' BL, Cotton MS, Otho C.X, fo. 209v; Singer (1827), pp. 458–9.

35 Amyot (1831), p. 64.

36 Merriman (1902), II, p. 12; *Lisle Letters*, III, no. 694; Amyot (1831), p. 65 (where 'Thursday afore May Day' is a transcription or printer's error for '*after* May Day'); Bodleian, Folio.Δ.624, facing p. 384; *LP*, X, nos. 865, 909; BL, Harleian MS 78, fo. 12; Muir (1963), p. 201. See also Friedmann (1884), II, Appendix F, pp. 348–9. Henry Knyvet, who served in the privy chamber, was Edmund's younger brother. Cromwell had him released within a few days. See *LP*, X, nos. 865, 870, 871; *Lisle Letters*, III, no. 695; NA, E 101/420/1, no. 8.

37 BL, Cotton MS, Otho C.X, fo. 229r–v; Singer (1827), pp. 452–3.

38 BL, Cotton MS, Cleopatra E.IV, fo. 110; *LP*, X, nos. 865, 1256 (39); Muir (1963), p. 201; *LP*, XIII, i, no. 981 (2), [14]; *Lisle Letters*, III, no. 6943.

39 *Lisle Letters*, III, nos. 694, 695.

40 *Lisle Letters*, IV, no. 846; Robison (1984), I, pp. 193–4. Page was back as sheriff of Surrey within months.

41 NA, SP 1/103, fos. 251, 266, 278; NA, SP 1/104, fos. 165, 166; NA, SP 3/13, fo. 46; *LP*, X, nos. 819, 840, 1131, 1135; *LP*, XI, no. 107; BL, Royal MS, 20 B.XXI (unfoliated); Nichols (1857), I, pp. xxx–xxxi; Bryson (2001), pp. 11, 49; Brigden (2012), pp. 280–1. Page had recently become Seymour's stepfather-in-law, after he married Elizabeth Stanhope (*née* Bourchier), the mother of Anne Stanhope, who married Seymour as his second wife.

42 Singer (1825), p. 35; *LP*, X, no. 1256 (8, 29); *LP*, XI, no. 1024; Thornton (2000), pp. 204–10; Ives (1976), pp. 36–41; Ives (1992), pp. 651–62; Ives (2004); pp. 347–8.

43 BL, Cotton MS, Otho C.X, fos. 209v–10; Singer (1827), p. 458.

44 NA, SP 1/87, fo. 35; *LP*, VII, no. 1446 (misdated); MacCulloch (2018), p. 316.

45 Merriman (1902), II, p. 12.

46 Schmidt (2009), pp. 126–8; Ascoli (1927), pp. 242–3 (ll. 339–74); BL, Lansdowne MS 105, no. 6 (fo. 19r–v); Pocock (1870), II, pp. 574–5; Ives (1972), p. 176; Ives (1992), pp. 656, 658; Clark (2018), p. 126; Bernard (2010), pp. 151–60.

47 *Lisle Letters*, III, no. 703a; *Lisle Letters*, IV, no. 847.

48 NA, SP 1/103, fo. 252; *LP*, X, nos. 820, 870.

49 *Lisle Letters*, III, no. 695; *LP*, I, ii, no. 3348 (p. 1409); *LP*, IV, i, no. 895 (p. 392); *PPE, Henry*, pp. 97, 112, 168; NA, E 179/69/27; NA, E

179/69/28; BL, Additional MS 71,009, fo. 40v; Ives (2004), pp. 328, 417, n. 51.

50 *Lisle Letters*, II, no. 260.

51 *LP*, X, nos. 1010, 1015 (21); BL, Additional MS 71,009, fos. 37–44 (especially fo. 42r–v); BL, Cotton MS, Vespasian, F. XIII, fo. 199; Ellis, 1st Series, II, pp. 67–8.

52 *Lisle Letters*, III, nos. 846, 846a.

53 NA, KB, 8/8; Wriothesley (1875–77), I, pp. 189, 196; NA, SP 1/105, fo. 5; NA, SP 1/110, fo. 28; NA, SP 1/112, fos. 162–3; NA, SP 1/125, fo. 1; BL, Cotton MS, Vespasian F.XIII, fo. 162; *LP*, XI, nos. 17, 202 (3), 926, 1277; *LP*, XII, ii, nos. 580, 722. The brief calendared abstracts do not do justice to the tone of the handwritten letters.

28 THE TRIALS BEGIN

1 Sylvester (1959), p. 179.

2 *Lisle Letters*, III, no. 698.

3 NA, SP 1/103, fo. 269; *LP*, X, no. 843.

4 *CSPSp*, V, ii, no. 55 (p. 131), where the original French is given.

5 BL, Cotton MS, Otho C.X, fos. 225, 228v, 229v; Strype (1822), I, i, pp. 435–6; Singer (1827), pp. 453, 454, 457; Beer (2018b), p. 44.

6 NA, SP 1/130, fo. 121; NA, STAC 2/15/213–28; NA, STAC 2/25/52; NA, STAC 2/26/127; *LP*, VII, nos. 497, 923 (p. 345); *LP*, X, no. 1091; *LP*, XII, ii, no 1060 (p. 374); *LP*, XIII, i, no. 586; *LP*, XV, no. 436 (48); HEH, Ellesmere MS 2652, fo. 14; BL, Additional MS 71,009, fo. 42v; *SR*, III, pp. 433–4; Fortescue (1869), II, pp. 156, 170, 254; Parker (1983), no. 51.

7 BL, Cotton MS, Otho C.X, fos. 225, 228v; Singer (1827), pp. 454, 457.

8 BL, Cotton MS, Otho C.X, fo. 229; Singer (1827), p. 451.

9 BL, Cotton MS, Otho C.X, fo. 228v, 229; Singer (1827), pp. 451–2, 456.

10 BL, Cotton MS, Otho C.X, fo. 229; Singer (1827), pp. 451–2; Stow (1580), p. 1006; Wriothesley (1875–77), I, p. 36.

11 BL, Cotton MS, Otho C.X, fo. 229r–v; Singer (1827), pp. 452–3.

12 BL, Cotton MS, Otho C.X, fos. 228v, 229; Singer (1827), pp. 452, 456–7.

13 BL, Cotton MS, Otho C.X, fos. 225v; Singer (1827), p. 455.

14 BL, Cotton MS, Otho C.X, fos. 225r–v, 229r–v; Singer (1827), pp. 452–3, 454–5.

15 BL, Cotton MS, Otho C.X, fos. 228v, 267v; Singer (1827), p. 457; *LP*, X, nos. 835, 908, 942.

16 *Lisle Letters*, III, no. 695; Schmid (2009), p. 50; Ascoli (1927), p. 257 (ll. 801–8); BL, Cotton MS, Otho C.X, fo. 225; Singer (1827), pp. 453–4.

17 *CSPSp*, V, ii, no. 55 (p. 128).

18 BL, Cotton MS, Otho C.X, fo. 230r–v; Cox (1846), pp. 323–4; *LP*, X, no. 792.

19 *CSPSp*, V, ii, nos. 54 (p. 121), 55 (pp. 125–8); *LP*, X, nos. 908 (p. 378), 909.

20 BL, Cotton MS, Otho C.X, fo. 228v; Singer (1827), pp. 456–7.

21 BL, Cotton MS, Otho C.X, fos. 225, 228v; Singer (1827), pp. 454, 456; *LP*, XI, no. 381.

22 BL, Cotton MS, Otho C.X, fos. 225, 228v; Singer (1827), pp. 454, 456.

23 BL, Cotton MS, Otho C.X, fo. 232r–v; BL, Hargrave MS 225, fos. 40v–2; BL, Stowe MS 151, fo. 1; BL, Harleian MS 1323, fo. 35; BL, Harleian MS 4031, fo. 15v; BL, Additional MS 22,587, fo. 22. Printed in Herbert (1649), pp. 382–4; *Scrinia Sacra* (1654), pp. 9–10; Burnet (1820), I, ii, pp. 225–6; Savage (1949), pp. 53–6. For a full analysis, see Smith (2018), pp. 86–116.

24 John Foxe, in his account of Anne in his *Acts and Monuments*, does not have it, nor does William Camden or the Elizabethan antiquary, John Stow.

25 Herbert enjoyed privileged access to Henry VIII's State Paper collection in Whitehall and to Sir Robert Cotton's library, first held in Lambeth, later at Ashburnham House, and now in the British Library. Where Cotton acquired the letter is unknown but as he died in 1631, it was either in existence before his death or was added to the library by his son. The most reliable text is bound into one of Cotton's manuscripts which we know for sure Herbert consulted in 1636. Although later damaged in the Ashburnham House fire, this was another document fully transcribed in 1714 by Gilbert Burnet, as a handwritten note on the next folio testifies. See BL, Cotton MS, Otho C.X, fo. 233v; Smith (2018), p. 96; Tite (2013), p. 154.

26 Herbert (1649), pp. 382–4.

27 BL, Cotton MS, Otho C.X, fo. 232v.

28 Special commissions were issued in the wake of revolts, riots or other outbreaks of disorder, or else in preparation for state trials to be held

(usually) in Westminster Hall or London's Guildhall. The king's signature was not necessary: Audley's approval only was required. See Wriothesley (1875–77), I, pp. 189–91, 205; NA, KB 8/8–9; NA, C 193/3, fo. 76v; *DKR*, 3rd Report, Appendix II; *LP*, X, no. 848 (1, 6).

29 These and subsequent details of the trials are taken from NA, KB 8/8–9; fully transcribed and printed in Wriothesley (1875–77), I, pp. 189–226. See also *DKR*, 3rd Report, Appendix II; *LP*, X, no. 876.

30 Ives (1992), pp. 653–64; Baker (2022), II, pp. 222–6.

31 NA, SP 3/12, fo. 64; *Lisle Letters*, IV, no. 845a.

32 In 1341, Edward III had learned of the misdeeds of Chief Justice Willoughby 'by the common fame and clamour of our people, as well as by divers petitions presented to us and our council', on which basis he was put on trial. See *CW*, X, p. 121; Thorne (1977), II, p. 398; Plucknett (1942), pp. 60–1, 63–8; Harris (1995), pp. 191–203.

33 Schmid (2008), pp. 145–8; Ascoli (1927), pp. 254–5 (ll. 717–76).

34 Wriothesley (1875–77), I, pp. 204–5; *LP*, VI, no. 728 (wrongly dated); Ives (2008), p. 339.

35 *CSPSp*, V, ii, no. 55 (pp. 125–6); *LP*, X, no. 908 (pp. 377–8); Spelman (1976–77), II, p. 71. For procedure in treason trials, see Elton (1972), pp. 293–326.

36 NA, KB 8/8; KB 29/169, m. 7v; Wriothesley (1875–77), I, p. 198 (where the Latin is rendered erroneously); Spelman (1976–77), I, pp. 70–1. See also Elton (1972), p. 386.

37 *CSPSp*, V, ii, no. 55 (p. 125); *LP*, X, no. 908 (p. 377); Wriothesley (1875–77), I, p. 36.

38 *Lisle Letters*, III, no. 695.

29 THE FALCON AT BAY

1 Wriothesley (1875–77), I, p. 214; *CSPSp*, V, ii, no. 55 (p. 125); Friedmann (1884), II, p. 275; Fonblanque (1887), II, p. 438.

2 Wriothesley (1875–77), I, p. 37; Bodleian, Folio.Δ.624, facing p. 385; Baker (2003), pp. 520–1; *CSPSp*, V, ii, no. 55 (p. 125); *LP*, X, nos. 908 (p. 377), 956.

3 Baker (2003), pp. 520–1; Harris (1986), pp. 196–7.

4 Merriman (1902), II, p. 21.

5 *CSPSp*, V, ii, no. 55; *LP*, X, no. 908; Amyot (1831), pp. 65–6; *Lisle Letters*, III, nos. 695, 698, 770, 845a, 846, 847; Spelman (1976–77), I,

pp. xvii–xxxii, 70–1. Burnet confirms that he saw Spelman's original 'writ with his own hand': Burnet (1820), I, i, pp. 305–7.

6 In his capacity as a herald, Wriothesley had an inside knowledge of the workings of the Lord Steward's Court. Wriothesley (1875–77), I, pp. 37–40; Hall (1809), p. 819.

7 An Oxford scholar with social pretensions, Turner was elected President of Corpus Christi College in 1688 and called himself 'Tourneur'.

8 Bodleian, Folio.Δ.624, facing p. 385; Burnet (1820), I, i, p. 306. Turner's notes, interspersed with comments of his own, are interleaved with his copy of Herbert (1649). For Stow's access to Anthony Anthony's journal, see Stow (1580), verso of the title page.

9 BNF, MS Dupuy 373, fos. 111v–12. De Carle is the likely author of a second, shorter poem on Rochford's death. See BMS, MS 202, fos. 137v–40v, and Ascoli (1927), pp. 274–8. The correlation between lines of the second poem and the notes in the Dupuy MS strongly implies de Carle's authorship of both. A close similarity also exists between Anne's scaffold speech in the first poem and in the notes.

10 The discovery that, despite Cromwell's strict cordon, some foreigners did slip through to witness Anne's execution makes it theoretically possible that de Carle or a compatriot could have been among them. See Bodleian, Folio.Δ.624, facing p. 384.

11 [Bentley] (1831), pp. 260–5; BL, G.6122; BL, 10806.b.51; Hamy (1898), pp. ccccxxxi–ccccxxxvi. The Italian edition, printed in Bologna, has the mouthful of a title *Il successo in la morte della Regina de Inghilterra: con il consenso del Consiglio di S. M. y la morte di quattro gran Baroni del Regno consentienti al delitto commesso da essa Regina con el proprio fratello*, and purports to be a letter from London.

12 Gachard (1885), I, p. 17, n. 1; *LP*, X, no. 911 (1, 2); Froude (1861), pp. 116–17.

13 NA, C 193/3, fo. 80.

14 Wriothesley (1875–77), I, pp. 37, 38, 213–18; Bodleian, Folio.Δ.624, facing p. 385.

15 In Hales's view, such a gift exchange constituted the 'overt act' involved in 'compassing' the king's death that the law had required in treason trials since 1351.

16 *CSPSp*, V, ii, no. 55 (pp. 125–6), the original French can be seen on p. 126; *LP*, X, no. 908 (pp. 377–8). For the correct punctuation and translation, see *Lisle Letters*, III, p. 363, and n. 3.

17 Spelman (1976–77), I, p. 71; *SR*, III, pp. 473–4.

18 Spelman (1976–77), I, p. 71.

19 Ibid.; Burnet (1820), I, i, p. 307; Ives (2004), p. 330.

20 *HC, 1509–1558*, III, pp. 500–2.

21 Burnet (1820), I, i, p. 307.

22 Ibid., p. 314.

23 Wriothesley (1875–77), I, pp. 38–9; Bodleian, Folio.Δ.624, facing p. 385; *CSPSp*, V, ii, no. 55 (pp. 125–6); *LP*, X, 908 (pp. 377–8); Ives (2004), p. 340.

24 Bodleian, Folio.Δ.624, facing p. 385; Stow (1580), p. 1007.

25 In his poem, de Carle reverses the order of Anne and George's trials for dramatic effect.

26 *CSPSp*, V, ii, no. 55 (p. 126), original French from Friedmann (1884), II, p. 277, n. 1; *LP*, X, no. 908 (p. 378).

27 Schmid (2009), pp. 156–7; Ascoli (1927), p. 261 (ll. 947–50).

28 Friedmann (1884), II, p. 278.

29 Wriothesley (1875–77), I, p. 38; Bodleian, Folio.Δ.624, facing p. 385.

30 Wriothesley, Chapuys, Spelman, Anthony Anthony, Stow, de Carle, Constantine and Husee are all silent on the point.

31 NA, KB, 8/9; Wriothesley (1875–77), I, pp. 38, 223.

32 Spelman (1976–77), I, p. 71; Bodleian, Folio.Δ.624, facing p. 385.

33 *CSPSp*, V, ii, no. 55 (pp. 126–7), original French from Friedmann (1884), II, p. 278, n. 1; *LP*, X, no. 908 (p. 378); Schmid (2009), p. 160; Ascoli (1927), p. 263 (ll. 1001–14).

34 NA, KB 8/9; Wriothesley (1875–77), I, pp. 223–4. Contrary to tradition, the official court record says that Percy collapsed after Anne's sentence had been handed down.

35 Wriothesley (1875–77), I, pp. 223–4.

36 *LP*, X, no. 908 (p. 378); *LP*, V, ii, no. 55 (p. 126).

37 NA, KB 8/9; *LP*, VIII, no. 826; *LP*, X, no. 876; *CSPSp*, V, i, no. 170.

38 *LP*, V, ii, no. 55 (p. 126); *LP*, X, no. 908 (p. 378); Wriothesley (1875–77), I, p. 39.

39 Schmid (2009), p. 154; Ascoli (1927), pp. 259–60 (ll. 882–6).

40 Mackay (2018a), pp. 116, 188; Ives (2004), pp. 341–2.

41 *LP*, V, ii, no. 55 (p. 126); *LP*, X, no. 908 (p. 378).

42 NA, KB 8/9; Wriothesley (1875–77), I, pp. 39, 224; *LP*, V, ii, no. 55 (p. 126); *LP*, X, no. 908 (p. 378).

43 Schmid (2009), p. 153; Ascoli (1927), p. 259 (ll. 861–4).

44 Amyot (1831), p. 66.

45 [Bentley] (1831), pp. 261–2.

46 BL, Harleian MS 283, fo. 134; Singer (1827), p. 460; Ellis, 1st Series, II, pp. 62–3; Starkey (2004), pp. 580–1.

47 BL, Cotton MS, Otho C.X, fo. 224; Hearne (1716), p. 113.

48 BL, Harleian MS 283, fo. 134.

49 Ibid.; NA, SP 1/103, fo. 30; *LP*, X, no. 902 (misleadingly calendared and wrongly dated). For the correct date, see *LP*, X, p. 644.

50 BL, Harleian MS 283, fo. 134.

51 Spelman (1976–77), I, p. 59; NA, SP 1/103, fo. 30. Cromwell's letter is lost, but its contents can be inferred from Kingston's reply.

52 NA, SP 1/103, fo. 30.

53 NA, C 193/3, fo. 80. Spelman, Wriothesley and Husee also say that Smeaton was beheaded on Tower Hill, but this has been repeatedly questioned. See Spelman (1976–77), I, p. 59; Wriothesley (1875–77), I, p. 39; *Lisle Letters*, III, no. 698.

54 The carving is found on the west wall of the main chamber on the first floor of the Beauchamp Tower, immediately below an extensive carving dated 1581. See Ives (2004), pp. 364, 424.

55 NA, SP 1/103, fo. 280v; *LP*, X, no. 869.

56 Nicholas Wotton and John Barbour, two rising church lawyers, were sent to represent Anne, while Dr Richard Sampson was Henry's proctor. Closely watching were Cromwell, Audley, the Duke of Suffolk, Fitzwilliam and Paulet. Neither Wotton nor Barbour was anything other than Henry's placeman. See Friedmann (1884), II, pp. 289–90 and Appendix G, pp. 351–5.

57 Wilkins (1737), III, pp. 803–4; Spelman (1976–77), I, p. 59; Wriothesley (1875–77), I, p. 41, n. 1; *LP*, X, nos. 896, 909. Wriothesley, who also gives the reason as a precontract between Anne and Percy, misreports that the hearing was in the afternoon. Others claimed the reason was Henry's affair with Mary Boleyn. See Friedmann (1884), II, pp. 289–90 and Appendix G, pp. 351–5.

58 *Lisle Letters*, III, no. 698; Schmid (2009), pp. 165–6; Ascoli (1927), pp. 266–7 (ll. 1115–1124); Amyot (1831), p. 65.

59 *Calais Chronicle* (1846), p. 46; BNF, MS Dupuy 373, fo. 111v. Confirmation comes from Wriothesley (1875–77), I, pp. 39–40; *Lisle Letters*, III, no. 770; [Bentley] (1831), pp. 262–3; Amyot (1831), p. 65.

60 BNF, MS Dupuy 373, fo. 111v; *Chronicle of Calais* (1846), pp. 46–7; Wriothesley (1875–77), I, pp. 39–40; NLW, MS 3054D, vol. 2, fo. 511; Carley (1998), p. 277, n. 43; *CSPSp*, V, ii, no. 55 (p. 128); *LP*, X, no. 908 (p. 379). See also Schmid (2009), pp. 163–5; Ascoli (1927), pp. 265–6 (ll. 1076–114).

61 *CSPSp*, V, ii, no. 55 (p. 128); *LP*, X, no. 908 (p. 379).

EPILOGUE

1 Rebholz (1978), no. 197.
2 *Lisle Letters*, IV, no. 848a.
3 *Lisle Letters*, III, no. 713.
4 NA, SP 60/3, fos. 38–9, 40, 46–7, 57, 59–60, 73; *St. Pap.*, II, pp. 315–16, 316–18, 318–21, 330–1.
5 *LJ*, I, p. 84.
6 *SR*, III, pp. 655–6.
7 Ibid., pp. 955–8; Guy (2013), pp. 91–8.
8 *SR*, III, pp. 657–68; Wriothesley (1875–77), I, p. 53. In the privy council, Robert Radcliffe, Earl of Sussex, one of the original gang of four who had plotted to replace Katherine and overthrow Wolsey in 1527, backed Fitzroy's nomination. If it came to a choice between a bastard daughter or a bastard son, he said, 'it was advisable to prefer the male to the female for the succession to the crown.' See *CSPSp*, V, ii, no. 61 (p. 139).
9 Wriothesley (1875–77), I, p. 53.
10 Cromwell, in a letter to Stephen Gardiner, describes Jane as 'the most virtuous lady and the veriest gentlewoman that liveth and one that varieth as much from the conditions of the other as the day varieth from the night'. See BL, Additional MS 71,009, fo. 37v; Merriman (1902), II, p. 21.
11 *St. Pap.*, I, p. 552; *LP*, XI, no. 1250.
12 *Lisle Letters*, IV, nos. 895, 896, 900.
13 BNF, MS FF 2997, fo. 3; BL, Additional MS 71,009, fos. 37–44v.
14 Griffey (2020), pp. 188, 193–4; Guy (2004), pp. 353–70.
15 Walker (2002), pp. 2–3; Lexton (2015), pp. 222–41.
16 *CSPSp*, V, ii, no. 55 (p. 125); *LP*, X, no. 908 (p. 377).

17 BL, Additional MS 25,114, fo. 267; *LP*, XII, ii, no. 78; Harmer (1937), pp. 1–160; Harmer (1939), pp. 443–74. The Lyon version appeared under the title *Epistre contenant le proces criminel faict à l'encontre de la royne Anne Boullant d'Angleterre*: BNF, Rés.YE.3668; BL, 11474.a.14. A doctored version attributed to 'Anthoine de Crespin, Seigneur de Miherne' (aka 'Crispin') is a corrupted text of de Carle's original: BMV, MS 419, fos. 1–26. De Crespin himself is a phantom. See Harmer (1937), pp. 132–3; Ascoli (1927), pp. 1–32. The most recent attempt to treat de Crespin as genuine is Weir (2009), pp. 219, 242–3, 245–6, 262, 266–7.

18 AGR, MSS Divers, 174/4; *LP*, X, no. 965.

19 *CSPSp*, V, ii, no. 55 (p. 127); *LP*, X, no. 908 (p. 378); Amyot (1831), p. 64; Wriothesley (1875–77), I, pp. 39, 41; Friedmann (1884), II, pp. 276, 294.

20 Singer (1827), pp. 445–6.

21 *St. Pap.*, V, pp. 58, 62; *LP*, XI, nos. 994, 1373, 1396; Wood (1846), II, pp. 288–91.

22 *Lisle Letters*, IV, no. 902; Wriothesley (1875–77), I, p. 54.

23 Ellis, 3rd Series, III, pp. 136–8; BL, Additional MS 71,009, fo. 42; *SR*, III, pp. 680–1; *LP*, XI, no. 294 (wrongly dated); *Lisle Letters*, IV, p. 181.

24 Out of duty, Henry paid for Masses for Thomas Boleyn's soul; *LP*, XIV, ii, no. 781, (p. 309). Information on Anne's mother's funeral is from NA, SP 3/12, fo. 42; *Lisle Letters*, V, nos. 1137, 1139.

25 Fox (2007), pp. 291–314.

26 Wriothesley (1875–77), I, p. 52; Logan (1988), pp. 658–67; MacCulloch (2018), pp. 363–71, 410–21, 448–52, 492–3, 515–16, 524–5, 542–3.

27 Ellis, 3rd Series, III, p. 77; Brigden (2012), pp. 536–48.

28 *ODNB*, s.v. 'Howard, Mary, Duchess of Richmond'.

29 NA, PROB 11/30/376; NA, SP 1/233, fo. 36; *LP*, XXI, i, no. 1426; *LP*, XXI, ii, no. 332 (91); Blomefield (1739–75), III, p. 62; Sessions (1999), pp. 301–4. As Mary survived until 1571, she lived through the scandal of Amy Robsart's unexplained death with a broken neck and two deep gashes in her skull after mysteriously falling down a staircase while lodged at Cumnor Place, near Oxford. See Skidmore (2010), pp. 203–306, 377–8. Shelton sued Clere's elder brother in the Court of Chancery when he contested the will: NA, C 1/1156/33.

30 Aylmer (1559), sig. [B4v].

31 The Chequers Trust.

32 Schmid (2009), p. 160; Ascoli (1927), p. 263 (ll. 1001–14). As elsewhere, we have amended the translation better to reflect the sense of the French original.

33 *CSPSp*, V, ii, no. 61 (pp. 137–8), where the original French is given.

34 Schmid (2009), p. 124; Ascoli (1927), p. 241 (ll. 281–7). 'Biens' in this context means 'worldly good' rather than just 'things'.

35 One inscription faintly reads, 'Mine own good niece Joanna, I require ye to pray for your aunt with this here prayer / Elizabeth Shirley': Hever Castle, *Hore beate Marie virginis ad usum ... Sarum*, sig. hiii. See McCaffrey (2021a), at https://www.the-tls.co.uk/ articles/inscriptions-discovered-in-a-book-owned-by-anne-bol eyn-essay-kate-e-mccaffrey.

36 Hurren (2013), p. 67.

37 Rebholz (1978), no. 123. See also Brigden (2012), pp. 274–6.

38 *Lisle Letters*, III, no. 798.

APPENDIX I: ANNE BOLEYN'S DATE OF BIRTH

1 Camden (1615), pp. 12–13.

2 NA, SP 12/264, fos. 186–7.

3 Blacker (1890), pp. 665–6; BL, Harleian MS 1,233, fo. 8.

4 The Queen's College, Oxford, MS 71, fos. 8, 40, 44. The authors thank Dr Matthew Shaw, the Librarian at Queen's, and his colleagues for supplying photos of MS 71. As was the custom among the heralds at the College of Arms at this date, George Boleyn, being male, and therefore the undisputed heir, is named first in the pedigree in conformity with the rule of primogeniture.

5 For accessible summaries of the modern controversy, see Round (1886), pp. 12–23; Paget (1981), pp. 163–4; Ives (2004), pp. 14–17. Starkey (2004), p. 258, agrees with Ives and Paget, although he places the dates a year or so later. Warnicke disagrees, defending Camden and arguing that Anne was the elder daughter, born in 1507: Warnicke (1985a), p. 942.

6 NA, SP 1/105, fos. 5–6; Ellis, 3rd series, III, pp. 22–3.

7 Stephenson (1926), pp. 236, 251.

APPENDIX 2: SOURCES FOR ANNE'S MOVEMENTS IN FRANCE

1 Michaud and Poujoulat (1836–39), V, pp. 85–93.
2 Orth (1982), pp. 55–66.
3 Ives (2004), pp. 30–1.
4 Barrillon (1897–99), I, pp. 56–327; ibid., II, pp. 1–191; and see Bibliography.

APPENDIX 3: SOURCES FOR THE TRIALS OF ANNE AND
GEORGE BOLEYN

1 NA, KB, 8/9; Wriothesley (1875–77), I, pp. 37–9, 207–24; Spelman (1976–77), I, p. 71; *CSPSp*, V, ii, no. 55 (pp. 125–7); *LP*, X, no. 908 (pp. 377–8).
2 *St. Pap.*, I, pp. 431–6; NA, SP 1/167, fos. 110–13, 117–20v, 131, 132, 133–4, 136–8, 140, 142–3, 144, 146; *LP*, III, i, no. 1284 (2, 3, 5); Thurley (1999), p. 49; Starkey (2004), pp. 575–6; Elton (1972), pp. 298–326.
3 *St. Pap.*, I, pp. ix–xxiv; Johnson (2003), pp. 22–42.
4 NA, SP 45/1, fos. 1–21. An assertion in *DKR*, 30th Report, Appendix VII (p. 224) that Sadler compiled the inventory is negated by the handwriting, which is that of Honnyngs. It should also be noted that the inventory lists no document of a later date than April 1544. Thomas Wriothesley is referred to as 'my lord Wriothesley' and not 'my Lord Chancellor', the office to which he was appointed in May 1544. For Honnyngs as clerk of the privy council, see *LP*, XIX, ii, nos. 216, 800 (10); SRO, HD 1538/113/1/7.
5 NA, SP 45/1, fos. 1v, 2, 18v, 19v.

APPENDIX 4: THE IDENTITY OF THE WOMAN GIVING
EVIDENCE AGAINST GEORGE BOLEYN

1 *Lisle Letters*, III, no. 703a; *Lisle Letters*, IV, no. 847. See also, *Lisle Letters*, III, pp. 378–84.
2 Spelman (1976–77), I, p. 71. See above, pp. 389–90.
3 For the classic exposition of this approach, see Weir (2009), pp. 114, 223–7.
4 The *Spanish Chronicle* claims merely that George had been seen going in and out of his sister's room 'dressed only in his night-clothes'. See

Spanish Chronicle (1889), p. 65. The so-called Portuguese gentleman refers only to 'that person': see above, pp. 387–8.

5 Leti (1694), I, p. 145. For his forgeries of letters said to be by Anne, see Wood (1846), II, pp. 15–16, 48–9.

6 Weir (2009), pp. 114, 287.

7 LPL, Shrewsbury MS 707, fos. 221–2.

8 NA, PROB 11/101/154.

9 NA, C 1/1110, fos. 65–9.

10 NA, C 54/418 (entry no. 18). See also Fox (2007), pp. 247–8.

11 Fox (2007), pp. 321–3, 367. On this point, Ives (2004), pp. 331–2 and n. 68, was misled by the research assistant he used to examine Turner's notes.

12 Fox (2007), pp. 315–17, 367.

13 Singer (1827), p. 446.

14 Ibid., p. 422.

15 NA, PROB 11/39/128; Julia Fox at https://www.theanneboleynfiles. com/jane-boleyn-the-infamous-lady-rochford-guest-post.

16 BL, Stowe MS 956; Nott (1816), II, p. xxv; Marsham (1874), pp. 259–72; *HC, 1509–1558* (1982), II, pp. 505–6; MMA, Accession Number: 14.40.637. See also NA, PROB 11/33/371. It should be noted that the miniature portrait of Henry VIII in the Stowe MS derives from Holbein's image of Henry made for the dynastic wall fresco at Whitehall in 1537, by which time Anne was already dead.

17 Singer (1827), pp. 446–7.

18 Singer (1825), II, pp. 71–4.

19 Burnet (1820), I, i, pp. 306, 484–5. In 1989, such beliefs sparked an unproven suggestion that George was a homosexual, whose 'buggery with a male friend' left Jane determined to be revenged on him. See Warnicke (1989), pp. 216–17.

20 Amyot (1831), p. 66; Fox (2007), pp. 324–5.

Dates, Spellings, Units of Currency

Dates are given in the Old-Style Julian Calendar, but the year is assumed to have begun on 1 January, not on Lady Day or the Feast of the Annunciation (25th March), which by custom was the first day of the calendar year in the sixteenth century. The New-Style Gregorian Calendar, advancing the date by ten days, was issued in Rome in 1582 and adopted in Italy and by Philip II throughout Spain, Portugal and the New World in October that year. France followed in December, as did much of the Netherlands. The Catholic states of the Holy Roman Empire followed in 1583. England, Scotland, Ireland, Denmark and Sweden retained the old calendar until the 1700s.

Spelling and orthography of primary sources in quotations are given in modernised form, except in book titles or quotations from the Devonshire Manuscript. Modern punctuation and capitalisation have also been provided where none exists in the original manuscript. Italian names are given in their original, and not anglicised format, for example, Lorenzo Campeggi, not Campeggio.

Units of currency appear, in the case of English money, in the pre-decimal form in use until 1971. There are twelve pence (12d) in a shilling (modern 5p), twenty shillings (20s) in a pound (£1 or US $1.25), and so on. A mark was a monetary unit worth 13s 4d sterling. English crowns were usually worth 5s 0d, and florins around 3s 3d. The gold noble was usually valued at 6s 8d, the 'riall' or royal at 10s. The Venetian ducat usually meant the gold ducat, worth about 4s 6d sterling. The pound sterling was worth between 9 and 10 French *livres tournois*. The *livre tournois* was divided into 20 *sous*, each *sou* worth 12 *deniers*. The main gold coin in France was the *écu d'or au soleil* or gold crown of the sun (named after the sunburst placed above the royal arms), worth around 4s 6d sterling. A pound in Brussels or Antwerp meant the Flemish pound, made up of 20 shillings, each of 12 groats or pence. Depending on rates of exchange, its value fluctuated between 15s or 16s and 22s 6d sterling. No actual pound coins were in circulation: the pound was a unit of reckoning devised by accountants, but one Flemish pound was equivalent to six Carolus guilders. The main unit of currency in the Low Countries, the guilder or florin, was a silver coin worth 40 Flemish pence.

Modern purchasing equivalents for sixteenth-century sums are given in parenthesis only where it seems helpful to readers. The effects of inflation and huge fluctuations in relative values render accurate conversions intractable. Henry VIII paid £4 for two acres of land to enlarge the Little Park at Windsor. He paid his gardeners salaries of between £4 and £12 a year depending on their location. He paid his principal falconers £10 a year. A farm at Greenwich, purchased for Anne Boleyn in February 1531, cost £66 13s 4d but we have no idea of its size. In November 1530, fourteen loads of hay and six loads of oats cost, with the carriage to Greenwich Park, £6 2s 8d. In July 1530, two men were paid 13s 4d for ten days' work in mowing. In February 1532, the hire of seven horses and the costs of the same number of men for sixteen days sent into Wales and other places came to £9 6s 8d. In July the same year ten men were paid 8d per day each for three days to drain the fishponds at Ampthill. We provide occasional rough estimates of minimum modern purchasing equivalents to guide readers by multiplying all the numbers by a thousand. We believe this, on average, to yield credible results based on the values of contemporaries.

Sources and Bibliography

PRINTED PRIMARY SOURCES

[Académie des sciences, belles lettres et arts de Besançon] (1806–1975). *Mémoires et documents inédits pour servir à l'histoire de la Franche-Comté*, 80 vols, Besançon

[Académie des sciences, belles lettres et arts de Marseille] (1803–1925). *Mémoires*, 114 vols, Marseilles

[Académie royale des sciences, des lettres et des beaux-arts de Belgique] (1919–69). *Bulletin de la Classe des lettres et des sciences morales et politiques*, 5th Series, 75 vols, Brussels

Allen, P. S., ed. (1906–58). *Opus Epistolarum Des. Erasmi Roterodami*, 12 vols, Oxford

Ambassades (1905). *Ambassades en Angleterre; la première ambassade, septembre 1527–février 1529: Correspondance diplomatique*, ed. V.-L. Bourrilly and P. de Vaissière, Paris

Amyot, T. (1831). 'Transcript from an Original Manuscript, containing a Memorial from George Constantyne to Thomas Lord Cromwell', *Archaeologia*, 23, pp. 50–78

Anon. (1517). *L'entrée de la royne de France a Paris faicte le mardy xij. iour du moys de may*, Paris

Anon. (1538). *The Courte of Venus. Newly and diligently corrected with many proper Ballades newly amended, and also added therunto which have not before bene imprinted*, London

Antiquarian Repertory (1807–9). *The Antiquarian Repertory*, ed. F. Grose, 2nd edn, rev. by E. Jeffery, 4 vols, London

Apian, P. (1527). *Eyn Newe unnd wolgegründte underweysung aller Kauffmanß Rechnung in dreyen buechern mit schoenen regeln und fragstucken begriffen*, Ingolstadt

Aylmer, John (1559). *An Harborowe for Faithfull and Trewe Subiectes* [London]

Baker, J. H., ed. (2022). *Reports from the Notebooks of Edward Coke*, 2 vols, Selden Society, London

Baroni, P. G. (1962). *La Nunziatura in Francia di Rodolfo Pio, 1535–1537*, Bologna

Barrillon, J. de (1897–99). *Journal de Jean Barrillon, secrétaire du chancelier Duprat, 1515–1521*, 2 vols, Paris

Bell, R., ed. (1854). *Poetical Works of Henry Howard, Earl of Surrey, Minor Contemporaneous Poets and Thomas Sackville, Lord Buckhurst*, London

[Bentley, S.] (1831). *Excerpta Historica, or Illustrations of English History*, London

Berwick y de Alba, Duque de, ed. (1907). *Correspondencia de Gutierre Gomez de Fuensalida*, Madrid

Blomefield, F. (1739–75). *An Essay towards a Topographical History of the County of Norfolk, containing a Description of the Towns, Villages, and Hamlets*, 5 vols, London

Bonnardot, F. (1833). *Registres des délibérations du bureau de la ville de Paris*, 2 vols, Paris

Bourbon, N. (1536). *Opusculum puerile ad pueros de moribus, sive paedagogion*, Lyon

— (1538). *Nugarum Libri Octo*, Lyon

Bourdeille, P. de (1912). *Illustrious Dames at the Court of the Valois Kings*, trans. K. Prescott Wormeley, New York

Bourdigné, J. de (1842). *Chroniques d'Anjou et du Maine*, Angers

Bradford, W. (1850). *Correspondence of the Emperor Charles V and his Ambassadors at the Courts of England and France: from the Original Letters in the Imperial Family Archives at Vienna*, London

Brown, R. (1854). *Four Years at the Court of Henry VIII. Selection of Despatches Written by the Venetian Ambassador, Sebastian Giustinian, and Addressed to the Signory of Venice, January 12th 1515 to July 26th 1519*, 2 vols, London

Bruce, J., Perowne, T. T., eds (1853). *Correspondence of Matthew Parker*, Parker Society, Cambridge

Bryan, F. (1548). *A dispraise of the life of a courtier, and a commendacion of the life of the labouryng man*, London

Burnet, G. (1820). *History of the Reformation of the Church of England*, new edn, 6 vols, London

Caius, John (1552). *A boke, or counseill against the disease commonly called the sweate, or sweatyng sicknesse*, London

Calais Chronicle (1846). *The Chronicle of Calais in the Reigns of Henry VII and Henry VIII to the Year 1540*, ed. J. G. Nichols, Camden Society, 1st Series, vol. 35, London

Camden, William (1615). *Annales rerum Anglicarum, et Hibernicarum, regnante Elizabetha*, London

— (1870). *Remains Concerning Britain*, ed. T. Moule and M. A. Lower, London [reissue of the edition of 1674]

Castiglione, B. (1928). *The Book of the Courtier*, ed. W. H. D. Rouse, London

Collins, A. J. (1955). *Jewels and Plate of Queen Elizabeth I: The Inventory of 1574*, London

Corrie, G. E., ed. (1845). *Sermons and Remains of Hugh Latimer*, Parker Society, Cambridge

Cotgrave, R. (1611). *A Dictionarie of the French and English Tongues*, London

Cox, J. E., ed. (1846). *Miscellaneous Writings and Letters of Thomas Cranmer*, Parker Society, Cambridge

Dallington, R. (1604). *The View of France*, London

Davis, N., ed. (2004). *Paston Letters and Papers of the Fifteenth Century*, 3 vols, Oxford

Desjardins, A. (1861–72). *Négociations diplomatiques de la France avec la Toscane*, 4 vols, Paris

Dowling, M., ed. (1990). 'William Latymer's Chronickille of Anne Bulleyne', in Camden Miscellany 30. Camden Society, 4th Series, vol. 39, pp. 23–65, 501–3

Dreux du Radier, J. F. (1808). *Mémoires historiques, critiques et anecdotes de France*, 10 vols, Paris

Du Bellay, M., Du Bellay, G. (1908–19). *Mémoires de Martin et Guillaume Du Bellay*, ed. V.-L. Bourrilly and F. Vindry, 4 vols, Paris

Ehses, S., ed. (1893). *Römische Dokumente zur Geschichte der Ehescheidung Heinrichs VIII. von England 1527–1534*, Zweigniederlassung

Elyot, T. (1533). *Pasquil the Playne*, London

Fiddes, R. (1724). *The Life of Cardinal Wolsey*, London

Florange, Seigneur de (1913). *Mémoires du Marchéchal de Florange*, ed. R. Goiubaux and P.-André Lemoisne, 2 vols, Paris

Forrest, W. (1875). *The History of Grisild the Second*, ed. W. D. Macray, London

Fortescue, T. (1869). *Sir John Fortescue, Knight. His Life, Works and Family History*, 2 vols, London

Foxe, John (1570). *Ecclesiasticall history contaynyng the actes and monumentes of thynges passed in euery kynges tyme in this realme, especially in the Church of England*, 2 vols, London

— (1583). *Actes and monuments of matters most speciall and memorable, happenyng in the Church: with an universall history of the same*, 2 vols, London

— (1843–49). *The Acts and Monuments of John Foxe*, ed. G. Townsend, 8 vols, London

Froude, J. A., ed. (1861). *The Pilgrim. A Dialogue on the Life and Actions of King Henry the Eighth*, London

Gachard, L-P., ed. (1874). *Collection des voyages des souverains des Pays-Bas*, 2 vols, Brussels

— ed. (1885). *Analectes historiques*, 5 vols, Brussels

Gardiner, Stephen (1930). *Obedience in Church and State*, ed. P. Janelle, Cambridge

Gringore, Pierre (2005). *Les entrées royales à Paris de Marie d'Angleterre (1514) et Claude de France (1517)*, ed. C. J. Brown, Geneva

Guillemeau, J. (1612). *Child-birth or, the happy deliverie of women wherein is set downe the government of women. In the time of their breeding childe ... and of their lying in*, London

Gutch, J., ed. (1781). *Collectanea Curiosa*, 2 vols, Oxford

Hall, E. (1809). *Hall's Chronicle Containing the History of England ... to the End of the Reign of Henry VIII*, ed. H. Ellis, London

Halliwell, J. O. (1848). *Letters of the Kings of England*, 2 vols, London

Hansische Geschichtsblätter (1871–2006). *Hansische Geschichtsblätter*, 124 vols, Leipzig and Lübeck

Harington, J. (1792). *Nugae Antiquae. Being a Miscellaneous Collection of Original Papers in Prose and Verse, Written ... by Sir John Harington*, 3 vols, London

Harpsfield, N. (1878). *A Treatise on the Pretended Divorce Between Henry VIII and Catherine of Aragon*, Camden Society, New Series, 21, pp. 1–302

— (1932). *The life and death of Sir Thomas Moore, knight, sometymes Lord high Chancellor of England, written in the tyme of Queene Marie*, ed. E. V. Hitchcock, EETS, Original Series, 186, London

Hasted, E. (1797). *The History and Topographical Survey of the County of Kent*, 2nd edn, 12 vols, Canterbury

Hayward, M., ed. (2004). *The 1542 Inventory of Whitehall: The Palace and its Keeper*, Society of Antiquaries, 2 vols, London

Hearne, T. (1716). *Titi Livii Foro-Juliensis, Vita Henrici Quinti, Regis Angliae. Accedit, Sylloge Epistolarum, a Variis Angliae Principibus Scriptarum*, Oxford

Henne, A. (1858–60). *Histoire du Regne de Charles-Quint en Belgique*, 10 vols, Brussels and Leipzig

Herbert of Cherbury, E. (1649). *The Life and Raigne of King Henry the Eighth*, London

Household Ordinances (1790). *A Collection of Ordinances and Regulations for the Government of the Royal Household*, Society of Antiquaries, London

Hovenden, R. (1898). *The Visitation of Kent, Taken in the Years 1619–21*, Harleian Society, 42, London

Howard, L., ed. (1753). *A Collection of Letters, from the Original Manuscripts of Many Princes, Great Personages and Statesmen. Together with some Curious and Scarce Tracts, and Pieces of Antiquity, Religious, Political and Moral*, London

Hoyle, R. W., ed. (1992). 'Letters of the Cliffords, Lords Clifford and Earls of Cumberland, c.1500–c.1565', Camden Society, 4th Series, 44, pp. 3–189

Ives, E. W. (1976). *Letters and Accounts of William Brereton of Malpas*, Record Society of Lancashire and Cheshire, 1st Series, 116, Woking

Kingsford, C. L., ed. (1905). *Chronicles of London*, with an introduction and notes, Oxford

Kipling, G., ed. (1990). *The Receyt of the Ladie Kateryne*, EETS, New Series, 296, Oxford

Le Glay, A. J. G., ed. (1839). *Correspondance de l'Empereur Maximilien Ier et de Marguerite d'Autriche, Gouvernante des Pays-Bas, de 1507 à 1519*, 2 vols, Paris

— (1845). *Négociations diplomatiques entre la France et l'Autriche durant les trente premières années du XVIe siècle*, 2 vols, Paris

Le Grand, J. (1688). *Preuves de l'histoire du divorce, de la défense de Sanderus, et de la refutation de M. Burnet*, 3 vols, Paris

Le Laboureur, J., ed. (1731). *Les mémoires de Messire Michel de Castelnau, Seigneur de Mauvissière*, 3 vols, Brussels

Le Roux, J. (1715). *Recueil de la noblesse de Bourgogne, Limburg, Luxembourg, Gueldres, Flandres, Artois ... et autres provinces commençant en l'an 1424 et continué jusqu'à l'an 1714*, Lille

Leland, J (1774). *Joannis Lelandi antiquarii de rebus Britannicis collectanea*, ed. T. Hearne, 3rd edn, 6 vols, Oxford

Lestocquoy, J., ed. (1961). *Correspondance des nonces en France, Carpi et Ferrerio, 1536–1540*, Paris

List of Sheriffs (1963). *List of Sheriffs for England and Wales from the Earliest Times to AD 1831*, ed. H. C. Maxwell Lyte, London and New York

Lodge, Edmund (1838). *Illustrations of British History, Biography and Manners in the Reigns of Henry VIII, Edward VI, Mary, Elizabeth, and James I*, 2nd edn, 3 vols, London

LP Richard III and Henry VII (1861–3). *Letters and Papers, Richard III and Henry VII*, ed. J. Gairdner, 2 vols, London

Lull, R. (2015). *The Book of the Order of Chivalry*, ed. Antonio Cortijo Ocaña, Amsterdam and Philadelphia

Lyell, L., Watney, F. D., ed. (1936). *Acts of Court of the Mercers' Company, 1453–1527*, Cambridge

Lysons, D., Lysons, S. (1806–22). *Magna Britannia, Being a Concise Topographical Account of the Several Counties of Great Britain*, 6 vols, London

Machiavelli, N. (1988). *The Prince*, ed. Q. Skinner and R. Price, Cambridge

Malory, T. (1967). *The Works of Sir Thomas Malory*, ed. E. Vinaver, 2nd edn, 3 vols, Oxford

Maquéreau, R. (1838). *Chronique de la maison de Bourgoigne*, in *Choix de chroniques et mémoires sur l'histoire de la France*, ed. J. A. C. Buchon, Paris

Marguerite of Angoulême (1984). *The Heptaméron*, trans. P. A. Chilton, London

Marot, Clément (1879), *Oeuvres complètes de Clement Marot*, 2 vols, Paris

Marshall, W. (1535a). *A Goodly Prymer in Englyshe, Newly Corrected and Printed, with Certeyne Godly Meditations and Prayers Added to the Same*, London

— (1535b). *The Forme and Man[n]er of Subvention or Helpyng for Po[o]re People*, London

Memorials of Henry VII (1858). *Memorials of Henry VII*, ed. J. Gairdner, London

Merriman, R. B. (1902). *Life and Letters of Thomas Cromwell*, 2 vols, Oxford

Michaud, J-F., Poujoulat, J. J-F., eds (1836–39). *Nouvelle collection des mémoires pour servir l'histoire de France*, 1st Series, 6 vols, Paris

Morant, P. (1768). *The History and Antiquities of the County of Essex. Compiled from the Best and Most Ancient Historians*, 2 vols, London

Muir, K., ed. (1963). *Life and Letters of Sir Thomas Wyatt*, Liverpool

Muir, K., Thomson, P., eds (1969). *Collected Poems of Sir Thomas Wyatt*, Liverpool

Murphy, V. M., Surtz, E. (1988). *The Divorce Tracts of Henry VIII*, Angers

Narratives (1859). *Narratives of the Days of the Reformation*, ed. J. G. Nichols, Camden Society, 1st Series, 77, London

Nichols, J. G., ed. (1857). *Literary Remains of King Edward VI*, Roxburghe Club, 2 vols, London

Northumberland Book (1905). *The Regulations and Establishment of the Household of Henry Algernon Percy, the Fifth Earl of Northumberland etc.*, New edition, London

Nott, G. F., ed. (1816). *The Works of Henry Howard, Earl of Surrey, and Sir Thomas Wyatt, the Elder*, 2 vols, London

Ordonnances (1902–40). *Ordonnances des rois de France. Règne de François Ier*, 6 vols, Paris

Parker, K. T. (1983). *The Drawings of Hans Holbein in the Collection of Her Majesty the Queen at Windsor Castle, with an Appendix by Susan Foister*, London

Perrenot, Antoine de, Cardinal de Granvelle (1841–52). *Papiers d'État du cardinal de Granvelle: d'après les manuscrits de la Bibliothèque de Besançon*, 9 vols, Paris

Pocock, N. (1870). *Records of the Reformation: The Divorce, 1527–1533*, 2 vols, Oxford

Pole, R. (1555). *Pro ecclesiasticae unitatis defensione, libri quatuor*, Rome

Porcacchi, T. (1571). *Lettere di XIII. huomini illustri, allequali oltra tutte l'altre fin qui stampate, di nuovo ne sono state aggiunte molte*, Venice

Procédures politiques (1885). *Procédures politiques du règne de Louis XII*, ed. R. de Maulde La Clavière, Paris

Pronay, N., Cox, J., ed. (1986). *The Crowland Chronicle Continuations: 1459–1486*, London

Puttenham, R. (1589). *The Arte of English Poesie*, London

Rebholz, R. A., ed. (1978). *Sir Thomas Wyatt: The Complete Poems*, London

Reiffenberg, F. de (1836). *Chronique métrique de Chastellain et de Molinet*, Brussels

Renaudet, A. (1916). *Préréforme et humanisme à Paris pendant les premières guerres d'Italie (1494–1517)*, Paris

Revell, T. (1536). *The Summe of Christianitie gatheryd out almoste of al placis of Scripture by that Noble and Famouse clerke, Francis Lambert of Avynyon*, London

Robinson, H., ed. (1846–47). *Original Letters relative to the English Reformation ... Chiefly from the Archives of Zurich*, Parker Society, 2 vols, Cambridge

Rogers, E. F. (1947). *The Correspondence of Sir Thomas More*, Princeton, NJ

— (1961). *St Thomas More: Selected Letters*, New Haven, Conn.

Roper, William (1935). *The Lyfe of Sir Thomas Moore knighte, written by William Roper*, ed. E. V. Hitchcock, EETS, Original Series, 197, London

Rutland Papers (1842). *Original Documents illustrative of the Courts and Times of Henry VII and Henry VIII*, ed. W. Jerdan, Camden Society, 1st Series, 21, London

Rye, W., ed. (1891). *The Visitation of Norfolk Made and Taken by William Hervey, Clarencieux, King of Arms, Anno 1563*, Harleian Society, 32, London

Rymer, T., ed. (1704–35). *Foedera, Conventiones, Litterae et Cuiuscunque Generis Acta Publica*, 20 vols, London

Sanuto, M. (1824–84). *I Diarii di Marino Sanuto (MCCCCXCVI–MDXXXIII)*, 58 vols, Venice

Savage, H., ed. (1949). *The Love Letters of Henry VIII*, London

Scrinia Sacra (1654). *Scrinia Sacra: Secrets of Empire in Letters of Illustrious Persons. A Supplement of the Cabala*, London

Singer, S. W., ed. (1825). *The Life of Cardinal Wolsey ... and Metrical Visions*, 2 vols, London

— (1827). *The Life of Cardinal Wolsey by George Cavendish*, rev. edn in 1 vol., London

Skemp, M., Cholakian, R., ed. (2008). *Marguerite de Navarre: Selected Writings*, Chicago

Smyth, J. (1883). *The Berkeley Manuscripts. Lives of the Berkeleys ... in the County of Gloucester from 1066 to 1618*, 2 vols, Gloucester

Spanish Chronicle (1889). *Chronicle of King Henry VIII of England ... Written in Spanish by an Unknown Hand*, ed. M. A. S. Hume, London

Spelman, Sir John (1976–77). *The Reports of Sir John Spelman*, ed. J. H. Baker, 2 vols, Selden Society, London

Starkey, D. R., Ward, P., Hawkyard, A., eds (1998). *The Inventory of King Henry VIII. Vol. I: The Transcript*, Society of Antiquaries, London

Starkey, Thomas (1989). *A Dialogue between Pole and Lupset*, ed. T. F. Mayer, Camden Society, 4th Series, 37, London

Stephenson, M. (1926). *A List of Monumental Brasses in the British Isles*, London

Stow, John (1580). *The Chronicles of England*, London

— (1631). *Annales or a Generall Chronicle of England*, London

Strype, John (1821). *The Life and Acts of Matthew Parker*, 3 vols, Oxford

— (1822). *Ecclesiastical Memorials Relating Chiefly to Religion and the Reformation of it*, 3 vols in 6 parts, Oxford

— (1840). *Memorials of Thomas Cranmer*, 2 vols, Oxford

Surtz, E., Murphy, V. M., ed. (1988). *The Divorce Tracts of Henry VIII*, Angers

Swinburne, H. (1686). *A Treatise of Spousals or Matrimonial Contracts, wherein all the Questions relating to that Subject are Ingeniously Debated and Resolved*, London

Sylvester, R. S., ed. (1959). *The Life and Death of Cardinal Wolsey by George Cavendish*, EETS, New Series, 243, Oxford

Theiner, A. (1864). *Vetera Monumenta Hibernorum et Scotorum Historiam Illustrantia, 1216–1547*, Rome

Thomas, A. H., Thornley, I. D., eds (1938). *The Great Chronicle of London*, London

Thorne, S. E., ed. (1977). *Bracton: De Legibus et Consuetudinibus Angliae*, 4 vols, Cambridge, Mass.

Tottel, R. (1557). *Songes and Sonettes, written by the ryght honorable Lorde Henry Haward late Earle Surrey, and other*, London

Tudor Tracts (1903). *Tudor Tracts, 1532–1588*, ed. A. F. Pollard, London

Van Ortroy, F. (1893). 'Vie du bienheureux Martyr Jean Fisher, Cardinal', *Analecta Bollandiana*, 12, pp. 97–287.

Vergil, Polydore (1950). *The Anglica Historia of Polydore Vergil*, ed. D. Hay, Camden Society, 3rd Series, 74, London

Villasancta, Alfonso de (1523). *Problema indulgentiarum quo Lutheri errata dissoluuntur*, London

Vocht, H. de (1947). *Acta Thomae Mori. History of the Reports of his Trial and Death with an Unedited Contemporary Narrative*, Louvain

Wakefield, R. (c.1534a). *Kotser codicis*, London

— (c.1534b). *Syntagma de hebraeorum codicum incorruptione*, London

Walker, H., ed. (1848). *Doctrinal Treatises and Introductions to Different Portions of the Holy Scriptures by William Tyndale*, Parker Society, Cambridge

Weaver, J. (1631). *Ancient Funerall Monuments within the United Monarchie of Great Britain, Ireland, and the Islands Adjacent*, London

Wickham Legg, L. G., ed. (1901). *English Coronation Records*, London

Wilkins, D. (1737). *Concilia Magnae Britanniae et Hiberniae*, 3 vols, London

Wood, A. (1691). *Athenae Oxoniensis: An Exact History of all the Writers and Bishops who have had their Education in the Most Ancient and Famous University of Oxford*, 2 vols, Oxford

Wood, M. A. E., ed. (1846). *Letters of Royal and Illustrious Ladies of Great Britain*, 3 vols, London

Wright, H. G. (1943). *Forty-Six Lives, Translated from Boccaccio's De Claris Mulieribus by Henry Parker, Lord Morley*, EETS, Original Series, 214, London

Wriothesley, Charles (1875–77). *A Chronicle of England during the Reigns of the Tudors, from AD 1485 to 1559*, 2 vols, Camden Society, New Series, vols 11, 20, London

Wyatt, George (1968). *The Papers of George Wyatt, Esquire, of Boxley Abbey in the County of Kent*, ed. D. M. Loades, Camden Society, 4th Series, vol. 5, London

Wyatt, Thomas (1528). *Tho. wyatis translatyon of Plutarckes boke, of the quyete of mynde*, London

SECONDARY SOURCES

Anglo, S. (1969). *Spectacle, Pageantry, and Early Tudor Policy*, Oxford
— (1992). *Images of Tudor Kingship*, London
Aram, B. (1998). 'Juana "the Mad's" Signature: The Problem of Invoking Royal Authority, 1505–1507', *SCJ*, 29, pp. 331–58
Arnaud, J.-P. (1987). 'La mythologie dans les entrées royales à Angers de 1518 à 1619', *Bulletin de la société nationale des antiquaires de France*, no. 1985, pp. 137–61
Ascoli, G., ed. (1927). *La Grande-Bretagne devant l'opinion française depuis la guerre de Cent ans jusqu'à la fin du XVIᵉ siècle*, Paris
Astor, G. (1975). *Hever Castle and Gardens*, Norwich
Atance, F. R. (1969). 'Marguerite de Navarre et la Réforme', Western Ontario PhD
Attreed, L. (2012). 'Gender, Patronage and Diplomacy in the Early Career of Margaret of Austria (1480–1530)', *Mediterranean Studies*, 20, pp. 3–27
Austin, W., Blundell, J. H. (1928). *The History of Luton and its Hamlets*, 2 vols, Luton
Axton M., Carley, J. P. (2000). *Triumphs of English: Henry Parker, Lord Morley, Translator to the Tudor Court, New Essays in Interpretation*, London
Baker, J. H. (2003). *The Oxford History of the Laws of England: Vol. VI, 1483–1558*, Oxford
— (2012). *The Men of Law, 1440–1550*, 2 vols, Selden Society Supplementary Series, no. 18, London
Bapst, E. (1891). *Deux gentilshommes-poètes de la cour de Henry VIII*, Paris
Baron, M. (1994). 'Mary (Howard) Fitzroy's Hand in the Devonshire Manuscript', *Review of English Studies*, 45, pp. 318–35

Baux, E., Bourrilly, V.-L., Mabilly, P. (1904). 'Le voyage des reines et de François 1er en Provence et dans la vallée du Rhône (Décembre 1515–Février 1516)', *Annales du Midi*, 16, pp. 31–64

Bayley, J. (1821). *The History and Antiquities of the Tower of London, with Memoirs of Royal and Distinguished Persons, deduced from Records, State Papers and Manuscripts*, 2 vols, London

Beer, M. (2018a). 'A Queenly Affinity? Catherine of Aragon's Estates and Henry VIII's Great Matter', *HR*, 91, pp. 426–45

— (2018b). *Queenship at the Renaissance Courts of Britain: Catherine of Aragon and Margaret Tudor, 1503–1533*, London

Bell, D. C. (1877). *Notices of the Historic Persons buried in the Chapel of St. Peter ad Vincula in the Tower of London*, London

Bernard, G. W. (1981). 'The Rise of Sir William Compton, Early Tudor Courtier', *EHR*, 96, pp. 754–77

— (1991). 'The Fall of Anne Boleyn', *EHR*, 106, pp. 584–610

— (1992). 'The Fall of Anne Boleyn: A Rejoinder', *EHR*, 107, pp. 66–74

— (1993). 'Anne Boleyn's Religion', *HJ*, 36, pp. 1–20

— (1996). 'The Fall of Wolsey Reconsidered', *JBS*, 35, pp. 277–310

— (2005). *The King's Reformation: Henry VIII and the Remaking of the English Church*, New Haven and London

— (2010). *Anne Boleyn: Fatal Attractions*, New Haven and London

Biddle, M. (2000). *King Arthur's Round Table: An Archaeological Investigation*, Woodbridge

Bietenholz, P. G., Deutscher, T. B. (1985–7). *Contemporaries of Erasmus: A Biographical Register of the Renaissance and Reformation*, 3 vols, Toronto

Biggs, E. (2016). 'The College and Canons of St Stephen's, Westminster, 1348–1548', 2 vols, York PhD

Blacker, B. H., ed. (1890). *Gloucestershire Notes and Queries*, IV, London

Blezzard, J., Palmer, F. (2000). 'King Henry VIII: Performer, Connoisseur and Composer of Music', *AJ*, 80, pp. 249–72

Blumenfeld-Kosinski, R. (1994). 'Jean Le Fèvre's *Livre de Leesce*: Praise or Blame of Women?', *Speculum*, 69, pp. 705–25

Bolland, C. (2011). 'Italian Material Culture at The Tudor Court', Queen Mary University PhD

Bouchard, M. (2018). 'The Power of Reputation and Skills according to Anne de Graville', in *Women and Power at the French Court, 1483–1563*, ed. S. Broomhall, Amsterdam, pp. 241–59

Brandi, K. (1965). *The Emperor Charles V*, London

Brigden, S. (1988). 'Thomas Cromwell and the Brethren', in *Law and Government under the Tudors*, ed. Claire Cross, D. M. Loades and J. J. Scarisbrick, Cambridge, pp. 31–50

— (1989). *London and the Reformation*, Oxford

— (2012). *Thomas Wyatt: The Heart's Forest*, London

— (2019). 'Thomas Wyatt among the Florentines', *EHR*, 134, pp. 1406–39

Brigden, S., Woolfson, J. (2005). 'Thomas Wyatt in Italy', *RQ*, 58, pp. 464–511

Broomhall, S. (2018). 'In the Orbit of the King: Women, Power, and Authority at the French Court, 1483–1563', in *Women and Power at the French Court, 1483–1563*, ed. S. Broomhall, Amsterdam, pp. 9–32

Brown, C. J. (2007). 'From Stage to Page: Royal Entry Performances in Honour of Mary Tudor', in *Book and Text in France, 1400–1600*, ed. A. Armstrong and M. Quainton, Farnham, pp. 49–72

— (2010). *The Queen's Library: Image-Making at the Court of Anne of Brittany, 1477–1514*, Philadelphia

Brown, M. C. (1911). *Mary Tudor, Queen of France*, London

Bryson, A. (2001). '"The Speciall Men in Every Shere". The Edwardian Regime, 1547–1553', St Andrews PhD

Buettner, B. (2001). 'New Year's Gifts at the Valois Courts, c.1400', *Art Bulletin*, 83, pp. 598–625

Buskirk, J. (2013). 'Portraiture and Arithmetic in Sixteenth Century Bavaria: Deciphering Barthel Beham's Calculator', *RQ*, 66, pp. 35–80

Butterworth, E. (2016). *The Unbridled Tongue: Babble and Gossip in Renaissance France*, Oxford

— (2018). 'Scandal and Narrative in the Heptaméron', *French Studies*, 72, pp. 350–63

Button, V. (2013). 'The Portrait Drawings of Hans Holbein the Younger: Function and Use Explored through Materials and Techniques', Royal College of Art/Victoria and Albert Museum PhD

Byrom, H. J. (1932). 'Nicholas Grimald as Editor of *Tottel's Miscellany*', *Modern Language Review*, 27, pp. 125–43

Cameron, E. (1991). *The European Reformation*, Oxford

Cameron, R. M. (1970). 'The Charges of Lutheranism Brought against Jacques Lefèvre d'Étaples (1520–1529)', *Harvard Theological Review*, 63, pp. 119–29

Campbell, L., Foister, S. (1986). 'Gerard, Lucas and Susanna
    Horenbout', *Burlington Magazine*, 128, pp. 719–27
Campbell, T. P. (2007). *The Art of Majesty: Henry VIII's Tapestry
    Collection*, New Haven and London
Carley, J. P. (1989). 'John Leland and the Foundations of the Royal
    Library: The Westminster Inventory of 1542', *Bulletin of the Society for
    Renaissance Studies*, 7, pp. 13–22
— (1998). ' "Her moost lovying and fryndely brother sendeth
    gretyng": Anne Boleyn's Manuscripts and their Sources', in
    Illuminating the Book: Makers and Interpreters, ed. Michelle P. Brown
    and Scot McKendrick, London and Toronto, pp. 261–80
— (2000). *The Libraries of King Henry VIII*, London
— (2002). 'Religious Controversy and Marginalia: Pierfrancesco di
    Piero Bardi, Thomas Wakefield and their Books', *Transactions of the
    Cambridge Bibliographical Society*, 12, pp. 206–45
— (2004a). 'Le livre évangélique en français avant Calvin: études
    originales, publications d'inédits, catalogues d'éditions anciennes',
    Nugae humanisticae, 4 (2004), pp. 131–46
— (2004b). *The Books of King Henry VIII and his Wives*, London
Castelain, M-F. (1986). *Au pays de Claude de France*, Société d'histoire et
    d'archéologie de Sologne, Romorantin-Lanthenay
Chamberlin, F. (1932). *The Private Character of Henry VIII*, London
Chambers, D. S. (1965). 'Cardinal Wolsey and the Papal Tiara', *BIHR*,
    38, pp. 20–30
Chatenet, M. (1992). 'Le logis de François Ier au Louvre', *Revue de l'Art*,
    97, pp. 72–5
— (2002). *La Cour de France au XVIe siècle. Vie social et
    architecture*, Paris
Chatenet, M., Whiteley, M. (1992). 'Le Louvre de Charles
    V: dispositions et fonctions d'une résidence royale', *Revue de l'Art*,
    97, pp. 60–71
Cholakian, P. F. (1991). *Rape and Writing in the Heptaméron of
    Marguerite de Navarre*, Carbondale, Illinois
Cholakian, P. F., Cholakian, R. (2005). *Marguerite de Navarre, 1492–
    1549: Mother of the Renaissance*, New York
Christoffersen, P. W. (1994). *French Music in the Early Sixteenth Century*,
    2 vols, Copenhagen

Clark, N. (2018). *Gender, Family, and Politics: The Howard Women, 1485–1558*, Oxford

Colvin, H. M., Brown, R. A., Crook, J. M., et al. (1963–82). *The History of the King's Works*, 8 vols, London

Cooper, J. P. (1957). 'The Supplication Against the Ordinaries Reconsidered', *EHR*, 72, pp. 616–41

Crawford, K. (2010). *Sexual Culture of the French Renaissance*, Cambridge

Cruickshank, C. G. (1969). *Army Royal: Henry VIII's Invasion of France, 1513*, Oxford

— (1971). *The English Occupation of Tournai, 1513–1519*, Oxford

Cunningham, S. (2009). 'Loyalty and the Usurper: Recognizances, the Council and Allegiance under Henry VII', *HR*, 82, pp. 459–81

Da Costa, A. (2012). *Reforming Printing: Syon Abbey's Defence of Orthodoxy, 1525–1534*, Oxford

Davis, F. (1855). *The History of Luton with its Hamlets*, Luton

De Boom, G. (1935). *Marguerite d'Autriche et la pre-renaissance*, Paris

De Jonge, K. (1989–90). 'Der herzogliche und kaiserliche Palast zu Brüssel und die Entwicklung des höfischen Zeremoniells im 16. und 17. Jahrhundert', *Jahrbuch des Zentralinstituts für Kunstgeschichte*, 5–6, pp. 253–82

De Jongh, J. (1953). *Margaret of Austria, Regent of the Netherlands*, New York

Dean, W. H. (1987). 'Sir Thomas Boleyn: The Courtier Diplomat, 1477–1539', West Virginia PhD

Decrue, F. (1885). *Anne de Montmorency, grand-maître et connétable de France*, 2 vols, Paris

Dekker, E., Lippincott, K. (1999). 'The Scientific Instruments in Holbein's Ambassadors: A Re-Examination', *Journal of the Warburg and Courtauld Institutes*, 62, pp. 93–125

Derrett, J. D. M. (1960). 'Neglected Versions of the Contemporary Account of the Trial of Sir Thomas More', *BIHR*, 33, pp. 202–23

— (1964a). 'The Trial of Sir Thomas More', *EHR*, 79, pp. 449–77

— (1964b). 'The "New" Document on Thomas More's Trial', *Moreana*, 3, pp. 5–19

Devereux, E. J. (1966). 'Elizabeth Barton and Tudor Censorship', *Bulletin of the John Rylands Library*, 49, pp. 91–106

Dietz, F. (1921). *English Government Finance, 1485–1558*, Urbana, Illinois

Dodds, M. H. (1916). 'Political Prophecies in the Reign of Henry VIII', *Modern Language Review*, 11, pp. 276–84

Doucet, R. (1921). *Étude sur le gouvernement de François I dans ses rapports avec le Parlement de Paris*, 2 vols, Paris

Dowling, M. (1984). 'Anne Boleyn and Reform', *JEH*, 35, pp. 30–46

— (1986). *Humanism in the Age of Henry VIII*, Beckenham

Dowling, M., Shakespeare, J., eds (1982). 'Religion and Politics in Mid-Tudor England through the Eyes of an English Protestant Woman: the Recollections of Rose Hickman', *BIHR*, 55, pp. 94–102

Duffy, E. (1992). *The Stripping of the Altars: Traditional Religion in England, 1400–1580*, New Haven and London

— (2013). 'Hampton Court, Henry VIII and Cardinal Pole', in *Henry VIII and the Court: Art, Politics and Performance*, ed. T. Bedderidge and S. Lipscomb, Farnham, pp. 197–213

Dumitrescu, T. (2017). *The Early Tudor Court and International Musical Relations*, London

Dyer, A. (1997). 'The English Sweating Sickness of 1551: An Epidemic Anatomized', *Medical History*, 41, pp. 362–84

Eichberger, D. (1996). 'Margaret of Austria's Portrait Collection: Female Patronage in the Light of Dynastic Ambitions and Artistic Quality', *Renaissance Studies*, 10, pp. 259–79

— (2002). 'The Habsburgs and the Cultural Heritage of Burgundy', in *The Age of Van Eyck: The Mediterranean World of Early Netherlandish Painting, 1430–1530*, ed. T. H. Bochert, London, pp. 185–94

— (2018). '"Women Who Read are Dangerous": Illuminated Manuscripts and Female Book Collections in the Early Renaissance', in *Antipodean Early Modern: European Art in Australian Collections, c.1200–1600*, ed. A. Dunlop, Amsterdam

Ellis, S. G. (1976). 'The Kildare Rebellion and the Early Henrician Reformation', *HJ*, 19, pp. 807–30

— (1995). *Tudor Frontiers and Noble Power: The Making of the British State*, Oxford

— (2019). 'Siegecraft on the Tudor frontier: the Siege of Dublin, 1534, and the Crisis of the Kildare Rebellion', *HR*, 92, pp. 705–19

Elton, G. R. (1953). *The Tudor Revolution in Government*, Cambridge

— (1972). *Policy and Police: The Enforcement of the Reformation in the Age of Thomas Cromwell*, Cambridge

— (1973). *Reform and Renewal: Thomas Cromwell and the Common Weal*, Cambridge

— (1974–92). *Studies in Tudor and Stuart Politics and Government*, 4 vols, Cambridge

Ferguson, G., McKinley, M. B., eds (2013). *A Companion to Marguerite de Navarre*, Leiden

Fideler, P. A. (1974). 'Christian Humanism and Poor Law Reform in Early Tudor England', *Societas: A Review of Social History*, 4, pp. 269–85

Flannigan, L. (2020). 'Justice in the Court of Requests, 1483–1538', Cambridge PhD

— (2021). 'Signed, Stamped, and Sealed: Delivering Royal Justice in Early Sixteenth-Century England', *HR*, 94, pp. 267–81

Fletcher, C. (2012). *Our Man in Rome: Henry VIII and his Italian Ambassador*, London

Flood, J. L. (2003). '"Safer on the Battlefield than in the City": England, the "Sweating Sickness", and the Continent', *Renaissance Studies*, 17, pp. 147–76

Floyer, J. K. (1913). 'English Brick Buildings of the Fifteenth Century', *Archaeological Journal*, 70, pp. 121–32

Foister, S. (1978). *Holbein and the Court of Henry VIII*, London

— (2004). *Holbein and England*, New Haven and London

— (2006). *Holbein in England*, London

— (2012). 'Holbein, Antonio Toto and the Market for Italian Painting in Early Tudor England', in *The Anglo-Florentine Renaissance: Art for the Early Tudors*, ed. C. M. Sicca and L. A. Waldman, New Haven and London, pp. 281–306

Foister, S., Roy, A., Wyld, M. (1997). *Making and Meaning: Holbein's Ambassadors*, London

Fonblanque, E. B. de (1887). *Annals of the House of Percy*, 2 vols, London

Foyle, J. (2002). 'An Archaeological Reconstruction of Thomas Wolsey's Hampton Court Palace', Reading PhD

Fox, A., Guy, J. (1986). *Reassessing the Henrician Age: Humanism, Politics, and Reform*, Oxford

Fox, Julia (2007). *Jane Boleyn: The Infamous Lady Rochford*, London

— (2011). *Sister Queens: Katherine of Aragon and Juana, Queen of Castile*, London

Frangenberg, T. (1992). 'The Angle of Vision: Problems of Perspectival Representation in the Fifteenth and Sixteenth Centuries', *Renaissance Studies*, 6, pp. 1–45

Freeman, A. (2007). 'To Guard His Words', *Times Literary Supplement*, issue 5463 (14 Dec. 2007), pp. 13–14

Freeman, T. S. (1995). 'Research, Rumour and Propaganda: Anne Boleyn in Foxe's "Book of Martyrs"', *HJ*, 38, pp. 797–819

Friedmann, P. (1884). *Anne Boleyn: A Chapter of English History, 1527–1536*, 2 vols, London

Gairdner, J. (1893). 'Mary and Anne Boleyn', *EHR*, 8, pp. 53–60, 299–300

— (1896). 'New Lights on the Divorce of Henry VIII', *EHR*, 11, pp. 673–702

— (1897). 'New Lights on the Divorce of Henry VIII continued', *EHR*, 12, pp. 1–16, 237–53

Gardiner, L. R. (1984). 'Further News of Cardinal Wolsey's End, November–December 1530', *BIHR*, 57, pp. 99–107

Grant, L. (2019). *Latin Erotic Elegy and the Shaping of Sixteenth-Century English Love Poetry*, Cambridge

Gray, J. M. (2012). *Oaths and the English Reformation*, Cambridge

Green, H. J. M., Thurley, S. (1987). 'Excavations on the West Side of Whitehall 1960–62, Part 1: From the Building of the Tudor Palace to the Construction of the Modern Offices of State', *Transactions of the London and Middlesex Archaeological Society*, 38, pp. 59–130

Griffey, E. (2020). 'Express Yourself? Henrietta Maria and the Political Value of Emotional Display at the Stuart Court', *Seventeenth Century*, 35, pp. 187–212

Guépin, M. A. (1839). *Histoire de Nantes*, 2nd edn, Nantes

Gunn, S. J. (1986). 'The Duke of Suffolk's March on Paris in 1523', *EHR*, 101, pp. 596–634

— (1988). *Charles Brandon, Duke of Suffolk, 1484–1545*, Oxford

— (1996). 'Henry VIII's Foreign Policy and the Tudor Cult of Chivalry', in *François Ier et Henry VIII, deux princes de la renaissance, 1515–1547*, ed. C. Giry-Deloison, Centre d'histoire de la région du Nord et de l'Europe du Nord-Ouest, Collection 'Histoire et littérature régionales', 13, Lille and London, pp. 25–36

— (2016). *Henry VII's New Men and the Making of Tudor England*, Oxford

Gunn, S. J., Lindley, P. G., eds (1991). *Cardinal Wolsey: Church, State and Art*, Cambridge

Guy, J. (1980). *The Public Career of Sir Thomas More*, New Haven and Brighton

— (1982). 'Henry VIII and the *Praemunire* Manoeuvres of 1530–1531', *EHR*, 97, pp. 481–503

—, ed. (1997). *The Tudor Monarchy*, London

— (2004). *'My Heart is My Own': The Life of Mary, Queen of Scots*, London

— (2008). *A Daughter's Love: Thomas and Margaret More*, London

— (2013). *The Children of Henry VIII*, Oxford

— (2019). *Gresham's Law: The Life and World of Elizabeth I's Banker*, London

Gwyn, P. (1980). 'Wolsey's Foreign Policy: The Conferences at Calais and Bruges Reconsidered', *HJ*, 23, pp. 755–72

Haas, S. W. (1980). 'Martin Luther's "Divine Right" Kingship and the Royal Supremacy: Two Tracts from the 1531 Parliament and Convocation of the Clergy', *JEH*, 30, pp. 317–25

Hammond, E. A. (1975). 'Doctor Augustine, Physician to Cardinal Wolsey and King Henry VIII', *Medical History*, 19, pp. 215–49

Hamy, A. (1898). *Entrevue de François Iᵉʳ avec Henry VIII à Boulogne-sur-Mer, en 1532*, Paris

Harmer, L. C. (1937). 'The Life and Works of Lancelot de Carle', Cambridge PhD

— (1939). 'Lancelot de Carle: Sa Vie', *Humanisme et Renaissance*, 6, pp. 443–74

Harrier, R. C. (1954). 'Notes on Wyatt and Anne Boleyn', *Journal of English and Germanic Philology*, 53, pp. 581–4

Harris, B. J. (1986). *Edward Stafford, Third Duke of Buckingham, 1478–1521*, Stanford, CA

— (1997). 'The View from My Lady's Chamber: New Perspectives on the Early Tudor Monarchy', *Huntington Library Quarterly*, 60, pp. 215–47

— (2002). *English Aristocratic Women 1450–1550: Marriage and Family, Property and Careers*, Oxford

Harris, E. K. (1995). 'Evidence Against Lancelot and Guinevere in Malory's *Morte D'Arthur*: Treason by Imagination', *Exemplaria*, 7, pp. 179–208

Harrison, C. J. (1972). 'The Petition of Edmund Dudley', *EHR*, 87, pp. 82–99

Hawkyard, A. (2016). *The House of Commons, 1509–1558: Personnel, Procedure, Precedent and Change*, Parliamentary History Yearbook Trust, London

Hayward, M. (1998). 'The Possessions of Henry VIII: A Study of the Inventories', LSE PhD

— (2005). 'Gift Giving at the Court of Henry VIII: The 1539 New Year's Gift Roll in Context', *AJ*, 85, pp. 125–75

— (2007). *Dress at the Court of Henry VIII*, Leeds

— (2016). '"We should dress us fairly for our end": The Significance of the Clothing Worn at Elite Executions in England in the Long Sixteenth Century', *History*, 101, pp. 222–45

Heller, H. (1972). 'The Evangelicism of Lefèvre d'Étaples: 1525', *Studies in the Renaissance*, 19, pp. 42–77

Hervey, M. F. S. (1900). *Holbein's Ambassadors: The Picture and the Men*, London

— (1904). 'A Portrait of Jean de Dinteville, One of Holbein's Ambassadors', *Burlington Magazine*, 5, pp. 412–13

Highley, C. (2005). '"A Pestilent and Seditious Book": Nicholas Sander's *Schismatis Anglicani* and Catholic Histories of the Reformation', *Huntington Library Quarterly*, 68, pp. 151–71

Higman, F. M. (1983). 'Luther et la piété de l'Église Gallicane: *le Livre de vraye et parfaicte oraison*', *Revue d'Histoire et de Philosophie Religieuses*, 63, pp. 91–111

— (1984). 'Les traductions françaises de Luther', in *Palaestra Typographica*, ed. J.–F. Gilmont, Aubel, pp. 11–56

— (2016). *Piety and the People: Religious Printing in French, 1511–1551*, London

Hochner, N. (2010). 'Imagining Esther in Early Modern France', *SCJ*, 41, pp. 757–87

Holban, M. (1935). 'François Du Moulin de Rochefort et la querelle de la Madeleine', *Humanisme et Renaissance*, 2, pp. 26–43, 147–71

Holder, N. (2011). 'The Medieval Friaries of London: A Topographic and Archaeological History, before and after the Dissolution', Royal Holloway PhD

Hook, J. (1969). 'The Sack of Rome, 1527', Edinburgh PhD

Horowitz, M. (2018). *Daring Dynasty: Custom, Conflict and Control in Early-Tudor England*, Newcastle

Hoyle, R. W. (1995). 'The Origins of the Dissolution of the Monasteries', *HJ*, 38, pp. 275–305

— (2001). *The Pilgrimage of Grace and the Politics of the 1530s*, Oxford

Hunt, A. (2008). *The Drama of Coronation: Medieval Ceremony in Early Modern England*, Cambridge

Hurren, E. T. (2013). 'Cultures of the Body, Medical Regimen and Physic at the Tudor Court', in *Henry VIII and the Court: Art, Politics and Performance*, ed. T. Betteridge and S. Lipscomb, Farnham, pp. 65–89

Irish, B. J. (2011). 'Gender and Politics in the Henrician Court: The Douglas-Howard Lyrics in the Devonshire Manuscript', *RQ*, 64, pp. 79–114

Ives, E. W. (1972). 'Faction at the Court of Henry VIII: The Fall of Anne Boleyn', *History*, 57, pp. 169–88

— (1981). 'Crime, Sanctuary, and Royal Authority under Henry VIII: The Exemplary Sufferings of the Savage Family', in *Of the Laws and Customs of England*, ed. M. S. Arnold, T. A. Green, S. A. Scully and S. D. White, Chapel Hill, NC, pp. 296–320

— (1983). *The Common Lawyers of Pre-Reformation England*, Cambridge

— (1992). 'The Fall of Anne Boleyn Reconsidered', *EHR*, 107, pp. 651–64

— (1994a). 'Anne Boleyn and the Early Reformation in England: The Contemporary Evidence', *HJ*, 37, pp. 389–400

— (1994b). 'The Queen and the Painters: Anne Boleyn, Holbein and Tudor Royal Portraits', *Apollo*, 140, pp. 36–45

— (1996). 'Anne Boleyn and the "Entente Évangélique"', ed. C. Giry-Deloison, Centre d'histoire de la région du Nord et de l'Europe du Nord-Ouest and Institut Français, Collection 'Histoire et littérature régionales', 13, Lille and London, pp. 83–102

— (1998). 'A Frenchman at the Court of Anne Boleyn', *History Today*, 48:8, pp. 21–6

— (2004). *The Life and Death of Anne Boleyn*, 2nd edn, Oxford

James, S. E. (2021). 'The Horenbout Family Workshop at the Tudor Court, 1522–1541: Collaboration, Patronage and Production', *Cogent Arts and Humanities*, 8:1, 1915933, DOI: 10.1080/23311983.2021.1915933

Johnston, A. (2003). 'William Paget and the Late-Henrician Polity, 1543–1547', St Andrews PhD

Jollet, E. (1997). *Jean et François Clouet*, Paris

Jones, M. (2003). 'The Rituals and Significance of Ducal Civic Entries in Late Medieval Brittany', *Journal of Medieval History*, 29, pp. 287–314

Jones, M. K., Underwood, M. G. (1992). *The King's Mother: Lady Margaret Beaufort, Countess of Richmond and Derby*, Cambridge

Kaufmann, M. (2017). *Black Tudors: The Untold Story*, London

Keay, A. (2001). *The Elizabethan Tower of London: The Haiward and Gascoyne Plan of 1597*, London

Kelly, H. A. (1976). *The Matrimonial Trials of Henry VIII*, Stanford, CA.

Kelly, M. (1965). 'The Submission of the Clergy', *TRHS*, 5th Series, 15, pp. 97–119

Kipling, G. (1997). 'He That Saw It Would Not Believe It: Anne Boleyn's Royal Entry into London' in *Civic and Ritual Drama*, ed. A. F. Johnson and Wim Hüsken, Atlanta, GA, pp. 39–79

Kisby, Fiona (1999). 'Kingship and the Royal Itinerary: A Study of the Peripatetic Household of the Early Tudor Kings 1485–1547', *Court Historian*, 4, pp. 29–39

— (2000). 'Officers and Office-holding at the English Royal Court. A Study of the Chapel Royal, 1485–1547', *Royal Musical Association Research Chronicle*, 32, pp. 1–61

— (2001). '"When the King Goeth a Procession": Chapel Ceremonies and Services, the Ritual Year, and Religious Reforms at the Early Tudor Court, 1485–1547', *JBS*, 40, pp. 44–75

Knecht, R. J. (1972). 'The Early Reformation in France and England: A Comparison', *History*, 57, pp. 1–16

— (1994). *Renaissance Warrior and Patron: The Reign of Francis I*, Cambridge

— (1998). *Catherine de' Medici*, London

Knowles, D. (1958). 'The Matter of Wilton, 1528', *BIHR*, 31, pp. 92–6

— (1959). *The Religious Orders in England, III, The Tudor Age*, Cambridge

Kolata, G. (1987). 'Wet-Nursing Boom in England Explored', *Science*, New Series, 235, pp. 745–7

Kolk, C. Z. (2009). 'The Household of the Queen of France in the Sixteenth Century', *The Court Historian*, 14, pp. 3–22

La Saussaye, L. de (1866). *Histoire du Château de Blois*, Paris

Laynesmith, J. L. (2004). *The Last Medieval Queens: English Queenship, 1445–1503*, Oxford

Lebey, A. (1904). *Le Connétable de Bourbon, 1490–1527*, Paris

Lehmberg, S. E. (1970). *The Reformation Parliament, 1529–1536*, Cambridge

— (1977). *The Later Parliaments of Henry VIII, 1536–1547*, Cambridge

Lerer, S. (1997). *Courtly Letters in the Age of Henry VIII: Literary Culture and the Arts of Deceit*, Cambridge

L'Estrange, E. (2016). ' "Un étrange moyen de séduction": Anne de Graville's Chaldean Histories and her Role in Literary Culture at the French Court in the Early Sixteenth Century', *Renaissance Studies*, 30, pp. 708–28

Leti, G. (1694). *La Vie d'Elizabeth, reine d'Angleterre*, 2 vols, Amsterdam

Levine, M. (1973). *Tudor Dynastic Problems, 1460–1571*, London

Lexton, R. (2015). 'Reading the Adulterous/Treasonous Queen in Early Modern England: Malory's Guinevere and Anne Boleyn', *Exemplaria*, 27, pp. 222–41

Lingard, J. (1878). *A History of England from the First Invasion by the Romans to the Accession of William and Mary in 1688*, 10 vols, London

Lloyd Jones, G., ed. (1989). *Robert Wakefield: On the Three Languages*, New York

Loach, J. (1994). 'The Function of Ceremonial in the Reign of Henry VIII', *PP*, 143, pp. 43–68

Loades, D. M. (1986). *The Tudor Court*, London

— (2008). *The Life and Career of William Paulet, c.1475–1572*, Aldershot

Logan, F. D. (1988). 'Thomas Cromwell and the Vicegerency in Spirituals: A Revisitation', *EHR*, 103, pp. 658–67

Lowinsky, E. E. (1969–70). 'MS 1070 of the Royal College of Music in London', *Proceedings of the Royal Musical Association*, 96, pp. 1–28

MacCulloch, D. (1995). 'Henry VIII and the Reform of the Church' in *The Reign of Henry VIII: Politics, Policy and Piety*, ed. D. MacCulloch, London, pp. 159–80

— (1996). *Thomas Cranmer: A Life*, New Haven and London

— (2018). *Thomas Cromwell: A Life*, London

MacDonald, D. (2002). 'Acknowledging the "Lady of the House": Memory, Authority and Self-Representation in the Patronage of Margaret of Austria', McGill PhD

Mackay, L. (2018a). *Among the Wolves of Court: The Untold Story of Thomas and George Boleyn*, London

— (2018b). 'The Life and Career of Thomas Boleyn (1477–1539): Courtier, Ambassador, and Statesman', Newcastle (Australia) PhD

McCaffrey, K. (2021a). 'Hope from Day to Day', *Times Literary Supplement*, issue 6164, 21 May 2021, at https://www.the-tls.co.uk/articles/inscriptions-discovered-in-a-book-owned-by-anne-bol eyn-essay-kate-e-mccaffrey/

— (2021b). 'Do We Have to Be "Team Catherine" or "Team Anne" when it comes to Henry VIII's Wives?', *History Extra*, 27 October 2021, at https://www.historyextra.com/period/tudor/team-cather ine-team-anne-why-choose/

McEntegart, R. (2002). *Henry VIII, the League of Schmalkalden and the English Reformation*, Woodbridge

McGlynn, M. (2003). *The Royal Prerogative and the Learning of the Inns of Court*, Cambridge

McIntosh, J. L. (2002). 'Sovereign Princesses: Mary and Elizabeth as Heads of Princely Households and the Accomplishment of the Female Succession in Tudor England, 1516–1588', Johns Hopkins PhD

Madden, F., ed. (1834–43). *Collectanea Topographica et Genealogica*, 4 vols, London

[Maddison, J., Newman, J.] (1987). *Blickling Hall, Norfolk*, National Trust [n.p.]

Marshall, P. (2003). 'Forgery and Miracles in the Reign of Henry VIII', *PP*, 178, pp. 39–73

— (2008). '"The Greatest Man in Wales": James Ap Gruffydd Ap Hywel and the International Opposition to Henry VIII', *SCJ*, 39, pp. 681–704

— (2017). *Heretics and Believers: A History of the English Reformation*, London

Marsham, R. (1874). 'On a Manuscript Book of Prayers in a Binding of Gold Enamelled, said to have been given by Queen Anne Boleyn to a Lady of the Wyatt Family', *Archaeologia*, 44, pp. 259–72

Marvin, M. B. W. (1977). 'Regret Chansons for Marguerite d'Autriche', *Bibliothèque d'humanisme et renaissance*, 39, pp. 23–32

Masson, G. (1868). 'L'Histoire du Protestantism Français', *Bulletin historique et littéraire*, 17, pp. 542–55

Mattingly, G. (1950). *Catherine of Aragon*, London

Mayer, C. A. (1965). 'Le sermon du bon pasteur: un problème d'attribution', *Bibliothèque d'humanisme et renaissance*, 27, pp. 286–303

— (1986). 'Anne Boleyn et la version originale du "Sermon du bon pasteur" d'Almanque Papillon', *Bulletin de la Société de l'histoire du protestantisme français*, 132, pp. 337–46

Mayer, T. F. (2000). *Reginald Pole, Prince and Prophet*, Cambridge

Miller, H. (1962). 'London and Parliament in the Reign of Henry VIII', *BIHR*, 35, pp. 128–49

— (1986). *Henry VIII and the English Nobility*, Oxford

Mirabella, B. (2012). '"In the sight of all": Queen Elizabeth and the Dance of Diplomacy', *Early Theatre*, 15, pp. 65–89

Montagu, W. D. (1864). *Court and Society from Elizabeth to Anne from the Papers at Kimbolton*, 2 vols, London

Müller, C., Kemperdick, S. (2006). *Hans Holbein the Younger: The Basel Years, 1515–1532*, Munich and New York

Murphy, B. A. (2003). *Bastard Prince: Henry VIII's Lost Son*, Stroud

Murphy, N. (2015). 'Henry VIII's First Invasion of France: The Gascon Expedition of 1512', *EHR*, 130, pp. 25–56

Murphy, V. M. (1984). 'The Debate over Henry VIII's First Divorce: An Analysis of the Contemporary Treatises', Cambridge Ph.D.

— (1995). 'The Literature and Propaganda of Henry VIII's First Divorce', in *The Reign of Henry VIII: Politics, Policy and Piety*, ed. D. MacCulloch, London, pp. 135–58

Murray, J. (2009). *Enforcing the Reformation in Ireland: Clerical Resistance and Political Conflict in the Diocese of Dublin, 1534–1590*, Cambridge

Néret, Jean-Alexis (1942). *Claude de France: Femme de François I*, Paris

Neville, P. A. (1990). 'Richard Pynson, King's Printer (1506–1529): Printing and Propaganda in Early Tudor England', Warburg Institute PhD

Nicholson, G. D. (1988). 'The Act of Appeals and the English Reformation', in *Law and Government under the Tudors*, ed. Claire Cross, D. M. Loades and J. J. Scarisbrick, Cambridge, pp. 19–30

Nitti, F. (1892). *Leone X e la sua politica secondo documenti e carteggi inediti*, Florence

Orme, N. (1996). 'John Holt (d. 1504), Tudor Schoolmaster and Grammarian', *The Library*, 6th Series, 18, pp. 283–305

Orth, M. D. (1982). 'Francis Du Moulin and the *Journal* of Louise of Savoy', *SCJ*, 13, pp. 55–66.

Page, W., ed. (1904–12). *A History of the County of Bedford*, VCH, 3 vols, London

Paget, H. (1981). 'The Youth of Anne Boleyn', *BIHR*, 54, pp. 162–70

Paisey, D., Bartrum, G. (2009). 'Hans Holbein and Miles Coverdale: A New Woodcut', *Print Quarterly*, 26, pp. 227–53

Palmer, R. C. (2002). *Selling the Church: The English Parish in Law, Commerce and Religion, 1350–1550*, Chapel Hill and London

Parker, G. (2019). *Emperor: A New Life of Charles V*, New Haven and London

Parker, K. T. (1983). *The Drawings of Hans Holbein in the Collection of Her Majesty the Queen at Windsor Castle*, with an appendix by Susan Foister, London and New York

Parkinson, J. A. (1958). 'A Chanson by Claudin de Sermisy', *Music and Letters*, 39, pp. 118–22

Plucknett, T. F. T. (1942). 'The Origin of Impeachment', *TRHS*, 24, pp. 47–71

Pollard, A. F. (1929). *Wolsey*, London

Pollnitz, A. (2015). *Princely Education in Early Modern Britain*, Cambridge

Porrer, S. M., ed. (2009). *Jacques Lefèvre d'Étaples and the Three Maries Debates*, Geneva

Powell, J. (2005). '"For Caesar's I Am": Henrician Diplomacy and Representations of King and Country in Thomas Wyatt's Poetry', *SCJ*, 36, pp. 415–31

— (2016). 'The Network Behind *Tottel's Miscellany*', *English Literary Renaissance*, 46, pp. 193–224

— (2019). 'Secret Writing or a Technology of Discretion? Dry Point in Tudor Books and Manuscripts', *Review of English Studies*, New Series, 7, pp. 37–53

Prescott, W. H. (1854). *History of the Reign of Ferdinand and Isabella, the Catholic, of Spain*, 7th edn, London

Pugh, T. (2005). 'Christian Revelation and the Cruel Game of Courtly Love in *Troilus and Criseyde*', *Chaucer Review*, 39, pp. 379–401

Purdy, R. J. W. (1901). 'Mannington Hall', *Norfolk Archaeology*, 14, pp. 321–8

Quinn, D. B. (1961). 'Henry VIII and Ireland', in *Irish Historical Studies*, 12, pp. 318–44

Rasmussen, M. (1995). 'The Case of the Flutes in Holbein's *The Ambassadors*', *Early Music*, 23, pp. 114–23

Rawcliffe, C. (1978). *The Staffords, Earls of Stafford and Dukes of Buckingham, 1394–1521*, Cambridge

Raymond, P. (1859). 'Nouvelles des affaires de France (1521)', *Bibliothèque de L'École des chartes*, 20, pp. 369–80

Redworth, G. (1990). *In Defence of the Church Catholic: The Life of Stephen Gardiner*, Oxford

Reid, J. A. (2001). 'King's Sister, Queen of Dissent: Marguerite of Navarre (1492–1549) and her Evangelical Network', Arizona State PhD

— (2013). 'Marguerite de Navarre and Evangelical Reform', in *A Companion to Marguerite de Navarre*, ed. G. Ferguson and M. B. McKinley, Leiden, pp. 29–58

— (2018). 'Imagination and Influence: The Creative Powers of Marguerite de Navarre at Work at Court and in the World', in *Women and Power at the French Court, 1483–1563*, ed. S. Broomhall, Amsterdam, pp. 263–83

Remley, P. G. (1994). 'Mary Shelton and her Tudor Literary Milieu', in *Rethinking the Henrician Era: Essays on Early Tudor Texts and Contexts*, ed. P. Herman, Urbana and Chicago, pp. 40–77

Rex, R. (1989). 'The English Campaign against Luther in the 1520s', *TRHS*, 5th Series, 39, pp. 85–106

— (1991). *The Theology of John Fisher*, Cambridge

— (1993). *Henry VIII and the English Reformation*, London

— (1996). 'The Crisis of Obedience: God's Word and Henry's Reformation', *HJ*, 39, pp. 863–94

— (2003). 'Redating Henry VIII's *A Glasse of the Truthe*', *The Library*, 7th Series, 4, pp. 16–27

— (2014). 'The Religion of Henry VIII', *HJ*, 57, pp. 1–32

Richardson, G. (1995). 'Anglo-French Political and Cultural Relations during the Reign of Henry VIII', LSE PhD

— (1999). 'The Privy Chamber of Henry VIII and Anglo-French Relations, 1515–1520', *Court Historian*, 4, pp. 119–40

— (2008). 'The French Connection: Francis I and England's Break with Rome', in *The Contending Kingdoms: France and England, 1430–1700*, ed. G. Richardson, Aldershot, pp. 95–115

— (2013). 'Hunting at the Courts of Francis I and Henry VIII', *Court Historian*, 18, pp. 127–41

— (2014a). 'Boys and their Toys: Kingship, Masculinity and Material Culture in the Sixteenth Century', in *The Image and Perception of Monarchy in Medieval and Early Modern Europe*, ed. S. McGlynn and E. Woodacre, Cambridge, pp. 183–206

— (2014b). *The Field of Cloth of Gold*, London

Richardson, W. C. (1970). *Mary Tudor: The White Queen*, London

Ring, M. (2017). *So High A Blood: The Life of Margaret, Countess of Lennox*, London

Robertson, M. L. (1975). 'Thomas Cromwell's Servants: The Ministerial Household in Early Tudor Government and Society', UCLA PhD

Robinson, J. Armitage (1915). 'Thomas Boleyn, Precentor of Wells', *Proceedings of the Somersetshire Archaeological and Natural History Society*, 4th Series, 61, Part II, pp. 1–10

Robison, W. B. (1984). 'The Justices of the Peace of Surrey in National and County Politics, 1481–1570', 2 vols, Louisiana State PhD

Rollins, H. E., ed. (1928). *Tottel's Miscellany (1557–1587)*, Cambridge, Mass.

Rossiter, W. (2009). '"I know where is an hynde": Sir Thomas Wyatt and the Transformation of Actaeon', in *Ovid's Metamorphoses in English Poetry*, ed. S. Coelsch-Foisner and W. Görtschacher, Heidelberg, pp. 69–88

Round, J. H. (1886). *The Early Life of Anne Boleyn: A Critical Essay*, London

Rowlands, J. (1985). *Holbein: The Paintings of Hans Holbein the Younger*, Oxford

Rowlands, J., Starkey, D. (1983). 'An Old Tradition Reasserted: Holbein's Portrait of Queen Anne Boleyn', *Burlington Magazine*, 125, pp. 88, 90–2

Royal Collection (1978). *Holbein and the Court of Henry VIII*, London

Sadlack, E. A. (2011). *The French Queen's Letters: Mary Tudor Brandon and the Politics of Marriage in Sixteenth-Century Europe*, London

Samman, N. (1988). 'The Henrician Court during Cardinal Wolsey's Ascendancy', Cardiff PhD

Saunders, J. W. (1951). 'From Manuscript to Print: A Note on the Circulation of Poetic Manuscripts in the Sixteenth Century', *Proceedings of the Leeds Philosophical and Literary Society*, 6, pp. 507–28

Scarisbrick, J. J. (1956). 'The Pardon of the Clergy, 1531', *HJ*, 12, pp. 22–39

— (1968). *Henry VIII*, London

Schilling, E. (1937). *Drawings of the Holbein Family*, London

Schmid, S. W. (2009). 'Anne Boleyn, Lancelot de Carle and the Uses of Documentary Evidence', Arizona State PhD

Sergeant, P. (1923). *The Life of Anne Boleyn*, London

Sessions, W. A. (1999). *Henry Howard: The Poet Earl of Surrey: A Life*, Oxford

Sharkey, J. (2004). 'Thomas Wolsey: The Influence of the Ideal of a Roman Cardinal on an English Prince of the Church', Cambridge MPhil

— (2008). 'The Politics of Wolsey's Cardinalate, 1515–1530', Cambridge PhD

— (2011). 'Between King and Pope: Thomas Wolsey and the Knight Mission', *HR*, 84, pp. 236–48.

Shaw, C., Mallett, M. (2019). *The Italian Wars, 1494–1559*, 2nd edn, London

Siemens, R. G. (1997). 'The English Lyrics of the Henry VIII Manuscript', University of British Columbia PhD

— (2009). 'Henry VIII as Writer and Lyricist', *Musical Quarterly*, 92, pp. 136–66

Skidmore, C. (2010). *Death and the Virgin*, London

Smith, A. R. (1982). 'Aspects of the Career of Sir John Fastolf, 1380–1459', Oxford PhD

Smith, J. C. (2011). 'Albrecht Dürer as Collector', *RQ*, 64, pp. 1–49

Smith, S. R. (2018). 'Unlocking *Cabala*, Mysteries of State and Government: The Politics of Publishing', Birkbeck College PhD

Southall, R. (1964). 'The Devonshire Manuscript Collection of Early Tudor Poetry, 1532–41', *Review of English Studies*, Old Series, 58, pp. 142–50

Stamatakis, C. (2012). *Sir Thomas Wyatt and the Rhetoric of Rewriting: 'Turning the Word'*, Oxford

Stanley-Millson, C., Newman, J. (1986). 'Blickling Hall: The Building of a Jacobean Mansion', *Architectural History*, 29, pp. 1–42

Starkey, D. R., ed. (1987). *The English Court from the Wars of the Roses to the Civil War*, London

— (1991). *Henry VIII: A European Court in England*, London

— (1998). 'King Arthur and King Henry', in *Arthurian Literature, XVI*, ed. J. P. Carley and F. Riddy, Woodbridge, pp. 171–96

— (2002). *The Reign of Henry VIII, Personalities and Politics*, 2nd edn, London

— (2004). *Six Wives: The Queens of Henry VIII*, London

— (2008). *Henry: Virtuous Prince*, London

Stephenson, B. (2000). 'Patronage, Piety and Politics in the Correspondence of Marguerite of Navarre', Rutgers PhD

— (2004). *The Power and Patronage of Marguerite de Navarre*, London

Stevens, J. (1961). *Music and Poetry in the Early Tudor Court*, London

Sutton, A. F. (2005). *The Mercery of London: Trade, Goods and People*, Aldershot

Szkilnik, M. (2010). 'Mentoring Noble Ladies: Antoine Dufour's *Vies des femmes célèbres*', in *The Cultural and Political Legacy of Anne de Bretagne: Negotiating Convention in Books and Documents*, ed. C. J. Brown, Cambridge, pp. 65–80

Taylor, A. (2012). 'John Leland's Communities of the Epigram', in *Neo-Latin Poetry in the British Isles*, ed. G. Manuwald and L. B. T. Houghton, Bristol, pp. 15–35

Thirsk, J., ed. (2006). *Life, Land and People in a Wealden Parish, 1400–1600*, Kent Archaeological Society, Maidstone

Thornton, T. (2000). *Cheshire and the Tudor State, 1480–1560*, London

Thurley, S. (1993). *The Royal Palaces of Tudor England: Architecture and Court Life, 1460–1547*, New Haven and London

— (1999). *Whitehall Palace: An Architectural History of the Royal Apartments, 1240–1698*, New Haven and London

— (2017). *Houses of Power: The Places that Shaped the Tudor World*, London

— (2020). 'Tudor Ambition: Houses of the Boleyn Family', Gresham College Lecture, 16 Sept. 2020, at https://www.gresham.ac.uk/lectures-and-events/boleyn-houses

Thwaites, G., Taviner, M., Gant, V. (1997). 'The English Sweating Sickness, 1485–1551', *New England Journal of Medicine*, 336, pp. 580–2

— (1998). 'The English Sweating Sickness, 1485–1551: A Viral Pulmonary Disease?', *Medical History*, 42, pp. 96–8

Tite, C. G. C. (2013). *The Early Records of Sir Robert Cotton's Library: Formation, Cataloguing, Use*, London

Trapp, J. B. (1992). 'Erasmus and His English Friends', *Erasmus of Rotterdam Society Yearbook*, 12, pp. 18–44

Travers, N. (1836–41). *Histoire civile, politique et religieuse de la ville et du comté de Nantes*, 4 vols, Nantes

Ullmann, W. (1979). 'This Realm of England is an Empire', *JEH*, 30, pp. 175–203

Urkevich, L. (1997). 'Anne Boleyn, a Music Book, and the Northern Renaissance Courts: Music Manuscript 1070 of the Royal College of Music, London', Maryland PhD

— (2009). 'Music Books of Women: Private Treasures and Personal Revelations', *Early Modern Women*, 4, pp. 175–85

Varlow, S. (2007). 'Sir Francis Knollys's Latin Dictionary: New Evidence for Katherine Carey', *HR*, 80, pp. 315–23

Venn, J., ed. (1897–1901). *Biographical History of Gonville and Caius College, 1349–1897*, 3 vols, Cambridge

Walker, G. (1989). 'The "Expulsion of the Minions" of 1519 Reconsidered', *HJ*, 32, pp. 1–16

— (2002). 'Rethinking the Fall of Anne Boleyn', *HJ*, 45, pp. 1–29

Warner, C. (2013). *The Making and Marketing of Tottel's Miscellany, 1557: Songs and Sonnets in the Summer of the Martyrs' Fires*, Farnham

Warner, M. (1996). 'Des Hermines et Fleurs de Lys: l'importance politique de l'entrée muncipale bretonne, 1491–1532', *Bulletin de la Société archéologique et historique de Nantes et de la Loire-Atlantique*, 131, pp. 87–105

Warnicke, R. M. (1985a). 'Anne Boleyn's Childhood and Adolescence', *HJ*, 28, pp. 939–52

— (1985b). 'The Fall of Anne Boleyn: A Reassessment', *History*, 70, pp. 1–15

— (1986). 'The Eternal Triangle and Court Politics: Henry VIII, Anne Boleyn, and Sir Thomas Wyatt', *Albion*, 18, pp. 565–79

— (1987). 'Sexual Heresy at the Court of Henry VIII', *HJ*, 30, pp. 247–68

— (1989). *The Rise and Fall of Anne Boleyn*, Cambridge

— (1993). 'The Fall of Anne Boleyn Revisited', *EHR*, 108, pp. 653–65

— (1998). 'The Conventions of Courtly Love and Anne Boleyn', in *State, Sovereigns and Society in Early-Modern England: Essays in Honour of A. J. Slavin*, ed. C. H. Carlton et al., Stroud, pp. 103–18

Waterton, E. (1879). *Pietas Mariana Britannica*, London

Watt, D. (1997). 'Reconstructing the Word: the Political Prophecies of Elizabeth Barton', *RQ*, 50, pp. 136–63

Wedgwood, J. C., Holt, A. D. (1936). *Biographies of the Members of the Commons House, 1439–1509*, History of Parliament, London

Weir, A. (2009). *The Lady in the Tower: The Fall of Anne Boleyn*, London

Whiteley, C. B., Kramer, K. (2010). 'A New Explanation for the Reproductive Woes and Midlife Crisis of Henry VIII', *HJ*, 53, pp. 827–48

Willoughby, H. R. (1936). 'Current Errors concerning the Coverdale Bible', *Journal of Biblical Literature*, 55, pp. 1–16

Wilson-Chevalier, K. (2007). 'Claude de France', in *Encyclopaedia of Women in the Renaissance*, ed. D. Robin, A. R. Larsen and C. Levin, Santa Barbara and Oxford, pp. 80–1

— (2010). 'Claude de France: In her Mother's Likeness, a Queen with Symbolic Clout?', in *The Cultural and Political Legacy of Anne de Bretagne: Negotiating Convention in Books and Documents*, ed. C. J. Brown, Cambridge, pp. 123–44

— (2015). 'Denis Briçonnet et Claude de France', *Seizième Siècle*, 11, pp. 95–118

— (2018). 'Claude de France and the Spaces of Agency of a Marginalized Queen', in *Women and Power at the French Court, 1483–1563*, ed. S. Broomhall, Amsterdam, pp. 139–72

Woods, R. L. (1974). 'The Amicable Grant: Some Aspects of Thomas Wolsey's Rule in England, 1522–1526', UCLA PhD

Yates, F. (1947). 'Queen Elizabeth as Astraea', *Journal of the Warburg and Courtauld Institutes*, 10, pp. 27–82

Zell, M. (1974). 'Church and Gentry in Reformation Kent, 1533–1553', UCLA PhD

Zupanec, S. S. (2017). 'An Overlooked Connection of Anne Boleyn's Maid of Honour, Elizabeth Holland, with BL, Kings MS 9', *Electronic British Library Journal*, article 7, at https://www.bl.uk/eblj/articles/2017-articles

Acknowledgements

Although for the last twenty-five years we have usually had to some degree a collaborative role in each other's books, this is the first that we have written together. And it could never have been completed without help from so many different people and institutions.

Since we always start from the original manuscripts and earliest printed sources rather than relying on the more familiar nineteenth- or early twentieth-century abstracts of documents or on secondary works, we had intended to begin by spending six months or so in Paris immersed in the archives, a task which in the spring of 2020 suddenly became impossible as the various pandemic lockdowns took hold. Fortunately, the wonderful curators of the Bibliothèque Nationale de France and Centre des Archives diplomatiques du ministère des Affaires étrangères came to our rescue by sending us digitised copies of the manuscripts we so desperately needed. Luckily, with the helpful cooperation of (especially) the curators of the British Library and National Archives in Kew, we had photographed or obtained digital copies or microfilms of the main UK source materials in the summer of 2019. This book could not have been written during the worst of the Covid experiences without these facilities.

Heartfelt gratitude is due to our UK agent, Natasha Fairweather, and her assistant, Matthew Marland, and to our agent in the United States, Gráinne Fox, and her team for believing in this project from the beginning and for their unceasing encouragement and suggestions. Our editors at Bloomsbury, Alexis Kirschbaum and Jasmine Horsey, and Jonathan Jao at HarperCollins, have been magnificent. They all deserve our thanks for supporting us unreservedly, trusting us to work without interference, but being there when we needed them. Then, their close attention to the text and insightful edits were invaluable in making us question, rethink and rewrite our first draft: the book would be infinitely poorer without their assistance. We must also thank Lauren Whybrow, the Senior Managing Editor at Bloomsbury, who helped us see the book through its final stages so smoothly, especially when we were struck down ourselves by severe bouts of Covid at a crucial time. Ben Brock, our copy-editor, worked tremendously hard on the text to make it the best we could produce and we thank him unreservedly. Emma Brown, our picture researcher, came up trumps as she always does and helped us source the images we needed. We would also like to thank Dr Jonathan Foyle, who so willingly gave of his time to assist us with some points of architectural and furniture detail, and Dr Matthew Shaw, the librarian at The Queen's College, Oxford, and his colleagues for sending us cameraphone photos of some key documents we were unable to consult during the lockdowns. We gratefully acknowledge the assistance of staff of the National Archives at Kew, the London Library, the Cambridge University Library, the Bodleian Library and the British Library, with special thanks as always to Dr Andrea Clarke in the Medieval and Early Modern Manuscripts Department, and to the curators of half a dozen or more French municipal archives, the archives in Brussels and elsewhere, and those of the Vatican Apostolic Archives and Library. Warm thanks are due to John's colleagues and especially students at Clare College, Cambridge, who contributed to our book in ways often beyond what they might have imagined.

Finally, but most importantly, nothing could have been done without the constant love and support of our friends and family (human, feline and canine) who were with us throughout the whole process. We can never repay them.

Researching and writing together has been a joy. We both worked independently over the entire book rather than each handling specific sections before pooling our resources; we have spent hours (often in the middle of the night over tea and digestive biscuits) agonising and discussing the motivations, pressures and fates of the various characters, and we have enjoyed every minute of it. Would we do it again? Watch this space!

London
25 April 2023

Illustration Credits

1. View of the Tower of London from the south bank of the Thames, c.1544. By Anthonis van den Wyngaerde. Ashmolean Museum, Oxford. Heritage Image Partnership Ltd. / Alamy Stock Photo.

2. Henry aged about 18 shortly before he married Katherine of Aragon. The Picture Art Collection / Alamy Stock Photo.

3. While the identity of the sitter is unproven, the fact that she wears a collar depicting the letter 'K' and Tudor roses, and a 'C' for 'Catalina' (her Spanish name) on her dress, suggests that she is the young Katherine of Aragon. By Michel Sittow. Kunsthistorisches Museum, Vienna. Photo © AKG Images / Erich Lessing.

4. Hever Castle, the Boleyn seat in Kent where Anne spent her childhood after 1505. © John Bethell. All rights reserved. 2023 / Bridgeman Images.

5. Margaret of Austria. Portrait after Bernard van Orley. The Royal Monastery of Brou, Bourg-en-Bresse, France. Photo: John Guy and Julia Fox.

6. Claude, Queen of France. By an unknown artist. © 2023 Louvre, Paris (Cabinet des Dessins) / RMN Grand Palais. Michèle Bellot / Photo Scala, Florence.

7. Louise of Savoy, mother of Francis I. By Jean Clouet. Gallery of Portraits, Chateau de Beauregard, Cellettes, Loire Valley, Centre, France. Photo © AKG-Images / Manuel Cohen.

8. Francis I, King of France, aged about 32. By Jean Clouet. Louvre, Paris. Incamerastock / Alamy Stock Photo.

9. Marguerite of Angoulême, sister of Francis I, aged about 35. By Jean Clouet. Walker Art Gallery, Liverpool. Heritage Image Partnership Ltd / Alamy Stock Photo.

10. Anne de Graville presenting a copy of her French adaptation of Boccaccio's *Teseida* to Claude, watched by the queen's *demoiselles* (detail). Bibliothèque Nationale de France, Paris. Reference MS Arsenal 5116, fo. 1v.

11. Letter from Anne to her father from Tervuren, 1513. The Parker Library, Corpus Christi College, Cambridge. Reference CCCC MS 119, fo. 21.

12. Henry's younger sister Mary, briefly queen of France, and Charles Brandon, duke of Suffolk. By an unknown artist. From the Woburn Abbey Collection.

13. Charles of Ghent (later King of Spain, and Holy Roman Emperor as Charles V). By Bernard van Orley. Louvre, Paris / Bridgeman Images.

14. Princess Mary aged about 6, when betrothed to Charles V, c.1522. By Lucas Horenbout. National Portrait Gallery. Album / Alamy Stock Photo.

15. The challenge at the 'Castle of Loyalty', organised by Thomas Wyatt and his friends for the celebrations at Christmas 1524. College of Arms, MS M. 6, fol. 57v. Reproduced by permission of the Kings, Heralds and Pursuivants of Arms.

16. Thomas Wyatt. By Hans Holbein the Younger. Royal Collection Trust © His Majesty King Charles III, 2023 / Bridgeman Images.

17. Henry's suit of armour, 1527, made in the royal workshops in Greenwich and presented to François de la Tour, Viscount de Turenne. Metropolitan Museum of Art, New York. Agefotostock / Alamy Stock Photo.

18. Mary Boleyn. By an unknown artist. Hever Castle, Kent / Bridgeman Images.

19. Katherine of Aragon aged about 41. By Lucas Horenbout. National Portrait Gallery. Heritage Image Partnership Ltd / Alamy Stock Photo.

20. Henry VIII aged about 35. By Lucas Horenbout. The Royal Collection, The Royal Library, Windsor. Heritage Image Partnership Ltd / Alamy Stock Photo.

21. Anne Boleyn, Hever Castle version. By an unknown artist. Hever Castle, Kent / Bridgeman Images.

22. Henry's love note in French to Anne, scribbled beneath a miniature of Christ as the 'Man of Sorrows': 'If you remember my love in your prayers as strongly as I adore you, I shall hardly be forgotten, for I am yours, Henry R always'. British Library, London. © British Library Board. All Rights Reserved / Bridgeman Images.

23. Anne's response to Henry's love note, written beneath a miniature of the Annunciation: 'By daily proof you shall me find

/ To be to you both loving and kind'. British Library, London. © British Library Board. All Rights Reserved / Bridgeman Images.

24. One of Henry's love letters to Anne, written in French after learning that she had the sweating sickness. Biblioteca Apostolica Vaticana, Rome. Reference MS Vat.lat.3731.pt.A, fo. 11r. All Rights Reserved.

25. Joint letter of Henry and Anne (partially charred in a fire of 1731) to Wolsey, early August 1528, expressing concern at the slow progress of Cardinal Lorenzo Campeggi on his journey from Italy to London. British Library, London. © British Library Board. All Rights Reserved / Bridgeman Images.

26. Pope Clement VII, c.1531. By Sebastiano del Piombo. J. Paul Getty Museum, Los Angeles, 92.PC.25.

27. Cardinal Wolsey. By an unknown artist. National Portrait Gallery. Keith Corrigan / Alamy Stock Photo.

28. Anne's specially commissioned psalter, c.1529–30, showing her monograms and the black lion of Rochford. Copyright the Trustees of the Wormsley Fund and reproduced with permission from the Wormsley Estate.

29. Anne's illuminated Book of Hours produced in Bruges, c.1450, with her message: 'Le temps viendra / Je anne boleyn' ('The time will come / I Anne Boleyn'). Christie's sale, Wednesday 26 November 1997, lot 3, fo. 99v. All Rights Reserved / Hever Castle Ltd, Kent / Bridgeman Images.

30. The seating plan for Anne's coronation banquet in Westminster Hall. British Library, London. © British Library Board. All Rights Reserved / Bridgeman Images.

31. Anne's falcon badge, sceptred and bearing an imperial crown, set within an illuminated initial letter 'T' from *The Ecclesiaste*. Alnwick Castle, Percy MS 465, fo 23r (detail). © Collection of the Earl of Northumberland / Bridgeman Images.

32. Hans Holbein the Younger's design for a pageant on the theme of Mount Parnassus staged for Anne's coronation celebrations. Staatliche Museen zu Berlin, Kupferstichkabinett. Axis Images / Alamy Stock Photo.

33. The Ambassadors, Jean de Dinteville and Georges de Selve. By Hans Holbein the Younger. The National Gallery, London. Ian Dagnall Computing / Alamy Stock Photo.

34. A badly defaced proof version of Anne's portrait medal of 1534, struck (but apparently not issued) to celebrate the son she believed she was expecting. © The Trustees of the British Museum / All Rights Reserved.

35. A design for jewellery for Anne. By Hans Holbein the Younger. © The Trustees of the British Museum / All Rights Reserved.

36. The front cover of Volume II of Anne's copy of the French translation of the Bible by Jacques Lefèvre d'Étaples. British Library, London. © British Library Board. All Rights Reserved / Bridgeman Images.

37. Hans Holbein the Younger's design for a table fountain which Anne commissioned as a New Year's gift for Henry. Kunstmuseum, Basel, Kupferstichkabinett. Art Heritage / Alamy Stock Photo.

38. Lady Mary Howard, Duchess of Richmond, Anne's cousin and lady-in-waiting. By Hans Holbein the Younger. Royal Collection Trust © His Majesty King Charles III, 2023 / Bridgeman Images.

39. Mary Shelton, one of Anne's gentlewomen. By Hans Holbein the Younger. Royal Collection Trust © His Majesty King Charles III, 2023 / Bridgeman Images.

40. Margery Horsman, one of Katherine's maids, later Anne's gentlewoman. By Hans Holbein the Younger. Royal Collection Trust © His Majesty King Charles III, 2023 / Bridgeman Images.

41. 'Mistress Zouche', a gentlewoman wearing Anne's trademark French hood. By Hans Holbein the Younger. Royal Collection Trust © His Majesty King Charles III, 2023 / Bridgeman Images.

42. Unknown woman, later inscribed 'Anna Bollein Queen'. By Hans Holbein the Younger. The Royal Collection, The Royal Library, Windsor. Art Collection 2 / Alamy Stock Photo.

43. Three gentlewomen performing the chanson 'Jouyssance vous donneray' for their private entertainment, c.1520. By the Master of the Female Half-Lengths. The Harrach Collection, Schloss Rohrau, Austria. Album / Alamy Stock Photo.

44. Tablet miniature on the theme of 'King Solomon and the Queen of Sheba', commissioned by Anne for Henry as a New Year's gift. By Hans Holbein the Younger. The Royal Collection, The Royal Library, Windsor. Art Collection 2 / Alamy Stock Photo.

45. Thomas Cromwell. By Hans Holbein the Younger. The Frick Collection, New York. Ian Dagnall Computing / Alamy Stock Photo.

46. The 'Chequers' ring. The Chequers Trust. All Rights Reserved.

47. Jane Seymour, one of Katherine's maids, later Anne's gentlewoman, depicted as Henry's third wife. By Hans Holbein the Younger. GL Archive / Alamy Stock Photo.

Index

A Note on the Authors

John Guy is a historian, author and broadcaster and one of the world's leading scholars of Tudor history. Guy received his Bachelor's and PhD from Cambridge University. The author of sixteen books, he is a regular guest on multiple BBC radio shows and a BBC documentary contributor. Julia Fox is a teacher and author. She taught history at schools throughout London, having obtained her degree in history from the University of London. She is the author of two books, *Jane Boleyn* and *Sister Queens*.